Global Critical Race Feminism

Critical America
General Editors: RICHARD DELGADO and JEAN STEFANCIC

White by Law:
The Legal Construction of Race
Ian F. Haney López

Cultivating Intelligence:
Power, Law, and the Politics of Teaching
Louise Harmon and Deborah W. Post

Privilege Revealed:
How Invisible Preference Undermines America
Stephanie M. Wildman
with Margalynne Armstrong, Adrienne D. Davis, and Trina Grillo

Does the Law Morally Bind the Poor?
or What Good's the Constitution When You Can't Afford a Loaf of Bread?
R. George Wright

Hybrid:
Bisexuals, Multiracials, and Other Misfits under American Law
Ruth Colker

Critical Race Feminism: A Reader
Edited by Adrien Katherine Wing

Immigrants Out!
The New Nativism and the Anti-Immigrant Impulse in the United States
Edited by Juan F. Perea

Taxing America
Edited by Karen B. Brown and Mary Louise Fellows

Notes of a Racial Caste Baby:
Color Blindness and the End of Affirmative Action
Bryan K. Fair

Please Don't Wish Me a Merry Christmas:
A Critical History of the Separation of Church and State
Stephen M. Feldman

To Be an American:
Cultural Pluralism and the Rhetoric of Assimilation
Bill Ong Hing

Negrophobia and Reasonable Racism:
The Hidden Costs of Being Black in America
Jody David Armour

Black and Brown in America:
The Case for Cooperation
Bill Piatt

Black Rage Confronts the Law
Paul Harris

Selling Words:
Free Speech in a Commercial Culture
R. George Wright

The Color of Crime:
Racial Hoaxes, White Fear, Black Protectionism, Police
Harassment, and Other Macroaggressions
Katheryn K. Russell

The Smart Culture:
Society, Intelligence, and Law
Robert L. Hayman, Jr.

Was Blind, but Now I See:
White Race Consciousness and the Law
Barbara J. Flagg

The Gender Line:
Men, Women, and the Law
Nancy Levit

Heretics in the Temple:
Americans Who Reject the Nation's Legal Faith
David Ray Papke

The Empire Strikes Back:
Outsiders and the Struggle over Legal Education
Arthur Austin

Interracial Justice:
Conflict and Reconciliation in Post–Civil Rights America
Eric K. Yamamoto

Black Men on Race, Gender, and Sexuality:
A Critical Reader
Edited by Devon Carbado

When Sorry Isn't Enough:
The Controversy over Apologies and Reparations for Human Injustice
Edited by Roy L. Brooks

Disoriented: Asian Americans, Law, and the Nation State
Robert S. Chang

Rape and the Culture of the Courtroom
Andrew E. Taslitz

The Passions of Law
Edited by Susan Bandes

Global Critical Race Feminism:
An International Reader
Edited by Adrien Katherine Wing

Global Critical Race Feminism

An International Reader

Edited by
Adrien Katherine Wing

Foreword by
Angela Y. Davis

 NEW YORK UNIVERSITY PRESS • New York & London

NEW YORK UNIVERSITY PRESS
New York and London

Library of Congress Cataloging-in-Publication Data
Global critical race feminism : an international reader / edited by
Adrien Katherine Wing ; foreword by Angela Y. Davis.
p.   cm. — (Critical America)
Includes bibliographical references and index.
ISBN 0-8147-9338-X (paper : acid-free paper) — ISBN 0-8147-9337-1
(cloth : acid-free paper)
1. Minority women—Legal status, laws, etc.   I. Wing, Adrien
Katherine. II. Title. III. Series.
K644 .G59 2000
346.01'34—dc21   00-008391

New York University Press books are printed on acid-free paper,
and their binding materials are chosen for strength and durability.

Manufactured in the United States of America

10 9 8 7 6 5 4 3 2 1

Contents

Foreword   xi
Angela Y. Davis

Acknowledgments   xv

Introduction: Global Critical Race Feminism
for the Twenty-First Century   1
Adrien Katherine Wing

PART 1   Encounters with the "F" Word: Responses to Feminism

1   Turning the Gaze Back on Itself: Comparative Law,
        Feminist Legal Studies, and the Postcolonial Project   27
        Brenda J. Cossman

2   Toward a Feminist Internationality: A Critique of
        U.S. Feminist Legal Scholarship   42
        Vasuki Nesiah

3   Themes for a Conversation on Race and Gender
        in International Human Rights Law   53
        Celina Romany

4   Comparative Analysis of Women's Issues: Toward a
        Contextualized Methodology   67
        Antoinette Sedillo Lopez

5 Féminismes sans Frontières? The Cuban Challenge—
Women, Equality, and Culture 81
Berta Esperanza Hernández-Truyol

6 Women (Under)Development: Poor Women of Color
in the United States and the Right to Development 95
Hope Lewis

PART 2 Third World within the First: On Being "Othered"

7 Motherhood and Work in Cultural Context:
One Woman's Patriarchal Bargain 115
Devon W. Carbado

8 Discrimination in New Zealand: A Personal Journey 129
Mai Chen

9 African Women in France: Immigration, Family,
and Work 141
Judy Scales-Trent

10 Filthy, Old, and Ugly: Gypsy Women from Serbia 160
Zorica Mrsevic

PART 3 From Pathbreakers to Founding Mothers:
Historical Perspectives

11 Josephine Baker, Racial Protest, and the Cold War 179
Mary L. Dudziak

12 United States Foreign Policy and Goler Teal Butcher 192
J. Clay Smith, Jr.

13 Founding Mothers and Contemporary Latin American
Constitutions: Colombian Women, Constitution
Making, and the New Constitutional Court 204
*Martha I. Morgan with the collaboration
of Mónica María Alzate Buitrago*

PART 4 Human Rights Confronts Culture, Custom, and Religion

14 Deconstructing Patriarchal Jurisprudence in
Islamic Law: A Faithful Approach 221
Azizah Y. al-Hibri

15 For the Sake of the Country, for the Sake of the Family:
The Oppressive Impact of Family Registration
on Women in Japan 234
Taimie L. Bryant

16 Female Infanticide in China: The Human Rights Specter
and Thoughts toward (An)Other Vision 251
Sharon K. Hom

17 Bridges and Barricades: Rethinking Polemics and
Intransigence in the Campaign against
Female Circumcision 260
Leslye Amede Obiora

18 Uneasy Alliances and Solid Sisterhood: A Response to
Professor Obiora's "Bridges and Barricades" 275
Isabelle R. Gunning

19 Families, Fatherlessness, and Women's Human Rights:
An Analysis of the Clinton Administration's Public
Housing Policy as a Violation of the Convention
on the Elimination of All Forms of Discrimination
against Women 285
Lisa A. Crooms

PART 5 Violence against Women: Family Terrorism, Rape,
and Sexual Harassment

20 Violence against Aboriginal Women in Australia:
Possibilities for Redress within the International
Human Rights Framework 303
Penelope E. Andrews

21 Domestic Violence in Ghana: An Initial Step 317
Rosemary Ofeibea Ofei-Aboagye King

22 A Critical Race Feminist Conceptualization of Violence:
South African and Palestinian Women 332
Adrien Katherine Wing

23 Puerto Rico's Domestic Violence Prevention and
Intervention Law: The Limitations of
Legislative Responses 347
Jenny Rivera

24 Sexual Harassment and Human Rights in Latin America   362
Gaby Oré-Aguilar

PART 6 The Global Workplace

25 (Dis)Assembling Rights of Women Workers along
the Global Assembly Line: Human Rights and
the Garment Industry   377
Laura Ho, Catherine Powell, and Leti Volpp

26 Holding Up More Than Half the Sky: Marketization
and the Status of Women in China   392
Anna M. Han

27 Still Office Flowers: Japanese Women Betrayed by
the Equal Employment Opportunity Law   409
Kiyoko Kamio Knapp

Selected Bibliography   425
Contributors   437
Index   445

Foreword

Angela Y. Davis

The largest women's prison in Australia, located near Melbourne, is owned and operated by Corrections Corporation of America (CCA), based in Nashville, Tennessee. CCA, the largest of a rising number of private prison companies, might conceivably argue that punishment structures linked to the political history of the United States have been exported to other countries for the last two centuries. However accurate this observation, the context within which CCA and other transnational corporations conduct their business has been radically transformed over the last decades of the twentieth century. CCA's work is facilitated today by the rapid migration of capital, information, and ideas, as well as the attendant processes of privatization and structural adjustment promoted by the International Monetary Fund, the World Bank, and other global financial establishments. Within this new context, such peculiarly American institutions as the prison have become a major feature of the landscape in many countries that previously relied on more humane means of managing their social problems.

During a 1999 visit to a women's prison in Sydney, I was struck not only by the architectural similarities with women's prisons in the United States, but also by the patterns of racialization that appeared to define who goes to prison and who does not. When I talked to a number of young Aboriginal women incarcerated on charges connected with drug use, these conversations reminded me of similar exchanges with Black and Latina women in prison on drug charges in the United States. I also thought about the Latin American and Caribbean women I had interviewed at a prison in the Netherlands, many of whom were incarcerated in connection with drug-trafficking charges. The globalization of the U.S. war on drugs and its attendant demonization of people of color furnishes a striking example of the ease with which contemporary forms of racism move across national borders. Today, one of the most ominous instances of the dissemination of U.S. prison practices is the growing adoption of supermax prisons, even in countries like the Netherlands and the new South Africa, which we associate with historical or recent progressive social experiments.

While U.S. hegemony continues to be cause for great concern—especially given the speed with which repressive institutions and conservative ideas travel to the most far-flung areas of the globe—it is the homelessness of global capital that poses the greatest threat to women throughout the world. Garments bought by U.S. consumers are increasingly produced by women and girls in Asia, Central America, South America, and the Caribbean under conditions that fall far below the putative minimum labor standards in the United States. This, in turn, impels garment manufacturers, who proudly exhibit the "made in the U.S.A." label to rely on the sweatshop labor of immigrant women and girls who have frequently traveled to the United States in order to escape the economic dislocation caused by transnational corporations in their home countries. A recent campaign by Asian Immigrant Women's Advocates revealed that Jessica McClintock, Inc., sold prom dresses for $175, for which the women who produced them received a meager five dollars. It is not surprising that twenty years after the United Nations Convention on the Elimination of All Forms of Discrimination against Women, the U.S. Senate still has not seen fit to ratify this treaty.

Adrien Wing's *Global Critical Race Feminism* draws upon various theoretical and organizing traditions to help counter the egregious effects of globalization on women throughout the world and to affirm the possibilities of building feminist community around struggles of poor women of color in the North and women throughout the Southern countries. This work is the most recent of a series of anthologies organized around themes related to women of color in North America and Europe and/or women of the South. It takes its place alongside such important works as *This Bridge Called My Back: Writings by Radical Women of Color,* edited by Cherríe Moraga and Gloria Anzaldúa (2d ed., Kitchen Table, Women of Color Press, 1983); *Third World Women and the Politics of Feminism,* edited by Chandra Mohanty, Ann Russo, and Lourdes Torres (Indiana University Press, 1991); and *Feminist Genealogies, Colonial Legacies, Democratic Futures*, edited by M. Jacqui Alexander and Chandra Talpade Mohanty (Routledge, 1997). *Global Critical Race Feminism* goes beyond Wing's first anthology, *Critical Race Feminism* (New York University Press, 1997), in linking research and activism by lawyers and legal academics around women of color within a domestic U.S. context to a range of global issues. Wing's first anthology may be considered a point of departure. In fact, some of the key articles in the earlier work that urged us to internationalize our thinking about race and gender reappear in the present volume.

Many of the articles in this anthology explore possibilities of progressive legal practice informed by understandings of the cross-cutting and overlapping relationships of gender, class, race, and sexuality. In this sense, it charges lawyers and legal academics with the awesome task of translating the complicated theoretical relationships among these categories into transformative legal practice. As proponents of Critical Race Theory have often dramatically demonstrated, this is no easy task, given the various power dynamics deeply embedded in Western legal traditions. A number of the contributors to *Global Critical Race Feminism* point out that the contemporary urgency of forging feminist community around transnational legal projects vastly increases the magnitude of these difficulties.

The articles included in this collection reveal that global sisterhood in the twenty-first century will be a failed venture if it is imagined primarily as a project of generating knowledge—whether anthropological or legal—about similarities and differences among northern and southern women. In emphasizing the role of social activism, emerging scholar/activists, whose contributions play a significant role in this anthology, ask us to consider organizing strategies, which have grown out of many local contexts, as a starting point for productive forms of feminist solidarity. Readers will appreciate the provocative multigenerational conversations in *Global Critical Race Feminism* around such widespread problems as public and private violence against women. This work urges us all to imagine new, nonexploitative border crossings between countries, cultures, and ethnicities as well as between research, legal practice, and social activism.

Acknowledgments

First, I would like to sincerely express my gratitude and thanks to all the wonderful contributors to this volume for enabling me to share their work with a wider audience. Their words inspire me to produce my own modest contributions to this emerging genre. I must especially thank my friend Angela Y. Davis for taking time from her own amazingly busy schedule to write the foreword to this collection. I also acknowledge the special assistance of University of Iowa research assistants Armikka Bryant, Thushentha Devan, Anel Dominguez, Eric Hallstrom, Wendy Howza, Mary Kimani, Mahal Montoya, Adam Rodriguez, and Wael Wahbeh, as well as my very able, hardworking former secretary, Beverly Heitt. My dean, N. William Hines, has supported all my scholarly, teaching, and service efforts for more than a decade. I truly could not have accomplished all I have as a professor without him.

I have been fortunate enough to have had several mentors who greatly influenced my career as a student of international affairs. They include Joseph Borlo of Newark Academy in Livingston, New Jersey, who made sure my French was presentable; the Angolan specialist and professor Gerald Bender, formerly of the UCLA African Studies Program; and Stanford law professor John Merryman, one of the fathers of comparative law in the United States. When I worked as an international lawyer for five years in New York, my mentors included Keith Highet and the late Laishley Peter Wragg, both formerly of the Curtis, Mallet-Prevost et al. firm in New York. My principal mentor at the University of Iowa has been Professor Burns Weston, former director of the international and comparative law program. I have been proud to be a part of the phenomenal growth of international law in the wilds of Iowa under his energetic direction. Additionally there are several colleagues at other schools who have helped me find my way as an international law scholar and activist: Temple Law School professor Henry Richardson;

the late dean of the City University Law School at Queens Haywood Burns, who died in South Africa while fulfilling his mission as an international scholar/activist; and the late Howard Law School professor Goler Butcher, whose life work is featured in this volume.

Of course the true core of my success rests with my family. My mother, Katherine Pruitt Wing, made many sacrifices to assist me in obtaining the excellent educational foundation that has enabled me to soar beyond the borders of the United States. My father, the late Dr. John E. Wing, Jr., taught me that I would not be limited by racialized patriarchy in my choice of careers. Other influential family members in my choice of career include my uncle James Pruitt, whose African slide show way back in 1963 implanted a vision of Africa in my head that has lasted a lifetime; and my aunt Bess Pruitt, whose managerial representation of African dance companies further solidified my dreams of a career involving Africa. There is a granduncle I never met, Bob Grière, whose exciting career abroad in France and francophone Africa underlay our family lore. I imagine him in his jaunty French beret, living in the France of Josephine Baker and other Black American expatriates. Perhaps he once sat in a café with Paul Robeson, a role model I gained in college, whose global career in the face of injustice inspired me to name one of my sons in his honor, a son who was also born on his birthday.

At the foundation of everything, I must thank my partner, James C. Sommerville, for his unflagging support, patience, and love now spanning two decades. And finally it is my sons, Nolan, Ché-Cabral, Charles, Brooks, and Willie, and now grandson Isiah, who will all hopefully make it worthwhile in the twenty-first century.

Introduction

Global Critical Race Feminism
for the Twenty-First Century

Adrien Katherine Wing

In this introduction I hope to identify the intellectual threads that have contributed to this loosely woven tapestry I am labeling Global Critical Race Feminism (GCRF). The volume expands upon the issues addressed in my well-received first anthology, *Critical Race Feminism: A Reader* (New York University Press, 1997). That original book was the first collection predominantly focusing on the legal status of women of color living in the United States, that is, African Americans, Latinas, Asians, and Native Americans. In the words of CRF foremother Professor Mari Matsuda, these women can experience "multiple consciousness," an awareness of oppression they face based simultaneously on their race/ethnicity and gender.[1] The volume emphasized not only the experience of discrimination, but also resilience, resistance, and the formation of solutions. It covered such diverse areas as anti-essentialism, education, mothering, employment, welfare reform, criminality, domestic violence, and sexual harassment. The final part of the volume introduced global themes.

In my travels I am frequently asked the meaning of this odd term "Critical Race Feminism." Some people have wondered whether CRF adherents are "male-hating, bra-burning feminazis in blackface." Some men of color have asked whether we are race traitors who give greater priority to gender than to racial solidarity. Professor Richard Delgado of the University of Colorado Law School coined the term CRF in the first edition of his anthology *Critical Race Theory: The Cutting Edge* (Temple University Press, 1995). The beauty of the strange expression is that each word represents one of the primary legal traditions from which it derives— Critical Legal Studies (CLS), Critical Race Theory (CRT), and feminist jurisprudence. The word "global" added to the title of this collection implies the embrace of strands from international and comparative law, global feminism, and postcolonial theory as well.

1

When I explain the derivation of CRF in some circles, I am sometimes met by a stony silence or a condescendingly polite response, "Oh, that's very nice," as the conversation returns to "real law." Implicit in the exchange or lack of exchange may be skepticism on several levels. Isn't the concept of "women of color" nonviable as an organizing principle for scholarly work or activism, whether U.S. or internationally focused? Isn't the situation of minority group women in the United States categorically different from the status of "Third World" women in the countries of origin of their families or ancestors? Aren't the concerns of this subcategory of people covered adequately by "real law," that is, race- and gender-neutral law? If not, doesn't the U.S. race and gender discrimination law that has evolved primarily from the 1960s civil rights movements adequately protect women of color? Doesn't the post–World War II international legal regime that has developed principally since "First World" decolonization of most of the "Third World" encompass the legal problems of "Third World" women?

Critical Race Feminism is evolving as a richly textured genre interwoven with many areas of jurisprudence because the answer to all the above questions is a resounding "No!" As the articles in both my anthologies illustrate, existing legal paradigms under U.S., foreign, and international law have permitted women of color to fall through the cracks—becoming literally and figuratively voiceless and invisible. This volume attempts to not only identify and theorize about those cracks in the legal regime, but to formulate relevant solutions as well. Sometimes a little mortar will suffice, while in other instances an entire wall of a legal edifice must come down.

First, what about the validity of the term "women of color" as an organizing principle? Chandra Mohanty describes it as a sociopolitical designation for women of African, Caribbean, Asian, Latin American, and indigenous descent. Despite constituting a plurality of the world's people, women of color are usually situated on the bottom rung of each society, whether they live in developed or developing countries. The concept goes beyond mere color or racial identification. What all these women may have in common is their potential political relationship— likely an oppositional one—to sexist, racist, and imperialist structures.[2]

The authors in this collection are consciously engaged in revealing and challenging such discriminatory structures. As editor, I have deliberately chosen to feature predominantly the words of women of color themselves in an effort to break the silence and invisibility of such women in legal discourse. By foregrounding women of color, I am not saying that others can not write about the plight of these women. Men and Anglo women can certainly do so, and in this collection several of the contributors fall into one of these categories, most notably Professors Devon W. Carbado, J. Clay Smith, Jr., Taimie L. Bryant, Brenda J. Cossman, Mary L. Dudziak, Martha I. Morgan, and Zorica Mrsevic.

I do endorse, however, Mari Matsuda's notion of a "distinctive voice" that some (but certainly not all) people of color may possess in discussing the terms of their own oppression.[3] For example, in this volume Kiyoko Kamio Knapp, a Japanese scholar who came to the United States to earn her law degree, reveals a perspective in her essay on Japanese women that is informed to a large degree by her own status as a Japanese female. The distinguished UCLA professor Taimie Bryant also writes in these pages on Japanese women, but it cannot be from the same perspective as Knapp's. This is not to say that there is one essential Japanese view on an issue or that Bryant's views are wrong. They may even be similar to those of Ms. Knapp.

A more nuanced example of "distinctive voice" presents itself when two authors are both women of color, but from different ethnicities. For instance, I have written on the legal rights of both Black South African and Palestinian women, even though I belong to neither group. As an African American whose people have suffered discrimination for nearly four hundred years in the United States, I can empathize with the struggles of these women to confront various forms of oppression. I do not delude myself, however, that my perspective would be identical, much less superior, to that of a South African or a Palestinian woman.

All the authors in this collection are lawyers, and most are legal academics as well. Thus this book does not purport to directly represent the voices of the poorest women of color. The very notion of a "distinctive voice" for people of color has been attacked on class grounds by such conservative scholars as U.S. federal judge Richard Posner. He has challenged the validity of "elite" law professors like Richard Delgado who "claim" to speak on behalf of disenfranchised people of color.[4] I agree with Posner that we law professors of color are an elite, a tiny portion of groups disproportionately impoverished. I disagree wholeheartedly, however, with Judge Posner's inference that we therefore have no commonalities with the most oppressed people from our groups. I am quite certain that when Rodney King was beaten up by the Los Angeles police force, the officers did not ask him whether he was a lawyer. He was Black and animal-like, which justified their behavior in their own eyes. Elite class status as intellectuals does not shield people of color from racial attacks. Similarly, with respect to my gender, my job as a law professor does not shield me from the threat of rape.

As individuals writing about the concerns of disproportionately poor people of color, most authors in this collection have chosen to "look to the bottom" and identify with the oppressed, in the words of Mari Matsuda.[5] The assassinated African revolutionary leader Amilcar Cabral went even further and called for "class suicide" by intellectuals of color.[6] These concepts may characterize an aspect of what made the middle-class Reverend Dr. Martin Luther King sacrifice himself for the rights of the many poor Blacks. They may have influenced the Caribbean psychiatrist Frantz Fanon to write about the "wretched of the earth," and the lawyer Mohandas K. Gandhi to identify with the most despised class of Indians. The South African Xhosa tribal royal member/lawyer Nelson Mandela gave up the potential relative comfort of his privileged positions and said, "the struggle is my life." All these comparatively privileged individuals felt a tremendous sense of obligation and served as "translators" between the invisible, voiceless oppressed of their people and the power elite—the men who were the captains of industry, politics, and society. The weapons of communication varied from the pen to the sword, from nonviolent protest to armed struggle.

In this volume we are consciously attempting to translate between cultures—the cultures of privilege of those who have the luxury of time and capacity to read a book like this and the cultures of those who will never have the opportunity to enjoy such intellectual largesse. As translators, we therefore are assisting in demarginalizing the lives and legal concerns of women of color.[7]

GENESIS

GCRF originates from a collection of interrelated intellectual trends that emerged at the end of the twentieth century. It is my fervent hope that these colorful threads will continue to evolve into an increasingly interwoven tapestry that will have a place in global academic discourse in the twenty-first century. It is not that GCRF is a simple hybrid, but that the trends are "elements in the conditions of its possibility."[8] The three strands I will now briefly discuss are CLS, CRT, and feminism.[9]

The Conference on Critical Legal Studies was organized in the late 1970s by a "collection of neo-Marxist intellectuals, former New Left activists, ex-counter-culturalists, and other varieties of oppositionists in law schools."[10] Like these men, Critical Race feminists endorse a progressive perspective on the role of law in American society. We critique both conservative orthodoxies and legal liberalism. We challenge the notion of law as neutral, objective, and determinate. We may also use the deconstruction methodology of European postmodernists like Jacques Derrida and Michel Foucault to expose how law has served to perpetuate unjust class, race, and gender hierarchies.

As part of CRT, CRF extends beyond the intellectual borders of CLS. According to Harvard professor Cornel West, "CRT is a gasp of emancipatory hope that law can serve liberation rather than domination."[11] CRT constitutes a race intervention in leftist discourse and a leftist intervention in race discourse.[12] In illuminating the racist nature of the American legal system, CRT adherents are particularly interested in legal manifestations of white supremacy and the perpetuation of the subordination of people of color. While we are concerned with class issues since the majority of people of color are impoverished, we realize that poor communities of color have never been treated the same as the white underclass. Although CRT endorses the CLS notion that legal rights are indeterminate, we vehemently disagree that rights are therefore not important.[13] Indeed, the struggle to attain human rights remains critical for American minorities who have never had the luxury of taking such rights for granted.

In addition to challenging leftist discourse, CRT proponents also simultaneously engage in a leftist critique of liberal civil rights paradigms. We believe that racism has been an integral part of the American legal system since its founding, rather than an aberrational spot on the pristine white body politic. Racial progress is not necessarily inevitable, but may be cyclical. Gains often occur only if they are compatible with the self-interest of the white power elite.[14] We thus reject the notion that the legal system has ever been color-blind, and specifically embrace color consciousness and identity politics as the way to rectify today's racist legal legacies.[15] If racism was merely a spot, it could be cured with band-aid approaches like affirmative action, whose real purpose in the United States "is to create enough exceptions to white privilege to make the mythology of equal opportunity seem at least plausible."[16] Instead racism is like a cancer that permeates the body. It must be tackled with comprehensive approaches like the surgical, chemical, and/or radiation therapy of fundamental socioeconomic change. Despite the massive blitzkrieg, racism may persevere, spread, appear to be in remission for a while, only to reappear in a more virulent form. Some of the CRT adherents may even agree with a CRT founder, Professor Derrick Bell of New York University Law School, that racism is a permanent condition that can never be truly eradicated.[17]

Cornel West has carefully articulated some of the existential questions engaging CRT.

> How do we candidly incorporate experiences of intense alienation and subordination into the subtle way of "doing" theory in American academy? What are the new constructive frameworks that result from the radical critiques of the prevailing paradigms in United States legal education? What is our vocation as oppositional intellectuals who choose to stay in a legal academy of which we do not feel fully a part? How can liberation-minded scholars of color engage with white radical intellectuals without falling into the pitfalls of coalitions between such groups in the sixties?[18]

CRT also has begun to make contributions to international and comparative law discourse. For example, UCLA law professor Kimberlé Crenshaw has addressed the timely topic of globalization, which constitutes a racialized massive redistribution of wealth, power, and resources from the developing world to the developed—a form of economic apartheid. Richard Delgado has compared the treatment of hate speech in the United States with other constitutional systems where such speech is legally limited. Temple law professor Henry Richardson used a comparative analysis of international responses to the 1992 Los Angeles riots to show the poverty of American racial discourse. He and Villanova law professor Ruth Gordon have tackled the notion of "failed states," and shown how the espousal of a doctrine that would permit recolonization of failed states would be destructive to peoples of color internationally.[19]

As Critical Race theorists, CRF adherents sometimes use the controversial narrative or storytelling technique as methodology. Opponents have attacked this approach as nonlegal, lacking intellectual rigor, overly emotional, and subjective.[20] This methodology, however, has significant value. Many of us prize our heritages in which the oral tradition has had historical importance—where vital notions of justice and the law are communicated generation to generation through the telling of stories. Also, using stories enables us to connect to those who do not understand hypertechnical legal language, but may nonetheless seek understanding of our distinctive voices.[21] In this volume several authors use narrative techniques. For example, the Chinese lawyer Mai Chen details the multiple forms of discrimination she confronted growing up as a minority female in New Zealand. The Serbian feminist law professor Zorica Mrsevic uses the voices of Gypsy women in Serbia to illustrate the nature of their multilayered oppression.

We also believe in using critical historical methodology to demarginalize the roles people of color have played, usually outside the scope of the traditional historian's interests. In this volume, for example, the USC law professor Mary Dudziak explores the transnational fight waged by the entertainer Josephine Baker against U.S. racial injustice prior to the 1960s civil rights movement. Howard law professor J. Clay Smith, Jr., presents the global public service of the late Goler Butcher, an early Black female law professor.

Additionally, we endorse a multidisciplinary approach to scholarship in which the law may be a necessary, but not sufficient basis to formulate solutions to racial dilemmas. This book features significant citation to disciplines such as history, sociology, political science, economics, and anthropology, as well as African American studies and women's studies.

Although CRF proponents endorse Critical Race *Theory*, we wholeheartedly embrace critical race *praxis* as well.[22] Since many of us come from disenfranchised communities of color, we feel compelled to "look to the bottom," to involve ourselves in the development of solutions to our people's problems. We cannot afford to adopt the classic, detached, ivory tower model of scholarship when so many are suffering, sometimes in our own extended families. We do not believe in praxis instead of theory, but believe that both are essential to our peoples' literal and figurative future. For example, in this collection, the attorney Laura Ho combines her voice with those of law professors Catherine Powell and Leti Volpp to focus on the role of grassroots organizations as well as lawyers in assisting garment workers globally.

There are many forms that praxis can take. In addition to working with various public interest and nongovernmental organizations, Critical Race feminists have engaged in law reform in the United States and internationally. Coalition building, political activism, board memberships, speeches, and even writing can all be forms of praxis. My own attempts at praxis have included working with the actor and former star athlete Jim Brown's Amer-I-Can Program, a rehabilitative and preventive self-esteem curriculum ideally suited for youth at risk, ex-offenders, gang members, and others. This praxis enabled me to enrich my own efforts at theorizing about gang life. Internationally, I have advised the African National Congress Constitutional Committee on options for the democratic South Africa, as well as the Palestinian Legislative Council as it drafted the first constitution. Once again, these efforts enriched my subsequent scholarship and teaching on these topics.

Another jurisprudential tradition that CRF draws from is feminism. CRF constitutes a race intervention in feminist discourse, in that it necessarily embraces feminism's emphasis on gender oppression within a system of patriarchy. But most CRF proponents have not joined the mainstream feminist movement. While reasons vary, in some cases the refusal to become associated is due to that movement's essentialization of all women, which subsumes the variable experiences of women of color within the experience of white middle-class women.[23] Mainstream feminism has paid insufficient attention to the central role of white supremacy's subordination of women of color, effectuated by both white men and women. Nevertheless, some of the authors featured herein, such as St. Johns law professor Berta Esperanza Hernández-Truyol, pull from various prominent threads in feminism that may have relevance for their analysis, such as notions of formal equality, dominance/inequality, socialism, hedonic feminism, pragmatic feminism, radical feminism, and liberal feminism.

In developing our critiques of feminist jurisprudence, we have been influenced by feminists of color outside the legal academy. For example, scholars such as Patricia Hill Collins, Angela Davis, bell hooks, the late Audre Lorde, and Alice Walker have developed Black feminist or "womanist" notions that we have attempted to apply in legal contexts.

In addition to rejecting essentialism in feminism, Critical Race feminists reject CRT's essentialization of all minorities. As the experiences of males may differ significantly from those of females, we are thus a feminist intervention within CRT. Our anti-essentialist premise is that identity is *not* additive. In other words, Black women are not white women plus color, or Black men plus gender.

Through this volume, CRF goes beyond the domestic focus on the United States that is typical of most scholarship on CLS, CRT, and feminism, and embraces global or transnational perspectives. We are extending the narrow U.S. notion of race to examine the legal treatment of women of color, whether they are living in developing or industrialized societies. I hope that the works in this collection will inspire scholars to engage in looking at multiple levels of discrimination and privileging that women may simultaneously face globally, not only on the basis of their race and gender, but also due to their nationality, ethnicity, color, class, sexual orientation, age, disability, religion, primary language, minority status, pregnancy status, and marital status.

GLOBAL MULTIPLICATIVE IDENTITIES

As previously stated, Mari Matsuda coined the term "multiple consciousness" to describe the intersectional identities of women of color. In earlier scholarship, I have chosen to use the word "multiplicative" to configure identity. As a simplistic example, I am Black X female. If you multiply my identities, you have one indivisible being. You cannot subtract out any part of my identity, and ask me to pretend I am only a woman today or only a Black. Currently, I am in the beginning stages of developing a global perspective on identity that I would like to share here.[24] My initial premise is that everyone has multiple identities, not just women of color in the United States. Anglo-Saxon American males have multiple identities, and in a global context, most of their identities may privilege them. Women of color, on the other hand, may primarily possess a cluster of identities that lead them to face multiple forms of discrimination. But the analysis must become more complex. Even women of color, who are disproportionally impoverished, may have some identities that relatively privilege them. To assist women of color, we need to delineate their multiple identities, examine how those identities intersect to privilege or lead them to face discrimination, and then design multidimensional programs that would enhance their life situations.

I will now detail a number of identities that everyone has and, for simplicity's sake, discuss them separately. In reality, the impact of the intersection of the identities should be elaborated simultaneously.

For instance, one of the major identities we have is our nationality. While we are in our home country, that status might not be central to us on a daily basis. On the other hand, when I am traveling abroad, my American identity may privilege me or lead me to face discrimination. For example, every summer I teach in South Africa. When I go shopping in the stores, the white shopkeepers often frown at my brown face. As soon as I speak in my American accent, their faces beam and they are most helpful. I represent the almighty dollar. That same status has caused me to fear being robbed or ripped off, since I might be regarded as a "rich American." It took me a number of trips before I realized that indeed I am a rich American, at least as juxtaposed to the majority of Africans.

Even in the United States, my U.S. nationality may matter in many situations. I know that I can theoretically receive many benefits not open to "illegal aliens," legal tourists, foreign students, or even permanent residents.

Another central identity is race, which CRT and CRF naturally highlight. One tenet of CRT is that race is socially constructed, rather than biologically determined.[25] As a matter of fact, scientists have shown that there are often more genetic similarities across different so-called racial groups than within them. To illustrate how race is socially constructed globally, in the United States I am considered a member of the Black race. Both my parents and both sets of grandparents are African Americans. In South Africa, because of my light skin tone, shape of nose, and wavy hair texture, I am regarded as a Colored or mixed-race person. I am far too light to be considered Black. When I walk down the street there with my partner, who is a dark-skinned Black American, we are considered an interracial couple. In Brazil I discovered I am considered white! Only the darkest people of relatively unmixed African descent are considered Black in that country.

This example also illustrates the importance of an identity based on skin color. My skin tone has caused me to be called Latina, Indian, Arab, mulatto, biracial, and so forth. Within the Black American group, my coloring has historically led to a privileged position, because I am something known as "high yellow." The lighter-skinned Blacks have received benefits dating back to slavery, often because they were the master's illegitimate progeny. They may have become "house niggers" instead of field hands. Apparently the only slaves Thomas Jefferson freed upon his death were the children of his longtime slave mistress Sally Hemings. Several of these children immediately passed over into the white world, and the whereabouts of many of their descendants are unknown.

Today, lighter-skinned African Americans remain overrepresented in the numbers of Blacks who have attended college and attained professional status.[26] In my own maternal family's case, I am a third-generation college graduate in part because of the actions taken by my maternal great-great-grandfather, Confederate General Pierre Gustave Toutant Beauregard, who apparently set his quadroon daughter Susan on the path of higher education.[27] Paradoxically, we even have Blacks who are white in color, such as my former colleague, Dean Gregory Williams of Ohio State University Law School, who has written about his identity in his autobiography, *Life on the Color Line: The True Story of a White Boy Who Discovered He Was Black*. Internationally, I believe my skin tone has contributed to my warm acceptance in many countries. "You look just like my sister, mother, or aunt," I am often told.

Ethnicity is an interesting aspect of identity, but one that may be too often conflated with race, even in CRT-oriented scholarship. Although my skin color indicates many possible ethnicities, I am Black American or African American. Blacks who are from the Caribbean or Africa living in the United States may not consider themselves part of the same group to which I belong. At one law school in Florida there is a Black Law Students Association and a Caribbean student group as well. Imagine a white South African who moves to the United States and becomes a citizen. Isn't she an African American? I have cousins who are Jamaican Americans and Liberian Americans. Some consider themselves Black Americans and some do not.

Another identity can be one's status as a member of a minority group. While a Nigerian American is a minority in the United States and may be subjected to some discrimination or relative privileging, in Nigeria this person is obviously not a minority. Instead it may be their ethnic status as Yoruba or Hausa that helps or hinders them.

Religious affiliation is an important aspect of identity for many people. In the U.S. context, I am a secular mainstream denominational Protestant, and I do not often think about this status. When I travel to the Middle East, my identity as a Christian is juxtaposed with those around me who are mainly Muslim or Jewish. During the Palestinian uprising from 1987 to 1993, I visited the Gaza Strip several times. At one point, Islamic fundamentalists were stoning or throwing things at women who were not wearing a *hijab*, or head scarf. Even though I was a Christian and thus technically not subject to the admonition against bare heads, I put on the *hijab*.[28] Since my coloring and facial features indicate that I could be mistaken for a Palestinian, I was not willing to take a chance of trying to reason with a stone thrower.

With respect to gender, I will not belabor the point here since this identity is a central focus of this book. On a personal note, I recall amusedly the numerous incidents where people have visited my office, looked at me behind my desk, and asked, "Where is Professor Wing, where is he?" The assumption of many men and women is still that only men can be professors.

Interestingly, when traveling globally I am usually considered an "honorary male" and invited to dinners where no other women may be present. I have been served meals by women, who then retreat to a back room to eat with other women and children, as their men and I discuss politics, business, or international relations. My efforts to bridge the chasms of class, ethnicity, and culture that divide us are often defeated by our inability to speak the same language. Many wives have not had the same educational opportunities as their husbands to learn an international language like English. When I can communicate directly or through translation, I find that my identity as a mother is very valuable. As a mother of many sons, I am often considered multiply blessed and conversation may focus on the accomplishments of my fine young men.

My monolingual identity is a major inhibitor to my communication internationally, and that of most Americans. The hodge podge of French, Portuguese, Swahili, Spanish, and Arabic that I can utter does not substitute for the multilingual fluency needed for nuanced discourse. For example, if I must use male translators to ask uneducated Palestinian women how they feel about their lives, how am I to judge the filtered responses? What editing has occurred? What facial and tonal nuances have I missed because of my primary English-speaking identity? What fears do they have that I will get them in trouble with their menfolk as I satisfy my outsider curiosity?

Sexual orientation is an identity that heterosexuals rarely think about, since they are privileged on this basis. I did not realize how much my heterosexuality was part of my identity until lesbian friends pointed out the privileges I enjoyed every day: feeling free to talk about my partner, hold hands in public, place his picture in my office, slow dance at a club, and so forth. Thus even though I have felt discrimination as a Black woman, my situation is not the same as that of a Black lesbian. It is the work of such lesbians, like the late Audre Lorde, that helped me understand the holistic nature of identity:

> As a Black lesbian feminist comfortable with the many different ingredients of my identity, and a woman committed to racial and sexual freedom from oppression, I find I am constantly being encouraged to pluck out some one aspect of myself and present this as the meaningful whole, eclipsing or denying the other parts of myself. But this is a destructive and fragmenting way to live. My fullest concentration of energy is available to me only when I integrate all the parts of who I am, openly, allowing power from particular sources of my living to flow back and forth freely through all my different selves, without the restrictions of externally imposed definition. Only then can I bring myself and my energies as a whole to the service of those struggles which I embrace as part of my living.[29]

Marx, Engels, Lenin, and their followers developed socialist theory and left the world the legacy of class analysis. In the legal academy, CLS has developed a literature that addresses this aspect. Much of CRT focuses implicitly or explicitly on class, but sometimes conflates lower or working class with minority racial/ethnic status. As previously noted, some of the attacks on CRT criticize it for essentializing minorities, and have pondered how upper-class law professors of color dare speak for poor, oppressed masses.

Age is another aspect of identity, one that obviously changes over time. In some careers such as athletics, modeling, or acting for women, youth is a privileging identity. In other fields such as law, senior people may be accorded a respect and stature that elude the young. I keep thinking that one day when I go totally gray I will be treated with respect. My senior female colleagues assure me that this is definitely not the case for them as women. I also suspect that my relatively youthful appearance has exacerbated the voluminous amount of what is now termed "sexual harassment" in the United States, but is even more likely to still be viewed as good-natured, harmless fun abroad. My nationality and ethnicity intersect here to apparently lead some foreign men to blatantly ask me to go to bed with them. They think they know that American women are very promiscuous, and they have heard that Black American women are the sexiest. In my youth, I deeply resented the insinuation of American promiscuity. It took me a number of trips to realize that these leering men were at least partially correct. At the risk of "essentializing," American women as a class are more likely to engage in premarital sexual activity than can be the case for women in many developing countries, where virginity and chastity are highly valued and tightly controlled. Maybe my new status as a "bifocal granny" will confer more respect, and the harassment may decrease.

There are a number of other identities that may have important consequences at different stages of one's life. Anyone may join the ranks of the disabled on short notice. The stigma that still surrounds being mentally or physically disabled is often so profound as to cause those affected to hide or deny the status if they are able.

Marital status is a variable identity that has particular consequences for women. In the United States a woman's marital status may be instantly known if she uses Mrs. or Miss. I am sometimes asked if I married a Chinese man, because my surname is Wing. This name is my father's name and thus my "maiden" name, which I have never changed, despite being married. The divorced, widowed, single, or never married statuses can imply certain stereotypes about the desirability of a woman.

In delineating all these identities, I am not calling for balkanization ad infinitum. Strategic essentialism can be theoretically useful and practically necessary, particularly when the goal is to enhance our ability to design solutions for those subordinated in society. For example, current U.S. welfare reform efforts focus on class and gender—specifically poor women of color. Often implicit in the analysis is race, that is, concern for the Black "welfare queen." Yet there are many different types of welfare recipients. The needs of a minimum-wage Black lesbian single parent may be very different from those of a single white male who is mentally disabled and homeless. A Latina migrant worker, speaking very little English, married to an illegal alien who is battering her would have different requirements as well. These last examples have just highlighted several identities we have not mentioned previously, including immigration status.

Through this discussion of global multiplicative identity, I have provided a small example of what global CRF can bring to preexisting CRF concepts such as multiple consciousness. CRF also enhances the development of international and comparative law, which includes the subfields of public international law, human rights, international business transactions, and the comparative law of different countries. These are fields that developed primarily based on principles first enunciated by

American and European white male scholars. Men of color from the developing world did not become involved until their respective nations gained independence or sufficient clout in entities like the United Nations. Their voices are still muted, but often rise in discussions of cultural relativism and human rights. Western women have only recently become involved in attempting to reconceptualize international law from feminist perspectives.[30] Global feminists have noted that international law has failed to address what takes place in the private sphere of the family, where most women spend a significant part of their time.

One final thread contributing to the GCRF tapestry is postcolonial theory, which "is marked by a dialectic between Marxism, on the one hand, and poststructuralism/postmodernism, on the other . . . manifesting itself in an ongoing debate between the competing claims of nationalism and internationalism, strategic essentialism and hybridity, solidarity and dispersal, the politics of structure/totality and the politics of the fragment."[31] According to Leela Gandhi, postcolonialism's constituency is the "western academy and it enables nonwestern critics located in the west to present their cultural inheritance as knowledge."[32] Several authors featured in this volume fit into this latter category, including the Nigerian Lesyle Amede Obiora, the South African Penelope E. Andrews, Ghanaian Rosemary Ofeibea Ofei-Aboagye King, and the Japanese Kiyoko Knapp.

GCRF contributes to the development of international law, global feminism, and postcolonial theory by demarginalizing women of color in a theoretical and practical sense. Women of color may be simultaneously dominated in the context of imperialism, neocolonialism, or occupation as well as local patriarchy, culture, and customs. They have often had to choose between the nationalist struggle for independence or self-determination and the women's struggle against patriarchy. The nationalist struggle usually has prevailed, and the women who have just helped throw off the yoke of outsider oppression have then been forced back into the "women's work" of taking care of the house and children. Open acceptance of feminism can be seen as an unpatriotic embrace of Western values that may be regarded as inimical to local culture. One of the dilemmas for those who do choose to be known as feminists is how to embrace the universality of women's international human rights in their own cultural context. Despite the various difficulties, these women continue to insist on the complex interrelationships between feminist, antiracist, and nationalist struggles.[33]

THE ANTHOLOGY

Now that I have identified the intellectual threads that have contributed to the development of Global Critical Race Feminism, I will briefly introduce each part of the anthology and make a few comments about each contribution. When originally undertaking this project, I thought there would barely be enough material for one volume. I was pleasantly surprised to learn that I had enough material for several volumes. Unfortunately, space limitations do not permit such treatment at this time.

Thus I have carefully selected the pieces featured here as representative of some of the themes that GCRF is addressing.

Part 1 focuses on encounters with the "F" word: responses to feminism. The authors explore such questions as how to make the feminist theories developed primarily by white North American academics have relevance for women of color. What kinds of methodologies will enhance our understanding of their lives? Can liberation have different meanings in different cultural contexts? Can First World and Third World women collaborate effectively on feminist projects?

The Canadian Brenda Cossman situates her feminist analysis within the new approaches to comparative law movement and postcolonial theory. She explores "the possibilities of renegotiating the Anglo-American moorings of feminist legal studies, by displacing the unstated [Western] norms and center in favor of multiple norms and frames of reference." Her perspective has been influenced by her frequent collaboration with the Indian feminist lawyer Ratna Kapur.

New Mexico law professor Antoinette Sedillo Lopez is also a comparativist, and she calls for a clearly articulated methodology of feminist analysis in her contribution. Using her own research on abortion laws in Mexico and the United States, she develops a multipronged Critical Race feminist approach involving an assessment of both the relevant cultural and legal contexts. Sedillo Lopez's proposal dovetails with the "world traveling" methodology of Isabelle R. Gunning featured in her seminal article on female genital surgeries excerpted in the original *Critical Race Feminism* reader.[34] World traveling demands that we see ourselves in historical context, see ourselves as the "other" might see us, and see the "other" within her own complex cultural and legal context.

The prolific St. Johns Law School professor Berta Esperanza Hernández Truyol turns her gaze on the land of her birth and uses a contextualized methodology to deconstruct the nature of feminism in the Cuban context. In earlier work, she concluded that gender equality was a myth in that country. Here she reevaluates that position because gender equality in the Western feminist sense was never a goal of Cuban women's groups. While the Cuban movement has been very successful in its own cultural context, she ends with the question of whether a feminist movement can exist independent from notions of true equality. Her concluding query has implications for the research of the Islamic feminist scholar Azizah Y. al-Hibri, featured later in the collection.

While Cossman, Sedillo Lopez, and Hernández-Truyol concern themselves with comparative law, the young scholar Vasuki Nesiah boldly criticizes traditional feminist international human rights scholarship for its insularity, and calls for increased engagement between Third World and First World women. Nesiah anticipates my notions of multiplicative identity discussed above and desires to work toward "gendered understandings of the regulation of sexuality, class, race, nationality, and ethnicity."

The Puerto Rican feminist Celina Romany calls for international human rights law to use an intersectional approach to demarginalize the plight of Black women around the world. She also illustrates the "incoherence of a system of international protection built from the perspective of compartmentalized selves" that manifests itself in several major international agreements, including the Women's Convention and the Race Convention.

The international law scholar Hope Lewis is best known for her work on female genital surgeries that was excerpted in *Critical Race Feminism: A Reader.*[35] She ends the first part of the collection on a different note. She turns her gaze inward as Cossman suggests and overtly attempts to apply the hazily defined international right of development within the boundaries of the United States to the most disenfranchised groups of women of color. Endorsing the importance of rights discourse that characterizes Critical Race Theory, Lewis implicitly calls for a feminism that embraces transformative coalition building to reconceptualize women's economic development projects.

Part 2 continues Lewis's focus on the Third World that exists in the First World. While she was concerned with the United States, the primary locus for most CRT and CRF theorists, the authors in part 2 demarginalize the treatment of minorities in Europe and New Zealand. Questions for the reader to ponder include, What similarities and differences in oppression do these minorities face as compared to U.S. based groups? Does American antidiscrimination law or affirmative action policy have anything to offer to societies with different conceptualizations and awareness of discrimination? Could culturally relevant forms of feminist theory and praxis evolve in these societies that would assist the women in helping themselves and pressuring majority group male power elites?

In the context of British postcolonialism, UCLA law professor Devon Carbado tackles the question of whether the oppressed are oppressed, even if they do not feel their own oppression. He deconstructs the nature of motherhood, work, and patriarchy—effectively interspersing the narrative voice of his Jamaican immigrant mother. Despite the patriarchal bargain she has made that mandates work inside and outside the home, she maintains a positive self-image as she struggles to raise nine children in the belly of the former colonizer Great Britain. She does not consider herself a multiply oppressed victim. "A lived my life de wey A wanted to." Yet her "freedom" in the context of their family life was really her husband's.

We turn from the concerns of a poor female immigrant of color to a privileged woman in the chapter by Mai Chen, a Chinese lawyer and professor who movingly recounts her spirit injuries in simultaneously confronting race and sex discrimination growing up "down under." Spirit injury is a Critical Race feminist notion that connotes the psychological consequences of discrimination.[36]

Returning to the European context, the senior scholar Judy Scales-Trent conducted exciting original research demarginalizing the little known lives of immigrant women in France in the postcolonial period. These women must simultaneously confront race/ethnicity, gender, class, religious, and customary law restrictions in a country that has never exorcised all its demons from the colonial era. The multiplicative and nuanced nature of their oppression has been revealed in such well-publicized episodes as whether young Muslim girls can wear head scarves in French public schools. It is to be hoped that this article will be the basis for a book-length treatment of the subject by Scales-Trent, the author of the compelling autobiography *Notes of a White Black Woman: Race, Color, Community*.

The final selection in part 2 presents another piece of original research conducted for this anthology. The Serbian feminist Zorica Mrsevic illustrates a CRT tenet on the social construction of race in her chapter on Gypsy women in Serbia. From an American racial perspective, the Gypsies would be considered "white." Yet in the Serbian context, they are literally considered "Black," and treated in all the derogatory ways that this status prompts in the United States. Mrsevic's work benefits from the voices of abused Gypsy women, who also reveal how Gypsy patriarchy intersects with Serbian societal oppression. An interesting follow-up study would be to attempt to chart the impact of the Bosnian and Kosovo conflicts on how Serbians treat Gypsy women.

Part 3 illustrates the use of critical theory historical method to reveal women of color who have been pathbreakers and founding mothers. The work of the three scholars featured here raises the question of how history can be more than accolades to male power elites. Can these women be role or goal models for everyone, especially other women of color? How can their stories be taken from the margins to the center of historical discourse? The legal historian Mary Dudziak is best known for her article "Desegregation as a Cold War Imperative."[37] In this collection she produces another piece of Cold War scholarship focusing on the Black American entertainer/activist Josephine Baker. Dudziak meticulously combed U.S. government archives to portray the threat that Baker was felt to represent to American interests as she boldly denounced U.S. race discrimination laws in her travels to foreign countries. Baker did not wallow in victimhood, even when her livelihood and home were threatened. She waged her struggle in the private sphere as well, raising a "Rainbow Tribe" of twelve children.

J. Clay Smith, Jr., another legal historian, is the editor of *Rebels in Law: Voices in History of Black Women Lawyers*. Here he brings us a more contemporary and less well known example of a "(s)he-ro." He explores the unsung role that the late Goler Teal Butcher, international lawyer and Howard law professor, played with respect to shaping U.S. foreign policy on Africa.

Alabama law professor Martha Morgan collaborates with her former student Mónica María Alzate Buitrago to take us beyond the U.S. context. They highlight a society in which there were founding mothers as well as fathers of a constitution. They explore how Colombian women managed to play both formal and informal roles in the attainment of progressive gender provisions, despite conditions of machismo and narcotrafficking violence. American feminists may have much to learn from the Colombian experience in the event that the question of constitutionally enshrined gender equality is tackled again in the United States.

Part 4 expands on the concerns raised by Morgan and various authors who grapple with the question of how law can successfully challenge the entrenched norms that prevent women, especially women of color, from reaching their full human potential.

The Islamic scholar Azizah al-Hibri produces a provocative contribution that challenges the Western notion that Islamic law must be patriarchal, oppressive, and incompatible with human rights. Additionally, it challenges Islamic interpretations that assume that patriarchy is divinely ordained. Al-Hibri's feminist intervention posits that Islam can be stripped of its false patriarchal presumptions in a way that permits women to remain true to their faith and achieve equality as well.

UCLA law professor Taimie Bryant takes us to Asia for the first time in the collection in her extensively researched work on the Japanese family registration system. She explicates the patriarchal nature of the regime, which is shored up by deeply rooted hierarchical Confucian ideology, despite the post–World War II imposition of more egalitarian constitutional norms. To alter the system, Bryant radically calls for a praxis based on Japanese majority group women working in coalition with other disadvantaged groups, including the shunned *burakumin* minority, immigrant Koreans, and out-of-wedlock children.

In her chapter on female infanticide in China, Sharon K. Hom speaks from the postcolonial borderlands: "an American by citizenship; a British colonial subject by birth; a Chinese American by culture." She immerses us in the custom that has been exacerbated as China attempts to impose the one-child policy on a society with a historical preference for boys: female infanticide. Interspersing narrative in her analysis of the Women's Convention, Hom looks toward a twenty-first-century future in which all children would be valued, and human rights conventions would be "superfluous anachronisms of a more primitive time."

The next two selections tackle the universalism versus cultural relativism debate in international human rights law within the context of female genital surgeries (FGS), alternatively known as female circumcision or female genital mutilation. Is FGS an outright abomination and violation of the human rights of women and girls that must be universally condemned or is there room for various cultural practices like FGS to continue, especially if they are endorsed by many of the "oppressed" women who have undergone them?

The discussion represents a dialogue between two prominent legal academics in the field. The Nigerian scholar Lesyle Obiora calls for medical clinicalization of the practice. In her view, performing a relatively symbolic procedure under hygienic circumstances would constitute a middle course between absolute universality (ban it altogether) and absolute relativity (leave us alone).

The African American professor Isabelle Gunning agrees with Obiora that there are "racist and hypocritical manipulations of the imagery and lives of African women" in the anti-FGS campaign. Nevertheless, she finds Obiora's clinicalization approach insufficient without a broader context of opposition to FGS practices. Additionally, Gunning posits that Obiora essentializes the views of Western feminists in the same way that she claims that Western feminists monolithically portray the lives and views of African women.

Lisa A. Crooms addresses cultural relativism in the United States in the closing selection. Although the United States has not yet signed the Women's Convention, the author brings its refreshing perspectives to the public housing problem, which has heretofore been regarded only through the U.S. law lens. "Unless and until the United States abandons its reactionary and conservative brand of cultural relativism, the integrity of the rights of women within its borders, particularly poor women, will remain compromised."

Part 5 presents another example of the clash between custom and human rights: violence against women, whether it be family terrorism, rape, or sexual harassment. While the O. J. Simpson trial and the Anita Hill–Clarence Thomas hearings popularized these issues in the United States, these contributors illustrate the universality of the problem in culturally specific contexts. Penelope Andrews speaks from the borderlands of multiplicative identity mentioned by her colleague Sharon Hom. But in Andrews's case, she is a South African–born Coloured woman who lives in New York and holds Australian citizenship as well. She demarginalizes the nature of violence against the minority Aboriginal women in Australia. She then creatively speculates about the possibilities for redress within human rights paradigms for this multiply oppressed group of women who must deal with the legacy of Anglo colonialism and patriarchy coupled with Aboriginal patriarchal practices as well.

Another borderlands scholar, the Canadian-based Ghanaian professor Rosemary Ofei-Aboagye King draws our attention to domestic violence in postcolonial Ghana, "The largest problem in (not) talking about domestic violence is its nonproblem status." She provides us with narrative analysis on two levels. First, we hear the voices of the abused women themselves, who were surveyed as clients of the Legal Aid Clinic of the International Federation of Women Lawyers. King also critically analyzes Ghanaian folk tales to reveal how they continue to support women's mistreatment. Her proposed solutions include further research, teaching methods of self-help, and communal education that can acknowledge and incorporate tradition.

My own contribution to the discussion is a comparative analysis of the violence problem in South Africa and Palestine. I speculate about the feasibility of using international human rights agreements, such as the Women's Convention coupled with the incorporation of gender equality on the constitutional level, and implementing legislation as well. South Africa can serve as a model for the world since its 1996 constitution even contains a clause prohibiting both public and private violence. Praxis must be based on effectively linking grassroots organizations with the police, legal system, academy, and family.

City University of New York law professor Jenny Rivera then returns us to the North American context and her homeland as she analyzes our "pseudocolony" Puerto Rico's Ley 54, the Domestic Violence Prevention and Intervention Law. She hopes her preliminary assessment of the case law, illustrating the limited efficacy of this "model" statute battling machismo, will be useful in other jurisdictions.

Finally, the young lawyer Gaby Oré-Aguilar looks at sexual harassment and human rights in Latin America. Her brief visionary exegesis advocates that sexual harassment be characterized as a gender-based act of violence under international human rights law and national legislation in the countries of the region.

Part 6 ends the collection with a focus on the global workplace. It illustrates that those concerned with the rights of women of color, who constitute the most subordinated groups of workers, cannot limit their vigilance to their local or national boundaries. As the new century commences, global capitalism appears triumphant over socialism. Is it possible for national legislation and international law to work together to police multinational corporations that are richer than many developing nations? What can be done to enhance the economic opportunities for women of color with safe, well-paid working conditions? How can we prevent the last hired, first fired syndrome that seems to plague women the world over?

The attorney Laura Ho and Professors Catherine Powell and Leti Volpp collaborate to address some of these questions in their chapter on women workers in the world-wide garment industry. They confront those of us in the North with the query, "My sister makes my blouse. Are my hands clean?" The chapter examines the challenges that U.S.–based female garment workers face in asserting their human rights since U.S. labor law is unable to effectively serve their needs. The authors present multiple, al-ternative global strategies to spur creative thinking on building "transnational soli-darity among workers, among women, and among communities."

The former law firm partner Anna M. Han provides a comparative law perspective on her homeland in her chapter on marketization and the status of women in China. Although the implementation of capitalist economic principles may be positive for the largest communist country as a whole, it has had an unanticipated impact on female workers. Whatever its political shortcomings, communism greatly enhanced women's economic status and ability to transcend deeply rooted patriarchal norms. The author leaves us with the question of how Chinese women will regain the lost ground and continue forward on the long march toward gender equality.

The attorney Kiyoko Kamio Knapp ends the collection with another foreign law selection in her essay on Japanese Equal Employment Opportunity Law (EEOL). Japan's global economic success has not included transcendence of cultural norms that regard women as "office flowers." In her analysis, the EEOL emerges as a mere ornament totally inadequate to the enormity of the task. She calls for Japan to one day become a society where "harmonizing work life with family life should be a true goal for both men and women."

NOTES

At the end of this introduction I have included a brief bibliography of some general sources on feminist approaches to international/global legal issues. The bibliography at the end of the book contains a large number of additional works that focus on the legal status of women of color globally. It also contains the full citations to the articles in this collection that have been previously published. Due to space limitations, I had to severely edit many of these wonderful pieces, deleting much text and many of the rich endnotes to which American legal scholarship is addicted. These deletions are not indicated in the edited text. I encourage you to seek the unedited versions. One advantage of the editing process is that almost all au-thors had a chance to review the edited versions, and some chose to update their previous work. Since the previously published articles came from a wide variety of sources, I decided to standardize the citations to conform to *The Bluebook: A Uniform System of Citation* (16th edition). The *Bluebook* font styles are not followed, however.

1. Mari Matsuda, *When the First Quail Calls: Multiple Consciousness as Jurisprudential Method*, 11 Women's Rts. L. Rep. 7 (1989).

2. Chandra Mohanty, *Introduction: Cartographies of Struggle, in* Third World Women and the Politics of Feminism 7 (Chandra Mohanty et al. eds., 1991).

3. Mari Matsuda, *Looking to the Bottom: Critical Legal Studies and Reparations*, 22 Harv. C.R.-C.L. L. Rev. 323 (1987).

4. Richard Posner, book review of Daniel A. Farber and Suzanna Sherry, Beyond All Reason: The Radical Assault on Truth in American Law, New Republic, Oct. 13, 1997, at 40.

5. Matsuda, *supra* note 3.

6. *Identity and Dignity in the Context of the National Liberation Struggle, in* Return to the Source: Selected Speeches of Amilcar Cabral 57 (Africa Information Service ed., 1973).

7. *See* Kimberlé Crenshaw, *Demarginalizing the Intersection of Race and Sex: A Black Feminist Critique of Antidiscrimination Doctrine, Feminist Theory, and Antiracist Politics*, 1989 U. Chi. Legal F. 139.

8. Kimberlé Crenshaw, *Introduction* to Critical Race Theory: The Key Writings that Formed the Movement xix (Kimberlé Crenshaw et al. eds., 1996).

9. For sample publications on CLS, see, e.g., Critical Legal Studies (James Boyle ed., 1992); Critical Legal Studies (Peter Fitzpatrick and Alan Hunt eds., 1987); Critical Legal Studies (Alan Hutchinson ed., 1989); Mark Kelman, A Guide to Critical Legal Studies (1987). For anthologies on CRT, see Crenshaw, *supra* note 8 and Critical Race Theory: The Cutting Edge (Richard Delgado ed., 1995).

There are affiliated critical networks, such as Critical White Studies, Critical White Studies: Looking Behind the Mirror (Richard Delgado and Jean Stefancic eds., 1997); Lat-Crit Theory, The Latino Condition: A Critical Reader (Richard Delgado ed., 1998); Symposium, *Lawyering in Latina/o Communities: Critical Race Theory and Practice*, 9 La Raza L.J. (1996); Symposium, *Lat-Crit Theory: Naming and Launching a New Discourse of Critical Legal Scholarship*, 2 Harv. Latino L. Rev. (1997); Colloquium, *International Law, Human Rights and LatCrit Theory*, 28 U. Miami Inter-Am. L. Rev. 177 (1996–97); as well as Asian crits, Robert S. Chang, *Toward an Asian American Legal Scholarship: Critical Race Theory, Post-Structuralism, and Narrative Space*, 81 Cal. L. Rev. 1244 (1993). Articles on Queer legal theory include Francisco Valdes, *Queers, Sissies, Dykes, and Tomboys: Deconstructing the Conflation of "Sex," "Gender," and "Sexual Orientation" in* Euro-American Law and Society, 1995 Cal. L. Rev. 1; Elvia Arriola, *Gendered Inequality: Lesbians, Gays, and Feminist Legal Theory*, 9 Berkeley Women's L.J. 103 (1994).

For collections on feminism, see, e.g., Feminist Legal Theory (Frances E. Olsen ed., 1995); Feminist Legal Theory: Foundations (D. Kelly Weisberg ed., 1993); Matthew H. Kramer, Critical Legal Theory and the Challenge of Feminism: A Philosophical Reconception (1995); Lisa R. Pruitt, *A Survey of Feminist Jurisprudence*, 16 U. Ark Little Rock L.J. 183 (1994).

10. Crenshaw, *supra* note 8, at xvii.

11. Cornel West, *Foreword* to Crenshaw, *supra* note 8, at xii.

12. Crenshaw, *supra* note 8, at xix.

13. *See* Patricia Williams, *Alchemical Notes: Reconstructing Ideals from Deconstructed Rights*, 22 Harv. C.R.-C.L. L. Rev. 401 (1987).

14. *See* Derrick Bell, *Brown v. Board of Education and the Interest Convergence Dilemma*, 93 Harv. L. Rev. 518 (1980).

15. *See* Neil Gotunda, *A Critique of "Our Constitution Is Color-Blind,"* 44 Stan. L. Rev. 1 (1991); Gary Peller, *Race Consciousness*, 1990 Duke L.J. 758.

16. Crenshaw, *supra* note 8, at xxix.

17. *See* Derrick Bell, Faces at the Bottom of the Well: The Permanence of Racism (1992).

18. West, *supra* note 11, at xi.

19. *See* Crenshaw, *supra* note 8, at xxx, *citing* Arjun Makhijani; Richard Delgado, *Words That Wound: A Tort Action for Racial Insults, Epithets, and Name Calling, in* Critical Race Theory: The Cutting Edge, *supra* note 9, at 159; Henry J. Richardson III, *The International Implications of the Los Angeles Riots*, 70 Denv. U. L. Rev. 213 (1993); Henry J. Richardson III, *"Failed States," Self-Determination and Preventative Diplomacy: Colonialist Nostalgia and Democratic Expectations*, 10 Temp. Int'l and Comp. L.J. 1 (1996); Ruth E. Gordon, *United Nations Intervention in International Conflicts: Iraq, Somalia and Beyond*, 15 Mich. J. Int'l L. 519 (1994). Richardson discusses these citations in *Dinner and Self Determination*, a paper presented at the Critical Race Theory Conference, November 15, 1997.

20. For examples of the narrative technique, see, e.g., the works of Derrick Bell, such as And We Are not Saved: The Elusive Quest for Racial Justice (1987); and Richard Delgado, such as the Rodrigo Chronicles (1995). For critics, see, e.g., Daniel A. Farber and Suzanna Sherry, Beyond All Reason: The Radical Assault on Truth in American Law (1997).

21. Matsuda, *supra* note 1; Richard Delgado, *When a Story is Just a Story: Does Voice Really Matter*, 76 Va. L. Rev. 95 (1990).

22. *See, e.g.,* Adrien Katherine Wing, *Brief Reflections toward a Multiplicative Theory and Praxis of Being*, 6 Berkeley Women's L.J. 181 (1990–91).

23. *See* Angela P. Harris, *Race and Essentialism in Feminist Legal Theory*, 42 Stan. L. Rev. 581 (1990); Crenshaw, *supra* note 7.

24. Some of this section was initially delineated in Adrien Katherine Wing, *Violence and State Accountability: Critical Race Feminism*, 1 Georgetown J. Gender, Sexuality and L. 95 (1999).

25. For an analysis of the American social construction of race, see Ian Haney Lopez, White by Law (1997).

26. *See* Kathy Russell, Midge Wilson, and Ronald Hall, The Color Complex: The Politics of Skin Color among African Americans (1992).

27. For more on Beauregard, see T. Harry Williams, P. G. T. Beauregard: Napoleon in Gray (1955).

28. I have written extensively on Palestine. *See, e.g.,* Adrien Katherine Wing, *Custom, Religion, and Rights: The Future Legal Status of Palestinian Women*, 35 Harv. Int'l L.J. 149 (1994); and items listed in the bibliography to this volume.

29. Audre Lorde, *Age, Race, Class and Sex: Redefining Difference, in* Out There: Marginalization and Contemporary Cultures 285 (Russell Ferguson et al. eds., 1990).

30. For examples of global feminist jurisprudence, see the bibliography at the end of this introduction.

31. Leela Gandhi, PostColonial Theory: A Critical Introduction viii–ix (1998).

32. *Id.* at ix.

33. Mohanty, *supra* note 2.

34. Isabelle Gunning, *Arrogant Perception, World Traveling, and Multicultural Feminism: The Case of Female Genital Surgeries, in* Critical Race Feminism: A Reader 352 (Adrien Katherine Wing ed., 1997).

35. *See* Hope Lewis, *Between Irua and "Female Genital Mutilation": Feminist Human Rights Discourse and the Cultural Divide, in* Critical Race Feminism, *supra* note 34, at 352.

36. Wing, *supra* note 22. The term derives from spirit murder, coined by CRF foremother

Patricia Williams in *Spirit Murdering the Messenger: The Discourse of Fingerpointing as the Law's Response to Racism,* 42 U. Miami L. Rev. 127 (1987).
    37. 41 Stan. L. Rev. 61 (1988).

BIBLIOGRAPHY ON WOMEN'S INTERNATIONAL HUMAN RIGHTS

Amnesty International. Women in the Front Line: Human Rights Violations against Women (1991).

Arzt, Donna. *The Application of International Human Rights Law in Islamic States,* 12 Hum. Rts. Q. 202 (1990).

Askin, Kelly D. War Crimes against Women: Prosecution in International War Crimes Tribunals (1997).

Askin, Kelly D., and Dorean Koenig. Women's International Human Rights: A Reference Guide (4 vols.) (1999).

Bouvard, Marguerite Guzman. Women Reshaping Human Rights: How Extraordinary Activists Are Changing the World (1996).

Bunch, Charlotte. *Women's Rights as Human Rights: Toward a Re-Vision of Human Rights,* 12 Hum. Rts. Q. 486 (1990).

Byrnes, Andrew, and Jane Connors. *Enforcing the Human Rights of Women: A Complaints Procedure for the Women's Convention?,* 21 Brook. J. Int'l L. 679 (1996).

Charlesworth, Hilary. *A Feminist Critique of the Right to Development,* 12 Austl. Y. B. Int'l L. (1992).

————. *Feminist Critiques of International Law and Their Critiques,* 1995 Third World Legal Studies 1 (1994–1995).

————. *The Public/Private Distinction and the Right to Development in International Law,* 12 Austl. Y. B. Int'l L. (1992).

Charlesworth, Hilary, Christine M. Chinkin, and Shelley Wright. *Feminist Approaches to International Law,* 85 Am. J. Int'l L. 613 (1991).

Coliver, Sandra. *United Nations Commission on the Status of Women: Suggestions for Enhancing Its Effectiveness,* 9 Whittier L. Rev. 435 (1987).

Cook, Rebecca J. *International Protection of Women's Reproductive Rights,* 24 N.Y.U. J. Int'l L. and Pol. 645 (1992).

————. *The International Right to Nondiscrimination on the Basis of Sex: A Bibliography,* 14 Yale J. Int'l L. 161 (1989).

————. *Women's International Human Rights: A Bibliography,* 24 N.Y.U. J. Int'l L. and Pol. 857 (1992).

————. *Women's International Human Rights Law: The Way Forward,* 15 Hum. Rts. Q. 230 (1993).

————, ed. Human Rights of Women: National and International Perspectives (1994).

Copelon, Rhonda. *Introduction: Bringing Beijing Home,* 21 Brook. J. Int'l L. 599 (1996).

Daley, Caroline, and Melanie Nolan. Suffrage and Beyond: International Feminist Perspectives (1995).

Dallmeyer, Dorinda. Reconceiving Reality: Women and International Law (1993).

Dolgopol, Ustinia. *Women's Voices, Women's Pain,* 17 Hum. Rts. Q. 127 (1995).

Engle, Karen. *International Human Rights and Feminism: When Discourses Meet,* 13 Mich. J. Int'l L. 517 (1992).

Gallagher, Anne. *Ending the Marginalization: Strategies for Incorporating Women into the United Nations Human Rights System*, 19 Hum. Rts. Q. 283 (1997).

Grewal, Inderpal, and Caren Kaplan. *Transnational Feminist Practices and Questions of Postmodernity, in* Scattered Hegemonies: Postmodernity and Transnational Feminist Practices (1994).

Halberstam, Malvina, and Elizabeth F. Defeis. Women's Legal Rights: International Covenants an Alternative to ERA? (1987).

Hauge, H. *Prostitution of Women and International Human Rights Law: Transforming Exploitation into Equality*, 8 N.Y. Int'l L. Rev. 23 (1995).

Hernández-Truyol, Berta Esperanza. *Sex, Culture and Rights: A Reconceptualization of Violence for the Twenty-first Century*, 60 Albany L. Rev. 607 (1997).

———. *Women's Rights as Human Rights—Rules, Realities and the Role of Culture*, 21 Brook. J. Int'l L. 605 (1996).

Higgins, Tracey. *Anti-Essentialism, Relativism, and Human Rights*, 19 Harv. Women's L.J. 89, 104 (1996).

International Human Rights Law Group. *No Justice, No Peace: Accountability for Rape and Gender Based Violence in the Former Yugoslavia*, 5 Hastings Women's L.J. 89 (1994).

International Women's Tribune Centre Staff. Rights of Women: A Guide to the Important United Nations Treaties for Women's Human Rights (1998).

Kim, Nancy. *Toward a Feminist Theory of Human Rights: Straddling the Fence between Western Imperialism and Uncritical Absolutism*, 25 Colum. Hum. Rts. L. Rev. 49 (1993).

Langley, Winston E. Women's Rights in International Documents: A Source Book with Commentary (1991).

MacKinnon, Catharine A. *Rape, Genocide, and Women's Human Rights*, 17 Harv. Women's L.J. 5 (1994).

Mahoney, Kathleen. *Theoretical Perspectives on Women's Human Rights and Strategies for Their Implementation*, 21 Brook. J. Int'l L. 799 (1996).

Martin, J. P. Women and Human Rights: The Basic Documents (1996).

McConnell, Moira L. *Violence against Women: Beyond the Limits of the Law*, 21 Brook. J. Int'l L. 899 (1996).

Mehra, Madhu. *Exploring the Boundaries of Law, Gender and Social Reform*, 6 Feminist Legal Stud. 59 (1998).

Moon, Gillian. Making Her Rights a Reality: Papers in Women's Human Rights and Development (1997).

Morgan, Robin. Sisterhood Is Global: The International Women's Anthology (1984).

Morsink, Johannes. *Women's Rights in the Universal Declaration*, 13 Hum. Rts. Q. 229 (1991).

Neft, Naomi, and A. Levine. Where Women Stand: An International Report on the Status of Women in Over 140 Countries 1997–1998 (1997).

Olsen, Frances E. Feminist Legal Theory (The International Library of Essays in Law and Legal Theory) Vols. 1 and 2 (1995).

Orford, Anne. *Contesting Globalization: A Feminist Perspective on the Future of Human Rights*, 8 Transnat'l L. and Contemp. Prob 171 (1998).

Packer, Corinne A. A. The Right to Reproductive Choice: A Study in International Law (1996).

Peters, Julie Stone, and Andrea Wolper, eds. Women's Rights, Human Rights: International Feminist Perspectives (1995).

Poe, Steven C., Dierdre Wendel-Blunt, and Karl Ho. *Global Patterns in the Achievement of Women's Human Rights to Equality,* 19 Hum. Rts. Q. 813 (1997).

Rassam, A. Yasmine. Women in Domicile: The Treatment of Women's Work in International Law (1994).

Ray, Amy E. *The Shame of It: Gender Based Terrorism in the Former Yugoslavia and the Failure of International Human Rights Law to Comprehend the Injuries,* 46 Am. U. L. Rev. 793 (1997).

Rhoodie, Eschel. Discrimination against Women: A Global Survey (1989).

Romany, Celina. *Women as Aliens: A Feminist Critique of the Public/Private Distinction in International Human Rights Law*, 6 Harv. Hum. Rts. J. 87 (1993).

Rupp, Leila J. Worlds of Women: The Makings of an International Women's Movement (1998).

Shohat, Ella, ed. Talking Visions: Multicultural Feminism in a Transnational Age (1998).

Stark, Barbara. *Nurturing Rights: An Essay on Women, Peace and International Human Rights,* 13 Mich. J. Int'l L. 144 (1991).

Thomas, Dorothy. *Advancing Rights Protection in the United States: An International Advocacy Strategy*, 9 Harv. Hum. Rts. J. 15 (1996).

Thomas, Dorothy, and Michele E. Beasley. *Domestic Violence as a Human Rights Issue,* 15 Hum. Rts. Q. 36 (1993).

Tomasevski, Katarina. Women and Human Rights (1993).

Tomasevski, Katarina, and Gudmundur Alfredsson. Thematic Guide to Documents on the Human Rights of Women: Global and Regional Standards Adopted by Intergovernmental Organizations, International Non-Governmental Organizations and Professional Associations (1995).

Wetzel, Janice Wood. The World of Women: In Pursuit of Human Rights (1992).

Wolper, Andrea, and J. S. Peters. Women's Rights, Human Rights: International Feminist Perspectives (1995).

Woo, Margaret. *Biology and Equality: Challenge for Feminism in the Liberal and Socialist State*, 42 Emory L.J. 143 (1993).

1 | Encounters with the "F" Word

Responses to Feminism

1

Turning the Gaze Back on Itself

Comparative Law, Feminist Legal Studies, and the Postcolonial Project

Brenda J. Cossman

The Canadian filmmaker Atom Egoyan has described his recent production of Richard Strauss's operatic libretto *Salome* with the Canadian Opera Company as an exploration of "the danger of looking when the gaze is not returned."[1] The exotic young woman Salome desires the gaze of others. John the Baptist, who refuses to give Salome the gaze she so desires, pays with his life. Her stepfather, Herod, who cannot stop looking at Salome, and who makes her dance the Dance of the Seven Veils, must pay by fulfilling Salome's wish of revenge: he must order the prophet killed and his head delivered to Salome on a silver platter. Ultimately, Salome's obsession with being looked at, John the Baptist's refusal to look, and Herod's inability to stop looking lead to Salome's own death.

The gaze in Egoyan's *Salome* is not a simple one. Salome is not passively objectified, but seemingly empowered through the gaze of others. She, too, is obsessed with gaze—of others looking at her, valuing her, and desiring her. But this too has a price. In the end, the power she apparently acquires from the gaze of others cannot save her from her own act of transgression—she desires too much and ultimately brings about her own death. In *Salome,* the power of the gaze is ambivalent. Is it objectifying or empowering? Is the recipient of the gaze a desiring subject or a passive object? And what is the danger of looking when the gaze is not returned? Is it simply that we will not see all there is to see? Is it that we assume that the other is observable, knowable in an objective and quantifiable way? Is it that we force the other to pay for our desire to look? Or is it that we will pay for our voyeurism? Egoyan provides no simple answers, but tells us only that our voyeuristic desires can lead us to dangerous places.

Comparative law can be seen to be haunted by the ghosts of Salome. The danger of looking when the gaze is not returned is indeed a real danger for comparative

Reprinted by permission from 1997 *Utah Law Review* 525.

law. To state the obvious, comparative law invariably involves comparison—something is always being compared to something else. It therefore invariably encounters all the dilemmas of comparison—of unstated norms against which difference is viewed and judged. In the context of comparative law, the geopolitical location of the author becomes the unstated norm against which the exotic "other" is viewed. It is a project that is perhaps inherently ethnocentric—there is no way to escape or transcend the ethnocentric gaze. If this gaze is inescapable, some might be tempted to abandon it altogether. After all, in *Salome,* the ultimate act of resistance was to refuse to look—to deny Salome the gaze that she so desired. And so, in comparative law, would the ultimate act of resistance be the refusal to look, to compare? It is an act of resistance, however, that comes with an extraordinary price: comparative law, like John the Baptist, would pay with its life.

But, if, as *Salome* also suggests, the power of the gaze is ambivalent, then perhaps we need not demand that comparative law sacrifice itself so completely. There may be different ways of negotiating the ethnocentric gaze of comparative law without falling into a cultural relativism that would abandon the very project of looking beyond. Such a refusal to look outside ourselves and our culture would after all undermine one of the most basic objectives of the postcolonial project, that is, exploring the transnational flows of culture and the ways the colonial binaries—us/them, here/there, West/non-West, colonizer/colonized—have long been mutually constituting.

In this chapter I explore some of the ways the ethnocentric gaze of comparative law might be negotiated in the specific context of comparative law's encounter with feminism. The challenge of ethnocentrism is a familiar one in the feminist project in recent years. On the one hand, the unstated norms of feminist theory and practice have become the site of intensive contestation from within—women whose lives do not accord with these norms have demanded that the partiality of feminism's vision be recognized and then radically transformed. On the other hand, feminism has also been a site of contestation from without—from those who endeavor not to expand its embrace, but to radically curtail it. It has been denounced as quintessentially Western and therefore utterly devoid of cultural legitimacy in non-Western contexts.

The feminist project in recent years has become increasingly adept at negotiating this hazardous terrain somewhere in between un–self-critical ethnocentrism and hyper–self-critical cultural relativism. While not always avoiding the pitfalls, feminist theory in general and feminist theorizing about law in particular have become increasingly self-conscious of the dangers of either extreme, and have attempted to create new paths somewhere in between. Feminist theory may thus provide a rich resource from which new approaches to comparative law can draw in their efforts to renegotiate the comparative gaze.

In the remarks that follow, I consider not how the ethnocentric gaze of comparison might be transcended, but rather how it might be differently inhabited. If the danger lies in a gaze that is not returned, then we might try to find ways of returning it. I explore the potential of a strategy of turning the gaze back on itself. I argue that this strategic intervention may help in the project of negotiating the challenge of comparison without falling into the traps of either ethnocentrism on one side or cultural relativism on the other.

In order to do so, I use some of my recent collaborative work—ambivalently related to the comparative project—to explore the general dilemmas of feminism's encounter with the comparative project. I use my collaborative work *Subversive Sites: Feminist Engagement with Law in India* as a text to explore some of these dilemmas and the way this strategic intervention of turning the gaze back on itself may help negotiate those dilemmas.[2] I begin with a general reflection on our ambivalent relationship with comparativism, at the same time as I reflect on some of the ways our project could be seen as comparative and might contribute to a comparative methodology. While the purpose of the essay is to locate this work within new approaches to comparative law, I would more broadly frame the process as one of situating the work within the project of postcolonialism—or more specifically, feminism and law in a postcolonial context. It is part of a larger project on scattering feminist legal studies,[3] that is, on the possibilities of renegotiating the Anglo-American moorings of feminist legal studies,[4] by displacing the unstated norms and center in favor of multiple norms and frames of reference.

I. TO BE OR NOT TO BE A COMPARATIVIST

I begin with considerable trepidation about my own relationship to the comparative project. While others claim that I am a comparativist, and locate my work within comparative law, I am somewhat skeptical. My work is about women and law in India. I work and write with an Indian feminist lawyer and researcher, Ratna Kapur. And we write primarily, but not exclusively, for an Indian audience. The work is not comparative in any traditional sense. We are not comparing Indian law and legal discourse to any other legal system. While some might cast our work under the umbrella of "foreign law," when I hesitantly put this suggestion to my coauthor, she sarcastically retorted, "Why, because you're a foreigner?" For my colleague, who lives and works in India, the only thing remotely foreign about our work is me. Her response underscores the extent to which the very category of "foreign law," alongside that of comparative law, begins from a very particular geopolitical location. It begins from an unstated norm of "us/here" against which others—"them/there"—are to be measured. It is an unstated norm that my colleague wants no part of.

I say this not to belabor the point of comparative law's ethnocentrism, but to emphasize our own unease with being cast as comparative or foreign lawyers. And I say it to raise questions about what it is about our work that makes others say, with such apparent certainty, that we are comparativists. Is it no more than my identity that makes it comparative? Was my colleague right in saying that it is only because I am a foreigner to the subject of our study? It strikes me as odd that in these days of post–identity politics my identity alone could make or break "us" as comparativists.[5]

Yet much of it does seem to revolve around who you are, who you write about, and who your audience is. Perhaps the issue should be recast not as one of identity, but of location. A politics of location or positionality insists on the historical, geographic, and cultural specificity of political definition and the production of knowledge.[6] It is location—defined not as a fixed and static point but a "temporality of struggle"—that shapes our knowledge of the world. As Chandra Mohanty argues, "My location forces and enables specific modes of reading and knowing the dominant. The struggles I choose to engage in are then the intensification of these modes of knowing."[7] It is our location that shapes not only our modes of understanding the world and the work we produce, but also, as Lata Mani has argued, the way that work will be received. She describes this as "the politics of simultaneously negotiating not multiple but discrepant audiences, different 'temporalities of struggle.'"[8] A politics of location could allow us to situate our work in different temporalities of struggle, such that in some locations it could be understood within a comparative project, whereas in others it could be framed otherwise. Indeed, a politics of location, and its insistence on the temporality of modes of knowledge and cultural production, might vindicate my coauthor's disavowal of the comparative project at the same time as it could situate my authorship within it.

Having asked these somewhat existential questions about whether to be or not to be a comparativist, and expressed my own sense of ambivalence, I will speculate on how our text can perhaps be cast as comparative. It is perhaps appropriate to cast our work within the emerging project of comparative legal feminism(s), or comparative feminist legal studies. In our study we borrow heavily from the methodologies and theoretical frameworks of Anglo-American feminist legal studies. This process of borrowing presents a number of theoretical and methodological challenges, which warrant further reflection, and which may reveal some insight for others engaged in similar comparative projects—feminist or otherwise.

II. SUBVERSIVE SITES AS COMPARATIVE METHODOLOGY

Our book *Subversive Sites* explores the ideological assumptions that inform the legal regulation of women in India and the ways law subordinates women. It examines the complex and subtle forms in which law constitutes and reinforces deeply gendered assumptions, relations, and roles. It explores the multiple ways legal discourse is constitutive of women's subjectivities as wives and mothers, as passive and weak, as subordinate and in need of protection. At the same time, law is a site where these roles and identities have been challenged—where social reformers and feminist activists have sought to displace previously dominant understandings of women's appropriate roles and identities and sought to reconstruct women's identities as more full and equal citizens. We argue that law is a site of discursive struggle where competing visions of the world, and women's place therein, are fought out.

We focus on the extent to which the legal regulation of women is informed by and serves to reinforce familial ideology. By familial ideology, we refer to a set of norms, values, and assumptions about family life and how it should be organized. It is a set of ideas that has been so naturalized and universalized that it has come to dominate commonsense thinking about the family.[9] In the Anglo-American context, familial ideology refers to the way the nuclear, heterosexual, patriarchal family—with very particular roles for women as wives, mothers, economic dependents—is naturalized and comes to represent commonsense thinking about the family. In our work, we try to show how ideas about the Indian family shape and inform the legal regulation of women, how these ideas appear throughout legal discourse as self-evident, and how this legal regulation operates to reinforce these assumptions about the family and women's roles therein. We examine a broad range of legal regulation—from family law to criminal law to employment law—and attempt to reveal the multiple and often contradictory ways familial ideology shapes legal discourse. We consider, for example, how assumptions about women's "natural" roles as wives and mothers are the measure against which courts judge women: women whose lives most closely conform to these assumptions are more likely to have their claims vindicated than are women whose lives have deviated from these ascribed roles.[10] We also examine how these assumptions about women's natural roles in the family have operated to undermine women's equality claims.[11]

But as mentioned, this concept of familial ideology is an idea taken from Anglo-American feminist legal studies. Some critics would reject the validity of the study on this basis alone, that is, on the outright rejection of the cultural legitimacy of feminism. This is not a position that we take very seriously insofar as it denies the historical legacy of feminist struggle in India,[12] renders invisible the vibrant feminist scholarship that is being produced by Indian women, both in and outside India,[13] and is premised on the very notions of cultural authenticity that we reject. Other somewhat more sympathetic critics might be less concerned with universal claims to feminism's cultural illegitimacy, but would nevertheless raise objections to the Anglo-American bias of the feminist analysis. We share this concern and take as axiomatic that the concepts of Anglo-American feminism cannot simply be mechanically applied to other contexts. As Chandra Mohanty's work has persuasively argued, concepts like the sexual division of labor and economic dependency cannot be used "without their specification in local and historical contexts."[14] Throughout our work, we have thus attempted to interrogate the explanatory nature of the concepts in the historically and materially specific context of the legal regulation of women in India. This process requires that theoretical concepts like familial ideology be adapted to this context.

But, lest we be mistaken for what Gunter Frankenberg describes as a fragile and tragic self, fearful of treading into the uncharted terrain of the other, afraid of going native and, simultaneously, of not going native—suffice it to say for the moment that we are not.[15] Although we believe that we need to tread cautiously on this journey, we do forge ahead. Moreover, the journey has much to offer those courageous enough to set off on it. The process of adaptation is, I will argue, simultaneously a process that can transform the very nature of the concepts themselves.

To illustrate the transformative nature of this process, I return to the concept of familial ideology. It is a simple observation that familial ideology in the context of Anglo-American feminist legal studies developed in relation to the nuclear family that is said to be the dominant household arrangement in industrialized, capitalist societies.[16] But in India the nuclear family is not the dominant ideological form. The joint family is the household structure that is commonly believed to be the dominant form. The tragic self might at this point simply abandon ship, fearful of applying a concept that is so clearly foreign to Indian culture.[17] But if we cautiously forge ahead and consider whether the concept of familial ideology might nevertheless have some explanatory potential, we begin an interesting and transformative process.

On one hand, if familial ideology is to have any explanatory value at all, it must be reconstructed around this concept of the joint family and the gendered roles and identities therein. However, further investigation into the nature of the joint family is illuminating. The joint family—the idea that represents the essence of Indian family culture—was a term first coined by Sir Henry Maine in 1863. Maine, the Law Member of the Government of India from 1862 to 1869, believed that he had discovered "a living example of the patriarchal family in ancient times."[18] As a result of his influential position as Law Member, his view of the joint family came to be accepted by the colonial government as an accurate representation of the most common Hindu family form—a form that was then used in government censuses.[19] The joint family is thus illustrative of how the colonial past is always indelibly present in ostensibly pure Indian cultural forms. The example of the joint family reveals how the assumption by the tragic self of the purity of Indian cultural and legal forms obscures the already ever present West and its deep influences on the very construction of tradition. As postcolonial theory has insisted, there is no place of pure Indianness, no place that exists in a pure form prior to the moment of colonial intervention.[20] This strategy of historicization begins to reveal the extent to which Indian culture is very much a hybrid cultural form—produced in and through the colonial encounter. It helps refute the idea of cultural authenticity, displacing it with an insistence on cultural hybridity.[21]

Moreover, as Indian sociologists have revealed, while the idea of the joint family dominates popular thinking about the family, the majority of Indians do not live in joint families.[22] The joint family is neither purely Indian nor descriptive of how millions of Indians live in families. Nevertheless, the joint family and its very particularized roles for women as wives, mothers, daughters, and daughters-in-law continues to operate as a dominant normative ideal of family—a dominant normative ideal that continues to inform judicial discourse. We try to illustrate, throughout the work, the extent to which this dominant ideology about the family operates in law: the way this ideology is partially constitutive of women's identities and the way it operates to limit efforts to destabilize these identities.

This idea of the joint family is but one of the most obvious ways the concept of familial ideology needs to be reframed and recast in the context of the legal regulation of women in India. It is this process of interrogating, reframing, and recasting that is particularly interesting from the point of view of comparative legal feminism. The process begins to transform the concept itself. Familial ideology looks very different in the Indian context than in the Anglo-American context. And this difference can begin to tell us something interesting about the concept itself. This is where the direction of the flow of analysis and comparison can begin to shift. Instead of understanding the flow of the comparative analysis as unidirectional, we might begin to displace the hegemonic discourses of the West if we insist that the flow of comparative analysis be multidirectional. Recent cultural studies and post-colonialism have emphasized and examined the transnational and multidirectional flow of culture, traveling theory, and the syncretism and hybridity in contemporary mass culture.[23] Borrowing these insights, we might begin to deconstruct the monolithic categories of Anglo-American legal feminism by turning the gaze of comparison back on itself. We can move from the question of what is culturally specific about familial ideology in India (which retains the West as the unstated norm) to the question of what is culturally specific about familial ideology in Anglo-American legal systems—a question within which non–Anglo-American contexts can become a stated norm. We can begin to shift in subtle ways what is being compared to what and begin to displace unstated and monolithic norms in favor of stated and multiple ones.

When we turn the gaze back on itself, we are not so much escaping the colonial or imperial gaze as finding different ways to inhabit the space of that gaze. When we turn the gaze back on the unstated norm and reveal its own specificity, we might begin to find and inhabit, in the words of Homi Bhabha, "the in-between space" between West and non-West, an in-between space "through which the meanings of cultural and political authority can be negotiated."[24] It is an in-between space that can recognize and nurture cultural hybridity. When the gaze is turned back on itself, the gaze might thus become something other than what it was; it is reconfigured in a way that it might become the "beyond" or the "in-between" that the "post" in the postcolonial signifies. As a comparative methodology, turning the gaze back on itself can help make explicit the seemingly inescapable risk of ethnocentrism in the comparative project, while at the same time deploying the comparison to challenge that ethnocentrism. It can assist in what Frankenberg has described as the challenge of seeing ourselves as exotically as we see the "other."[25]

The risk—and there are always risks—is that in turning the gaze back on itself, we (the us/here comparativists located in the West) simply end up back where we started—focusing on ourselves. Ruth Frankenberg and Lata Mani have astutely made this point in critiquing the work of Robert Young on the impact of the Algerian War of Independence on French political theory and philosophy.[26] They have argued that although Young's work, on one hand, constitutes "a powerful critique of ethnocentrism," it is, on the other hand, undermined by "his general tendency to read anti-colonial movements as primarily engaging the logic of Western philosophy."[27] They observe, "One is tempted to wonder whether we have merely taken a detour to return to the position of the Other as resource for rethinking the Western Self, only this time, it is not the Other as 'ourselves undressed' so much as 'ourselves disassembled.'"[28] We need, then, to be attentive to the risk of reducing the comparative analysis to an analysis that is "primarily and fundamentally a critique of the West."[29] In turning the comparative gaze back on itself, we must remain committed to finding the space in between West/non-West, colonizer/colonized, us/them, here/there, and not simply refocusing our attention back onto ourselves. We must, in other words, not simply gaze into a mirror but retain a keen focus on the kaleidoscope that a postcolonial lens of comparison can provide.

Further, it is in this kind of strategic intervention that comparative feminist legal studies can begin to become part of the postcolonial project and assist in what I describe as scattering feminist legal studies, that is, displacing the Anglo-American center of feminist legal studies. First, turning the gaze back on itself, alongside other postcolonial strategic interventions, can help defend the feminist emancipatory project against those who would deny its cultural legitimacy and authenticity. In breaking the here/there, us/them cultural binaries and revealing the hybridity of Indian culture, we can begin to disrupt the very assumptions on which claims of feminism's cultural inauthenticity are based. And in its place, we can defend not feminism's authenticity (for that would be to reinvoke the very binaries we have tried to displace), but simply its political legitimacy and relevance in the analysis of contemporary gender relations.

Second, turning the gaze back on itself can help multiply the norms, perspectives, and frames of reference in and through which feminist legal studies is constructed. For example, in the context of our work, the analysis of the historically and materially specific context of feminist engagement with law in India can become a stated norm against which the assumptions of Anglo-American feminist legal studies are viewed, judged, and—potentially—rethought. Moreover, the strategy can be seen to move beyond the mere call for a recognition of difference. Caren Kaplan writes of the problem of Western feminist theorists simply "calling for inclusion of 'difference' by 'making room' or 'creating space'" rather than paying attention to the politics of "the production and reception of feminist theories in transnational cultural exchanges."[30] As Kaplan argues, this politics of location in the production and reception of theory can turn the terms of inquiry from desiring, inviting, and granting space to others to becoming accountable for one's own investments in cultural metaphors and values. Such accountability can begin to shift the ground of feminist practice from magisterial relativism (as if diversified cultural production simply occurs in a social vacuum) to the complex interpretive practices that acknowledge the historical roles of mediation, betrayal, and alliance in the relationships between women in diverse locations.[31]

The strategy of turning the gaze back on itself can help shift attention to this politics of location in feminist legal studies. Instead of simply calling for an attention to difference within a preordained theoretical framework, the strategic intervention subjects the theoretical concepts themselves to interrogation and renegotiation and then redeploys them against the initial framework. It is an intervention that can help bring the issue of accountability into sharper relief. Not only does it require that the Anglo-American feminist legal scholar recognize the partiality of her perspective, but it also directs her attention to the way that partial perspective shapes how the comparative knowledge is received and interpreted. Not only can a multiplicity of stated perspectives be brought to the center of the project, but the relationship between these perspectives and the construction of knowledge can be recognized as one that is indeed "fraught with history, contingency and struggle."[32] "Difference" thus arrives on stage not simply as the empirical raw material to be theorized or as its own theoretical perspective or epistemological claim, but as simultaneously shaping the very interpretive terrain of the feminist project.

Turning the gaze back on itself can assist in bringing a politics of location to feminist legal studies, which as a project can in turn begin to be freed from its Anglo-American moorings. Feminist legal studies can be rendered more complex, more global, more local, more transnational. It is a project in which the unstated norms and frames of reference of Anglo-American feminist legal studies must be stated and revealed on the one hand and challenged as contingent, temporal, and partial on the other. It is a project that refuses the simple binaries of here/there, us/them (alongside a host of other binaries that the postcolonial project refutes: past/present, modern/tradition, global/local) by insisting on the hybridity of culture, on theory's travels, and on the transnational flow of theory/culture. It is a project that attempts to locate feminist legal studies within postcolonial projects in which Western hegemony is displaced by scattered hegemonies and in which feminist legal studies is itself located within the transnational flow of culture. It is neither here nor there, but caught up, in Stuart Hall's words, in the dizzying "two way cultural traffic"[33] located in the postcolonial space somewhere in between.

It is perhaps prudent to conclude this discussion by noting that the strategic intervention of turning the gaze back on itself can hardly be expected to accomplish the task of scattering feminist legal studies on its own. We will have to deploy a host of other postcolonial strategic interventions to move this project forward. For example, the strategies of both historicization and disrupting the tradition/modernity opposition can assist in revealing cultural hybridity, refuting assertions of cultural authenticity, and revealing the extent to which discursive struggles over women's rights in India (and elsewhere) have been located within the colonial encounter, and continue to be constituted in and through the postcolonial moment. Historicizing the struggle for women's rights helps locate the feminist project within Indian history, and thus as partially located within the culture rather than as transposed at the end of the twentieth century. At the same time, disrupting the tradition/modernity binary and historicizing cultural nationalism as a product of the colonial and postcolonial encounter help undermine the claims of cultural authenticity, by partially locating "tradition" as emanating from outside the culture. Thus we disrupt the very binaries of inside/out, further revealing the hybridity of culture, including the constructions of gender relations, the efforts to subvert these gender relations, and the resistance that such efforts have encountered. Scattering feminist legal studies will require that a multiplicity of these postcolonial strategic interventions be deployed. Turning the gaze back on itself, although perhaps particularly well suited to the development of new approaches to comparative law, can be but one of the many strategies that will need to be pursued if feminist legal studies is indeed to be relocated within the postcolonial project.

III. COLLABORATION, POLITICS, AND OTHER STORIES

The collaborative nature of our work has been an important methodological component of the project of scattering feminist legal studies. This process of collaborative work has paralleled, in at least some ways, the insights of postcolonial theory that disrupts the here/there, us/them, colonizer/colonized binaries, and insists on the mutual and multidirectional flow of knowledge and analysis; that is, on the "two-way cultural traffic."[34] Our collaboration has very much been one of two-way cultural traffic. It has helped us in displacing the unidirectionality of the perspective and the flow of analysis, as well as in breaking the "us 'n them" framework. The collaborative nature of our work instantiates, with a certain materiality, the postcolonial insight that theories, and theorists, travel.[35] As authors, we travel back and forth, to and from each of our respective worlds in a manner that begins to complicate any simple effort to locate us as here or there.[36] But, more significantly, it is our ideas and our texts that really rack up frequent flyer points. Our ideas travel back and forth, often with dizzying speed, to the point that they no longer belong to either one of us. They are neither here nor there.[37] But, having said this, I must add that we make no claims to have actually accomplished the project of inhabiting the postcolonial space in between in our work. Our claim is rather more modest—to contribute to the development of feminist legal studies in India and to do so in a way that we hope begins to displace the Anglo-American moorings.

Finally, I would add a word about politics. I very much appreciated Fran Olsen's words, putting the question of political agendas onto the agenda of comparative law.[38] We do have a political agenda, but we have only thought of it as a domestic agenda for one of us. It is, as our title suggests, an agenda of subversion. We are attempting to contribute to the debate about how law can be used, if at all, in women's struggle for social change, how law can be used to begin to destabilize hierarchical gender identities in India. We make no claims to neutrality in our work, but rather begin from an explicitly and unapologetically political location. And we have made no claims to a political agenda outside the Indian context. It is this insistence on a domestic political location that has complicated our relationship with the traditional comparative project, a project that (mis)cast itself as transcendent, that is, as without either a political agenda or a geopolitical location. But as new critical approaches to comparative law begin to shatter these myths of geopolitical neutrality, our political commitments need no longer exclude us from the comparative project.

Moreover, we will need to think harder about the postcolonial implication of our politics of location for the location of our politics. If we take seriously the idea of the dizzying exchange of ideas, then we can hardly confine our political agendas to a single location—to a "here," not "there," or depending on your perspective, a "there," not "here." If we take seriously the postcolonial refutation of these cultural binaries, then we need to complicate our own understanding of the location of our politics. My own political visions, struggles, and contingencies have been shaped and transformed by this work in multiple and subtle ways. My own cultural and intellectual terrain has been reconfigured in ways that may be difficult to quantify, but that need to be subjected to the same postcolonial interrogation of transnational cultural flows.[39] The imperative of turning the gaze back on itself, after all, is born of political commitments. And to suggest that one's political agenda could somehow be cut off from one's intellectual project is to fall back into the very dichotomous thinking that "new approaches" scholarship categorically rejects.

IV. CONCLUSION

Turning the gaze back on itself may be a way of renegotiating the dangers of the ethnocentric gaze of comparative law. In the spirit of Egoyan's *Salome,* we might renegotiate the dangers of obsessive voyeurism by reimagining the project of looking. Turning the gaze back on itself may help the new comparativist inhabit the gaze differently, by recognizing that in looking at others we are always also looking at ourselves. And as in *Salome,* the gaze may be dangerous, but it is not unambivalently so; it is multiple and contradictory and complicated. The gaze of comparative law is dangerous, but it too can be rendered multiple, contradictory, complicated. Turning the gaze back on itself is but one of a range of postcolonial strategic interventions that may assist the new comparativist to locate the project of new approaches to comparative law as a site of transnational discursivity, as a site of contradiction, contestation, grafting, and subversion.

But the methodological intervention of turning the gaze back on itself will not allow us to escape all of comparative law's perils. The ghosts of *Salome* will continue to haunt even the "new" comparative lawyer, and we should take heed of its cautionary tale. Voyeurism is indeed seductive, and the new comparativist must remain vigilant to the dangers that may lie hidden within this contradictory practice. The desire to know the other, to possess the other without disrupting its purity, and to do so without being seen may be irresistibly intoxicating to voyeur and comparativist alike. And as in *Salome,* neither resistance nor transgression comes without peril and sacrifice. Turning the gaze back on itself may help us reimagine the act of looking beyond ourselves and back at ourselves, but it will not allow us to escape all the dangerous seductions of doing so.

NOTES

1. Interview with Atom Egoyan (CBC Arts Report radio broadcast, Oct. 1996).
2. Ratna Kapur and Brenda Cossman, Subversive Sites: Feminist Engagement with Law in

India (1996) (exploring ideological assumptions that inform legal regulation of women in India and ways law subordinates women).

3. I have borrowed the concept of scattering from the work of Inderpal Grewal and Caren Kaplan. *See* Inderpal Grewal and Caren Kaplan, *Introduction: Transnational Feminist Practices and Questions of Postmodernity* (using the term "scattered hegemonies" to refer to "the effects of mobile capital as well as the multiple subjectivities that replace the European unitary subject"), *in* Scattered Hegemonies: Post Modernity and Transnational Feminist Practices 1, 7 (Inderpal Grewal and Caren Kaplan eds., 1994). I am using the term to refer to the process of displacing a vast array of unstated Western norms in favor of multiple norms and frames of reference.

4. The term "feminist legal studies" corresponds to the term more commonly used in American literature on feminism and law, that is, "feminist legal theory." "Feminist legal studies," although hardly a term of art, has gained in popularity in British, Canadian, and Australian circles, as witnessed by the emergence of journals, conferences, and institutes under its general rubric. In my view, the term "studies" is better suited to describe the area of inquiry than "theory," insofar as it can begin to displace the idea that there is a single theoretical narrative to tell about feminism and law. Carol Smart makes a similar observation about the concept of "feminist jurisprudence." *See* Carol Smart, Feminism and the Power of Law 66, 66–89 (1989) (stating that the concept of "feminist jurisprudence" needs to be problematized as it suggests general, total, and homogeneous theory of law that simply replaces traditional legal abstractions about law). The term "studies" better captures the multiplicity of perspectives and frameworks that characterize contemporary theorizing around feminism and law.

5. Gunter Frankenberg's essay, *Stranger Than Paradise: Identity and Politics in Comparative Law*, suggests that comparative law is still a relative newcomer to the realm of identity politics and that questions of identity, along with a host of other critical theoretical interrogations, have only very recently arrived on the stage of the comparative project. *See* Gunter Frankenberg, *Stranger Than Paradise: Identity and Politics in Comparative Law*, 1997 Utah L. Rev. 259. These new approaches to comparative law, although interrogating notions of identity, are doing so within a range of anti-essentialist or post-essentialist narratives. On essentialism and anti-essentialism, see generally Diana Fuss, Essentially Speaking (1989) (deconstructing opposition between essentialism and constructionism) and Angela P. Harris, *Race and Essentialism in Feminist Legal Theory*, 42 Stan. L. Rev. 381 (1990) (using racial critique to attack gender essentialism in feminist legal theory). This post-essentialist exploration of identity in comparative law is perhaps another example of what Nathanial Berman has described as "aftershocks." Nathanial Berman, *Aftershocks: Exoticization, Normalization, and the Hermeneutic Compulsion*, 1997 Utah L. Rev. 281.

6. *See* Chandra Talpade Mohanty, *Feminist Encounters: Locating the Politics of Experience* (calling for politics of location that includes "historical, geographical, cultural, psychic and imaginative boundaries which provide the ground for political definition and self-definition"), *in* Destabilizing Theory: Contemporary Feminist Debates 74, 74 (Michele Barrett and Anne Phillips eds., 1992); *see also* Lata Mani, *Multiple Meditations: Feminist Scholarship in the Age of Multinational Reception* (stating that feminist theory on the politics of location now calls for a revised politics of location "because, unlike its initial articulation, the relationship between experience and knowledge is now seen to be one not of correspondence, but fraught with history, contingency and struggle"), *in* Knowing Women: Feminism and Knowledge 306, 308 (Helen Crowley and Susan Himmelweit eds., 1992).

7. Mohanty, *supra* note 6, at 74.

8. Mani, *supra* note 6, at 309 (citation omitted); *see also* Caren Kaplan, *The Politics of Location as Transnational Feminist Critical Practice* (emphasizing the importance of focusing on both "the production and reception of feminist theories in transnational cultures of exchange"), *in* Scattered Hegemonies, *supra* note 3, at 137, 138.

9. *See* Kapur and Cossman, *supra* note 2, at 88–99.

10. For example, we consider divorce petitions where husbands have alleged cruelty on the grounds that their wives did not discharge their marital duties. Women who are able to demonstrate that they have lived up to the ideal of the good wife may be able to defeat their husband's claim. Compare Vimlesh v. Prakash Chand Sharma, A 1992 All 260 (holding that the wife's letters to her husband were sufficient evidence that she was a "totally devoted Hindu wife") with Santana Banerjee v. Sachindra Nath Banerjee, A 1990 Cal 367 (holding that the wife failed to establish that she led the life of a traditional Bengali married woman); *see also* Kapur and Cossman, *supra* note 2, at 105–12 (examining common ground of cruelty for divorce in India).

11. In chapter 3, "Constitutional Challenges and Contesting Discourses: Equality and Family," we examine the ways familial ideology has informed the judiciary's approach to gender difference and the ways this ideology has often operated to limit the attempts to use constitutional equality rights to challenge laws that discriminate against women. We attempt to reveal the role of familial ideology in the way legal discourse constitutes women as "different" and thus effectively disqualified from equal treatment. *See* Kapur and Cossman, *supra* note 2, at 173–222.

12. *See generally* Radha Kumar, The History of Doing: An Illustrated Account of Movements for Women's Rights and Feminism in India 1800–1990 (1993) (discussing in detail the history of women's rights movements in India); Janaki Nair, Women and Law in Colonial India: A Social History (1996) (examining impulses behind and effects of legislation passed in colonial period aimed at ameliorating legal position of women in India).

13. *See, e.g.,* Bina Agarwal, A Field of One's Own: Gender and Land Rights in South Asia (1994) (examining the link between property and gender relations in South Asia); Ratna Kapur, Feminist Terrains in Legal Domains: Interdisciplinary Essays on Women and Law in India (1996); Archana Parashar, Women and Family Law Reform in India: Uniform Civil Code and Gender Equality (1992) (analyzing governmental conduct with regard to reform of religious personal laws in India); Rajeswari Sunder Rajan, Real and Imagined Women: Gender, Culture and Postcolonialism (1993) (providing collection of feminist critical essays attempting to map the space of the postcolonial female); Recasting Women: Essays in Indian Colonial History (Kumkum Sangari and Sudesh Vaid eds., 1989) (providing collection of essays analyzing the reconstitution of patriarchies in the colonial period).

14. Chandra Talpade Mohanty, *Under Western Eyes: Feminist Scholarship and Colonial Discourses, in* Third World Women and the Politics of Feminism 67 (Chandra Talpade Mohanty et al. eds., 1991).

15. *See* Frankenberg, *supra* note 5, at 266–70.

16. *See* Michele Barrett and Mary MacIntosh, *The Anti-Social Family* 8 (1982) ("The stereotypical nuclear family accounts, roughly, for only a third of households in Britain today. Yet the media gives the impression that the entire population is securely bound up in it.").

17. *See* Frankenberg, *supra* note 5.

18. Patricia Uberoi, Family, Kinship and Marriage in India 31 (1993).

19. *See* N. J. Uash Rao, *Gaps in Definitions and Analysis: A Sociological Perspective*

("[T]he Indological views regarding the concept of the Hindu family were popularized by the British administrators and are reflected in many of the definitions of 'joint family' formulated by anthropologists and sociologists."), *in* Finding the Household: Conceptual and Methodological Issues 49, 56 (K. Saradamoni ed., 1992).

20. The hybridity of Indian cultural forms is made particularly evident in our work in relation to the family, which became an intensely contested terrain in the Hindu revivalist movement and the nationalism struggle. The family was claimed by revivalists as precisely this space of pure culture, uncontaminated by the public nature of colonialism. During the late nineteenth century, political nationalists sought to redefine the domestic realm as a pure space of Hindu culture and tradition, untouched by colonial oppression. *See generally* Kapur and Cossman, *supra* note 2, at 45–52 (discussing the first wave of social reform in nineteenth-century colonial administration); Tanika Sarkar, *Rhetoric against Age of Consent: Resisting Colonial Reason and Death of a Child-Wife*, Economic and Political Weekly, Sept. 4, 1993, at 1869, 1869 (contending that colonial power structures retained considerable hegemony even when faced with indigenous patriarchy and caste systems).

21. On hybridity, *see* Homi K. Bhabha, The Location of Culture (1994), particularly his essay *Signs Taken for Wonders: Questions of Ambivalence and Authority under a Tree outside Delhi, May 1817.*

22. *See* A. M. Shah, The Household Dimension of the Family in India (1974) (stating that even after a century of British surveys and census reports showing otherwise, most Indians believe that joint families are the norm). *See generally* Pauline Kolenda, Regional Differences in Family Structures in India (1987) (providing collection of papers attempting to understand causes, correlates, or conditions of joint-family living in India).

23. *See generally* Bhabha, *supra* note 21; Grewal and Kaplan, *supra* note 3 (emphasizing the importance of postmodernity and transnational flow of culture in feminist practices); Catherine Hall, *Histories, Empires and the Postcolonial Moment* (rethinking the history of the British Empire in a postcolonial framework), *in* The Post-Colonial Question: Common Skies, Divided Horizons (Iain Chambers and Lidia Curti eds., 1996); Stuart Hall, *When Was the Post Colonial? Thinking at the Limit* (exploring "the interrogation marks which have begun to cluster thick and fast around the question of 'the post-colonial' and the notion of post-colonial time"), *in* The Post-Colonial Question: Common Skies, Divided Horizons, *supra* (hereinafter Hall, *When Was the Post Colonial?*). On traveling theory, *see* Edward Said, Traveling Theory, the World, the Text and the Critic (1983) (mapping theory's location and displacement—its travels—through space and time); and James Clifford, *Notes on Travel and Theory*, 5 Inscriptions 177, 184 (1989) (critiquing Said's four stages of travel "on origin, a distance traversed, a set of conditions for acceptance or rejection, and finally a transformed idea occupying 'a new position in a new time and place' (Said (1983) at 227)" as "a linear path [that] cannot do justice to the feedback loops, the ambivalent appropriations and resistances that characterize the travels of theories, and theorists, between places in the 'First' and 'Third' Worlds").

24. Homi K. Bhabha, *Introduction: Narrating the Nation, in* Nation and Narration 1, 4 (Homi K. Bhabha ed., 1990).

25. Frankenberg, *supra* note 5.

26. *See generally* Robert Young, White Mythologies: Writing History and the West (1990) (examining the relation of history to theory and of politics to knowledge).

27. Ruth Frankenberg and Lata Mani, *Crosscurrents, Crosstalk: Race, "Postcoloniality" and the Politics of Location*, 7 Cultural Stud. 292, 300 (1993).

28. *Id.* at 301 (citation omitted).

29. *Id.*

30. Kaplan, *supra* note 8, at 138–39.

31. *Id.* at 139.

32. Mani, *supra* note 6, at 308.

33. Hall, *When Was the Post Colonial?*, *supra* note 23, at 251.

34. *Id.*

35. *See* Clifford, *supra* note 23.

36. Without going into excruciating biographical detail, a few words about location may be appropriate. Although I live in Canada, and Ratna lives in India, we have each lived for extended periods in each other's context. I have spent several years in India, and Ratna has both studied and worked in North America and England. She, more than I, in many ways represents the postcolonial intellectual—a transient in many diasporic spaces, while reversing the more common diasporic path, in moving from "there" to "here" at a young age, and then choosing to move from "here" to "there" as a young adult. Our histories only further refuse the notion of authentic and separate identities/locations and underline the extent to which these identities/locations are inescapably mutual and multidirectional.

37. We do not mean to suggest that collaboration is essential to the project of scattering feminist legal studies (for that would be far too essentialist a claim, and indeed would be an exclusionary move that would preclude scholars without transnational collaborators), but simply, that it is a methodology that seems particularly well suited to the task at hand. Feminist legal scholars engaged in the project of scattering have already begun, and will no doubt continue, to develop other methodologies that will help displace the Anglo- American moorings of feminist legal studies. *See, e.g.*, Vasuki Nesiah, *Towards a Feminist Internationality: A Critique of U.S. Feminist Legal Scholarship*, 16 Harv. Women's L.J. 189 (1993) (also chapter 2 in this volume) (referring to struggles of female factory workers in Sri Lanka as an example of the failure of American feminist legal analysis to theorize international contradictions).

38. Frances Olsen, *The Drama of Comparative Law*, 1997 Utah L. Rev. 275.

39. I am indebted to Fran Olsen, who has encouraged me to think harder about the potential implications of our work for feminist politics in North America.

2 Toward a Feminist Internationality
A Critique of U.S. Feminist Legal Scholarship

Vasuki Nesiah

> In the context of the West's hegemonic position today . . . Western feminist scholarship cannot avoid the challenge of situating itself and examining its role in [the] global economic and political framework. To do any less would be to ignore the complex interconnections between first and third world economies and the profound effect of this on the lives of women in all countries.
> —Chandra T. Mohanty, "Under Western Eyes"

Factories operated by transnational corporations (TNCs) in "Third World" countries have been a crucial avenue for the appropriation of surplus capital from the "Third" to the "First World."[1] These export-oriented factories employ women primarily; roughly a half million women work in TNC factories under oppressive conditions.[2] The struggles of these women against gendered and neocolonial exploitation form a critical fault line in the global map of imperialism.

This chapter examines how American feminist legal analysis has dealt with the global contradictions that Sri Lankan factory workers address in their struggles.[3] I also explore how American legal feminism itself could work to disrupt the imperialist map. I argue that although feminist legal scholars have provided a powerful critical voice in a number of arenas, they have not challenged global contradictions in their efforts to articulate a feminist project. Moreover, when they have addressed the struggles of women in the "Third World," their analysis has often worked to erase the structural contradictions that separate women across the globe.

The chapter is mapped in the following manner: In section 1, I note the sheer invisibility of global contradictions in feminist legal scholarship in the United States. Section 2 explores conceptions of internationality in that narrow strand of feminist legal analysis that does explicitly include women all over the globe in the feminist project: feminist human rights analysis. Here I take apart and examine the conceptions of internationality entailed in what Gayle Rubin has described as theory that

Reprinted by permission from 16 *Harvard Women's Law Journal* 189 (1993). © 1993 by the President and Fellows of Harvard College.

"accounts for the oppression of women in its endless variety and monotonous similarity."[4] I suggest that most feminist human rights work locates the foundation of
feminist internationality in women's shared experience of male oppression. In section 3, I problematize this approach by bringing together American scholars' struggles in the legal academy and Sri Lankan factory workers' struggles in transnational
corporations to explore some of the fault lines of feminism in an international
frame. My primary goal is not to investigate the practical legal problems of Sri
Lankan factory workers and American legal academics, but rather to work toward
a feminist internationality by interrogating both situations simultaneously.[5] While
this project partly involves appreciating and challenging the political strategies of
the factory workers, I focus primarily on the legal academics. I build upon my criticisms of experiential discourse to suggest an alternative way of thinking about feminist internationality.

I. GLOBAL CONTRADICTIONS AND AMERICAN FEMINIST
LEGAL ANALYSIS

Feminist legal theory in the United States remains remarkably insular. For the most
part, the theoretical and practical preoccupations of feminist legal scholarship have
been informed and bounded by a United States–centered vision. In mainstream
American legal analysis, such intense internal preoccupation would not be surprising given its narrow conception of the scope and object of legal scholarship. Feminist legal analysis, on the other hand, has often pushed and challenged such nar-
rowness; it has provided a vigilant, critical voice to combat efforts to effect closure
on the social concerns with which legal academics "legitimately" engage.

In light of this critical history, it is all the more telling that global contradictions
have remained virtually invisible in the politics of American feminist legal analysis. The struggles privileged by these feminists have seldom included the challenging of global contradictions that are fundamental in structuring the realities of
women in the "Third World"—and, indeed, of women everywhere.[6] This absence
conveys a loaded presence. What Cherríe Moraga said of the invisibility of
women of color in white feminist groups also speaks to the invisibility of "Third
World" women in the conversations of American feminists in the legal academy:
"[S]o often the women seem to feel no loss, no lack, no absence when women of
color are not involved; therefore, there is little desire to change the situation. This
has hurt me deeply."[7]

When posed in the most abstract form, my arguments for recognizing and challenging global contradictions echo the arguments raised by Moraga and others for
working through the institutional arrangements and practices that structure the
reality of women of color in the United States. The questions are unhappily familiar: Who is included and excluded in the "women" who are the subjects of American feminist legal analysis? Whose interests are erased from the political consciousness of this feminism? In this context, I am repeatedly disappointed that

global contradictions have been ignored even by feminist legal theorists sensitive to the multiplicity of social relations that situate women's lives along axes such as gender, class, race, and sexual orientation. Even as I learn from their acute political sensitivity in invoking multiple struggles with a radical simultaneity, I am struck by their failure to recognize the critical links between the struggles within the United States and the struggles contesting imperialism on the global map.

II. GROUNDING FEMINIST INTERNATIONALITY IN THE PERVASIVE EXPERIENCE OF OPPRESSION

Feminist human rights scholarship is the one arena where feminist legal theorists have made an attempt to engage in contestations outside the United States and to speak of a feminist internationality.[8] Even here, however, there is very little work, and most of the work is relatively recent. The human rights framework has special relevance for the women who constitute the TNC labor force. Efforts to improve working conditions have often involved both international labor regulations and international human rights law.

Most feminist legal theorists who invoke the human rights framework to confront women's struggles across the globe ground their analysis in the pervasive experience of women's oppression. This experiential approach to understanding oppression and identity construction is dominant in American feminist jurisprudence in general. Most feminist human rights theorists posit the experience of the denial of women's human rights across the globe as proof of, and grounds for, an international sisterhood. They emphasize that although women are "one half of humanity," they suffer oppression all over the world.[9] They thus illustrate a gendered gap between human rights theory and action. The attraction of the human rights framework is notable. On the one hand, it has been an enabling framework, internationalizing rights discourse and thereby opening space to engage with the struggles of "Third World" women. On the other hand, it has been restrictive. The struggles of "Third World" women have been conceptualized only within the narrow vocabulary and institutional framework of rights discourse.

Catharine MacKinnon's argument that violence against women is "torture" is paradigmatic of this approach. Her identification of oppressive features of women's lives across the globe—"rape, domestic battery, and pornography"—is used to frame the universal "realities of women's condition."[10] For MacKinnon, this "universal" reality of sex-based torture must form part of the human rights agenda. Her vision is grounded in the idea that women's rights as human beings are threatened because all women's lives are structured by gender—the most deep and pervasive contradiction of human relations. By understanding oppressive aspects of women's lives primarily, and sometimes exclusively, in terms of gender, this approach produces a sweeping vision of women's internationality. MacKinnon, like most feminist legal scholars, sees no differences among women that are significant enough to trip the analysis.

When writers do recognize differences in institutional arrangements and ideological systems, they usually find that gender overdetermines all other differences in constituting the identity of those oppressed. They see differences as running along the gender continuum rather than reflecting structures, such as nationality and class, that overlap with and contest gendered processes.

In asserting the primacy, and perhaps sufficiency, of gendered ideologies and institutional arrangements to explain oppression, feminist human rights scholars construct a transnational identity as woman. For some of these feminists, this identity is also essentialist, and therefore prior to male-dominated social conditions; for all of them, this identity is coherently rooted in the shared experience of gendered oppression. The difficult question of a transnational subject class is clarified in this experiential understanding of gender. While they may disagree about whether to understand experience solely in terms of structures of oppression or also in terms of authenticity, they do see experience as speaking fairly clearly about the coherence of women as a universal category.

The production of a transnational feminist agenda is grounded in this transnational identity as woman. Experience thus becomes the most critical touchstone of the feminist project in two senses: determining the subject of feminism and determining the agenda of feminism. By focusing on experience, feminist theorists produce an international subject class and contend that this focus also produces a shared international agenda.

III. PROBLEMATIZING THE IDEA OF "WOMEN" AS A TRANSNATIONAL SUBJECT CLASS

In this section I problematize the use of experiential discourse in the context of two related sets of concerns: first, that a discourse about universally shared oppression can obfuscate global contradictions, and second, that a discourse about the experience of oppression often participates in the imperially charged agenda of defining "Third World" women as victims of oppression. In laying out my criticisms of American feminist legal scholars, I draw heavily on the political interventions of Sri Lankan women who labor in transnational factories.

Increasingly, factories owned by transnational corporations are among the largest nonagrarian employers of young women in Sri Lanka. Women constitute 86 percent of the workforce in these factories, which are located in the free trade zones.[11] They work on assembly lines carrying out small, repetitive tasks such as sewing on shirt buttons.[12] Working conditions are marked by hard-line antiunionism, abysmal occupational health and safety standards, routine sexual harassment, and intense regulatory scrutiny of worker performance. Taking five minutes to visit the rest room can involve lengthy negotiations with the supervisor. The lack of health and safety standards often results in physical problems, ranging from eyestrain to birth defects, that ensure fast labor turnover. Employers have the prerogative to hire and fire at will. There are virtually no avenues established to remedy unfair labor practices and sexual harassment. Attempts to unionize are brutally crushed; organizers are fired and blacklisted. Labor and other government ministries have proven unsympathetic to workers' claims. In fact, the country commits to "discouraging" worker militancy so as to entice transnational companies with the promise of a docile workforce.[13]

Despite this oppressive working environment, the coupled phenomena of spiraling unemployment and inflation ensure that jobs in these firms are in high demand.[14] The TNC is able to hire nearly the cheapest factory labor in the world. At the same time, the factory worker receives higher wages than women workers in other sectors of the economy. Even in the industrial sector, TNC employees earn slightly more than workers in the better-regulated local factories outside the free trade zone.[15]

A. EXPERIENTIALIST DISCOURSE AND THE FOUNDATIONALIST ERROR OF NEGATING STRUCTURAL CONTRADICTIONS

The situation of the Sri Lankan free trade zone worker emphasizes the inadequacy of merely positing the experience of gender as an all-consuming analytic category. By examining ethnicity and class, we can obtain a more complex understanding of how these women negotiate gender. While the situation of the free trade zone worker is deeply oppressive, she may be relatively privileged because of ethnicity—a critical issue in the context of Sri Lanka's ethnic conflict. In the southwestern part of the country, where the free trade zones are located, the Sinhalese constitute 78 percent of the population.[16] However, the ethnic composition of the free trade zone labor force is 97.6 percent Sinhalese, 1.2 percent Moor, and 1.2 percent Burgher.[17] These women enjoy not only the broad privileges of the dominant ethnic group but also the concrete gains that stem from work in the factories. Recruitment into the free trade zone takes place primarily through patronage networks, such as those established by local members of parliament. Given a patronage system, membership in the dominant ethnic group and, more importantly, ties to the Sinhala-dominated ruling party often translate into rewards such as sought-after job opportunities. The disparity between the diverse ethnic composition of the country and the near monolithic composition of the free trade zone workforce illustrates this point forcefully. The homogenization of Sri Lankan women that results from purely gendered lenses obscures power relations along the axis of ethnicity. These unequal power relations play a fundamental role in structuring the options and opportunities of Sri Lankan women.

While ethnic injustice has remained a dormant issue among free trade zone workers, their statements reflect a concern for questions of class. These women do not articulate their claims solely through the frame of gender. When speaking to women organized as feminists, the TNC workers refer to themselves not simply as women but as "female employees."[18] Despite their goal of building links with feminists, they are quite insistent on invoking both class and gender oppression. If terminology can be taken as symptomatic of a broader theoretical and political commitment, the TNC workers convey the simultaneity of class and gender through their refusal to call themselves "female" except when the word is coupled with "worker" or "employee."

The danger of basing feminist internationality on experiential discourse is that American feminists simply assume an international feminist community without interrogating their own investment in obscuring the structural contradictions that separate women. The global class privilege that these women enjoy as members of the American legal academy forces on them a particular responsibility to interrogate their own complicity in the global economic and political framework.

We can see this masking of global contradictions by feminist scholars when we locate the American legal profession in an international frame. This erasure is particularly ironic since the export of the "rule of law," with the freedom and democracy it is said to safeguard, is the frequently heard campaign cry of America's imperialistic adventures. Law is often the touchstone of the crude "orientalist" dichotomy that portrays the "Third World" as shackled to brutal chaos and the industrialized North as the embodiment of secured freedom and ordered democracy under the rule of law.[19] In this context, the prestige and identity of the legal profession are invested in the vision and the projects of American imperialism.

If American feminist legal analysis is to contribute to a feminist internationality, it must interrogate critically the complexities of a world in which women's realities, be they Sri Lankan factory workers or American academics, are constructed along lines not only of gender, but also of nationality, ethnicity, class, race, and sexuality. There is a marked need in feminist human rights analysis, and in feminist legal scholarship more generally, to engage in a socially located discussion of internationality. It must speak to the specific political realities that divide women as much as it does to those that may bring women together.

Feminists cannot invoke "women" without speaking to the specific politics and conditions of struggle through which women are socially constructed and against which women are socially situated. This is not to say that we should not generalize but rather that generalization must always be hesitant and politically grounded.[20] The signification of "women" can be understood more fully in terms of the contingent politics that inform and constitute such identity.

My emphasis on socially located analysis is not a celebration of localism, nor is it a celebration of cultural relativism. In attempting to understand and contest oppressive structures, feminists cannot sidestep the difficulties of negotiating power relations merely by focusing on the local. As suggested by the tensions of ethnicity, class, and gender in the interventions of the Sri Lankan workers, socially located analysis calls for sensitivity to the particular power structures implicated in a given situation. Certainly such sensitivity demands generalization in some cases. However, "we do not need 'easy generalizations,' [but] we do need difficult ones."[21] It is this "difficult generalization" that will help us struggle toward a feminist internationality. Even when feminists deconstruct the presupposed commonality of women's experience, they must seek to hold on to the possibility of a strategic feminist internationality. By contesting global contradictions, feminist theorists may contingently construct a transnational community of women, based on "a political constituency, not a biological or even sociological one."[22] Such a community will be fraught with instability, but it can be a politically enabling instability if difference is confronted and negotiated.

B. THE EXPERIENTIAL DISCOURSE OF OPPRESSION AND THE COLONIALIST PROJECT OF DEFINING "THIRD WORLD" WOMEN

Intimately related to feminist theory's tendency to obscure structural contradictions among women is the ideological production of "Third World" women through experiential discourse on women's universal oppression. As discussed above, the traditional orientalist move used by "First World" feminists to comment on the "Third World" essentializes, homogenizes, and erases these communities. Here, the orientalism is retained to exact a slightly different move; "Third World" women are not erased from the picture but are defined by "First World" feminists. The emphasis on women's oppression becomes a neocolonialist project in which the invocation of the "shared oppression of women" translates into the power to define and produce "Third World" women—typically, as passive victims of male oppression.

A narrative of victimization operates in the context of the Sri Lankan free trade zone worker. Much of the literature on the subject produces an image of a helpless worker, an oppressed cog in the wheel of global capital. Although I acknowledge the harshly oppressive working conditions, I urge against the passive recording of women only as objects of capital, as traces of patriarchy. Women resist despite huge constraints and penalties. Although nonunionized and unorganized in "traditional" terms, women have carried out work stoppages and other oppositional action in a number of factories.[23] It is speculated, for example, that the extraordinarily frequent medical complaints by free trade zone workers are nontraditional forms of protest. Undoubtedly, these complaints, which have no apparent somatic basis, disrupt the efficient functioning of the factory. In addition, efforts to unionize persist despite continued harassment from management.

We need a contextual analysis to resist the modeling of "Third World" women as victimized and to acknowledge the complexity of Sri Lankan women's work in TNCs. While factory work is undoubtedly oppressive, transnational factories are the one form of economic development that not only creates employment disproportionately for women, but also offers higher wages. Wage labor has likely had a significant impact in disrupting the gendered political economy of the household and the agrarian sector. The fact that women have had to leave their homes and live in hostels on the outskirts of the free trade zones, albeit in horrifying conditions, has inevitably allowed them greater independence. Thus many young women may choose employment in transnational factories as a ticket out of a socially suffocating and financially less lucrative political economy. It is a difficult ticket, but such employment is in high demand given structural constraints on available options.

This victimization narrative is coupled invariably with a contrasting story about comparatively privileged Western women. In an approach whose subtext sees Western women as having a patent on feminism, the benevolent Western feminists provide theory that is useful for "Third World" practice, that rescues "Third World" women. American feminist theorists thus produce an international division of labor that says Western feminists theorize, and "Third World" feminists struggle. This narrative in some sense reenacts the colonial project in which the "white man's burden" of carrying Christianity and civilization to the heathens is now the Western woman's burden of carrying feminism and civilization to victimized "Third World" women. To contest this narrative, we must problematize the "First World" feminists' sense that they are privileged as women and its concomitant colonialist claim to cultural superiority.

When feminists assert and explore the differences between women—for example, between the feminist legal scholar in the United States and the free trade zone factory worker in Sri Lanka—they should not reinscribe difference in neocolonialist ways. In confronting global contradictions, "First World" legal feminists must not assume the privileges of modernity and Western cultural location relative to orientalist tradition, of theoretical insight as opposed to practice in the trenches, of emancipatory feminism as opposed to false consciousness and victimization.

Sensitivity to structural privilege and discursive ruptures in "women" should not be the reinscription of an orientalist dichotomy that now, in a call to modernity, appropriates the discourse of feminism to produce a neocolonialist difference.

IV. CONCLUSION

In this chapter I have problematized a dominant strand of American feminist legal scholarship and, more particularly, a dominant strand of feminist human rights work. The identification of a dominant tendency, however, should not preclude an acknowledgment of American feminist legal analysis as heterogeneous, complicated, nuanced, and dynamic. In fact, part of the agenda of an expansion of this essay should be the exploration of the marginal strands of feminist legal scholarship that do speak of the lives of "Third World" women in ways that engage in analyzing the complexity of their goals and strategies. These strands are located primarily, but not entirely, in feminist legal writing that addresses race and racism, and in some feminist human rights scholarship, such as this anthology represents.[24] The unexplored possibility of using debates within American feminist legal analysis may provide an avenue to understanding feminism in the context of international structures and social relations.

Similarly, theorists must resist a homogenization of feminists and feminist struggles in the "Third World." The repetitive uniformity of conditions in transnational factories in Sri Lanka and, for example, the Philippines bears out the claim of the homogenizing power of global capital. Yet the specific social relations into which transnational factories intervene are vastly different. The deeply pervasive structural contradictions between the North and the South may locate different women within Sri Lanka, and even Sri Lanka and the Philippines, similarly in the international division of labor. This similarity of location, however, says nothing about the very complex, highly textured differences in the particular contexts in which different women imagine, theorize, fight for, and occasionally even succeed in shaping a more equitable, emancipatory reality.

American feminist legal academics must critically examine issues central to feminist theory and practice in an international context. They need to acknowledge and confront the theorizing, the struggles, and the lives of "Third World" women. To do so, they must situate feminist scholarship and political intervention in the global framework and examine tensions, and also shared understandings, between "Third World" and "First World" women. Finally, American feminist legal scholars must explore the centrality, and simultaneously the deconstruction and fragmentation, of various identities, beginning with the logic that produces the category "women." As we work towards gendered understandings of the regulation of sexuality, class, race, nationality, and ethnicity, feminist internationality demands that, in turn, we examine how gender is itself implicated by these other discourses of power.

NOTES

1. I am uncomfortable with the use of terms such as "Third World," "First World," "underdeveloped," and "developed." Historically, the term "Third World" has often been used in paradigms that invoke orientalist conceptualizations of the countries or regions to which they refer. They have negative essentialist connotations that imply a bipolar, adversely hierarchical relationship between the "developed First World" and the "underdeveloped Third World." They group together a number of countries as if they were homogeneous with no regard to their diversity and complexity. The terms "North" and "South," although not as hierarchical, are equally homogenizing. Moreover, even a work that speaks critically of "Third World" resistance runs the risk of implying untenable links between identification as a "Third Worlder" and political commitment to anti-imperialist struggle. Nevertheless, I use this terminology because I want to address certain commonalities that arise from the impact of colonial and postcolonial domination without negating the historical specificity that conditions the experience of each country and each community in the "Third World." In addition, some writers have suggested that the term "Third World" could be recaptured in oppositional political interventions akin to the appropriation of terms such as "Black" and "queer." *See, e.g.*, Chandra T. Mohanty, Ann Russo, and Lourdes Torres, *Preface* to Third World Women and the Politics of Feminism ix, x (Chandra T. Mohanty et al. eds., 1991). To convey my continued discomfort with the terminology, I awkwardly use the terms in quotation marks.

2. Linda Y. C. Lim, *Women's Work in Export Factories: The Politics of a Cause, in* Persistent Inequalities: Women and World Development 101, 101–02 (Irene Tinker ed., 1990).

3. Although the term "American" refers broadly to North and South America, I use it, absent a more precise term, to refer to the United States. The designation "American feminist legal analysis" is not intended as an empirically descriptive category, but as a category

that signifies the privileges of readership and publication in academia in the United States. In examining American feminist legal analysis, I focus on its most dominant voice—dominant in the sense that it is both pervasive and attributable to scholars who may be labeled elite. I do not intend to imply that American feminist legal scholarship speaks with one voice. In fact, the critical but marginal voices have significantly influenced the critique I offer in this chapter.

4. Gayle Rubin, *The Traffic of Women: Notes on the "Political Economy" of Sex, in* Toward an Anthropology of Women 157, 160 (Rayna R. Reiter ed., 1975).

5. I use the term "feminist internationality" (it is a borrowed term, but I am not sure of its original usage) in contrast to terms such as "global sisterhood" that speak only of a universal alliance of women. "Feminist internationality" functions as a shorthand for a transnational political alliance of women whose differences are acknowledged. While difference remains a potent tension that threatens a comfortable sense of community, it is confronted rather than ignored, thus becoming rich and productive.

6. The critical international lens helps to illuminate the structural realities of women in the "First World" as well as the "Third World." Indeed, the luxury of thinking of global contradictions as a "Third World" issue is a potent statement of the structural privileges enjoyed by mainstream American feminists. In commenting on race, Ann Russo writes, "Not seeing race as a white issue is part of the privilege of being white. Understanding the impact of race on our lives—what we gain and what we lose—would encourage us to see the issue of racism as our issue." Ann Russo, *"We Cannot Live without Our Lives": White Women, Antiracism, and Feminism, in* Third World Women and the Politics of Feminism, *supra* note 1, at 297, 300.

7. Cherríe Moraga, *La Guera, in* This Bridge Called My Back: Writings by Radical Women of Color 27, 33 (Cherríe Moraga and Gloria Anzaldúa eds., 1981).

8. *See* Karen Engle, *International Human Rights and Feminism: When Discourses Meet*, 13 Mich. J. Int'l L. 517 (1992) (analyzing feminist theorists' engagement with human rights discourse).

9. *See, e.g.*, Riane Eisler, *Human Rights: Toward an Integrated Theory for Action*, 9 Hum. Rts. Q. 287, 303 (1987).

10. Catharine A. MacKinnon, *On Torture: A Feminist Perspective on Human Rights, in* Human Rights in the Twenty-first Century: A Global Challenge (Kathleen Mahoney and Paul Mahoney eds., 1993).

11. Voice of Women, Women Workers in the Free Trade Zone of Sri Lanka: A Survey 85 (1983).

12. The host countries advertise the particular aptness of their labor force for such tasks in heavily gendered and racially charged terms. For instance, the Malaysian government boasts in its brochure that "[t]he manual dexterity of the Oriental female is famous the world over. Her hands are small, and she works fast with extreme care. . . . Who, therefore, could be better qualified by nature and inheritance, to contribute to the efficiency of a bench-assembly production line than the Oriental girl?" Barbara Ehrenreich and Annette Fuentes, *"Life on the Global Assembly Line" Exposes "Ms.-Treatment" of Women Workers*, AFSC Women's News l. (Women and Global Corporations Project Insert), Winter 1981, at 12.

13. Voice of Women, *supra* note 11, at 51.

14. The rise in rural poverty provides one explanation for the attraction of TNC employment. According to the International Fund for Agricultural Development (IFAD), Sri Lanka is one of the five countries in the world that has experienced the sharpest increase in rural

poverty over the last twenty years. *Trickle-Down Economics Hurt Rural Poor in Third World*, Reuters, Nov. 23, 1992, available in Sri Lanka Net.

15. Asoka Bandarage, *Women and Capitalist Development in Sri Lanka, 1977–87*, Bulletin of Concerned Asian Scholars, Apr.–June 1988, at 57, 68.

16. The ethnic composition of the southwestern region of Sri Lanka is as follows: 78 percent Sinhalese, 11 percent Tamil, and 11 percent Muslim and others. Stanley J. Tambiah, Sri Lanka: Ethnic Fratricide and the Dismantling of Democracy 10 (1986).

17. Voice of Women, *supra* note 11, at 87.

18. *Id.* at 78.

19. The term "orientalism," popularized by Edward Said, has come to refer to the colonial and neocolonial project of Western writers, from academics to journalists to foreign policy bureaucrats. Their imaginative discursive production of "the Orient," defined in opposition to "the Occident," is crucially linked to the power configurations of imperial dominance. *See generally* Edward W. Said, Orientalism (1979).

20. Such generalization should be in the spirit of what Gayatri Spivak refers to as strategic, not ontological, essentialisms. Judith Butler, *Gender Trouble, Feminist Theory, and Psychoanalytic Discourse, in* Feminism/Postmodernism 324, 325 (Linda J. Nicholson ed., 1990) (citing Gayatri Chakravorty Spivak, Address at the Center for the Humanities, Wesleyan University (Spring 1985)).

21. Bruce Robbins, *Comparative Cosmopolitanism*, 31–32 Social Text 169, 175 (1992).

22. Chandra T. Mohanty, *Introduction* to Third World Women and the Politics of Feminism, *supra* note 1, at 1, 7.

23. Voice of Women, *supra* note 11, at 51–54.

24. *See, e.g.*, Critical Race Feminism: A Reader (Adrien K. Wing ed., 1997).

3 | Themes for a Conversation on Race and Gender in International Human Rights Law

Celina Romany

I. INTRODUCTION

In the past few decades, a concerted women's movement has seized the international human rights arena in an effort to make these rights responsive to the realities of gender inequality. The Rio, Vienna, Cairo, Copenhagen, Beijing, and Istanbul conferences presented opportunities for translating women's claims into rights and into policy-oriented platforms for action. The incorporation of women's rights as human rights was clearly recognized in these conferences' blueprints.

Women's marginalization, however, wears many faces around the globe. Black women are marginalized by virtue of their membership in a historically subordinated racial group. Regardless of demographic realities, Black women are treated as members of national minorities.[1]

The reality of compounded subordination experienced by Black women, indigenous women, and "women of color" in the American region has grown in serious proportions. If we talk about the feminization of poverty without realizing how such feminization gains intensity when racialized, we would distort gender analysis.

Throughout this region, Black women are national minorities and are located at the bottom of the social and economic ladder. They experience poverty at higher levels than other women's groups. They confront higher health risks, are affected by the lack of adequate reproductive rights policies, and are severely isolated when subject to violence. For all these women the lack of an adequate national policy, as well as the inadequate implementation of services, is severely affecting their chances to escape poverty and discrimination.

Reprinted by permission of the author.

53

As a tool of empowerment and as a discourse with its own set of remedial strategies, international human rights law can begin to make visible the compounded social marginalization these women experience. The incorporation of their voices into the international human rights framework will result in tremendous gains in such areas as violence, reproductive rights, and the economic and social rights of women.

Women who become social minorities via multiple discriminations have been more isolated and thus less able to coalesce in networks that are catalysts for the new conceptual frameworks required to make their needs visible and properly heard. Equally difficult is their national and regional participation in discussions that revolve around ethnic and racial discrimination. The latter has an androcentric focus that obscures the gender dimension.[2] That is, racial and ethnic oppressions seem to affect only men. Such isolation and compartmentalization are furthered by the failure of international and regional institutional forums and nongovernmental organizations (NGOs) to incorporate an integrated race/ethnic/gender perspective.

Women who experience multiple forms of discrimination in their public and private lives need to participate in the redefinition of human rights law. Both race and ethnic subordination compound the way women experience devaluation and invisibility in society. To ask an Afro-Latina or an African American woman to neatly compartmentalize and dissect each source of oppression is to ask her to deny her life experiences.

It is time to redefine, in the concrete scenario of the experiences of Black women, a feminist theoretical model of international human rights law, which, although acknowledging diversity, is still far from recognizing and addressing its implications in both theory and practice. In this chapter I will sketch the themes for the beginning of a conversation on race and gender in international human rights law. Extrapolating from the insights of critical race theory, critical race feminism, and postmodernist feminism, I aim to chart a methodological course for thinking about Black women in international human rights law and for devising legal strategies that better respond to their compounded sources of oppression.

The analysis of the intersection of race and gender in the context of Black women can hopefully be extrapolated for issues involving the international human rights of women of color in general.[3] I thus hope this chapter will be a contribution toward the theoretical and practical re-vision of international human rights law that can be adapted to the country-specific realities of women's simultaneous experience of racism and sexism.

In suggesting themes for an ongoing conversation on the incorporation of race and gender, we must take notice of the multiplicity of conversations that revolve around this one. Issues of poverty and the very concept of "minority" in international human rights law are key components of these conversations. As a tool to redress compounded marginality, the incorporation of the intersection of race and gender in international human rights law requires the isolation of race as one category that is inferiorized and stigmatized by social actors in power. Thus, a conceptualization of minoritization in international human rights law must accompany an analysis of the intersection of race and gender as a compounded manifestation of devaluation.[4]

First, I will provide a brief overview of the marginalization of Black women in the gendered critique of the international human rights framework. The work of most scholars and activists in the human rights field does not sufficiently problematize the realities of diversity, nor does it examine the political and legal effects of such diversity. The marginalization of Black women will be introduced through two prisms: the examination of the foundational feminist assumptions mostly used for the feminist reconceptualization of international human rights law, and the actual practical-political strategies of visibility explored by women's nongovernmental organizations in the male-dominated NGO world.

Second, alternative accounts for the construction of a racialized feminist subject, devalued by dominant discourses and practices, must be part of the proposed conversation. The theoretical work of Black feminists in the United States and South Africa can offer insights for a more encompassing critique.

Third, the incoherence of a system of international protection built from the perspective of compartmentalized selves must be challenged. The pitfalls of a system that offers a different set of protections (with its concomitant system of hierarchies) to Blacks *and* to women needs to be exposed through a comparative examination of the Race Convention (CERD), the International Covenant on Civil and Political Rights (ICCPR), and the Women's Convention (CEDAW).

Finally, there is the need to "bring home" to the national legal framework an international human rights law framework that adopts the intersection model.

II. THE RESILIENCE OF ESSENTIALISM IN THE FEMINIST CRITIQUE OF INTERNATIONAL HUMAN RIGHTS LAW

The incorporation of diversity in the social critique that aims to unveil the androcentric character of global society presents significant conceptual challenges. There is the need to recognize that categories of legal protection reflect power differentials. International human rights law is no exception. Thus, in devising ways to incorporate marginalized voices, we must direct our efforts to reveal the devices deployed for inclusion and exclusion, the systems of domination/subordination that remain entrenched.

Black feminist thought has challenged the essentialist impulse of such conceptual order in feminism. In doing so, however, it has had to prevent itself from slipping into new paths of essentialism. In this regard, international human rights law presents a bigger challenge, given the magnitude of the political and cultural diversity of Black women around the globe. The commonalities that we must seize in order to expose the limited view of a feminist critique of international human rights law cannot pretend to be the foundation for any grand theory of a global and totalizing account of the intersection of race and gender. The task is more modest. Such commonalities will merely expose the incomplete picture.

The redefinition of international human rights law from a Black feminist perspective cannot assume the existence of a monolithic Black feminist standpoint. It rather opens the door for the recognition of an oppositional consciousness that engages both the feminist and the phallocratic establishments. It recognizes that within the national, ethnic, and cultural diversity that the globe inscribes into Blackness, a consciousness begins to emerge that is privy to contradictions, fallibility, and the nuances of colored voices in colored bodies.

A. SCANNING FEMINIST THEORY IN INTERNATIONAL HUMAN RIGHTS LAW

As a feminist woman of color, I have found that the experience of using an essentialist detector in the United States, although painful and often frustrating, has been rich in educational rewards. To see a consistent pattern of exclusion (and/or inclusion in footnotes that remind us of the "diversity question") re-created in feminist reconceptualizations at an international level, however, sends frustration to new heights. Theoretical insights coming from a discourse and reality of multiple consciousness have yet to fully inform feminist scholarship and practice in international human rights law. Although feminist scholars and activists have had a significant impact on the lives of all women throughout the world, the white-essentialist dimension of feminist critiques still has to undergo substantial revisions.

With very few exceptions, feminist critiques of the male-centered character of international law rely on a core of feminist work that essentializes gender as its axis-category of analysis. Regardless of the school of feminism subscribed to, a feminist construction of identity primarily revolves around gender. A "generic woman" category is elaborated in feminist critiques of the androcentric framework of international human rights law. Often the feminist critique looks like a battle between the generics: the generic male versus the generic female subject of international human rights law. Black women, along with other women of color, have been quick to point out how such a view compounds exclusion and also gets played out in the context of North-South political divisions within the global women's movement.

Critiques of the androcentrism found in the public/private distinction, in the dichotomy between civil and political rights and their social and economic counterparts, and in the centrality of the state are made against the backdrop of feminist scholarship that is primarily focused on gender.

Angela Harris has aptly described the effects of essentialist feminism:

> Essentialism in feminist theory has two characteristics that ensure that Black women's voices will be ignored. First, in the pursuit of the essential feminine Woman leached of all color and irrelevant social circumstance, issues of race are bracketed as belonging to a separate and distinct discourse—a process which leaves Black women's selves fragmented beyond recognition. Second, feminist essentialists find that in removing issues of "race" they have actually only managed to remove Black women, meaning that white women now stand as the epitome of Woman.[5]

As a critique grounded on a construction of contextual identities, Black feminism particularly targets the Enlightenment project and its influence in international human rights law. However, unlike white feminists, Black feminists find that it is not enough to challenge the male-centered assumptions hiding beneath the "human self." The problematization of the "human self" must engage the world of differences within those who, in theory and practice, are excluded from that categorization. The aspiration is one that aims to develop a set of rights and guarantees that properly accounts for the diversity of the human paradigm.

B. SCHOOLS OF FEMINIST THOUGHT IN THE CRITIQUE OF INTERNATIONAL HUMAN RIGHTS LAW

Hilary Charlesworth's analysis of the presence of different schools of feminist jurisprudence in international human rights law is sensitive to its lack of diversity when she describes how these strands interact with a human rights discourse and practice throughout its "generational" framework. The liberal school, advocating a notion of equality that maintains the structural status quo unaltered, has focused its critique on carving an equal niche for women on the basis of sameness. Cultural feminists have advocated a women-based conceptualization of rights that allows for an expanded version that acknowledges differences and thus recognizes the importance of the private realm as a framework of regulation. Radical feminists have centered on the principle of sexual inequality and have advocated an encompassing antisubordination principle that eradicates pervasive entrenched male forms of social domination.

Each critique comes with its strengths and weaknesses inasmuch as their theoretical foundations stem from partial constructions of gender relations in patriarchal societies. The liberal critique unleashed a debate around difference and sameness, picked up by cultural feminists, who aimed to transcend it by not only celebrating difference but also devising normative frameworks that did not devalue them. Radical feminists went for the roots of patriarchal society and critiqued both the liberal and cultural approaches for not attacking core foundations of domination, which remain ensconced in women's advocacy for sameness or the respect for difference within a system of subordination.

From a strategic standpoint, all these critiques have proven helpful in the overall challenge to the androcentric character of international human rights law. For Black women, however, there is the need to approach international human rights discourse and practice from a decompartmentalized location that politicizes the criteria for the theoretical knowledge upon which it is based. It is, then, with the benefit of such knowledge that we can talk of common grounds—common grounds that challenge the androcentric character of human rights law.

Theoretical reconceptualizations that stem from experience must engage in dialogues that do not re-create male hierarchies. The resilience of essentialist feminism is far from engaging women of color equally, at both theoretical and practical levels. Women of color are still, when invited, asked to fill the gaps, asked to "make revisions" to the central criteria when "such criteria seem ethnocentric and arrogant." The politicization of the criteria for theoretical knowledge, one of the most significant achievements of Black feminist discourse, is wasted along the way. As Nancie Caraway aptly notes,

> the questions of who is "authorized" to create theory, in what voice and from what spaces of life, become powerful interventions enabling Black feminists to reject the policing authority of both the feminist and the phallocratic establishments. Through strategies which both appropriate modes of abstract intellectual analysis and shatter their boundaries, Black feminist theory redefines the variegated forms in which "knowledge" is conveyed.[6]

There is an increasing chorus of the voices of women of color that narrate, theorize, and trace a transformative agenda toward the eradication of racism and sexism. The chorus underscores the linking nature of oppressions experienced in scenarios as diverse as family, food, shelter, employment, civil liberties, reproduction, and sexuality. It is a chorus with wounds inflicted by hollow concepts of sisterhood when, individually or through associations, women play a role in the maintenance and perpetuation of the inferior status of women of color in their respective countries.

The reality for women of color in societies where they are minoritized is that they fare much worse than white women. Regardless of whether patriarchy is ultimately responsible for all the oppression in the world, white women have been privileged by their white skin vis-à-vis Black women. Thus, to establish a strategy for social transformation in which international human rights law can play a key role, a feminist critique has to address the racial face of the gender subordination that Black women experience. To retain its emancipatory character, it must transcend the single focus on gender. A feminist critique must take into account discourses such as gender, race, and class so that colonization maneuvers, which keep Black women subordinated, can be unveiled.

C. THE INTERSECTION OF RACE AND GENDER IN THE CRITIQUE OF THE LIBERAL FOUNDATIONS OF INTERNATIONAL SOCIETY

1. Liberal Foundations

In developing a critical framework for a reconceptualization of international human rights law that properly addresses the realities of Black women, the genealogy of liberalism and its construction of the human rights field must not only expose the male supremacy[7] of such construction, but also the intersection of the latter with other forms of subordination such as race.

As I have pointed out in earlier works, a feminist critical analysis of the sources and process doctrines that give legitimacy to international human rights law must recognize that women are the paradigmatic aliens of international society.[8] A centerpiece of any critical challenge to the alienation of women must be the historicization of human rights. We must develop a framework that places in a political-historical dimension the political and moral choices embedded in the conceptions of justice, equality, and dignity that are present in human rights. The historical record of power struggles in international society is thus recognized in an effort to see how changes in discursive and nondiscursive conditions both keep the status quo intact and bring about new forms of legitimation.

2. The Intersection Model

For Black women, the story of the original contract in modern patriarchy's history must unveil the hidden existence of a sexual and racial contract, which operates to compound their multiple sources of oppression. For Black women, the paradox of a social contract that constructs political rights on the basis of equality, while separating spheres on the basis of a natural division, raises questions that require the exploration of the interaction of race and gender in the formation of social identity.

3. Generations Framework

An examination of the generations framework in international human rights law reveals that notwithstanding the development of classical civil and political rights into a more comprehensive vision of citizenship encompassing the social and economic realm, women's experiences are still relegated to the margins. The principles of discrimination contained in both the ICCPR and the International Covenant on Economic, Social and Cultural Rights (ICESCR) advocate for a notion of equality where men are the norm. Despite provisions addressing formal and de facto equality, the same can be said of CEDAW. Discrimination is still narrowly tailored to accepted norms of human rights and freedoms. All primarily refer to the public realm, thus neglecting fundamental protections that should accompany the private lives of women.

Rights as crucial as the right of liberty and security are, in the first generation of civil and political rights, framed as applying only in the public sphere. The "state" as the paradigmatic public sphere remains central to a second generation of rights that require a more affirmative state responsibility for the protection and exercise of civil and political rights.

This generation of rights still lags behind in protecting women from the economic, social, and cultural context in which most women live. The third and fourth generations of human rights, which are concerned with collective rights, are no exception. A strong global women's movement has indicted women's invisibility in peace, development, and environmental issues. Discourses that range from a romantic eco-lyricism to correlations of poverty, population control, pollution, and gender subordination are at the forefront of such critiques.

If we examine equality provisions in human rights law through the lens of a woman who assumes her identity through the filter of compounded inferiorization, we quickly notice the significant need to document and analyze the adequacy of those provisions. This requires a dual challenge, which is both theoretical and factual. On the one hand the challenges must—at a normative level—incorporate the intersection of race and gender, bringing about core reconceptualizations. On the other hand, there is an urgent need to document with factual data women's racial experiences. Otherwise, both the theoretical and factual developments emerging as the result of the women's international lobby would further conceal the realities of Black women vis-à-vis women who enjoy racial privileges.[9]

III. THE INTERSECTIONAL MODEL: A COMPARATIVE EXPERIENCE

South Africa's constitutional experience has provided an ideal platform to translate the intersectional model.[10] In South Africa, women bore the brunt of the apartheid regime, filling the ranks of the unskilled and lowest-paid jobs. Plagued by violence and serious health issues in the midst of institutional terror, women had to be acknowledged by the new constitution serving as the blueprint of hope and reconciliation.

The debate around the promulgation of the South African Constitution incorporated the multiple subordinations experienced by South African women. From the outset, the constitutional agenda had to recognize how a gender-essentialist critique fell short and did not adequately conceptualize a regime of rights and protections responsive to the realities of Black women.

The critique of the demarcations of the public and private lives was different. Prohibitions against inequality and discrimination had to incorporate adequate ways to redress the compounded nature of discrimination. A social and economic framework that laid the foundation of a redefined citizenship had to be seriously considered.

The South Africa experience has shown that the public/private split is not static. Given the history of state intervention, abuse, and repression experienced in South Africa, a "universal-gender-essentialist" critique of such a split could only advance a hollow/abstract framework that re-creates the limitations of a liberal self that feminist critique has targeted.

The equality paradigm was questioned in the context of the South African experience also. A liberal model that hides an assimilationist framework under the mask of neutrality was critiqued as well for failing to address the compounded nature of gender and racial inequalities.

In the design of a framework that recognizes systematic social marginalization of groups such as Blacks, women, and Black women, a contextual balance between individual and group rights was a clear objective. As a right with a very concrete historical consciousness, affirmative action became a basic platform of redress.

With due acknowledgments of sociopolitical differences, women of color in the United States have elaborated similar critiques of the liberal foundations of equality and nondiscrimination. The intersectional lens exposes the arbitrariness of the demarcation of social spheres and shows not only how the dichotomy hides the ways the self becomes gendered, but also how it becomes simultaneously racialized and engendered—that is, how the psychological and political barriers imposed on Black women by the social division of labor affect them as women and as Blacks.

Violence against women provides an example. In the United States, Black women have critiqued the way states extend protections to women without properly acknowledging cultural and racial differences. The ways Black women respond to the criminal justice system, to the criminalization of violence, to shelters that fail to recognize cultural differences are considerations that an effective public policy against violence must take into account when properly addressing multiple forms of subordination. In South Africa the institutionalization of violence during the apartheid regime made it particularly difficult to measure the actual extent of violence, given the inadequate response of a criminal justice system that was itself a component of state repression.

Sociocultural representations with distinct constructions of a Black woman's body—a colored body—must also be taken into account when we formulate a discourse of rights affecting violence and health concerns. Black women's vulnerability to rape and to the absence of adequate legal protections is different from that experienced by white women. A significant difference is Black women's unique ambivalence toward a construction of rape that does not adequately factor multiple victimization.

Slavery offers a historical backdrop for these differences, since rape was a centerpiece of slavery. Black men were castrated when they raped a white woman, while the rape of a Black woman by a white man could not be penalized since he was disposing of his property.[11] Rape was an "institutional crime, part and parcel of the white man's subjugation of a people for economic and psychological gain."[12]

Dorothy Roberts's work provides an excellent account of the social subordination of Black women, while properly documenting the racialization of the welfare face of a liberal state. In documenting the genesis of a welfare state that excludes Black women from "citizenship," Roberts shows how immigrant white women were the primary beneficiaries of a race-conscious welfare state.

In 1931 the first national survey of mothers' pensions along race classifications reported that only 3 percent of Black women were receiving benefits. Their approach to welfare differed dramatically from that adopted by white women, since Black women accepted married women's employment as a reality and a necessity and thus advocated for welfare assistance as working mothers.[13] According to Linda Gordon,

> For the white northern reformers early in this century, the primary fact was that they did not notice these minorities—did not imagine them as indicated objects of reform. For the southerners, the immigrants appeared reformable and integratable as Blacks did not. Their maternalist legislation was intended to assimilate women who had the potential of becoming citizens. Blacks lacked this potential, stood entirely outside the elite white women's paternalistic concept of national community.[14]

At the centerpiece of rights discourse around women's issues we find notions of "family." A critique of such notions (if proper account is to be given to the racialization of gender relations) must be able to discern that "family" is a unit of social life that is clearly affected by the uneven distribution of social advantages and social costs. It is also affected by the way the racial and cultural values informing its organization get devalued by dominant discourses and political practices.

In South Africa, Black women fought for the survival of their families given the assault they experienced at the hands of apartheid. Disrupted families, through forced migration and the imprisonment and death of many men were realities that a process of social and political reconstruction could not elude.

In the United States the relationship between social labor organization and the family has been documented. Unlike white migrants, Blacks were brought to the United States to meet the need for cheap labor and to work under exploitative conditions. Little attention was given to family life and to the cultural assaults Black families were experiencing as a result of the organization of the labor system where Blacks participated.

The acknowledgment of Black women's experiences and the sociohistorical realities in which they live provides an initial framework in the formulation of a critique of multiple subordination. Commonalities found in comparative experiences not only buttress feminist critiques of international human rights law, but also strengthen the impact international human rights law has on national rights and policies.

IV. THE INTERSECTION OF RACE AND GENDER: DEMOCRACY, CITIZENSHIP, AND HUMAN RIGHTS (SOME NOTES ON INTERPRETATION)

A conversation about the ways the international human rights framework can better respond to the realities of Black women, at a minimum, requires a feminist methodology of interpretation that incorporates the intersection model. To acknowledge the racialization of gender stratification, we need to deploy critical models of interpretation.

The structure of international human rights discourse and its offspring forms of rationality, scientificity, objectivity, and cultural and aesthetic ideals should be challenged. The controlling metaphors and the categories that develop and delimit the conceptions of truth and knowledge within the discourse are main targets. Furthermore, a feminist methodology that destabilizes frozen versions of social life and human association that exclude the way Black women experience social marginalization must be enlisted in preparation of a deconstructive and reconstructive critique. A critical, political-historical assessment of both the emergence and hierarchization of human rights is an important foundation that demonstrates how accepted notions of legitimacy in the human rights field embrace political and moral choices played out through historically specific conceptions of justice, equality, and dignity.

The historicization of human rights opens the door for the incorporation of notions of multiple and compounded subordination, and for the exposure of social and political racialization maneuvers. It shows how core concepts of human rights law, such as the dignity and personal integrity of human beings, have the imprint of historical struggles of groups and individuals that bring about realignments of power structures and thus legitimate new legal rules.

With the deployment of critical methodologies, we should be able to identify key principles and provisions of international conventions that, subject to re-visions and reinterpretations, can better guarantee the rights of Black women via an intersectional approach. A series of key questions for the proposed conversation must be kept in mind. We need to better analyze the impact of an intersectional analysis on basic notions of international human rights law that deems racial equality, and not gender equality as *jus cogens*, that is, binding upon all actions. Similarly, we need to address the privileging of race discrimination within the customary norm framework of international law.

V. INTERNATIONAL CONVENTIONS: A SAMPLE OF FUTURE DISCUSSIONS

Our attempts to guarantee the international human rights of Black women require a dual journey along radical and reformist paths. The reformist path requires an expansive interpretation of applicable international conventions, so that they properly address and incorporate Black women's experience.

For example, under the equality provisions of the ICCPR, ICESCR, CEDAW, and CERD, Black women could be viewed as a separate group entitled to a greater protection than that offered to white women and Black men. In the United States, a constitutional argument developed in the context of equal protection offers guidance as to the possibilities of advocating for expansive interpretations under the above conventions.

It has been argued that for equal protection purposes Black women in the United States can be categorized as a subset of Blacks or of women, or as a separate group characterized as being excluded from the benefits of full citizenship. They can constitute a "discrete and insular minority"—that is, a group possessing immutable characteristics (such as race) that has been the subject of historical prejudice and political powerlessness.[15] This argument is one that could be successfully explored in the international arena because, as in the United States, race discrimination enjoys a higher level of protection than its gender counterpart.[16]

The Race Convention provides a framework with much potential for the application of the intersection analysis. Narrow positivist constructions of the Convention support the view of some commentators that "sex" is outside its parameters. An expansive reading, rid of such constraining baggage and in tune with the proposed intersection methodology, can support a different conclusion. The fact that race discrimination is considered a *jus cogens* norm and has a customary genesis can indeed constitute a springboard for broader interpretations that better reflect historical realities for Black women. Moreover, such a broader interpretation would be in sync with the emergence in the last decade of nonpositivist interpretations of human rights.

An international human rights convention prohibiting race discrimination must be treated as a living document. It is a document imbued with the "strong moral force of virtual universality rooted in the overriding principle (*jus cogens*) that racial discrimination should be eliminated everywhere."[17] What legitimate justification can be offered for excluding Black women from such a universal condemnation?

An intersectional methodology directs us to ask the woman/race question. Ask such a question when reading the Race Convention preamble, which is the outcome of many intense debates, and one that incorporates the Universal Declaration of Human Rights, which talks about the human person. Ask such a question in the context of a preamble that recognizes how any doctrine of superiority based on racial differentiation is an obstacle to peace, and is "capable of disturbing peace and security among peoples and the harmony of persons living side by side." Or ask the woman/race question in the context of a gender-neutral definition that prohibits racial discrimination in the enjoyment of human rights and fundamental freedoms in the political, economic, social, cultural, or any other field of public life. Ask such a question in light of a legislative history (*travaux preparatoire*) that shows an international society barely beginning to grapple with emerging international actors in a postcolonial world.

While the main subject matter of CERD and CEDAW (that is, race and sex, respectively) gets full explicit attention in both preambles, such emphasis does not preclude an understanding of multiple subordinations. The Vienna Convention on the Interpretation of Treaties is relevant. Article 31(1) allows room for the formulation of the woman/race question that encourages expansive readings. But Article 31 underscores the importance of referring to the ordinary meaning of a term in its context and in light of its object and purpose.

The inclusion in the preamble of CERD of notions of equality stemming from the United Nations Charter and the Universal Declaration supports a prohibition against multiple discrimination. Equality, as espoused in such documents, is not an enclosed room full of compartments. Rather, it is an open and encompassing concept—with race and gender among its categories. Furthermore, in alluding to the UN Charter, the Race Convention refers to the "equality inherent in all human beings," a clear recognition that both men and women are entitled to be free of race discrimination. Finally, the preamble states that one of the purposes of the United Nations is to "promote and encourage universal respect for an observance of human rights and fundamental freedoms for all, without distinction as to race, sex, language or religion." To ask the woman/race question in light of this background can only show that the "sex" omission is either a question of emphasis, a product of the UN historical moment, or just simply an inadvertent omission.

It is important to ask the woman/race question in order to foster an integrated and more coherent use of international instruments. Unlike the Women's Convention, the Race Convention provided for the scrutiny of state action not only via national reports, but through an individual complaint mechanism that facilitates a more textured presentation of alleged violations.

VI. CONCLUSION

Although I am cognizant of the limitations of a rights discourse that is based on equality notions that suppress differences and that stem from a male norm, the rights framework continues to be an important tool, given the high moral and emotional legitimacy of human rights.

There is a crucial need for the gathering of disaggregated data that properly document the social and economic realities of Black women. The available data are scarce and fragmented. Equally important is to assess the ways national legislation specifically impacts these women. A comparative framework of the lack of protection available at the more formal legislative levels must be examined. In the same vein, there is the need to document, against the backdrop of de jure equality, the presence of de facto inequalities.

A way to walk reformist paths while simultaneously waging more radical battles is to keep a contextualization critique of international human rights law alive and well. The move from equality to antisubordination, a paradigm better suited to deal with intersection and multiple sources of oppression, then finds its breathing space.

A conversation among those who usually do not sit on the same platform is long overdue. The phallocratic establishment of the Race Convention as well as the more gender-essentialist focus of the Women's Convention must be receptive to interpretations that address the multiple subordinations that a "human person" endures. The more experienced networks under the ICCPR should join in and enrich the dialogue. Only then can the dialogue begin to address the unique situation of women who experience multiple forms of discrimination.

NOTES

This chapter was originally presented at a panel entitled "Challenging Boundaries: International Human Rights," at a symposium sponsored by the Yale Journal of Law and Feminism (Yale Law School) in November 1996.

1. The term "minority" and "minoritized" are used to capture a situation of social powerlessness.

2. "Androcentric" refers to an emphasis on masculine interests.

3. This chapter focuses on Black women. The application of the intersectional model suggested to other women of color is beyond the scope of this essay.

4. Minoritization, inferiorization, and devaluation are mechanisms for the assignment of social location that do not depend on numbers. As the history of apartheid in South Africa clearly reveals, majority in numbers can, in terms of power, be highly irrelevant. A full dis-

cussion of the construction of minoritization in international human rights law is beyond the scope of this chapter. Yet the discussion can shed light on how other "minorities" can begin to address human rights law from a compounded perspective.

5. Angela Harris, *Race and Essentialism in Feminist Legal Theory, in* Critical Race Theory: The Cutting Edge 257 (Richard Delgado ed., 1995).

6. Nancie Caraway, Segregated Sisterhood: Racism and the Politics of American Feminists 35 (1994).

7. Celina Romany, *Women as Aliens: A Feminist Critique of the Public/Private Distinction in International Human Rights Law*, 6 Harv. Hum. Rts. J. 87, 90 (1993).

8. "Women are aliens within their states and aliens within an international society defined by participation doctrines which do not deem them to be actors." *Id.* at 95.

9. These realities can open the door for multiple correlations to appear; in particular, race superiority can join ranks with its economic counterpart to create subordinated economic classes or underclasses.

10. A more thorough exploration of the theory and arguments surrounding the constitutional process in South Africa appears in Celina Romany, *Black Women and Gender Equality in a New South Africa: Human Rights Law and the Intersection of Race and Gender,* 21 Brooklyn J. Int'l L. 857 (1996).

11. Adrien Wing, *Race, Ethnicity, and Culture: Spirit Injury from Bosnia to Black America, in* Critical Race Theory, *supra* note 5, at 520–21.

12. *Id.* at 521.

13. Dorothy Roberts, *Welfare and the Black Citizenship,* 105 Yale L.J. 1563, 1570 (1996).

14. Linda Gordon, *cited in id.* at 1575–76.

15. Judy Scales-Trent, *Black Women and the Constitution,* 24 Harv. Civ. Rts. Lib. L. Rev. 9 (1989).

16. Judy Scales-Trent notes,

the level of protection granted Black women will differ depending upon whether they are placed in the Black group or the female group. Yet the notion that the level of protection would change depending upon which way they are classified is bizarre since Black women are always both Black and women. To the extent that they are always burdened by both classifications, the level of protection should be constant. Moreover, since Black women are always stigmatized by the race classifications, they should always be provided the highest level of protection available under the Constitution.

Id. at 24.

17. Natan Lerner, citing the UN Secretary General in a report on the implementation of the Program of Action for the Second Decade to Combat Racism and Racial Discrimination, at 70.

4 Comparative Analysis of Women's Issues

Toward a Contextualized Methodology

Antoinette Sedillo Lopez

> The very notion that there exists a prototypical woman who can be described in ways that reflect and have meaning for the lives of the many different women living in very different geographical, economic, political and social settings needs to be challenged.
> —Ruth Hubbard, *Women's Nature:*
> *Rationalizations of Inequality*

I. INTRODUCTION

Despite a global feminist movement, feminists have not developed a clearly articulated methodology of comparative analysis. Such an analysis shows how problems faced in one jurisdiction are addressed in another. Comparing women's rights can provide important cultural insights on the various ways women's issues have been addressed. A difficult issue comparativists face, however, is a tendency to be ethnocentric when studying another nation's legal system.

Comparative analysis by a Western scholar must reconcile a perspective developed in the United States with respect for another culture. In discussing women's rights, lawyers, judges, students, and sociologists have justified certain women's situations as an inherent aspect of culture. For example, traditional "female genital surgery" has been defended as a "mere bodily mutilation" that is the "sine qua non of the whole teaching of tribal law, religion, and morality."[1] In Mexico "machismo" has been justified as an immutable characteristic of Mexican culture that should be respected.[2] Cultural relativists maintain that criticizing cultural norms is akin to advocating cultural genocide.[3] Thus, comparative analysis faces the challenge of respecting cultural differences.

Feminists have confronted the issue of respect for diversity and respect for other

Reprinted by permission from 10 *Hastings Women's Law Journal* 101 (1999). © 1999 by University of California, Hastings College of Law.

cultures.[4] Although the feminist movement in the United States has been dominated by white middle-class feminists, feminists of color have criticized white feminists for ignoring their needs and perspectives.[5] Similarly on a global level, the feminist movement has been dominated by U.S. and other Western feminists but challenged by Third World feminists for excluding or essentializing the perspectives and needs of women of color and Third World women.[6] The United Nations Fourth World Conference on Women, held in Beijing, illustrated the difficulty of communicating across cultural differences to articulate a common statement on women's rights.[7] Western feminists are now attempting to include women of color and women from other countries and cultures as part of their intellectual and activist movement.[8] Such inclusiveness can help white feminists see their own ethnocentricity and understand their privileged position as compared to that of Third World women and women of color.[9]

Just as inclusivity works to overcome narrow perspectives, using a range of theoretical perspectives helps to broaden comparative analysis. Liberal feminism teaches about the value of autonomy and independent moral agency.[10] Radical feminism articulates the limits of liberalism and autonomy, especially for those women not in a position to exercise autonomous choice.[11] Cultural feminism instructs us about the possibilities of alternative women's values.[12] Postmodern feminists and feminists of color teach us about the falsity of overgeneralizing about women's experiences, values, and needs.[13] No single feminist approach to analyzing women's legal status appropriately draws comparisons about women's legal status across cultures in different legal systems.

It is important to evaluate the effect of laws on the quality of women's lives. Does the law open opportunities for women? Does it treat women fairly? What do women need to pursue their needs, their lives, their dreams? In what ways does law circumscribe women's lives? Do the culture and legal system value autonomy? If so, are women in a position to exercise autonomous choice? If not, how do women feel about their position in society? How do feminists and women who belong to the culture prioritize and conceptualize their own agenda for social change?

This chapter will begin to construct a feminist method of comparing women's legal status using insights from feminism and critical race theory. Adrien Wing has labeled theories at the intersection of feminism and critical race theory "Critical Race Feminism."[14] The framework should evaluate the progress in improving women's lives and legal status in another country while being sensitive to that country's cultural values. The comparative methodology proposed involves the following three steps: First, the comparativist must look for and perceive cultural context, which can be discovered in a variety of ways, including travel, reading, interviewing, listening, observing, ethnography and demographic interpretation. Second, the comparativist must develop a framework for identifying the legal context. For example, the status of the legal system as civil, common law, socialist, Islamic, and so forth, is very important to understanding the legal context. Third, the comparativist should use feminist theories and critical race insights to consider the implications of the legal issues for women. The comparativist should find women's stories in the culture and listen to their stories. By using the proposed methodology, the comparativist will be able to draw meaningful comparisons and contrasts in legal status while recognizing cultural context. The analysis helps comparativists broaden perspective and minimize ethnocentricity. The proposed methodology recognizes the importance of understanding how women view their own legal status and situation. Finally, the chapter will discuss abortion law in Mexico and the United States to illustrate the comparative method proposed.[15]

II. THE PERILS OF COMPARING: DECONSTRUCTING DIFFERENCES AND CONSTRUCTING FALSE DICHOTOMIES

A growing body of literature compares laws affecting women. A problem in attempting such analysis is a failure to understand differences in cultural values. Thus, the comparisons made are incomplete. A feminist comparativist must be open to the possibility that women in a particular society might be empowered by different cultural approaches to gender.[16] Although feminists are concerned with deconstructing patriarchal legal systems and social structures that disadvantage women, they must also be wary of imposing their own values on others—ironically one of the very things feminists have resisted about patriarchy. It is important that a feminist who chooses to engage in comparative analysis learn to suspend judgment in analyzing differences. Differences should be viewed in their cultural context. This is not to say that feminists should not examine the ways in which women are disadvantaged in cultural systems. A global universal truth is that women are disadvantaged socially, politically, legally, and educationally in most cultures. However, the nature of the disadvantage will not be the same as that experienced by white, liberal, middle-class feminists in the United States. Rather, women's oppression may be linked to broader social, political, and cultural issues. For example, poor women in Third World countries who are interested in obtaining credit for their microbusiness for their economic survival are more interested in the availability of credit on their terms. Credit problems faced by middle-class divorced women in the United States focus on their problems establishing credit because their husbands paid the bills during their marriage.

Thus, it is important that a comparativist perceive social and cultural context. A major comparative work on family law and abortion is Mary Ann Glendon's *Abortion and Divorce in Western Law*.[17] Glendon surveys the legal principles in European countries and the United States. Unfortunately, the work suffers from a failure to perceive the cultural context and women's role in that cultural context. After admitting that the legal "story" is not the whole "story," Glendon proceeds to summarize and categorize the types of abortion laws and family laws in the nation-states of Europe and the United States. She alludes to a cultural context, but she fails to include a description of the role of women in society and in creating social and cultural advances in women's rights. For example, she glosses over the feminist litigation responsible for much of the transformation of the abortion law and family law in the United States and Europe. She places the judge-made and legislature-created legal "stories" in philosophical and theoretical constructs created by Toqueville, Hobbes, and John Stuart Mill in the United States and Rousseau and Kant in Europe.[18] While these philosophers had an important impact on liberal intellectual discourse, and Mill and Rousseau created important intellectual foundations for feminist theory, it was the more textured changes wrought by feminist activists and their political will that resulted in the profound transformation of women's legal status throughout both Europe and the United States. Ironically, while Glendon professes to be interested in the educational function of the enactment of legal norms, she ignores the educational role of feminist consciousness raising that resulted in an awareness of law as a source of women's oppression and the impact of that awareness on culture. Her conclusion that a mediated approach like that of the European nations might satisfy the needs of both abortion advocates and opponents[19] misses the points raised by women on both sides of the question and tells an incomplete story.[20] A feminist comparative analysis should avoid such omissions.

III. PROPOSED ANALYSIS

A. PERCEIVING CULTURAL CONTEXT

As illustrated by Glendon's book, a major difficulty in comparative analysis is the perception of cultural context. Culture has been almost exclusively studied by white First World anthropologists who attempt to describe societies and social ways of doing things. Of course, the nature of culture can vary from subgroup to subgroup and even from individual to individual. Culture is also affected by political development and stability as well as economic status. Unfortunately, anthropologists' descriptions of culture may suffer from the distorted lenses that even the best-trained observer can bring to the study of people who are different. On the other hand, people of a particular culture have difficulty describing their cultural norms except as being different from others with which they might be familiar. In other words, culture is often invisible to those who are within the culture. Interaction of people from different cultural backgrounds reveals the differences. Interaction makes people notice different values, beliefs, and customs. Cross-cultural interaction makes the previously invisible visible, which is one of the reasons international travel is so valuable. Other sources of cultural context are critical readings of popular culture, history, literature, ethnography, interviews, and experiences. In addition, a review of demographics and social and educational data enhances understanding. Comparative analysis that ignores social and cultural context risks painting an incomplete picture.

B. IDENTIFYING CONTEXT IN LEGAL NORMS

Of course, a comparativist must also perceive legal context. The development of legal systems is as varied as the number of systems that exist. Some systems evolved from cultural and political self-development, other legal systems were transplanted, some systems were borrowed, others were imposed. All legal regimes are fluid, changing in response to social, political, or cultural pressure. Further, the application and interpretation of legal norms vary with social contexts, political systems, and cultural norms. It is possible that laws that look startlingly different on their face may be very similar in application. Other laws may look similar on the books but be applied quite differently. The context of the legal system as part of the civil law tradition or as part of the common law tradition will mean that the methods of enforcement and interpretation will be quite different. A cursory comparison then might deconstruct differences that are not really there or create false dichotomies. For example, while Mexico's constitution looks like that of the United States, it is quite different in history, purpose, and application. Thus, the comparativist needs to understand the law's history, intended purpose, and application in order to have a complete picture of the culture studied.

C. USING FEMINIST THEORIES TO CONSIDER IMPLICATIONS FOR WOMEN

A feminist comparative analysis of laws affecting women should use critical race and feminist insights to help draw comparisons in women's legal status and to understand the implications for women. These insights will help identify subtle issues confronting women in the culture studied. Patricia Cain has classified the various writers on contemporary U.S. legal feminist thought into four main categories: liberal feminism, radical feminism, cultural feminism, and postmodern feminism.[21] Liberal feminists believe that women should be treated by the legal system as autonomous, independent rights-bearing individuals (just like men).[22] The quest for equal treatment has been criticized because in some situations men and women are not equal. Treating men and women as equals results in women losing ground in rights and privileges previously accorded to women.[23] Radical feminists tend to stress women's subordination as a class, not as individuals.[24]

Cultural feminists, like radical feminists, focus on women's differences from men, but they believe that women's special nurturing orientation should be valued by the law. For example, divorce and custody law are examples in which women's differences should be recognized positively.[25] Cultural feminists have relied on work such as Gilligan's theory of women's different "voice" to support their theories.[26]

Postmodern feminists and critical race feminists do not believe in an "essential" quality of woman; they seek to discover the diverse realities of women's experience.[27] Women of color, poor women, and lesbian women, for example, have experiences that are different from the "essential characteristics" of the abstract woman described in previous schools of feminism. Minority and poor women have always faced the challenge of working to survive and caring for their children. Their experiences in the workplace and the political realm are different from those of middle-class white women.[28] All these theories are useful when we consider the implications of laws affecting women. We learn about the positive aspects of autonomy, but also its limitations. We learn about the value and uniqueness of women's experiences, and we learn to respect and appreciate the diversity of women's experiences. My own view is that feminist insights all reveal male/female complexities; however, feminism does not present a coherent approach to those complexities. This failure, in my view, stems from the fact that feminist theory is in its infancy. While we have learned to deconstruct and criticize patriarchy, we have not convincingly created an alternate view. Comparative work can help us learn about other cultures and can help us become more sophisticated in developing a coherent alternative vision.

IV. APPLYING THE PROPOSED ANALYSIS: ABORTION IN MEXICO AND THE UNITED STATES

A. PERCEIVING CONTEXT: SOCIAL AND DEMOGRAPHIC CONTEXT

The United States and Mexico have vastly uneven economic resources. Since 1940 Mexico has steadily grown (albeit unevenly) economically. Postwar development has been pronounced in the manufacturing sector. Agricultural development under the "green revolution" has been channeled into the capital-intensive production of export crops such as cotton and coffee at the expense of subsistence crops that have traditionally supported farm workers. The population has grown from 19.6 million in 1940 to an estimated 73 million in 1982, to about 90 million in 1990. The population of Mexico is projected to be more than 100 million by the year 2000.[29] Demographic movement depicts a pattern of migration from rural areas to the cities. Massive urban growth has put a burden on the poor. Housing is grossly inadequate to meet their needs. This is in sharp contrast to the United States, the most wealthy and powerful country in the world. This social and demographic context explains potential priorities for a women's agenda in Mexico. It is predictable that women in Mexico will be concerned with social and economic justice rather than more middle-class concerns.

B. CULTURAL DIFFERENCES IN VALUES

One way to understand cultural context is to observe popular culture. The popular Mexican film *Like Water for Chocolate* has been subtitled in English and screened in an edited version in art theaters throughout the United States.[30] It is based on the best-selling novel by Laura Esquibel.[31] She tells the story of a family living near the U.S./Mexican border in turn-of-the-century Mexico. In that particular family, a tradition dictated that the youngest daughter could not marry, but had to remain at home to care for her mother. Tita, the youngest daughter, falls in love with a handsome young man named Pedro. Her mother does not permit her to marry him but arranges for Tita's older sister, Rosaura, to marry Pedro. He agrees to marry the older sister in order to be near Tita. He moves in with the family, thus setting up the sexual tension, repression, and rage that bubble within the household.

At one point, Tita suffers a breakdown; an American doctor nurses her back to the vibrant, vivacious woman she had been. The American physician falls in love with Tita and asks her to marry him. At first she agrees, but she ultimately decides not to marry him and engages in an illicit affair with her first love, her brother-in-law. The movie also involves the magical nature of Tita's cooking. The wedding cake Tita bakes for her sister's wedding causes the guests to become affected by great waves of melancholy; they remember lost loves, and become ill with pain and nausea. Her quail in rose petal sauce produces sexual desire and longing in everyone who partakes of it. The mix of magic, passion, and beauty is compelling.

I had the unique opportunity of seeing the film in Mexico at the height of its popular run and then about a year later seeing the shortened version that ran in the United States. I saw it with Mexicans in Mexico and with Americans in the United States. Mexicans loved the stunning photography, the fine acting, and the actors' sensuality. Mexican feminists were interested in the portrayal of passion from a woman's perspective. They discussed the triangular conflict between mother, daughter, and sister. They were intrigued by the symbolism in the use of cooking and the kitchen. They discussed the sexual repression and the family rage.

In the United States, Americans with whom I discussed the film also enjoyed its beauty and many other aspects. But while they accepted the film's magical moments as characteristic of Latin American literature, some found the plot wholly unbelievable. Several of my friends could not understand how Tita could acquiesce to her mother's wishes. In other words, my American friends could not understand how Tita could put her family ahead of her own wishes. Others did not understand how an intelligent woman could reject the security of a marriage with the American doctor. They could not see how an intelligent, beautiful, and vibrant woman could make the "irrational" choice of rejecting a solid, well-to-do physician in order to pursue a doomed love affair with her sister's ineffectual husband.

The different reactions I was exposed to illustrate some differences in perspectives between Mexican culture and Anglo-American culture. Devotion to family has traditionally been a very important cultural value in Mexican society. Individuals often sacrifice their needs for the needs of the family. While it is not exactly a Mexican cultural trait to put passion before security in matters of marriage, I think the American view that marriage to the doctor would have been the more "rational" choice illustrates a perspective on the values of American culture. While both countries have experienced profound societal changes wrought by economics, technology, and education, each country has retained distinct cultural values: the United States values individualism and autonomy; Mexico values a strong tradition and the family. It is important to keep these differences in mind in comparing and contrasting these two countries, since values underlie legal systems.

C. PERCEIVING LEGAL CONTEXT

On the surface, Mexico's legal system seems much like that of the United States. Mexico's constitution (especially the provisions of the 1917 constitution that survive from the 1824 and 1857 constitutions) was modeled, in many respects, on that of the United States. Mexico has a Senate and a House of Representatives, a Supreme Court, circuit courts, district courts, the appearance of checks and balances, and a federal system as well as a state system of jurisdiction. However, although much was modeled on North American legal forms, Mexico did not adopt the English common law, but instead continued with the Roman and European civil law tradition.

The civil law tradition largely operates without juries. Judges rely on the written code to render decisions. They do not engage in a search for judicial interpretation of a statute to resolve ambiguities. For example, a Mexican district court is not bound by a previous Supreme Court interpretation of a statute in a case unless the Supreme Court has created binding precedent by ruling the same way in five consecutive cases. Mexican lawyers rarely cite cases in their legal briefs. If they cite anything other than the code, they will cite a treatise or other writing by a legal scholar. The power of the judiciary is limited as compared to the power of the judiciary in the United States. Judges do not have the power to declare statutes unconstitutional and thus void. If a litigant has a claim based on a deprivation of a right guaranteed by the constitution, the litigant may use the *amparo* process.[32] However, this proceeding is binding on only the litigants before the court. A statute, even if found by the judge to be inconsistent with the constitution, stays on the books and continues to be enforced until the legislature changes it. Thus rulings such as the *Roe v. Wade* decision declaring restrictions on a woman's right to abortion unconstitutional are not possible under the Mexican system. In practical effect, the judiciary has been accused of being a rubber stamp for the policies and legislation of the powerful executive branch.[33]

Meaningful comparisons between laws of the two countries and especially those laws affecting women also require an understanding of the distinctions between legal and social phenomena. In Mexico it is often said that there is a huge gap between *el derecho y el hecho*, the law and the deed. That is, laws may envision a set of consequences flowing from a law, but citizens may experience those consequences quite differently. The law professor Alicia Elena Pérez of the Universidad Nacional Autónoma de México (UNAM) believes that since the Spanish colonization of Mexico began in the sixteenth century, it has been inherent in Mexico's culture to have a deep distrust of government and the judicial process. She believes that feminists in Mexico more than share this distrust.[34] Thus, women have not used the judicial process of *amparo* to challenge obvious discriminatory laws that are not consistent with the constitutional equal rights amendment guaranteeing equality to men and women. In contrast, resort to the courts has been a powerful method for feminists to challenge gender discriminatory laws in the United States.

D. MODERN MEXICAN FEMINISM

In Mexico there seem to be many more feminist activists than feminist academics. Some academics write about women in literature, others focus on reproductive rights, others on feminist and social theory. The activists work in rape crisis centers and actively organize demonstrations. Urban poor women have fought to improve their lives and the lives of their children. Community-based female activists have pursued change. Some of them have used rather interesting strategies. Learning about their mutual concerns about inadequate services, inflation, alcoholism, and family violence, women have banded together to petition the government and stage demonstrations. However, in their public and political work they often present their demands as a struggle to fulfill their traditional family role as mother. For example, in Guadalajara women have protested chronic water shortages by bathing their children in the ornamental fountain in front of city hall. They chastised state officials for choosing to allocate water for a public fountain over providing water for basic human needs. These women did not challenge the culture's traditional gender roles. Rather, they viewed themselves as being forced to take public and political action in order to fulfill their traditional roles. These political and community activities are in a sense transforming the role of mother to include activism in order to further their maternal impulses. Their objective of improving the daily lives and the quality of life of children does not rely on asking to be treated "equally." They seek to change the values of government and to place their needs on the governmental agenda.

This approach is consistent with Mexican cultural support for the family and thus is more likely to be accepted by society. It also values a feminine perspective on achieving structural change that can transform society. They seek improvement for their communities rather than enhancement of individual rights. They thus seek the opportunity to create new societal norms that value community and human needs.

Although some Latin American feminists have drawn parallels between authoritarian governments and families, in Mexico there does not seem to be a unified feminist movement seeking to change the traditionally gendered family roles.[35] This is true despite the fact that women's work outside their homes serves to change traditional gender role allocations.[36] In meeting the challenge of economic survival, many Mexican women are not seeking "individual rights" for women, but instead seek basic improvement in the quality of life for all.

E. COMPARING ABORTION LAW IN MEXICO AND THE UNITED STATES

The laws on abortion in the United States and Mexico are completely different. Generally, Mexico prohibits abortion while the United States permits it. The Mexican conceptual approach focuses on morality, the sanctity of the family and new life. The conceptual approach in the United States focuses on a woman's right to autonomy in decision making. Mexico's constitution provides that all families have the right to control the number and spacing of their children.[37] North Americans who are accustomed to thinking about individual rights and autonomy tend to think of this as a guaranteed constitutional right to family planning. Abortion, however, is not considered a method of family planning under Mexican law, because from the moment a person is conceived, she comes under the protection of the law and has the same protection as one who is born.[38] Mexican states generally permit abortion and make it available to women only in cases of rape or to protect women's health. In Yucatán, the criminal law excuses the crime of abortion for serious economic reasons if the woman has at least three children.[39] The vast majority of Mexican citizens are Catholic—retaining the religion brought by the Spanish colonizers. Thus, their belief in the teaching of the Church affects their positions on abortion.

In 1990 there was an attempt to liberalize the abortion laws in the state of Chiapas.[40] Interestingly, the Chiapas story illustrates the power of the federal executive and the problems feminists have in Mexico. According to Alicia Pérez, the federal family planning authorities approached the executive about considering abortion as a method of family planning. This would probably have a dramatic effect on population control in that if abortions were considered a method of family planning, they could be performed for free or at very low cost in well-run government clinics. The officials wanted to see whether the people of Mexico would accept this drastic change from previous policy before announcing it as federal policy. They then persuaded the Chiapas legislators to amend the criminal law in Chiapas and decriminalize abortion. The Chiapas legislature responded with the usual accommodation of requests from the federal executive and made the desired changes. Upon publicizing the changes, the government discovered extreme opposition and intense national debate on the issue. Liberalization of abortion law was widely blasted as immoral and destructive of the family.

Mexican feminists, while clearly not the impetus for the change, felt obligated to support it since reproductive rights had been on their agenda for some time. Many feminists, however, had private reservations about the change, because they feared that if abortions became legal, overly aggressive government clinics might engage in forced abortions in the same manner in which they had performed unconsented sterilizations.[41] The national debate in opposition became so intense that the Chiapas legislature revoked its legalization of abortion. On a side note, it is reported that some of the most vigorous opponents of legalization are gynecologists who are rumored to perform clean, skilled, but illegal abortions (disguised as dilation and curettage) for hefty fees.

Finally, abortion laws in Mexico are not vigorously enforced. Only two women in the last twenty years have been prosecuted for obtaining illegal abortions, yet many illegal abortions are performed throughout Mexico. Numerous women suffer complications from botched illegal abortions. A report from a public hospital in Durango indicated that in 1990, 1,200 women received medical care after suffering complications from botched abortions. This was a 153 percent increase over 1989.[42] In practice, abortion is available to women with funds to pay for it. Most of these women travel to a different state and pay a gynecologist to perform their dilation and curettage for a large fee.[43]

In contrast, the United States was slowly moving to legalize abortion in various states until the famous case of *Roe v. Wade* legalized abortion for any reason during the first trimester of pregnancy.[44] In the context of reproductive rights, individual rights have been perceived as a sphere of autonomy in which the individual has the right to exercise choices about familial relationships.[45] Building on earlier cases giving individuals the right to use contraception without state interference,[46] the *Roe v. Wade* case focuses on an individual woman's autonomy and her right to choose whether or not to terminate her pregnancy. The Court limited states' ability to legislate in this area. A woman has the right to make this decision without the consent of her husband.[47] However, subsequent cases about this right have ensured that it is not available to poor women,[48] and subject to state regulation as to parental consent and waiting periods.[49] Although the government will not pay for or counsel about abortions,[50] generally, abortions are available to middle-class women without "undue burdens" by the state.[51] Reproductive rights are seen as an aspect of individual autonomy. However, the issue has proven to be extremely controversial. Feminists in the United States have found that the autonomy, rights-based approach to abortion has limitations.[52] Laurie Schrage has pointed out that the abortion debate in the United States has polarized women. According to Schrage, women on opposite sides of the abortion debate in the United States have different views of motherhood. Pro-choice women see the demands of motherhood as unreasonable, unfair, and sometimes unmanageable if a woman is not ready for motherhood. For pro-life women, motherhood is an essential aspect of a woman's existence. When a woman marries or has sex she implicitly agrees to take on this role. The demands of motherhood are seen as reasonable and fair if she has the proper attitude.[53] These perspectives are obscured in the rhetoric about "women's right to choose" or "pro-life." Religious convictions play an important role in values concerning the morality of abortion. In addition to the theoretical and religious differences between pro-choice advocates and pro-life advocates, the abortion issues have become part of the political discourse. I think the issue reflects deeply held views about women's self-perception and men's perception of their reproductive role in society.

Despite the difference in abortion theory and politics, in practice, abortions are available in both countries to middle-class women with money to pay for the procedure. However, given the countries' different economic situations, more women in the United States have the financial ability to access the procedure. The implications of the above comparative analysis are complex. Of course, Mexican and Mexican American women in the United States find themselves caught in a clash of cultural and legal norms.[54] Allowing absolute individual autonomy (as in the United States) can help women in a position to exercise choices to make those choices. However, autonomy theory does not help women (e.g., minorities, poor) who are *not* in a position to exercise choices. And there are real questions about how much "choice" women really have in a patriarchal society, where expectations about women's proper roles limit women's opportunities. Feminist successes in the United

States seek to further individual choice. Individual choice, however, evades the morality questions. Laws in Mexico support traditional cultural gender roles and religious moral values. The approaches to abortion reveal how autonomy is an important value in the United States and family and religious values are deeply held in Mexico.

A contextualized comparative analysis of women's rights reveals that the abortion issue is conceptualized differently in Mexico and the United States. Context helps comparativists studying women's rights to draw meaningful comparisons and contrasts in legal status while recognizing cultural contexts. The proposed methodology helps broaden perspective and minimize ethnocentricity. The methodology draws on feminist insights to evaluate implications of the law for women. Finally, it recognizes the importance of understanding how women perceive their own legal status in their own cultural context. There is much comparative work to be done; the proposed methodology helps to organize this work.

NOTES

1. Jomo Kenyatta, Facing Mt. Kenya 129 (1965) *cited in* Hope Lewis, *Between Irua and "Female Genital Mutilation": Feminist Human Rights Discourse and the Cultural Divide*, 8 Harv. Hum. Rts. J. 1, 1 (1995).

2. Octavio Paz, The Labyrinth of Solitude: Life and Thought in Mexico 81–88 (1961).

3. *See* Elisabeth Bumiller, May You Be the Mother of a Hundred Sons 72 (1990).

4. *See* Isabelle R. Gunning, *Arrogant Perception, World-Traveling and Multicultural Feminism: The Case of Female Genital Surgeries*, 23 Colum. Hum. Rts. L. Rev. 189 (1991–92). As a Latina, I am particularly sensitive to the dangers of forced acculturation by a dominant group. *See* Latinos in the United States: History, Law and Perspective (Antoinette Sedillo Lopez, ed., 1995).

5. *See, e.g.*, articles collected and cited in Latina Issues: Fragments of Historia (Ella) (Herstory) (Antoinette Sedillo Lopez, ed., 1995).

6. *See, e.g.,* Third World Women and the Politics of Feminism (Chandra Talpade Mohanty et al. eds., 1991).

7. *See, e.g.*, Patrick E. Tyler, *Forum on Women Agrees on Goals*, N.Y. Times, Sept. 15, 1995, at A1, col. 1.

8. *See, e.g.*, Ellen Carol Dubois and Vicki Ruiz, Unequal Sisters: A Multi Cultural Reader in U.S. Women's History (1990); Martha I. Morgan and Mónica María Alzate Buitrago, *Constitution-Making in a Time of Cholera: Women and the 1991 Colombian Constitution*, 4 Yale J.L. and Feminism 353 (1992).

9. Antoinette Sedillo Lopez, *"On Privilege,"* 2 Am. U. J. Gender and the Law 217 (1994).

10. Deborah L. Rhode, *Perspectives on Professional Women*, 40 Stan. L. Rev. 1163 (1988).

11. Christine A. Littleton, *Reconstructing Sexual Equality*, 75 Cal. L. Rev. 1279 (1987).

12. *See, e.g.*, Martha Fineman, *Dominant Discourse, Professional Language and Legal Change in Custody Decision-Making*, 101 Harv. L. Rev. 727 (1988); Carol Gilligan, In a Different Voice: Psychological Theory and Women's Development (1982).

13. *See* Patricia J. Williams, Alchemy of Race and Rights (1991); Carrie Menkel-Meadow, *The Power of Narrative in Empathetic Learning: Post Modernism and the Stories of Law*, 2 UCLA Women's L.J. 287 (1992).

14. *See* Critical Race Feminism: A Reader (Adrien Katherine Wing ed., 1997).

15. *See, e.g.*, Antoinette Sedillo Lopez, *Two Legal Constructs of Motherhood: "Protective" Legislation in Mexico and the United States*, 1 S. Cal. Rev. L. and Women's Stud. 239 (1992) (comparing protective legislation in Mexico and the United States).

16. *See, e.g.*, Gloria Valencia-Weber and Christine Zuni, *Domestic Violence and Tribal Protection of Indigenous Women in the United States*, 69 St. Johns L. Rev. 69 (1996) (discussing the importance of respecting culture as opposed to Western feminism in crafting legal solutions for Native people).

17. *See* Mary Ann Glendon, Abortion and Divorce in Western Law (1987).

18. *Id.* at 112–34.

19. *Id.* at 58–62.

20. *See* Heleen F. P. Ietswaarrt, *Book Review: Incomplete Stories,* 69 B.U. L. Rev. 257 (1989) (reviewing Mary Ann Glendon, Abortion and Divorce in Western Law (1987)) (criticizing Glendon for failing to perceive the social ramifications of abortion and divorce law).

21. Patricia A. Cain, *Feminism and the Limits of Equality*, 24 Ga. L. Rev. 803 (1990).

22. *See id.* at 829.

23. *See* Littleton, *supra* note 11.

24. *See* Cain, *supra* note 21, at 832.

25. *See* Fineman, *supra* note 12.

26. Gilligan, *supra* note 12.

27. *See, e.g.*, Angela P. Harris, *Race and Essentialism in Feminist Legal Theory,* 42 Stan. L. Rev. 581 (1990).

28. *See, e.g,* Williams, *supra* note 13.

29. Mexico: A Country Guide XIX (Tom Barry ed., 1992).

30. Like Water for Chocolate, Miramax (1991).

31. Laura Esquibel, Like Water for Chocolate (1989).

32. Richard D. Baker, Judicial Review in Mexico: A Study of the Amparo Suit (1971).

33. Interviews with Mexican lawyers who prefer to remain anonymous (1994).

34. Alicia Pérez, Condición jurídica de la mujer (1992) (on file with the author).

35. Sandra McGee Deutsch, *Feminist Studies, in* Latinas of the Americas: A Sourcebook 129–52 (K. Lynn Stoner ed., 1988).

36. Soledad González Montes, *Los ingresos no agropecuario, el trabajo renumerado femenino y la transformación de las relaciones intergenericas e intergeneracionales de las familias campesinas, in* Textos y pretextos: Once estudios sobre la mujer, El Colegio de Mexico (1991).

37. Mexico Const. art. IV.

38. Código civil, para el Distrito Federal [C.C.D.F.] art. 167 (Mexican Civil Code).

39. This was true in Chihuahua before 1987 and in Chiapas before 1984. Alicia Elena Pérez Duarte y Norona, La maternidad: Relato de una contradicción (unpublished manuscript, on file with the author).

40. *State of Chiapas Backs Down from Attempt to Decriminalize Abortion,* SourceMEX, Jan. 16, 1991.

41. Sara Lovera, *Sterilization Pushed without Women's Consent,* March 16, 1989 (citing a study by the College of Mexico that denounced the abusive way women were sterilized in

public hospitals and clinics: describes the plight of Dulce Maria González, who was sterilized without her consent in a government hospital at the age of twenty-two; and women's groups mounting 1984 protests against the sterilization of women against their will or without their informed consent) Reuters, Oct. 11, 1996, available in Lexis-Nexis, Academic Universal.

42. *Complications from Botched Abortions in Durango: One Hundred fifty-three Percent Increase over 1989*, SourceMEX, Jan. 16, 1991.

43. Interview with Mexican female professional who prefers anonymity (June 1994).

44. Roe v. Wade, 410 U.S. 113 (1973).

45. Planned Parenthood v. Casey, 505 U.S. 833 (1992); Antoinette Sedillo Lopez, *The New Reproductive Technology: A Decisionmaking Approach*, 28 Fam. L. Q. 173 (1988).

46. Eisenstadt v. Baird, 405 U.S. 438, 443 (1972).

47. Planned Parenthood v. Danforth, 428 U.S. 52 (1976).

48. Harris v. McCrae, 448 U.S. 297, 325 (1980).

49. Bellotti v. Baird, 443 U.S. 622, 643–44 (1979).

50. Rust v. Sullivan, 500 U.S. 173 (1991).

51. Webster v. Reproductive Health Services, 492 U.S. 490 (1989).

52. Reva Siegel, *Reasoning from the Body: A Historical Perspective on Abortion Regulation and Questions of Equal Protection*, 44 Stan. L. Rev. 262 (1991–92); Sylvia Law, *Rethinking Sex and the Constitution*, 132 Penn. L. Rev. 998 (1984).

53. Laurie Shrage, Moral Dilemmas of Feminism: Prostitution, Adultery and Abortion 60 (1994).

54. Alfredo Mirandé, Evangelina Enríquez, La Chicana (1979); Margaret E. Montoya, *Máscaras, Trenzas y Greñas: Un/Masking the Self While Un/Braiding Personal Experience in Latina Stories and Legal Discourse*, 15 Chicano-Latino L. Rev. 1 (1994); Sedillo Lopez, *supra* note 5; Berta Esperanza Hernández-Truyol, *Building Bridges—Latinas and Latinos at the Crossroads: Realities, Rhetoric and Replacement*, 25 Col. Hum. Rts. L. Rev. 369 (1993); Lawrence Mosqueda, Chicanos, Catholicism and Political Ideology (1986). I myself have deeply ambivalent views about abortion. While I believe that a woman should not be forced to bear a child against her will, the moral and psychological issues trouble me. Further, abortion can be used as a form of genocide. As a society, we should not be cavalier about the implications of these painful choices.

5 Féminismes sans Frontières?

The Cuban Challenge—Women, Equality, and Culture

Berta Esperanza Hernández-Truyol

> *El hombre está hecho para la calle y la mujer para la casa.*
> —Cuban adage, quoted in K. Lynn Stoner,
> *From the House to the Streets*

> *En un mundo hecho a la imagen de los hombres la mujer es sólo un reflejo de los hombres. Pasiva, se convierte en diosa, ser que encarna los elementos estables y antiguos del universo: la tierra, madre y virgen; activa es siempre función, medio, canal.*
> —Octavio Paz, *El laberinto de la soledad*

I. INTRODUCTION

Not all feminisms are alike. The question is whether all women's liberation movements are feminist. Can a women's movement be feminist without having defined borders, such as the goal of eradicating women's inequality in the state, society, and even the home? Can a movement be feminist if it embraces a culture's, gender-subordinating norms and roles?

In the United States there are diverse feminist approaches, such as formal equality feminism, dominance/inequality feminism, hedonic feminism, and pragmatic feminism.[1] All these feminisms seek to better the condition of women's lives. The various approaches, however, have varied means of and philosophies concerning the attainment of the desired end.

For instance, formal equality, the favored approach in the early years of feminism, challenged classifications based on sex as perpetuating sex norms and stereotypes. This approach urged adjudicators to reject laws that treated men and women differently, thus eschewing any legal basis for distinguishing between the sexes based on traditionally assigned roles. On the other hand, unlike the formal equality perspective, the dominance analytical approach focuses on the inequality between the sexes, particularly the power differential between men and women. Thus, in the context of sex, where men and women are (or may be) different—such as the pregnancy conundrum—the goal of formal equality "becomes a contradiction in terms, something of an oxymoron."[2]

As these two approaches reveal, a dialectic tension permeates the sex-liberating goals of feminism and the jurisprudential borderlands of the equality-as-sameness judicial approach. Thus, diverse feminist perspectives and approaches seem appropriate to grapple with the complexities of women's inequality and subordinated status. However, some approaches, while seeking to establish certain rights for women in public life, embrace gendered cultural norms that continue to subordinate women in both the public and private spheres. The issue then arises whether a cultural feminism that is premised upon the validity of traditional sex/gender roles that entrench and perpetuate the subordination of women can be deemed feminist. For example, the goals and perspectives of women's movements in Cuba are not identical to those of Western feminists. Although the Cuban women's movements sought rights to participate in the country's governance and protections for and achievement of certain rights—particularly with respect to education and work—Cuban feminists' goals were never formal equality, sameness, or the eradication of sex roles. Rather, Cuban women's movements operated within "traditional" social roles and mores, always revering motherhood—which is seen as giving women social status and as a stepping-stone to power—and seeking to preserve femininity.

This chapter will trace the struggles and achievements of Cuban women from the turn of the century to the present. Throughout history—be it from the first call for independence from Spain in 1868 to the socialist revolution of 1959—Cuba's laws and constitutional provisions affecting women and establishing and protecting women's rights have always been among the most progressive in the world. The reformist nature of the laws and legal system is related to and reflects appreciation and respect for women's participation in all of Cuba's liberation struggles.

To convey the role of Cuban women in society, this chapter presents first the history and background of Cuban "feminism" and evaluates the changes in the role and status of women in postrevolution Castro's Cuba according to existing rules and laws. However, notwithstanding the formal rights of Cuban women, a review of the reality of their lives reveals persistent inequality—a condition that in an earlier work led me to conclude that in Cuba gender equality is a myth.[3] However, further and more recent interrogation leads me to reevaluate that position because gender equality in the sense understood in Western feminism was never the goal of the Cuban women's *feminine* movements. Rather, the focus was on pressing for and achieving legal changes that would enable, encourage, and facilitate woman's natural role as, and calling to be, a mother and wife, a nurturer.[4] The *grupos femeninos*, with their marianista model,[5] were since their early days (and continue to be at present) unquestionably successful movements—as the State's progressive laws attest.

In the end, one may question whether the acceptance of patriarchal, women-subordinating cultural norms within some women's movements—movements in which women's citizenship is full de jure but second-class de facto because of its gender-stereotyping and subordinating core—makes the feminist label an oxymoron. While the tremendous successes of the Cuban *grupos femeninos* must be recognized and applauded, it might be appropriate not to label them *feminista*. It could make better sense either to call the Cuban women's movement something other than feminism or to contest whether equality and nonsubordination need be central foundations of feminisms. In short, rather than conclude with an answer, this chapter concludes with the question whether a feminist movement can exist outside, extrinsic to, independent of, divorced from notions of true in/equality; can we have *féminismes sans frontières?*

II. THE EARLY CUBAN WOMEN'S MOVEMENT

A. HISTORICAL BACKGROUND: THE MAMBISAS— FIGHTING FOR INDEPENDENCE

The first Cuban women who broke from the mold established by society, church, and state dictating that women are to be weak, dependent, and submissive were the *mambisas*—woman warriors.[6] These women—wives and mothers—redefined the borders of womanhood by leaving the safety of their *hogares* (homes) to join in the fight for Cuban independence from Spain. They also challenged the traditional female spaces of weakness and submissiveness and embraced strength and leadership.

Considering their active role in battle as well as their continued domestic duties, the *mambisas* may well have been the precursors of today's superwoman who does it all—working full-time both in and outside the home. But careful scrutiny reveals that even their role in battle was appreciated in the context of their exalted natural role as mothers. Indeed, Mariana Grajales, the mother of ten soldiers, including Antonio Maceo, one of Cuba's best-known, loved, and respected heroes, fought alongside her sons in war and thus became the archetype and exemplar of motherhood.[7] Such an image of the *madre patriota* became an emblem of Cuban sacrifice and endurance[8]—traits demanded of women in all events by the culture, which requires that its female ideal, *marianismo*, be modeled after the "Catholic Virgin Madonna, and prescribes dependence, subordination, responsibility for all domestic chores, and selfless devotion to family and children."[9]

B. POST-INDEPENDENCE WOMEN'S MOVEMENT: ORGANIZATIONS AND GOALS

In the twentieth century women benefited from the passage of progressive laws regarding property rights, divorce, maternity, and decriminalization of adultery.[10] Significantly, women obtained these broad rights without any acknowledgment of, aspiration for, or desire to attain women's equality. Moreover, the Cuban feminists who fought for these rights were far from representative of Cuban society as a whole. The Cuban feminists were white, middle- to upper-class, educated women, about 40 percent of whom were mothers, 42 percent of whom were married, 60 percent of whom had, at some time, been employed, 75 percent of whom had graduated from a university, 33 percent of whom had postgraduate degrees, and every single one of whom had at least one domestic servant who was expressly excluded from the protection of the maternity law.[11]

On the other hand, these cultural aspirations and expectations were different for and foreign to Black, *mulata*, and poor white women. These women had no option but to leave home and work. So when only a small number of women were employed during the early years of Cuban independence, approximately three-quarters of the employed women were Black, and most were engaged as domestics (some of whom were serving the feminists), laundresses, and tobacco plantation workers.[12] These women, in contrast to the educated feminists, faced poverty, ill health, sexual exploitation, and disrespect for their race and/or class. They were viewed by all as inferior, and, pursuant to the *machista* society, they were objectified even to the extent that they were expected to be sexually available to the men with or for whom they worked.[13] Despite the reforms effected under the auspices of the women's movement, the women who most needed legal protection did not get it.

C. THE 1940 CONSTITUTION: THE RIGHTS TO VOTE AND TO EQUALITY

Beyond the passage of the property, divorce, and maternity laws and the abolition of the adultery law, a main goal of the early women's movement was to secure the vote for women. Although President Grau San Martín granted the vote to women in the provisional constitution of 1934, that right, together with the right to be elected to public office, became a confirmed reality in the constitution of 1940, one of the most progressive for women. Like the right to own property, however, neither the right to vote nor the express constitutional provisions regarding gender equality signified an acknowledgment of women's equality.[14] However, the provisional constitution and its permanent successor effected a change in the discourse by couching, casting, and contextualizing women's rights and conditions within an equality paradigm.

The 1940 constitution had several noteworthy progressive provisions regarding technical legal rights to equality. For example, Article 23 provided that "All Cubans are equal before the law. The state does not recognize special privileges or status. It is illegal and punishable by law to discriminate based on sex, race, color, class, and any other prejudice against human dignity." In addition, Article 62 provided equal pay for equal work, regardless of sex, race, or nationality. Article 68 made it illegal to distinguish between married and single women in the workplace. Yet Article 77 mandated an eight-and-a-half-hour work day, restricting night work for women.[15] Significantly, the protective (paternalistic) nature of the Article 77 provisions reflects the reality that inequality for women persisted, largely based on cultural and gender roles and stereotypes.

Finally, women may have had constitutionally dictated equal rights to be elected to public office, but, consistent with their second-class citizenship, they rarely ran for office and few were elected.[16] Thus, although women apparently had very strong paper legal rights, these were aspirational as the reality did not comport to the technical rules. Moreover, once these extensive gender-based legal rights were achieved, the feminist movement in Cuba basically died and no version reemerged until after the socialist revolution.

D. CULTURAL PERSPECTIVES ON GENDER

Notwithstanding the *mambisas'* deviation from the classic sex role mold by joining in the battle for liberation, and later the feminists' insistence on laws that would promote women's rights, Cuban feminism before the Castro revolution stands out as a movement that simply did not challenge the cultural conceptions, perceptions, and expectations of women's proper location and space in society. Motherhood, submissiveness, purity, and weakness were central features of a woman's life as defined by the church, state, and culture.[17] This *familismo* narrowly located women in society, the family, the home—and together with *marianismo* dictated women's conduct "by Church teaching, social custom, and man-made laws."[18] Although, as discussed in the preceding sections, women's struggles effectively changed some of the laws, the cultural norms were never challenged.

Moreover, Cuban feminism was essentialist. The participants in the movement were generally white, middle- and upper-class women who sought power for themselves and did not hesitate in claiming it in the name of all women. The feminists were set apart from poor women and women of color, but they were aware of race and class issues and sought to speak on behalf of all women. The aspirations were to focus on and advance the position of women in society, claiming power and entitlements within the varied communities, within the accepted cultural location of women as mothers and keepers of the family and morality. Indeed, Cuban feminists often viewed the status of motherhood as an entrée to power. The traditional epistemology of *marianismo* was not challenged. Even as they challenged church practices, women, in seeking liberation and culturally contextualized emancipation and participation, aspired to the impossible—to attain the image and virtues of the Virgin Mary, including her mystical (mythical) purity and morality as defining of the feminist cause—even as they challenged church practices.

III. THE SOCIALIST REVOLUTION AND BEYOND

A. THE ASPIRATIONS: EQUALITY AS A GOAL OF THE REVOLUTION

The foundation of Castro's 1959 socialist revolution was the concept of egalitarianism, particularly class-based—a new concept in the Cuban model. In fact, in a statement that makes patent the intersection of sex and class, Castro's first address to the nation noted the need to end discrimination against women's participation in the labor force. Shortly after that declaration not only did the Labor Ministry start to enforce labor legislation regarding women more strictly, but the state passed new regulations regarding rights of pregnant women to their jobs.[19] Similarly, in Castro's September 26, 1960, address to the General Assembly, he clearly stated that one of the aims of the revolution was to eradicate inequality and discrimination. He specifically noted that one of the principles of the Cuban revolution was the condemnation of discrimination against Blacks and Indians, and inequality and exploitation of women.[20] Castro designated this move toward equality for women as a revolution within a revolution.[21]

The 1976 constitution reiterated this right to equality. Like its 1940 predecessor but reflecting the socialist position concerning the correlative rights and duties of a citizenry, Chapter 5 of the 1976 constitution expressly provided that "all citizens enjoy equal rights and are subject to equal obligations."[22] Again, like the 1938 provisional constitution and the 1940 permanent constitution, the 1976 constitution framed the discourse of the rights of women within the borderlands of an equality paradigm.

Reflecting this revolutionary philosophy of sex equality, and following the example (tradition?) of the *mambisas* in the war to free Cuba from Spanish domination, in the revolution of 1959 women again fought alongside their male comrades. Further reflecting the gender equality foundation of the revolution movement, and in order to institutionalize women's place in it, Castro created the Federación de Mujeres Cubanas (Federation of Cuban Women)—the FMC. By the mid-1980s, 80 percent of Cuban women over the age of fourteen were dues-paying members of the FMC.[23]

The goals of the FMC have been to prepare women educationally, politically, and socially to participate in the revolution, as well as to incorporate women into the workforce and raise their educational consciousness.[24] Significantly, the head of the FMC was Vilma Espín, Castro's former sister-in-law and the only woman to serve in the Politburo, albeit for a very short time. Also interesting is that Espín as the leader of the FMC, while waging a national campaign to retrain and reeducate domestic workers, enjoyed domestic help paid for by the FMC.[25]

B. THE REALITY: WOMEN'S ADVANCEMENT

The 1993 United Nations Human Development Report labels women "a non-participating majority" because while they are "a majority of the world's population [they] receive only a small share of developmental opportunities. They are often excluded from education or from the better jobs, from the political systems or from adequate health care."[26] Contrary to the global reality, this section reveals that women's advancement in Cuba was significant in health, education, and employment largely because of programs instituted during Castro's rule with active FMC participation.

For example, the FMC figured prominently in the literacy campaign mobilizing women, who constituted 55 percent of the volunteers (*brigadistas*).[27] The campaign succeeded in reducing illiteracy from 23.6 percent to 3.9 percent of the population, making approximately three-quarters of a million persons, 56 percent of whom were women, literate.[28] Another major undertaking of the revolution that expressly concerned women and in which the FMC played a major role was the reeducation or retraining of domestic servants and prostitutes.[29]

Beyond the specialized retraining programs, women also fared well in formal education. With the socialist revolution making education free for everyone, women's educational attainment quickly progressed. Current education figures show that females are on par with, if not ahead of, males.[30] Today women number about 50 percent of the medical students, and 90 percent of the students in education.[31] However, such progress has not consistently translated to full equality. Indeed, while Castro recognized that women's equality was not a reality, the government imposed quotas limiting women's enrollment in medical schools. The twofold explanation for the quotas involved the critical role played by civilian medical assistance in Cuba's foreign policy. First, expressly recognizing women's *in*equality in the home by citing women's greater family responsibilities, the government justified limiting women's enrollment in medical school by stating that domestic responsibilities would make it difficult for women to travel overseas for extended periods to deliver medical assistance. Second, the state reasoned that male doctors were needed to deliver medical services because the countries receiving assistance had not recognized (as Cuba did) the changing role of women in society. Thus, notwithstanding Cuba's enlightenment regarding women even within their own country's borders, foreign sexist attitudes prevailed in the formation of foreign policy. Women's equality and self-determination were negated and paternalism reigned. Women were denied access to a profession, and deemed unable to decide for themselves whether to travel and/or to put up with sexist attitudes; the notion of equality ceded to the governmental policy to deliver aid.

C. EMPLOYMENT AND REPRESENTATION

Beyond increasing their labor market participation, women also have broadened their role. They now hold many jobs that had exclusively been done by men, such as cane cutters, citrus fruit packers, auto mechanics, dentists, doctors, engineers, and traffic police. Such changes notwithstanding, female participation in the labor force still predominantly follows traditional gendered patterns and continues in the pink ghetto tradition. However, women comprise 56 percent of all working professionals and constitute the majority in some "nontraditionally female" fields such as medicine[32] and increasingly in law[33]—there are more female than male doctors and judges.[34]

Women in Cuba have also made great strides in parliamentary representation. In 1991 the percentage of parliamentary seats occupied by women in Cuba was 22.8

percent, behind only Norway, Romania, and the then Soviet Union.[35] However, it was not until 1986 that a woman became a full Politburo member. Nevertheless, women lag far behind in the "more powerful and prestigious occupational levels in revolutionary Cuba. Although one out of every three workers is a woman, less than one in five directors of state, political and economic organizations is female. This female under-representation in the pinnacles of political and economic power . . . remains puzzling if one is to accept the official rhetoric calling for equality between the sexes."[36]

IV. IS THIS EQUALITY?

The revolutionary equality notions, mostly encoded in law, were noble and perhaps partly realized insofar as one considers the improvements in health, education, and welfare discussed above. In reality, however, the notions of gender equality are plagued with deeply embedded cultural sex roles and stereotypes and relegate even Cuban women who enjoy broad de jure equality rights to second-class citizenship. The pattern evident in the above discussion of high levels of women's representation but only at the lesser levels of government is emblematic and reflective of their second-class citizenship. This pattern repeats itself in the labor force.

Cuba, as a socialist state, guarantees employment to every citizen who wants to work.[37] Notwithstanding this guarantee, the state's habitual influencing of the size of the labor force by policy proclamations provides strong evidence that true equality in the marketplace is but aspirational.[38] One of the ways that Cuba has manipulated the size of the labor force is "by granting or removing economic and other incentives for female labor force participation or by changing the regulations under which women are allowed to work."[39] As in other cultures, women are considered a supply of labor when there are labor shortages.[40] On the other hand, when the state has found it necessary, it has taken measures to discourage female employment. Arguably, one such measure is the difference in retirement ages for women (fifty-five) and men (sixty),[41] which has the effect of removing women from the labor force at an earlier age than men, in spite of the fact that women's life expectancy is greater than men's.[42] In order to manipulate the labor force, the state also has classified some jobs as male only.[43]

Historically government regulations have limited women's access to certain jobs. These restrictions, supposedly aimed at protecting women's health, are in reality pretexts for resolving employment problems—usually labor surpluses. To be sure, the FMC objected to the work restrictions as violative of principles of equality. Nevertheless, there are still some job categories that are off limits to women, although the list now only numbers approximately twenty-five jobs, whereas in the 1970s it numbered about three hundred.

Effectively, the so-called equality rights women enjoy are no more than a state-supported reinforcement and perpetuation of traditional gender roles, including one that presumes that work outside the home is more important for men, the execution of which is facilitated by state policies, as evidenced in the foreign policy. As late as its 1990 congress the FMC still was noting the obstacles to gender equality posed by the double burden of work and home. The FMC also noted the continued discrimination in job promotions, the lack of promotions of women to leadership positions, and the significantly lower earnings of women as compared to men even when women were better educated, despite the various constitutional equality provisions, including equal pay for equal work.

Even in the midst of revolutionary changes, women are not represented in many areas because they are subject to a double burden. Pursuant to the socialist obligation to work, women worked outside the home all day in record numbers. Yet not even the constitutional mandate of equal responsibility for men and women in maintaining the household changed the traditional gendered roles, patterns, and expectations. Thus, after putting in a full day at work outside the home, women then continued to work inside the home caring for their children and husbands at night. Studies reveal that women working outside the home had an average of only two hours and fifty-nine minutes of free time a day. Women spent six hours and twenty-nine minutes at their job, and then four hours and four minutes in domestic chores. On the other hand, men, on the average, spent seven hours and forty-eight minutes working at their jobs, but then only thirty-two minutes on housework.[44] This reality hardly comports with the equal domestic partnership for which the constitution and the Family Code expressly provide.

In fact, reflecting the depth of cultural gendered expectations, the revolutionary messages regarding sex equality were often inconsistent. The revolution provided that women should work outside the home in order not to deprive the state of "productive" labor and because engaging in paid employment is key to women's emancipation.[45] Indeed, the revolutionary government deems housewives to be "unintegrated."[46] Yet state employment policies, depending on the state's need, often discourage women from participation in the labor force and thus reinforce traditional domestic arrangements. Moreover, while domestic tasks are seen as unproductive and unpleasant, the state has failed to provide the means to relieve women of their double duty. After almost forty years of equality rhetoric, the state has failed to change the reality of women's traditional culture-defined roles: women continue to be seen primarily as mothers. The result is simultaneously to praise motherhood and devalue it as unproductive. This attitude reveals the deeply rooted view of the maternal role as the primary and quintessential role of women, and the subordinated status of that role, which is seen as not *real* but rather "unproductive" work. Moreover, notwithstanding the state's formal pronouncements concerning the need for men's equal participation in housework and child care, it incorporates and reinforces the cultural view of men as inherently unreliable regarding family responsibilities. Consequently the state's policies reinforce women's domestic roles, entrenching, as a matter of practice, traditional roles and placing primary family care burdens on women.

In sum, it is plain, forty years after a revolution based on egalitarianism, that women have not met stated equality goals. Although women have made some praiseworthy gains, they have largely been excluded from centers of power. More-over, notwithstanding consistent pronouncements about de jure equality of men and women in private and public life, women's status remains second-class. Much of the attitudes remain grounded in prerevolutionary cultural traditions and expectations.

V. CONCLUSION

Women in Cuba have enjoyed a long history of participation in liberation struggles as well as enjoyment of progressive laws. Yet throughout several revolutions it appears that for women not much has changed with respect to social, cultural, and family roles, patterns, and expectations. The *mambisas'* insistence on feminine accoutrements while wearing combat attire reflected an acceptance of the system and a concept of feminism that does not operate along a binary model. Later, the way Castro in 1960 addressed the issue of discrimination evidenced a similar cultural tension. He seemed to view racial discrimination—against Blacks and Indians, probably men—as different from gender discrimination. He implied as much when he said that one of the principles of the Cuban revolution is the condemnation of discrimination against Blacks and Indians and inequality and exploitation of women. Castro declared "the right of Blacks and Indians to the 'full dignity of *man*'; the right of women to civil, social and political equality."[47] Women do not get the "dignity of man"—whatever that may be—or, apparently, even economic or cultural equality.

This sense of a less equal—or at least "different"—"equality" for women can pose a challenge to the true equality of the *mambisas* and the egalitarianism of the revolution. On the other hand, the challenge can be viewed as one posed to feminism. This latter challenge interrogates the meaning of feminism and, at its most difficult, asks whether a notion of a cultural feminism that accepts traditional gender roles, and thus implicitly if not explicitly eschews the goal of equality, can coexist with the existing paradigms of feminism.

To be sure, it is incontrovertible that Cuban women—from the *mambisas* to the FMC activists–have not only participated in emancipatory struggles, but also attained laudable advances. Women have been beneficiaries of these advancements, although the benefits have not included attaining equal participation or representation in government, nor have they included a termination or an even significant departure from or restructuring of traditional gender roles.

The tension in Cuba between equality and feminism, offers a good point of departure from which to re-interrogate, re-create, and re-present the equality paradigm also the meaning of feminism. The progress made with respect to women's social, educational, and welfare positions are by any measure feminist advances. This and other forms of cultural feminisms should be embraced. Yet the quandary posed by the Cuban model is that in the cultural contextualization of the movement, an intellectual analysis requires accommodation of the cultural norms that include *marianismo*, the underpinnings of which are most charitably described as being on a direct collision course with nondiscrimination principles as they are designed and inspired by and dependent on gender hierarchy. The results are ostensibly incongruous and inconsistent—a de jure equality mandate coexists with the de facto gender role divide that permeates Cuban society.

Given both the incontrovertible successes and stresses of the roles, goals, and participations of women in the cultural context, when viewed through a gendered lens, the Cuban condition presents a starting point for discursive developments concerning women's rights and feminism. These developments provide opportunities and possibilities to explore strategic alliances with the goal of developing a *féminisme sans frontières* that sharpens the understanding of the way law, society, and culture have collaborated in the production of sex subordination. The achievements also expand the possibilities and understandings as well as clarify the limitations of law and culture in an emancipatory project.

NOTES

The translations of the epigraphs at the beginning of this chapter are as follows:
 "Men are made for life in the streets, women for life within the home."
 "In a world created in the image of men, woman is only a reflection of man. Passive she becomes a goddess, a person who embodies the stable and ancient elements of the universe; earth, mother and virgin; active she is always duty, means, conduit."

 1. Mary Becker, *Strength in Diversity: Feminist Theoretical Approaches to Child Custody and Same-Sex Relationships*, 23 Stetson L. Rev. 701, 704–15 (1994) (describing formal equality as requiring "that similarly situated individuals be treated similarly regardless of their sex or gender," thus seeking the invalidation of laws that mandated differential treatment on the basis of sex and therefore entrenched gender/sex roles and stereotypes; dominance feminism as a rejection of formal equality because it can help women only when they are similarly situated with men and that "the systematic disadvantaging of women is most likely to be operating when women and men do not seem similarly situated" but rather when women are in a subordinated status; hedonic feminism as recognizing the importance of power but suggesting that the focus should be "[a] critical legal method which aims directly for women's subjective well being" and the bettering of "women's lives as actually lived"; and pragmatic feminism, which recognizes that there is no one-size-fits-all answer to human problems and thus "feminists [need] to make pragmatic decisions based on our best guess . . . of what is likely to work best"; choices are to be made in the context of "the concrete reality of women's daily lives").
 2. Catharine A. MacKinnon, Feminism Unmodified: Discourses on Life and Law 33 (Harvard University Press 1987).
 3. *See* Berta Esperanza Hernández-Truyol, *Women in Castro's Cuba: A Myth of Equality*, *in* Encyclopedia of Third World Women (Nelly P. Stromquist ed., 1998).
 4. *See* K. Lynn Stoner, From the House to the Streets: The Cuban Woman's Movement for Legal Reform 1 (1991) (demonstrating "how feminism, emerging in Cuban society during the formative years of the republican period, drew from traditional notions of femininity and

a rejection of gender equality to advance a cause that assumed that women's roles were necessary for social progress"); *see also* Berta Esperanza Hernández-Truyol, *Borders (En)Gendered: Normativities, Latinas, and a LatCrit Paradigm*, 72 N.Y.U. L. Rev. 882 (1997) (discussing Latinas' gendered roles and the culture's reverence and respect for, veneration and adoration of, and deference to motherhood); Berta Esperanza Hernández-Truyol, *Las Olvidadas—Gendered in Justice/Gendered Injustice: Latinas, Fronteras, and the Law*, 1 Iowa J. Gender, Race and Just. 353 (1998) (discussing Latinas' traditional gendered roles).

5. *See* Gloria Bonilla-Santiago, Breaking Ground and Barriers 4, 11 (1992) (noting that "typical sex-role stereotypes of the macho male and the submissive female still pervasive in society today seem even more powerful in Latina/o culture [and the persistence of these stereotypes] hinders and precludes Latina women from leaving the domestic domain of home and family, entering the labor force, gaining leadership roles, or acquiring a formal education" and that the female role is modeled after the Virgin Mary); Rosa María Gil and Carmen Inoa Vázquez, The María Paradox 7 (1996) ("[M]arianismo defines the ideal role for woman. And what an ambitious role it is, taking as the model of perfection the Virgin Mary herself. *Marianismo* is about sacred duty, self-sacrifice, and chastity. About dispensing care and pleasure, not receiving them. About living in the shadows, literally and figuratively of your men—father, boyfriend, husband, son—your kids, and your family. Aside from bearing children, the *marianista* has much in common with *una monja de convento*, a cloistered nun—but the order she enters is marriage, and her groom is not Christ but an all too human male who instantly becomes the single object of her devotion for a lifetime."); Pierrette Hondagneu-Sotelo, Gendered Transitions: Mexican Experiences of Immigration 9 (1994) (noting that the female ideal, *marianismo*, is modeled after the "Catholic Virgin Madonna, and prescribes dependence, subordination, responsibility for all domestic chores, and selfless devotion to family and children").

6. *Mambí*, a term originally derogatorily used to refer to Blacks from Santo Domingo, was appropriated by Cubans to refer to themselves during the wars of independence. *Mambisas* was the term used to refer to the women who fought in the war. *See* Stoner, *supra* note 4, at 201–02.

7. *See id.* at 20.

8. *See id.* at 19.

9. Hondagneu-Sotelo, *supra* note 5, at 9.

10. Women earned the right to own property early in the century. The divorce laws of 1918, 1930, and 1934 were very progressive as far as grounds. In 1928 the crime of adultery was abolished. The 1934 maternity leave granted benefits.

11. *See* Stoner, *supra* note 4, at 78.

12. *See* Margaret E. Leahy, Development Strategies and the Status of Women 93 (1986).

13. *See* Stoner, *supra* note 4, at 3, 78, 85–86.

14. *See generally* Constituciones Cubanas: Desde 1812 hasta nuestros días 242–311 (1974)(reprinting the Cuban Constitution of 1940).

15. *See id.*

16. *See* Leahy, *supra* note 12, at 92.

17. *See generally* Hernández-Truyol, *Borders (En)Gendered, supra* note 4 (reviewing in depth the impact of cultured gendered expectations).

18. *Id.* at 14.

19. *See* Marifeli Perez-Stable, The Cuban Revolution: Origins, Course and Legacy 76 (1993).

20. *See* Fidel Castro, The Case of Cuba Is the Case of All Underdeveloped Countries, Address to the UN General Assembly (Sept. 26, 1960), *in* To Speak the Truth: Why Washington's "Cold War" against Cuba Doesn't End 91–92 (Mary-Alice Waters ed., 1992).

21. *See* Susan Kaufman Purcell, *Modernizing Women for a Modern Society: The Cuban Case, in* Female and Male in Latin America 258 (Ann Pescatello ed., 1973).

22. Juan Clark, Mito y realidad: Testimonios de un pueblo 434 (2d ed. 1992) (citing Constitucion de la República de Cuba 35–36 (1976)). Significantly, Chapter 5 of the 1976 Constitution provides for equal access to employment, services, military rank, salary for equal work, education (primary through university), medical assistance, housing, restaurants, transportation, and beaches and other public places. *See id.* at 435.

23. *See Working Women, in* Socialist Countries: The Fertility Connection 201 (Valentina Bodrova and Richard Anker eds., 1985).

24. *See* Purcell, *supra* note 21, at 263.

25. *See* Andres Oppenheimer, Castro's Final Hour 460, 487 (1992).

26. Human Development Report, United Nations Development Programme (1993).

27. *See* Purcell, *supra* note 21, at 264.

28. *Id.* at 264.

29. *Id.* In 1961 there were sixty schools for domestic servants and by 1967 there were only about 5,500 women left in these schools. Many of the women who graduated (in total about 50,000 domestic servants graduated from the schools) went on to other areas of employment. *See* Purcell, *supra* note 21, at 264.

30. Cuba's literacy rate for adult women is 94.6 percent. *See* Human Development Report, United Nations Development Programme 139 (1996)[hereinafter UNHDR, 1996].

31. *See* Purcell, *supra* note 21, at 266.

32. *See* Sarah M. Santana, *Whither Cuban Medicine? Challenges for the Next Generation, in* Transformation and Struggle: Cuba Faces the 1990s 251, 253 (Sandor Halebsky and John M. Kirk eds., 1990).

33. Debra Evenson, *The Changing Role of Law in Revolutionary Cuba, in* Transformation and Struggle, *supra* note 32, at 63.

34. *See* Robert W. Benson, *An Island on the Way to Ectopia: Cuba's Human Rights Record Compares Well to Mexico and Others,* L.A. Times, Mar. 29, 1992, at 5.

35. *See* UNHDR, 1996, *supra* note 30, at 142 (citing 1995 figures).

36. *See* Sergio Diaz-Briquets, *The Cuban Labor Force in 1981 and Beyond, in* The Cuban Economy: Dependency and Development 107, 108 (Antonio Jorge and Jaime Suchlicki eds., 1989).

37. *See id.* at 99.

38. *See id.* at 102 (citing Carmelo Mesa-Lago, The Economy of Socialist Cuba: A Two Decade Appraisal (1981)). Examples of state policies that affect the labor participation rate include "enforcement of existing school attendance laws and the expansion of the national education system . . . relaxation of retirement requirement for older workers . . . [c]ontracting or expanding the size of the armed and paramilitary forces." *Id.* at 102.

39. *Id.* at 102.

40. Diaz-Briquets relates that a good example in Cuba was during the "agricultural push of the late 1960s . . . [when] [w]omen were . . . called to replace male urban workers that had gone to labor in the fields, and also to directly contribute their input to the sugar harvest." *Id.* at 102.

41. *See id.* at 103–04 (discussing age-specific labor patterns in Cuba).

42. *See* UNHDR, 1996, *supra* note 30, at 139 (stating that life expectancy for Cuban men is 73.6 years, while the life expectancy for Cuban women is 77.4 years).

43. *See* Diaz-Briquets, *supra* note 36, at 102–03.

44. *See* Diana Riveira, Women's Legal Advances in Cuba 34 (1989) (unpublished master's thesis, University of Miami) (on file with the author).

45. *See* Lois M. Smith and Alfred Padula, *The Cuban Family in the 1980s, in* Transformation and Struggle, *supra* note 32, at 177.

46. *See id.* at 177.

47. *See* Castro, *supra* note 20, at 91–92.

6 | Women (Under)Development

Poor Women of Color in the United States and the Right to Development

Hope Lewis

This right to development I have defined as "the recognized prerogative of every individual and every people to enjoy in just measure the goods and services produced thanks to the effort of solidarity of the members of the community."

> —Keba M'Baye, Opening remarks at 1981 conference
> on development and human rights

Nobody cares and has ever cared for the poor Black woman in America. . . . I have learned to fight and to get information nobody intended for me to have. I have learned how to use that information, and share it with other people in my community. I have also learned that I have to make connections with people outside my community. . . . My sewing shop is a place where people know they can come when they do not know what else to do. We make answers.

> —Cora Lee Johnson, testimony at 1995 UN summit
> on social injustice

I. INTRODUCTION

Some might view the right to development as an anachronism in the face of the globalization of market-based economic systems. However, "development"—in the form of a thriving industrial sector, reliable infrastructure, and steady economic growth—remains beyond the reach of many nations, especially the poorer nations of Africa. Moreover, the broader goals of social development—access to basic needs and an improved quality of life—are denied to millions of people in "developed" nations as well. Nevertheless, we may well feel a sense of reluctance before discarding completely a concept that inspired progressive postcolonial movements. If this

Reprinted by permission from 18 *Law and Policy* 281 (1996). © 1996 by Blackwell Publishers Ltd.

right to development is to extend beyond rhetoric, then poor and disadvantaged groups and individuals, including those in the United States, must find it a useful tool.

Women of color who are poor in the United States struggle with the effects of underdevelopment while surrounded by the resources of the most economically developed nation on earth.[1] These women experience violations of their social and economic human rights that are strikingly similar to those affecting poor women of color in the rest of the Global South.[2] They face limited access to affordable health care; encounter discrimination in education and employment; lack access to credit; cannot obtain affordable housing; and do not receive equal protection from public and private violence. "Development" implies progress toward better living conditions; instead, the well-being of many poor women of color, and of those they care for, grows more precarious.

The reinvigoration of right-wing ideology in the United States has made, for some, an already desperate situation an intolerable one, as policies resulting in the elimination or drastic reduction of basic services are implemented. In the most ironic sense of the words, poor women of color in the United States live "under" development. Still, many poor women of color are not simply passive victims of the crushing effects of class, gender, and ethnic discrimination and exploitation—they actively resist these conditions and struggle to maintain the well-being of their families and their communities. The activism of such women has been a central (if underrecognized) base of support for the U.S. civil rights movement, the women's rights movement, and struggles for economic equity.

The language of rights has been a key tool of empowerment for many disadvantaged groups, including people of color, women, and the women of color who intersect both groups. As part of a larger strategy, leaders of minority ethnic groups in the United States have based their appeals for social justice on human rights concepts and have appealed to international institutions to assist in publicizing or supporting their struggles. Civil rights and pan-Africanist leaders have attempted to present violations of the human rights of African Americans before the United Nations.[3] The indigenous peoples of the Americas also have looked to the international human rights system as an alternative means of redressing harms not adequately addressed under domestic law.[4]

This chapter explores whether the call for a right to development that originated in Third World nationalism and non-aligned movements has relevance for communities of poor women of color in the developed North. In particular, it raises questions about the implications of certain development strategies for poor women of color in the United States. Could they claim the right to development while geographically located within a highly developed national economy? If they were to do so, what pragmatic use could be made of such a claim?

As imagined in this essay, such groups could claim a right to (alternative) development. However, implementing the right could not depend solely on government ratification of human rights treaties or on the passage of implementing legislation by Congress and state legislatures. If it is to have effective, substantive impact for poor women of color, they must also be able to deploy the concept as a basis for transformative coalition building and a weapon of political strategy. The right to development could be creatively used to reconceptualize the implementation in the United States of women's economic development projects.

Women-in-development programs in the United States, like those in Africa, Asia, the Caribbean, and Latin America, are often characterized as humanitarian efforts to uplift the poor while relieving state actors from the burden of providing basic services to the "undeserving" poor. As conceived by many government officials and international aid agencies, the purpose of such programs is to "empower," as if by magic, women to maintain themselves and their families with minimal state or charitable assistance. Underlying that discourse is the belief that poor women of color are poor because they (or the men in their communities) lack initiative; they need only take advantage of a mythic national and local economy bursting with opportunities for newly empowered female entrepreneurs. The effects of inequitable educational, wage, and benefits systems; structural unemployment and underemployment; violence against women; race, gender, and class discrimination; inadequate child care, elder care, and health services; and the global movement of capital—all are to be overcome by making poor women more efficient producers in the informal economy.[5]

What might happen were poor women of color in the United States to claim development and their full participation in that process as a human right? Rights-based calls for basic needs are not novel in the United States,[6] although public support for such approaches has waxed and waned in the last two decades.[7] Despite the limitations of rights discourse, rights talk can be an integral part of effective strategies for influencing states and other powerful actors to create the conditions necessary for true development.[8]

II. DEFINING DEVELOPMENT—AND THE RIGHT TO IT

Implementing the right to development is problematic, in part, because the term "development" defies universal definition. The relationship between development and human rights had been referenced at least since the adoption of the Universal Declaration of Human Rights in 1948.[9] By most accounts, however, the right to development, as such, first came into widespread international prominence as a result of an influential speech by Keba M'Baye in 1972.[10] M'Baye and other scholars of international human rights envisioned the right and its corresponding duties as relevant not only to states and institutions, but also to peoples and individuals.[11] By 1979 the UN secretary general issued a formal report on the dimensions of a right to development.[12] The report found that the legal basis for an international human right to development already existed in the instruments constituting the International Bill of Human Rights:

Articles 55 and 56 of the UN Charter; the Universal Declaration of Human Rights, especially Article 22 (the right to social security and to the realization "of the economic, social and cultural rights indispensable to [human] dignity and the free development of [the human] person") and Article 26(2) ("education shall be directed to the full development of the human personality . . ."); Article 1 of both International Covenants on Human Rights (the right to self-determination); and the International Covenant on Economic, Social and Cultural Rights, especially Article 2(1) (the obligation to implement progressively the enumerated rights) and Article 11 ("the right of everyone to an adequate standard of living").[13]

The Declaration on the Right to Development, adopted by the General Assembly in 1986, builds on these previously elaborated human rights obligations. According to James Paul, the declaration encompasses three important elements of the right:[14] (1) people-centered development;[15] (2) the promotion and protection of all human rights in and through development processes;[16] and (3) the adoption and promotion of legal measures designed to ensure popular participation and the protection of human rights in and through development.[17]

III. FEMINIST CRITIQUES: WOMEN IN/AND/UNDER DEVELOPMENT

A. FEMINIST INTERVENTIONS IN INTERNATIONAL DEVELOPMENT AGENDAS

Since the early 1970s, feminist development experts such as Ester Boserup[18] have argued persuasively that international development efforts are destined for failure if they ignore or underestimate the role of women as economically productive in both "public" and "private" sectors.[19] Women are farmers as well as mothers, market women as well as housewives. The long-term success of any development project is therefore threatened if women do not have equal access to education, training, and entrepreneurial credit.

One could track changes in approach to development policy by tracking changes in terminology. The term "women-in-development" (WID) came into common usage as a result of Boserup's influence on feminist development experts within and outside the U.S. Agency for International Development. For USAID, women-in-development was an aspect of development policy, "the underlying rationale of which was that women are an untapped resource who can provide an economic contribution to development."[20] In this sense, WID was primarily an add-on to existing development policies. WID programs first attempted to increase the number of women in large-scale development projects (referred to disparagingly as the "add women and stir" approach). Later, such programs began to target women for specialized training and credit programs in order to more efficiently exploit their contributions to economic growth.[21] The related term "women *and* development" seems to recognize the concerns of women as occupying a separate, but overlapping, space with the concerns of development. Some approaches therefore focused on examining the effects of development (or the lack thereof) on women and on women's rights.

In current development policy discourse, the preferred term is "gender and development" (GAD), which focuses on aspects of women's lives that are implicated by gender (social relations between men and women) rather than by sex (biological differences between men and women). Carolyn Moser notes that "[t]he focus on gender rather than women makes it critical to look not only at the category 'women'—since that is only half the story—but at women in relation to men, and the way in which relations between these categories are socially constructed."[22] She argues that the fundamental goal of GAD is emancipatory, while WID takes an add-on approach to women that takes economic development as its fundamental goal. Official World Bank policy statements now reflect development goals that have been broadened from mere economic efficiency to include social goals such as "improving the economic and social status of women."[23] However, some human rights activists view the stated commitment of international aid agencies to the advancement of women with suspicion, in that relatively few resources from mainstream projects are devoted to the needs of women.

Based largely in the informal sector, the businesses developed under the rubric of "microenterprise for women" take a wide variety of forms. True microenterprise ventures involve very small capital investments (generally under $1,000) and employ fewer than five persons each. Producer cooperatives are structured to vest ownership and control of management in the workers. Self-employment training seeks to provide low-income women with skills in business development and management so that participants can create their own jobs. The success of many such small businesses depends on increasing women's access to alternative sources of credit such as community development banks and peer lending circles.

Microenterprise programs took on fully global significance with the advent of a World Summit on Microcredit in 1997. The World Summit also illustrated the manipulability of development strategies. The Washington, D.C., summit was chaired by Hillary Rodham Clinton and was attended by more than two thousand delegates from one hundred countries. Ironically, the U.S. administration's support for microenterprise took place against the backdrop of President Clinton's signing of controversial welfare "reform" legislation. The enactment of welfare reform and praise for U.S. microenterprise projects were argued to be consistent. Microenterprise programs were touted as ameliorative of the harsher effects of reductions and alterations of public benefits. Whether microenterprises could provide a sufficient level of income to replace the lost subsistence benefits of poor women and children remained unexamined. Further, the excitement surrounding microenterprise as an escape hatch for welfare mothers belied the difficulties associated with successfully starting and maintaining any small business in the United States (many of which initially lose money or fail). Despite the problematic manner in which microenterprise can be applied in the United States, it was at least encouraging to note that the world summit recognized the existence of Third World conditions within the First World.[24]

B. WOMEN AND THE U.S. COMMUNITY ECONOMIC DEVELOPMENT MOVEMENT

The discourse of development is no stranger to the U.S. context. The long history of domestic efforts to achieve economic development in low-income communities has its modern origins in the Johnson-era War on Poverty. These efforts focused on community projects intended to address the provision of basic needs such as housing, education, food, and access to health care through government-sponsored social service structures. However, these programs were not supported through the legal implementation of economic rights. Rather, Supreme Court decisions supported due process in the administration of social services, but they did not characterize access to economic or social opportunities and services as fundamental rights.[25]

As a correlative to direct social welfare transfers, U.S. community development corporations have engaged in work that parallels Third World development efforts. Policy makers are increasingly attempting to strengthen ideological and methodological linkages with international development programs to address "Third World" problems in U.S. urban centers (and poor rural communities).[26] Nowhere is this connection more evident than with respect to the recent mushrooming of women's economic development programs. Such programs range from efforts to increase the number of women-owned businesses, regardless of the economic circumstances of the owners, to microenterprise programs that specifically target women living on welfare.[27]

As in the Third World, WID/GAD programs in the United States can be simultaneously part of a destructive economic agenda as well as the expression of an indigenous form of survival and resistance. There are now hundreds of programs in the United States that are described as an alternative to "welfare dependency" among poor women.[28] Many train women to start small independent businesses (such as hairdressing or home-based sewing). There is support for these programs from among both conservatives and liberals. Some project organizers emphasize the ability of such programs to empower women who were formerly "dependent" by creating work opportunities or by training them to enter mainstream labor markets. The projects appeal to the popular perception that what women on welfare need is to be forced to work harder. There is little discussion of the fact that microenterprise and small business projects alone cannot address structural underemployment and unemployment. Further, while federal welfare reform legislation makes it easier for states to adjust limits on recipient asset levels to accommodate microenterprise projects, it also encourages state governments to see WID/GAD as an easy way to reduce their public benefits budgets.

Some activists in the United States caution against seeing WID/GAD as a wholesale solution to the problem of the poverty of women and children in the United States. They note that women and men in urban and rural poor communities in the United States have had a long history of working cooperatively for survival. Their efforts have ranged from the occupation and restoration of abandoned buildings for housing and community centers to the organization of community patrols aimed at reducing crime and reporting police brutality. Some activists fear that WID/GAD programs in the United States, by contrast, will be imposed in a top-down manner that lacks community accountability. They argue that such programs must be de-linked from punitive approaches to welfare reform.[29] Rather, GAD should be one element of a comprehensive approach to implementing fundamental human rights.

C. WOMEN, DEVELOPMENT, HUMAN RIGHTS: COMPATIBLE OR INCOMPATIBLE?

Rhoda Howard, among others, has been critical of the idea that the right to development is necessarily emancipatory for women in the developing world. According to Howard, "the agenda of women's rights intersects, but is not synonymous with, the agenda of development."[30] Howard's concerns that the individual rights of African women will tend to be trumped by the agendas of nondemocratic African governments, private interests, and international development agencies are well taken. Resources allocated to improve the status of poor women have been cynically diverted to further line the pockets of those in power in both the North and the South.

Other feminists, many among them women of color, find it ironic that the *inclusion* of women in certain forms of development contributes to the violation of their human rights.[31] Merely recognizing that women play an important role in the economy does not lead to more equitable development policies of benefit to women and their communities.

Instead of development programs focused primarily on channeling "women's labour and produce through national and international businesses,"[32] many women of color are exploring ways to achieve alternative forms of development that prioritize the survival of poor peoples. Some poor women have refused to be co-opted as passive participants in projects intended to keep them only marginally less poor. They have begun to recognize that the solidarity created among grassroots women in collective economic enterprises contributes to political activism as well.

Just as "integrating women into development" in Africa, Asia, the Caribbean, and Latin America often has translated into the exploitation of women as the targets of top-down development policies, similar dangers exist for poor women of color in the United States. It is not in their interest to be passive recipients of either development projects or welfare benefits. The limitations of top-down women's economic development programs were presaged by Martin Luther King's critique of poverty programs. He understood that breaking free from poverty and the effects of gender and racial discrimination requires more than the recognition of formal rights; it requires affirmative actions on the part of those whose policies contribute to underdevelopment. It therefore necessitates struggle by those who make the claim in order to motivate those actions. The international community faces a similar conundrum in that implementation of the right to development for peoples and nation-states requires not only a demand from the rights-claimant, but also the power to influence the duty-bearer to meet that demand. King recognized that it is only through the exercise of community-based power that these programs can be successfully implemented. For poor women of color in the United States, the right to development will not be a "bestowed gift of freedom"—it will be a hard-won victory.

IV. "WE MAKE ANSWERS": COULD A RIGHT TO DEVELOPMENT BE MEANINGFUL FOR COOPERATIVE ECONOMICS FOR WOMEN?

A. COOPERATIVE ECONOMICS FOR WOMEN

We can illustrate the problems and opportunities facing poor women of color in the United States by exploring what the right to development might mean to a group of women who participate in a women's economic development organization. Cooperative Economics for Women (CEW) is a grassroots community development organization that assists poor women in creating producer cooperatives in and around Boston, Massachusetts.[33]

CEW provides technical and other assistance to help women organize business cooperatives to meet their own economic needs and those of their communities. The emphasis is on building those survival skills necessary for the women to generate income for themselves and their families rather than on entrepreneurship per se. Based on popular education models developed in both the North and South, CEW assists the women's co-ops through a three-part training process. In phase 1, women who are interested in forming co-ops meet each other, identify their own goals and needs, identify their existing skills, and work with organizers trained in feminist popular education methodology to learn more about the principles of cooperative business and the impact of the economy on their communities. Once the women as a group determine that they wish to work together, they decide how their unique set of skills could translate into products and services that could fill unmet needs in their communities. Among the needs co-op members have identified are child care, food catering, and cleaning services.

The members learn the basics of savings, business planning, marketing, and other business operations (some while learning how to read and write). Throughout, however, the focus is on critical analysis of the negative roles that business enterprises can sometimes play in poor communities (for example, in promoting negative images of women of color in advertising). During this phase, CEW provides necessary technical and financial assistance in the form of child care and other reimbursements.

The co-ops enter phase 2 (which can last up to three years) when they begin practice work in their communities. They learn basic office skills, how to make phone calls, plan a job, and evaluate the results of a job. In addition, with the aid of translators, women learn basic arithmetic and how to read in English. Significantly, co-op members are involved in the management structure of CEW in that at least one-third of them fill board seats. The process also involves political education (on welfare reform and immigration policy, for example), external technical assistance (such as that available from law school clinics), and intergroup education (for example, by educating each other about the different cultures from which the members come). In phase 3, the co-ops are able to sustain themselves and become independent of CEW.

What if CEW was to encounter a U.S.–recognized right to development? This requires a significant stretch of the imagination on at least two levels: (1) that the United States would ratify a Convention on the Right to Development; and (2) that the right would be interpreted to require the implementation of the social and economic rights of poor women of color within U.S. borders.

Formal ratification and implementation of a convention on the right to development would be a significant problem. At the international level, the United States and other Western nations likely would object to adoption of such a convention. In addition, the United States has a poor record of ratifying human rights treaties.

The possibility of implementing in the United States the rights under the Economic, Social, and Cultural Covenant (which lay the groundwork for any meaningful right to development) has been analyzed elsewhere.[34] It is my purpose here to begin imagining how poor women of color could engage a right to development in ways that have relevance prior to ratification of the required covenants, conventions, and implementing provisions; that are relevant in advocating ratification; and that are relevant once formal laws recognizing such a right are enacted. Certainly, this state of affairs does not appear to be on the legal or political horizon in the near term—but perhaps it is only by such acts of imagination that one can move forward.

Before CEW could use the human rights framework as a transformative tool for achieving alternative development, the tools of the international human rights system must be made accessible to them. Current barriers to international human rights structures prevent grassroots women in development organizations from effectively using these tools in their struggles. CEW is a group of grassroots women who hope to secure women's right to development on the domestic front. How do they begin to take ownership of the right to development if it is shaped primarily by lawyers and policy makers within elite UN and human rights organizations? The answer may lie in the cross-fertilization of grassroots development organizing with human rights legal and theoretical strategies in determining whether and when traditional, modified, or alternative human rights frameworks will be useful to poor women of color.

An example of such cross-fertilization has occurred in recent tribunals on violations of women's human rights. In tribunals held at the Vienna Human Rights Conference, the Copenhagen Conference on Social Development, and the Beijing Conference on Women, grassroots women's rights activists worked with human rights lawyers to present testimony on the violations prioritized by the women who testified.[35]

In order to make such an approach work for the women of CEW, they, and those who work with them, must begin by addressing two issues: first, the problems of definition associated with development; and second, the problems associated with the various actors involved in the implementation of the right.

B. SOMETHING OUT OF NOTHING? ENGAGING THE RIGHT TO DEVELOPMENT

1. What Content Could Be Embedded in the Right to Development?

> [D]evelopment is a comprehensive economic, social, cultural and political process, which aims at the constant improvement of the well-being of the entire population and of all individuals on the basis of their active, free and meaningful participation in development and in the fair distribution of benefits resulting therefrom.[36]

To achieve the implementation of their right to development, the women of CEW's co-ops would have to engage in struggle over the content of the right. Assuming that the political will to implement a right to development existed, would implementation take, for example, the currently popular form of workfare? Will poor women be made a more efficient low-wage, non-unionized labor pool? Does the right to development simply mean that poor women would be expected to lift themselves and their communities out of poverty by their bootstraps?

Rebecca Johnson, the lead organizer of CEW, has spoken with hundreds of poor women of color about the needs on which they place priority. She summarizes their definitions of "development" as follows:

> Poor women feel their economic and human development needs will begin to be addressed when they have access to affordable child care close to home, affordable transportation and universal health care; when they have the ability to generate and control income and to make work decisions based on the needs of the family rather than out of fear of public welfare or the desperate inadequacy of multiple-job, minimum-wage work; and when they are active participants in renewing the communities where they live and work.[37]

The women of CEW already have taken significant steps toward defining the content of their own right to development. They identify their development goals based on intimate knowledge of the social and economic needs of their communities. They provide for themselves and their families by relying on complex networks of support through cooperation with other members, family, friends, and their communities to make limited resources stretch as far as possible. They learn about each other's similarities and differences and about how to resist threats to their survival.

2. To Whom Should the Right Belong and Who Could Make the Right Have Meaning?

If the right to development belongs to the nation-state, then the United States certainly seems to have taken full advantage of it. As envisioned in the declaration, however, the right belongs to individuals and groups as well. The declaration does not exclude those living in a highly developed nation-state and envisions equitable distribution of the benefits of development such as fair access to housing, food, education, and health care. In fact, as the purported central subjects of development, the women of CEW should be the direct beneficiaries of development since they are among those most in need. All are poor; most rely on public social welfare programs for subsistence income. Some are immigrants or refugees from political or social violations at home; others are survivors of domestic violence in this culture. The declaration also provides that individuals are entitled to "contribute to" development.[38] Despite media images to the contrary, poor women already contribute a great deal to development. Both the public and private sectors depend on the formal and informal work of poor women, including the enormous burdens of housework, child care, elder care, and domestic and other service sector employment they take on.

The language in the declaration providing for state responsibility for the creation of national as well as international development policies that are aimed at the entire population seems promising. However, it may have little impact in a domestic environment of drastic cuts in social welfare entitlements and when it has become commonplace to replace those entitlements with coercive behavior modification programs. As envisioned here, the implementation of a right to development would require the U.S. government to take specific, concrete steps, legislative and otherwise, to implement the right. If it did not do so, the women of CEW could conceivably submit complaints, for informational or recourse purposes, to an international body that could sanction or condemn the U.S. government's failure to comply.

These efforts would likely rely on the "embarrassment effect" of having the actions of the U.S. government toward women within its borders condemned at a global level. In the Cold War context, some have argued that the embarrassment of the U.S. government over international condemnation of its treatment of African Americans influenced the elaboration and implementation of some U.S. civil rights.[39] But the Cold War is over. Can the United States still be embarrassed on the world stage over its treatment of the poor? The practical difficulties associated with placing pressure on the most economically and militarily powerful nation on earth might appear overwhelming to the women of CEW individually. However, the right to development, a quintessentially collective right, requires some form of group-based solidarity or coalition building to implement. One such potential coalition is among poor women of color, but there are many others. It is still possible that the United States would respond to the exposure of the fact that the richest nation on earth tolerates grinding poverty in its midst.

Nevertheless, CEW cannot merely be a pawn of the state in the process of implementing such a right to development. Women must be active participants in shaping implementation strategies and in the actual process of implementation. If they were to claim their participation in the right to development, the right of CEW members to obtain basic needs would not be based on the benevolence of the state, nor on whether members were recognized as deserving and efficient economic producers. CEW would need to demand the right to development and demand participation in the implementation of the right. To effectively accomplish this task, CEW not only must have the knowledge as an organizing tool to constitute a grassroots movement, powerful enough to exercise the leverage needed to effectively make that demand, it must also have access to human rights nongovernmental organizations and individual acti ists who could share their knowledge of the human rights framework and its scope with CEW and with similarly constituted organizations. Such a collaborative effort must also focus on finding ways of teasing out how grassroots concepts of rights or justice relate to the established human rights concepts.

The process of consciousness raising cannot itself be effective or lay the groundwork for future claims to the right if it does not involve grassroots participation. In the already rarefied atmosphere in which human rights discourse and instruments exist, the right to development is truly without content absent the substantive right of participation. Often, however, "participation," as UN bureaucracies and member states define it, means the participation of elite women and organizations in defining the human rights agenda independent of grassroots women. Increasingly, grassroots organizations have pressed for greater participation in UN and other international fora that define the agenda on economic development. Language in the Declaration provides that development should be a broadly participatory right, and one that requires the state to take special, effective measures to ensure the active role of women. The responsibility to ensure such grassroots participation in defining and shaping the international agenda and development of rights lies not only with the states, but also with the more prominent international human rights organizations.

How would a grassroots, democratic form of participation be implemented? It would require grassroots participation in the governmental structures set up to administer development programs. It also would require more equitable representation of poor women of color even in the community development organizations that have tended to take a top-down approach to their concerns. Further, the women themselves would have to identify the goods and services they need to support their participation. Certainly, current discussions and debates on welfare reform and community development rarely include the poor women of color who are the subjects of the proposed legislation or programs. Congress, the state house, and the nonprofit organizations that may administer the programs rarely look to the women for their visions of economic development. For the co-op members, as for many poor women around the world, the lack of true participation in the creation of development policies is likely to remain a significant barrier to implementation of the right to development.

Furthermore, although states have a responsibility for the fair and equitable distribution of resources, state action alone is not enough. The private and nonprofit sectors have a responsibility as well because fair and equitable distribution of resources among the people of a state cannot be accomplished without their participation in the process. Equitable distribution of resources in itself is not development. Rather, development is a dynamic process that requires the participation of all, including the private sector, nongovernmental organizations, and governments, toward the goal of ensuring equality of opportunity for all in their access to resources. To successfully realize the right to development, CEW and other grassroots organizations could use human rights strategies as an organizing tool.

V. CONCLUSION

As a relic of the traditional human rights system, the right to development is so far a failure in the international arena—it has not yet gone beyond rhetoric. Economic and social development remains a prisoner of the political will of the dominant national economies and of the old international economic order.

Nevertheless, even this failed rights claim has opened space for alternative, even revolutionary, forms of organizing and empowerment. In the United States the call for a right to such an alternative development could provide additional support for women to press their goals at levels over, under, and through national governments. Such alternative visions of development by no means relieve the state of its responsibility toward the poor. Rights-based claims have energized grassroots, community-based organizations to make claims that cannot effectively be made on mere humanitarian terms. And it creates room, however small, for direct advocacy in domestic legislative fora and judicial interpretation. Most important, poor women of color are using opportunities to reach out to each other—to share similarities, differences, and solutions. CEW's co-ops, for example, are enriched by the experiences and knowledge of women from Ethiopia, Cape Verde, and Cambodia, as well as from rural and urban America. Their worker cooperatives are modeled on groups in the Caribbean and Zimbabwe.

The economic role of women is now widely recognized to be central to the development of poor communities, and to the ability of women to organize around other issues of concern to them, such as political and educational participation, and reproductive and health-related rights. However, as long as the focus of U.S. WID remains on replacing one stereotypical image of poor women of color as lazy and dependent with another stereotype of poor women of color as independent, free-standing mini-capitalists, U.S. WID will not be about the empowerment of women. Programs that focus solely on "motivating" poor women to pull themselves up by their bootstraps could lead to more of the top-down, ineffective approaches that have characterized some efforts in developing countries. Instead, U.S.-based women's development programs could create legal and political spaces that support women's efforts to seek truly transformative development for themselves and their communities.

NOTES

A version of this chapter appeared previously as *Women (Under)Development: The Relevance of the "Right to Development" to Poor Women of Color in the United States,* in 18 Law and Policy 281 (1996) and was presented at the 1995 Annual Meeting of the Law and Society Association in Toronto, Canada, in a session titled, "Beyond Rhetoric: Implementing the Right to Development."

1. Poor women of color experience the triple threat of gender, racial, and class discrimination. They often constitute the poorest members of poor communities, and they currently are the focus of particularly abusive legal and social policies in the United States. Wilhelmina Leigh notes that "of the nearly 249 million people counted as U.S. residents in the 1990 census, 51.3 percent of them were women, and over 31 million were women of color." Wilhelmina A. Leigh, The Health Status of Women of Color: A Women's Health Report of the Women's Research and Education Institute 3 (1994). Chandra Mohanty describes the term "women of color" as having significant political content in an international context as well:

> This is a term which designates a political constituency, not a biological or even sociological one. It is a sociopolitical designation for people of African, Caribbean, Asian, and Latin American descent, and native peoples of the U.S. . . . What seems to constitute "women of color" or "third world women" as a viable oppositional alliance is a *common context of struggle* rather than color or racial identifications. Similarly, it is third world women's oppositional *political* relation to sexist, racist, and imperialist structures that constitutes our potential commonality.

Chandra Mohanty, *Introduction: Cartographies of Struggle, in* Third World Women and the Politics of Feminism 7 (C.T. Mohanty et al. eds., 1991).

2. The term "Global South" is used to convey the fact that poverty, unfair terms of trade, colonialism, and neocolonialism are not confined to the geographic South. I occasionally use the problematic term "Third World" in this chapter to refer to peoples, whether located in the North or South, who are affected adversely by those conditions. I recognize, however, that no such term could fully comprehend the variety of conditions experienced by Third World peoples.

3. Bert B. Lockwood, Jr., *The U.N. Charter and United States Civil Rights Litigation: 1946–1955,* 69 Iowa L. Rev. 90 (1984).

4. Robert A. Williams, Jr., *Redefining the Terms of Indigenous Peoples' Survival in the World,* 1990 Duke L.J. 660.

5. Shelley Wright, *Interdisciplinary Approaches to International Economic Law: Women and the Global Economic Order: A Feminist Perspective,* 10 Am. U. J. Int'l L. and Pol'y 861 (1995).

6. Edward V. Sparer, *The Right to Welfare, in* The Rights of Americans (N. Dorsen ed., 1971).

7. Joel Handler notes that the "ideology of entitlements" has been attacked from the Left ("for further dividing the poor, for failing to protect welfare recipients from substantive cut-

backs in benefits and for contributing to the legalization of welfare. . . . At the same time, conservatives . . . have used entitlements to justify the new efforts at social control in welfare, namely 'workfare'"). Joel F. Handler, *Constructing the Political Spectacle: Interpretation of Entitlements, Legalization, and Obligations in Social Welfare History*, 56 Brook. L. Rev. 899 (1990).

8. Critical legal theorists have identified a number of weaknesses in liberal rights discourse. Two such examples are "the embrace of the public/private distinction," in which rights discourse focuses primarily on the relationship between the individual and the state, and the indeterminacy of rights, which, some critics believe, may "turn out to be dependent on controversial assumptions and arguments of political philosophy." Karl Klare, *Legal Theory and Democratic Reconstruction*, 25 U. Brit. Colum. L. Rev. 69 (1991).

9. Ved P. Nanda, *Development and Human Rights: The Role of International Law and Organizations, in* Human Rights and Third World Development 295–96 (G. W. Shepherd, Jr., and V. P. Nanda eds., 1985).

10. M'Baye has been a Chairman of the Commission on Human Rights and a member of the International Court of Justice. He discussed the concept of a right to development in a lecture to the International Institute of Human Rights in Strasbourg. Jack Donnelly, *In Search of the Unicorn: The Jurisprudence and Politics of the Right to Development*, 15 Cal. W. Int'l L.J. 473, 474 (1985). *See also* Mohammed Bedjaoui, *The Right to Development, in* International Law: Achievements and Prospects 1178 (M. Bedjaoui ed., 1992).

11. Jack Donnelly, *The "Right to Development": How Not to Link Human Rights and Development, in* Human Rights and Development in Africa 261, 264 (C. E. Welch and R. Meltzer eds., 1984).

12. Donnelly, *supra* note 10, at 474–75.

13. *Id.* at 479.

14. James C. N. Paul, Incorporating Human Rights into the Work of the World Summit for Social Development (1995).

15. According to Article 2(1), "The human person is the central subject of development and should be the active participant and beneficiary of the right to development."

16. Article 1 notes that the full realization of all human rights and fundamental freedoms can be achieved only in the context of the implementation of an inalienable right to development. Article 6 notes that implementation of this right requires cooperation among states to promote observance of all human rights and fundamental freedoms without distinction as to race, sex, language, or religion and that "All human rights and fundamental freedoms are indivisible and interdependent; equal attention and urgent consideration should be given to the implementation, promotion and protection of civil, political, economic, social and cultural rights."

17. The Vienna Declaration of the 1993 UN World Conference on Human Rights confirmed these goals and principles in Art. 10.

18. Ester Boserup, Woman's Role in Economic Development (1970).

19. Barbara Herz, *Bringing Women into the Economic Mainstream: Guidelines for Policymakers and Development Institutions*, 266(4) Fin. and Dev. 22 (1989).

20. Carol O. N. Moser, Gender Planning and Development: Theory, Practice and Training 2 (1993).

21. Herz, *supra* note 19.

22. Moser, *supra* note 20, at 3.

23. Wright, *supra* note 5, at 881–84.

24. According to media reports, "the Summit will set the decade-long goal of getting 100 million of the world's poorest families on microcredit. Of that total, . . . 4 million will come from industrialized countries, 2 million of them from the U.S." Nichole Gaouette, *Mini Loans Help Welfare Mothers to Create Their Own Jobs*, Christian Science Monitor, Jan. 31, 1997, at 4.

25. Goldberg v. Kelly, 397 U.S. 254 (1970) (granting due process protections to welfare recipients). The Court stated that "statutory welfare grants were legal entitlements; as such, they could only be withheld or terminated according to due process of law"). However, it must be noted that the Supreme Court's support for due process in the administration of social services was limited to certain programs. In particular, subsequent to *Goldberg v. Kelly,* the Court refused to extend due process protections to administration of Social Security benefits.

26. For example, USAID consulted with the city government of Baltimore with regard to addressing that city's infant mortality and other poverty-related problems. *U.S. Development: USAID Brings Development Techniques Home*, Interpress Service, Jan. 16, 1995, *available in* 1995 WL 2259402 (noting an illiteracy rate of 14 percent, 45 percent unemployment rates in some neighborhoods, and infant mortality rates in some areas as high as 19 per 1,000 live births—higher than the rates in some developing countries).

27. June K. Inuzuka, *Women of Color and Public Policy: A Case Study of the Women's Business Ownership Act*, 43 Stan. L. Rev. 1215 (1991).

28. One source, citing a 1994 Aspen Institute Study, noted that 64 percent of U.S. microlenders lend to recipients of AFDC (Aid to Families with Dependent Children); 78 percent of the borrowers are women, and 62 percent are members of a racial or ethnic minority. Jo-Ann Johnston, *To Boldly Loan Where No Banker Has Loaned Before*, Bus. Ethics 45 (Nov.–Dec. 1995).

29. Rebecca Johnson, *Letter from the Lead Organizer*, 1 CEW's News 2 (Winter 1994).

30. Rhoda Howard, *Women's Rights and the Right to Development, in* Human Rights and Governance in Africa 115, 119 (R. Cohen et al. eds., 1993).

31. Pam Simmons, *Women in Development: A Threat to Liberation?*, Ecologist, Jan.–Feb. 1992, at 16; *see also* TransAfrica Forum, *Seminar Proceedings—Development Policy: Black Female Perspectives,* 4(3) TransAfrica Forum 69, 84–90 (Spring 1987) (remarks of Loretta Ross).

32. Simmons, *supra* note 31.

33. Although I was a member of the CEW board between 1994 and 1996, the positions taken in this essay do not reflect formal positions of the organization or its members. Rather, this discussion reflects my own exploration of whether the rarefied world of international human rights theory can be reconciled with the practical concerns of a grassroots women's organization. See Hope Lewis, *From Beijing to Chelsea: Poor Women and the "Right to Development,"* 2 CEW's News 1, 5 (Fall 1995). The following description of CEW's structure and activities is based on CEW organizing documents prepared by its lead organizer, Rebecca Johnson.

34. Barbara Stark, *Economic Rights in the United States and International Human Rights Law: Toward an "Entirely New Strategy,"* 44 Hastings L.J. 79 (1992).

35. Center for Women's Global Leadership, From Vienna to Beijing: The Copenhagen Hearing on Economic Justice and Women's Human Rights at the United Nations Summit on Social Development (1995); Without Reservation: The Beijing Tribunal on Accountability for Women's Human Rights (Niamh Reilly ed., 1996).

36. UN Declaration on the Right to Development 1987: preamble.
37. Johnson, *supra* note 29, at 2.
38. UN Declaration, *supra* note 36, art. 1.
39. Lockwood, *supra* note 3.

2 | Third World within the First

On Being "Othered"

7 | Motherhood and Work in Cultural Context

One Woman's Patriarchal Bargain

Devon W. Carbado

> Of course, your mother is not only that woman whose womb
> formed and released you. . . . But naming your own mother (or her
> equivalent) enables people to place you precisely within the univer-
> sal web of your life, in each of its dimensions: cultural, spiritual,
> personal, and historical.
> —Paula Gunn Allen, *Who Is Your Mother?*

I. ON THE CONSTRUCTION OF MOTHERHOOD

My mother "mothered." That is to say, she not only physically bore us, she sustained us—spiritually, emotionally, and (along with my father) economically. She
was our primary parent.[1]

(My father had an invisible presence. Emotionally, he was disconnected from us.)

But you are probably thinking that my construction of "mothering" acquiesces
in the image of women as nurturers and emotional givers. Perhaps it does. However, some cultural feminists such as Carol Gilligan maintain that the image of
women as "givers" and "nurturers" is real and results from women's tendency to
view the world through relationships and through an existential sense of connection.[2] Significantly, Gilligan and many other cultural feminists do not base their
"connection thesis" (that "[w]omen are actually or potentially materially connected to other human life [in a way that men are not]")[3] on notions of biological essentialism.[4] Rather, their argument is that "women are more 'connected' to
life than men are because it is women who are the primary caretakers of young
children."[5]

Gilligan's attribution of "care," "responsibility," and "nurturing" to women certainly applies to my mother. She was more connected to us than my father was and

Reprinted by permission from 21 *Harvard Women's Law Journal* 1 (1998). © 1998 by the President and Fellows of Harvard College.

more responsible for our day-to-day existence. She knew what was happening at school, what we liked to read, how we liked our hair cut.

And we knew her.

But my interaction with my parents need not have been gendered that way. My father could have been our primary parent. He could have been the "emotional giver," the "nurturer." He could have "mothered." That is why "mothered" is in quotes—to convey the idea that there is no a priori reason or biological basis for the gendered construction of the characteristics I ascribe to my mother. My father could have exhibited an "ethic of care."

The question then becomes, why didn't he and why don't many other men? It is here that I think Gilligan's analysis is truncated. While she is careful to point out the difference between the male moral imperative and the female moral imperative, and how this difference is manifested in family life,[6] she does not answer the more fundamental question about the gendered allocation of family responsibilities: "[W]hy do women, rather than men, raise, nurture, and cook for children? What is the cause of this difference?" If my essay had begun with the statement, "My father 'fathered,'" the subsequent explanation would not have been that he emotionally and spiritually sustained us.

To be sure, there were external factors operating on our family life that contributed to my father's invisibility. It was not simply a matter of him not wanting to connect with us. He was a factory worker for British Leyland. He worked six nights a week lubricating machines. His days were spent sleeping. The extent to which he could interact with us was necessarily circumscribed.

And yet I do not think that issues of class or socioeconomic-status explain completely the patriarchal aspects of my family life, the extent to which my mother was responsible for family-centered work. Patriarchy operates across class boundaries. The allocation of work in our family would not have been terribly different if we had been upper- or middle-class. Jamaican cultural norms with respect to domesticity are gender- but not class-determinative: women, and not men, "raise" children. My mother raised us.

II. ON MOTHER AND FEMINISM (THE "F" WORD)

There were nine of us to raise—five boys, four girls. One through six were born in Jamaica; seven, eight, and nine were born in Birmingham, England. I was number eight. West Indians are famous for having lots of kids.

The house in which I grew up was No. 15 Railway Side, a two-story semidetached house in Smethwick, Birmingham, that has since been condemned. It was a large enough house, I suppose, affording nothing more or less than any other house on our street; there were a bathroom, a kitchen, a den downstairs, and three rooms upstairs where we all slept.

Attached to the kitchen was a "side-house," the functional equivalent of a basement. Kim, our dog, spent most of his time there digging the chalk out of the walls;

my mother did "her" laundry there every Saturday morning; my father used it principally as an entrance to the backyard; my brothers and I went fishing there—for cod from my mother's stainless steel washing bowls. Carbolic soap was our bait. The soaking clothes (placed there one or two days, as a sort of prewash, before my mother scrubbed them) made our waves.

We all loved Railway Side: my siblings and I because we could watch the trains go by from our living room, experiencing an earthquake-like jitter each time; my father because it had a fairly large yard in which he could store all his electrical paraphernalia; my mother because it symbolized her hard work. Because she owned it. She made a point of always telling us that "non-a my kids kyan sey dat dem grow-up inna council [government] property. I werk too hard fa dat."[7]

I think before I ever understood what feminism means or what it might mean, I knew that women were as capable as and often more capable than men because of my mother and her work. My mother never knew how to spell the word "lazy." That is what she used to tell us. It was not in her vocabulary. "Work," however, was. She would always say there is dignity in work; that it teaches us humility; that it is its own good; that it emancipates us. I never doubted any of this. Mother's aphorisms were the stuff we were made of. We grew up on them.

"Sometime yuh have to leave de nest to fine de worm." That was the aphorism my mother invoked to explain her decision to immigrate to England in 1961, initially without my father. Explains my mother, "money was hard in Jamaica." Like many other West Indians, my mother was "pushed" and "pulled" to England.[8] The ideology of migration was ubiquitous. Poor economic conditions in Jamaica and the shortage of labor in Britain after World War II caused many Jamaicans to think of Britain as the land of opportunity—and for many Jamaicans it was. Of course, Jamaican workers, as a replacement labor force, were being exploited in England. But they were being exploited in Jamaica as well. There was more money to be made under British exploitation and there were more opportunities, including educational opportunities, in Britain. At age forty-six, after having the nine of us, my mother was able to earn her only postsecondary degree in England, a Management Certificate in catering from Birmingham's College of Food and Domestic Arts.

My mother's "passage" to England by herself, as a woman, was not the norm. As a general matter, men went first and subsequently "sent" for their families.[9] My mother had decided, however, that notwithstanding my father's hesitance, she had to "beat the ban on immigration."[10] With the steady flow of "coloureds" to Britain after World War II,[11] British politicians, in response to strong public pressure, began discussing the need to restrict immigration.[12] The following provides an indication of the then-emerging anti-Black immigration sentiment:

We cannot overwhelm ourselves with large numbers of people who, however worthy, are alien, have alien cultures, different temperaments, totally different backgrounds and habits and different ways of life. If we allow them to come in at a rate faster than we can absorb them, we will create a growing fear in the minds of our own people who, rightly or wrongly, say that before the end of the century there will be large minorities of alien people in various parts of the country, and they fear that the British way of life will change. That fear exists in the minds of many people and, for this reason, entry must be regulated.[13]

I suppose it is ironic that between 1958 and 1961 West Indians were rushing to England in increased numbers for fear that Britain would close its doors to immigration, and it was precisely their increased numbers that became a catalyst for the government's formalization of immigration controls.

As "colonial subjects," West Indians, to the extent they had the economic means, could, for the most part, travel to and from Britain as they desired. The British Nationality Act of 1948 granted citizens of the United Kingdom and colonies and citizens of the Commonwealth unrestricted entry to, and the right to work in, Britain.[14] Even though this statute did nothing more than formalize what, for some time, had been de facto British immigration policy, the passage of this act was not uncontroversial. While the Conservative Party and the Labour Party understood that the development of the British economy required the British government to encourage immigration, both parties were also sensitive to the desire on the part of white British people to "admit a migrant type that conformed in their racial and religious characteristics to the majority population of Britain."[15] Perhaps not surprisingly, then, in 1949 the Royal Commission on Population issued a report that in part foreshadowed the racialization of British immigration laws: "Immigration on a large scale into a fully established society like ours could only be welcomed without reserve if the immigrants were of good human stock and were not prevented by religion or race from intermarrying with the host population and becoming merged in it."[16] While the Flemish and French Protestants were considered immigrants of "good human stock," West Indians were not. Concerns about crime, about employment, and about rioting were invoked to prompt government intervention to prevent or reduce nonwhite immigration to Britain.[17] By the late 1950s it became perfectly clear that the British government would enter the business of racially regulating immigration.

The battle cry to "keep Britain White" was answered in 1962 with the passage of the Commonwealth Immigrant's Act (the "Act").[18] The Act officially ended Britain's open-door immigration policy vis-à-vis "Her Majesty's subjects." Though not racially discriminatory on its face, the Act had a racially discriminatory effect. It called for "special entry" regulations for all Commonwealth and Colonial immigrants with two notable exceptions—the Irish (mostly white)[19] and Citizens of the Commonwealth holding passports issued by the British government[20] (again, mostly white). However, the Act was unable to "keep out" Kenyans of Indian ancestry, whose British passports were issued by the British High Commission. This caused Enoch Powell, a very influential Member of Parliament, to refer to the Kenyans as a "loophole" in the Act.[21] The anti–Black/people of color immigration ideology had taken hold.

Had my mother entered England after 1962, she would have had to qualify for one of three types of vouchers issued by the Ministry of Labour: (1) Voucher A, issued to persons who are coming to England for a specific job; (2) Voucher B, issued to persons with "training skills," or educational qualifications likely to be useful in Britain; or (3) Voucher C, issued to all other persons.[22]

My mother would not have been issued a Class A Voucher; she had no specific job in England. Nor would the Ministry of Labour have issued her a Class B Voucher; she was not a doctor, a nurse, a teacher, a dentist, or a lawyer. With respect to obtaining a Class C Voucher, she would have had to compete with almost every other West Indian attempting to immigrate to Britain, since most of them also would have been unlikely candidates for Class A or Class B Vouchers.[23]

Yet my father's hesitance was understandable. Racism was very real in England. The *Jamaican Weekly Gleanor* reported on discriminatory experiences West Indians endured in Britain. Jamaicans wrote home about the riots in Birmingham, London, and Nottingham, about police brutality,[24] about employment discrimination,[25] about how difficult it was to get housing.[26]

And there was a gendered component to British racism. Black men and Black women experienced British racism differently. My mother would not have to worry much about experiencing police abuse. Mostly, that was a problem for West Indian men. But she would have to worry about housing and employment discrimination, and I don't think she was fully prepared for either. "Dem couldn't tell me anyting about racism in Englan'. I see it in Jamaica all de time." But as a light-skinned biracial woman, my mother was the beneficiary of Jamaica's racism. If my mother applied for a job in Jamaica and didn't get it, she could take comfort in the fact that it was not because she was "Black" (read: dark-skinned). Colorism—intraracial distinctions among Black people based on skin tone, hair texture, and facial features— was a common social practice in Jamaica.

My mother's unpreparedness for British racism was not solely, or predominantly, a function of skin-privilege and colorism, however. Like many Jamaicans who immigrated to England, she had an awful lot of faith in the Union Jack, notwithstanding what she read about in the *Jamaican Weekly Gleanor* and what she heard from friends who had immigrated to England before her. This was not a matter of naïveté on my mother's part. It was a matter of her needing to believe in the promise of a better life. My mother had deeply internalized the ideology of migration. If things did not work out, she knew that she could always return home; "if worse comes to worse, A can jus' pack-up an' leave. Afta Jamaican not going anywhere."

Furthermore, and as my mother often says, "Englan' was not a stranger to me." For my mother, going to England was not the same as, say, going to America. She knew very little of America and even less about Americans. But England (she thought) she knew and the British (she thought) she understood. England was, after all, the motherland and she was a British subject. In school she sang "God save the Precious Queen" and saluted the British flag. She, like many other West Indians, invested a lot of psychological capital believing that they belonged to Britain, that their status as colonial subjects—subjects of the Crown—meant that England was also home. My mother would come to learn that not even the fact of birth in Britain renders a West Indian British. As Enoch Powell observed, "the West Indian does not, by being born in England, become an Englishman. In law, he becomes a UK citizen by birth; in fact, he is a West Indian . . . still."[27] There is "no Black in the Union Jack."[28]

My mother arrived in Birmingham, England, via a ship (it was cheaper than air travel) in January 1961 with two suitcases and very little money. Birmingham was cold and damp and dreary. The houses were like "chicken coops." The streets were narrow. The pavement was often strewn with trash. The people were unfriendly.

But it was England.

My mother had arranged to stay with a friend until she found a job, which would not be easy. It was not that my mother had difficulty getting a job, but rather that her race and gender circumscribed the kinds of jobs she could obtain. Although my mother could do basic bookkeeping and knew a little shorthand, she could not get a secretarial job or a job as an administrative assistant. Those were reserved for white women. Jamaicans functioned as a "replacement population" for only certain kinds of jobs. My mother had two options: she could work as a cook or a domestic. Significantly, neither of these jobs involved public contact. According to my mother, "dem [white people] doe waunt Black people wey [white] people can see dem. Dem jus waunt we fi cook dem food and clean dem house." West Indian men were not required to cook white people's food or clean white people's homes. They got the "better-paying" jobs—with British Railways, in the steel factories, and on the buses. My mother "chose" to work as a cook in a hospital, Dudley Road Hospital. She would work at Dudley Road for the next sixteen years.

As you might imagine, my mother did not make much money as a cook. But it was more money than she had ever earned before, and it was enough money for her to rent a room in an "Indian man's house." My mother had attempted to find temporary government housing ("I came to Englan' to werk, not fe mek government mind me"), but she had poor luck. The problem for my mother and many other West Indians was twofold. For one thing, there was very little information available to immigrants about how they might access government housing—where to apply, what the criteria were, how involved the process was. For another, the public housing sector was locally based, oriented toward "its own people," "good families, i.e., quiet, clean, regular-earning families with not too many children."[29]

In the private sector, many whites were not willing to rent rooms in their homes to West Indians. It would not be uncommon to see advertisements in the papers that read, "Room for rent. Outdoor bathroom. No kitchen. Preferably white."[30] No legislation prohibited private housing discrimination.[31] The fact that there was a housing shortage throughout Britain compounded the problem. Those whites who did rent rooms, cellars, and attics to the growing West Indian population were often bigoted. Not only did they charge over-market rents, they also took great care to keep their West Indian tenants out of the neighborhood's eye. The following account from one West Indian in Leicester was not atypical:

There is one thing that I will never forget. I was standing at the bedroom window looking out one afternoon. As "the gaffer" walked across the yard, he looked up and saw me. Within two minutes he rushed into the room. "Don't you ever do that again" he said. "What will the people think if they see you looking out from one of my rooms." They didn't want us to be seen in their house.[32]

Many West Indians, including my mother, ended up renting from East Indians.

After living in England for six months, my mother concluded that "things not so bad." My father joined my mother in England in August 1961. Over the next few years, they would "skimp an' save" to send for my six siblings. My brothers and sisters came to England one at a time. Except for my youngest sister and my oldest brother, each arrived in England before the age of thirteen. Thirteen was the cut-off age for discount airfares: children thirteen and over paid full fare, children under thirteen paid half fare. Two of my siblings arrived in England the day before their thirteenth birthday.

My mother does not think that there was anything particularly courageous about her decision to go to England before my father. I doubt that she would consider it an act of feminism. Generally speaking, "feminism" in Jamaican culture is a dirty word, just as it is in mainstream American culture.[33] Calling a Jamaican woman a "feminist" at once undermines her racial and cultural loyalty (since feminism is associated with white European and white American women)[34] and her identity as a woman (since feminism is associated with women who want to be men).

Nor do I think many people would consider my mother a feminist, given her views about family life, the who-is-supposed-to-do-what issues. She believes that women "kyan du anyting dey waunt." But there is a proviso: "so long as dey does keep up de house, do de cookin', and tek care a de kids." My mother never tires of asking my wife, "What yuh cooking for Devon's and Asmara's [my daughter's] dinna?"

Based on this gendered construction of family responsibility (that it attaches to women and not men), one could certainly argue that my mother wittingly or unwittingly acquiesces in sexist, essentialist notions of manhood and womanhood: namely, that men don't do housework—women do. But my mother has to be looked at in her own social context, a Caribbean context. To understand my mother one would have to, borrowing a term from Isabelle Gunning, "world travel" and situate oneself squarely within her social reality.[35]

III. ON MOTHER IN CULTURAL CONTEXT AND THE PARTICULARIZATION OF PATRIARCHY

Women are perceived simultaneously as workers and mothers in Jamaican culture. They are patriarchally suited for both. Thus, regardless of the extent that a woman works outside the home, she is still expected to perform all the duties inside the home. This my mother did as a matter of course. If she considered this a burden, we would not have known. If she considered this oppressive, we would not have known. She never complained. Seemingly, she was being a mother and a wife in the only way she knew how. She lived to work for her family. My mother is now seventy-one years old. One of the few things she regrets about growing old is that "A doe have de strent fi help unu [you all] no more."

My mother grew up understanding that her social context imposed real limitations on her ability to transcend the gendered expectations of how she would live her life. She knew that her social existence would have to be organized around a socially constructed, existential given: that housework and child rearing were "her" responsibilities. Her mother wanted her to be a schoolteacher because that would not interfere with her ability to be a housewife and mother. Her father wanted her to be a "good" housewife, which, in his mind, precluded her from being much of anything else. These expectations were not simply the private, familial expectations having to do with what-we-want-our-kids-to-be-when-they-grow-up; they were public expectations as well, socially and culturally informed and intimately wound up with family life and relationships. Fighting these expectations required one to fight with one's self, one's cultural identity, as much, or more so, than it required one to fight with one's family and society as a whole.

And my mother did fight. Her way of fighting was to demonstrate that women could perform all that was required of them in the home and still pursue opportunities outside the home. In this sense, she engaged in micro-aggressive politics, undertaking to transform the very personal and private aspects of her social life. Somewhere along the line, though, I think my mother normalized her fight, so that it was no longer a fight as such and became instead her way of life. She invested her identity in it.

My mother would always praise my father for never trying to "rule" or "dominate" her. "A spen money as A see fit," she always used to say (and still does). "If A wha go out anywey, George does drop me off and pick me up. I am a free woman."

My mother's statements concerning my father are certainly true. He did "permit" her to live her life as she saw fit. He never insisted, for example, that my mother cook. And my sense was that if she had given up the responsibility of cooking, my father would simply have assumed it. I honestly do not think my mother wore so many hats because she thought my father would have been angered if she decided not to. Still, my father probably harbored an expectation that my mother would cook. Jamaican cultural and social norms required him to. It was probably one of his many silent, culturally informed expectations of my mother.

Presumably, my mother knew that my father had unarticulated expectations about family life and responsibilities. She must have known. Every Jamaican grows up knowing who is "supposed" to do the cooking and who is "supposed" to take care of the kids. Our culture, like most other cultures, is rather noisy about issues of family life.

Indeed, I think, in part, it is precisely because my mother knew about my father's expectations, and because of other patriarchal expectations of Jamaican women, that she juggled so many roles and responsibilities. Doing extra- and intra-household work was her way of negotiating her conception of what women could do with what Jamaican cultural conceptions required women to do: housework and child rearing. This negotiation gained her a certain amount of autonomy outside the home. It was not a cost-free negotiation, however. It resulted in her having a greater stake in the patriarchal aspects of her life than my father: whatever she chose to do outside the home could not interfere with what she (felt she) had to do inside the home. Yet she considered herself free!

I remember when I was about twelve, my mother asked my brothers and me whether we were troubled by the fact that she worked so hard and whether we would be happier if, like my aunt, who lived just down the road from us, she became a homemaker. I remember the moment very well because it was the only time that my mother looked to us, her three youngest ("the boys," as we were called), to affirm her decision to exist as a woman outside of her role as mother. My brothers and I understood this. We knew that my mother's concerns were not simply about work; they were also about her sense of identity as a Jamaican woman, about having a public identity that transcended traditional motherhood, about composing her life.[36] Of course, we did not think about the matter in precisely those terms. All we knew was that mother would always talk about how maddening it would be for her to stay home every day, and that she could not understand how my aunt spent "my uncle's" money so freely: "how she spen Ustas' money when she doe mek none, I jus doe no." My mother, like many other people, has a very narrow conception of what constituted income- producing work and it did not include what my aunt was doing at home with her kids. That kind of work could never "buy" her freedom. We knew that my mother could not survive the life of a housewife. Her question was disingenuous, but she needed to ask it and she needed us to answer.

"No, we don't mind that you work so much, and we don't want you to stay home like Aunt Tancy."

We spent the rest of our adolescence proving to mother that we meant those words, that we were prepared to live by them. Rather than allocate some of "her" family responsibilities to my father (which, presumably, would have reflected badly on her motherhood), my mother involved us in her housework rituals. In this way, she retained the responsibility for homemaking. Work became an essential part of our lives. Each evening, my mother dished out our chores after grace with dinner.

"Devon, A season de meat fa tomorrow dinna. Put it in de oven at half-pass-five. Let it cook fa a-houa-an-a-half. Den, cova it up and turn off de oven. Colin, bring unu clothes from upstairs and put dem fi soak so A can wash dem. Lenny, sweep wey di mess dat Kim mek in di outhouse. A kya bare fi see dat mess when a-doing mi washin."

We performed our chores religiously (most of the time). And when we were not doing chores, we spent our time "sensibly." At thirteen, I could make a decent pot of curry, and my fourteen-year-old brother could bake an apple pie from scratch.

IV. ON FATHER AND PATRIARCHY

I do not think I fully understood how my father was implicated in my mother's assertion that she is "a free woman" until I started reading bell hooks. According to hooks, Black male sexism is not limited to explicit attempts to discriminate against women.[37] It includes "romantic visions of black men lifting black women to pedestals," protecting the "femininity" of Black women, maintaining social inequality of Black women, and failing to unburden the family responsibilities of Black women.

I see my father's failure to unburden "my mother's" family responsibilities as patriarchy—passive or unconscious patriarchy.[38] hooks does not use either of these terms, but I think this is what she has in mind when she tells the story of Ida B. Wells, whose husband supported her work outside the home as a political activist but did not relieve her of the family responsibilities assigned to her as a woman; on various occasions Wells appeared at public engagements with her small children.[39]

The patriarchy is passive in the sense that women who experience it are not told, for example, that they cannot perform work outside the home. There is no obvious resistance to the woman's decision to do extra-household work. Indeed, such work might even be encouraged. It is, or can be, unconscious in the sense that "the man of the house" does not necessarily actively erect barriers to prevent women (or make it difficult for them) to work outside the home. The barriers (for example, child care responsibilities and homemaking more generally) exist because men unconsciously acquiesce in the "natural" female-gendered allocation of family responsibilities.[40] They do little to challenge them. They accept them as the "what is" of family life, necessarily incidental to motherhood.

Unconscious patriarchy definitely applies to my father. His conduct in the context of our family life and vis-à-vis my mother was never overtly sexist. He never told my mother what to do. He never made any demands. But he need not have done either; whatever his burdens were, they did not include the day-to-day responsibilities of child care and housework. My mother (with our help) made sure of it. My father "did not have to" tell my mother what to do. It went without saying that the second shift was my mother's.[41]

Because my father was not responsible for our day-to-day existence, I never really got to know him—beyond knowing who he was. I have no childhood memories of real intimacy with him. On those rare evenings he was home, he avoided us and we avoided him. (I tell myself that his avoidance came first.) I got better and better at avoiding him as I got older. I spoke to him only when it was necessary: "Daddy, mommy said to ask you for some lunch money," or "Daddy, mommy said to tell you to pick her up at six o'clock." I spoke to my father with the authority of mother behind me. My brothers did the same. Mostly my father spoke to us when we needed to be disciplined: "Colin, how much time A must tell yuh not to trouble mi speakers," or "Lenny, turn off dat television and go to yuh bed," or "Devon, tek-up a book an' read and leave dat dog alone." I wish I could say that, despite our avoidance of each other and our functional conversation, I knew that my father was as concerned about our well-being as my mother was.

But as I have already said, and want to say more directly here, our family life did not exist in an economic, cultural, or social vacuum. We were working-class. And we were West Indians in Britain. These "externalities" acted upon all of us, including my father. In a sense, he was being a father in the only way that he knew how—as a financial provider. That was his socially constructed, existential given. There was no cultural precedent for him to be actively involved in parenting, or for him to cook,[42] or for him to do housework. Every Jamaican grows up knowing what men, as a general matter, do not do.

And maybe my father knew that there was a certain amount of power inherent in housework and child rearing (the ability to define the character of the home and shape the development of life) and that my mother had invested her identity in both. Maybe my father "fathered" so that my mother could "mother."

Still, my father was a beneficiary of my mother's double work. We all were. And the issue of agency (the extent to which he was individually responsible for the allocation of work in our family and the question of whether he could have transcended West Indian cultural norms) is, on some level, not important. The reality is that my mother was burdened with housework and child care responsibilities because she is a woman and because family responsibilities are gendered. My father is not completely to blame for this. There was a cultural/functional dimension to the patriarchal aspects of our family life that all of us, including my mother, internalized and re-created. He is nevertheless culpable. Unlike my mother, he rarely came home to work.

If you were to ask my mother what she regrets about her life, she would probably say, "not a ting. I lived my life de wey I wanted to." But I think my mother knows she made a patriarchal bargain. Her "freedom" required it. Though I doubt my mother would openly admit it, her "freedom," in the context of our family life, was really my father's.

NOTES

An earlier version of this chapter appears in Critical Race Feminism: A Reader 339 (Adrien Katherine Wing ed., 1997).

1. For a discussion of the ways motherhood has been constructed so that women bear the brunt of child-rearing responsibilities, see Nancy Chodorow, *Mothering, Male Dominance, and Capitalism, in* Capitalist Patriarchy and the Case for Socialist Feminism 83, 86 (Zillah R. Eisenstein ed., 1979). For a discussion of how motherhood has been configured to subordinate Black women, see Dorothy Roberts, *Racism and Patriarchy in the Meaning of Motherhood,* 1 Am. U.J. Gender and L. 1, 6 (1993). Roberts's point, with which I agree, is that whiteness is normalized in the construction of motherhood and to the extent that Black women "diverge from" or "contradict" the white, middle-class, heterosexual married woman, they are perceived as deviant. *See also* Nathalie A. Augustin, *Learnfare and Black Motherhood: The Social Construction of Deviance, in* Critical Race Feminism: A Reader, *supra* at 144 (discussing the degree to which Black mothers are considered deviant in the context of Learnfare). For a discussion of motherhood and work in the context of Indian culture, see Mitu Gulati (with Leela Gulati), *Female Labor in the Unorganized Sector: The Brick Worker Revisited*, 32 Economic and Political Weekly 968 (1997).

2. *See* Carol Gilligan, In a Different Voice: Psychological Theory and Women's Development (1982). According to Gilligan, "women's [description of identity] is . . . judged by a standard of responsibility and care." *Id.* at 160. Not all feminists agree with Gilligan's "different voice" thesis. *See, e.g.*, Catharine A. MacKinnon, *Difference and Dominance: On Sex Discrimination, in* Feminism Unmodified: Discourses on Life and Law 33–34 (critiquing Gilligan). For a discussion of the various strands of feminism, see Cass R. Sunstein, *Feminism and Legal Theory*, 101 Harv. L. Rev. 826–28 (1988) (reviewing MacKinnon, Feminism Unmodified, *supra*), *cited in* Daniel R. Ortiz, *Feminisms and the Family*, 18 Harv. J.L. and Pub. Pol'y 523, 523, and n.1 (1995).

3. Robin West, *Jurisprudence and Gender*, 55 U. Chi. L. Rev. 1, 14 (1988).

4. *But see* Nel Noddings, Caring: A Feminine Approach to Ethics and Moral Education 128 (1984) (maintaining that biology does play a role in shaping the identities of men and women).

5. West, *supra* note 3, at 16.

6. Gilligan, *supra* note 2, at 100.

7. I have chosen not to translate my mother's Patois into (standard) English. Patois is my mother's language. It is a part of her identity. My mother rarely speaks (standard) English to us, even though we rarely speak to her in Patois.

8. For a discussion of the literature concerning the extent to which it is useful to analyze West Indian immigration to Britain in terms of "push" and "pull" factors, see Margaret Byron, Post-War Caribbean Migration to Britain: The Unfinished Cycle 6–12 (1994).

9. *See* Aubrey W. Bonett, *The New Female West Indian Immigrant Dilemma of Coping in the Host Society, in* In Search of a Better Life: Perspectives on Migration from the Caribbean 140 (Ransford M. Palmer ed., 1990).

10. Jamaicans interested in immigrating to Britain were also concerned about the political discussions in Jamaica about independence. It was unclear what relationship Jamaica would have with Britain if Jamaica became an independent state. Jamaica did gain its independence in 1962, attaining "fully responsible status within the Commonwealth." Jamaica Independence Act, 1962, ch. 40 (Eng.). My mother continues to think that "independence was de worse thing that could happen to Jamaica." She attributes Jamaica's present standing in the world to its dissociation from Britain.

11. For a discussion of West Indian immigration to Britain after the Second World War, see James Walvin, Passage to Britain: Immigration in British History and Politics 182–98 (1984). *See also* Ceri Peach, West Indian Migration to Britain (1968).

12. *See* Gary P. Freeman, Immigrant Labor and Racial Conflict in Industrial Societies: The French and British Experience 1945–1975, at 261–62 (1979). *See also* Frank Reeves, British Racial Discourse 94 (1983).

13. Robert Miles and Annie Phizacklea, White Man's Country: Racism in British Politics 63 (1984) (quoting John Hall).

14. British Nationality Act, 1948, 11 Geo. 6, ch. 56 (Eng.).

15. Byron, *supra* note 8, at 81.

16. *Id.* at 82.

17. Ian R. G. Spencer, British Immigration Policy since 1939, at 63, 109–11 (1997).

18. Commonwealth Immigrants Act, 1962, ch. 21 (Eng.).

19. *See* Richard T. Schaefer, The Extent and Content of Racial Prejudice in Great Britain 31 (1976).

20. Commonwealth Immigrants Act, *supra* note 18.

21. *See* Miles and Phizacklea, *supra* note 13, at 59.

22. Commonwealth Immigrants Act, *supra* note 18, at pt. 2, Section 3.

23. *See* Shiela Patterson, Immigration and Race Relations in Britain 1960–1967, at 142–43 (1969) (discussing the "voucher system" and the extent to which it affected immigration of people of color from the Commonwealth). No class C vouchers were issued after 1965. *See id.*

24. *See, e.g.*, John R. Lambert, Crime, Police, and Race Relations: A Study in Birmingham (1970); Martin Adeney, *Police Accused of Violence against Blacks*, Guardian, Sept. 25, 1971, at 5.

25. *See, e.g.*, Bob Hepple, Race, Jobs and the Law in Britain (1968).

26. *See generally* Marie Jahoda and Patricia Salter West, *Race Relations in Public Housing*, 7 J. Soc. Issues 132 (1951). In 1965 Parliament passed the Race Relations Act, which, among other things, prohibited discrimination in "places of public resort." Patterson, *supra* note 23, at 87.

27. Claire E. Alexander, The Art of Being Black: The Creation of Black British Youth Identities 2 (1996).

28. *See* Paul Gilroy, There Ain't No Black in the Union Jack (1987) (discussing, among other things, the discriminatory experiences of West Indians in Britain).

29. Patterson, *supra* note 23, at 211. In the application process, my mother was required to inform the housing authorities of my father's intention to immigrate (as an unskilled laborer) with the rest of the family, my six siblings who were born in Jamaica.

30. *See* Byron, *supra* note 8, at 139 (observing that "[b]y 1961, 74 percent of Caribbeans were occupying privately rented property").

31. One of the criticisms leveled at the Race Act was that it did not cover housing discrimination. *See* Patterson, *supra* note 23, at 85–86.

32. Byron, *supra* note 8, at 146.

33. *See, e.g.*, Leslie Bender, *A Lawyer's Primer on Feminist Theory and Tort*, 38 J. Legal Educ. 3, 3 (1988) ("Feminism is a dirty word. . . . Feminists are portrayed as bra-burners, men haters, sexist, and castrators. . . . No wonder many women . . . struggle to distance themselves from the opprobrium appended to the label. 'I am not a feminist; I'm safe; I'm ok,' is the message they seek to convey."); Louise Bernikow, *Let's Hear It for the "F" Word*, Newsday, June 18, 1993 at 62 ("It's a touchy word, 'feminist.' . . . But [Ruth Bader Ginsburg] is an unabashed feminist. For every Ginsburg, there are many women who harbor feminism in their hearts but dare not speak its name.").

34. Several Black American feminists have critiqued the extent to which feminism in the United States has been a movement mostly concerned with white women's issues. *See, e.g.*, Alice Walker, In Search of Our Mothers' Gardens (1983) (preferring to use "womanist" rather than "feminist"); Kimberlé Crenshaw, *Demarginalizing the Intersection of Race and Sex: A Black Feminist Critique of Antidiscrimination Doctrine, Feminist Theory and Antiracist Politics*, U. Chi. Legal F. 139 (1989); Angela P. Harris, *Race and Essentialism in Feminist Legal Theory*, 42 Stan. L. Rev. 581 (1990); Deborah K. King, *Multiple Jeopardy, Multiple Consciousness: The Context of a Black Feminist Ideology*, 14 Signs 265 (1981); Audre Lorde, *Age, Race, Class and Sex: Women Redefining Difference, in* Sister Outsider 114 (1984).

35. *See generally* Isabelle R. Gunning, *Arrogant Perception, World Traveling and Multicultural Feminism: The Case of Female Genital Surgeries*, 23 Colum. Hum. Rts. L. Rev. 189 (1992) (arguing that, to avoid cultural and political imperialism, Western feminists, as

outsiders, should "world travel" before formulating policy initiatives to address female genital surgeries).

36. *See generally* Mary Catherine Baterson, Composing Life (1990) (using the lives of five women to discuss how life is composed through work).

37. *See* bell hooks, Ain't I a Woman: Black Women and Feminism 89 (1981).

38. I use "unconscious" with respect to patriarchy here in the same way that Charles Lawrence uses "unconscious" with respect to racism. *See* Charles Lawrence, *The Id, the Ego, and Equal Protection: Reckoning with Unconscious Racism*, 39 Stan. L. Rev. 317 (1987) (arguing that the Supreme Court's focus on intent in the context of Fourteenth Amendment jurisprudence is inadequate to combat racism that is not explicit or manifest but latent and implicit—a part of our cultural norm).

39. hooks, *supra* note 37, at 90. hooks's reading of Wells's appearance in public with her children might well say something about our expectations for political discourse—that it doesn't include children.

40. My use of "unconscious" in this context is not meant to suggest that men don't actively engage in sexist conduct that limits women's ability to work outside the home. "Unconscious" here is intended to apply to men whose conduct functions to subordinate women but who would say either that their conduct is not the result of any antiwoman animus and that they do not believe in inequality between the sexes or that they are not intentionally conducting themselves to subordinate women in the context of family life. *See generally* Lawrence, *supra* note 38 (discussing racism as an unconscious internalization process, which is not necessarily related to racial animus but has the effect of subordinating minorities).

41. For a discussion of the working mother's continued role as primary homemaker in two-career families, see Arlie Hochschild, The Second Shift (1989).

42. I make a distinction here between cooking as a part of one's family responsibility and cooking more generally. I would imagine that most West Indian men can cook and that many do in fact cook. I suspect, though, that few would consider cooking a part of their parental or family responsibility, West Indian cultural norms being what they are. *See* Chodorow, *supra* note 1, at 86 ("[A]ll societies do have a sexual division of labor. These include women's involvement in routine daily cooking for their immediate families (festive cooking, by contrast, is often done by men).").

8 | Discrimination in New Zealand
A Personal Journey

Mai Chen

I. INTRODUCTION

This is an essay about a Taiwanese immigrant woman in New Zealand. It concerns my experiences of discrimination, which impelled me to become a law teacher and to take an academic interest in the law relating to discrimination. It is part of my personal story, but it also offers lessons for antidiscrimination law and an understanding of the pervasiveness of discrimination in New Zealand.

The methodology used in this essay to make these points is not a traditional legal criticism of antidiscrimination laws and comparative analysis to make the case for reform. Rather, it uses experiences as a basis for analyzing the law. Some would argue that telling "stories" is not scholarship; that as a method, it is biased, emotive, and not value-neutral. However, others (including those in critical race theory, feminist legal theory, and critical legal studies) would argue that it is false to presume the validity of traditional methods of legal analysis that have always claimed to be objective and value-neutral. Winter argues that the recent *return* to narrative in the United States is occurring because the legal community is coming "increasingly to doubt its former confidence in the neutrality and objectivity of standard legal analysis [and that] as it retreats from its faith in abstractions, it inevitably seeks solace in the more concrete."[1]

Using experiences as a basis for analyzing the law can challenge prevailing legal ideologies; it can "enlist empathy and understanding from [people] whose own experiences do not ordinarily lead them to challenge official views";[2] and it can introduce perspectives that are usually excluded. Furthermore, experiences of discrimination can

Reprinted by permission from 23 *Victoria University of Wellington Law Review* 137 (1993).

illuminate particular values and suggest particular solutions to the problems of discrimination. As Mari Matsuda states,

> [o]utsider scholars have recognized that their specific experiences and histories are relevant to jurisprudential inquiry. They reject narrow evidentiary concepts of relevance and credibility. They reject artificial bifurcation of thought and feeling. Their anger, their pain, their daily lives, and the histories of their people are relevant to the definition of justice. . . . If you have been made to feel, as I have, that such inquiry is theoretically unsophisticated, and quaintly naive, resist! . . . These proposals add up to a new jurisprudence—one founded not on an ideal of neutrality, but on the reality of oppression.[3]

It is impossible to separate out my experience of sex discrimination and race discrimination since they often intersect to create a set of experiences unique to immigrant Chinese women.[4] Thus, I will deal with these experiences together. The focus of this chapter is the richness that experiences of discrimination can bring to writing in antidiscrimination law, primarily in understanding that discrimination attacks the victim's spirit (by which I mean the sense of identity and individuality) as much as the victim's pocket. Thus, any remedies for such actions must act to revive and promote the spirit as well as redress damage to property through loss of employment or accommodation.[5] It is on this basis, among others, that I reject arguments for self-regulation in discrimination and support the need for antidiscrimination laws.

Recounting my experiences of discrimination is difficult since it means reflecting on experiences that have caused me pain. In addition, there is the fear that such significant and disturbing personal experiences may not be believed by others, or their significance disputed. It is difficult to bear the insult this can add to injury. As a six-year-old newly arrived from Taiwan, I recall that my teachers at Christchurch primary school, where my sisters and I were the only Chinese, would say, "Oh I don't believe that. The other children would not treat you like that just because you're a Chinese girl. Now run along and don't be silly."

Despite the risks in recounting my experiences, I think that it is important to describe the crippling impact that discrimination can have, and the extent of that intolerance in New Zealand society, even to members of "successful" minorities like Chinese immigrants. Such a growth in understanding would be timely as Asia becomes an increasingly significant source of immigrants and refugees to New Zealand,[6] and as our economic future increasingly lies in Asia and the South Pacific.[7]

II. THE EXPERIENCES THAT SHAPED ME

I was born in Taiwan into a family of four daughters. Chinese value sons more than daughters,[8] and my mother always told me, the youngest, that I was their last attempt to have a son. They had been so sure that I was going to be a boy because I had kicked a lot in the womb. My parents gave up trying to have a son after I was born. My sisters and I grew up constantly hearing the extended family and my parents' friends saying, "Four daughters, huh, what bad luck. Well at least you will have someone to look after you in your old age." My uncle (who had four sons) took pity on my parents and offered to give them their youngest son in exchange for me. Thankfully, my parents turned down his generous offer.

My family emigrated to New Zealand in 1970, settling first in Christchurch and then in Dunedin. There were few colored minorities in the South Island. On the first day we were in New Zealand a kindly neighbor offered to take the girls on a walk down to the park. While the neighbor was trying to explain to us how to push the button at the pedestrian crossing, we heard an almighty crash. The neighbor later told my father, who spoke some English, that the offending driver had been so amazed by the sight of four Chinese girls dressed in identical red Chinese suits that he had not noticed the red light and had plowed into the car in front of him, triggering a series of crashes down the line of traffic.

There were Chinese people in Dunedin, many being offspring of those who had come to Otago during the gold rush in the nineteenth century, but they were mostly immigrants from China, and relations between China and Taiwan were, and still are, hostile.[9] They also spoke Cantonese or Hockien, while we spoke Mandarin. We became New Zealand citizens in 1974. Until 1975 there was no other Taiwanese family we knew of in the South Island. By 1980 we knew of only two Taiwanese families apart from our own. My father taught physical education at Teachers' College, so I spent a lot of my childhood taking part in sporting activities. My mother gave up her teaching career to raise us, but continued to work part-time at various jobs to keep the family afloat financially.

There was a great deal of ignorance about Taiwan in Christchurch and Dunedin in the 1970s. The children at school used to ask me if we wrote in the sand in Taiwan and if we lived in tents. "Did you have television?" "Did you eat rats?" There was derision and a sense of smug superiority in their voices. I had never had to deal with these insinuations of inferiority before. They teased us about the way we looked, and about our inability to speak English. We were ugly, slit-eyed, squashed-nose, and yellowy-brown. Somehow being Chinese made us so different, so "bad" that the other children did not want to be our friends.

I remember seeing my reflection and that of Elizabeth, a blond, blue-eyed *pakeha* (white) girl, in the lavatory mirrors as we went to fetch our play lunch from our satchels. She looked so white, so fair, and all the other children thought she was beautiful. I looked almost muddy in comparison. So dark, such funny slitty eyes and a squashed nose. Even at the age of seven, I realized that I could never aspire to look like Elizabeth, and that realization made me resent being Chinese.[10] I concluded that I could not compete on the grounds of beauty because being beautiful meant being white, having a pointy nose and thin lips. So I moved to a basis where I could compete on an equal footing—academic achievement. To me, academic achievement was race- and gender-neutral. I may be dark and ugly, I may be just a girl, but you had to credit me with worth because I was smart. I dressed like a boy. I hid my femininity. I decided that I was not interested in boys.

As I grew older, I learned to stick up for myself. I now spoke English well. If I could not stop the teasing any other way, I would punch the offender and make a run for it. My parents, however, spoke with a strong accent and it hurt me deeply when people said, "What's that you're saying, I can't understand you" or gestured at my parents as if they were deaf, mute, or stupid.[11] I will always remember the time my proud parents accompanied me to the South Island finals of a national speech competition for secondary school students and were challenged (when nobody else was) by the usher as to their right to be present. Most of those attending were parents and relatives of the contestants and the usher obviously never thought that there could be a Chinese contestant in an English speech competition. Immigrant children have a difficult time in a new country, but parents also suffer. They often experience a usurpation of their parental role since their children learn the new language, culture, and etiquette faster and soon overtake their parents.

I observed that I was not given the same treatment as *pakeha* around me and had to work harder to get helpful or polite treatment. I found that I was far less likely to suffer discrimination if I was with my British-born, white husband or with his family. It was as if their whiteness gave me legitimacy. However, when I was on my own or with members of my family, the difference in treatment was marked. The contrast helped me to understand why white New Zealanders find it difficult to comprehend that shop assistants, among others, could be rude and unhelpful to colored minorities just because of their race. The world is a very different place for them—it is generally full of polite people, who try to be friendly and helpful. They find it difficult to believe that there could be another side to people when they are dealing with colored minorities.

The message I received from these and other experiences was clear. Being Chinese was a handicap. Since I was Chinese, I was inherently handicapped. I responded by overcompensating, by throwing off every vestige of "Chineseness" and fully embracing New Zealand culture. I wanted people to know that I was not really Chinese because I did not want to be treated like a Chinese. For me, becoming Kiwi was the path of least resistance. It was a way of surviving.

At the age of twenty-four, I had just returned from postgraduate studies overseas and a stint at the International Labour Office in Geneva. My parents wanted to take me to get *paua* from the sea, as they had when I was younger. It was a beautiful day. My father set up his fishing gear and my mother and I started poking about in promising-looking places among the rocks. We had not been there long when a man in his mid-twenties strode toward us and started shouting and gesturing with his hands. He accosted my mother first. "Not more than ten *pauas*," he was saying, and then held up ten fingers since he presumed she did not understand English. My mother tried to respond politely, which sent the man into a tirade: "You Asians come in and take all the *paua*! We have laws, you know, and you can only take ten." Unable to keep quiet any longer, I informed the man that we were perfectly able to understand English and to count without visual aids, so he could put his fingers down. I was well aware of the Fisheries (Amateur Fishing) Regulations 1983, and what authority did he have to harass people going about a lawful activity in a public place?

Not surprisingly to me, the man was not a fisheries officer. But my response just made him angrier. He wanted to continue arguing and he insisted on inspecting our buckets. I told him he had no right to look. Throughout, my parents looked mortified and my father kept telling me that they did not want any trouble. My father then started packing up his fishing gear and my mother gathered up our scattered coats and picnic goodies to go. They almost ran out of that place with me in tow raving that the man had no right to talk to us that way and that we should stand our ground because the beach was a public place. Our happy outing had been ruined and in the car on the way home, my mother tried to change the subject. All I could think of was how, after twenty years in New Zealand, after all the struggles and the eventual triumphs to thrive and succeed in this new country, our legitimacy to be here could still be challenged by one insignificant racist.

I also realized that, while discriminatory behavior may not take the form of an actual refusal to allow a person to use a public place (in our case, the beach), the effect can be the same: the racial minority is made to feel so ashamed by the discriminatory treatment that they will relinquish the right to avoid prolonging the treatment. Discrimination has the effect of bruising the psyche so that people submit more easily to this type of degrading treatment.

This incident particularly stood out in my mind because of my recent arrival back from overseas. I remembered saying to my husband that it was really good to be home. While we waited at Christchurch airport for our flight to Dunedin to be reunited with our families, my husband stretched out on seats some distance away to sleep. I was left to guard all the hand luggage, of which there was a great deal after two years abroad. Some White New Zealanders came and sat a short distance from us. A woman said, "Look at that Chinese woman with all that hand luggage. God, they're taking over the country. I wouldn't be surprised if she's just arrived from Hong Kong and is going to stay. Probably bring her whole family out next." She made no attempt to lower her voice and they all stared at me and nodded in agreement.

I felt an overwhelming desire to retaliate by telling them that I spoke English and understood what they were saying, that I was a law academic who had just come back from postgraduate studies overseas, that I understood what this country had given me and wanted to make a contribution in return, and that I came from a family who were all making a significant contribution to their society. However, my experience has been that achievements do not provide full protection from discrimination. No amount of education, achievement, contribution to society, or acculturation can make you legitimate, because some people do not respect achievements. Anyway, why should it make any difference that I could speak English and was a law academic? What if I had just arrived from Hong Kong and could not speak English? What if I was about to try to bring out my family? I understand that some New Zealanders are nervous about Asian immigrants taking their jobs in the current economic climate,[12] but surely all people are worthy of respect regardless of their color, achievements, or abilities because of the inherent dignity of human be-ings. This principle is so fundamental that it underlies all major international human rights documents. For example, Article 1 of the Universal Declaration of Human Rights states, "[a]ll human beings are born free and equal in dignity and rights. They are endowed with reason and conscience and should act towards one another in a spirit of brotherhood [and sisterhood]."

I considered marching over and punching the woman, my successful childhood strategy; but having just said how nice it was to be home, the sad irony of the whole situation hit me, and I suddenly felt very tired by my inability to escape discrimination.

My mind cast back to other instances of discrimination. I remembered how a classmate had said to me when I won a major scholarship to study abroad that it should have gone to a "real" New Zealander. After my first week in a constitu-tional law course at Harvard Law School, I went to see the professor to get permis-sion to tape his classes until I had adjusted to his American accent and the new vo-cabulary of American constitutional terms. He talked very fast. His secretary an-nounced my name and my inquiry, so I did not have a chance to speak. The professor took one look at me, presumed I was a postgraduate student from China for whom English was a struggle, and said to me, "If you are finding the lectures difficult to understand now, then you will never last the distance. From my experi-ence, it would be much better if you just dropped the course right now." I tried to explain that I was a graduate student from New Zealand and that English was not a problem. He just held up his hands in protest, said that he was too busy to talk, and put his head down to continue with his work. It took a long time to recover my confidence in his class. I also felt ashamed that I had been put in the position of having to effectively say that I was not really Chinese (in terms of language ability), that I just looked like it. What if I had really been a Chinese postgraduate student from China with language difficulties?

No matter how much I achieved, the cloud of suspected incompetence never seemed to go away. When I was accepted into Harvard Law School, a New Zealand law professor remarked that he had heard they were "looking for women." When I returned from working at the International Labour Office in Geneva to take up a lectureship at Victoria University, an academic from another institution asked me if I had been hired because the Law Faculty was looking for women.

After recounting many of her experiences of discrimination as a Black woman, Adrien Wing states that:

> [t]o some people, such incidents of micro-discrimination may appear trivial and not worthy of discussion, especially in a law journal. After all, I should be thankful that I haven't been raped, beaten or lynched as were countless numbers of my people. Yet the cumulative impact of hundreds or even thousands of such incidents has been dev-astating to my spirit. . . . [B]lack women are lifelong victims of . . . "spirit-murder."[13] [Patricia] Williams only addresses the racial aspect, noting that racism is "a crime, an offence . . . deeply painful and assaultive . . ." I would go further and add sexism

to her characterization by saying that the combined impact of racism/sexism "is as devastating, as costly, and as physically obliterating as robbery or assault; indeed they are often the same." Racism/sexism "resembles other offences against humanity whose structures are so deeply embedded in culture as to prove extremely resistant to being recognized as a form of oppression. It can be as difficult to prove as child abuse or rape, where the victim is forced to convince others that he or she was not at fault, or that the perpetrator was not just 'playing around.' As in rape cases, victims of racism must prove that they did not distort the circumstances, misunderstand the intent or even enjoy it." To me, spirit-murder consists of hundreds, if not thousands, of spirit injuries and assaults —some major, some minor—the cumulative effect of which is the slow death of the psyche, the soul and the persona. This spirit-murder affects all blacks and all black women, whether we are in the depths of poverty or in the heights of academe. [footnotes omitted][14]

The worst effect of discrimination is self-hatred, hatred of what you inherently are, and rejection of those things that make you less worthy in the eyes of others. This is compounded for colored women by the combination of racism and sexism. You suffer low self-esteem and a loss of confidence. Since the offenses are primarily to the spirit and not necessarily to the pocket, remedies must address the first mischief and not just the grievances to property. This does not mean that, in itself, passing antidiscrimination laws will result in victims of discrimination moving beyond self-hatred to a love of self, to an understanding that they will never win acceptance from those outside, but that love must come from within. But the passage of such laws can help, as I argue below.

III. THE BENEFITS OF EXPERIENCE

Lawyers who have experienced discrimination can bring a unique and valuable contribution to the law. It was my experiences of discrimination that first attracted me to the law. I studied law because I saw it as a tool to redress the powerlessness and discrimination that I, and those I loved, had experienced. I also wanted to prevent others from suffering the same experience. I came to the law, not to perpetuate the status quo but to change it, and so I chose an academic career where I could write and think about how the law could be reformed for the better. I also wanted to teach so I could support students who did not fit the traditional lawyer mold and encourage them to hang in there and to make a difference.

A. MENTORING STUDENTS

My own experience of legal education had been difficult. The struggles of minority women, especially those who are immigrants, to achieve legitimacy makes it difficult for them to assert their difference.[15] For me, this meant that even when I wanted to question the impact of certain laws on the oppressed, and to query the "fairness" of laws, I sometimes said nothing.[16] When you are naturally an outsider, the desire to conform and to be one of the crowd is very strong. Fear of rejection and discrimination provides a strong incentive. Yet I found the cultural context in which the law is developed and practiced very different from the one I had grown up in. I did not fit the mold and I agonized over whether I had any contribution to make to the law. Ten years after I started my law degree, the realization dawned on me that much of the contribution I have been able to make to the law is directly due to my difference.[17] It is that realization that made me determined to return to the university to encourage students who did not fit the traditional lawyer stereotype that they could make a contribution to the law, that they can survive law school and make a difference. I was an advisor to women students in the law faculty from 1990 to the end of 1992 and I have mentored, and continue to mentor, women students, many of whom are colored.

B. LEGAL RESEARCH AND WRITING

My experiences of discrimination have brought insights to my work that I would not otherwise have found and have particularly enhanced, I believe, my research on anti-discrimination law. The article I wrote on discrimination seeks to refute the case to repeal all employment discrimination laws in the private sphere such as is propounded by Richard Epstein in *Forbidden Grounds: The Case against Employment Discrimination Laws*.[18] It is partly on the basis of my experiences of discrimination that I conclude that Epstein's arguments are flawed. He takes no account of the cost that discrimination inflicts on the spirit and of the benefits that antidiscrimination laws can have in reviving and promoting the spirit.[19]

Epstein argues that discrimination in the private sphere of employment holds little risk of social or private peril and should be permitted since free entry into the market and multiple employers provide ample protection for all workers. If 90 percent of employers do not want to hire you, then you can concentrate on doing business with the other 10 percent. Although the universe of potential trading partners is smaller, Epstein states that the critical question for my welfare is not which opportunities are lost but which are retained.[20] There are many problems with his arguments even if traditional methods of criticism are used. For example, why should victims of discrimination have to incur greater information costs to find the 10 percent of "willing" employers? Their range of choices is also diminished, along with their bargaining power, since the employer knows that 90 percent of the other employers would not hire such a person.

My experience of discrimination adds a further dimension to my analysis in leading me to argue that the effect of being turned away nine times may well devastate the spirit and undermine a person's confidence so that they may not try a tenth time. There is no point saying that the victim should not give up. People do get dispirited, and who could blame them? Those who are discriminated against are often "discrete and insular" minorities, or from groups who have a long history of discrimination and are relegated to the position of political powerlessness, even though the characteristic that is their badge of distinction may bear no relation to ability to perform or contribute to society, and is an immutable characteristic that is either inherent or uncontrollable.[21] Conditioning and experience from a very young age tell these groups that the world is hostile, and it may well be self-preservation for them not to try again. The fear of rejection may be an invisible "barrier to entry" for victims of discrimination. The barrier is strengthened by the unpredictability of discrimination. What if the next employer is not part of the 10 percent who will be willing to employ you? The effort of bracing yourself for discrimination and rejection may defeat your will to try at all. Epstein's arguments for repealing antidiscrimination laws in employment are flawed because he fails to factor damage to the spirit and the ability of antidiscrimination laws to revive the spirit into his cost/benefit analysis of such laws.

Antidiscrimination laws can revive and promote the spirit by reaffirming the principle that discriminatory treatment on the basis of characteristics such as race or sex is wrong, that it is contrary to the public interest and censured by the state. Such laws can aid discriminated groups to move beyond self-hatred to a love of self, and may also encourage those who believe themselves to be vulnerable to discrimination to assert their rights. As Fiss states, "[r]eliance on self-regulation entails a silence that may be pregnant with contrary implications for the likely victim."[22]

Antidiscrimination laws also provide a necessary minimum safeguard to ensure that minorities are able to exercise and enjoy their rights on an equal basis with other New Zealanders. On returning from overseas, my husband and I went looking for a flat in Wellington. We had followed up an address in Mt. Victoria that was a vacant flat under the landlord's house. We had come from work, so we were smartly dressed. While my husband parked the motorbike, I walked toward the flat and greeted the Greek landlord, who was sitting on the veranda. He stared at me very disapprovingly and did not respond to my greeting. When my husband arrived, the landlord removed his gaze from me for the first time and said to my husband, "The flat is gone." He then entered his house, slamming the door behind him. The flat was not taken—I checked.

Although I was furious about the incident, the shame of having to confront my suspicion of being rejected on the basis of my race held me back from complaining to the Race Relations Conciliator. My earning ability allowed me to get accommodation elsewhere, so I justified my inaction on the basis of not compounding the difficulties of settling into a new city and a new post at Victoria University Law Faculty. I understood that my privileged position allowed me at least to mitigate my powerlessness to some extent. I thought hard about what I would have done if we had been desperate to find accommodation and how much more, in those circumstances, that discriminator's treatment would have knocked my confidence.

To the critics of antidiscrimination legislation who argue that we can never change people's prejudices, I respond that that is not the whole aim of such legislation. Landlords may continue to think racist thoughts, but the law can prevent them from acting on those prejudices to prevent colored minorities from getting accommodation. As Maya Angelou states, "you cannot legislate love, but what one can do is legislate fairness and justice. . . . Legislation affords us the chance to see if we might love each other."[23]

IV. VALUING DIFFERENCE

New Zealand needs to maintain effective antidiscrimination laws as a minimum safeguard of people's ability to exercise and enjoy their rights without discrimination, and to reaffirm the principle that discriminatory treatment on the basis of characteristics such as race or sex is wrong. This is important for affirming and reviving the spirit, damage to which is a major cost of discrimination. Such laws can encourage groups that are discriminated against to express their differences without fear of denigrating and humiliating treatment, to be proud of their differences instead of responding to the incentives that discrimination creates to conform with the Kiwi majority. Antidiscrimination laws may also bring people together by challenging the basis of people's prejudices and showing them up for what they really are—unfounded.

When I was growing up, I resented my "differentness" because being an immigrant Chinese female brought discrimination and that made life hard. But the passage of time has brought the realization that what may be perceived by others to be weaknesses can be turned into strengths. It is these differences and the experiences that stemmed from them that have enriched my research on antidiscrimination law.

Well-meaning people often say to me that they do not notice that I am Chinese. They think of me as one of them. As much as I appreciate the sentiment, the fact is that I am not the same. We are all different, one from the other, and that is something to be valued, not denigrated.

POSTSCRIPT

It has been six years since I wrote this essay. I have now left academia to found New Zealand's first public law specialist firm with another academic colleague and former New Zealand Prime Minister, the Rt Hon Professor Sir Geoffrey Palmer. Americans would call Chen and Palmer Australasia's first "Washington" law firm. The focus is on Government, policy, and legislation. The firm's philosophy is that litigation is the last resort. Despite skepticism from colleagues in the profession that there was no market for public law, the vision of the firm has been vindicated and the firm has flourished. By New Zealand standards, the firm is now almost middle-sized. I still teach part-time at Victoria University Law Faculty and I have a weekly television program, where I talk about topical public law issues. I sit on boards, I still try to write. But most important, I am happy and content. I have found what I most love to do, and although I have days when the discrimination I encounter still makes me despair, I try not to dwell on it. I look at my lot in the round and I count myself fortunate. I do not resile from anything I wrote all those years ago about my experience of discrimination in New Zealand, but my thoughts have evolved. Ultimately the decision must be made whether to expend our energy feeling angry and victimized or to move on to fulfill our potential as best we can and to try and change the world in our own way. Antidiscrimination laws aid the latter goal by changing societal norms of behavior over time and easing the barriers. But most important, my experience has been that retaining a victim mentality is antithetical to conquering the world. We must not forget our roots. We must not forget our experiences and the suffering. But we need to transcend those experiences if we are to do any good. The best way to bring about a brave new world without unfair discrimination is to live your life *now* as if that were the fact; to transcend stereotypes, thereby risking humiliation and discrimination, but to stand your ground because you believe that people should be judged on merit and not on race and gender.

NOTES

1. S. L. Winter, *The Cognitive Dimension of the Agon between Legal Power and Narrative Meaning*, 87 Mich. L. Rev. 2225, 2227 (1989).

2. K. L. Schelleple, *Foreword: Telling Stories*, 87 Mich. L. Rev. 2073, 2074 (1989).

3. Mari J. Matsuda, *When the First Quail Calls: Multiple Consciousness as Jurisprudential Method*, 11 Women's Rts. L. Rep. 7 (1989).

4. *See, for example*, M. Hong-Kingston, The Woman Warrior: Memoirs of a Girlhood among Ghosts (1975); and Amy Tan, The Joy Luck Club (1989).

5. See, for example, the very broad remedies in section 88 of the Human Rights Act 1993.

6. 1991 New Zealand Census of Population and Dwellings: Provisional National Summary 11 (Dept. of Statistics, Wellington, 1991). New Zealand Official Yearbook 1998, at 101 tbl. 5.15 (Dept. of Statistics, Wellington, 101st ed. 1998). New Zealand Working Party on Immigration, Report of the Working Party on Immigration 5 (Govt. Printer, Wellington, 1991).

7. New Zealand Official Yearbook 1998, at 522 tbl. 25.20 (Dept. of Statistics, Wellington, 101st ed. 1997); R. D. Cremer and B. Ramasamy, Tigers in New Zealand? The Role of Asian Investment in the Economy (1996).

8. *See* Hong-Kingston, *supra* note 4, at 45, 53.

9. Raj Vasil and Hong Key Yoon, New Zealanders of Asian Origin (1997); Malcolm McKinnon, Immigrants and Citizens: New Zealanders and Asian Emigration in Historical Context (1996).

10. Angela P. Harris, *Race and Essentialism in Feminist Legal Theory*, 42 Stan. L. Rev. 581, 597–98 (1990).

11. *See* Mari J. Matsuda, *Voices of America: Accent, Anti-discrimination Law, and a Jurisprudence for the Last Reconstruction*, 100 Yale L.J. 1329 (1991).

12. *See* R. Gordon, *The Asian Invasion,* Metro 150, 154, Auckland, New Zealand, July 1988; *see* McKinnon, *supra* note 9.

13. Patricia J. Williams, *Spirit-Murdering the Messenger: The Discourse of Finger Pointing as the Law's Response to Racism,* 42 U. Miami L. Rev. 127 (1987).

14. Adrien K. Wing, *Brief Reflections toward a Multiplicative Theory and Praxis of Being,* 6 Berkeley Women's L.J. 181, 185–86 (1991).

15. *See* Mai Chen, Drawbacks of the Tough Law School Environment in New Zealand and the United States: Is Reform Women's Work? (1987) (unpublished paper prepared for a Comparative Legal Education course at Harvard Law School, on file with author).

16. *See* Matsuda, *supra* note 3. *See also* Matsuda, *supra* note 11, at 1330.

17. *See* Mari J. Matsuda, *Affirmative Action and Legal Knowledge: Planting Seeds in Plowed Up Ground*, 11 Harv. Women's L.J. 1 (1988).

18. Mai Chen, *Law and Economics and the Case for Discrimination, in* The University, Ethics and Society 27 (1995).

19. Matsuda, *supra* note 3, at 11.

20. Richard A. Epstein, Forbidden Grounds: The Case against Employment Discrimination Laws 30 (1992).

21. *See* United States v. Carolene Products Co., 304 U.S. 144, 152, note 4 (1938). *See* W. Sadurski, *Judicial Protection of Minorities: The Lessons of Footnote Four*, 17 Anglo-Am. L. Rev. 163 (1988).

22. O. M. Fiss, *A Theory of Fair Employment Laws*, 38 U. Chi. L. Rev. 235, 249 (1971).

23. Brian Laker, I Dream a World: Portraits of Black Women Who Changed America 162 (1986).

9 African Women in France

Immigration, Family, and Work

Judy Scales-Trent

I. INTRODUCTION

In the fall of 1997 much of the news in France seemed to lead back to Africa—back to reminders of French colonization on that continent, back to the painful memories of those years. Most of this news centered on Algeria.

It was a time when waves of terrorism were sweeping Algeria. As residents of entire villages were being slaughtered at random, the world began to wonder who those terrorists were: were they fundamentalist insurgents? Or agents of the current government trying to maintain its power? Shock waves from Algeria spread north to France as more and more terrified Algerians moved there for safety. There were bombings and assassinations in French cities; French soldiers in camouflage patrolled metropolitan areas with machine guns.

As they struggled with the impact of terrorism in Algeria, the French were also trying to figure out what to do about their high rate of unemployment, especially among the youth. And for weeks and weeks, the news was full of stories about the forty-five-day hunger strike of the sons of the "harkis," those Algerian men who had fought for the French during the Algerian war for independence. After the war, France moved the harkis and their families to special government camps in the French countryside, where they were supposed to live temporarily under military authority. However, the harkis and their families remained isolated in these rural camps from the early 1960s until the early 1980s, during which time their sons were given only two hours of schooling a day. It was not surprising, then, that the sons of the harkis were on a hunger strike, because for this group of French-Algerian youth, the unemployment rate was a staggering 80 percent.[1]

Reprinted by permission from 24 *Brooklyn Journal of International Law* 705 (1999).

And even when the media were reporting on the trial of Maurice Papon for war crimes committed against French Jews he had deported to Nazi Germany during World War II, Algeria surfaced once again. For Maurice Papon, the mayor of Bordeaux during World War II, had been head of the Paris police in the early 1960s during Algeria's war for independence. And in October 1997, as Papon's trial began, and as the French Jewish community gathered before the court in Bordeaux to remind France of their loss, representatives of the Algerian community in France demonstrated at their side: they were there to remind France that this man who had signed the deportation orders for French Jews was the same man who, some twenty years later, had encouraged and supported the police as they murdered hundreds of Algerians who were gathering for a peaceful demonstration back in October 1961.[2]

At the same time, in the fall of 1997, one could hear, in a much lower tone, the complaints of some French women protesting inequality between men and women in France. Some protested salary inequities: in 1991 French working women earned only 67 percent of the salary of French men.[3] Others protested the fact that although 56 percent of French voters were women, only 6 percent of the deputies elected in 1995 were women. Why should the political parties be allowed to present slates of only male candidates? France was far behind most of the countries in the European Union in this regard. In Sweden, for example, 40.4 percent of the deputies were women. Some French women were suggesting modifying the Constitution in order to authorize the creation of a form of affirmative action (*discrimination positive*) that would lead to the proportional representation of women in French elective bodies.[4]

And finally, during the month of October 1997, a major research institute at the University of Paris held a two-day conference on African immigrant women and work, thus addressing both of these questions in tandem—the issues raised by the legacy of France's colonial empire in Africa and gender inequalities in France.[5]

I spent October 1997 in France exploring the intersection of race/ethnicity and gender in that country. My plan was to explore the parameters of a future study of the lives of immigrant African women in France. Certainly it must be very hard to be an African immigrant in France; how much harder would it be if the immigrant were a woman? What social and legal consequences might appear when the issues of gender were added on to the issues posed by ethnicity?

Before traveling to France, I spent several months reading about immigration and gender issues in France, as well as relevant current events. While in France, I interviewed activists, lawyers, and researchers, who explored ideas with me, put me in touch with others, and recommended much helpful material.[6] I also spent several days in Paris at the Agence pour le Développement des Ressources Interculturelles (ADRI), a private organization that specializes in issues involving immigrant communities in France.[7] And my overall education was enhanced by general conversations with the French and African workers and students I met during that five-week period.

This chapter will thus provide a brief overview of some of the issues that face many African women in France. It will address three principal questions:

(1) Who are these women who are stigmatized by both their African origins and their gender?

(2) What do they bring with them from their homeland that might create social and legal problems for them when they arrive in France?

(3) What will they find when they arrive in France that might make their lives difficult?

II. WHO ARE "AFRICAN IMMIGRANT" WOMEN IN FRANCE?

In 1990 there were 56.6 million people living in metropolitan France.[8] The percentage of foreigners in this group has been particularly stable: in 1982 there were 3.68 million foreigners, and in 1990 there were 3.6 million.[9] In 1990 the largest group of immigrants from any one particular country was from Portugal, a fellow member of the European Union.[10] One would think therefore that the French would not be particularly troubled about immigration. But they are. Because what has changed in France is both the increasing number of African immigrants and their immigration pattern, for it now appears that these African immigrants are planning to stay in France.

In 1946 the immigrant population in France was as follows: Europeans, 88.7 percent; North Africans, 2.3 percent; other Africans, 0.8 percent. The 1990 census shows a much different picture of who is moving to France: Europeans, 40.6 percent; North Africans, 38.7 percent; other Africans, 11.8 percent.[11] Clearly, the increase in both sub-Saharan and North African immigration is marked, as is the 50 percent decrease in European immigration.

There are several reasons for the increasing number of African immigrants to France—France's recruitment of African soldiers from its colonies during World War I and World War II, France's palpable presence in Africa based on its control of a large part of the African economies since their independence, the continued drought in the Sahel region, and worldwide recession.[12] Another reason is France's recruitment of African workers.

France has historically invited immigrants to its shores when it needed labor, labor it then exploited in the most devalued sectors of the industrial labor market. Cycles of expansion and economic crisis have thus provoked corresponding cycles of encouraging immigration, then discouraging immigration and sending foreign workers home. As a general rule, then, France has considered immigrants transient workers.[13]

During the economic boom after World War II, France encouraged foreign workers—including workers from Africa—to immigrate to France. Even more workers came from Africa and Asia after the period of decolonization in the 1950s and 1960s. During this same period, fewer workers came from Western Europe, as living standards in those countries were increasing.[14] In 1974, as the French economy went into decline, France banned the continued immigration of unskilled foreign workers.[15] However, this ban included only non-European workers, since European workers had right of entry as members of the European Union. As a result, every year since 1974, France has admitted approximately 100,000 European Union nationals, as well as approximately 100,000 others who were not banned from entry: this number includes spouses of French citizens, families of foreign residents, political refugees, and skilled workers.[16] It does not include the many immigrants who enter France illegally.[17] Thus, even though many African workers were excluded in 1974, the flow of immigrants from Africa has not stopped.

These are some of the reasons for the increased number of Africans among the immigrants to France. But it is important to notice that the proportion of women among those immigrants is also increasing. In 1962 only 15 percent of the immigrants were women, but by 1990 that percentage had doubled to 30 percent.[18] In 1990, of the 1,614,250 foreign women in France, 19 percent were from Portugal; 15.73 percent and 15.55 percent were from Algeria and Morocco respectively; 5.26 percent came from Tunisia; and 4.25 percent emigrated from sub-Saharan Africa.[19]

The regulatory framework for immigration that the French set up after World War II permitted families to join the workers though the program of *regroupement familial*. However, when France banned further immigration of unskilled foreign workers in 1974, it also banned the immigration of their families. The ban on family reunifications, however, was held unlawful by the Conseil d'Etat, France's highest administrative court.[20] As a result, even though no more unskilled African men could come to France, wives and children of male African workers already in France could still join them there. This has led not only to the increased percentage of women immigrants, but also to a major structural change in the African population in France.[21] No longer primarily single male workers thinking of one day returning to their homelands and their families, these immigrant Africans are now families with children who were born in France and who are being educated in French schools: it appears that they might well stay. And it is this shift that troubles many French, leading to heightened racism and xenophobia.[22]

Although my plan here is to discuss issues affecting "African immigrant women" in France, the apparent simplicity of that phrase is misleading. I use the phrase in order to count and think about those women who may face discrimination in France based on their African ethnicity. However, because the French government has not created and does not use classifications of "race," scholars and policy makers use immigrant status as a proxy for determining who is likely to face discrimination in France.[23] Immigrant status, however, is a very clumsy proxy.[24]

For example, the census defines "foreigner" as someone who is a permanent resident in France and who does not have French nationality, whether that person was born in France or not.[25] However, some "Africans" may have immigrated to France, become citizens, and still often may be treated as a "foreigner" in France because of their appearance. Similarly, the children or grandchildren of African immigrants may well be French, but are still often treated as "foreigners."[26] Indeed, many in France call the children of immigrants "second generation immigrants."[27]

And finally, some French citizens have been born and raised in France and never "immigrated" to France, but will still be treated as "foreigners," as "Africans," once they go to the mainland: these are the French citizens of African ancestry who live in French *départements* of Réunion, Guadeloupe, Martinique, and French Guiana.[28] If it is true, as one commentator has noted, that in France "some foreigners are more foreign than others,"[29] then it is also sadly true that in France some citizens are more "foreign" than others.[30]

Nonetheless, although it is not a very precise term for what I am trying to discuss, I use here the term "immigrant," the one that is used in France to both capture and symbolize ethnicity or "race."[31]

III. WHAT CUSTOMS AND TRADITIONS DO "AFRICAN" WOMEN BRING WITH THEM FROM THEIR HOMELAND THAT MIGHT CREATE SOCIAL AND LEGAL PROBLEMS FOR THEM WHEN THEY ARRIVE IN FRANCE?

Immigrants take to their new country the cultural and religious practices of the old one. Because so many of the African immigrants are Muslim, Islam is now the second largest religion in France.[32] Thus, many African immigrant women bring Muslim traditions with them to France.

Several commentators have suggested that Islam often takes on more importance to Muslim immigrants in France than it did in their home country, for it plays an important role in the maintenance of culture, language, and identity. Immigrant parents often exaggerate their attachment to Islam in order to keep their children from straying too far from them into an alien European culture. Young women play an important role in maintaining these newly accentuated Muslim traditions, since communities often control group identity by controlling choices with respect to marriage and reproduction. Thus, the control of young Muslim girls and women becomes even more important once their families immigrate to France.[33]

This section of the chapter explores the problems that arise at the intersection of the African and French religious and cultural practices. How might Koranic and customary rules about women's sexuality and marriage—excision, clitoridectomy, and infibulation;[34] style of dress; polygamy; dowry; repudiation— complicate the lives of African women once they immigrate to France? How are these practices interpreted by the French social and legal systems? What happens when these practices collide with French immigration and social welfare laws? What is the effect of bilateral conventions between the home country and France on these practices?

It is not surprising that the incident to raise the most questions about the place of Islam in France involved three young Muslim schoolgirls who were suspended when they wore the Muslim headscarf to school in September 1989. According to the school principal, the girls were violating fundamental principles of separation of church and state, principles embodied in a regulation that forbade proselytism in French schools. Within several months, however, France's highest administrative court, the Conseil d'Etat, ruled that it was not the girls who were at fault, but rather the principal, who had violated their freedom of religion as guaranteed by the French Constitution.[35] The girls must be allowed to wear the headscarf.

This incident sparked what one commentator calls a national psychodrama, a debate way out of proportion to the incident itself, for there had always been girls wearing Muslim headscarves to school in France.[36] But the issue provoked a crisis at this moment because of the contemporaneous rise of radical Islam in the international context. Thus, three young girls wearing the headscarf in France immediately became confused with the chador, ayatollahs, and fundamentalism.[37]

Another reason that many French were troubled about girls wearing the Muslim headscarf in school is that many had seen these young girls, rather than their brothers, as the principal agents of Muslim integration into French culture: if the girls weren't taking on that role, then who would?[38] And finally, the French were more troubled about these young girls than they had ever been about their grandmothers wearing headscarves to go to the market, because scarves in school suggested that Muslim girls were somehow not willing to be completely assimilated even though France was educating them to be "French." Muslim grandmothers were living the old way, and probably hoping to return home; but their granddaughters would likely stay in France, yet still be "different."[39] To many French, then, this raised troubling questions about changes in France's national identity.

In 1994 the appearance of numerous headscarves in the schools led the Minister of Education to issue a statement banning ostentatious religious symbols in public schools.[40] His statement led to so many confrontations and refusals to remove headscarves that the Minister appointed two mediators, women of North African origin, to intervene in the schools.[41] Through this work, one of the mediators learned that many of the young women were wearing the headscarf to school not because of family pressure, but on their own initiative, as a way to find a positive identity in a hostile country, and as a way to separate from their parents. In her view, then, wearing the headscarf was merely a tool of emancipation: if the girls were left alone, the headscarf would ultimately facilitate their integration into French society, not alienate them.[42]

The 1989 national psychodrama about the headscarves, then, was an important marker of questions in the French population about the role of Islam in France, a marker mediated through the lives of young African women: it put in relief problematic questions of "race," difference, and national identity.[43] And the debate continues. In July 1996 the Administrative Court in Paris upheld a rule of the lycée Albert-Schweitzer that forbade all "ostentatious" religious signs, such as the Islamic headscarf. Samira Kherouaa's refusal to remove her headscarf was, therefore, held a valid reason for her permanent removal from the school.[44] Later that year, in a case involving another school, the Conseil d'Etat stated that merely wearing a headscarf was not, in and of itself, an ostentatious religious sign, and therefore not necessarily incompatible with the principle of secular schools.[45] Because of this confusion, some have suggested the enactment of a law on religious neutrality in public schools; others suggest a referendum on this issue, in order to forbid all religious signs in schools. At least one commentator thinks that such acts would be immediately struck down as either unconstitutional or violative of international law.[46]

Other commentators have wondered why the debate over the Islamic headscarf focuses so specifically on the question of religious freedom, and not on gender equality, since France's constitution provides for equality between men and women. And why does the Conseil d'Etat repeatedly emphasize Article 9 of the European Convention on the Rights of Man, which protects the right to express one's religion, without mentioning Article 5 of the Convention on the Elimination of All Forms of Discrimination against Women, which requires signatories to modify cultural patterns of conduct in order to eliminate discrimination?[47] Although it is clear that the problem raised in France by the Islamic headscarf in schools is one that implicates issues of both religion and gender equality, the gender issue has simply not been addressed as prominently.[48]

Like the custom of covering their heads, other cultural and religious practices that some African immigrant women bring with them to France implicate issues of sexuality, marriage, and reproduction. And again, as with discussions over the headscarf, the debate in France over these practices focuses on the extent to which a different culture can be assimilated into the French national identity: questions of patriarchy and equality between men and women remain in the margin.

[Editor's note: The author next discusses how the French legal system addresses some of those religious and cultural practices, including genital excision, polygamy, dowry requirements, and the Islamic divorce known as repudiation.]

IV. WHAT IS ALREADY IN PLACE IN FRANCE THAT MIGHT MAKE THE LIVES OF IMMIGRANT AFRICAN WOMEN DIFFICULT?

From the first, African women will find racism in France. In a 1990 survey, 90 percent of the French interviewed said that racism in France was "rather" or "very" widespread. According to 83 percent of those surveyed, the major targets are the North Africans, followed closely by young French men and women of North African ancestry, then sub-Saharan Africans.[49] Two years later, 65 percent of the French surveyed said that there were too many Arabs in France;[50] 38 percent said there were too many Black people; and 31 percent said there were too many Asians.[51]

It is not surprising that North Africans are the chief targets of racism in France, for, as noted earlier, the Algerian war is apparently not yet over for many French. As one commentator has noted, France doesn't have a problem with immigration. It has a problem with its colonial past in general, and with its Algerian past in particular.[52]

France's control over Algeria began in 1830 and lasted 130 years. In 1947 France made Algeria an integral part of the country. As a result, anyone born in Algeria after 1947 was automatically a French national.[53]

The beginning of the Algerian war of independence in December 1954 was a powerful blow to France: only four months earlier, it had lost its colonies in Indochina after an eight-year war.[54] And Algeria was unique in France's empire: only five hundred miles south of Marseilles, Algeria was France's closest and largest trading partner, as well as the French colony with the largest European settler community. It had unique political ties to France, and had proven its strategic value during World War II.[55] The loss of Algeria would be thus an important economic, political, and symbolic loss. Finally, after eight years of war, with atrocities and 400,000 deaths on each side, Algeria gained its independence in 1962.[56]

In 1994, some thirty years after the peace accord was signed, there was still a large group of the French population—over five million people—who had been directly affected by the war: three million of them had been soldiers; one million were European settlers who left Algeria after the war; and another one million were Algerians who had moved to France.[57] Even if we do not count the families of the three million soldiers, this means that over 10 percent of the people in France are directly implicated in the war. Thus, there are many French who remember the war and their losses, and fix their memories and rage on anyone who might be Algerian. And unfortunately for the Tunisians and Moroccans, they often are considered Algerian by the French.[58]

Racism in France is reflected in many ways, including violence. Racist violence rose sharply in France in the 1980s.[59] Between 1990 and 1991, threats against North Africans increased by 25 percent.[60] Racism is reflected in housing discrimination in both public and private sectors.[61] It is also reflected in the national debates on immigration and citizenship bills, as well as the rise of the extreme right-wing party, The National Front, which campaigns on an anti-immigrant platform.[62]

Racism coalesces with other factors in French society to make it often very difficult for African immigrant women to get a job. One of those factors is a sluggish economy.

The period from 1955 through 1975 was a period of great economic expansion in France, an expansion that led France to invite worker immigrants, especially from Algeria. In 1975, one-quarter of all workers in the construction and car industries were immigrants.[63] Since 1975, however, France has been beset by a profound reorganization of its economy, including the increasing use of robots, and subcontracting work. Work is disappearing most in those areas where foreigners were heavily employed, such as industry and construction. The gains made in the economy have been in precarious areas such as textile and clothing manufacture, food preparation, cafés, and restaurants.[64]

The sluggish economy has led to a high unemployment rate, which doubled between 1980 and 1990.[65] If one factors in the hostility toward Africans noted earlier, it is not surprising that African immigrants have a higher rate of unemployment than the French. And because both France and the sending African countries value women less than men, it is also not a surprise that the unemployment rate for African women is even higher than that of African men.[66]

Table 1. Unemployment Rates in France in 1990

	Men	Women
French	7.5%	14.1%
Algerian	23.1%	42.3%
Moroccan	20.7%	42.5%
Tunisian	22.0%	41.7%

SOURCE: Alec G. Hargreaves, Immigration, "Race" and Ethnicity in Contemporary France 41 (1995)

For sub-Saharan women, the unemployment rate was a staggering 45 percent to 50 percent for Senegalese women, 46 percent for women from Mali, 46.7 percent for women from the Ivory Coast, and 36 percent for Camerounian women.[67]

There is no doubt that a significant part of the reason for the high unemployment rate for African women is that many of them immigrate to France with little formal education, an inability to speak French, or both. However, this is not the whole answer to the high unemployment rate, for employment discrimination against Africans is rampant in France.[68] One study showed, for example, that even controlling for all relevant variables, the risk of unemployment was eighty times higher for immigrants from North Africa than for the French.[69] Thus, African women who apply for jobs for which they are well qualified are often rejected.[70]

Indeed, in a stunning example of the irrelevance of "qualifications," a study of a company that places cleaning women in businesses showed that its customers refused to accept African women. Instead, they asked the company to send them French women to clean their offices. Indeed, some customers insisted that both the first and last name of the cleaning woman be French, so that they could be sure that they were not hiring by mistake an African woman who might have acquired a French last name through marriage.[71] Similarly, the French are more likely to hire Spanish and Portuguese immigrant women to clean their homes than they are to hire African immigrant women.[72]

One would think that this situation would improve for the children of these immigrants. Unfortunately, it appears that this is not true for this group of youth, which has markedly less likelihood of upward mobility than do French nationals of the same age and class. And the problem is exacerbated for girls in this group, who face discrimination as women, as migrants, and as youth, yet often receive educational "training" in areas such as sewing, which give them little preparation for the workforce.[73]

African women immigrating to France will also find that although French law prohibits employment discrimination, enforcement of that law is almost nonexistent. France's Criminal Code makes it unlawful to refuse to hire or to punish or fire a person or subordinate a job offer to a discriminatory condition because of that person's origin, or the fact that he belongs to, or doesn't belong to a particular ethnic group, country, race, or religion.[74] A violation of this law carries a penalty of up to two years in prison and a fine of 200,000 francs. If the violation is committed by someone in the public sector, the punishment is increased to three years in prison and 300,000 francs.[75] France's Labor Code also prohibits an employer from adopting internal policies that would penalize employees based on their nationality or religion.[76] However, the laws are rarely enforced because, according to the French, such discrimination is almost impossible to prove, as employers can escape liability simply by denying any racist motivations.[77] Some victims of discrimination are too ashamed or frightened to file a lawsuit; some find it difficult to find witnesses who will testify on their behalf.[78] Still others know that if they lose the lawsuit, they could be sued for defamation.[79]

Immigrant African women will also discover that French citizenship requirements will make it difficult for them to find jobs. Many public sector jobs that women might be interested in—teaching in a public school, clerical jobs with the government—are generally open only to French citizens.[80] This is especially problematic in France, where approximately one-third of all jobs are in the public sector or in private sector jobs with some public authority.[81] It is important to note, however, that since French nationals from France's *départements* in the Caribbean, South America, and Indian Ocean (Martinique, Guadeloupe, French Guiana, and Réunion) are entitled to hold the jobs of citizens, many jobs in the public sector in metropolitan France are filled by French citizens with brown or black skin. Indeed, the majority of those who move to the metropole from the Antilles work in the public sector.[82]

Finally, immigration issues can also make it difficult for African women to find work. Women who are entitled to come to France to join their husbands under the system of family regroupment (*regroupement familial*) don't have their own independent immigration status: they take the same status as their husbands. Because their rights are derivative, if the husband has no right to work, neither does the wife.[83] And it is often difficult to obtain a work authorization permit in France.[84]

V. CONCLUSION

France has put many resources into incorporating migrants into the French community. The major state agency with this responsibility is the Fonds d'Action Social pour les Travailleurs Immigrés et leurs Familles (FAS), which manages the money allocated for state and private programs that facilitate the integration of migrants.[85] In 1989, 43.3 percent of the FAS budget went to housing, 27.6 percent went to education, and 26.8 percent went to social and cultural activities.[86] France's Ministry of Work and Solidarity develops government policy on immigrants; and the International Migration Office tries to facilitate the reception of migrants in France. The Association of Social Assistance for Migrants uses its local offices to deliver social services to them.[87]

Before 1981, noncitizens did not have the right to organize associations in France. As a result, French nationals created the associations designed to fight racism and improve the lives of immigrants.[88] Three of the most important are le Mouvement contre le Racisme et pour l'Amitié entre les Peuples (MRAP), le

Groupe d'Information et de Solidarité auprès des Travailleurs Immigrés (GISTI), and SOS-Racisme. They are also authorized to file suit in cases of discrimination, thus playing a role similar to that of American public interest law firms.[89]

Since 1981 the number of associations created by noncitizens has skyrocketed. By the mid-1980s there were over four thousand such groups, mostly concentrated in Paris. These groups tend to mobilize around specific political issues, through activities such as demonstrations, expositions, and marches.[90]

The government has also put resources into improving the lives of women in France. One of the most important is the Service des Droits des Femmes, a bureau in the Ministry of Work and Social Affairs, which has twenty-seven offices throughout France, including several in its overseas *départements*. Its goals are to help women to get better trained for jobs; to get businesses to open up more jobs for women; to promote women's rights, including health and reproductive freedom; and, especially for foreign women, to facilitate their access to citizenship and their protection against abuses of authority. One of its specific goals is to fight against the various forms of exclusion that face women who have several "handicaps," such as long-term unemployment, isolation, inadequate training, and poor mastery of French.[91] This national bureau thus recognizes the issues of immigrant African women and is putting some resources toward solving their problems. One of the ways it carries out its mission is by supporting other groups, such as Planning Familial and the Centre d'Information sur les Droits des Femmes (CIDF). With offices throughout the country, CIDF networks between individual women who come to its offices for help and support groups in the community, providing women with information and advice on a wide range of issues, such as divorce, retirement, alimony, housing, finding work, training, and health.[92] The Marseilles office of CIDF now houses a regional office (Bureau Régional des Ressources Juridiques Internationales) (BRRJI), which provides advice on those complex questions of international law that affect immigrant women and their children.[93] Between June 1996, when the office began operation, and June 1997, the BRRJI staff researched and answered 190 legal questions. Many of the questions concerned issues noted earlier in this chapter, issues such as the effect of repudiation on a wife and children, and the problem of who gets a widow's pension where there are several widows.[94] BRRJI provides this advice to other associations, and works as well with attorneys, judges, the Ministry of Justice, and private groups, such as a group of mothers of abducted children.[95]

France also has several university research centers that focus on women's issues, such as the Centre d'Enseignement, de Documentation et de Recherche des Etudes Féministes, an important research center for the past twenty-five years; and it has other university research centers such as URMIS, which sometimes addresses women's issues in tandem with its major focus.[96]

And finally, there are a plethora of African women's organizations in France. Those with a feminist orientation generally work in association with other international groups of African women to increase their autonomy by ending, for example, female circumcision and polygamy.[97] Then there is the much larger group of

African women's organizations, most of which were created to help new immigrant women adjust to the social and legal systems in France, to facilitate the daily life of the immigrant woman and her family, and to help French institutions such as hospitals and schools better understand the African population there.[98]

Indeed, some localities find the assistance of women in these groups so helpful that they have formalized the role of "intercultural mediator" or *femme relais*: these are women from North or West Africa who work out of, for example, a school, hospital, or social services office to facilitate communication between African immigrant women newly arrived in France and French social workers, medical staff, and teachers.[99]

Many of these African women's groups are also trying to change the system of derivative rights, which limits their autonomy. As noted earlier, both immigration and citizenship rights, as well as rights to social benefits, go directly to the husband, then indirectly to the wife. There has been some action on this issue at the international level. Groups have asked the European Parliament to ensure that immigrant women in Europe be given legal status independent of their spouse after a two-year stay in the European country. Specifically, they have asked that these women be given work and residence permits in their own name, which would make them much less vulnerable in cases of divorce or spousal abuse. In a report issued in 1993–94, the European Parliament took note of this problematic situation of immigrant women.[100]

However, even if these rights were granted tomorrow, this would improve the lives of African women with respect to issues of sexism and patriarchy, but not with respect to the racism that they face every day. What good would it do a new immigrant from Mali to have her own work papers if employers refuse to hire anyone from Africa? In order to make her life substantially better, France must substantially reduce both sexism and racism within its borders.

France has created many tools to eliminate racism and sexism, not the least of which is a centralized education system: the power to decide what each child in the country learns on any particular day about history and about people from different parts of the world is not negligible. France also has legal tools. There are laws that make it a criminal offense to discriminate in employment or in furnishing goods or services such as housing. Sanctions include a fine, jail, and/or the closing down of the establishment in question. French law also proscribes hate speech.[101] The only question is how aggressive the French will be in using these tools to meet their own goals of civil equality. I spent October 1997 in France, and now, at the end of June 1998, I am finishing this essay. The news from France these days sounds familiar.

A court in Aix-en-Provence has just given a fifteen-year prison sentence to a Frenchman who killed Ibrahim Ali, a young man from Comoros, off the east coast of Africa. The attorney for the murderer, a billposter for the right-wing National Front, said that his client was defending himself from attack, the prosecutor pointed out that young Ali was shot in the back.[102]

There are demonstrations in France and riots in Algeria because of the assassination of Lounès Matoub, a popular Berber Algerian singer who took a strong stance against Islamic fundamentalism.[103] Matoub had moved with his family to France after having been kidnapped by the Groupe Islamique Armée in 1994. Upon his return to Algeria last week for a visit, that same group assassinated him on a country road as he was driving home.[104] In the last weeks of June, terrorists killed 260 people in Algeria.[105]

The Assemblée Nationale has just adopted, by a vote of 94-0, a constitutional amendment that establishes parity between men and women on the candidates' lists for regional office.[106] This amendment must now be approved either by the Parliament (National Assembly and Senate together), or by referendum.[107]

There is nothing in the news about African women, except for television pictures of grieving mothers and wives and sisters. But, as we have seen here, African women are very present in France. They are making their way as students, as *femmes relais*, as workers, wives, and mothers. Some go to France because they have no choice but to follow their husband, but most go to make their lives better. Many take with them cultural and religious traditions and educational weaknesses that will make their lives complicated in France; and when they arrive in France these women will find problems with racism and sexism, as well as a high rate of unemployment. But still they go to France because, even under these conditions, they expect that life there will be better. As we have seen, the French government and private associations have created a plethora of programs to improve their lot.

We in America know only too well how hard it can be to eliminate deeply entrenched biases, as well as those structural weaknesses in the economy that can limit so severely the opportunities for women harmed by both racism and sexism. Hopefully, those in France who are working on these issues will make progress there that will inspire our own.

NOTES

1. *See* Dalila Kerchouche, *Harkis: Le droit à l'histoire*, L'Express, Oct. 9, 1997, at 49.

2. *See* Jean-Luc Einaudi, *Le papon des ratonnades*, L'Express, Oct. 2, 1997, at 52–53.

3. Conversations with French graduate students at Ecole Supérieure de Commerce, in Paris (Oct. 20, 1997) and at Faculté de Droit et de Science Politique, in Aix-en-Provence (Oct. 28, 1997); Rachel Silvera, *Les inégalités des salaires entre hommes et femmes, in* l'Etat de la France 91 (1997).

4. *See* Annie Labourie-Racapé, *Oser la parité, pour l'égalité, in* L'Etat de la France 86, 86 (1997).

5. Interview with Catherine Quiminal, researcher, Group for the Study of Migrations and Society (Unité de Recherches Migrations et Société) (URMIS), Université Paris VII, in Paris (Oct. 22, 1997).

6. My research was made much easier by the help of Prof. Catherine Raissiguier, Chair of the Department of Women's Studies, University of Cincinnati, who encouraged this work and shared her French contacts with me. I take this opportunity to thank her, and to thank as well the many French scholars, lawyers, and activists who were so generous with their time

and knowledge: Béatrice Borghino, Anne Lespinat, Catherine Quiminal, Mady Vetter, Claude Zaidman, Liliane Zandel.

For their patient French lessons during the spring and summer of 1997, I thank Agnès de-Carlo, Fabienne DuBois, and Malha Zerouki of the Alliance Française of Buffalo. I also owe a debt of gratitude to the colleagues who provided many helpful comments on earlier drafts of this chapter: Sessi Aboh, Béatrice Borghino, Hichem Kefi, Estelle Lau, Isabel Marcus, Mady Vetter, and Malha Zerouki. And finally, I appreciate the continued support of the Baldy Center at SUNY at Buffalo, which provided funding for a week's research in Paris.

7. Although ADRI is an independent organization, like many other associations in France, it receives public funding. *See* Letter from Béatrice Borghino, Délégation Régionale Chargée des Droits de la Femme, Marseilles, to Judy Scales-Trent (Mar. 12, 1998) (on file with author).

8. *See* Philippe Bernard, L'immigration 44, 47, 60–61 (Le Monde-Editions 1993).

9. *Id.*

10. *Id.* at 61.

11. *See* Alec G. Hargreaves, Immigration, "Race" and Ethnicity in Contemporary France 11 (1995).

12. *See* Christian Poiret, *Le phénomène polygamique en France*, 91 Migrants-Formation 26, 26 (Dec. 1992).

13. *See* Gérard Noiriel, *Difficulties in French Historical Research on Immigration, in* Immigrants in Two Democracies: French and American Experience 66, 67–68 (Donald L. Horowitz and Gérard Noiriel eds., 1992) [hereinafter Immigrants].

14. *See* Hargreaves, *supra* note 11, at 10–12.

15. *Id.* at 17.

16. *See* Patrick Weil, *Pour une nouvelle politique d'immigration,* 220 Esprit 136, 138 (Apr. 1996). There are also bilateral and multilateral agreements between France and African countries that modify the 1974 ban on the immigration of unskilled foreign workers. *See* Letter from Mady Vetter, Director, Bureau Régional de Ressources Juridiques Internationales, Marseille, to Judy Scales-Trent (Feb. 25, 1998) (on file with author).

17. *See* Hargreaves, *supra* note 11, at 52–53.

18. *See* André Lebon, *La composante féminine de la population étrangère. Quelques données de cadrage*, 105 Migrants-Formation 6, 8 (June 1996).

19. *See* Annette Goldberg-Salinas, *Femmes en migrations: Une réflexion sur l'état de la question en France,* 105 Migrants-Formation 31, 36 (June 1996). Some 12 percent of the remaining women came from various Asian countries, and 6 percent came from Turkey. *Id.*

20. *See* Hargreaves, *supra* note 11, at 18–19.

21. African women have migrated to France, of course, in other contexts than that of *regroupement familial*. Some have gone alone as students, workers, or political refugees; some went legally, and others, illegally. Many migrated to France to gain more personal freedom than they had in their home country. *See* Goldberg-Salinas, *supra* note 19, at 31, 37.

22. *See* Catherine Raissiguier, Becoming Women, Becoming Workers: Identity Formation in a French Vocational School 133 (1994). *See also* Etienne Balibar, *Is There a "Neo-Racism"?, in* Etienne Balibar and Immanuel Wallerstein, Race, Nation, Class: Ambiguous Identities 21 (1988) (conceptualizing "new racism" in France as "the reversal of population movements between the old colonies and the old metropolises").

23. France does not collect statistical data on race, ethnicity, or religion, based on its notion that each citizen has a direct connection with the nation-state that is not mediated

through group identity. *See* Noiriel, *supra* note 13, at 69–72. *But see* Roxane Silberman, *French Immigration Statistics, in* Immigrants, *supra* note 13, at 119–23 (arguing that disguised ethnic categories diffused throughout the French census have a strong racist and colonial character).

24. The socially constructed notion of "race" is, however, no less clumsy. *See, e.g.,* Judy Scales-Trent, Notes of a White Black Woman: Race, Color, Community 2–3 (1995).

25. *See* Bernard, *supra* note 8, at 43.

26. *Id.* at 135.

27. Raissiguier, *supra* note 22, at 50. In very much the same situation, Germans call this phenomenon "immigration by birth." Alan Cowell, *Like It or Not, Germany Becomes a Melting Pot,* N.Y. Times, Nov. 30, 1997, at A3.

28. *See* Bernard, *supra* note 8, at 143. In 1990 these four islands had close to one and a half million inhabitants. *See Les Possessions d'outre-mer, in* l'Etat de la France 633–34 (1997).

29. Tahar Ben Jelloun, Hospitalité Française 131 (Éditions du Seuil 1997).

30. The right-wing National Front party counts as "foreigners" all of these groups, thus radically increasing the count of "foreigners" who live in France. *See* Silberman, *supra* note 23, at 113.

31. *See* Raissiguier, *supra* note 22, at 49.

32. *See* Sophie Body-Gendrot, *Pioneering Muslim Women in France, in* Mobilizing the Community: Local Politics in the Era of the Global City 276 (Robert Fisher and Joseph Kling eds., 1993). Note, however, that many immigrants are not Muslim. For example, many francophone Africans are Catholic. *Id.* at 275. Also, practically all the French who "immigrate" from the Antilles to the metropole are Catholic. *See* Claudie Beauvue-Fougeyrollas, *Femmes antillaises en métropole,* 84 Migrants-Formation 96 (Mar. 1991).

33. *See* Ben Jelloun, *supra* note 29, at 150–56.

34. Excision involves removing the hood of the clitoris; clitoridectomy involves removing the clitoris and the labia minora; and in infibulation, the clitoris, labia minora, and labia majora are removed. *See* Gregory A. Kelson, *Gender-Based Persecution and Political Asylum: The International Debate for Equality Begins,* 6 Tex. J. Women and L. 181, 185 (1997). In this chapter I will use the term "excision" to refer to all three procedures.

35. *See* Hargreaves, *supra* note 11, at 125–26. It was apparently not problematic to the school officials that some Catholic students wore crucifixes, and that some Jewish boys wore yarmulkes. *Id.*

36. Bernard, *supra* note 8, at 135.

37. Françoise Gaspard, *De l'invisibilité des migrantes et de leurs filles à leur instrumentalisation,* 105 Migrants-Formation 15, 21–22 (June 1996).

38. *See* Jacques Barou, *Sous le voile,* 102 Migrants-Formation 82, 86 (Sept. 1995). This notion is based, in part, on the essentialist notion that facilitating relationships is a female task. *See* Gaspard, *supra* note 37, at 24. It is also very likely based in part on the fact that many African women are indeed taking on the role of intercultural mediator in their communities. Perhaps some think that young girls should be even better at this task than their mothers, since these girls are being raised and educated in France.

39. *See* Barou, *supra* note 38, at 86.

40. The Conseil d'Etat had previously ruled that students' free expression rights could be limited in situations where they infringed on the religious freedom of others or worked to the detriment of the educational program of the schools. *See* Michel Bouleau, *Port du Foulard*

Islamique: Remise en cause de la jurisprudence du Conseil d'Etat, 106 Les Petites Affiches 10, 12 (Sept. 3, 1997).

41. *See* Hanifa Chérifi, *Jeunes filles voilées: Des médiatrices au service de l'intégration,* 1201 Hommes et Migrations 25 (1996).

42. *Id.* at 27–30.

43. For an explanation of the problematic nature of ethnic communities given France's "unitarist" political framework, see Rogers Brubaker, Citizenship and Nationhood in France and Germany 105–06 (1992).

44. *See M. et Mme Kherouaa,* 106 Les Petites Affiches 18 (Sept. 3, 1997).

45. *Ligue Islamique du Nord, M. et Mme. Chabou et autres,* 30 Les Petites Affiches 10 (Mar. 10, 1997).

46. *See* Nguyen Van Tuong, *Note,* 30 Les Petites Affiches 11 (Mar. 10, 1997).

47. *See* Guy Coq, *Foulard Islamique: Pour un retour à la loi républicaine,* Libération (Nov. 6, 1996).

48. *See* Gaspard, *supra* note 37, at 23.

49. *See* Stéphane Rozès, *La France est-elle raciste?, in* l' Etat de la France 44 (1997).

50. In conversations, discussions, and texts on immigration in France, there is much slippage between the term "North African" and "Arab." There are, of course, ethnic groups in North Africa that are not Arabic, such as the Berbers, the indigenous people of North Africa. In Algeria, for example, Berbers comprise approximately 25 percent of the population. *See Une marée humaine à l'enterrement du chanteur Lounès Matoub* (visited June 28, 1998) <http://www.yahoo.fr/actualité/980628/culture/899057760-yahoo138.html>.

51. *See* Bernard, *supra* note 8, at 140. Some 22 percent also thought there were too many Jews. *Id.*

52. Ben Jelloun, *supra* note 29, at 21; *see also* Body-Gendrot, *supra* note 32, at 274–75 (observing that the Algerian war is still one of greatest influences upon racial attitudes in metropolitan France).

53. *See* Hargreaves, *supra* note 11, at 166. "Nationality" was not the same as "citizenship," which authorizes full political rights. France granted French citizenship to only a small elite of its colonial subjects. *Id.* at 162, 165.

54. *See* Tony Smith, The French Stake in Algeria, 1945–1962, at 31 (1978).

55. *Id.* at 22.

56. *See* Bernard, *supra* note 8, at 140–41.

57. *See* Yvan Gastaut, *Le racisme anti-maghrébin et les séquelles de la guerre d'Algérie,* 1174 Hommes-Migration 35, 36 (1994).

58. *Id.* Tunisia and Morocco were protectorates of France. *See* Ann Roze, La France Arc-en-Ciel 282 (Éditions Julliard 1995). The French presence in these two countries was less intimate, and less violent; thus, decolonization took place with less resentment. *See* Ben Jelloun, *supra* note 29, at 27.

59. *See* Hargreaves, *supra* note 11, at 157. For a powerful chronology of attacks on and murders of Algerians in France during a seventeen-month period in the early 1980s, see Ben Jelloun, *supra* note 29, at 71–76.

60. *See* Bernard, *supra* note 8, at 143.

61. *See* Hargreaves, *supra* note 11, at 68, 72.

62. *Id.* at 151.

63. *See* Bernard, *supra* note 8, at 95.

64. *Id.* at 97.

65. *Id.* at 98.

66. *See* Véronique De Rudder et al., *La prévention du racisme dans l'entreprise en France,* Unité de Recherche Migrations et Société, Jussieu VII 12, 39 (1996) (observing that discrimination against women in France is so widespread as to be considered the social norm). For studies on how traditional African culture and Arab and French colonization have made the lives of African women difficult, see generally Barbara Callaway and Lucy Creevey, The Heritage of Islam: Women, Religion, and Politics in West Africa (1994), and Nancy J. Hafkin and Edna G. Bay, Women in Africa: Studies in Social and Economic Change (1976).

67. *See* Catherine Quiminal et al., *Mobilisation associative et dynamique d'intégration des femmes d'Afrique subsaharienne en France,* 61 Migration Etudes 1, 133 (Oct.–Dec. 1995).

68. *See generally* Hargreaves, *supra* note 11, at 65–66. Employers in France use familiar explanations to justify their discrimination against qualified African job applicants—an inability to "control" them; the racism of other workers; the refusal of the French to patronize a business with African workers. *See* De Rudder et al., *supra* note 66, at 36.

69. *See* De Rudder et al., *supra* note 66, at 11. Also, the French press publishes blatantly discriminatory employment announcements such as "White woman wanted to care for elderly lady," and "No persons of colour." U.N. Comm. on Human Rights, Report of the Special Rapporteur on His Mission to France from 29 September–9 October 1995, at 6 (1996).

70. Interview with Anne Lespinat, Centre d'Information sur les Droits des Femmes, in Aix-en-Provence (Oct. 6, 1997).

71. *See La Rayonnante,* 226 CFDT Magazine 36–37 (Mar. 1997). Some businesses apparently use the phrase BBR (*bleu-blanc-rouge*) ("blue, white, red" is a synonym for the French flag) as a code for "French only." *Id.* They also use other covert ways to discriminate—by requiring job applicants to provide pictures of themselves, by hiring only the children of current workers, and by refusing to hire workers from neighborhoods that are heavily immigrant. *Id.* Some French immigrants have apparently carried this prejudice with them to the United States. A random glance at the Help Wanted notices in the weekly French American newspaper *France-Amérique* shows that although fully half of the requests for positions as baby-sitters were from women from North Africa, West Africa, or Haiti, three of the five requests for a baby-sitter requested "French women." France-Amérique, Oct. 11–17, 1997, at 34. Refusing to hire a job applicant because of her ethnicity is, of course, a violation of both Title VII of the 1964 Civil Rights Act, 42 U.S.C. 2000e et seq. (1981) and the Immigration and Reform Control Act of 1986, 8 U.S.C. 1324(a) et seq. (Supp. 1996).

72. *See* Hargreaves, *supra* note 11, at 76–77.

73. *See* Raissiguier, *supra* note 22, at 40.

74. *See* Ministère de la Justice, Guide des lois antiracistes 16 (1994) [hereinafter Guide des lois antiracistes].

75. *Id.* At the time of this writing, 200,000 francs is the approximate equivalent of $33,245.00.

76. *See* Danièle Lochak, *Discrimination against Foreigners under French Law, in* Immigrants, *supra* note 13, at 392.

77. *See* Zouhair Aboudahab, *Face à la discrimination; le droit et ses limites,* 79 Ecarts d'Identité 2, 3 (Dec. 1996). Conversation with class of lawyers at Ecole Supérieure de Commerce in Paris (Oct. 20, 1997).

78. *See* Aboudahab, *supra* note 77.

79. *See* Gaspard, *supra* note 37, at 27.

80. *See* De Rudder et al., *supra* note 66, at 41.

81. *See* Lochak, *supra* note 76, at 401–04. These include jobs with France's electric company, gas company, railway system, the Paris transportation system, and Air France. Except under certain international agreements, foreigners are not allowed to run tobacco shops or liquor stores or manage an entertainment business or a private technical school. Certain jobs in insurance, business, and the stock market are closed to them. With respect to professions, one must be French to be an architect, lawyer, surveyor, accountant, pharmacist, dentist, doctor, or veterinarian. *Id.* Thus, one can remove whole categories of jobs from the reach of immigrants simply by nationalizing them. For example, in 1976 the Paris city government stopped recruiting foreigners to sweep the streets as "temporary auxiliaries." As a result, the proportion of foreigners in that job classification dropped from 72 percent in 1975 to 32 percent in 1985. At the same time, the city upgraded those jobs with respect to both pay and working conditions. *See* Hargreaves, *supra* note 11, at 50.

82. *See* Beauvue-Fougeyrollas, *supra* note 32, at 96.

83. *See* Poiret, *supra* note 12, at 33.

84. *See* Gaspard, *supra* note 37, at 27.

85. *See* Yasemin Nuholu Soysal, Limits of Citizenship: Migrants and Postnational Membership in Europe 76 (1994).

86. *Id.* at 60.

87. *Id.* at 75–76. Like ADRI, this latter organization is an *association* that has been delegated a public function. *See* Letter from Béatrice Borghino, *supra* note 7. ADRI is also charged with improving communication between the French and foreigners. One of its tasks is to develop training programs for police, judges, teachers, and social workers in order to make them more sensitive to the diverse populations they serve. *See* De Rudder et al., *supra* note 66, at 41.

88. *See* Soysal, *supra* note 85, at 104.

89. *See* De Rudder et al., *supra* note 66, at 29, 31.

90. *See* Soysal, *supra* note 85, at 104–06.

91. See Service des Droits des Femmes, Une administration au service des Femmes (1993) (pamphlet on file with author).

92. Lespinat, *supra* note 70.

93. *See* Mady Vetter, *Le B.R.R.J.I., un nouvel outil pour les droits des femmes étrangères,* 79/80 Femmes Info 20–21 (Summer–Fall 1997). BRRJI serves a support function for the Regional Delegation on the Rights of Women. *See* Letter from Mady Vetter, *supra* note 16.

94. *See* Mady Vetter, *L'action du B.R.R.J.I. Juin 1996–Juin 1997: Un an d'activité* 5 (June 1997) (report on file with author).

95. *Id.* at 7.

96. *See, e.g.,* Quiminal, *supra* note 5.

97. *See* Quiminal et al., *supra* note 67, at 7.

98. *Id.* at 8.

99. *See generally* Catherine Delcroix, *Médiatrices socioculturelles, citoyennes innovantes!, in* Les Femmes de l'Immigration au Quotidien 41 (1997).

100. *See* Mady Vetter, *Situation juridique et sociale des femmes âgées étrangères* 12, 13 (1997) (paper on file with author).

101. *See* Guide des lois antiracistes, *supra* note 74. French law also makes it unlawful to deny the existence of crimes against humanity, or to wear uniforms or insignia that resemble those of the groups that committed those crimes. *Id.*

102. *Fifteen Years in Prison for National Front Murderer*, Agence France Presse, June 22, 1998, *available in* LEXIS, News Library, curnws File.

103. *See* Craig R. Whitney, *Lounes Matoub, 42, Is Killed; Sang to Promote Berber Cause*, N.Y. Times, June 27, 1998, at B8.

104. *Id.*

105. *See Des manifestations dégénèrent à Tizi-Ouzou—Un mort*, Agence France Presse, June 27, 1998.

106. *See Scrutin région-l'Assemblée établit la parité hommes-femmes*, Agence France Presse, June 24, 1998.

107. *See Parité hommes-femmes: Lionel Jospin renvoie la balle dans le camp de Jacques Chirac*, Agence France Presse, June 24, 1998.

10 Filthy, Old, and Ugly

Gypsy Women from Serbia

Zorica Mrsevic

> My husband always beats me. When he loses on gambling and
> when he wins. He beats me when he gets a job but also when he is
> fired. He beats me when he drinks and when he hasn't anything to
> drink. I am always guilty for everything. He beats me because I am
> "filthy, old, and ugly" and make his life "contaminated by my ugli-
> ness," as he usually says. Fortunately, he is rarely at home. In a
> month he is at home maybe two to three days.
>
> —Gypsy woman, Belgrade, 1993

I. INTRODUCTION

The narrative methodology of Critical Race Feminism is particularly appropriate
for an analysis of the position of Romani or Gypsy women in Serbia because statistics, social science research, books, and articles about various aspects of Gypsy
life in that particular region are rare. This chapter demarginalizes these women by
using stories I gathered over three years while serving as a volunteer for SOS Hotline and the Autonomous Women's Center against Sexual Violence in Belgrade.
Their stories reflect not only the patriarchy of Gypsy and broader Serbian society,
but also deeply rooted social and racial discrimination against Gypsies, who remain mired in pervasive poverty. In the American racial classification scheme, the
Gypsies would be considered "white"; their color resembles the swarthier skin
tones of Sicilians, Greeks, or maybe some Hispanic groups. But in the Serbian
context they have been socially constructed as unwanted, racially different
"Blacks." For example, when a Gypsy boy was recently beaten to death, the head-
lines read, "Death of Black Boy"; these stories were followed by articles on
"Protest from the Black Community." This essay hopes to enhance transnational
understanding of racial/gender oppression by providing general background information about Serbian Gypsies and the racial/social discrimination they face, analyzing the role of Gypsy women in the economy of survival, and examining vari-

Reprinted by permission of the author.

ous aspects of "domestic" or family violence. My analysis is preliminary here. It is my hope in offering these stories that some of you will be interested in learning more, in doing additional research to make the plight of Romani women visible to the international community. Perhaps some of you will join us in designing solutions, legal and otherwise, for this oppressed group. I leave to others the important task of cross-cultural comparisons, a major project to which this anthology contributes.

II. BACKGROUND: GYPSIES IN SERBIA

Gypsy people, properly known as Romani, are now estimated to number six to ten million worldwide. They began a slow migration from northern India some two thousand years ago, and entered Europe through Turkey and Spain somewhere between the twelfth and fourteenth centuries, perhaps earlier. They are distributed throughout the globe, but half live in Europe, and almost two-thirds of these are concentrated in Eastern Europe, including the Balkan states.[1] They have preserved their own language, which is different from any other European language, but it has become mixed with words from local languages. Gypsies are known for their colorful clothes with flower patterns, jewels, bandannas, earrings, and kerchiefs.[2] They are thought to excel at music and sports.[3]

It is not possible to say how many Gypsies live in Serbia today.[4] Officially less than 2 percent of the population are Gypsies. But they are often not apparent to authorities because they have historically embraced a survival strategy of secrecy. Gypsies usually adopt the names and religion of the majority ethnicity or nationality.[5] So Gypsies in Hungary call themselves Hungarians and belong to the Catholic church. Gypsies who live in Muslim areas like Kosovo or Sandzak in southern Serbia have Muslim names and practice Islam. Therefore, official papers and documents do not reveal how many Serbs are in fact Gypsies. This tactic of strategic assimilation has created identity formation problems for young Gypsies. A twenty-three-year-old female student at Belgrade University, whose features and dark (in the Serbian context) skin indicate a Gypsy heritage, said, "I am not a Gypsy, not at all. Gypsies are thieves and smugglers, street beggars and singers. But I am a decent student and my parents have a big house."

Physically, the Gypsies are usually people of dark skin and black, often curly, hair. An increasing number are racially mixed, and are called Mandovs. They may have honey light skin and light brown hair, and it is not possible to tell by their appearance that they are Gypsies. Usually, the Mandov's non-Gypsy parent is western European, from countries where the Gypsy family went in search of work, such as Germany, Austria, Switzerland, or Scandinavia. Some Mandovs are very proud of their heritage. "I am proud to be a Gypsy. Everyone is against us, but I don't care. I need only my people and my nation, where I know who I am," said a seventeen-year-old female smuggler traveling on a train with her mother and two aunts. This pride is far from universal. The young woman's darker-skinned mother warned her to be silent and apologized to the other passengers: "She is still a child and she doesn't know what she is speaking about."[6]

Marriage often occurs very early. Usually parents buy twelve- to fifteen-year-old girls as brides for their sons. These are not official marriages, partly because minors are not legally permitted to marry, and partly because Gypsies do not like to deal with the state authorities, whom they perceive as enemies. They often prefer to live according to their own customs and habits, ignoring state laws and formal procedures.

Educational achievement is often de-emphasized or impossible. Absenteeism and early dropouts are acute problems, even at the primary school level. Very few ever attend university.[7] Many Gypsy children must drop out of school because they are needed to help financially support their families. Their achievement of working status enhances their prestige in their own community. Young teenage brides also do not have time for school books.

A disproportionate number of Gypsy children who do stay in school are shunted to special institutions for the disabled. Some of them are genuinely disabled because of the debilitating effects of insufficient prenatal care, nutrition, and medical care, as well as poverty and poor housing conditions. Other children are not disabled at all, but merely speak inadequate Serbian, so they cannot keep up in regular classes.

There are some Gypsy parents who deliberately enroll their normal child in the disabled school, telling the child to pretend she is deaf or mentally retarded. The motive may be that the students will get a free meal or reduced-price textbooks. Since academic requirements are significantly lower, Gypsy teenagers can thus have more time to help their parents earn a livelihood. The irony is that only a bright child can perform the fake disability well enough to deceive the experts, consisting of physicians, psychologists, teachers, and social workers, who determine who can attend the special schools.

Emir Kusturica, a well-known film director from Sarajevo who has won several awards at the Cannes festival, has stated that Gypsies survived as a people through the centuries because of their ability to respond to force and violence against them with nonviolence.[8] They are endlessly ready to defeat all misfortune by reducing their own demands. They also channel their feelings through art, humor, and songs.

A. RACISM

Romani are tolerated in Belgrade and throughout Serbia. Their existence is accepted as an inevitable fact. Usually they are not expelled, removed, or exposed to physical threats.[9] The pejorative word *cigan* was even replaced by "Rom" during the 1970s.[10] A recent survey found that very few Serbs considered Gypsies to be a hostile minority—only 3.5 percent, compared to 77.9 percent for Albanians, 54.4 percent for Muslims, 36.5 percent for Croats, and 12.9 percent for Hungarians.[11]

Although Gypsies have formal equality under the constitution, they have not achieved this status in reality. They thus face the types of problems of de facto discrimination that African Americans face today in the United States. There are many different types of prejudice against Gypsies, whose social status is lower than that of any other group in Serbian society. Part of the problem in remedying the discrimination is that so much is unrecognized. Many ordinary Serbian people would be very offended at being accused of racism or discrimination against Gypsies. In their own defense, they would say that in Serbia all people, including Gypsies, are equal according to the constitution and the laws. If Gypsies have problems, it is due to their own behavior and not discrimination.

The stereotypes about the Romani are numerous. "Gypsy" is an epithet, an offensive word, which means a filthy and ugly villain, usually a smuggler or a thief. Gypsies are regarded as lazy, bad workers, thinking only about having fun. They have too many children, and are incestuous, polygamous, promiscuous, immoral, natural prostitutes, and child sellers. Gypsies have unstable families. They are short-sighted, cowardly, and bad soldiers. They are slow, stupid, wasteful, dropouts, and simple. Gypsies are unnatural, unhealthy, drug abusers, alcoholics, nomads, magicians, superstitious, liars, and disease-ridden. They mutilate their own children to make them better beggars. The list is endless.

Gypsies are regarded as "dirty" people, a stereotype that is exacerbated by the fact that many live in housing without running water. Also, the perceived "dirtiness" of Gypsies is considered to be the direct result of their dark, "unclean" skin. For example, a thirty-nine-year-old computer analyst from Belgrade said, "I don't want to swim in the same swimming pool with Gypsies, and that's all. This is not because I am a racist. I am certainly not. I haven't anything against Gypsies; I think they are great singers and I like Gypsy music the best. I also honestly believe in equal political rights for all people, including Gypsies. But simply, I am disgusted with their dirty skin and I don't feel comfortable sharing the same water with some of them." I have been told that this same viewpoint was held by many white Americans toward African Americans when official segregation still existed in the United States. While I did not stay in the United States a long time, it appears that some whites still hold this racist view, nearly forty years after de jure apartheid has ended.

Children in Serbia are usually taught not to express hatred for other peoples. Despite official pronouncements, even children know that there are some who can be hated with impunity: Gypsies and homosexuals. Even when children do not know who Gypsies really are, and what the term really means, they know that it is permitted to hate them and they are encouraged to express this hatred publicly and openly. Gypsies are to be disdained, ridiculed, and rejected. I have heard angry people say "go back to Africa" to Gypsies. When it is pointed out that the Romani originally came from India, the response might be "What's the difference, Africa or India? They are all Black, and we don't need any of them."

B. HOUSING

One common stereotype about Gypsies is that they are wandering nomads. Whatever truth there may have been to this notion in the past, it is clear that those days are gone. Gypsies in Serbia no longer wish to move and are anxious to be able to stay in one place and find stability.[12] In towns, they tend to live in the poorest parts, lacking the basic facilities and other essentials necessary for decent living. In villages, they live even more strictly separated from other inhabitants in areas that are called *cigan mala,* meaning "gypsy streets." They are often not permitted to build their houses outside *cigan mala.*

Most Gypsies usually live now in two types of settlements, the old ones and the new ones. The older Gypsy settlements are called "yards" (in Serbian *dvoriste*) or "gardens" (*basta*), and are situated mainly in the city areas. The new ones, "wild" settlements, are built on town edges, along with new workers' residential blocks of skyscrapers. Both types of settlements are well below the average standard of housing in Serbia.

1. The *Dvoriste,* or Life around a Mulberry Tree

Some of these slums date back to the nineteenth-century early industrial era. Their purpose was to squeeze in as many new workers flocking to the cities as possible. The life was often communal. People may have lived there as one big family, helping each other as much as possible, especially when somebody was sick or unemployed. Some workers were able to move out of the crowded conditions, while others had to stay.

To make their living conditions better, the tenants usually planted flowers or vegetables in the middle area of the yard. There were also benches for sitting, drinking coffee, and chatting. Even now there is also a big tree, by tradition usually a mulberry tree, for providing shade during the summer. Living in a "yard" is thus sometimes called "living around a mulberry tree" (*ziveti oko duda*). There is even an expression, "you have eaten too many mulberries in your childhood," which means that you grew up in the poverty of the "yards."

After the Second World War, the new socialist government wanted to eradicate certain "yards" as a shameful relic of the capitalist, exploitative past. The government quickly built new flats for workers, mostly in blocks of skyscrapers, and provided them with central heating, bathrooms, cold and hot water, and toilets. Most of the dilapidated "yards," especially in the central, downtown areas, were razed and replaced with new buildings for workers. The "yards" still exist in some poorer Belgrade suburbs such as Cukarica, Vracar, Zvezdava, Palilula, and Dusanovac. I was born in such a yard in Palilula, and spent the first seven years of my life there, when it was still inhabited by Serbians. The former owners of some "yards," afraid of being prosecuted by the communist regime, abandoned their property or sold them cheaply to the tenants who lived in them. As workers got new flats, practically the only people with any interest in living in such conditions were unemployed Gypsies, who previously did not have any permanent houses.

A "yard" consists of five to ten little units. Each apartment has a small kitchen and one or two tiny rooms. There is no running water. Each unit has an entrance from the same shared "yard." In the middle of the area, there is a shared water pipe with cold water that is usually frozen during the winter. In one corner of the yard there is a wooden outhouse, a shared toilet. There are also a few wooden huts for the coal and wood necessary for heating in the winter. Some of the better *dvoriste* contain a *vesernica,* which is a separate hut for washing laundry that is equipped with a big cauldron and an open fireplace. Since there are no bathrooms, the *vesernica* may be used as a bathroom sometimes, mostly for children.

Gypsies sometimes name their yards and settlements. Interestingly, the names may be those of African towns or countries. In Belgrade you can find areas known as Addis Ababa, Katanga, Angola, and Cairo. Perhaps the names represent a recognition of mutual hardship. Perhaps they represent creative defiance against a system that assigns only numbers instead of names to buildings.

Living in a *dvoriste* means minimum privacy or no privacy at all. Also, the shared spaces and structures are permanent sources of conflict and disputes. Any violence that happens in a family is visible and audible to all the inhabitants of the yard and even a few of the neighboring areas. Since only Gypsies now live in the *dvoriste,* their conflicts are thus more visible than those of other families. This may be one of the reasons Gypsies are perceived as more violent than other groups. Other social problems, such as discrimination and poverty, which force Gypsies into such living conditions and keep them there, and which cause an increase in all kinds of violence among them, are simply overlooked.

Neighbors are usually upset at living near Gypsies. "There is always somebody screaming and always somebody beats somebody, but I guess, this probably is regular Gypsy life," explained one retired teacher from Palilula in Belgrade, who lives in the neighborhood of two "yards." "They don't know any better than to beat their wives and children, but this is because they are Gypsies," said a saleswoman in a grocery store near some "yards" in the Zvezdava area of Belgrade.

2. The *Divlje Naselje*

The new settlements are far away from downtown areas, mostly in residential blocks, but also in newly built suburbs such as Resnick, Surcin, Banjica, and Miljakovac. Sometimes they are built at the edges of town, usually after a new housing block for workers has been finished. Gypsies may take abandoned construction materials or steal what they need to build shelter. Thus, the new type of typical Gypsy settlements are shacks made of various materials, such as plastic, wood, tin metal plates, and even cardboard. These settlements are "wild" (in Serbian *divlje naselje*) because they are built without permits from city authorities, who sometimes try to eradicate them. But since people from those agencies do not know what to do with the inhabitants, mostly unemployed Gypsies who are not entitled to get flats from the town, the authorities often ignore them. They may issue warnings from time to time, but do not usually expel the Gypsies by force. As one forty-one-year-old Gypsy woman said, "We came only for one winter, only to save our children and elders from cold weather. But then, we didn't know where to go and stayed there almost ten years. We still don't know where to go."

In the new settlements there is no running water, no sewage system, no electricity, no telephones, and no streets. There are usually fifty to a hundred shacks inhabited by hundreds, who live in conditions impossible for decent living. The hovels usually consist of only one or two rooms, which are shared by members of one family. Most families consist of three generations, with between five and eight members.

Their neighbors in the residential blocks accept the services of Gypsies but do not like them at all. Gypsy women clean their flats, building entrances, and corridors, and take care of babies and cook in families where women work. "Gypsies are dirty and smell like animals," said a fourteen-year-old girl living near Addis Ababa, a wild Gypsy settlement.[13]

A man who works in a post office and lives in Block 45 thought Gypsies should go live somewhere else:

> We were so happy when we moved into the new flat. But the next month there came those Gypsies, who built something like stables and began to live there. From that moment there is no peace for us. They attack our children when they return from school, take money and jackets from them. They commit burglaries in our flats and in our cellars when we work or when we are on holiday. I reported several times all those problems to the police. They usually come and arrest some of them, and that's all. But the problems continue and the only solution is not putting some of them in jail but removing them completely from our neighborhood. Where will they go? I don't know and this is not my business. What have we done to be so cursed by this Gypsy settlement here?

Listening to the conversation, a woman who worked in a shoe factory added, "You won't believe, but they have there, in their very houses, if we can call those cabins houses at all, pigs and chickens! They live with animals and they are nothing else but animals."

A group of male teenagers who had gathered on the basketball court in Block 45 were asked about Gypsies.[14] "Where are they? I don't see any," said the leader.

"They are not permitted to play here or even to appear here. We don't want them to spoil everything," explained another.

"They are cowards, those poor things living over there in the mud. We beat them several times. Yes, older Gypsies are dangerous, they have knives and even guns, but they are rarely at home. Adult men are always somewhere else, doing business. Only women and kids are there and we can deal easily with them," added a third.

"I don't understand them at all," another man said. "Sometimes they burn down their own houses. I live on the seventeenth floor and from there we can see their entire settlement, and once or twice in a month, some of the houses simply disappear in a fire! They do it when they are angry or sad, at least that's what our cleaning woman explained. But who is so crazy to burn down his own house, especially if you are poor as they are? This is what I can't understand."

This section has provided the socioeconomic context of modern Romani life. They remain subject to multiple levels of discrimination, entrenched at the bottom or in the margins of Serbian society. Gypsy women simultaneously suffer from gender discrimination as well. Yet they must often carry the economic burden of the entire family.

III. THE ROLE OF GYPSY WOMEN IN THE ECONOMY OF SURVIVAL

The Romani are usually poorer than members of the Serbian majority because many are unemployed or employed at low-paying jobs. Their lower educational level exacerbates their plight. Some earn their livelihood through illegal trade and agriculture. Some men pass the time gambling, drinking, playing or singing, chasing women, or dreaming of "big" money and how to attain those dreams quickly. Young, unemployed Gypsy men may join criminal gangs, even at very early ages. They may join gangs because they do not have enough to eat and are out of their mothers' control (mothers who work all day to provide them with the basics). They do not begin as full members of the gang, but as messengers or lookouts for the bosses. Eventually they rise in the gang hierarchy and get used to the "easy" money.[15] For many others, smuggling and illegal trade across the borders into neighboring countries are the only way to earn a living. This is a difficult and insecure business, with small profits and many risks. Gypsies are not protected from brutal raids by the police, who deprive them of their goods, fine them, and subject them to a higher level of various types of maltreatment than Serbs in the same position. It is accepted as "normal" that Gypsies must suffer more. Since many men do get caught in criminal activities or as members of criminal gangs, they end up in prison in disproportionate numbers.[16]

Women are thus left to maintain their families alone, and in appalling conditions. Yet due to prejudice about Gypsy lazy and/or criminal natures, few employers want to hire them. For example, in one research institute in Belgrade, two cleaning women retired in 1991. According to internal regulations, a primary school education is required of cleaning workers. When the job openings were announced, a few dozen Gypsies applied. The director of the institute said that he did not want to hire Gypsies "when so many Serbian women are unemployed," although no Serbians had applied. To solve the "problem," he decided to change the internal regulations by requiring a high school education. Most of the Gypsy women who applied had only a primary school education and they were automatically rejected. Yet three of the Gypsy women had the required high school level, while still no Serbian women appeared. Usually, Serbian women with high school educations try to find better jobs than cleaning, such as administrative or secretarial work. Instead of hiring one of these overqualified Gypsy women, the institute annulled the entire search. Then the salary for the cleaning job was upgraded, and a Serbian woman who would accept the job was found through alternative means. She was promised that she would be supported in her efforts to resume her university studies! Such an incentive was not offered to the Gypsies, who would have been satisfied with the original lower salary. They did not have a chance. They were Gypsies.

Many Gypsy women thus end up accepting all kinds of odd jobs and physical labor. Cleaning buses, factories, corridors, and entrances are the usual jobs "dedicated" to Gypsies. A high school teacher whose daughter brought home bad grades threatened her, "If you don't get better grades in school, you will end up as a corridor cleaner, along with Gypsies."

The women are well known as the cheapest workers. They go from door to door offering their services to working women by saying, "Nobody will clean your place for such a small sum of money as I will." They are expected to accept the heaviest odd jobs for the lowest wages. "If I have to pay more, then I will hire somebody else, but not you, a Gypsy," said the owner of a café to a Gypsy woman who cleans the place.

Gypsy women are also known as the skillful makers of useful things for households, such as garden grills, children's toys, pots and pans, chairs and tables, bookshelves, lamp shades, bags, baskets, and brooms. They make these things practically from nothing, using abandoned materials. They sell their products cheaply at the markets or offer them in the streets.

Some women also work for Gypsy "bosses"; they sell smuggled cigarettes or change foreign currency in the street or near the green markets. Kalenic market is the best-known place where many Gypsy women work. They are notorious because of their tireless soliciting of customers. "Be always my customer. I have the best offer for you. And you will recognize me easily: I have blue eyes! I am the only Gypsy with blue eyes, look!" says Slavica, a Gypsy woman with dark blue eyes, who changes foreign currency in the Kalenic market.

Slavica mentioned the dark side of her job. "Police officers come and take whatever they want. We can't do anything. Moreover, we have to smile and pretend we are happy to be robbed. If not, the officers will arrest us, take all our goods and accuse us of 'public disorder.' We will then be fined, put in prison, or forbidden to work in Kalenic market. It's the destiny of Gypsies, to be cursed forever."

Another type of work, mostly unpaid and unrecognized, involves the collection of firewood. Older Gypsies still believe that "big water will eat them" and have traditionally had a fear of rivers and lakes. In spite of this fear, Gypsy women (but never Gypsy men) spend many hours during summer and autumn on the banks of rivers tirelessly gathering pieces of wood, branches, and stumps that drift by in the currents. Some of them carry those pieces of woods in small trolleys, but more often they carry them in heavy bundles on their shoulders. For many Gypsy families, this will be the only source of heating during cold winter days. How many hundreds of those bundles are necessary for only one month of heating? For the whole winter?

Romani women often have little gardens in "no-one's land," around their shacks, or outside the residential blocks. They plant some essential vegetables, such as potatoes, onions, peppers, and tomatoes. Sometimes they sell their products at the green markets, but in most cases they produce only enough for their families' own needs.

One traditional Gypsy women's activity, which has almost disappeared today, is bartering eggs for old clothes and shoes. Women, usually in late autumn, offered eggs from door to door, asking for old garments in exchange. The activity was treated more as begging than a real barter, in spite of the fact that the eggs had market value but the old clothes and shoes did not. As a child, I was always warned by my mother never to openly recognize my clothes if they turned up on Gypsy girls at school. She always gave old clothes and shoes to the Gypsy women and never "bargained" for the price, but took five to six eggs just to support the impression of an exchange.

And yes, some Gypsy women are reduced to beggars. They beg in the streets with their children, poorly dressed, unwashed, their hair uncombed, barefooted. Young mothers, still girls themselves, sit with their dirty babies on shabby blankets or cardboard. They stare at pedestrians with their big, sad, beautiful black eyes. They beg, speaking nasally, "Udelite koji dinar za hleb. Deca mi gladuju." (Dole out some coins for bread. My children are starving.) Many Serbs believe that this is only the "Gypsy theater of poverty," just another survival technique.[17]

Gypsy women are excluded from participating in the upper echelons of the most lucrative businesses—smuggling scarce goods from foreign countries, reselling fruits and vegetables at the green markets, foreign currency exchange, and even music. In all those activities Gypsy women are only the workers—never or rarely the negotiators, middlemen, or bosses. Women are rarely paid musicians, although many Gypsies like music and enjoy performing it. Being a player is "only for men." Gypsy women singers do exist, but are restricted to the lowest-level establishments. When Gypsy bands play in any better restaurants or hotels, they tend to have white (preferably blonde) singers. Gypsy women are treated as "too ugly or too vulgar" and as such, improper for this more prestigious line of work.

Job discrimination exists even for highly skilled Gypsy women. Ljubica is a dark-skinned Gypsy woman who obtained a law degree with excellent grades. She had dreamed of becoming a court clerk, but was rejected by all the places where she applied. During an interview in one public prosecutor's office, she was told that women of her kind usually do not like to work, but just wanted to have children. Because this office needed somebody to work, they would not hire her. Ljubica soon realized that despite her impressive credentials, as a Romani she would never be offered any government job. She is now a very reputable attorney who has her own law firm in a Gypsy "yard" in Vracar. She restored the buildings, and now works and lives there as a single parent with her teenage daughter. She earns a good income and says that her clients do not discriminate against her because she is a Gypsy woman; they know that she will do her job properly.

Despite their heavy work responsibilities in dealing with the majority culture, Gypsy women must also face the patriarchy of their own culture, doing the double duty that women are accustomed to throughout the world. They are exploited by their own men, who may simply take their meager earnings from them by force.

Edvina's husband has family from Bosnia. Some of his cousins escaped from the battlefields and live with them. They are all men. Nobody works and nobody wants to work. They all wait for her to prepare their food, wash and iron their clothes, and clean the house. There is no washing machine or running water in the house.

Nobody gives her money. She has to earn money by cleaning the neighbors' houses. She has to do this secretly because her husband and his cousins take her money or beat her because of "shame." "What will people say seeing that a woman works? Will they think that the men are unable to provide enough money?" She has a little garden for vegetables, which is destroyed from time to time by some of the angry men in her family. They destroy her garden for the same reason: "What will people say, that the men do not provide enough?" And they certainly do not want to work in the garden—that is not work for men!

In Bozana's home, all four family members live on her salary. Her husband's money goes mostly for his own enjoyment. "A man has the right to have his own life," he explains. He has never given anything for household expenses. But he always has demands—to have beer, meat, and this and that for dinner. She even has to buy socks and shirts for him from her money. If she does not, he beats her or just takes clothes from their sons.

Another burden that Gypsy women face in addition to the economic tribulations described in this section is family violence. Conditions of racism, poverty, and social discrimination have contributed to the violence in their communities. Some of that violence is directed at them and their children.

IV. DOMESTIC VIOLENCE AGAINST GYPSY WOMEN

> Nobody can scream like a Gypsy woman. When some of them scream, we can hear it in the entire area, all over our block. I don't know why they scream, probably their men beat them. They become completely crazy when drunken, those Gypsy men. I saw once how one of them strapped a woman to a tree and beat her all day long with a stick. (Anonymous source)

The experience of a young Gypsy woman, who lived for eighteen months during 1995 and 1996 in the Autonomous Women's Center against Sexual Violence in Belgrade, typifies the nature of the problem. Abandoned as a baby, she was raised in an orphanage and by several foster families. As a teenager, she was raped by several boyfriends. She was also the victim of a gang rape. The perpetrators laughed at her threats to report the assaults to the police. "Nobody would believe you—you are a Gypsy." The police allegedly told her, "You Gypsies always ask for trouble, and you are particularly notorious. How many times do you think to come here reporting that you were raped? We have a lot of other things to do, besides taking care of your problems." Not one of the perpetrators has ever been caught, in spite of the fact that she provided some names, personal descriptions, and addresses.

This negative reaction from the police provides an illustration of why Gypsies loathe and fear law enforcement. The police are on the "other side"; officers are enemies, and they are not to be involved in a Gypsy's "internal matters." Thus for Gypsy women, the legal system is traditionally believed to exist to oppress and deny their rights.[18] Instead, some Gypsy women will approach centers for social work for assistance. Because they desperately need food, medicine, money, jobs, housing, or other "more important" (essential) services, the women do not want to bother social workers with more "trivial" problems, such as domestic violence. They guess that they will not be listened to because such problems would be thought of as "luxuries," not "real-life" problems. Since many Gypsy women do not buy newspapers or read, they may not know the numbers of organizations like SOS Hotline. Since many do not have telephones, their ability to report violence to SOS Hotline or any other group is hindered as well.

So how do we know anything about beaten Gypsy women? They occasionally come to some women's groups. They know by word of mouth that such groups disseminate humanitarian aid. When they come, they feel free to speak about their problems. I have discovered that virtually every Gypsy woman who has visited women's groups I work with in Belgrade has been a victim of domestic violence.

Anita, age forty, has been married for thirteen years.[19] Her husband is an alcoholic and has been in prison for assault. He beats her and her children regularly. Recently she was assaulted so badly that she needed emergency treatment for head injuries. She said, "He beats me as if he doesn't see me, as if I am a sack."

Another woman mentioned her abusive father and the long-term effects his violence has had on her:

Anger and violence is something I do well. I grew up with an abusive father. When he was at home I would take the beatings for my mother, who had bad kidneys, and for my disabled, paralyzed brother, until I got old enough to fight back. Then we would fight; I got into several fistfights until he realized I would not back down to him. One day he went away and never returned, but I am still all stuffed with anger. I don't want to be physically abusive to anyone. For a while I would hit brick walls and stuff like that. My anger is still there. I only know how to release it in a physical way.[20]

Prison often provides a release from violence, as one woman indicated:

I have four children. Their father was like a boy, he liked jokes, and games, music and alcohol. This part of my life, when we lived together, was full of joy. But at the same time, full of pain, because he beat me regularly, without any reason, just for fun, just because he liked action. Now he is in prison where he has to serve eleven more years. I still remember when my neighbor came to me and said, "Say *dragichka*: your husband is in prison! Now, you have one less mouth to feed."[21] First, I was crying but then I realized that it was the truth. Instead of five children, I now have to take care of four, plus nobody beats me.[22]

Another abused wife also commented on the effect of prison:

My husband is in jail for a crime he committed against me and our children. He bound his own daughter to a tree, cut her clothes with a knife and badly hurt her. He is confined for that. He sends threats that we will pay for every day he spends in prison, because he is the only Gypsy man in prison for doing anything to his family. I have no place to go with my children.[23]

Sometimes the death of the abuser finally frees the woman to seek help. Djurdjica had suffered her husband's violence for eighteen years. She endured terrible beatings, threats, and humiliations, but she did not have the courage, the support, or the opportunity to protect herself and her children. Her husband was killed by an unknown murderer several months ago. Then she called SOS Hotline for the first time and got help.[24]

While conditions of poverty may exacerbate violence, abuse exists even in wealthier Gypsy families. Dubravka has been married for seventeen years, has two children, and is unemployed. Her husband owns a small firm and often takes business trips. When he travels, he locks Dubravka and her children in the house without money. Sometimes he does not return for three weeks. He keeps her locked up "so the whore cannot cruise around." When he is at home, he beats her and will not let her get a job or even leave the house. She is divorcing him, but not because of the violence she suffers. He recently brought into their home a "new bride," a fifteen-year-old Gypsy girl whom he bought a few months ago. Therefore he is willing to let Dubravka go, but alone—without the children. "Children and the house are mine," he says.[25]

Another aspect of family violence is incest, which is believed to happen more frequently among Gypsies than among other groups. An enraged mother explained her reaction:

> He did everything he wanted to me: cut me with the knife, burnt me with cigarettes and beat me as if I was an animal. But when he came after my oldest daughter, when she was an eight-year-old, you know how, in "that" way, wanting sex from her, I felt as if a kind of darkness fell on my eyes. I grabbed the knife, the biggest we had in the house, and told him to go out of my house and never to return. This is something Gypsy women rarely say to their men. He shrugged and told me that there were many women who would be happy to live with him and that I would regret kicking him out. And then he went out and never returned, but I have never regretted it. Probably, some other women have to suffer him, but not me any more. I only regret I didn't do it earlier. You know, today it seems to me as if it was so easy, I just pulled the knife and said "out" to him, and suddenly I was free. But at that time, I was dying of fear even from his shadow.[26]

A childhood victim of incest also explained her situation and the long-term effect it has had on her:

> When I was ten years old my father replaced my mother with me, explaining that she was too ugly and too old for him and couldn't satisfy his needs. I spent all my childhood hating him, praying to God that one of us would die, it didn't matter which one. When he died, I continued to hate men. But I can't always see men as the enemy. It is too hard and scary and I don't really believe it is true. Still, whenever I am on the train, I find myself looking at the men on the train and I wonder who they have molested, their daughters or younger sisters? It is a very uncomfortable feeling. I guess maybe I am naive, but I can't believe that every man on the face of the earth is

a monster. It doesn't work for me. I'd be afraid to go out of the house if I really believed that.[27]

As the prior comment indicated, fathers are not the only perpetrators.

The first in my life was my oldest brother. It all started when I was three and finally stopped when I was ten—when he was sixteen and got married. Similar things were happening to a couple of friends in the yards where we lived, so I figured it was just part of growing up. Boys were expected to be experienced before marriage, but where could they find available girls? Sisters were the solution to the problem. But I was and I am the only one who felt the need to stay clothed, even when sleeping. I used to sleep clothed and I wore as many clothes as the temperature would allow—even shoes. I always got teased a lot for those, but I never really thought much about why I needed them.[28]

Some girls responded to the incest with violence of their own:

I used to get into fights. It began when I was a nine-year-old girl and I beat up the eleven-year-old leader of an all-boy gang in my yard. I became an honorary boy and used my height and my anger to my advantage. I think the fighting was the way I responded to the powerlessness I felt during the night. I couldn't stop my father at night but I could get back at the world by beating the shit out of the boys around me. After I left home, my fighting instincts helped me gain respect in the community I lived in.[29]

V. CONCLUSION: THE FOURTH WORLD

The disintegration of Yugoslavia's multicultural community has become the most dramatic and brutal event in post–World War II Europe. After several decades in which diversity was reasonably protected and fostered,[30] the ghosts of intolerance, ethnic hatred, and rejection of all who are "Others" have now reappeared. Gypsy women are obviously among those "Others." Their problems are ignored because of prevailing attention to "more important" issues such as conflict among Serbs, Muslims, Croats, and Albanians. Their problems are invisible not only because they are Gypsies, but also because they are women. Gypsies consider life to be a fight for common goals (survival problems), caused by common causes (poverty, discrimination), which does not leave much space for "separate" problems like gender issues. In a certain sense, the situation of Gypsy women is comparable to the general situation in Eastern Europe before the fall of the Berlin Wall, when women as citizens felt equally oppressed with their men and developed a kind of solidarity with them. Many women came to believe that their separate gender interests were less important until some broader political issues got resolved. Thus, the feeling of common engagement in the daily struggle for common goals and for universal values that are equally important to men and women has influenced Gypsies, male and female, to minimize and overlook manifestations of sexist aggression.

If the former socialist countries are so-called Second World, then the Gypsies, as their poorest and most oppressed and discriminated citizens, are the "Third World" inside it.[31] They were the first "Blacks" in Europe, rejected by the pillars of medieval society, the Church, the state, and the guilds,[32] and they are still discriminated against, ignored, and rejected. And if Gypsy men are the Third World within the Second World, then Gypsy women are its Fourth World. They are even more oppressed, more discriminated against, and poorer than their men, not only suffering discrimination because they are Gypsies, but also suffering from their own violent and negligent men or male violence in general.

Citizens can and should be equal in their civil liberties, economic potential, and civic responsibilities. But they cannot all speak the same language or have skin of the same color. Equal citizenship should belong to various ethnic groups who do not share the same history, legends, art, lifestyle, or literature, including those who are nothing but "filthy, old, and ugly" Gypsy women.[33]

NOTES

1. G. Puxon, On the Road, Gypsy People 10 (1968).

2. *Id.* at 4.

3. *See* G. Puxon, Rom: Europe's Gypsies 19 (1973).

4. *Id.* at 18.

5. *Id.*

6. I shared the train compartment with this family in June 1995.

7. Puxon, *supra* note 3, at 18.

8. This was in an interview for NIN (April 29, 1997), a weekly Belgrade magazine. He was speaking about his newest film project, which deals with Gypsy life.

9. In neighboring countries like Romania, pogroms against Gypsies occurred from 1898 to 1991, resulting in deaths, injuries, burned houses, and removals or migration. E. Gozdiak, *Needy Guests, Reluctant Hosts: The Plight of Rumanians in Poland,* 13 Anthro. East Eur. Rev. 9 (1995).

10. *See* Puxon, *supra* note 3, at 18.

11. In November 1996 Helsinki Watch in Serbia led research among Serbs about various aspects of their attitudes toward the minorities living in Serbia. The sample consisted of five hundred persons. Nasa Borba [independent daily Belgrade news], Feb. 17, 1997.

12. *See* Puxon, *supra* note 1, at 27.

13. The statements were made by neighbors of the Gypsy settlement Addis Ababa near New Belgrade's residential block known as Block 45. All these interviews with various persons from Block 45 were conducted by the author in November 1993.

14. The author was helping a Gypsy woman carry a bag of beans from the Autonomous Women's Center in November 1993. After visiting the woman's hut, the author asked several persons living in Block 45 (including the group of male teenagers playing basketball) about Gypsies.

15. Dealing with foreign currencies in the street is highly profitable for bosses, but not for street dealers. This business is allegedly almost completely controlled by the government agencies tightly connected with organized crime. While the real bosses and organizers are not

visible publicly, the lowest workers are mainly Gypsies. Thus the Gypsies are usually blamed for high exchange rates, and even for the very existence of the black market. The truth is that they are the only ones willing to stand all day long in the streets, in spite of all weather conditions, subject to abuse from the police and their bosses.

16. When I visited the main Serbian prison, Zabela, as a student of law, I was surprised to see that most of the inmates were Gypsies. Even the prison guards did not know how many they had.

17. *See* Gozdiak, *supra* note 9, at 16.

18. *See generally* European Roma Rights Center, The Misery of the Law: The Rights of Roma in the Transcarpathian Region of Ukraine (1997).

19. SOS Hotline file from 1993. This quotation from a Gypsy woman and other examples of domestic violence in this article are taken from the documentation of SOS Hotline in Belgrade. The author volunteered there from 1993 to 1996.

20. SOS Hotline file from 1994.

21. Shout of happiness caused by receiving some good news. *Dragicka* means something like "hurrah."

22. This was a thirty-one-year-old Gypsy woman. She sells lettuce, tomatoes, and peppers at Kalenic green market. She often speaks with the author, who lives in the neighborhood and buys at the market.

23. SOS Hotline file from 1995.

24. SOS Hotline file from 1996.

25. *Id.*

26. SOS Hotline file from 1995. The author dealt personally with this case.

27. A Gypsy woman who sells eggs at Kalenic green market recounted the story to the author, who is a regular customer of hers.

28. SOS Hotline file from 1996. The author dealt personally with the case.

29. She was a twenty-seven-year-old Gypsy woman who cleans in the Vracar sport center. She told her story to the author.

30. *See* T. Varady, *Minorities, Majorities, Law, and Ethnicity: Reflections of the Yugoslav Case*, 19 Hum. Rts. Q. 9, 10 (1997).

31. *See* Puxon, *supra* note 1, at 17.

32. *Id.* at 5.

33. *See* Varady, *supra* note 30, at 12.

3 | From Pathbreakers to Founding Mothers

Historical Perspectives

11 | Josephine Baker, Racial Protest, and the Cold War

Mary L. Dudziak

During the early 1950s Josephine Baker was an international star who lived in a castle in France and wore Dior gowns in concert, and whose most radical political idea seems to have been a hope that the world might some day live in racial harmony. She would hardly seem a threat to the national security of the United States. Nevertheless, during the early fifties the Federal Bureau of Investigation (FBI) kept a file on Baker, and the State Department collected data on her activities, using the information to dissuade other countries from allowing her to perform. Baker was seen as a threat because she used her international prominence to call attention to the discriminatory racial practices of the United States, her native land, when she traveled throughout the world.

Baker was caught in the cross fire of the Cold War in Latin America in the early 1950s. Her seemingly simple campaign for racial tolerance made her the target of a campaign that ultimately pushed her from the limelight of the exclusive club circuit to the bright lights of a Cuban interrogation room. The woman lauded in Havana and Miami in 1951 as an international star was arrested by the Cuban military police two years later as a suspected Communist, but she had undergone no radical political transformation in the interim. That Josephine Baker engendered an international campaign to mute her impact is a demonstration of the lengths to which the United States and its allies would go to silence Cold War critics. More important, however, Josephine Baker found herself at the center of a critical cultural and ideological weak point in American Cold War diplomacy: the intersection of race and Cold War foreign relations.[1]

In the years following World War II, the United States had an image problem. Gunnar Myrdal called it an "American dilemma." On one hand, the United States

Reprinted by permission from 81 *Journal of American History* 543 (September 1994).

claimed that democracy was superior to communism as a form of government, particularly in its protection of individual rights and liberties; on the other hand, the nation practiced pervasive race discrimination. Voting was central to democratic government, for example, yet African Americans were systematically disenfranchised in the South. Such racism was not the nation's private shame. During the postwar years, other countries paid increasing attention to race discrimination in the United States. Voting rights abuses, lynchings, school segregation, and antimiscegenation laws were discussed at length in newspapers around the world, and the international media continually questioned whether race discrimination made American democracy a hypocrisy.[2]

To raise the stakes even higher, as early as 1946 the American embassy in Moscow reported that several articles on American racial problems had been published in the Soviet media, possibly signaling more prominent use of the issue in Soviet propaganda. The Soviet Union and the Communist press in various nations used the race issue very effectively in anti-American propaganda. Meanwhile, allies of the United States quietly commented that Soviet propaganda on race was uniquely effective because there was so much truth to it.[3]

U.S. government officials were concerned about the effect of this international criticism on foreign relations. This concern permeated government-sponsored civil rights efforts in the late 1940s and early 1950s. The international implications of civil rights were continually noted in briefs in the United States Supreme Court and in government reports.[4]

In this environment, African Americans who criticized race discrimination in the United States before an international audience added fuel to an already troublesome fire. When the actor and singer Paul Robeson, the writer W. E. B. Du Bois, and others spoke out abroad about American racial problems, they angered government officials because the officials saw them as exacerbating an already difficult problem. The State Department could and did attempt to counter the influence of such critics on international opinion by sending speakers around the world who would say the right things about American race relations. The "right thing" to say was, yes, there were racial problems in the United States, but it was through democratic processes (not communism) that optimal social change for African Americans would occur. It would make things so much easier, however, if the troublemakers stayed home. Consequently, in the early 1950s the passports of Robeson, Du Bois, and Civil Rights Congress chairperson William Patterson were confiscated because their travel abroad was "contrary to the best interests of the United States."[5]

The entertainer Josephine Baker posed a special problem for the government. During her international concert tours in the 1950s, she harshly criticized American racism. The U.S. government could not restrict her travel by withdrawing her passport because she carried the passport of her adopted nation, France. The government had to employ more creative means to silence her.

Josephine Baker is best known as the young Black entertainer from St. Louis, Missouri, who took Paris by storm in the 1920s. In France there was great interest in African art and in jazz during the twenties, and, to French audiences, Baker seemed to embody the primitive sexual energy of Black art and music that would energize European culture.[6]

The primary roles available for Black entertainers in the United States at this time were heavily racially stereotyped. In France Baker also had to cater to white fantasies about race. In the Black review that brought her to Paris at the age of nineteen in 1925, Baker danced in a number called "Danse Sauvage," set in an African jungle. In her opening performance at the Folies Bergère the next year, Baker did the Charleston dressed only in a skirt of bananas, a costume that would become her trademark. Eventually, however, Baker was able to transcend racial stereotyping in France and to play the music halls descending long staircases in elegant gowns in the kind of role previously reserved for white stars.[7]

In Paris Baker was generally free of the day-to-day insults of American-style racism. She lived a glamorous lifestyle free from racial segregation. Like many other African Americans, she found the city a haven in the years between the two world wars. In 1937, after marrying a Frenchman, Baker finally adopted her new nation by becoming a citizen of France.[8]

In 1948 Josephine Baker sailed to New York, hoping to gain the recognition in the country of her birth that she had achieved in France. She did not find the critical acclaim she had hoped for; what she did find was racial discrimination. Baker and her white husband, Jo Bouillon, were refused service by thirty-six New York hotels. Baker then decided to see for herself what life was like for an average African American woman in the South. Leaving her husband behind, she traveled south using a different name, and she wrote for a French magazine about such experiences as getting thrown out of white waiting rooms at railroad stations. Becoming Josephine Baker again, she gave a speech at Fisk University, an African American school in Tennessee, and she told the audience that her visit to Fisk was the first time since she had come to the United States that she felt at home. After this trip, she told a friend that she would dedicate her life to helping her people.[9]

In 1950 and 1951 Baker was a smash hit on a tour of Latin American countries, and agents and club operators in the United States became interested in booking her. She declined their invitations, saying she was not interested in performing in theaters with racially segregated audiences. Ultimately, Baker's popularity enabled her to negotiate a contract with the Copa City Club in Miami Beach, Florida, before an integrated audience.[10] Following her success there, Baker always required that audiences be integrated and that she receive accommodations in first-class hotels.[11]

Baker's prominence sometimes shielded her from harsh discriminatory treatment, sometimes not. In October 1951 the *South Pacific* star Roger Rico and his wife took Baker and another guest, Bessie Buchanan, to New York's exclusive Stork Club for a late dinner. They were seated and Baker ordered a steak, but the waiters refused to serve her. Baker filed a complaint with the New York City police about the incident. Baker's wrath was not directed only at the Stork Club, however. The prominent New York gossip columnist Walter Winchell was at the Stork Club at the same time, although it is unclear whether he was aware of the discrimination against Baker. In interviews about the Stork Club incident, Baker criticized Winchell for failing to come to her assistance. Winchell responded by attacking Baker in his columns.[12]

Sharing Senator Joseph McCarthy's tendency to see the specter of communism in any adversary, Winchell had written to FBI director J. Edgar Hoover, asking him to check up on allegations that Baker was a Communist. The FBI began collecting derogatory information on Baker, paying close attention to the question of whether she was sympathetic to communism.[13] In fact, Baker preferred to distance herself from the Left. Although she took a strong interest in the case of Willie McGee, Baker backed out of a rally in support of McGee when she learned that it was sponsored by the American Labor Party and that Paul Robeson and the radical congressman Vito Marcantonio were also scheduled to speak. Baker was praised for this move by the staunchly anticommunist newsletter *Counterattack*. According to *Counterattack*, Baker, "unlike some other entertainers, . . . will not use her fight for justice and civil rights as an excuse for underhanded support of the CP."[14]

Meanwhile, the controversy surrounding the Stork Club incident affected Baker's ability to get and hold bookings in New York. She had become too controversial. Political activism in the entertainment industry at that time was tantamount to an invitation for an investigation by the House Committee on Un-American Activities, and controversy was not good for business.[15]

In 1952 Baker took her critique of American racial practices on the road on a tour of Latin America. In September 1952, after she had been in Uruguay for three weeks, the acting public affairs officer at the U.S. embassy in Montevideo reported to the State Department on her activities. The officer's interest in Baker stemmed from an appearance she made in that country on September 25, 1952. That evening Baker was scheduled not to sing, but to give a lecture. The event was organized by the World Cultural Association against Racial and Religious Discrimination, an association Baker founded to promote interracial understanding, and sponsored by the Uruguayan Cultural and Social Association and the Association of Bankers of Uruguay. According to the dispatch, "Before an audience of approximately 200 Uruguayans," Baker "stated that she felt impelled by God and her deep religious feelings to fight discrimination by stressing this problem in talks to people wherever she goes." Baker began by criticizing racial practices in South Africa and then turned to a lengthy discussion of race discrimination in the United States. The officer described Baker as a "staunch crusader for the elimination of racial and religious discrimination throughout the world" and he thought that her objective was "a most worthy one." Nevertheless, he was concerned about her activities because "her remarks concerning racial discrimination in the United States are wholly derogatory, thus presenting a distorted and malicious picture of actual conditions in the United States."[16] Consequently, the officer thought that the State Department would be "interested in following her campaign."[17]

Although the State Department was alarmed at Baker's harsh critique of American race relations, her notion of social change was not very radical. Baker's underlying philosophy was that education and respectful interaction among persons of different races and religions would overcome prejudice.

If American embassy officers seemed overly sensitive to Josephine Baker's crusade against racism, they had reason to be concerned. By 1949 American race relations were a "principal Soviet propaganda theme."[18] Race became a weapon in the Cold War, a weapon easily deployed against the United States. Government officials came to realize that if they wished to save Third World countries for democracy, they would have to improve the image of American race relations.

In this context, Josephine Baker was a threat. The United States had enough of a foreign relations problem from Soviet propaganda and from international media coverage of events at home. It did not help matters when individuals such as Baker actively sought to generate foreign interest in American racial discrimination. Consequently, the U.S. government did what it could to limit her activities and to respond to her accusations.

The State Department became increasingly concerned about Baker's actions when she traveled to Argentina in the fall of 1952 and her complicated politics, or perhaps her attraction to powerful people, led her into a close association with Juan Perón.[19] When Baker arrived in Buenos Aires, she received the sort of attention the embassy officer in Uruguay had been concerned about. Her statements about race discrimination were given "dramatic play" by most Buenos Aires newspapers. Baker also escalated the rhetoric in her critique of the United States. In a speech covered by the evening paper *Crítica*, Baker reportedly compared American racism to the Holocaust.[20]

The State Department was upset about the effect of Baker's speeches in Argentina. According to an internal memo on Baker's activities, "her work was welcomed in Argentina by the Perónistas who had been making much of the discrimination issue in their propaganda against the U.S." One staff member suggested that the department should do something "to counteract the effects of her visit. One of the most effective ways to my mind would be to have one or two outstanding negro intellectuals make trips through the southern part of the hemisphere." The staff of the United States Information Service (USIS), which was then part of the State Department, began to consider that strategy, involving such people as Ralph Bunche, Walter White, and Jackie Robinson.[21]

Although they had different ideas about strategy, USIS staff members were unanimous on one point. As one individual put it, "Naturally we should avoid any appearance of having sent someone to 'offset' J. Baker." According to another, "To put ourselves on the defensive in this case could serve to weaken our arguments. We should do nothing to directly refute Baker's charges." A third person noted that such a cautious approach was "in keeping with the Department's policy to avoid doing things which draw attention to the fact we have a problem in connection with the negro."[22]

While the State Department planned a propaganda response to Baker, embassy personnel also took steps to silence or discredit her. Baker found it increasingly difficult to perform in Latin American countries. She was unable to travel to Peru in

December 1952 because that country denied her request for a visa. A representative
of the theater in Lima, Peru, where Baker was scheduled to perform told the local
press that Baker's contract had been canceled because she insisted on using her performances not just for artistic purposes but also to express her views about racial
inequality. A scheduled trip to Colombia was called off for the same reasons. According to Baker, her Bogotá appearances were canceled when she refused to make
a written commitment to refrain from making speeches against racial discrimination while in that city.[23] A planned trip to Haiti was canceled as well.

In early 1953 Baker was scheduled to appear in Havana, Cuba. In late January
the American embassy in Havana, concerned about what it called "further anti-
American activity," urgently cabled the State Department for background information on Baker. Embassy officials wanted to know about her "anti-American statements" and the recent cancellations of appearances in Peru and Colombia; they
wanted quotations from African American newspapers criticizing Baker; and they
wanted personal data, including that she gave up her American citizenship. The information supplied included the fact that Baker had been married three times (it
was actually four) and that two of her husbands were white.[24]

Embassy officers then contacted Goar Mestre, who owned the theater where
Baker was scheduled to perform, and local newspapers. Embassy personnel "infor-
mally outlined to Mr. Mestre and to certain newspaper people that Miss Baker had
given statements to the Argentine press highly uncomplimentary to the United
States. The idea was planted discreetly that Miss Baker might use the Cuban press,
particularly its communistic elements, as a further sounding board for her accusations of the mistreatment of Negroes in the United States."[25]

The press reaction to Baker's anticipated visit was mixed. On January 27 *El
Mundo* reported a Baker interview in which she stated that she was fighting "not
only for the Negroes but for all persecuted people" and that her efforts were being
supported in Latin America. In contrast, the *Havana Herald*, an American-man-
aged paper, ran an editorial calling Baker "the darling of the Kremlin and of Perón"
and a "Kremlin propaganda transmission belt."[26] Baker did not arrive in Cuba in
time for her scheduled performances. She sent a wire from Rio de Janeiro requesting a later date. Instead, her performances were canceled. As Mestre put it, "We
know that Josephine Baker has terrific drawing power, but we can't keep adjusting
our business to her." According to an embassy officer, Baker's tardiness "may well
have provided her Habana employers with just the legal loophole they needed to
'get out from under' a ticklish situation."[27]

Baker showed up in Havana anyway. She gave a press conference on February 10
and blamed American influence for her contract cancellations. She claimed that
Teatro América had canceled a scheduled performance because the theater was
afraid of losing its American film franchise. According to the embassy, "failure to
arrive at a financial understanding is closer to the truth." Baker had a history of financial disputes with her employers, and at times she tried to hold out for more
money than had originally been agreed to; it is entirely possible that a disagreement
over her pay was an element in the cancellation of her Teatro América contract.

Nevertheless, it is also clear that the U.S. embassy took steps to show its displeasure over the possibility that Baker might perform in Cuba. Consequently, it is most likely that any disagreement over finances, like Baker's tardiness, provided the theater with an excuse to avoid a politically uncomfortable situation.[28]

Though Baker's other engagements in Havana had been canceled, an advertising agency scheduled a February 11 appearance for her on *Cabaret Regalias,* a popular evening television show. The agency did not, however, seek approval from Goar Mestre, the president of the television station. When she arrived at the studio on February 11 for an afternoon rehearsal, Mestre threw her out and ordered his doorman to bar Baker from reentering the television studio. As the American embassy reported it, "Adamant, Miss Baker, costume over her arm, stood outside the gate from 3:00 p.m. to 9:30 p.m. in an apparent effort to elicit sympathy." Mestre told the *Havana Herald* that Baker could stand there "'until hell freezes over' before he would permit her to perform." Mestre "would not permit Miss Baker or anyone else 'to order me around.'" He then "sent down a chair for her to sit down in and told her to make herself comfortable for she was in for a long wait if she thought she was going to be admitted into the building again." Meanwhile, the embassy reported, "'Cabaret Regalias' went on the air without her."[29]

After much effort, Baker finally was able to arrange an appearance in Cuba. On February 16 she opened a one-week run at the Teatro Campoamor, described in an embassy dispatch as "a down-at-the heels theater which last year was a burlesque house." The embassy reported that "there was no indication she . . . used the Campoamor stage for political purposes." Baker was warned not to. At 4:30 P.M. the day after her opening, Baker was taken into custody by the Cuban military police. They filed no charges against Baker, but they interrogated her for three hours about her political and social views. The military police reported that "the questioning was in response to a suggestion by the U.S. Federal Bureau of Investigation that Miss Baker might be an active Communist." Baker was photographed and fingerprinted. The military police asked her to sign a stenographic report of her interrogation, but she refused. Baker later wrote in an autobiography that the statement would have her admit to "being paid by Moscow and indulging in subversive activities." When she was fingerprinted, "the word 'Communist' was marked beneath my picture." Baker was warned to "stick to her art and refrain from any voicing of political views at the Campoamor." She was released in time for her evening appearance.[30]

Baker's visit to Cuba had far less artistic and political impact than she would have liked. After she left the country, the American embassy in Cuba concluded that "Miss Baker's visit to Cuba must be considered of little value to her cause." The embassy also felt that Baker had done little harm. "All in all, Miss Baker's influence on Cuban Negroes may well be appraised as negligible. The Negro press ignored her, and Negro societies made no fuss over her." The embassy reported that a Cuban newspaper editor "explained to an Embassy officer that the attitude of the Cuban Negro toward the United States has changed radically in the last few years and that the Cuban Negro is now aware that real progress is being made in the United States toward the elimination of racial discrimination."[31]

Clearly frustrated in her efforts to appear in Latin America and the Caribbean, Baker would soon be unable to turn to the United States as an alternative market for her performances. In 1954 Baker returned to the United States to file a libel action against Walter Winchell. She was able to enter the country because, according to the FBI, there was "insufficient derogatory subversive information to use as a basis for her exclusion." Her prospects for future entrances to the United States were lessened, however. According to an FBI internal memorandum of December 10, 1954, the commissioner of the Immigration and Naturalization Service (INS) had taken "a personal interest in the case of Josephine Baker and has directed that INS obtain sufficient information with which to order her exclusion from the U.S." The INS requested that the FBI review its files to ensure that "all pertinent derogatory information" had been forwarded to the INS. J. Edgar Hoover then sent a one-page document to the INS commissioner regarding Baker, most of which was deleted by the FBI when supplied to the author under the Freedom of Information Act on the grounds that it contained "material which is properly classified pursuant to an Executive order in the interest of national defense or foreign policy."[32]

Whatever was in the document seems to have been enough. On January 21, 1955, the *New York Herald Tribune* reported that Josephine Baker was detained by the INS at a New York airport, where she had stopped en route from Paris to Mexico City. She was held for four hours before being allowed to depart. No explanation was given for the INS action. While Baker's reaction to her exclusion is not reported, she had earlier stated, "If my entry into the United States is forbidden, for me this [will be] an honor because it will show that my work for humanity has been successful."[33]

The INS action was probably not necessary to keep Baker from performing in the United States in the mid-1950s. Theater owners were unlikely to book such an "un-American" figure. Nevertheless, Baker's literal exclusion from the United States capped government efforts to exclude her from the discourse on American race relations. She would return to perform in the early 1960s and to participate in the 1963 March on Washington, then a tired and aging, though still very popular, performer. And although she expressed regret for some of her harsh criticism in earlier years, by 1963 Baker's voice no longer stood out amid the chorus of critics of American race discrimination.[34]

Baker's detention by the INS brought government surveillance and harassment of the entertainer full circle. In 1951 the FBI had initiated its investigation after Baker publicly charged Walter Winchell with racism. The FBI could document no "subversive" acts on Baker's part and in fact had information that seemed to suggest that Baker may have been anticommunist. Nevertheless, the bureau passed on the derogatory information it had to the State Department, which in turn sent it on to the American embassies. Embassy staff members then engaged in behind-the-scenes negotiations to interfere with Baker's ability to speak out against race discrimination. The INS, in turn, restricted Baker's ability to travel freely, signaling to the world that she was considered to be too dangerous to tolerate. It is surely a mark of the government's sensitivity to charges of race discrimination and its concern about the impact of negative attention to American racial problems on foreign relations that the FBI, the State Department, and the INS felt they needed to spend so much time and effort to keep one woman from speaking out.

Although it seems that any critic of the U.S. government was summarily categorized as a radical in the context of Cold War politics, there was another dimension to Baker's challenge. Unpacking the reasons that Baker was viewed as threatening may help to explain more fully the travel restrictions placed on others.

The State Department put a lot of energy and resources into trying to shore up the image abroad of American race relations. Josephine Baker threw a wrench into this scheme. Instead of talking about progress, she talked about lynching. Instead of describing expanding employment opportunities, she described segregation. While the State Department tried to frame the debate as one about the nature of change within a democratic order, Baker and others argued that race discrimination called into question the nature of American democracy itself. At a time when world politics were seen as divided between the "free world" and communist nations, between liberty and tyranny, critics of American democracy were seen as aiding a vicious enemy. From the State Department's perspective, the stakes were too high to tolerate dissent.

The restrictions on Josephine Baker's ability to travel and perform did more than harm her career as an entertainer; they denied her the role she sought for herself as a personal ambassador for equality, furthering equal rights by winning the hearts of nations and their leaders. When Baker returned to France, she turned her focus on racial harmony inward. She sought to create at home the equality she hoped to see among the world's peoples. In 1954 Baker and Bouillon began adopting children of various races and religions. The "Rainbow Tribe," as she called them, grew to twelve children. Baker hoped that her family would demonstrate that people of different races and religions could live in harmony.[35]

Although the FBI ultimately concluded that Josephine Baker was not "procommunist" but "pro-Negro," bureau officials continued to pass derogatory information about her to the State Department and other sources for several years. She would ultimately be able to perform again in the United States and Latin America after adopting a more conciliatory posture toward the U.S. government. The restrictions placed on her during the 1950s, however, had a lasting impact on her life.[36] Josephine Baker's relative poverty in her later years was clearly attributable to poor financial management and her pursuit of expensive dreams such as the Rainbow Tribe. Still, following World War II she was a superstar with international appeal. Once she began criticizing American race relations, she lost valuable markets for her performances—both in the United States and, owing to the efforts of the embassies, in other countries sensitive to American influence.

Josephine Baker's ultimate embrace of domesticity as the locus of her politics in the late 1950s seems oddly consistent with the pre–*Feminine Mystique* status of women in the United States. While American women were forced out of the factories and encouraged into the maternity wards in the postwar years, Baker was ultimately blacklisted out of the international entertainment circuit. Without a public platform for her call for equality, she sought to promote racial justice through her own vision of motherhood. And just as the federal government had a hand in constructing the postwar culture of domesticity, it played a not-too-subtle role in ushering Baker off the stage.[37]

While "containment" of women in the home seemed an important Cold War value, as Elaine Tyler May has argued, "containment" of Josephine Baker within French borders, where she would no longer be a threat to the image of American democracy, was seen as a national security imperative. By the mid-1950s the government made some progress in ameliorating international criticism. The message of *Brown v. Board of Education*, that racial segregation in schools was unconstitutional, was the top priority of Voice of America programming for several days in May 1954. Even as massive resistance forces began to organize in the American South, American embassy personnel reported that *Brown* had softened criticism in India.[38] Through limited social change, advertised through American propaganda, there was a possibility of bolstering American prestige and credibility. Silencing Josephine Baker was simply a part of the propaganda campaign. Excluding her voice would make it easier to maintain a carefully crafted image of American democracy. And the image of race in the United States was no small matter. In the words of Ambassador Chester Bowles, its importance to the Cold War was "impossible to exaggerate."[39] In the face of the war between the superpowers, Josephine Baker's international crusade for racial harmony would have to wait.

NOTES

A longer version of this essay first appeared at 81 J. Amer. Hist. 543 (1994), and is reprinted with permission. Citations remain in their original form and have not been updated to reflect recent scholarship. This research is part of a broader project by the author, Cold War Civil Rights: Equality as Cold War Policy, 1946–1968 (forthcoming Princeton University Press).

1. There is a growing literature on the role of race in foreign relations. These works primarily consider the role of race in relations among different nations. *See, e.g.*, Paul Gordon Lauren, Power and Prejudice: The Politics and Diplomacy of Racial Discrimination (1988); John W. Dower, War without Mercy: Race and Power in the Pacific War (1986); Thomas Borstelmann, Apartheid's Reluctant Uncle: The United States and Southern Africa in the Early Cold War (1993); and Alexander Deconde, Ethnicity, Race, and American Foreign Policy: A History (1992). In contrast, this chapter is concerned with the intersection of domestic race politics and United States foreign relations. For related works, see Brenda Gayle Plummer, Castro in Harlem: A Cold War Watershed, paper presented at the conference "Rethinking the Cold War: A Conference in Memory of William Appleman Williams," University of Wisconsin, Madison, October 1991; Gerald Horne, Black and Red: W. E. B. Du Bois and the Afro-American Response to Cold War, 1944–1963 (1986); and Penny M. von Eschen, African Americans and Anti-Colonialism, 1937–1957: The Rise and Fall of the Politics of Diaspora (1994) (Ph.D. diss., Columbia University).

2. Gunnar Myrdal, An American Dilemma: The Negro Problem and Modern Democracy

(1944); Steven Lawson, Black Ballots: Voting Rights in the South, 1944–1969 (1976); James W. Ivy, *American Negro Problem in the European Press*, 57 Crisis 413, 416–18 (July 1950).

3. U.S. Embassy, Moscow to Secretary of State, Nov. 20, 1946, RG 59, 811.4016/11-2046, Records of the Department of State, National Archives; U.S. Embassy, The Hague, The Netherlands to Department of State, Feb. 13, 1950, RG 59, 811.411/2-1350, Records of the Department of State, National Archives. *See also* Mary L. Dudziak, *Desegregation as a Cold War Imperative*, 41 Stan. L. Rev. 61, 80–93 (1988).

4. For government concern about the impact of race relations on foreign affairs, see President's Committee on Civil Rights, To Secure These Rights (Washington, 1947); Brief for the United States as Amicus Curiae, Shelley v. Kraemer, 334 U.S. 1 (1948); Brief for the United States, Henderson v. United States, 339 U.S. 815 (1950); Memorandum for the United States as Amicus Curiae, McLaurin v. Oklahoma, 339 U.S. 637 (1950); and Brief for the United States as Amicus Curiae, Brown v. Board of Education, 347 U.S. 483 (1954).

5. Horne, *supra* note 1, at 212–18; Martin Duberman, Paul Robeson 389 (1988). On the choice of speakers by the State Department, see Dudziak, *supra* note 3, at 98–101; von Eschen, *supra* note 1, chapter 5. On passport confiscations, see Duberman, *supra,* at 389; Horne, *supra* note 1, at 212–18; Gerald Horne, Communist Front? The Civil Rights Congress, 1946–1956, at 167 (1988); and William L. Patterson, The Man Who Cried Genocide: An Autobiography 198–201 (1971).

6. As Josephine Baker constructed her stage image, she also reconstructed her personal history. Baker and those associated with her would at times commit versions of her life story to paper. On her work for the French Resistance, see Jaques Abtey, La guerre secrete de Josephine Baker (1948); for a memoir by Baker and her fourth husband, see Josephine Baker and Jo Bouillon, Josephine (Mariana Fitzpatrick trans., 1977). The groundwork for full-fledged biographies was laid by Lynn Haney, Naked at the Feast: A Biography of Josephine Baker (1981). An elegant volume that effectively evokes Baker as an artist is Phyllis Rose, Jazz Cleopatra: Josephine Baker in Her Times (1989). The most complete collection of photographs of Baker and Baker memorabilia is Ben Hammond, Josephine Baker (1988). The most comprehensive biography is Jean-Claude Baker and Chris Chase, Josephine: The Hungry Heart (1993). This work is full of previously unreported details about Baker's life. It is also an intensely personal portrait by a man who was taken under the entertainer's wing at the age of fourteen and who considers himself to be her son. Jean-Claude Baker speaks directly to Josephine Baker in the book and urges on the reader his interpretation of her complex personality. For a full bibliography of works by and about Josephine Baker, see *id.* at 506.

7. Rose, *supra* note 6, at 18–45, 121–22, 150–52.

8. *Id.* at 69–75.

9. Haney, *supra* note 6, at 247.

10. *Miami Success Climaxes Storybook Career*, Ebony, May 6, 1951, at 76. While most African American performers had to endure segregation if they wanted to work, Paul Robeson, like Baker, made a practice of demanding no segregation as a condition for his appearances. Duberman, *supra* note 5, at 256, 288.

11. *Miami Success Climaxes Storybook Career*, *supra* note 10, at 78.

12. Chicago Defender, Oct. 27, 1951, at 1. The NAACP backed her protest, sponsoring a star-studded picket line at the Stork Club. The executive secretary, Walter White, called on the FBI. He telegraphed a request that J. Edgar Hoover protest the Stork Club's refusal to serve Baker because "such discrimination . . . anywhere in the United States plays directly

into the hands of communists and other enemies of democracy. Disapproval of such policy by those who make Stork Club success it is . . . will demonstrate vitality and integrity of democracy." Hoover responded, "I don't consider this to be any of my business." Rose, *supra* note 6, at 218–19; National Association for the Advancement of Colored People to J. Edgar Hoover, telegram, Oct. 19, 1951, "Josephine Baker," Federal Bureau of Investigation file 62-95834 (J. Edgar Hoover FBI Building, Washington, D.C.) [hereinafter Baker FBI file]. On FBI surveillance of African Americans, see Kenneth O'Reilly, "Racial Matters": The FBI's Secret File on Black America, 1960–1972 (1989); David Garrow, The FBI and Martin Luther King Jr. (1981); Kenneth O'Reilly, Black Americans: The FBI Files (David Gallen, ed., 1994); and Michael Friedly and David Gallen, Martin Luther King, Jr.: The FBI File (1993).

13. Baker FBI file, *supra* note 12.

14. Counterattack, *Letter No. 200*, March 23, 1951, at 3–4, *in* Baker FBI file, *supra* note 12; Haney, *supra* note 6, at 258.

15. Haney, *supra* note 6, at 258; Stephen Papich, Remembering Josephine 176–77 (1976). *See* Victor Navasky, Naming Names (1980).

16. U.S. Embassy, Montevideo to State Department, Sept. 30, 1952, RG 59, 811.411/9-3052, Records of the Department of State, National Archives.

17. *Id.*

18. U.S. Embassy, Moscow to Secretary of State, July 27, 1949, RG 59, 811.4016/6-2749, Department of State Decimal File, Records of the Department of State, National Archives.

19. Haney, *supra* note 6, at 259–65.

20. U.S. Embassy, Buenos Aires to State Department, Oct. 6, 1952, RG 59, 811.411/10-652, Records of the Department of State, National Archives; Department of State, translation of article in *Buenos Aires Crítica*, Oct. 3, 1952, Buenos Aires, Argentina, TC 57594, T-19/R-1, RG 59, 811.411/10-352, Records of the Department of State, National Archives.

21. Raine to Haden, Oct. 20, 1952, RG 59, FW811.411/9-3052 CS/W, Records of the Department of State, National Archives.

22. *Id.*; Ordway to Reid, Dec. 30, 1952, RG 59, 811.411/12-3052 CS/W, Records of the Department of State, National Archives.

23. There is no direct, unclassified evidence of United States embassy involvement in the cancellation of Baker's visa and contracts in Peru and Colombia. In one unclassified dispatch, the American embassy in Lima, Peru, clearly showed satisfaction at the cancellation of Baker's appearances but noted that "some people in Lima will believe that this Embassy had something to do with the cancellation of her contract—which, of course, is not the case." The events in Peru and Colombia were so similar to what would later happen in Cuba, where State Department records clearly indicate embassy involvement, that it is likely the embassies in Peru and Colombia took similar actions to discourage Baker's visits. U.S. Embassy, Lima to State Department, Dec. 31, 1952, RG 59, 811.411/12-3152 LWC, Records of the Department of State, National Archives; U.S. Embassy, Buenos Aires to State Department, Dec. 29, 1952, RG 59, 811.411/12-2952, Records of the Department of State, National Archives; U.S. Embassy, Santiago to State Department, Dec. 30, 1952, RG 59, 811.411/12-3052, Records of the Department of State, National Archives; U.S. Embassy, Rio de Janeiro to State Department, Feb. 2, 1953, RG 59, 811.411/2-253, Records of the Department of State, National Archives.

24. U.S. Embassy, Habana to Secretary of State, Jan. 27, 1953, RG 59, 811.411/1-2753, Records of the Department of State, National Archives.

25. U.S. Embassy, Habana to State Department, Jan. 30, 1953, RG 59, 811.411/1-3053, Records of the Department of State, National Archives.

26. For quotations from *Havana Mundo* and *Havana Herald,* see *id.*

27. For quotation from Goar Mestre and embassy commentary, see *id.*

28. U.S. Embassy, Habana to State Department, Feb. 12, 1953, RG 59, 811.411/2-1253, Records of the Department of State, National Archives; U.S. Embassy, Habana to State Department, Jan. 30, 1953, RG 59, 811.411/3053, Records of the Department of State, National Archives.

29. U.S. Embassy, Habana to State Department, Feb. 12, 1953, *supra* note 28; *Josephine Baker Fails in Try to Force CMQ to Let Her Perform,* Havana Herald, Feb. 12, 1953, *in* Baker FBI file, *supra* note 12.

30. U.S. Embassy, Habana to State Department, Feb. 18, 1953, RG 59, 811.411/2-1853, Records of the Department of State, National Archives; U.S. Embassy, Habana to State Department, Feb. 19, 1953, RG 59, 811.411/2-1953, Records of the Department of State, National Archives; Baker and Bouillon, *supra* note 6, at 189.

31. U.S. Embassy, Habana to State Department, March 3, 1953, RG 59, 811.411/3-353, Records of the Department of State, National Archives.

32. N. W. Philcox to R. R. Roach, Re: Josephine Baker, Dec. 10, 1954, *in* Baker FBI file, *supra* note 12; Memo, Director, FBI, to Commissioner, INS, Re: Josephine Baker, Jan. 6, 1955, *in* Baker FBI file, *supra* note 12. A sheet entitled "Explanation of Exemptions" was provided to the author by the FBI along with Baker's FBI file. The relevant Freedom of Information Act exemption from full disclosure of the memo is 5 U.S.C. Sec. 552(b)(1).

33. N.Y. Herald Tribune report in teletype message to FBI, Jan. 28, 1955, *in* Baker FBI file, *supra* note 12; U.S. Embassy, Buenos Aires to State Department, Nov. 6, 1952, RG 59, 811.411/11-652, Records of the Department of State, National Archives.

34. As Ellen Schrecker has suggested, there were two steps to blacklisting; first the government identified individuals as subversive, and then private employers (in this case theater owners) made decisions against hiring them. Ellen W. Schrecker, No Ivory Tower: McCarthyism and the Universities 9 (1986).

35. Rose, *supra* note 6, at 231–38.

36. G. H. Scatterday to A. H. Belmont, Re: Josephine Baker, 10 Feb. 1960, *in* Baker FBI file, *supra* note 12; American Consulate, Bordeaux to State Department, Aug. 4, 1958, RG 59, 811.411/8-458 HBS, Records of the Department of State, National Archives.

37. Carolyn Jones, *Split Incomes and Separate Spheres: Tax Law and Gender Roles in the 1940s,* 6 L. and Hist. Rev. 259 (1988). *See* Betty Friedan, The Feminine Mystique (1963).

38. Elaine Tyler May, Homeward Bound: American Families in the Cold War (1988).

39. Bowles, Ambassador's Report 396 (1954).

12 United States Foreign Policy and Goler Teal Butcher

J. Clay Smith, Jr.

These are sobering times when the challenges of natural calamities as well as the crises of human uncaring, political miscalculations, military and economic opportunism cry out to us for our input. . . . [L]awyers must step forward to assist in the effort to address the challenge of the earth itself.
—Goler T. Butcher, "The Immediacy of International Law for Howard University Students"

INTRODUCTION

This chapter was inspired by the work of Goler Teal Butcher, who retired from the law faculty of Howard University School of Law in 1992. Professor Butcher, who was born in 1925, died in 1993 while the preliminary research for this essay was in progress. The tribute expanded as I learned more about Butcher's extraordinary career as a lawyer, public servant, and advocate for human rights, and about the significant role she played in developing United States policy in Africa.

This essay is not intended to be a full chronicle of Goler Teal Butcher's contributions to foreign and domestic policy. Rather, its purpose is to cast light on the prodigious life of a Black female law professor—a pioneer in academia whose writings, public statements, actions, courage, and ideals about international law merit closer attention by academics and makers of U.S. foreign policy.

Placing Butcher's life in context has been challenging. She left a rich and lasting legacy, one that she stamped on the White House after the election of President Clinton. One of Butcher's last projects was to head the Clinton-Gore transition team for the United States Agency for International Development (AID). She undertook the project even though she was suffering visibly from the effects of a stroke.

Butcher served as a full-time faculty member of the Howard University School of Law for eleven years, where she taught both core and advanced courses in international law. Much can be said about Butcher as a cherished colleague, master

Reprinted by permission from 37 *Howard Law Journal* 139 (1994).

teacher, and change agent. She was one of the handful of Black women whose career combined the practice of international law with the management of a federal agency that formulated policy issues on the development of African countries.

As a scholar, Butcher wrote about issues that consumed her professional career. The issues that she raised, the rights for which she vigorously agitated, the dreams and aspirations of the underclass that she adopted as her own, the responsibility that she undertook to change the world, and the ideas that she shared with students and the legal profession about the world mark Goler Teal Butcher as a progressive modern thinker. Indeed, her works make her an important contributor to the jurisprudential matrix, and a forerunner in an evolving world.

Although Butcher was a universal woman, she was concerned about the dearth of Black men and women in the field of international law. As a Black woman, Goler Teal Butcher was uniquely aware of the pervasiveness of racial and gender discrimination in the field of international law. When Butcher was employed at the Department of State in the 1950s, she "had tremendous difficulty getting to see [her] clients because the secretaries were primed not to allow a woman to see the male Foreign Service officers."[1] She was also a staunch advocate of dismantling the racist apartheid system in South Africa. Butcher thought, however, that Black lawyers in the field of international law should not confine their practice to African affairs, because she believed Black lawyers needed to be involved in the worldwide struggle for human rights.

LAW STUDENT AND JUDICIAL CLERK

Goler Teal Butcher was an extraordinary student from the time she entered Howard University School of Law in 1954. Endowed with a brilliant mind, a ferocious appetite for knowledge, and a keen competitive spirit, she earned the highest marks in several subjects. During the 1956–57 academic year, Butcher was elected editor in chief of the *Howard Law Journal,* the first woman to hold that post. She also published two student articles of her own, and graduated summa cum laude in 1957 as the sole female student. When she graduated from the law school, she was awarded a fellowship to study international law at the University of Pennsylvania School of Law, and received her LL.M. degree one year later.

Butcher then clerked for Judge William Henry Hastie of the Third Circuit Court of Appeals. She was one of the first women to serve as a judicial clerk in the U.S. federal system. She broke new ground by winning this clerkship: she is likely the first Howard Law graduate and the first Black woman to clerk at the federal circuit level.

BUTCHER ENTERS THE FIELD OF INTERNATIONAL LAW

Butcher's career in international law started when she joined the Office of Legal Counsel in the Department of State in 1963. When she joined the legal staff, "the

State Department announced that she was believed to be the first black person to serve in the legal unit."[2]

In 1971, when Congressman Charles Coles Diggs became the first Black to chair the House Subcommittee on Africa, Butcher became a consultant to the House Foreign Affairs Committee and counsel to the Subcommittee on Africa. In 1972, in her role as consultant to the subcommittee, Butcher accompanied Congressman Diggs to London, the Sudan, Zambia, and Botswana, a trip referred to as the "Study Mission to Africa." Butcher worked for the Subcommittee on Africa until 1974, when she went into private practice at the Washington, D.C., law firm of White, Fine and Verville. While there, she became involved in the important work of the Lawyers' Committee for Civil Rights under Law and was an AID subcontractor for the African-American Scholars Council.

In 1975 Butcher was one of the lawyers representing "members of the House of Representatives and four associations who represent the interests of black Americans" that appealed an order of the Civil Aeronautics Board (CAB) that authorized a new route for foreign airlines between New York and South Africa. Butcher argued that the order was constitutionally infirm.[3] The court affirmed CAB's order on the ground that the relevant statute barred judicial review.[4] Butcher testified before the Senate Subcommittee on African Affairs and asked Congress to "take the lead to end what is essentially a coverup of U.S. policy on southern Africa."[5] She claimed that the U.S. government had been hypocritical in its racial policies toward South Africa. She asserted that while the United States publicly denounced the racist regime, the country supported the status quo in its private dealings.

A target of Butcher's criticism was a recently disclosed policy position of the National Security Council Study Memorandum of 1969 (NSSM 39).[6] Butcher viewed South Africa as "a caldron of racism"; to her, support for this regime was inconsistent with the tenets of human rights.[7] Because Butcher believed that minority rule in South Africa could not last, she urged the United States not to cast its support with the minority regime in South Africa. She argued that such a policy would jeopardize "our substantially greater interest in black Africa; namely, access to raw materials, oil, minerals, commodities . . . and strategically, with respect to Africa as a whole."[8] Yet the American foreign policy view of NSSM 39, which Butcher opposed, was the so-called Tar Baby Option, premised on the view "that whites [were in South Africa] to stay and the only way that constructive change can come is through them."[9]

During the final days of the Ford administration, the U.S. foreign policy toward southern Africa began to change. In large part, this change was due to the "collapse of Portuguese colonial rule in 1974 when the mother country, weary of half a century of Fascist rule and weakened by three colonial wars, chose to turn its back on five centuries of empire."[10] In what became known as the Lusaka speech, Secretary of State Henry Kissinger announced the United States' intention to end institutionalized inequality in South Africa.[11] Kissinger encouraged South Africa to provide equal opportunity and human rights to all its citizens.[12]

Shortly after the Lusaka speech, a skeptical Goler Teal Butcher testified before Congress and questioned the Nixon-Ford administration's new policy toward South Africa:

This brings me to a major concern on the Lusaka speech of Secretary Kissinger. Of course his speech was welcome. For an administration that has placed Africa at the bottom of its priorities; for an administration that has not only had a devious policy, as finally revealed in NSSM-39 of actual support of the status quo and hence of the minority regimes in Africa, but has had the conviction that the white regimes are here to stay; for an administration which has had the insensitivity to appoint an official of some 30 years almost of high position with Union Carbide to the second highest position in the Department of State; and for an administration under which the former campaign manager of the President visited Rhodesia and endorsed the normalization of relations with the illegal Smith regime, [the Lusaka speech] is certainly welcome.[13]

In August 1976 Butcher again testified before the House Subcommittee on International Organizations regarding U.S. policy from the standpoint of U.S. interests.[14] Butcher argued that the people of the United States must better understand the common bond between African and U.S. interests. At this time, the United States imported "43 percent of its copper, 51 percent of its manganese, 28 percent of its platinum, 85 percent of its uranium oxide . . . 56 percent of [its] cocoa and 29 percent of [its] coffee from Africa." Butcher stressed that the American people had to realize that "the United States is not strong enough to assure [its own citizens] the kind of life and material goods and technological functioning of our society or our global security without the friendship of the majority of people of the world community."[15] She knew that if U.S. policy continued to tilt toward the white minority in South Africa, the vital interests of the United States would be threatened in places like Namibia.

Butcher again questioned the Department of State's emphasis on "minority rights" in South Africa. She urged an end to "the thoughtless use of shibboleths such as the protection of 'minority rights,' and such as 'peaceful progress.'"[16] Butcher concluded that the United States should continue to focus on the broader policy of human rights for all people, "lest the concept of the protection of minority rights become a mechanism for the preservation of majority privilege."[17]

BUTCHER AS ASSISTANT ADMINISTRATOR FOR AFRICAN AFFAIRS AT AID: THE CARTER YEARS

Jimmy Carter was elected President in 1976, about the time Goler Teal Butcher petitioned the court to prohibit the United States "from continuing to deal with the South Africans concerning the importation of seal furs from Namibia."[18] She and others argued that UN Resolution 301 prohibited this activity.

In his inaugural address, President Carter emphasized that the United States' "commitment to human rights must be absolute."[19] He declared that his administration had "a clearcut preference for those societies which share with us an abiding respect for individual human rights."[20] Carter also emphasized human rights in his "Day Message" to the people of the world.[21] Many African Americans welcomed these statements, and viewed them as an integral part of the Carter administration's foreign policy in Third World nations, particularly in southern Africa.

Soon after the inauguration, Cyrus Vance, Carter's secretary of state, concluded that the administration's foreign policy should not be limited to traditional Cold War concerns. Vance would later criticize previous U.S. policies for not understanding the explosive forces of change in the developing world.[22] Indeed, "[g]lobal interdependence, once a fashionable buzzword, had become a reality, [with the] future [of the United States] inextricably entwined with the economic and political developments of a turbulent Third World."[23]

Butcher had been a foreign policy adviser to the Carter presidential campaign. The announcement of the Carter foreign policy was exciting and prompted Butcher to accept a position as assistant administrator of the Agency for International Development (AID), with principal responsibility for Africa. Butcher was the first Black woman to hold this position.

The next four years tested Butcher's fortitude, as well as that of her colleagues, as she attempted to transform the words of President Carter's inaugural address into action. Armed with a mission to accomplish change in Africa, she traveled between Africa and Capitol Hill for numerous congressional hearings to fight for the Carter administration's development policies in Africa. Her encyclopedic knowledge of the region and her mastery of detail won her the respect of many senators and congressmen, including many who opposed her proposals.

BUTCHER FIGHTS FOR GREATER U.S. ECONOMIC ASSISTANCE FOR AFRICA

Significant international activity relevant to Africa occurred in 1977: the Reverend Leon H. Sullivan, a Black activist minister and director of General Motors, issued the Sullivan Principles;[24] Steve Biko, a popular Black activist, died as a result of a brutal beating suffered while in the custody of the South African police; and the Brandt Commission was established to further North-South dialogue.

It was in this political environment that Goler Teal Butcher returned to Congress to explain why the United States should be more responsive to Africa's development. Her reports to Congress were forthright, honest, and graphic because she saw firsthand the devastation and the progress. This knowledge increased her credibility and influence with Congress. The African countries for which she sought support could not have had a stronger champion.

Butcher asserted that "the African countries have been . . . the stepchildren of our foreign assistance program."[25] She voiced concern about the diminishing assistance being provided to Africa through AID since 1962, but stated that she was encouraged by the current $155 million in development assistance, "the highest amount since 1972."[26] Mindful that a decade earlier the United States was "far freer from commitments in Africa south of the Sahara than in any region of the world,"[27] Butcher hoped that the development assistance budget for 1978 would be over $200 million. This budget included funds for "the Sahel development program, and $115 million in security supporting assistance, the total of which will bring [AID] back to the 1962 [*sic*] level."[28] Butcher hoped that during the Carter presidency, aid to Africa would "build steadily [and] develop new and imaginative programs within the framework of a longer term commitment to assist the peoples of Africa."[29]

In early 1978 Butcher testified before the House Subcommittee on Africa on the need for economic and military assistance programs on the continent and requested $339 million in aid. This amount included "$294 million in development assistance and $45 million in security supporting [*sic*] to supplement our regular development assistance programs in southern Africa."[30] During these hearings Butcher began to map out her imaginative programs and her vision of enlarging the role of AID in assistance programs in Africa in three areas: food production, health services, and education and human resource development.

Butcher based her budget requests on two premises. First, AID's programs must "address the basic needs of the poor masses [and] impact immediately on these people." Second, the programs must contribute to "institution building [in Africa that will allow Africans to] determine the direction of their assistance needs."[31]

Professor Butcher was soon before the House Subcommittee on Appropriations, renewing her request for the funding of AID projects that supported "Sahelian governments' action to coordinate long-term comprehensive development planning in the post-drought period and to address the basic causes of the vulnerability of the Sahel to drought."[32] Butcher spoke frankly before the Subcommittee, contending "that the operating budget for [1978 had] been inadequate to staff support our field missions properly."[33] Butcher's goal was "[n]ot only [to] sustain our support for Sahel development, but we must increase our contributions" to develop infrastructure, stabilize production, achieve food self-sufficiency, inform American citizens of the plight of the Sahel countries, and provide technical assistance to speed the use of alternative energy sources.[34] In this, and other projects that were not co-funded by other nations, Butcher risked criticism by proclaiming that AID was "trying to [be] a forerunner in the Sahel Region."[35]

In 1980 Butcher testified regarding the success of AID's Sahel program. She reported that one-person field offices had been replaced with "full-scale bilateral missions in five countries, staffed more fully with the technicians and project managers to design, implement and monitor projects in the Sahelian countries."[36] Butcher proclaimed that donor assistance programs had positive effects on "the lives of people throughout the Sahel in such projects as the Bakel Small Irrigated Perimeters and the Sine Saloum Rural Health project in Senegal; the Women In Development project in Mauritania; the Eastern ORD Integrated Rural Development project in

Upper Volta; the Niamey Department Development project in Niger [and] Operation Millet in Mali."[37]

PROFESSOR BUTCHER AT HOWARD UNIVERSITY SCHOOL OF LAW

In 1981, just after the Reagan administration took office, Wiley Austin Branton, Sr., dean of Howard University School of Law, persuaded Butcher to join the law faculty to teach international law. She soon became director of the Master of Comparative Jurisprudence Program. As Butcher taught international law and increased the Howard legal community's awareness of South Africa's problems, the Reagan administration was creating a foreign policy friendly to the apartheid regime. The policy was known as constructive engagement. Chester Crocker, Assistant Secretary of State for Africa, was "the architect of the [Reagan] administration's southern Africa strategy . . . [and] contended that Washington could do more to encourage change [in southern Africa] by showing greater patience, understanding and willingness to help Pretoria shed its pariah image worldwide."[38]

On behalf of the Lawyers' Committee for Civil Rights under Law, Butcher presented testimony before Congress on enforcement of the arms embargo against South Africa. She outlined the legal justification for the arms embargo. She argued that

> any loosening of the policy, which prohibits "the export to South Africa and
> Namibia of certain arms and military equipment and materials used for their manu-
> facture and maintenance which are not in the State Department Munitions List . . ."
> would be a clear violation of the explicit injunction of [Security Council] Res. 418.[39]

Butcher concluded with a call for a congressional inquiry to ascertain "the extent to which the foreign subsidiaries of U.S. corporations in South Africa and in other countries are supplying the South African military or police with arms or related materials."[40]

Butcher's call for lawyers to "step forward to assist in the effort to address the challenge of the earth itself" commanded a response from the entire legal profession.[41] In addition, it was a call for future generations of lawyers, particularly Black lawyers, to carry on the tradition of reporting, protesting, litigating, teaching, and explaining why lawyers like Butcher took a stand against the pariahs of apartheid. She was one of the first arrested in November 1984 at the start of the Free South Africa Movement.[42]

Black lawyers voiced strong objections when members of the American Bar Association's legislative committee of young lawyers were about to pass a resolution supporting U.S. recognition for South Africa's "homelands" policy. The proposal, drafted in 1984, was squelched when Vincent Cohen, a Black lawyer in Washington, D.C., rallied Black bar groups and others to oppose the proposal.[43] Just prior to the ABA debacle, Gay J. McDougall, Henry J. Richardson III, and Professor Butcher filed a brief before the Commission of Inquiry into Kangwane (the Rumpff

Commission) opposing the cession of Kangwane to Swaziland under South Africa's Bantu Homelands Citizenship Act. They argued that the forced "homelands" policy violated international law.[44]

In 1985 Butcher made a motion on the resolution against apartheid before the ABA's House of Delegates.[45] As chair of the ABA's subcommittee on South Africa of the Section of Individual Rights and Responsibilities, Butcher was the ideal person to present the motion. It probably did not go unnoticed in the assembly that this historical motion was made by a Black woman law professor from Howard University. Butcher sought to persuade the ABA to adopt a position that made "an unequivocal, unambiguous statement opposing the evil of apartheid."[46] Although the House of Delegates adopted Butcher's motion, the ABA failed to give Butcher credit for her pivotal role when the vote was reported in its journal.[47]

CONCLUSION

Professor Goler Teal Butcher used law to advance human rights. As she fought her way through legal and political thickets, she was often underestimated by forces that were unable to stop her, or even to understand the complexity of her battle plan to help all the disadvantaged of the earth. Goler Butcher was better known in some African villages than in her own country. Curtis T. White, a Black lawyer and international traveler, reported that while he was in a restaurant during a trip to Africa, Butcher's name was mentioned. He recalled a person listening to the conversation enthusiastically asking, "Do you know Goler?" The person, though unaware of Goler's last name, knew of her good works.[48]

Butcher lived a full and rich life. She spared no time in idle or superficial activities. She proclaimed that she would push vigorously her human rights agenda "until I die."[49] She fulfilled this promise. She helped expose the plight of women of all races and classes, particularly in the United States and in Africa.

Butcher lived to witness great changes in the development of Africa, to see the product of her work and activism at AID blossom, and to participate in almost every major effort to free South Africa. Butcher lived to see Andrew Young and Donald F. McHenry represent the United States, as "successive black envoys," at the United Nations. She lived to see the divestiture movement and the fight that led to the passage of the Comprehensive Anti-Apartheid Act of 1986, which imposed economic sanctions against South Africa.[50] Butcher lived to see Clarence Clyde Ferguson, Jr., elected as the first Black president of the American Society of International Law in 1978, its seventy-second year.[51] In 1988 she was elected vice president of the same group, and later served as honorary Vice President until her death. In addition, she saw the Reverend Leon Sullivan abandon the Sullivan Principles, and Edward J. Perkins become the first Black U.S. Ambassador to South Africa.

During Butcher's lifetime, Congressman William H. Gray III, other members of the Congressional Black Caucus, and other Black Americans met in Abidjan and Libreville at economic summits to increase aid and to formulate an agenda in Africa.[52]

President Clinton appointed Clifton R. Wharton, Jr., the first Black American U.S. Deputy Secretary of State, the number two post at the Department of State, and Conrad K. Harper the first Black American Legal Adviser of the Department of State.

Butcher also saw the construction of buildings to house Africare, TransAfrica, and the Arthur R. Ashe Jr. Foreign Policy Library at TransAfrica. Butcher saw the release of Nelson Mandela from prison and the lifting of a thirty-year ban on anti-apartheid groups by the South African government.

Butcher worked hard in her quest to educate Howard law students, politicians, academicians, and the community about human rights and self-determination for southern Africa. She knew, as a report by the Joint Center for Political and Economic Studies revealed, that only "41 percent of the black Americans feel any really close connection to Africa. And 54 percent disagreed with the statement: 'Black Americans have more in common with Africans than they have in common with white Americans.'"[53]

Nonetheless, Butcher's unswerving faith was not bent or swayed by contrary opinions or bleak circumstances. She continued to work to achieve the principles in which she believed: economic development, human rights, and government policy to implement human rights in Africa. Goler Butcher loved Africa. Her determined efforts to assure that the majority of people in South Africa would one day be empowered by law to rule was realized within a year after her death. On April 27, 1994, the first all-races election was held and Nelson Mandela became the first democratically elected president of the republic.

In the words of Simon Rifkind,

> [M]orals have exerted a spell upon individuals enjoying a special grace, a more acute sensitivity. . . . It is these special individuals who have reached for norms of conduct more elevated than those that prevailed in the market place; they have acted beyond the call of duty. . . . The example of their rise has marked human progress in the scale of moral improvement.[54]

Goler Teal Butcher is the epitome of such a person endowed with "a special grace." In her invaluable work to further human rights in Africa, she placed an indelible mark on America's foreign policy. In so doing, she faithfully lived up to Dean George Marion Johnson's charge to graduates of Howard's law school to be the "core of the nation's civil rights specialists."[55] Butcher, in her usual fashion, exceeded Johnson's charge, and left the world with one of her own: that graduates of Howard University School of Law and lawyers across the world be the core of the world's human rights specialists. To further advance her dream, this chapter documents the critical foreign policy of Goler Teal Butcher.

NOTES

1. 1987 Am. Soc'y Int'l L. Proc. 517, 532 (remarks of Professors Henry J. Richardson III and Goler Teal Butcher).

2. Richard Pearson, *Goler Butcher Dies: Lawyer and Professor*, Wash. Post, June 13, 1993, at B5.

3. Diggs v. Civil Aeronautics Bd., 516 F.2d 1248 (D.C. Cir. 1975).

4. *Id.* at 1249.

5. U.S. Policy toward Southern Africa: Hearings before the Subcomm. on African Affairs of the Senate Comm. on Foreign Relations, 94th Cong., 1st Sess. 259, 262 (1975).

6. *Id.* at 263.

7. Faces of Africa: Diversity and Progress; Repression and Struggle, Report of the House Comm. on Foreign Affairs, Pursuant to H. Res. 109, 92d Cong., 2d Sess. 231, 265 (1972).

8. *Id.* at 266.

9. Walter Isaacson, Kissinger 687 (1992). NSSM 39 was prepared by Roger Morris. *Id.* at 686.

10. Colin Legum, *The End of Cloud-Cuckoo-Land*, N.Y. Times, Mar. 28, 1976, sec. 6 at 19, 52. *See* Jennifer S. Whitaker, *Introduction: Africa and U.S. Interests, in* Africa and the United States Vital Interests 1, 2–3 (Jennifer S. Whitaker ed., 1978).

11. Henry Kissinger, *United States Policy on Southern Africa*, 74 Dep't St. Bull. 672 (1976).

12. Don Oberdorfer, *Mondale to Warn South Africa: U.S. Sterner on Apartheid*, Wash. Post, May 14, 1977, at A1, A9.

13. Resources in Rhodesia: Implications for U.S. Policy: Hearings before the House Subcomm. on International Resources, Food, and Energy of the Comm. on International Relations, 94th Cong., 2d Sess. 62 (1976) (statement of Goler T. Butcher).

14. Namibia, the United Nations, and U.S. Policy: Hearings before the Subcomm. on International Organizations of the House Comm. on International Relations, 94th Cong., 2d Sess. 57 (1976) (statement of Goler T. Butcher).

15. *Id.* at 58.

16. *Id.* at 65.

17. *Id.*

18. Diggs v. Richardson, 555 F.2d 848, 849 (D.C. Cir. 1976).

19. Inaugural Address of President Jimmy Carter, Pub. Papers 1, 8 (Jan. 24, 1977).

20. *Id.* at 2.

21. United States Foreign Policy, Pub. Papers 4, 5 (Jan. 20, 1977).

22. Cyrus Vance, Hard Choices: Critical Years in America's Foreign Policy 23 (1983).

23. *Id.* at 27.

24. The Sullivan Principles, issued on March 1, 1977, were a six-point program of fair employment practices to be adopted by U.S. companies doing business in South Africa. Morton Mintz, *Activist Minister Took Bold Step at GM Annual Meeting in 1971*, Wash. Post, June 3, 1987, at G1. On September 9, 1985, President Reagan issued an executive order codifying the Sullivan Principles. Exec. Order No. 12,532, 50 Fed. Reg. 36,861 (1985). But six years later Sullivan abandoned these principles. John D. Batterby, *South Africa Reacts Angrily to Sullivan Call*, N.Y. Times, June 4, 1987, at D6; *Without Sullivan*, Wash. Post, June 5, 1987, at A26; *Tutu in Accord with Sullivan on S. African Withdrawal*, Chicago Defender, June 6, 1987, at 4.

25. Toward a More Responsive AID Policy for Africa: Hearing before the Subcomm. on Africa of the House Comm. on International Relations, 95th Cong., 1st Sess. 3 (1977) [hereinafter Responsive AID Policy].

26. *Id.* at 2.

27. Rupert Emerson, *American Policy in Africa*, 40 Foreign Aff. 303 (1962).

28. Responsive AID Policy, *supra* note 25, at 2.

29. *Id.* at 3.

30. Foreign Assistance Legislation for Fiscal Year 1979: Hearings before the Subcomm. on Africa of the House Comm. on International Relations, 95th Cong., 2d Sess. 2 (1978).

31. *Id.* at 4–5.

32. Foreign Assistance and Related Agencies Appropriations for 1979 Part 2: Hearings before a Subcomm. of the House Comm. on Appropriations, 95th Cong., 2d Sess. 304 (1978).

33. *Id.* at 306.

34. *Id.* at 306–07.

35. *Id.* at 344 (regarding population planning); *see also* Foreign Assistance and Related Programs Appropriations for Fiscal Year 1979: Hearings on H.R. 12931 before the Subcomm. of the Senate Comm. on Appropriations, 95th Cong., 2d Sess. 632 (1978). *Id.* at 573 (regarding disease control).

36. Foreign Assistance and Related Programs Appropriations for Fiscal Year 1980, First Sess. on H.R. 4473; Hearings before a Subcomm. of the Senate Comm. on Appropriations, 96th Cong., 1st Sess. 375, 376 (1980).

37. *Id.* at 376.

38. John M. Goshko, *After 7 Years, Africa Expert's Goal Is Near*, Wash. Post, Aug. 11, 1988, at A24.

39. Her testimony was published in the *Howard Law Journal*. Goler T. Butcher, Testimony before the House Foreign Subcommittee on Africa and International Economic Policy and Trade U.S. House of Representatives (Feb. 9, 1982), in 26 How. L.J. 153, 158 (1983).

40. *Id.* at 169.

41. Goler T. Butcher, *The Immediacy of International Law for Howard University Students*, 31 How. L.J. 435, 441 (1988).

42. Southern Africa Project, 1984 Annual Report South Africa 1984: Renewed Resistance, Increased Repression 39–40 (1984).

43. Ed Bruske, *ABA on "Homelands,"* Wash. Post, Dec. 17, 1984, at B2; Fred Strasser, *South Africa Proposal Is Dropped*, Nat'l L.J., Dec. 24, 1984, at 4.

44. Amicus Brief of the Lawyers' Committee for Civil Rights under Law, in re The Cession of Kangwane to Swaziland 3, 42 (1984) (on file with the Lawyers' Committee for Civil Rights under Law).

45. *See* Goler T. Butcher, *The Resolution of the American Bar Association against Apartheid*, 28 How. L.J. 649 (1985).

46. *Id.* at 651.

47. Faye A. Silas, *Anti-Apartheid: House Condemns Policy*, A.B.A. J., Apr. 1985, at 35.

48. Interview with Curtis T. White, former consultant to World Administrative Radio Conference, in Washington, D.C. (May 20, 1993). *See* Curtis T. White, *Uprooting the Squatters*, 9 Foreign Pol'y 148 (1979).

49. *Professor Goler Teal Butcher Receives Whitney North Seymour Award*, 2 Res Ipsa 1992, 2.

50. Comprehensive Anti-Apartheid Act of 1986, Pub. L. No. 99–440, 100 Stat. 1086.

51. *Ex-Howard Dean Named Law Society President*, Wash. Post, Apr. 29, 1978, at C4.

52. Neil Henry, *Meeting of Africans, U.S. Blacks Ends with Vow to Boost Aid, Ease Debt*, Wash. Post, Apr. 20, 1991, at A18; Keith B. Richburg, *Americans Bring an Agenda Out of Africa*, Wash. Post, May 30, 1993, at A39; *Afro-American Summit*, 30 Afr. Res. Bull. 11263

(1993); Jehron X. Hunter, *African Summit Ends with Agenda for Unity*, Crisis, Aug.–Sept. 1993, at 24.

53. Courtland Milloy, *A Fountain of All Things African*, Wash. Post, Sept. 15, 1993, at C1.

54. Simon H. Rifkind, *The Law as a Moral Force*, 4 How. L.J. 1, 7–8 (1958).

55. George M. Johnson, *The Law School*, 1 How. L.J. 86 (1955).

13 Founding Mothers and Contemporary Latin American Constitutions

Colombian Women, Constitution Making, and the New Constitutional Court

Martha I. Morgan with the collaboration of Mónica María Alzate Buitrago

INTRODUCTION

As women and other marginalized groups demand to have their voices heard in contemporary constitution making, they are changing traditional conceptions of "founding fathers" as well as of constitutions and the role they can play in the struggle for social change. In Latin America as elsewhere, an enormous gap still exists between formal guarantees of equality and other fundamental human rights and the harsh realities of women's daily lives. Seeking to close this gap between "law in the books" and "law in the streets," women's rights activists in Colombia have begun using their new charter to take *machismo* to court on a variety of charges.

This chapter continues the examination of founding mothers in contemporary Latin American constitution making begun in our article "Founding Mothers: Women's Voices and Stories in the 1987 Nicaraguan Constitution."[1] It focuses on the adoption of the 1991 Colombian Constitution and the early gender jurisprudence of the new Constitutional Court it created as a setting for examining questions about how, if at all, women's interests can be advanced through constitution making and how, if at all, formal constitutional guarantees can become more than "just words" in the struggle against *machismo* and other forms of oppression.[2] Written from a belief that feminists and other progressives in the United States have much to learn from Latin American women and their struggles, it combines portions of two earlier articles that treat these issues in much greater detail.[3]

204

I. COLOMBIAN WOMEN AND CONSTITUTION MAKING

Given the conservative attitudes that prevailed in the decades following independence in 1819 and the lack of feminist consciousness among women, Colombian women did not make real gains in their political and legal status until the twentieth century. Women were granted legal capacity to administer their property in 1932,[4] rights of access to higher education in 1933, and the right to hold nonelected public offices in 1936.[5] Women finally obtained the right to vote in 1954, during the country's only military dictatorship (1953–57).[6] Although women constitute approximately half of Colombia's voters and participate actively in political parties, few women have held elected offices. Colombian women's groups faced the recent constitutional process ill-prepared to play strong leading roles as "founding mothers."

As if lifting a page from the novel by Gabriel García Márquez, Colombians wrote their 1991 charter during a time of *cólera*[7]—both literally and figuratively.[8] Understanding the violence of Colombian society is crucial both to comprehending how, after more than one hundred years, Colombians came to frame a new constitution, and to recognizing the hurdles women faced in trying to influence its drafting. Amid the well-publicized exploits of drug traffickers and still-armed left- and right-wing guerrilla forces, seasoned politicians from the traditional liberal and conservative parties and new factions of these parties sat down with former guerrillas, indigenous leaders, and evangelicals in a desperate attempt to solve the problems facing this complex and contradictory country through dialogue rather than violence. The Constitutional Assembly was unlike anything Colombia had ever known; voices never before present were being heard in the seats of power.

Despite its diversity, the body was not fully representative of Colombian society. Latin America's third largest country, Colombia has a population of approximately thirty million people, of whom nearly 70 percent now live in urban areas. According to the Colombia Information Service, 60 percent of the population are *mestizos* (mixed Spanish and indigenous), 20 percent are Euro-American, 14 percent are mulattos, 4 percent are Afro-American, and 2 percent are indigenous peoples.[9] Although indigenous people elected two of their representatives to the Assembly, an organization representing the Black population of Colombia failed to elect any of its list of candidates.[10] Most strikingly underrepresented were women of any color—only four of the seventy-four members of the Assembly were women. Helena Herrán, the ex-governor of the province of Antioquia, was one of the Liberals elected to the Assembly. Aída Abella, a leader of the Central Workers Union, was one of the two representatives of the leftist Patriotic Union to win election. Two women were from the Alianza Democrática M-19 (AD M-19) list: María Teresa Garcés, a lawyer and magistrate on the Administrative Tribunal, and María Mercedes Carranza, a poet and journalist.

Outside the Assembly, women joined with other groups and sectors in heeding President Gaviria's invitation (which explicitly included "feminist and women's organizations") to present their proposals for constitutional reform before *mesas de trabajo* (literally, worktables) organized by region and sector. The Constitutional

Assembly received over 1,500 proposals through this process. The proposals of the Bogotá women's *mesa de trabajo* covered a wide range of topics including equality, right to life, protection of maternity, family, labor, social security, and education.

The Constitutional Assembly convened on February 5, 1991, to begin its five-month task. From February until the end of April, members met in five commissions that reviewed the draft reforms and prepared draft articles in their assigned subject areas to be submitted to plenary debate.

Many women were still lamenting their poor showing in the assembly elections while the Assembly members were at work in the commissions and subcommittees. After watching the process from outside and realizing that time was short, a group of women in Cali decided that organization was required if women hoped to influence the outcome of the Assembly's upcoming plenary sessions.

On May 4, women from seven cities responded to the call from Cali. They met there and formed a national pressure group, the Women and the Constituent Assembly National Network. The Network quickly grew to include over seventy organizations from various regions of the country. In addition to taking part in the Network's activities, women participated in other organizations attempting to influence the Assembly. These included the National Association of Indigenous and Campesina Women (ANMUCIC), organizations representing Colombia's Black population, and the "Viva la Ciudadanía" Campaign—a broad coalition of organizations supporting progressive constitutional reforms.

In interviews during the Constitutional Assembly, lobbyists for ANMUCIC and women from the national Black community revealed that while they shared many grievances with women from other organizations, their emphases differed. Indigenous and campesina women were particularly concerned about health, education, and employment issues.[11] The lives of rural women (who comprise 30.4 percent of the country's female population) differ dramatically from those of urban women.[12] The birthrate for Colombian women in rural areas still averages 4.7 children. They work between sixteen and eighteen hours a day, yet the number of rural women working in salaried positions decreased from 38 percent in 1978 to 28 percent in 1980. Succumbing to parental pressure, 61.73 percent leave school to help in agricultural work; 35 percent of campesina mothers are illiterate.[13] Black Colombian women face additional difficulties. Mercedes Moya Morena, a community leader from the cholera-plagued region of Chocó, contends that it is no coincidence that the regions populated by Black Colombians are the most underdeveloped regions of the country and emphasizes that Black women face exploitation based on class, gender, and race.[14]

Having debated over six hundred draft articles amid active lobbying from many sides, the assembly approved the new Constitution on July 4, 1991, and it took effect at midnight. With 380 articles, the new Colombian Constitution was one of the longest in the world. Among these articles, as will be seen, are provisions responding to many of the gender-related issues raised by Colombian women's organizations, providing the basis for subsequent legal challenges to a wide array of discriminatory and unfair laws and practices.

II. RIGHTS AND REMEDIES

A. THE CONSTITUTION'S SUBSTANTIVE GENDER-RELATED GUARANTEES

As a result of the efforts of women's organizations and the parallel efforts of supportive men and women in the Constitutional Assembly, the constitution contains several formal guarantees related to women's rights. First, in stark contrast to the 1886 Constitution it replaced, the 1991 Constitution expressly reflects both the Convention on the Elimination of All Forms of Discrimination against Women (CEDAW) prohibition on discrimination against women and its approval of special positive measures as a means of assuring substantive rather than merely formal equality. Article 13 of the new constitution incorporates these twin principles of equality:

> All persons are born free and equal before the law, will receive the same protection and treatment from the authorities, and will enjoy the same rights, liberties and opportunities without any discrimination for reasons of sex, race, national or family origin, language, religion, or political or philosophical opinion.
>
> The State will promote conditions so that equality will be real and effective and will adopt measures in favor of groups discriminated against or marginalized.
>
> The State will specially protect those persons who because of their economic, physical or mental condition find themselves in circumstances of manifest weakness and will punish abuses and mistreatment that are committed against them.

The new Constitutional Court's earliest decisions under Article 13 relied on principles of reasonableness and proportionality as employed in European law; more recently it has also employed a concept of levels of scrutiny, drawing on cases from both the European Court of Human Rights and the United States Supreme Court. Unlike the U.S. Supreme Court, however, the Colombian Court has applied "strict scrutiny" to laws discriminating based on "suspect categories" such as sex (and, more recently, sexual orientation) as well as when fundamental rights are infringed on.[15]

In addition to Article 13's general equality guarantee, Article 40 provides that "the authorities will guarantee the adequate and effective participation of women in the decision-making levels of Public Administration." Article 42 states that "family relations are based in the equality of rights and duties of couples and in reciprocal respect among all its members," and Article 43 declares, "Women and men have equal rights and opportunities. Women cannot be subjected to any type of discrimination." Finally, Article 53 includes equality of opportunity and special protection for women, maternity, and minors among the fundamental principles to be considered by Congress in enacting a labor law.

One of the most controversial features of the new constitution was its extension of civil divorce to religious marriages. According to Article 42, "The civil effects of all marriages will be terminated by divorce according to the civil law." Article 42 also recognizes that a family can be formed by "natural or judicial bonds, by the free decision of a man and a woman to contract marriage or by the responsible will to form it," and, as mentioned above, guarantees equality of rights among couples. It further provides that "Any form of violence within the family is considered destructive of its harmony and unity, and will be punished according to the law."

Although Article 42 also recognizes the right of couples "to freely and responsibly decide the number of their children," the Constitutional Assembly rejected demands of women's groups that free choice about motherhood, including the right to legalized abortion, be explicitly guaranteed. On the other hand, Article 43 guarantees special state assistance and protection to women during pregnancy and after birth, including "support benefits from it if they then become unemployed or abandoned." It further provides that the "State will provide help in a special manner to women heads of family." And, as mentioned above, protection for maternity is also among the fundamental principles that Article 53 directs lawmakers to consider in enacting a labor law.

Other articles that women have used in their legal attacks include Article 11's right to life; Article 15's guarantee to all persons of the "right to personal and family privacy and to their good name"; Article 16's recognition that "all persons have the right to the free development of their personality without limitations except those imposed by the rights of others and the legal order"; Article 18's guarantee of freedom of conscience; Article 21's right to dignity; and Article 67's right to education. Also significant are Articles 93 and 94 regarding international human rights law and unenumerated human rights. Finally, Article 85 provides that many of the constitution's fundamental rights, including those in Article 13, are of immediate application.[16]

B. THE CONSTITUTIONAL COURT, THE *TUTELA,* AND OTHER CONSTITUTIONAL PROCEDURES FOR PROTECTING FUNDAMENTAL RIGHTS

Three features of the 1991 Colombian Constitution provide important judicial mechanisms for the protection of its newly recognized fundamental rights and liberties. Two of these are new: the creation of a separate Constitutional Court and the introduction of the *tutela.* The third feature, the public action of unconstitutionality, existed under prior law, but has taken on new significance with the creation of the Constitutional Court.

Article 4 of the Constitution recognizes the supremacy of the Constitution as law, providing that it is *"norma de normas"* and that "[i]n all cases of incompatibility between the Constitution and the law or other legal norm, the constitutional dispositions shall be applied." Article 241 entrusts the Constitutional Court with the "safeguarding of the integrity and supremacy of the Constitution." Members of the Court are selected by the Senate from lists of three candidates submitted by the President, the Supreme Court, and the Council of State.[17] After interim one-year appointments under the Constitution's transitional provisions, judges serve eight year terms and are limited to a single term. The Court is currently composed of nine judges, or *magistrados*; all are males.

Colombia's *tutela* allows any person to seek immediate judicial protection of their fundamental constitutional rights. Article 86 provides that the action may be filed with any judge and must be ruled on within ten days. Although orders granting *tutelas* may be appealed and are subject to discretionary review by the Constitutional Court, they must be complied with within forty-eight hours of the initial order granting protection. Colombia's new writ of protection for fundamental rights was initially inspired by the Mexican *amparo*, an action that somewhat resembles but is broader than the writ of habeas corpus.[18] But as adopted by the 1991 Constitutional Assembly, after a study of various countries' mechanisms for protecting fundamental rights, the *tutela* is an entirely Colombian innovation.[19] Apart from its immediacy (requiring initial resolution within ten days), the most surprising aspect of the *tutela* to one accustomed to the U.S. legal system may be its broad availability against private entities and individuals. Following selection of the *tutelas* for review, the Constitutional Court generally sits in panels of three judges to hear and rule on them.

Another important procedure for protecting constitutional rights is Article 40(6)'s public action of unconstitutionality. Any citizen, regardless of whether they have any personal injury or stake in the controversy, can bring this action. One of the functions Article 241 entrusts to the Constitutional Court is "to decide on petitions of unconstitutionality that citizens present against laws, both for their substantive content and for procedural errors in their formation."

III. THE EMERGING GENDER JURISPRUDENCE

A. DOMESTIC VIOLENCE

In a society characterized by violence, one of the first uses of *tutelas* by Colombian women was to seek protection against violence in their homes. Women quickly began using *tutelas* to obtain orders against physical or psychological abuse by husbands or companions. As previously noted, *tutelas* can be filed not only against public authorities (and against private entities that provide public services or that seriously and directly affect the common interest), but also against private persons with respect to whom the petitioner is in a position of subordination or vulnerability. The Constitutional Court has recognized that physical or psychological violence against women violates their fundamental rights to personal integrity, health, and life. And while the relief is an order directing or prohibiting certain actions, fines and jail sentences may be imposed for noncompliance with such orders. Thus, husbands could be sent to jail for continuing to abuse their wives after being ordered to stop.

Until 1996, Colombia had no legislation specifically addressing domestic abuse. In July 1996, acting to comply with Article 42's direction that "[a]ll forms of violence in the family shall be considered destructive of its harmony and unity and shall be sanctioned according to the law," Congress enacted domestic violence legislation.[20] While Jacquin de Samper, wife of then President Samper, blamed the new law with contributing more to the disintegration of the family than to family unity and led a campaign to reform the law to make it less punitive and more rehabilitative, others believed the new law was too lenient.[21] Gloria Guzmán Duque brought a public action of unconstitutionality against the new legislation's Article 22 (Intrafamilial Violence) and Article 25 (Sexual Violence Between Spouses). Her complaint alleged that these articles violated Articles 42 and 44 (rights of children) of the constitution because of their lenient treatment of family violence.

On June 5, 1997, the Constitutional Court rejected the challenges to Article 22, which established a penalty of one to two years in prison for physical, psychological, or sexual abuse of any member of the nuclear family. In an opinion by Judge Carlos Gaviria Díaz, the court ruled that this provision was constitutional because it created a separate new offense and did not preclude application of the more severe punishment prescribed for other offenses if their elements are established.[22] Article 25, however, which treated marital rape as punishable by six months to two years imprisonment as opposed to sentences of up to eight years otherwise applicable to rape charges, was declared unconstitutional. The opinion concluded that providing more lenient penalties for rape against a spouse, cohabitant, or person with whom one had conceived a child violates Article 13's right to equality. Assigning different sanctions to the same act without legitimate reasons violated the principle of proportionality deducible from Article 13.

Judge Eduardo Cifuentes Muñoz has pointed to the intrafamilial violence law as an example of positive interaction between the Constitutional Court and Congress. He characterized the new law as a response to the Court's *tutela* jurisprudence involving domestic abuse. And, following the adoption of the law, the Court has ruled that it will no longer grant relief on such *tutelas* because there now is an alternative available judicial procedure that affords immediate protection for domestic violence victims.[23] Many lower courts have reacted negatively to the new law, however, and proposals have been made to "dejudicialize" domestic violence.[24]

B. SEXUAL AND REPRODUCTIVE RIGHTS

1. Pregnancy Rights

Colombian women also have used *tutelas* to raise issues of reproductive freedom related to pregnancy. For example, teenage mothers brought some of the first *tutelas*, successfully obtaining orders regaining admission to high schools after becoming pregnant.[25] The Court based its rulings in these cases on the new constitution's protections against discrimination and its protection of human dignity and the free development of personality, as well as its declaration of a right to education and its special protection of pregnant women.

Despite numerous rulings in favor of pregnant teenagers and teenage mothers, they continue to confront negative cultural attitudes in schools. On September 21, 1998, the Court granted a *tutela* on behalf of pregnant students and students in *uniones de hecho*, or de facto marriages, who were forced to wear red aprons or pinafores.[26] The Court ruled that the school's practices violated rights of the family as the basic institution of society, to equal protection, and to the free development of one's personality.

In the employment context, the Court has afforded protection to pregnant workers by recognizing a concept of *fuero de maternidad* (analogous to the long-standing concept of *fuero syndical* that protects the job security of union activists) to protect against loss of employment for reasons of pregnancy.[27] For example, in September 1997 the Court affirmed that women workers cannot be dismissed from their jobs without cause during pregnancy or within the first three months after giving birth and that employers who unlawfully terminate an employee during these periods are obligated to pay the employee sixty days' salary as provided in Article 239 of the labor code and to reinstate all employment rights. Judge Alejandro Martínez Caballero's opinion relied on Articles 13 and 43 and on Article 53's recognition of special protection for women, maternity, and minor workers as fundamental principles that must be taken into account in labor legislation, and supplemented Article 239 with a judicial gloss to deny all effect to such unlawful terminations of employment.[28]

In announcing the Court's decision, *El Tiempo* noted that, in Bogotá alone, an average of four women workers a day are fired from their jobs because they are pregnant. A leader of one women's rights organization, Olga Amparo Sánchez Gómez, Director of Equality for Women, praised the Court's opinion, telling the press that "To have a child should not be an obstacle to working. These barriers must begin to be torn down, because in Colombia to be a mother seems a punishment."[29]

2. Abortion

Not surprisingly in this overwhelmingly Catholic country, the other side of the coin in terms of reproductive freedom has met with less success in the Constitutional Court. In 1994 a majority of the Constitutional Court rejected a direct constitutional challenge to the country's strict criminal abortion law.[30] Article 343 of the penal code provides, "A woman who causes her abortion or permits another to cause it, will incur imprisonment for from one (1) to three (3) years." It recognizes no exceptions for therapeutic abortions. Over objections of three dissenting judges, the Court upheld the law as a protection of the right to life.[31] Judge Antonio Barrera Carbonell wrote the Court's opinion rejecting arguments that Article 343 violated the constitution's recognition of a couple's right to decide their number of children or constitutional guarantees of women's rights to equal protection, to personal and family privacy, and to the free development of their personality. In closing, the majority did suggest a role for the legislature in resolving possible conflicting rights of women and the unborn.[32]

On January 23, 1997, a day after the twenty-fourth anniversary of *Roe v. Wade*, the Colombian Constitutional Court again addressed the abortion issue. The case was an action of unconstitutionality filed by José Euripides Parra challenging the provisions of the penal code that provide criminal penalties for abortions in cases of pregnancies resulting from rape or involuntary insemination.[33] Article 345 of the penal code provides that "A woman pregnant as a result of violent or abusive carnal access or nonconsensual artificial insemination who causes her own abortion or permits another to cause it, will incur *arresto* of from four (4) months to one (1) year." The Court rejected the challenger's demand that it invalidate the code's recognition of "lesser" penalties in these cases and instead establish as uniformly applicable the even harsher penalties provided for other abortions. The majority upheld the legislative judgment about the appropriate severity of the penalty for abortions in such "attenuating circumstances." But the five justices joining the main opinion once again expressed their views about abortion as an attack on human life which they saw as beginning with conception. Their opinion included parts of papal encyclicals by Pope Paul VI and Pope John Paul II.

Four justices wrote separate opinions expressing their differing views on this matter. Judge Jorge Arango Mejía objected to the use of the papal encyclicals and made it clear that he believed that Congress could decriminalize abortion without running afoul of the new constitution. Three judges went further, writing a joint opinion dissenting from the majority's handling of the matter altogether. Judges Eduardo Cifuentes Muñoz, Carlos Gaviria Díaz, and Alejandro Martínez Cabellero rejected arguments that this was a matter for determination by the legislative processes. These three judges argued that it violated the constitution to impose criminal penalties on abortions by women who are pregnant because of rape or involuntary artificial insemination. They accused the judges in the majority of imposing their own moral and religious prejudices.

Today abortions are eight times more frequent than ten years ago. The latest studies show that in Colombia one in three women who have been pregnant has had an abortion. Twenty-six of every hundred women attending the country's universities have had an abortion. Of every one hundred women who have abortions, twenty-nine suffer complications, eighteen of which are very serious.[34] Despite these alarming statistics, on December 15, 1998, the Colombian Congress rejected a proposal to depenalize abortion in certain instances, including cases of rape.

C. DIVERSE FAMILY STRUCTURES

Several of the Constitutional Court's decisions have dealt with the constitution's recognition of Colombia's diverse family structures. As a result of factors such as war and other violence, poverty, and high rates of teenage pregnancy, over 25 percent of families are headed by single women. Women become heads of families less because of changes in roles in the family than because of changes in the status of men.[35] In addition, according to a study completed in July 1998 by the National Administrative Statistics Department, the number of Colombian families living in *uniones libres* or *uniones de hecho* has increased from 10 percent in 1983 to 35 percent in 1998.[36] The study also revealed an increase in the number of widows, corresponding to an increase in deaths, especially of men between twenty and forty-four years old, as a result of the intensification of the violence.

In an early case dealing with *uniones de hecho,* the Court protected the property rights of a woman upon the death of her companion in a de facto union.[37] It ruled that disregarding the value of the woman's domestic work in acquiring and improving the home where the couple had lived in favor of inheritance rights of the man's sister and only heir violated the companion's rights of equality and due process.[38]

The Court has also relied upon Article 42's recognition that the family can be formed by legal or natural bonds and its guarantee of equal rights and duties for all children whether born within marriage or not to invalidate numerous provisions of the Civil Code that discriminated against children born outside marriage.[39]

D. POSITIVE DISCRIMINATION

Article 13 textually enshrines the concept of positive discrimination or affirmative action. The Constitutional Court has taken seriously Article 13's requirement that "[t]he state will promote conditions so that equality is real and effective and shall adopt measures in favor of groups discriminated against or marginalized." In the realm of gender classifications, however, some of the Court's decisions have been criticized as perpetuating stereotypical views of women as economically dependent.[40] For example, in late 1992 the Court invoked both the positive and negative aspects of Article 13's concept of equality in a challenge to a law granting single (*célibes*, celibate or never married) daughters of military officials special social welfare rights.[41] In an opinion by Judge José Gregorio Hernández Galindo, the Court upheld the positive discrimination in favor of daughters over sons as a measure to make the principle of equality "real and effective," given the frequent economic dependency on men in Colombian society. On the other hand, it ruled that the discrimination between single and married daughters violated Article 13's protection against discrimination and the guarantee of the free development of one's personality, reasoning that "every person, in the exercise of their liberty, must be able to choose without coercion and in a manner free of stimulation established by the legislator, between contracting marriage or remaining single." Accordingly, the law was held valid except for the terms *"célibes"* and "remains in a state of celibacy," which were held unenforceable.

In the context of women's employment-related rights, the Court invoked this principle of "positive discrimination" or affirmative action in rejecting a challenge to differential retirement ages of fifty-five for women and sixty for men.[42] The Court requested and considered statistical evidence and opinions by social scientists before concluding that this positive discrimination in regard to pension rights was a rational, reasonable, and proportional measure designed to compensate for women's continuing inferior position in the labor force and for the physical and mental burdens placed on them because of their double workload as members of the paid labor force and as those responsible for the society's unpaid domestic work.

IV. COLOMBIAN PERSPECTIVES ON THE COURT'S GENDER JURISPRUDENCE

One of the limitations of comparative legal scholarship is the difficulty involved in attempting to assess the cultural impact of legal decisions from a distance and as an outsider. And it is far too early to fully assess how effective the new Colombian Constitutional Court will be in its mission, as described by Judge Gaviria, "to make sure that people's fundamental rights do not just stay on paper."[43] However, based on the available evidence from the media and my interviews, it appears that many Colombians' evaluations of the Constitutional Court's evolving gender jurisprudence, while mixed, are positive overall.

Socorro Ramírez, a Colombian feminist author and historian who has closely followed the development of women's rights under the new constitution, notes how widely women have resorted to the courts to protect their rights under the new constitution. Ramírez acknowledges that the Court's decisions in cases that have to do with women "on many occasions, have signified substantial advances. . . . There is, however, one matter, that of reproductive and sexual rights, where the majority of the judges and the Court have advanced only to a certain point."[44]

Judge Cifuentes also had mixed views on the Court's early work in the gender arena. Although his general view of the role of the Constitutional Court in protecting the rights of women and minorities was positive, he pointed to the absence of women on the Constitutional Court and their low numbers in other important positions as evidence of the persistence of *machismo* and intolerance.[45]

In a work in progress, Isabel Cristina Jaramillo, a professor of judicial theory at the Universidad de los Andes, chronicles and critiques the Court's jurisprudence on women. She examines a sample of 123 decisions—105 *tutelas* and 18 actions of unconstitutionality. Of the *tutelas*, 58.1 percent were resolved favorably to the complainant (as opposed to only 43.3 percent of all *tutelas*), but the results varied among the nine *tutela* panels. Jaramillo notes the existence of two contrasting images of the woman; as capable, strong, and equal to the man in the public sphere, and as weak, economically dependent, loving, sacrificing, fully a mother in the private sphere. She also notes a parallel tension between concepts of protection of women, one based on paternalism and the other based on a recognition of women as autonomous subjects. In addition, the perception that women must be protected as members of a less favored social group contrasts with the perception that women must not be given undeserved privileges.[46]

A group of women who suffer multiple burdens in Colombia are Africo-Colombian women. Senator Piedad Córdoba, herself an Africo-Colombian, spoke of the intersectionality of gender, race, and class discrimination and the resistance of these strains of discrimination to cure through formal legal guarantees.

> [Racism] is unarguably another of the conditions that weigh upon women. It is another discrimination. Beyond being a woman, to be a Black woman, and if she is poor, then it is a triple discrimination, still greater. . . . And you don't end this with articles in the Constitution. That is to say, it is all a joint effort of the society, which has to come to value a person because she is a person. Not because [the person] is Black, white, yellow, or because one is a man or woman, or because one is of some other color. But this is a society that discriminates, that is undeniable. Also, it is true that Africo-Colombians live in the poorest regions of the country. And their visible presence in positions of decision or direction, no, it is very clear, it is very evident you do not even see it and unarguably there continues to be a very wide sector of the population that discriminates, still, on the basis of color.[47]

Drawing on her former experiences as a Colombian judge, Luz Nagle offered this assessment of the significance of the *tutela* on gender issues in Colombia:

> In a country where the justice system is greatly inefficient, the courts have been unreachable and have reinforced the disaffection, discrimination, and subjugation of women; the law is the exclusive possession of the wealthy, the elite, the judges and the lawyers; sexism, patriarchy, and *machismo* are the rule, the *tutela* is the only hope for transformation. *Tutelas* have become a quick and friendly way for women to redress their issues. The "regular" system is still impregnated with bias and the social stereotype that women ought to be submissive, "walk behind their man," supporting him without complaint. To reach a resolution through a lawsuit takes too long. Now, with the *tutela*, women are heard.[48]

She cautioned, however, that the "possibility of imminent transformation" requires more than *tutela* decisions. "It requires more aggressive and meaningful approaches by women, more women in high and influential positions and a real commitment from men."[49]

NOTES

1. Martha I. Morgan, *Founding Mothers: Women's Voices and Stories in the 1987 Nicaraguan Constitution,* B.U. L. Rev. 1–107 (1990).

2. *See* Joel Balkan, Just Words: Constitutional Rights and Social Wrongs (1997). *See also* Martha I. Morgan, *The Bitter and the Sweet: Feminist Efforts to Reform Nicaraguan Rape and Sodomy Laws,* 26 U. Miami Inter-Am. L. Rev. 439 (1995).

3. Martha I. Morgan, with the collaboration of Mónica María Alzate Buitrago, *Constitution-Making in a Time of Cholera: Women and the 1991 Colombian Constitution,* 4 Yale J. L. and Feminism 353–413 (1992); Martha I. Morgan, *Taking Machismo to Court: The Gender Jurisprudence of the Colombian Constitutional Court,* 30 U. Miami Inter-Am. L. Rev. 253 (1999). The latter article contains a much more extensive discussion of the Colombian

Constitutional Court's gender jurisprudence. Of particular importance, though regrettably beyond the scope of this work, its discussion of sexual autonomy issues details the Court's seemingly contradictory early treatment of sexual orientation issues, including its September 1998 decision regarding gay and lesbian teachers in which it announced that laws discriminating based on sexual orientation, like laws discriminating based on sex generally, must be subjected to "strict scrutiny." Sentencia No. C-481/98.

4. *See generally,* Edith E. Scott, *Married Women's Rights under the Matrimonial Regimes of Chile and Colombia: A Comparative History,* 7 Harv. Women's L.J. 221 (1984).

5. Consejería Presidencial para la Juventud, la Mujer y la Familia, Lineamientos hacia una política integral para la mujer Colombiana 5 (1991).

6. Diana Medrano and Christina Escobar, *Pasados y presente de las organizaciones femeninas en Colombia, in* Mujer y familia en Colombia 231, 236–38 (Elssy Bonella ed., 1985).

7. The title of our earlier article on the 1991 constitution was inspired by the Colombian Nobel Prize–winning author Gabriel García Márquez's novel *El amor en los tiempos del cólera* (1985), which has been translated into English under the title *Love in the Time of Cholera* (1988).

8. In early June 1991, Colombian President César Gaviria's liberal government was feverishly engaged on at least four fronts: first, in Caracas, Venezuela, talking with the largest of Colombia's remaining armed guerrilla movements about the conditions for their disarmament and reentry into the civilian political processes; second, in Medellín, Colombia, negotiating with the druglord Pablo Escobar over the conditions of his surrender and the size and accommodations of the prison being prepared for him; third, in Bogotá, Colombia, dealing with the Constitutional Assembly charged with reforming the country's 1886 charter, now working late into the evenings to write a new constitution before its July 4 deadline; and, finally, on Colombia's Pacific Coast, coping with the deadly cholera epidemic that attacked the largely Black population of Buenaventura and threatened to spread to other sections of the country.

9. Colombia Information Service, Colombia: Land of Contrasts 4 (1990).

10. Interview with Mercedes Moya Morena, National Coordinator of Black Communities, Bogotá, Colombia (May 25, 1991).

11. Interview with ANMUCIC leader Leonora Cantiña and other members of ANMUCIC, Bogotá, Colombia (June 3, 1991).

12. These statistics on rural women come from a study by the Colombian Ministry of Agriculture and the Inter-American Institute for Agricultural Cooperation and are reported in Edmer Tovar M., *Mujer campesina: Líder, padre y madre,* El Tiempo, June 2, 1991, at 6C, col. 1.

13. *Id.*

14. Interview with Mercedes Moya Morena, Bogotá, Colombia (June 1, 1991).

15. *See, e.g.,* Sentencia No. C-481/98 (strict scrutiny is applicable to a law treating homosexuality as a grounds of misconduct for teachers because if sexual orientation is biologically determined the law is equivalent to a sex classification and if sexual preference involves personal choice, the law infringes on the right to the free development of one's personality). *See generally* César A. Rodríguez, *El test de razonabilidad y el derecho a la igualdad, in* Observatorio de justicia constitucional: Balance jurisprudencial de 1996 (1998).

16. Const. Pol. Col. art. 85: "The rights established in articles 11, 12, 13, 14, 15, 16,

17, 18, 19, 20, 21, 23, 24, 26, 27, 28, 29, 30, 31, 33, 34, 37, and 40 are of immediate application."

17. Const. Pol. Col. art. 239.

18. Article 30 of the 1991 Colombian Constitution guarantees the right to invoke habeas corpus and requires that once invoked it must be complied with within thirty-six hours.

19. Interview with Manuel José Cepeda, dean of the School of Law at the Universidad de los Andes and constitutional adviser to President Gaviria during the adoption of the 1991 constitution, Bogotá, Colombia (Dec. 15, 1998).

20. Ley de Violencia Intrafamiliar, Ley 294/96.

21. *Menos punitiva y mas rehabilitadora*, 193 Mujer/Fempress, Nov. 1997, at 20.

22. Sentencia No. C-285/97.

23. Interview with Judge Eduardo Cifuentes Muñoz, Bogotá, Colombia (Dec. 11, 1998). *See, e.g.,* Sentencia No. T-420/96.

24. Interview with María Isabel Plata, executive director of Pro-Familia and María Cristina Calderón, director of Pro-Familia Legal Services, Bogotá, Colombia (Dec. 15, 1998).

25. *E.g.,* Sentencia No. T-420/92; Sentencia No. T-292/94.

26. Sentencia No. T-516/98. *See* Adriana Palacio Garcés, *Damaris ya no es la chica de rojo*, El Tiempo, Sept. 24, 1998.

27. Interview with Catalina Botero, Auxiliary Magistrate (Dec. 16, 1998).

28. Sentencia No. C-470/97.

29. *No a despido de embarazadas: Corte*, El Tiempo, Sept. 26, 1997.

30. Sentencia No. C-133/94.

31. *Id.*

32. *Id.* Judge Barrera emphasized this portion of the opinion when questioned about his decision in this case. Interview with Judge Antonio Barrera Carbonell, Bogotá, Colombia (Dec. 11, 1998).

33. Sentencia No. C-013/97. The court also rejected the action's challenge to Articles 347 and 348 of the penal code, which provide lesser penalties for abandoning, abusing, or killing a minor under such circumstances (provided the act occurs within eight days of the child's birth). Cód. Pen. arts. 347 and 348.

34. *Aborto: Otra "moda" en la U.*, El Tiempo, Oct. 9, 1998. *See generally* Mónica María Alzate, Free Motherhood in Colombia: Between the Catholic Church and the Law, (1993) (M.A. thesis in Women's Studies, University of Alabama).

35. *See ¿Por que llega a ser jefa de familia?* 205 Mujer/Fempress, Nov. 1998, at 14 (reporting on recent research by the organizations Enda América Latina y Vamos Mujer in Medellín, which also pointed out the gender bias in the current concept of head of family that focuses on who is the principal economic provider, whose last name is used, and who has decision-making power).

36. Socorro Ramírez, *Revolución silenciosa*, 205 Mujer/Fempress, Oct. 1998.

37. *See, e.g.,* Juan Lozano, *Extraña reforma*, El Tiempo, Sept. 28, 1998.

38. Sentencia No. T-494/92.

39. Sentencia No. C-105/94.

40. Cepeda interview, *supra* note 19.

41. Sentencia No. C-588/92.

42. Sentencia No. C-410/94.

43. Carlos Gaviria Díaz, Judge and former President of the Colombian Constitutional

Court, quoted in Juanita Darling, *Colombians Happy to Tell It to the Judge*, L.A. Times, Dec. 22, 1996, at A39.

44. Socorro Ramírez, *La tutela*, 187 Mujer/Fempress, May 1997, at 6.

45. Interview with Judge Eduardo Cifuentes Muñoz, Bogotá, Colombia (July 5, 1995).

46. Isabel Cristina Jaramillo S., *Crónica de la jurisprudencia de la Corte Constitucional Colombiana sobre las mujeres* (work in progress).

47. Interview with Senator Piedad Córdoba de Castro, Bogotá, Colombia (July 4, 1995). In an earlier interview with the *New York Times,* Senator Córdoba de Castro spoke of the difficulties posed by the low level of identification among Black and mixed-race people in Latin America. She acknowledged the lack of reliable statistics because countries do not openly categorize by race; she estimated that Blacks represented 21 percent of Colombia's thirty-five million people. Karen De Witt, *Black Unity Finds Voice in Colombia*, N.Y. Times, Apr. 18, 1995, at A5. In a recent poll, 83 percent of Colombians interviewed said that they were not racist, but 85 percent believed that there is racism in Colombia and 78 percent had witnessed racial discrimination. Francisco Celis Albán, *Racismo a flor de piel*, El Tiempo, Oct. 12, 1998. *See generally* Peter Wade, Blackness and Race Mixture: The Dynamics of Racial Identity in Colombia x (1993) ("The official image of Colombia is that of a racial democracy, and even, in the new Constitution of 1991, of an ethnically plural society, but beneath or rather parallel to and integrated with this image is a pervasive, apparently self-evident social order in which Colombia is a mestizo, or mixed blood, nation that is gradually erasing Blackness (and indianness) from its panorama.").

48. Statement by Professor Luz Estella Nagle, Nov. 25, 1998.

49. *Id.*

4 | Human Rights Confronts Culture, Custom, and Religion

14 Deconstructing Patriarchal Jurisprudence in Islamic Law

A Faithful Approach

Azizah Y. al-Hibri

INTRODUCTION

Islamic law is viewed by the West as patriarchal, oppressive, and incompatible with basic Western values such as democracy and human rights.[1] In particular, it is viewed as hopelessly oppressive to women.[2] This attitude is partly rooted in our ignorance of the history of Islamic societies, especially the early ones. It is also rooted in our ignorance of the flexibility of and rich diversity within Islamic jurisprudence. To complicate matters, we are barraged in the West by news reports about oppressive practices against women in Muslim countries. From these instances we hasten to conclude unjustifiably that Islamic law itself must be discarded if our suffering sisters are to find relief.

This chapter will show that this conclusion is both unwarranted and unworkable. Briefly, it is unwarranted because it attributes to Islamic law problems that arise as a result of patriarchal local customs and patriarchal judicial perspectives. We cannot simply make these problems disappear by blaming them on Islamic law itself. They are just as likely to arise under a secular legal regime, and must be confronted directly. The conclusion is also unworkable because most Muslim women are serious about their religion and prefer to solve their problems from within that framework. So long as Muslim women are led by patriarchy to believe that their oppression was divinely decreed, they will hesitate to change the status quo, as oppressive as it may be. Therefore, it is important to unmask the patriarchal assumptions lurking within present laws in Muslim countries, and to reveal them for what they are, neither divine nor condoned by the Divine.

Reprinted by permission from 12 *American University Journal of International Law and Policy* 1 (1997).

Additionally, attempts to encourage Muslims to discard their religion are viewed in Muslim countries with extreme suspicion. They seem to continue in a new guise the concerted efforts of Western colonialists to achieve similar results in the last century. Not only was colonialism instrumental in weakening Muslim societies, it also played a very important role in the West. As a result of the colonialist heritage, Western views of Islam have been based on the works of Orientalists and Neo-Orientalists who built whole careers on "interpreting" Islam to the West.[3] Some succeeded in their endeavor, but most were unable to escape their culturally and religiously biased perspectives. Their conclusions unavoidably reflected these perspectives and resulted in a highly negative and distorted view of Islam.

The typical Orientalist view of Muslim women pictures them as passive, oppressed, and confined to the seraglio.[4] This theme has been circulated in the United States for at least two hundred years.[5] It can be argued that its most recent formulation uses the language of international instruments and universal human values. A prime example was offered by the Fourth World Conference on Women, held in Beijing, China. There, the Platform for Action originally contained language inconsistent with Islamic *Shari'ah* (basic law).[6] When the discussion of that language reached the floor, Muslim delegates refused to accept it, stating repeatedly that they regarded the law of God as superior to the law of the United Nations.[7]

This, then, is the crux of the issue: Is Islamic law oppressive to women? Furthermore, if the West believes it is, should it accept the religious choices of Muslim women, or should it liberate them against their own will? Because of limitations of space, this chapter will address the first question only. The second question is quite important; a positive answer to it underlines further the patriarchal/patronizing attitude adopted by the West generally, and the feminist movement specifically, toward Muslim women. We now turn to a quick introduction to Islamic law.

ISLAMIC LAW AND CUSTOM

To understand Islamic law, we need to understand its basic principles and its relation to local custom. Islamic law is based on Islamic *shari'ah*, which in turn is based on the Qur'an, the revealed word of God. To the extent that Qur'anic verses may need further illumination, Islamic *shari'ah* is also informed by the *sunnah* (life, words, and example of the Prophet Muhammad). Both sources are supplemented by *ijtihad* (juristic interpretation of text) whenever necessary, and by other sources of Islamic jurisprudence, such as *ijma'* (consensus) of the Muslims. Today there are five major schools of *ijtihad*. They are the Hanafi, Hanbali, Maliki, Shafi'i, and Ja'fari schools. All these schools were established between the seventh and eighth centuries A.D.

Ijtihad is open to all qualified Muslims, whether male or female. The qualifications concern the knowledge of the *mujtahid* (one engaging in *ijtihad*) of the Qur'an, the *sunnah*, important commentaries, and other related works.[8] They also concern the *mujtahid's* piety and fairness.[9] Furthermore, since it is a basic jurisprudential principle that Islamic law must be suitable for the society in which it is promulgated, it follows that the *mujtahid* must be familiar with the conditions of his or her society.[10] This principle was reflected in the practice of major jurists, such as al-Shafi'i, who revised his old school of jurisprudence when he moved from Iraq to Egypt.[11] Most important, this recognition was derived from the Qur'anic verse encouraging diversity.[12] This encouragement led Muslim jurists to develop or adopt the Islamic jurisprudence most suitable to their societies and to supplement that with local custom, so long as that custom did not conflict with Islamic law.[13]

This positive attitude toward judicial diversity within Islam was reflected in the past by the fact that Muslim individuals could adopt the jurisprudence of their choice, with no interference from the state. More recently, this state of affairs was replaced by the Napoleonic approach of codification. As a result, most Muslim governments selected a school of Islamic jurisprudence for their own citizens, which they then modified and codified. Of particular significance, as we shall see later, was the codification of personal status codes (family law). This interference by government in the religious affairs of Muslims is relatively recent.[14] It denied Muslims the right to freedom of conscience and allowed the state to propagate oppressive local customs in the name of religion. It also silenced the Muslim woman's voice, since those involved in the codification efforts were men.

For this reason, a quick overview of the personal status codes of Muslim countries reveals a very patriarchal view of the family and male-female relations. For example, most of these codes make a male (usually the father) the *wali* (guardian) of the adult woman, require the wife to obey her husband, and complicate divorce laws in favor of the male. It is important to note that some major Muslim jurists of prior centuries chose more equitable approaches. Modern Muslim jurists, however, have avoided some of these approaches by introducing the principle of *takhayur* (selectivity).[15] This principle allowed a lawmaker to discard from a selected school of thought those views he disagreed with, and replace them with preferred views from other schools. Given that the officials doing the *takhayur* were male, it is not surprising that the resulting modern codes were in certain respects more patriarchal than the original older schools of thought.

For example, despite the fact that Morocco is a Maliki jurisdiction, it states explicitly in its code that taking care of the house is part of the legal duties of the wife.[16] Imam Malik, however, rejected the view that the marriage contract was a service contract.[17] He concluded that the woman was not obligated to perform housework.[18] In fact, some jurists argued that the husband had a duty to bring to the wife prepared food.[19] Other jurists responded by arguing that their local customs required otherwise.[20]

PERSONAL STATUS CODES IN MUSLIM COUNTRIES

Before evaluating the validity of a response that defends patriarchal laws by relying on local custom, I would like to present one illustration of the common features of

Muslim personal status codes in Egypt, Syria, Jordan, Morocco, Algeria, and Kuwait (the "Codes"): the duty of the wife to obey her husband. After introducing this topic, I shall discuss the jurisprudence that supports it.[21]

Egypt, Syria, and Jordan follow the Hanafi school of thought, while Morocco, Algeria, and Kuwait follow the Maliki school of thought. Nevertheless, each one of these Codes lists or implies a duty of obedience (*ta'ah*) by the wife.[22] The duty of *ta'ah* is very important because it includes the duty not to leave the home without the husband's permission, and because violating the duty of *ta'ah* (*nushuz*) has financial repercussions. The Codes, however, expressly recognize customary limits for *ta'ah*. For example, the wife may leave the home without her husband's consent for a "legitimate reason," such as for visiting her family, working, and safety.[23] Most Codes permit the husband to cease his maintenance of a *nashiz* (disobedient) wife.[24]

THE JURISPRUDENCE OF TA'AH

As elaborated by traditional jurists of the various major schools, the *Ta'ah* concept is perhaps the most degrading to Muslim women. It diminishes their fundamental liberties as human beings worthy of equal status under the law. *Ta'ah* enables the husband to prohibit the wife from leaving her home, unless she is willing to risk loss of financial support and, in some cases, divorce. While many Codes contain a few carve-outs that permit legitimate exceptions to this rule, it shocks the conscience to have the rule in the first place. One wonders what Khadijah, the successful businesswoman and wife of the Prophet, would say to those medieval jurists who confined wives to their homes and permitted their unauthorized exit only in cases of extreme necessity.[25]

This power to confine the wife in her home was called by some traditional jurists *ihtibas* and was viewed as the quid pro quo for her maintenance.[26] Under this point of view, the woman was allowed to visit and receive her family a limited number of times during the year without her husband's consent, although other jurists argued even against this modest carve-out.[27] This traditional jurisprudence is not obsolete. The reason is that, unless a specific provision of traditional jurisprudence is explicitly ruled out by the Code, it is considered legally part of that Code by incorporation. Furthermore, every reference in the Code to "custom" is a reference to an anachronistic patriarchal custom that found its way into the code.

The concept of *Ta'ah* as now presented in the Codes is a patriarchal hierarchical construct that, as I shall argue later, contradicts the fundamental Islamic concept of *tawhid* (the unity of God). In fact, a critique of the *Ta'ah* concept would be very similar to a critique of the concept of *ta'ah* as used in the political arena. The notion of *Ta'ah* to the ruler has also been rendered extremely hierarchical and oppressive. Strict forms of *Ta'ah* are due only to God, and not to a ruler or husband. Human-oriented *Ta'ah* is a much more modest concept based on a variety of requirements, such as those of *shura* (consultation) and genuine consent whether in the public or private sphere. Furthermore, it is symmetrical in that the ruler is also required to obey the will of the people and serve them just as much as the people are required to obey the ruler.[28] The people's limits of their obedience are defined by God (as is the ruler's). The nature of that obedience is one that is more akin to self-discipline, collective organization, and mutual responsibility and advice than to hierarchy, oppression, and violence. The same is true of *ta'ah* in marriage.

The *Ta'ah* requirement was claimed to be based on the Qur'an. Later, I will focus on one major argument (involving the concept of *qiwamah*) used to justify this requirement. I shall argue that the argument is based on a patriarchal reading of a Qur'anic *ayah* (verse). At this point, however, I would like to present another argument that throws further doubt on the *Ta'ah* requirement. Muslim jurists have always recognized the validity of including conditions in the marriage contract.[29] These conditions tend to be protective of the woman; some of them, such as the woman's right to divorce her husband at will or the right to refuse to move with him away from her town, clearly limit the husband's traditional right to *Ta'ah* in the family. Therefore, even in traditional jurisprudence, the husband's right to *ta'ah* can be negotiated away, thus revealing its social as opposed to divine origin. It is interesting in this regard to mention the marriage contract of the third marriage of Sukaynah, the granddaughter of the Prophet who was known for her piety and independence. Supposedly, it included conditions that would be defined by most of the Codes today as *nushuz*. For example, Sukaynah included in the contract the condition that her husband may not prohibit her from doing what she wanted.[30] She also required him not to contradict her wishes.[31] A third condition was that he may not touch another woman while married to her.[32] If such reports were accurate, then it would appear that Sukaynah transferred contractually to her husband (at least partially) the duty of obedience.

The Prophet's *sunnah* itself indicates a lack of commitment to a gender-biased division of labor and hence to *ihtibas*. His wife Khadijah was a prominent businesswoman. After her death, the Prophet married A'isha, who became a distinguished political and religious leader. Both women enjoyed full freedom of movement, a fact that at several points caused A'isha problems in her society. The Prophet himself mended his own clothes, cut meat, and performed other household chores.[33] In short, as a husband, the Prophet did not demand "obedience" at home. Instead, his private life was characterized by cooperation and consultation, all to the amazement of some of the men who knew about it.[34] This egalitarian model is not the basis of the Codes that have departed from this *sunnah*.

We cannot correct the present situation merely by revising the Codes discussed here. Revision would be a good start, but much more is needed, such as the religious reeducation of Muslims. Muslims, both male and female, need to know what is the proper Islamic position with respect to the status of women. Muslims should be informed about the corruption of Islam by authoritarian/patriarchal cultural influences. Reeducation should be introduced in a well-conceived manner and synchronized with a plan to raise popular consciousness and create a new consensus. As a first step toward righting this monumental wrong against Muslim women, we must educate women and their parents about the necessity of including in the marriage contract conditions that would protect the wife.

THE QUR'ANIC VIEW OF GENDER RELATIONS

As stated earlier, laws oppressive to women were justified partly by reliance on local custom, and partly by reliance on Qur'anic verse. The latter type of justification is most powerful, since it claims to rely on divine revelation. Thus it is very important to evaluate carefully arguments claiming to be based on the Qur'an.

To do that, we must first understand the Qur'anic worldview. The central concept in the Qur'an is that of *Tawhid*, that there is only *one* supreme being and that being is God. This concept permeates the whole Qur'an. For our present purposes, it is instructive to approach it from the perspective provided by the story of the fall of Iblis (Satan).[35] According to the Qur'an, Iblis's fall from grace was the result of his vanity. He was the only one who refused to obey God's order to bow to Adam. Iblis objected to the order, saying to God, "I am better than him [Adam]; you created me from fire and created him from clay."[36] This statement captures the essence of Satanic logic, which is rooted in feelings of vanity and superiority. These feelings gave rise in Iblis to a hierarchical perspective of the world, in which he ranked high and Adam ranked low. Iblis was so committed to this perspective that he risked the wrath of God rather than violate the hierarchy. By doing so, Iblis ranked his own will as superior to that of God. In other words, he committed the sin of *shirk* (denial of *tawhid*).[37]

Muslims who are vain and arrogant, whether for individual, racial, economic, or gender-related reasons, engage in Satanic logic.[38] The Qur'an states clearly and repeatedly that we were all created from the same *nafs* (soul).[39] In particular, the very first *ayah* in *surat al-Nisa'* states, "O people! reverence God (show piety toward God) who created you from one *nafs* and created from her (the *nafs*) her mate and spread from them many men and women; and reverence God, through whom you demand your mutual rights, and the wombs (that bore you), (for) God watches you."[40]

The question presented by this *ayah* is this: if all humans are made of the same *nafs*, why did God create so many differences among us? The Qur'an again provides us with answers. On the question of race and ethnicity, it tells us that we were created as different genders, and made into nations and tribes, so that we may become acquainted with each other (i.e., to enjoy each other's differences and company, or to put it differently, "variety is the spice of life").[41] On the question of gender, the Qur'an informs us in *surat al-Rum* that God created for us from our *anfus* (plural of *nafs*) mates *so that we may find tranquility with them*, and God put affection and mercy between us.[42] "That," the Qur'an adds, "is a sign for those who ponder."[43] (I will refer to this *ayah* as the Equality Principle.) This *ayah* on gender relations is repeated in various forms in the Qur'an.[44] Consequently, we may justifiably conclude that it articulates a basic general principle about proper gender relations; namely, that they are relations between mates created from the same *nafs*, and that these relations are intended to provide tranquility and be characterized by affection and mercy. Such relations leave no room for Satanic hierarchies, which result only in strife, subordination, and oppression.[45]

One *ayah* appears to conflict with the Equality Principle. It is a highly controversial *ayah* that is often cited by some secular feminists as proof that Islam is structurally patriarchal. Because of this challenge, I have decided to address the first (and most cited) part of this *ayah* in this chapter. Again, the treatment can only be rudimentary because of space limitations. But I hope that this treatment would suffice to indicate the line of thought that needs to be adopted in explaining the rest of the *ayah* and other similar *ayahs* that are often cited in discussing this issue. It would also show the level of familiarity with Qur'anic philosophy and interpretation necessary for Muslim women to rebut patriarchal claims.

The first part of the thirty-fourth *ayah* of *surat al-Nisa'* (which I will refer to as the Complex Phrase) starts with the following (partially translated) statement, which has often been used to justify male dominance: (i) "Men are *qawwamun* over women *bima* God *faddala* some of them over others, and *bima* they spend of their own money." A modern patriarchal translation of this phrase is the following: (ii) "Men are the *protectors and maintainers* of women, because God has *given the one more (strength) than the other*, and because they support them from their means."[46] The problem with the modern translation of the words left in Arabic in (i) above, is that in each case it selects the meaning that supports a patriarchal interpretation.

For example, the word *qawwam* (singular of *qawwamun*) has been interpreted variously to mean "head," "boss," "leader," "protector," or even "manager," "guide," and "advisor." These meanings range from ones reflecting hierarchical assumptions to others that do not. Part of the reason for this discrepancy is rooted in the relational meaning of the word. One old Arabic dictionary defines the related word *qiyam*, specifically in the context of the *ayah,* as "having the meaning of preservation and betterment."[47] Another old dictionary defines the related word *qayyim* as "one who manages the people's affairs, leads and straightens them out."[48] Both meanings, while not necessarily hierarchical, are open to hierarchical authoritarian interpretations. So where a society was authoritarian, it made sense that interpreters colored these meanings with their own authoritarian perspective.[49] As the world changed, modern interpreters tried to regain for the word its original meaning. Given our bias in favor of democracy (which rejects inherent Satanic hierarchies), we may do well to opt for nonhierarchical interpretations of the word.

Also, the verb *faddala* is usually translated as meaning "being superior."[50] Linguistically, *faddala* is explained as having a distinction, a preferred difference over another, a feature or ability the other lacks.[51] At this point, I ask the reader to resist concluding prematurely that the Qur'an therefore states that men and women are essentially different, and that the man is superior. That is in fact the patriarchal conclusion; mine is different.

The word *bima* is the most complex in the above clause (i). Linguistically, it is composed of two parts: *bi* and *ma*. The first is a connector with more than one meaning. Among the most prevalent meanings of *bi* are (a) one that conveys a relation of causality (*sababiyah* or *'illiyah*); (b) one that conveys circumstantiality (*dharfiyah*); and (c) one that conveys a quantity that is less than all (*tab'idh*).[52] *Ma* acts here as a pure connector (*mawsuliyah*) but may have at times a more enhanced meaning (indicating a *masdar*).[53] It is used to refer to inanimate objects only.[54]

The critical meaning then of *bima* revolves mostly around the *bi* segment. As a result, *bima* could mean (a) "because"; (b) "in circumstances where"; and (c) "in that which," a meaning that indicates *tab'idh*, a portion or a part of, but not the whole.

Looking back at the above translation, we can now revise it to read: (iii) "Men are [advisors/providers of guidance] to women [because/in circumstances where/in that which] God made some of them different from some others and [because/in circumstances where/in that which] they spend of their own money."

A basic rule of Islamic jurisprudence is the following: where *ayahs* appear to conflict, they must be carefully studied in search of a meaning that makes them consistent with each other.[55] Another basic rule states that one way to resolve apparent conflict between *ayahs* is to check the scope of each.[56] If one is general and the other is particular, then the second may be an exception to or a carve-out from the first.

The Qur'anic phrase that articulates the Equality Principle is clearly general. It has no qualifiers, provisos, or carve-outs. It is also repeated in similar forms several other times in the Qur'an.[57] The second *ayah* is totally different in structure. In stating what appears to be a general statement, namely, that "men are *qawwamun* over women," the phrase immediately provides an explanation. The explanation acts as a limitation on the apparently general statement (*takhsis* of the *'aam*), by specifying the reasons (*'illahs*) or circumstances (as indicated by the various meanings of *bima*) that would entitle a male to be *qawwam*.[58] These include differences between some males and some females.[59]

The elements of this limitation are two. The first part of (iii), namely, that men are *qawwamun* over women, is a general statement. But it is operative only (1) where God has endowed a male (in a certain circumstance or at a certain time) with a feature, ability, or characteristic that a particular woman lacks (and presumably needs in that circumstance or at that time); *and* (2) where that male is maintaining that particular woman. Only under *both* of these conditions may the man presume to offer guidance or advice to the woman. The Qur'an clearly indicates that not all men satisfy both conditions.

In other words, the Qur'an was describing (and not recommending) in this *ayah* a situation akin to the traditional one existing at the time, where some women were financially dependent. In those circumstances, the *ayah* informs us, God gave the man supporting her the responsibility (*taklif*, not privilege) of offering the woman guidance and advice in those areas in which he happens to be more qualified or experienced.[60] The woman, however, is entitled to reject both (otherwise the advisory role is no longer advisory). This interpretation is consistent with another *ayah* in the Qur'an that states that Muslims, male and female, are each other's *walis* (allies, protectors, or even guardians).[61]

This analysis is a very truncated one because of space limitations. However, it suffices to illustrate the fact that the traditional approach of Muslim jurists toward women was often based, even in the case of Qur'anic interpretation, on patriarchal assumptions. These assumptions resulted in stripping Muslim women of their God-given rights. Furthermore, not only did traditional jurists espouse a patriarchal model of gender relations, they even worked actively at making it a social reality. They passed restrictive laws that were highly detrimental to women. They utilized the traditional stereotype of the woman as irrational, dependent, and impulsive, as well as their legal power, to assert the automatic superiority of all men over all women.[62] In doing that, they inadvertently violated a major Qur'anic principle, the Equality Principle discussed earlier. Consequently, thoughtful Muslims should no longer accept patriarchal interpretation, and Muslim women must rediscover the truth of the Qur'anic Equality Principle in order to achieve liberation and freedom without guilt.

CONCLUSION

In short, the solution to Muslim women's human rights problems is not to ask these women to cast away their deepest beliefs in search of a Western quick fix. Like their sisters in the West did before them, they simply must face the patriarchal behemoth in their own backyard and win on their own terms.

NOTES

This chapter is based on a longer contribution entitled *Islam, Law and Custom: Redefining Muslim Women's Rights*, 12 Am. U. J. Int'l L. and Pol'y 1–44 (1997). The reader is encouraged to consult the original article for detailed discussion of the statements made herein.

1. *See, e.g.,* Judith Miller, *The Challenge of Radical Islam*, Foreign Affairs 43, 50–54, Spring 1993 (quoting Bernard Lewis that Islam and liberal democracy do not make natural bedfellows and discussing human rights problems); John Esposito and John Voll, Islam and Democracy 23 (1996) (stating that non-Muslims and some conservative Muslims have argued that it is impossible to have an "Islamic democracy"); Kathryn Webber, *The Economic Future of Afghan Women: The Interaction between Islamic Law and Muslim Culture*, 18 U. Pa. J. Int'l. Econ. L. 1049, 1056–57 and n. 27 (1997) (referring to the ongoing debate over the compatibility of Islam and international human rights agreements); *Dressing Down*, Financial Times (London), Feb. 1, 1994, at 19 (announcing a debate at the Oxford Union on whether Islam and democracy are compatible); Ken Adelman, *Limits to Liberty Where Islam Reigns*, Washington Times, Apr. 3, 1996, at A15.

2. Movies and television programs, such as *I Dream of Jeannie, Not without My Daughter,* and the older *Omar Khayyam, The Sheikh,* and others, as well as the print media, have repeatedly depicted Muslim women as either oppressed, submissive, or sex objects. Recent articles have been more sensitive to this issue and have distinguished in their reports between the situation of women in a Muslim country and the claim that Islam is responsible for the

problem. *See, e.g.*, Monia Hejaiej, *An Intimate Peek behind the Veil: A Look at the Lives of Muslim Women*, Christian Science Monitor, Oct. 31, 1996, at B1; *see also* statement by Jay Leno about Islam and Muslim women's rights, *What's Up?* San Antonio Express News, Oct. 22, 1998, at 2F.

3. For more on "Orientalism," *see* Edward Said, Orientalism, *passim, esp.* 59–61 (1979). *See also* Rana Kabbani, Imperial Fictions (Pandor rev. and exp. ed. 1994); and Marnia Lazreg, The Eloquence of Silence, esp. 136, 224 (1994).

4. *See* discussion of this point by Kabbani, *supra* note 3, at viii–ix, and Lazreg, *supra* note 3, at 13–14.

5. *See* Timothy Worthington Marr, Imagining Ismael: Studies of Islamic Orientalism in America from the Puritans to Melville 103 (1997) (unpublished Ph.D. diss., Yale University) (on file with the Yale University Library).

6. The issue involved was that of inheritance. The original language spoke of equal shares of inheritance regardless of gender, in an apparent contradiction to a Qur'anic verse. The Qur'anic treatment of inheritance is quite complex and deserves a separate article.

7. The event was reported to us by a member of the Karamah delegation who attended the sessions. Karamah is a Muslim women lawyers' organization for human rights. *See also* the Karamah press release in Beijing on these issues. Web site: <karamah.org>. *See also* Bharathi Anandhi Venkatraman, *Islamic States and the United Nations Convention on the Elimination of All Forms of Discrimination against Women: Are the Shari'a and the Convention Compatible?* 44 Am. U. L. Rev. 1949 (1995).

8. 2 Wihbah Al-Zuhayli, Usul al-Fiqh al-Islami (2 vols.) 1043–51, 1066, 1092–93 (Damascus, Dar al-Fikr, 1986); *see also* Subhi Mahmassani, Muqaddimah fi Ihya' 'Ulum al-Shari'ah 30 (Beirut, Dar al-'Ilm li al-Malayin, 1962). *See also* Abdel Qader Abu al-'Ila, Buhuth fi al-Ijtihad 71–75 (Egypt, Matba'at al-Amanah, 1987) (discussing conditions of *ijtihad*).

9. *See, e.g.,* 2 Al-Zuhayli, *supra* note 8, at 1043–51, 1066, 1092–93; *see also* Mahmassani, *supra* note 8, at 30. *See also* Abu al-'Ila, *supra* note 8, at 71–75.

10. *See, e.g.,* 2 Al-Zuhayli, *supra* note 8, at 1116; Subhi Mahmassani, Falsafat Al-Tashri' Fi al Islam 201 (Beirut, Dar al-'Ilm li al-Malayin, 3d ed., 1961).

11. *See* Taha Jabir al-Alwani, Usul al-Fiqh al-Islami 33–36 (Y. T. DeLorenzo trans., International Institute of Islamic Thought, Herndon, VA, 1990); Mahmassani, *supra* note 8, at 40. Muhammad Abu Zahrah, Al-Shafi'i 145–46 (Dar al-Fikr al-'Arabi, 1948); 'Ala' al-Deen ae-Samarqandi, Tariqat al-Khilaf Bayn al-Aslaf (Beirut, Dar al-Kutub al-Ilmiyah, reprint, 11th century, 1992) 13.

12. Qur'an 49:13.

13. *See, e.g.,* Mahmassani, *supra* note 8, at 67–69; *see also* Mohammad Shalabi, Usul al-Fiqh al-Islami 325–28 (Beirut, al-Dar al-Jami'iyah, n.d.).

14. Subhi Mahmassani, Al-Awda' al-Tashri'iyah fi al-Duwal al-Arabiyah 192–205 (Beirut, Dar al-'Ilm li al-Malayin, 3d ed., 1965).

15. *Id.* at 179.

16. Moroccan Code, Royal Decree No. 343.57.1 (1957), *as amended by* Royal Decree No. 347.93.1 (1993) [hereinafter Moroccan Code], Bk. 1, Tit. 6, Ch. 36, Art. 4.

17. *See* Farida Bennani, Taqsim al-'Amal Bayn Al-Zawjayn 144 and related notes (Marakesh, Silsilat Manshurat Kuliyat al-'Ulum al-Qanuniyah wa al-Iqtisadiyah wa al-Ijtima'iyah, Jami'at al-Qadhi 'Iyadh, 1992). *See also* Muhammad Abu Zahrah, Muhadarat fi 'Aqd al-Zawaj wa Atharuh 197 (Egypt, Dar al-Fikr al-Arabi, 1958).

18. *See* Bennani, *supra* note 17, at 144 and related notes. *See also* Abu Zahrah, *supra* note 17, at 197.

19. *See* Bennani, *supra* note 17, at 144–45 and related notes, esp. n.148.

20. *See id.* at 147 and related notes, esp. n.167.

21. In the original version of this article, I also discuss the right of a woman to contract her own marriage and to initiate divorce. *See* Azizah al-Hibri, *Islam, Law and Custom: Redefining Muslim Women's Rights,* 12 Am. U. J. Int'l. L. and Pol'y 1–44 (1997).

22. Moroccan Code, Bk. 1, Tit. 6, Ch. 36, Art. 2; Family Law No. 84-11 (1984) [hereinafter Algerian Code], Bk. 1, Tit. 1, Ch. 4, Art. 39. The Egyptian code consists primarily of Act No. 25 (1920) in respect of Maintenance and Some Questions of Personal Status, and Act No. 25 (1929) regarding certain Personal Status Provisions, *as both were amended by* Act No. 100 (1985) [collectively, hereinafter, Egyptian Code], Ch. 2, Art. 11 Repeated Twice; Personal Status Code, Provisional Law No. 61 (1976) [hereinafter Jordanian Code], Ch. 7, Art. 39; Law No. 51 (1984) Regarding Personal Status [hereinafter Kuwaiti Code], Part 1, Bk. 1, Tit. 5, Ch 3, Arts. 84–91; Decree No. 59 (1953) regarding Personal Status Law, *amended by* Law No. 34 (1975) [hereinafter Syrian Code], Bk. 1, Tit. 4, Ch. 3, Art. 75, by implication and generally as a result of the doctrine of incorporation. Some of these provisions only partially address the *ta'ah* requirement simply because the codes make use of the doctrine of incorporation. This doctrine views the jurisprudence of the school to which a country officially adheres as an implicit part of its code, except with respect to the parts explicitly ruled out by the code through the adoption of a contrary provision.

23. Algerian Code, *supra* note 22, Bk. 1, Tit. 1, Ch. 4, Art. 38; Egyptian Code, *supra* note 22, Law No. 25 (1920) (amended 1985), Bk. 1, Part 1, Art. 1; Jordanian Code, *supra* note 22, Ch. 9, Art. 69; Kuwaiti Code, *supra* note 22, Part 1, Bk. 1, Tit. 3, Art. 89 (*see also* comments on this provision in the related Explanatory Memorandum); Moroccan Code, *supra* note 22, Bk. 1, Tit. 6, Ch. 35; Syrian Code, *supra* note 22, Bk. 1, Tit. 4, Ch. 3, Art. 75. The Kuwaiti, Egyptian, Syrian, and Jordanian provisions derive their full impact from their use of the doctrine of incorporation or reference to customary law.

24. Algerian Code, *supra* note 22, Bk. 1, Tit. 1, Ch. 4, Art. 37; Egyptian Code, *supra* note 22, Law No. 25 (1920) (amended 1985), Art. 1; Jordanian Code, *supra* note 22, Ch. 9, Art. 68–69; Kuwaiti Code, *supra* note 22, Part 1, Bk. 1, Tit. 5, Art. 87; Syrian Code, *supra* note 22, Bk. 1, Tit. 3, Art. 74.

25. *See* Abu Zahrah, *supra* note 17, at 196; *see also* Muhammad Zakariya al-Bardisi, Al-Ahkam al-Islamiyah fi al-Ahwal al-Shakhsiyah 330–32 (Egypt, Dar al-Nahda al-'Arabiyah, 1965) (providing reasons for restricting the wife's mobility); 2 Abu Hamid al-Ghazali, 'Ihya' 'Ulum al-Din (4 vols.) 58–59 (Egypt, Mustafa al-Babi al-Halabi Press, 11th century, reprint, 1939); 8 Muwaffaq al-din Ibn Qudamah, al-Mughni (12 vols.) 129 (Beirut, Dar al-Kitab al-'Arabi, 12th century, reprint, n.d.).

26. *See, e.g.,* al-Bardisi, *supra* note 25, at 292–93; 4 Kamal al-Din al-Siwassi, Sharh Fath al-Qadir 378–80 (Egypt, Mustafa al-Babi al-Halabi Press, 13th century, reprint, n.d.) (text and commentary).

27. *See* Abu Zahrah, *supra* note 17, at 196; *see also* 2 al-Ghazali, *supra* note 25, at 58–59; 8 Ibn Qudamah, *supra* note 25, at 129.

28. *See* Azizah al-Hibri, *Islamic Constitutionalism and the Concept of Democracy,* 24 Case W. Res. J. Int'l L. 1, 11–26 (1992).

29. Abu Zahrah, *supra* note 17, at 186; 4 Abdul Rahman al-Jaziri, Kitab al-Fiqh 'Ala

al-Mathahib al-Arba'ah (5 vols.) 85–89 (Beirut, Dar Ihya' al-Turath al-Arabi, 1969) (text and notes); Muhammad Jawad Maghniyah, Al-Fiqh 'ala al-Mathahib al-Khamsah 301–02 (Beirut, Dar al-'Ilm li al-Malayin, 6th ed., 1969).

30. 16 Abu al-Faraj al-Isbahani, Kitab al-Aghani 102 (Beirut, Dar al-Thaqafah, 9th century, reprint, 1959). *See* 'A'ishah Abd al-Rahman (Bint al-Shati'), Sukaynah Bint al-Hussain 106 (Egypt, Dar al-Hilal, 1965) (listing reported conditions in Sukaynah's marriage contracts).

31. Al-Isbahani, *supra* note 30, at 102.

32. Abd Al-Rahman, *supra* note 30, at 106. Al-Mansur, the famous Abbaside statesman, also entered a marriage contract that prevented him from additional marriages. Kahalah, Omar, Al-Zawaj 57 (Beirut, Mu'assassat al-Risalah, 1977).

33. 2 Al-Ghazali, *supra* note 25, at 354; *see also* Abu al-Hassan al-Nadawi, Al-Sirah al-Nabawiyah 370 (Jeddah, Dar al-Shuruq, 1977).

34. 2 Abd al-Halim Abu Shuqqah, Tahrir al-Mar'ah fi 'Asr al-Risalah (5 vols.) 147–49, 153 (Kuwait, Dar al-Qalam, 1990).

35. I would like to note that the significance of this story was first brought to my attention by Sheikh Hassan Khalid, the late Mufti of Lebanon, may God rest his soul in peace.

36. Qur'an 7:12.

37. *See* 3 al-Ghazali, *supra* note 25, at 326–43.

38. *Id.*, but al-Ghazali did not refer to gender in his discussion.

39. Qur'an 4:1, 6:98, 7:189.

40. Qur'an 4:1.

41. Qur'an 49:13.

42. Qur'an 30:21.

43. *Id.*

44. *See, e.g.,* Qur'an 35:11, 39:6; Bennani, *supra* note 17, at 27–28. Bennani, a Moroccan Muslim law professor, argues in this award-winning book that the Qur'an clearly states in several places that men and women are equal intellectually as well as physically. She also relates *hadiths* to the same effect, and cites other evidence.

45. Bennani, *supra* note 17, at 13–14 (noting that Muslim patriarchal societies used the concept of *qiwama* to create a hierarchical structure within the family, headed by the husband). She also argues that such hierarchy contradicts the basic principle of gender equality revealed in the Qur'an. *Id.* at 27–28.

46. Yusuf Ali, The Holy Qur'an: Text, Translation and Commentary 190 (Brentwood, Maryland, Amana Corp., 1983).

47. 11 Muhammad Ibn Manthur, Lisan al-'Arab (18 vols.) 355 (Beirut, Dar Ihya' al-Turath al-'Arabi, 12th century, reprint, 1992).

48. 5 Abu Abdul Rahman al-Farahidi, Kitab al-Ayn (8 vols.) 232 (Beirut, Mu'assasat al-A'lami li al-Matbu'at, 8th century, reprint, 1988).

49. *See, e.g.,* 2 Muhamad Rashid Ridha, Tafsir al-Qur'an al-Hakim (Tafsir al-Manar) (12 vols.) 380 (Beirut, Dar al-Ma'rifa, 1947); 5 Ridha, at 67–70; *see also* Muhammad Abdul Hamid, Al-Ahwal al-Shakhsiyah fi al-Shari'ah al-Islamiyah 122 (Cairo, Muhammad Sabih and Sons, 1966); 4 Abu Ja'far al-Tabari, Tafsir al-Tabari (16 vols) 60 (Beirut, Dar al-Kutub al-Ilmiyah, 9th century, reprint, 1992) (calling men "princes" over women).

50. *See, e.g.,* 5 Ridha, *supra* note 49, at 67; Ahmad Ghandour, Al-Ahwal al-Shakhsiyah fi al-Tashri' al-Islami 235–36 (Kuwait, Jami'at al-Kuwait Press, 1972).

51. 10 Ibn Manthur, *supra* note 47, at 280. Linguistically, the root verb *fadl* refers to "the opposite of deficiency," and *fudalah* means "remnant." *See* 7 al-Farahidi, *supra* note 48, at

43; 10 Ibn Manthur, *supra* note 47, at 281. Consequently, a secondary meaning of the word reduces *faddala* to mere difference, without ascribing any value to that difference.

52. These meanings can be found in a regular Arabic dictionary. *See, e.g.,* Muhammad Isbir and Bilal Junaidi, Al-Shamil 235–36 (Beirut, Dar al-'Awdah, 1981). *See also* 1 Fakhr al-Din al-Razi, al-Mahsul fi 'Ilm Usul al-Fiqh (6 vols.) 379, 381, n.3 (Beirut, Mu'assassat al-Risalah, 12th century, reprint, 1992) (for the meaning of *tab'idh*).

53. Isbir and Junaidi, *supra* note 52, at 764.

54. *See, e.g.,* 2 al-Razi, *supra* note 52, at 333–34.

55. 2 Al-Zuhayli, *supra* note 8, at 1177, 1182–83.

56. *Id.*

57. *See supra* note 39.

58. Shalabi, *supra* note 13, at 432–64.

59. Bennani, *supra* note 17, at 35–36. Bennani and others point out that the structure of the phrase permits the interpretation that the differences referred to there are not differences between men and women, but rather between men and other men. She argues that such differences are based on the man's ability to maintain his family.

60. *Id.* at 35 makes a similar point.

61. Qur'an 9:71.

62. For more on the traditional stereotype of women, see al-Hibri, *supra* note 21, at 16–17 and related notes. On the exercise of legal power, see Bennani, *supra* note 17, at 25 (alluding to this point when she wonders whether present gender differences were not artificially produced by patriarchal manipulation of the rules and laws of society and the family). *See* Fatimah Nasif, Huquq al-Mar'ah wa Wajibatuha fi Daw' al-Kitab wa al-Sunnah 238–40 (Jeddah, Tahamah, 1992), where the Saudi author argues that the husband is entitled to head his family by virtue of the natural capabilities with which God endowed all men. Among her reasons for giving men the leadership status are the following two: each organizational structure must have a head, and the husband is better suited to be that head, because of his physical strength and his role as maintainer and protector.

15 | For the Sake of the Country, for the Sake of the Family

The Oppressive Impact of Family Registration on Women in Japan

Taimie L. Bryant

The principle of hierarchy appears in virtually every description of Japanese society. Cast in the benign form of a status arrangement without assignment of worth, hierarchy has been used to explain everything from individual psychology to corporate organization to dispute resolution. It is also credited with generating national solidarity and societal stability in a world perceived as changeable and threatening. This picture is imbalanced, however, because negative social repercussions of this ubiquitous hierarchical principle have not been fully considered.

Legal regulation of the family through family registration, the requirement that family status events be registered with the government, has been an important means of generating and maintaining hierarchy in Japanese society. Various groups, including Koreans, the shunned *burakumin,* and "illegitimate" children, have fought against oppressive aspects of family registration since its establishment in 1872. The most recent protest against family registration comes from feminists.[1]

This chapter examines the operation of the family registration system in Japan and the costs it imposes on women. In increasing numbers, petitioners are seeking change in family registration to reduce its reinforcement of a patriarchal model of the family. Considered in isolation, these feminist voices seem puny and their issues trivial. Considered in the context of previous protests and governmental response to those protests, their strategies seem sensible, even inevitable.

Exploration of the patterns of activism and governmental response suggests reasons for the continued resilience of the current system of family registration. Some of these reasons are related to the government's consistent failure to respond effectively to many of the burdens generated by registration. The government's response provides only apparent relief, which fails to reach the deeper structure of family registration and the social structures with which it articulates. Other reasons are related to unconscious participation in oppression by majority Japanese. Finally, some reasons are related to the protesters themselves. For example, all protesters, but particularly women as primary caretakers of the family, have been sensitive to continuing support for the patriarchal family model underlying family registration. That support stems from the historical ideological linkage of family stability to national stability through the regulatory device of family registration. Family registration resulted in nationwide imposition of one (upper-class) family model, which in turn became the paradigm for a range of relationships such as employer/employee, teacher/student, government/citizen. Although diffuse, the belief is strong that Japan's domestic stability and international competitive success were achieved partially through adherence to norms and values associated with that family structure. For the sake of their country, for the sake of their families, those harmed by the system of family registration have been reluctant to engage in active protest.

Following an overview of the system of family registration, this chapter presents three controversies that highlight the centrality of women's issues in contemporary disputes about family registration. It then provides a more detailed analysis of the current controversy over women's issues before concluding with a comparison of protest strategies and majoritarian responses.

I. THE SIGNIFICANCE OF FAMILY REGISTRATION

The family registry (*koseki*) is fundamental to all aspects of all Japanese individuals' lives because it is the vehicle by which the state gives legal significance to personal status events such as birth, marriage, divorce, and death. An individual is not married legally unless and until registration is accepted by the local registrar. Each couple creates a new family registry, and subsequent personal status changes such as births of children, adoptions, and divorce must be recorded on the same family registry. An individual may not succeed to property through intestate succession, for example, without proper recordation on the family registry.

The family registry is of major importance in a Japanese individual's life because it is used to determine eligibility for basic government benefits such as education and income assistance. It provides a means of tracing an individual's movement in Japan not only because each personal status change must be registered, but also because requests for copies of the registry can be traced. Since copies of family registries are required for passport issuance and renewal, family registration also enables the government to control movement outside Japan.

The family registry is widely used in the private sector by employers, schools, and parents of potential spouses in order to learn more about an individual's background. As the subsequent examples will illustrate, information deemed relevant by the Japanese government for registration purposes takes on particular significance in labeling individuals as worthy of certain benefits and experiences in Japanese society. The *honseki,* the homesite of one's ancestors when family registration was instituted, marriages and divorces of other family members, whether one was adopted or born to married parents, even the spacing of children within a family are seemingly small pieces of information that carry significant weight when the government identifies that information as important enough to be registered. The Japanese government has consistently maintained that the information required for registration is relevant only for the purpose of legitimating the status events involved and that the family registry itself is a value-neutral document. However, the family registry cannot be value-neutral because value judgments adhere to the required information in ways that create and maintain hierarchies of worthiness and participation in Japanese society. Individuals are excluded, or restricted in participation, on the basis of others' knowledge of negatively valued elements of their family registries.

II. THREE RECENT CASES

The following three cases illustrate some of the issues around which protest against family registration has crystallized. All were causes célèbres in Japan; all provoked discussion of the impact on women's lives of this particular type of family registration as it articulates with social norms and values associated with the family.

In 1988 the Supreme Court of Japan rejected the last appeals of Noboru Kikuta, a doctor whose license was suspended because he falsified the birth records of 220 babies born to mothers who had initially sought abortions.[2] Kikuta issued false birth reports so that those babies could have family registries that disguised the circumstances of their births and adoptions; the birth reports enabled them to be registered as the legitimate offspring of their adoptive parents.

Despite much public acknowledgment that the false reports enabled the adoptive parents and children to escape the stigma associated with adoption under these circumstances, Kikuta's falsification of the birth reports was adjudged an offense serious enough to warrant suspension of his right to practice medicine. Appellate courts upheld the suspension on the grounds that the period of suspension was reasonable given the offense and that Kikuta's wrong was more serious than the harm he sought to prevent.[3] Although Dr. Kikuta did not accept any fees for the false registrations, the courts feared that exoneration could result in a gray market in babies. In addition to accepting arguments cast in terms of the best interests of the children,[4] the courts also feared that the failure to punish false registrations would cast doubt on the "purity" of the family registration system.

Despite the fact that most of those whom Kikuta assisted were married women unable to care for another child, debate about the case sidestepped that issue. Indeed, Kikuta's case was used to decry the alleged erosion of sexual morality; condemnation of Kikuta's actions was seen as necessary to prevent easy options for unmarried mothers.

As Kikuta's legal battle was winding down, another legal battle about family registration was just beginning. Reiko Sekiguchi began legal proceedings to secure the right to use her premarital surname in the course of her employment as a professor at a Japanese university.[5] As a requirement of legal marriage, Japanese couples must choose one of their surnames at the time they establish a family registry.[6] Although either surname may be selected, government statistics indicate that 97.8 percent choose the husband's name.[7] Sekiguchi, too, took her husband's surname upon marriage, although she had started her academic career three years previously under her premarital surname. However, Sekiguchi's employer at the time, another university, allowed her to continue to use her premarital surname. Sixteen years later, when Sekiguchi changed universities, her new employer required her to use her formally registered surname rather than her professionally established, premarital surname for all internal administrative matters.[8]

In the lawsuit, the university contended that Sekiguchi's legal obligation to use her husband's surname arose from her and her husband's decision to take his surname instead of hers; if she valued her surname so much, she should have protected it herself through the couple's choice of her surname upon marriage rather than expecting the university to use an unregistered surname. Sekiguchi contended that she should be able to use the name under which she had established her professional reputation, regardless of the fact of her marriage. As Sekiguchi pointed out, Japanese law disproportionately burdens marriages in which both spouses are professionals because one spouse is required to give up his or her surname at marriage. Sekiguchi argued that couples should not be put to the choice of whose surname to protect or left to the benevolence of employers who may or may not force use of the legally registered name.

In a third case, decided by the Tokyo District Court in 1989, Motoko Suzuki and six other women employees of Nissan Motor Company brought suit against Nissan for failure to pay them family allowances (*kazoku teate*).[9] Nissan, like most Japanese companies, provides family allowances to employees who are heads of households with children. Since the women employees were not registered as the heads of their households, their requests for family allowances were denied despite proof that they were supporting minor children. They argued that all employees supporting minor children should be entitled to a family allowance and that the "head of household" requirement has a discriminatory impact on women employees because registered heads of households are, overwhelmingly, husbands.

The Tokyo District Court held that it was reasonable for Nissan to use legal registration of head of household as exclusive proof of actual house headship. Moreover, the court held, there was no discrimination against women employees because women employees would be entitled to the family allowance if they were registered as heads of their households.[10]

III. THE IMPACT OF FAMILY REGISTRATION ON WOMEN

The governmental response to the dilemma posed by Kikuta's case illustrates a contemporary use of family registration as a means of social control of women. The other recent cases of Sekiguchi's fight to use her surname and the Nissan employees' argument of entitlement to family allowances rest on a related claim about the impact of family registration on women. These plaintiffs argued that family registration promotes a patriarchal model of the family that subordinates them in violation of the postwar constitution's insistence on individual dignity and autonomy.

One consistent response to this claim is that the system of family registration is gender-neutral because women can become legal household. This view credits post–World War II legal revision with elimination of the major gender-based legal impediments associated with the traditional hierarchal upper-class family structure known as the house system. Remnants of the house system are seen as fragmentary and insignificant. Skeptics also argue that the causal link between oppression and family registration is tenuous, particularly since there were sources of oppression in Japanese society, such as Confucian ideology, other than the use of a patriarchal model of the family. Finally, opposition to change in family registration in this as in other contexts stems from a belief in the basic neutrality of the document; discrimination results either directly from abuse by intentional discriminators or indirectly through failure to change social patterns associated with the family.

In order to understand the claim of gender neutrality, we must delve briefly into the historical development of family registration.[11] The Japanese government's explicit reason for instituting family registration in 1872 was to monitor population growth and movement, but by 1873 the government had removed the six-year reporting requirement for census purposes. Household registration was established for those purposes, but family registration was retained nonetheless.

The historian Einosuke Yamanaka suggests three reasons for requiring family registration after household registration replaced it as a means of census data collection.[12] One was crime control; individuals who might not consistently report their current residence might nevertheless register personal status changes. Another reason may have been the government's desire to break the spine of local communities' power.[13] Prior to legalization of personal status changes, communities as a whole had the power to validate events such as marriage and adoption.[14] Under the family registration system, the central government had the final say as to the validity of those events. A third reason for instituting family registration, as opposed to individual registration, is that it reinforced an ideology that was particularly useful to the government. If individuals could be made to answer to the heads of their families and family heads could be made to answer to the government, the government's need to control and monitor individual behavior would be reduced. Authorizing the family head to register status events gave the household power, but not enough power to threaten the stability of the government because that power was granted, and could be taken away, by the state.

The problem for the government was that only the families of landowners, wealthy merchants, and samurai were structured in a way that facilitated imposition of a hierarchy of accountability. While the notion of a senior male representative for the family was present for other classes, family life was characterized by more equality between the sexes and by a relatively high tolerance for movement in and out of family structures through divorce and remarriage.[15] Through its nation-wide institution of the family registry system, the government imposed the house system on commoners and made househeads the legal representative of the house to the government. The government also gave extensive power to the househead in running the house.[16] Family registration linkage between the househead and the ancestors before him, through identification of the *honseki,* validated and perpetuated ancestors' continuing influence in the decision of living generations.

If family registries were not widely used, or there were no value judgments associated with the registered events, the family model underlying family registration would have had relatively little impact. However, family registries are widely used, and there are negative value judgments associated with the registered events. Therefore it is, in fact, significant that the government validated the more rigidly patrilineal, patriarchal model of the house system of the upper class as the basis for the family registry. Typically, in that system of patrilineal linkage of the eldest sons of successive generations, the eldest son and his wife and unmarried children remained on the registry of his father (who was, in turn, the eldest son of the preceding generation). That son assumed responsibility for continuity of the house by adhering to rituals respecting the house ancestors and by ensuring the correct conduct of present members of the house. Other sons left the registry when they married and established their own or "branch" houses. Daughters remained on their fathers' registries until they married and entered their husbands' family registries.

Women could become househeads under certain circumstances,[17] but the stratum of society from which the house system was drawn, the samurai class, emphasized male control.[18] Whereas formerly women in the samurai class were much more restricted in autonomy relative to women in other classes, the imposition of the house system made that restriction generally applicable to all women. When they married, women married out of their fathers' house and into their husbands' house; they were insiders only if and when their husbands succeeded to headship of the house.[19]

Women experienced the insider/outsider distinction on a daily level because mothers-in-law frequently subjected their daughters-in-law to difficult tests of obedience and respect. They were outsiders also in relation to their own children. Children born to them during marriage were children of their husband's house and would remain with the father in the event of divorce; the husband's mother had more legal right to the children than did the mother.

If Japanese women were previously relatively powerless within the family, family registration that resulted in legal entitlement to protection by government officials might have benefited women by providing a means of equalizing power between the couple. However, not only did the law not provide for governmental intervention in the house, there is evidence that Japanese women of the lower classes were considered strong, respected family members prior to the imposition of the house system through the registration requirement.[20]

Subordination of women was exacerbated by use of the house system as a paradigm for other relationships, including the relationship between the emperor and Japanese citizens. The ideology of the Japanese nation as One Family was an important part of the Meiji government's attempt to consolidate power and unify the country. In that context of instilling commitment to strengthening the nation, certain aspects of the house system—the importance of duty, loyalty, and acceptance of hierarchical superiors' decisions—were amplified and became dominant aspects of the sociocultural content of the house. Because women were most often in tangential or structurally inferior positions within the houses they were born into or married into, an emphasis on those aspects of the house, which were amplified for nationalistic purposes, must have resulted in greater expectations of subservience than might have been the case had the model of the house not been used to strengthen commitment to the Japanese government.

In general, historical evidence about the imposition of family registration suggests governmental mindfulness of considerations other than overt discrimination against women. While changes in the Family Registration Law did result in some incremental improvements for women,[21] a concerted, explicit effort to equalize the treatment of men and women under the law did not emerge until post–World War II legal revision. During the postwar Occupation, the constitution and codes were revised with the goal of "democratizing" Japan, which was defined primarily as instilling values of equal treatment and respect for the individual.[22] Two of the most significant changes in the Family Registration Law at that time were elimination of the multigenerational house in favor of nuclear family registration[23] and the entitlement of individual men and women to establish their own separate family registries.[24]

Gradually other amendments were enacted to promote democratic values. Examples include the closure of the family registries in 1976, the right obtained by women in 1976 to retain their married surname or to return to their prior surname when establishing a family registry after divorce,[25] and the 1985 amendment that eliminated disparate treatment between Japanese men and women who marry non-Japanese.

Many Japanese believe that the postwar and subsequent changes in the Civil Code and the Family Registration Law, such as nuclearization of the registered family, removed the worst of the subordinating aspects of the family model underlying family registration. This belief rests partially on an assumption that approval by the Occupation legal advisors, those charged directly with democratizing Japan, meant that the Family Registration Law and Civil Code were basically as democratic as they needed to be. However, Occupation advisors were not fully aware of how certain legal rules (such as the retention of *honseki* and the specific provision for inheritance of religious paraphernalia associated with ancestor remembrance) permitted continuity of the hierarchical house system. Moreover, Japanese and Occupation jurists were incrementalists worried about the implementation of drastic change at a time of political and social chaos in postwar Japan. Nevertheless, the idea that the Occupation would not have left an inherently undemocratic institution in place is one source of majoritarian resistance to the call for sweeping change in the Family Registration Law and accompanying Civil Code provisions. Thus, a hallmark of postwar attacks on family registration, including contemporary attempts to push legal revision further in the direction of equalizing the impact of family registration on men and women, is a focus on specifically offensive features rather than a grand-scale attack.

A. THE REQUIREMENT OF ONE SURNAME AND ITS IMPACT ON WOMEN

Ms. Sekiguchi's dispute with her employer, Toshokan Joho University, over the use of her husband's surname is not the first time that the issue of wives' surnames has arisen. In the period immediately prior to the institution of family registration, peasants did not have surnames, and women lost even their first names upon marriage.[26] From marriage they were called simply by their title (bride, wife, mother, or widow).

When the present system of family registration was instituted in 1872, women were not allowed to adopt their husband's surname or *honseki* because it was considered important to preserve information regarding the mother's contribution to the "blood" of her husband's offspring.[27] Given this historical context, it was considered an elevation of women's status for them to be allowed to take their husband's surname and *honseki* upon marriage. This shift, which occurred at the time the civil code was promulgated in 1898, was perceived as part of a trend recognizing the importance of the present generation of the house, a trend that permitted more integration of wives as members.

The focus for the present debate over the selection of a surname at marriage, the Sekiguchi case, is couched in much different terms. Many who favor improvement of the status of women in Japanese society now argue in support of allowing each spouse to continue to use his or her premarital surname if he or she chooses. Absorption into the husband's house is viewed as a hindrance to the improvement of women's lives because it symbolizes their continued subservience to the demands of their husbands and their husbands' parents. The requirement that spouses select one of their surnames is particularly vexing for those women whose careers outside the home are important to their conception of self.[28]

The system of family registration is central to the debate about surnames. The choice of one of the spouse's surnames is required at the time of marriage, which is legally defined as the time of registration on a family registry. The family registry is accorded such weight that an individual cannot easily avoid the application of labels derived from it. Given the importance of the family registry in Japanese society, it is not surprising that Sekiguchi's employer required her to use the surname recorded on her family registry.

Sekiguchi's lawsuit against her employer over her right to use either surname brings into focus several issues that connect the system of family registry with the social unit it documents and legitimizes. One of the primary arguments against the required selection of one surname is the contention that the system of family registration reinforces the concept of the family, rather than the individual, as the smallest meaningful legal and social unit. This conflicts with the postwar constitution, which provides for protection of individual autonomy and dignity and for marriage based only on the mutual consent of the spouses. The unitary surname requirement illustrates this tension in that it requires some individuals to choose between marriage or protection of a professional reputation established under the premarital surname.

There is considerable support for this interpretation of the unitary surname requirement. The Tokyo Bar Association supports revision to permit retention of both surnames, and more legal scholars have focused attention on the benefits of revision and on resolving the administrative problems that would result from relaxation of the unitary surname requirement.[29] Nevertheless, there is also residual support for the unitary surname requirement that stems from a belief that it assists in the maintenance of a stable society.

The dispute over surname selection underscores the tension between those who view the family as the source of individual and societal stability and those who view it as a hindrance to the personal development of its members. That tension is evident also in the Nissan lawsuit about family allowances.

B. *SUZUKI V. NISSAN MOTOR COMPANY*: FAMILY ALLOWANCES, FAMILY REGISTRIES, HOUSEHOLD REGISTRIES

The legal registry of actual, current household residence and membership (*juminhyo*) is specifically at issue in the lawsuit seven women employees brought against Nissan.[30] The household registry is used for census purposes, and it is requested in many situations in addition to the family registry because it verifies current residence and household composition. A *buraku* leader has argued that the household registry is much more suitable than the family registry for verifying the identity and address of a job applicant, for example, because it provides current information that is registered according to legal procedures designed to insure veracity without including the *honseki*. The household and family registries are related, however, because both reify the same family structure; both identify the same individual as head of the family. Thus, while the *burakumin*'s problem would be eased by use of the household registry, the problem experienced by women who want to be treated without reference to their family roles would not be decreased by use of the household registry instead of the family registry. The Nissan dispute illustrates the problem of overlap in women's roles as employees and family members, a problem exacerbated by reliance on registries based on family units.

There is evidence that in 1977, long before the issue came before the courts in 1981, Nissan recognized a problem with its procedure of granting family allowances. Nissan had a rule (known as Rule A) that heads of households were entitled to a family allowance for each child they supported as long as the child was eighteen years old or younger. Only women employees who could prove that their husbands were deceased or disabled were eligible to receive family allowances for their children without being registered as heads of their households. In 1977 Nissan considered replacing Rule A with a new rule (Rule B) that would allow any employee to receive a family allowance if he or she were supporting children, regardless of whether the employee was the head of a household. However, Nissan never officially replaced Rule A with Rule B; registration of head of household continued as the determinative factor in providing family allowances.

Nissan did adopt a different rule (Rule C) that expanded the class of dependent relatives to include parents over the age of sixty. It also adopted the policy that single employees supporting siblings or parents would not necessarily be required to prove head of household status. However, Nissan left in place the rule that registered head of household status was a prerequisite for married employees.

The plaintiff women employees of Nissan wanted Nissan to pay family allowances to all employees who support minor children. They argued that Rule C was discriminatory because it used the legal registration of head of household to determine eligibility.[31] Since the overwhelming majority of Japanese couples register the husband as household, Nissan's reliance on household registries unfairly furthered the advantage men receive. While the plaintiffs also found fault with Rule B, at least Rule B eliminated the registration of household as a determining factor.

Although the court did not accept Nissan's argument that the "family allowance" was a gift (and therefore not subject to rules about fair distribution), the court did uphold Nissan's provision of family allowances under Rule C. First, the court held that deference should be accorded to a company's interpretation and execution of its own rules as long as there is a reasonable basis for the company's action. Second, Rule C was found to be a reasonable rule for accomplishing Nissan's goal of providing for employees' children because those registered as household heads usually are household heads, and heads of households are considered by most Japanese to be primarily responsible for supporting the couples' children.[32]

Finally, Rule C was not discriminatory, the court held, because the company was trying to match family allowances with the higher earner of the family. This was not because the size of the family allowance was related to the amount of salary. Rather, it was advantageous to give the family allowance to the higher wage earner who, as head of household, could receive tax deductions for dependents. If women earned more than men, it would be reasonable for them to receive the family allowance and to be treated as head of household for tax and other purposes. Among Nissan employees, more husbands than wives were the higher earner. Therefore, Nissan's identification of households through their registration comported with the reality of households among Nissan employees, and it was legitimate to use household registration to determine the family allowance. In other words, the court was most interested in protecting an efficient family income unit given the current tax regulations.

The court and Nissan shared the assumption that each family has one primary provider. Indeed, Nissan's argument for not putting Rule B into effect was that double income families would receive two family allowances; single income families would receive only one. The court unquestioningly accepted Nissan's argument that such a difference between families was inequitable and provided sufficient reason to retain Rule C. The plaintiffs' proposal that all employees supporting minor children receive family allowances was never seriously evaluated. The court's reliance on household or family registration, both of which identify only one househead, reinforced the assumption that each family has only one provider.

CONCLUSION

Some of the most recent challenges against family registration rest on a claim that although both men and women are vulnerable to disadvantages associated with the use and importance of family registration, women are affected negatively more often due to the confluence of social practices and regulations based on family registration. The underlying assertion in recent challenges is that the present system of family registration adversely affects women disproportionately because it reifies a family structure that subordinates them. Women's success or failure is closely connected to family role fulfillment, and, unlike men, they have few opportunities to expand the concept of self through a career outside the home. Their lack of access to the same educational and employment opportunities as men is directly related to the strength of a family structure that values women's participation in society only to the extent that they, as homemakers, smooth the way for their husbands and children.

This argument of disproportionate impact is strengthened by the government's linkage of national stability, the family registry, and the family model underlying the family registry. The government's use of the house system as a model of the relationship between government and citizens colored the sociocultural content of the house system through an emphasis on obedience, loyalty, and quiet acceptance of hierarchical superiors' decision making. That value content, which was part and parcel of the entire structure, adhered more to the status of women than to the status of men because of the undiluted hierarchical inferiority of women within the house.

The government's linkage of family and state has resulted also in a belief that the nation's stability is linked to maintenance of the house system. Those who seek change are seen as selfishly rocking the very boat that has provided domestic tranquility and national prestige abroad. In addition, the house system has become so entrenched as a model throughout society that it is difficult to stand outside it to grasp its ramifications or to launch a successful attack.

Some feminists have argued that the entire system of family registration is oppressive because of the centrality of ancestors and males. But the legal system does not provide many opportunities for sweeping attacks, and the political system is relatively impenetrable. Surely deep-seated pessimism about accomplishing such massive change is a major factor in the choice to pursue limited improvement. Women are also divided on the benefits and costs of challenging family registration. The high value placed on women's work within the home takes the edge off some women's discontent. Also, some compare themselves to other women in Asia and attribute their greater safety and affluence to a government that has done a good job of providing national security whether or not that security arose from the use of the house system as a model for governance. If they question family registration at all, some women consider its negative effects to be a small price to pay for overall stability and affluence.

Women face particular difficulty in demonstrating a causal link between subordination and family registration for two reasons. First, there are other sources of subordination, such as neo-Confucian ideas about women's supposedly negative or passive (yin) nature. Second, their situation seems different from that of other oppressed groups, such as *burakumin,* Koreans, or nonmarital children. For those latter groups, exclusion and negative valuation occur regardless of the context. Women, however, are treated with at least superficial respect if they stay within the family structure. Rather than the blanket negative valuation accorded the others, subordination of women takes the form of permission to participate in society only as support persons for their families. Because Japanese women are not consistently devalued in all areas of social life, it is difficult for them to argue, and perhaps believe, that partial exclusion, or inclusion only on someone else's terms, is as bad as total exclusion.

Majority Japanese responsiveness to those who would change family registration for the purpose of reducing discrimination is blunted by a belief that sufficient change has already occurred to permit protection. *Burakumin* can change their *honseki,* Koreans can naturalize (or perhaps soon establish family registries), nonmarital children can be adopted under the Special Adoption Law, and women can be registered as heads of households. Women have the most difficulty with this argument because of the number of sweeping postwar and subsequent incremental changes that have addressed inequities between men and women. However, in all cases under review previous changes have failed to reach deeply into the oppressive features of registration. In fact, as we have seen in each case of attempted amelioration, the changes themselves embed messages of subordination and lesser worth. The argument that subordinated groups can protect themselves fails to recognize the handicapping caused by lifelong participation in the subordinating structure.

Central to the problem of changing the family registration system is the Japanese preference for communitarian values despite respect for principles associated with an ideology of equality. Some indigenous support for individualistic principles is long-standing, and those ideals were incorporated into the postwar constitution and codes. Nevertheless, the ideals of individualism and equality are realized, if at all, in the context of communitarian values rather than as the primary concerns of the society and the legal system. The American example demonstrates that ideological commitment is not sufficient, but the absence of even rhetorical adherence to the primacy of equality is a stumbling block for those challenging family registration. In Japan hierarchical patterns of social and national organization combine with an ideology of homogeneity and its necessary counterpart, exclusivity, as bases of national solidarity. The assumptions that hierarchy is "natural," that the hierarchical categories are "natural," and that hierarchy is necessary for national stability result in placid tolerance of categories that restrict the opportunities of some

Japanese to participate in society. Majority descriptions of hierarchical ordering as value-neutral are belied by the experience of groups who have protested against family registration, but majority Japanese may not be able to see or understand that experience because of their privileged position in the hierarchy.

Majoritarian investment in family registration goes hand in hand with subordinated groups' difficulties in acquiring meaningful change in the basic structure of family registration. For the sake of national stability and the institutions that enhance it, challenges and responses to those challenges are limited to specifically offensive features. For the sake of their own family, not just for the sake of the institution, individuals are reluctant to challenge hierarchies in ways that will affect other family members. Women are relatively more burdened by the linkage of family, national stability, and family registration because, unlike the other subordinated groups, women's very reason for existence has been closely linked to supporting the family and, through the family, the country.

One way of furthering the feminist challenge would be to unite with others fighting against family registration. However, achieving a coalition would be difficult because members of one subgroup often participate in the subordination of other negatively valued groups. Moreover, some of the groups are associated with liberation tactics so heavily censured as to give rise to worry about a negative halo effect.[33] Nevertheless, in seeking a basis for joint protest, in finding commonality with others, feminists might break through the barrier of the family as the primary, if not exclusive, source of the definition of women. Through this redefinition and united protest, change in family registration could benefit women not only as women but as members of other subordinated groups.

NOTES

1. This is not to suggest that there is a united front against family registration. Indeed, many Japanese, including many Japanese women, believe that the family structure validated and reinforced by the government through family registration is a valuable source of women's protection. Thus, as will be discussed in the conclusion, those who seek social change through modification of family registration cannot call on a wide cross-section of the population of Japanese women.

2. Judgment of June 17, 1988, Saiko Saibansho [hereinafter Saikosai] (Supreme Court, 2d Petty Bench), 681 Hanrei Taimuzu 99 (1989) [hereinafter Hanta] (appealing the local medical association's revocation of his license to perform abortions); Judgment of July 1, 1988, Saikosai (Supreme Court, 2d Petty Bench), 723 Hanta 201 (1990) (appealing the Minister of Health and welfare's six-month suspension of his medical license). For descriptions of the dispute and its legal consequences, see Ishikawa, *Reform of the Adoption Law in Japan: The Legislative Creation of Special Adoption*, 32 Japanese Ann. Int'l L. 65, 67 (1989); Nakatani, *Kikuta ishi: Jitsuko assen jiken no keiji hoteki sokumen*, 665 Juristo 66 (1978); *Top Court Rejects Doctor's Appeal*, Japan L.J., Aug. 1988, at 1; *Court Dismisses Suit by Suspended Doctor*, Japan Times, June 29, 1983, at 2, col. 5.

3. It seems ironic that Kikuta would be prohibited from performing abortions since he is now prohibited from placing unwanted children by submitting fraudulent birth reports. However, the local medical association based its decision on the circumstances under which Kikuta had arranged the adoptions. Apparently he told pregnant women seeking abortions that he would place their children if they carried the children to term instead of aborting them. The local medical association believed that this was an inappropriate attitude for an abortionist. One would think that Kikuta's case would arouse less outrage since abortion is basically illegal in Japan, despite exceptions that swallow the rule, and that the search for alternatives to abortion would generally meet with approval. Therefore, the real issue must have been the fraudulent birth reports, which enabled everyone involved to escape stigma.

4. The best interests of the children included access to their biological parents' medical histories and prevention of subsequent inadvertent incestuous marriages.

5. For discussions of this case, see Sakakibara, *Kazoku no arikata no tayoka o motomeru*, 61 Horitsu Jiho, Apr. 1989, at 90; Kato, Hoshino, Torii, Toshitani, and Omori, *Fufu bessei no kento kadai*, 936 Juristo 90 (1989) [hereinafter *Fufu bessei*]; Zadankai, *Fufu besshi*, 37 Jiyu To Seigi, May 1986, at 85. English-language newspapers also carried the story. *See, e.g., Professor Files Suit to Use Maiden Name*, Japan Times, Jan. 4, 1989, at 2, col. 1; *Fight in Japan over Law on Married Names*, Sacramento Bee, Jan. 3, 1989, at A2, col. 1.

6. MINPO Section 750.

7. *Fufu bessei, supra* note 5, at 94; *see also* Chira, *What's in a Japanese Name? For Many Women, Obscurity*, N.Y. Times, Jan. 3, 1989, at A1, col. 3.

8. These included matters such as course listings, requests for funds to pay research assistants, publications submitted through the university, and applications for leaves to attend conferences abroad. The dispute reportedly reached the level of university officials tearing down lecture notices and refusing to transfer outside telephone calls if Sekiguchi's premarital surname were used.

9. Judgment of January 26, 1989, Chiho Saibansho [hereinafter Chisai] (Tokyo District Court), 1301 Hanrei Jiho 71 (1989) [hereinafter Hanji].

10. The plaintiffs appealed, but an agreement was reached whereby Nissan agreed to pay family allowances to employees supporting minor children, irrespective of the employees' status as head of household. Since the basis for the settlement is unclear, the Tokyo District Court opinion still stands as guidance to other companies. *Danjo sabetsu sosho ga wakai*, Rafu Shimpo, Sept. 19, 1990.

11. Cornell and Hayami report four conceptually distinct periods in the historical development of family registration. The Japanese government first instituted population recordation in 702 A.D., but the geographical area controlled by the government was limited and few of the records survived. In the late sixteenth century, central and local authorities again used population surveys, this time to ascertain the extent of labor power controlled by individual lords. They were also used to identify and persecute Christians, although compilation was irregular and geographically limited due to individual lords' inconsistent compliance with government directives. There was a third period, at the beginning of the eighteenth century, during which various forms of registration existed, but it was not until 1872 that the present comprehensive, nationwide system of family registration was established. By then the central government of Japan was becoming powerful enough to impose its control on the nation as a whole. Cornell and Hayami, *The Shumon Aratame Cho: Japan's Population Registers*, 11 J. Fam. Hist. 311 (1986).

12. E. Yamanaka, Nikon Kindai Kokka No Keisei To "Ie" Seido 41–44 (1988).

13. *Id.* at 115–16.

14. *Id.*

15. As Otake suggests, the greater equality may have stemmed from the overlap of work and family relationships rather than from the existence of a totally different family structure. H. Otake, Ie To Josei No Rekishi 233–34 (1977). In 1885 Yukichi Fukuzawa wrote of Japanese women prior to "samuraization" that "[p]articularly in marriage, they were very free, never restricted by the confining doctrines of later years. In those years, no one criticized a woman's remarriage." Fukuzawa, *On Japanese Women, in* Fukuzawa Yukichi on Japanese Women: Selected Works 25 (E. Kiyooka ed., 1988). Similarly, Yuzawa's analysis of historical patterns of divorce suggests that divorce was relatively frequent and not stigmatized except in those aristocratic families subscribing to the house system. Yuzawa, *Nihon: Kindaika no naka no konmei, in* Sekai No Rikon 170–202 (1979). Echoes of this flexibility exist in some accounts of rural, post–World War II communities in Japan, which suggests that attitudes toward marriage, divorce, and remarriage are more complex than current literature reflects. *See, e.g.,* R. Smith and E. Wiswell, The Women of Suye Mura 149–76 (1982).

16. A househead could control such things as the occupation, residence, and marriage partner of his children. He controlled his wife's property as well as the house property because she could not legally enter into contracts on her own. Househeads' authority was backed by the power to expel members of the house.

17. Section 736 of the Meiji Civil Code provided that a daughter could become the head of a house. If she married, her husband entered her house and became its head unless there was a contrary agreement that she would remain head of house. *See* J. E. de Becker's annotated version of the Meiji Civil Code for a discussion of Section 736. 2 J. de Becker, The Principles and Practice of the Civil Code of Japan 539 (1921).

18. William Hauser analyzed data about female heads of houses in Osaka before and after 1730. *See supra* note 11, for a discussion regarding population registries that preceded the 1872 registry system. He found increasing legal impediments to women becoming househeads. For example, for a woman to become a househead, a family representative had to ask for permission to register the woman as househead. The term was to last only until a man became househead or no longer than three years. Hauser suggests that such restrictions sprang from an interest in limiting competition among merchant houses. In those cases where the woman was succeeding to house property, that is, main house lines, special dispensations were made so that the main line of the house could continue. In those cases where the woman was succeeding to a house that rented property, that is, branch houses, the restrictions were applied such that it was harder for the house to survive. Thus, the rules restricting househeadship made it more difficult for branch houses, established by younger sons, to survive and compete with main house lines (established by eldest sons). Hauser, *Why So Few?: Women Household Heads in Osaka Chonin Families*, 11 J. Fam. Hist. 343–51 (1986). Two points in Hauser's analysis are particularly significant. First, women's roles in the upper-class house structure in some areas were already restricted well before the government made use of the house system for family registration. Second, the restrictions did not spring primarily from assumptions about women's inferiority.

19. Yamanaka contends that the classification of women as outsiders was the source of most of the status deterioration that attended imposition of the family registry. Yamanaka, *supra* note 12, at 260–61.

20. R. Ishii, Ie To Koseki No Rekishi 701–02 (1981) (lower-class women were tough and respected for their hard work and contributions to the family).

21. One was the right to use the husband's surname, which indicated an incorporation of the wife fully into the house. Another was elimination of the husband's right to unilateral divorce. In 1872 the government first recognized a wife's right to secure a divorce through judicial procedures. From 1919, administrative divorces would not be registered on the family registry without both spouses' consent. Ishii, *The Status of Women in Traditional Japanese Society*, 29 Japanese Ann. Int'l L. 10, 21 (1986).

22. An example of constitutional revision is Article 24, which provides that registration of marriage is to be the result of the individual spouses' choice and not that of their respective parents. An example of revised family law provisions is Civil Code section 770, which equalized the grounds for contested divorces.

23. According to Chizuko Ueno, the change to a nuclear family structure diluted the only form of power women exercised, the power of mistress of the extended house. While wives in nuclear households do retain considerable autonomy within that role, the role itself has been circumscribed by the nuclearization of the family. Ueno, *The Position of Japanese Women Reconsidered*, 28 Current Anthropology S75 (1987).

24. Not many Japanese women use this legal right to establish an independent family registry. This option is used primarily by those women who have divorced and prefer not to return to their family registries (or whose family prefers that they not return). This legal possibility is not exercised any more frequently than the legal opportunities to choose the woman's surname or *honseki* at marriage or to list her as the head of household. The law is gender-neutral on its surface, but the options it provides are not fully utilized. The mere fact of those legal rights does not penetrate to actual practice.

25. Civil Code section 767 allows retention of the marital surname, but the default rule is that the premarital surname will be resumed. Unless the individual actively seeks to retain the married name within three months of divorce, the premarital name will automatically become the legal name. Hisatake details the change in the rule. A. Hisatake, Uji To Koseki No Joseishi 197 (1988). According to Yamagawa, a legal historian, the change in rules concerning surnames arose out of concern for women who would have different surnames than their children if they were not allowed to keep the marital surname. Yamagawa, *Rikon no sai ni sho shite ita uji o sho shita tsuma to uji no henko*, in Kazoku Ho To Koseki 295, 301 (K. Hosokawa and Y. Ebihara eds., 1986).

26. Cornell and Hayami, *supra* note 11, at 319.

27. Yamanaka, *supra* note 12, at 257 (the rule amounted to establishing a pedigree and illustrates the negative effects of the house system on women's status).

28. According to a *Japan Times* report, articles about professional women who chose to use their premarital surnames began to appear in women's magazines around 1983, and many women, like Ms. Sekiguchi, began requesting permission to use their premarriage name despite having registered their marriages under their husbands' surnames. *Group Fighting to Let Couples Keep Own Surnames*, Japan Times, Oct. 22, 1988, at 3, col. 1.

29. Zadankai, *supra* note 5.

30. Judgment of January 26, 1989, Chisai (Tokyo District Court), 1301 Hanji 71, 694 Hanta 114.

31. The plaintiffs brought the case under sections 4 and 13 of the Labor Standards Law (antidiscriminatory provisions). They claimed that the basis for determining which employees could receive family allowances also violated the company's own rules against discrimination. Moreover, they argued, judicial validation of Rule C would violate section 90 of the Civil Code, which prohibits judicial validation of legal acts counter to public policy.

32. The court relies more on social custom than on the law. Under the Civil Code, both parents are equally responsible for supporting their minor children, regardless of who is the registered head of household. MINPO Sections 818, 820.

33. Members of the Buraku Liberation League, for example, have used public denunciation of those who have discriminated consciously or unconsciously against them. While Japanese courts have validated use of denunciation under limited circumstances, denunciation has done relatively little to improve majoritarian responses to *burakumin* and to the *buraku* liberation movement. *See* Upham, *Instrumental Violence and Social Change: The Buraku Liberation League and the Tactic of "Denunciation Struggle," in* Law and Society in Contemporary Japan: American Perspectives 289 (J. Haley ed., 1988).

16 Female Infanticide in China

The Human Rights Specter and Thoughts toward (An)Other Vision

Sharon K. Hom

A recurring story that my father tells is about the silent death of a girl infant from his village during the Second World War. Fleeing with a group of peasant families, my father took refuge under a bridge, huddled in the night. He was young, only a teenager, and it was so very long ago, but he remembers a family: a mother with an infant tied to her back and holding two small boys by the hands. The baby started to make crying sounds, perhaps sensing approaching danger, the sounds of war and death coming closer and closer in the darkness. The father of the family wrenched the baby from the mother's back and quickly submerged her in the waters, silencing any sounds that might endanger the survival of the group. My father, who takes pride in being tough, in being hard on his children, in order to survive at all costs, always pauses at the end of this story, and there is a moment when the past death of that nameless infant fills our silence and demands a response.

As I reflect on the literature on women in China and the inextricably connected literature on Chinese family and population policy, in an effort to understand something about the lives of women and the role that domestic and international law might play, I am haunted by that small infant's death.

Although female infanticide in China is arguably not a general norm of social practice but rather an extreme, persistent form of abuse and devaluation of female life, as a crime of gender it suggests disturbing insights into ideological, structural, and political factors that contribute to maintaining the inferior status of Chinese women. By underscoring the life and death consequences of ideology and contingent constructions of social life (e.g., law, government policy, or family), female

Reprinted by permission from 23 *Columbia Human Rights Law Review* 249 (1992).

infanticide provides a radical lens through which broader questions of social justice
and gender-based oppression can be analyzed.

FEMALE INFANTICIDE: SPHERES OF VIOLENCE AND GHOSTS AT THE WELL

OVERVIEW: FEMALE INFANTICIDE IN CHINA

Defined narrowly, infanticide is the deliberate killing of a child in its infancy; it
includes death through neglect.[1] It "has been practiced on every continent and by
people on every level of cultural complexity. Rather than being the exception, it has
been the rule."[2] Although not viewed as cruel or violent by the societies that practiced it in the past, infanticide is now considered a crime by national governments
all over the world.[3] Because there are very few cases of preferential male infanticide, as a universal social practice, female infanticide is a reflection of the deadly
consequences of the cross-cultural domination of patriarchal values and culture.

Although female infanticide[4] in China is arguably a crime within the existing
legal framework of domestic civil and criminal law, and is clearly officially condemned by Chinese leaders, the tendency to narrowly define female infanticide in
isolation from the broader question of gender inequality and violence against
women limits the analysis of the problem and the possible responses. Chinese literature and official rhetoric and the Western analysis of the problem focus on the
persistence of feudal thought and practices and reflect a tendency to characterize
female infanticide as the "unfortunate consequence" of Chinese population control and modernization policies. This narrow definition and its resulting explanations, however, need to be reexamined. How the problem is conceptualized filters
our capacity to imagine solutions and alternative visions that might inform these
approaches.

RECONCEPTUALIZING FEMALE INFANTICIDE AS SOCIAL FEMICIDE

The killing of girl infants is a form of violence against the infant herself, the
mother, and all women in the society in which the practice occurs. Female infanticide is no less than a gender-based discriminatory judgment about who will survive.
At the familial and societal level at which the mother is subjected to enormous pressure to bear a son or face the consequences of abuse and humiliation, female infanticide is a form of policing and terrorist practice of control over women to keep
them in their prescribed reproductive role as the bearers of sons.

At the same time, it is important to clarify the actors involved and not leave my
proposed reconceptualization adrift in a sea of unmediated social forces or faceless
individuals, institutions, or ideologies. If female infanticide is viewed narrowly as
the killing of female infants, the guilty responsible parties appear to be the mother
herself or the father, relatives, midwives, or medical workers who might get in-

volved. An appropriate "solution" to this privatized conception of the problem would be to criminalize this behavior and to focus on education, deterrence, and punishment of individuals. This "solution" in fact describes the Chinese government's approach.

Although legal prohibitions and protections are clearly significant in terms of building norms and contributing to a climate of equality for girls and women, the isolated privatized criminalization of the practice is not enough to eradicate the problem or its underlying ideological and structural causes. If viewed as a form of social femicide[5] that occurs as a result of the existence of spheres of violence against women, female infanticide would be viewed as more than a crime committed by individuals. Within a "spheres of violence conceptualization," female infanticide, the forced abortion of fetuses against the consent of pregnant women, the abortion of supernumerary children, the abuse of wives who "fail" to bear sons, suicides by despondent women, and malnutrition of female versus male children are all forms of the devaluation of female life.

All these forms of abuse against females are in fact inevitable and foreseeable gender-based consequences of official Chinese policies adopted in the context of the existing structural, ideological, and cultural realities. Government leaders cannot simply point to a formal system of law and policy to avoid responsibility for promulgating policies that have deadly gender-based consequences, and for failing to adequately plan for the inevitable resistance and reaction of the Chinese people.

As social femicide, these cultural practices and abuses implicate government policy makers and leaders at the institutional and ideological level, and raise questions about the locus of responsibility for the impact of these policy decisions. Reconceptualization of the problems as social femicide urges the framing of a more appropriate social response.

[Editor's note: Hom proceeds to analyze the background and implementation of China's One-Child Policy and the Household Responsibility System as two official policies that have contributed to the reemergence of female infanticide. She suggests that asking the "woman question" in the context of China might lead to a critique of the adequacy of the developing country rationale as justification for the deadly and gendered consequences of the actions of the predominantly male party leadership.]

INTERNATIONAL AND DOMESTIC NORMS: DISCOURSES OF UNIVERSALITY AND FALSE GENDER NEUTRALITY

[Editor's note: In this section, Hom discusses the relevance and potential impact of international and domestic legal norms in addressing the problem of violence against women in China. She suggests an analysis of women's human rights and Chinese women's rights in particular, within an international framework implicating two preliminary conceptual and political tensions: (1) the historically problematic, ideological, and marginalized political status of "women's rights" in the international human rights regime; and (2) the failure of a polar universalist/relativist debate and each position to provide an empowering rights framework. After an overview of the Women's Rights Convention (CEAFDAW)[6] and its implementation obstacles, Hom turns to a discussion of the legal, political, and ideological issues presented by China's implementation of CEAFDAW.]

Although China's signing of CEAFDAW may be a positive indication of its continued doctrinal commitment to a formal domestic policy of equality for women, and perhaps acceptance by the Chinese government that gender equality is not just a question of domestic policy but is subject to commitments made under international law, the implementation presents a continuing challenge to women's/human rights activists.[7] In its two Country Reports submitted to date for review by CEAFDAW, China has pointed to the body of domestic law that has been promulgated to address and protect the status of women. These include the 1982 Constitution;[8] the Marriage Law (1980);[9] and particular provisions of the Criminal[10] and Civil law.[11]

Despite the self-reported claims by China of formal compliance with the requirements of the Convention, a number of problems remain. First, although the Chinese legal system reflects a high degree of formal equality for women, the qualification of all rights in China by the 1982 Constitution[12] underscores the contingency of any rights and the subordination of rights to their usefulness to the state, the society, and the collective as determined by the Party. The exercise of these rights is entirely contingent on the party's definition of women's "real" needs and interests.[13]

Second, there is a gap between the formal guarantees and their actual impact on the lives of Chinese women, between the government's stated policy of equality and the reality of women's rights and status in China. Some factors that have been suggested as contributing to this gap between constitutional legal guarantees and social reality are the absence of an effective enforcement mechanism, the absence of an independent judiciary, and the absence of a rights consciousness. However, as the recent democracy movements demonstrate, the demand for rights is not foreign to Chinese citizens.

[Editor's note: Hom concludes that even with the development of formal legal institutions, there remain structural and ideological obstacles. She identifies some possible strategies that international NGOs and domestic Chinese women's organizations can explore, including monitoring China's country reports and using CEAFDAW's definition of discrimination as a "Trojan horse" to challenge conduct and policies formerly protected by a privileged "private" characterization.]

BEYOND HUMAN RIGHTS: THOUGHTS TOWARD AN(OTHER) VISION

Chinese scholars, feminists, activists, and government officials and policy makers face the difficult task of moving China into the twenty-first century with a vision of justice that is inclusive of the rights of all members of its society, including women. A proposal for a feminist reenvisioning of rights in the Chinese context is beyond the scope and goal of this chapter; it also may not be the political or ideological task of any individual scholar, Chinese, American, woman or man, or the perspective of any juxtaposition of these or other positive categories of experience. The goal of a feminist alternative framework should not be grand abstract theory building, but the weaving and living out of a vision shaped by the promises and contradictions inherent in the constraints of the present and the past, and the multiplicity of realities and aspirations of Chinese women and men. It might be a vision that recognizes the power and significance of law but would de-center law clothed in its Western rights-based hegemony as the exclusive social construction that will contribute to social transformation.

I begin thinking about the future by remembering a past journey. In 1987 I returned to my village in Guangzhou with my parents and my little boy. After forty years away from his home village, the hardest decision for my father was to return, but we made our way on the modern express train from Hong Kong, onto two ferry crossings, and along a dusty rural road. And there at the end of a cloud of dust of our approaching noisy van was a throng of several hundred people, all my relatives, all Homs (yes, a patrilocal village). We paid respects before the shrine of my great-grandfather, my ancestors, three generations of us: father, daughter, and grandson. With no running water or sewage system, the villagers still cleaned out the old stone well every spring. They still grew fish for market in the pond over which the village outhouse was situated. My cousin, one baby boy tied to her back, while two smaller children (a boy and a girl) ran around her legs, pointed to a huge mountain of grain that she had just harvested. My father said that nothing had changed except for the paved road into the village. I begin thinking about the future by remembering the unknown lives of millions of people who will never travel beyond these mountains, beyond that paved road.

What might Chinese society look like if the current male-dominated hierarchies of power and hegemonic narratives about women's realities were de-centered? What are strategies for rethinking existing "relations of ruling" and their attendant private and public violence? In locating the sites of resistance, we must recognize that resistance not only is present in organized movements, but "inheres in the very gaps, fissures, and silences of hegemonic narratives. Resistance is encoded in the practices of remembering, and of writing. Agency is thus figured in the minute, day-to-day practices and struggles of Third World women."[14] One way women can exercise this agency is to resort to the "ordered use of the power to disbelieve,"[15] to reject the definitions by the powerful of their/our realities, even in the midst of poverty, exploitation, or oppression. What if more and more Chinese women and men exercised their "power to disbelieve" the reified truths presented by the current patriarchs?

I frame these questions to suggest the centrality of alternative vision(s), values, and decision-making frameworks. The "intentionally provisional" framework suggested by this discussion is premised on a central recognition of Chinese women (and men) as human agents within (an)other vision of women as not only victims of the violence that pervades their/our lives, but also as already possessing the power to transform their/our lives and societies. This tentative framework is grounded in awareness of the powerful historical legacy[16] and glimpses of the daily and numerous ways Chinese men and women are already exercising this inherent power to disbelieve and to live, to construct alternative visions and realities in the face of an apparently hegemonic reality of power and control over every aspect of social life.

At a recent conference on women in China, Chinese women academics, researchers, and writers from China shared their work on sex education, population policy, Chinese rural women, Chinese families, literature, and perspectives on feminism with Western feminist scholars and activists.[17] In a panel on multiple perspectives on feminism, several Chinese women who had completed postgraduate studies in the United States powerfully shared their deep sense of despair and their awareness that they had become inhabitants of the borderlands between cultures, the forever "outsider" perspective. They/I went "home," but discovered it was no longer a place they/I could "fit in." Yet it is precisely from these borderlands, the margins, as it were, that it may be possible to develop a "consciousness of the borderlands,"[18] a plural consciousness necessitated by the internationalization of many of the issues affecting our lives in our different cultures. It is this outsider consciousness, the view from the borderlands, that may provide the images, the experiences that might shape (an)other vision(s) that will uproot dualistic consciousness and open the door to cross-cultural strategies. "It is only by understanding the contradictions inherent in women's location within various structures that effective political action and challenges can be devised."[19]

By engaging in the discursive arena(s) of feminism(s), I am also mindful of Rey Chow's critical reminder to non-Western but Westernized women to ask themselves/ourselves, "How do I speak? In what capacity and with whose proxy?"[20] I speak from the borderlands: an American by citizenship; a British colonial subject by birth; a Chinese American by culture. I do not speak on behalf of my Chinese comrades in China and here in this country. I do speak to encourage them/us to continue to exercise our "power to disbelieve." I imagine more Chinese women standing up and singing powerfully their own words and music. I imagine Chinese women in rural villages choosing to fight for the life of the girl child born, in loving their daughters, an honoring and claiming of themselves.[21] I imagine Chinese women writing women's scripts that will change the languages of power forever.

What vision(s) can guide our efforts? What might the world of the twenty-first century be like? What kind of country might China develop to be? What might our lives be like? Women have been conditioned in different societies to view themselves/ourselves as "the other." What might a vision of the future look like if the perspective of this marginalized "other" were included, if the vision not only began from the primacy and centrality of (an)other, but included the recognition of multiplicities of many possible subject "others"?

I would also envision a country where "human" rights unquestionably included the rights of women, perhaps a country in which the Convention on the Elimination of All Forms of Discrimination against Women is also taught in every school and

where the vision and principles of the convention shape the public and private domains of power and justice. It might be a country where the words "people," "citizens," and "individual" included women beyond linguistic gender neutrality, a
country in which a vision of equality and justice was present in the hearts and lives
of every man, woman, and child. It might be a country where the convention and
all such formal "rights" documents were superfluous anachronisms of a more primitive time. It might be a country where the birth of a female child as well as a male
child will be welcomed with tears of joy and pride. It might be a country where all
the adults, men and women, share equally the responsibility and gifts of raising
these precious charges. It is a country that may not exist anywhere in the world yet.
Or it may already exist. We may only have to recognize it in ourselves and in others. We may only have to continue to exercise our individual and collective power
to disbelieve the inevitability of existing "truths" and to call on ourselves to honor
and bear witness with our lives to the vision(s) we want to believe.

NOTES

1. Laila Williamson, *Infanticide: An Anthropological Analysis, in* Infanticide and the
Value of Life 62–63 (Marvin Kohl ed., 1978).

2. *Id.* at 61. Williamson points out that infanticide has satisfied important familial, economic, and societal needs. In Imperial China, Japan, and Europe, it has been practiced as a
method of controlling population growth and avoiding starvation and social disruption.

3. *Id.* at 72.

4. I use the term to mean the induced death (euthanasia) of infants by suffocation, drown-
ing, abandonment, exposure, or other methods. In China, reported methods also include
crushing the infant's skull with forceps as it emerges during birth or injecting formaldehyde
into the soft spot of the head. Maria Hsia Chang, *Women, in* Human Rights in the People's
Republic of China 260 (Yuan-li Wu et al. eds., 1988).

5. I use the term "social femicide" to suggest the implication of the role of an existing social order in practices that result in death and devaluation of female lives. For an international example of attention to the problem of the impact of social practices on women, see
Report of the Working Group on Traditional Practices Affecting the Health of Women and
Children, Working Group on Slavery of the Sub-Commission on Prevention of Discrimination and Protection of Minorities, U.N. Doc. E/CN.4/1986/42 (1986). The Working Group
on Slavery of the Sub-Commission on Prevention of Discrimination and Protection of Minorities of the UN Commission on Human Rights identified various traditional practices that
have an adverse impact on the health of women. These practices include female circumcision,
traditional birth practices, and preferential treatment for male children. In selecting these
practices as priority problems, the Working Group considered the extent of the phenomenon,
the mortality and morbidity rate, and other factors. The working group's report suggests a
clear link between preferential treatment of boys and the excess morbidity and mortality
among girls. It estimated that about one million female children per year die as the result of
neglect. As one of the consequences of son preference, female infanticide reflects the deadly
impact for female children of the value systems and "preferences" of patriarchal societies,
and thus is a form of social femicide.

6. UN Convention on the Elimination of All Forms of Discrimination against Women (CEAFDAW), opened for signature, Dec. 18, 1979, 34 U.N. GAOR Supp. No. 46 at 193, U.N. Doc. A/34/36 (1979).

7. Paul D. McKenzie, *China and the Women's Convention: Prospects for the Implementation of an International Norm*, 7 China L. Rep. 23 (1991). Since China's admission to the UN in 1979, it has ratified international treaties, used international standards to criticize other governments, and participated in UN human rights decisions to investigate human rights in other countries, including Afghanistan (1984) and Chile (1985). Roberta Cohen, *People's Republic of China, The Human Rights Exception*, 9 Hum. Rts. Q. 448, 536–37 (1987).

8. The 1982 constitution protects freedom of marriage and the duty of children and parents to support each other. Chin. Const. (1982) ch. II, art. 49. It also sets forth the duty to practice family planning. Chin. Const. (1982) ch. I, art. 2.

9. Although titled "Marriage Law," the scope of the law is broader and also addresses the regulation of the family. This law contains a marriage system based on free choice of partners, monogamy, and equality between the sexes.

10. Articles 179 through 184 set forth offenses against marriage and the family, for example, interference with the family, bigamy, spousal and child abuse, and child abduction. Rape (Article 139) is punishable by the death penalty. Prison terms of two to fourteen years may be imposed for a range of crimes against the family and marriage.

11. The General Principles of Civil Law of the People's Republic of China (1986) provide for civil rights and equality within the family.

12. For example, the preamble of the 1982 Chinese Constitution sets forth the guiding ideology, the Four Fundamental Principles: adherence to the socialist road; loyalty to the party; following through with the dictatorship of the proletariat; and adherence to Marxist/Leninist and Mao Zedong thought. Chin. Const. (1982) pmbl.

13. Chang, *supra* note 4, at 250–51.

14. Chandra T. Mohanty, *Cartographies of Struggle: Third World Women and the Politics of Feminism, in* Third World Women and the Politics of Feminism 38 (Chandra T. Mohanty et al. eds., 1991).

15. bell hooks, Feminist Theory: From Margin to Center 90 (1984) (citing Elizabeth Janeways, Powers of the Weak (1981)).

16. Chinese women have a long history of participation in rebellions and revolutionary struggle in China dating back to premodern China. There were secret all-women societies such as the White Lotus sect in the 1790s; all-women associations in the 1660s; women's units in the Boxer Rebellion of 1900; and outstanding women leaders and revolutionaries like Jiu Jin (1875–1907), who shocked and inspired a generation with her courage and personal life choices, including a life of fighting for national and women's liberation until her execution for plotting to overthrow the government. Jiu Jin urged her female compatriots to "hurry, hurry, women, save yourselves." Kumari Jayawardena, Feminism and Nationalism in the Third World 180 (1986).

17. *See* Engendering China: Women, Culture and the State, conference held Feb. 7–9, 1992, at Harvard University and Wellesley College.

18. I borrow the phrase from Chandra Mohanty's discussion of what Gloria Anzaldúa calls a "mestiza consciousness," "a consciousness born of the historical collusion of Anglo and Mexican cultures and frames of reference." Mohanty, *supra* note 14, at 36.

19. Chandra T. Mohanty, *Under Western Eyes: Feminist Scholarship and Colonial Discourse, in* Third World Women, *supra* note 14, at 66.

20. Rey Chow, *Violence in the Other Country: China as Crisis, Spectacle, and Woman, in* Third World Women, *supra* note 14, at 95.

21. *See Heart of the Dragon Mediating* (PBS television broadcast (1987)), depicting a young woman who demanded a divorce because she was convinced her husband wanted to murder their infant girl baby. After mediation among their respective work units, the couple, and their two families, the couple agreed to reunite and everyone agreed to honor and help raise the baby girl.

17 Bridges and Barricades

Rethinking Polemics and Intransigence in the
Campaign against Female Circumcision

Leslye Amede Obiora

I. INTRODUCTION: THE ANTI-CIRCUMCISION CAMPAIGN IN AFRICA

Western legislation and cultural criticism have placed female circumcision at the center of a worldwide controversy concerning how states may best act to protect the interests of women within a universal framework of human rights. Emotional charges and symbolism combined with an overwhelming emphasis on individualistic assumptions about the body lead critics to insist that all African practices of genital markings and reconstructions be designated a crime against women. The debate is divided between universalists, who invoke monolithic categories and constructions of dignity, integrity, and empowerment to condemn genital surgeries, and relativists, who argue for locally autonomous and culturally sensitive reformatory strategies.

Female circumcision does not easily fall within the traditional definition of a gender-specific human rights violation, nor does it seem completely analogous to violent coercion of women by men. It is usually performed for sociocultural reasons by predominantly female private actors with the apparent consent of the circumcised or her proxy. In moderate forms, only a drop of blood or the prepuce is extracted from the clitoris, and with medical supervision the procedure need not engender health complications.[1] Some efforts have been made in Egypt and Sudan to officially recognize these attenuated forms of the practice.[2] In the Netherlands, a Welfare, Health and Culture Ministry report recommended a comparable accommodation.[3]

Apparently some African immigrants in Holland circumcised themselves in often unhygienic and harmful circumstances because, while they could not afford the cultural alienation of not being circumcised, Dutch medical and social workers denied

Reprinted by permission from 47 *Case Western Reserve Law Review* 275 (1997).

them assistance with the procedure. To address the needs of these women, the Ministry, on the basis of the findings of a study it sponsored among five hundred Somali refugee women, recommended a distinction between mutilating or tissue-impairing circumcision and nonmutilating ritual incisions. The report further argued for official stipulation of conditions under which doctors might be allowed to perform simple incisions or ritual perforations of the clitoral covering as an alternative to infibulation. The report drew a storm of protests and was eventually superseded.[4]

In the opinion of Berhane Ras-Work, the Ethiopian chair of the Inter-African Committee (IAC), official approval of the Dutch compromise would have set a dangerous precedent, reconfirming the subjugation of women.[5] The IAC is one key organization facilitating the eradication of traditional practices negatively affecting women and children. To the credit of Ras-Work's dynamic leadership and good offices, the IAC has engaged and positively reoriented potentially volatile traditional issues. Nonetheless, Ras-Work's reaction to the Dutch proposal is somewhat misconceived and overbroad. Incidentally, Ras-Work's reaction has some resonance. The World Health Assembly as well as the International Federation of Gynaecology and Obstetrics are among other entities that have unequivocally condemned female circumcision and called for coalitions to abolish it.[6]

While the lessons of history counsel vigilance against state acquiescence in gender oppression, relief lies at the heart of the recommended Dutch compromise. Rejecting it as an option without critical evaluation of the merits of the voices it echoes is problematic. Any number of procedures could qualify as "incision," and where the benefits of a certain kind of incision outweigh the burdens, form need not occlude substance. To undermine the significance of the voices and agency of the women directly implicated by ritualized surgeries in the guise of protecting them is to erect obstacles to the development of pragmatic efforts to transform the manner and health consequences of the surgeries. A nuanced account of how indigenous participants understand female circumcision suggests the need to cede prominence to grassroots involvement in both the tailoring and implementation of reform. Reform strategies that prioritize notions of individual autonomy and choice must be rigorously attentive to the reality of what bodies, individuals, and communities are (and have been) in African societies and what they mean to women who participate in circumcision.

This chapter seeks to reconcile conflicting positions in the circumcision controversy by elaborating a middle course underscoring how an acute sensitivity to cultural context and indigenous hermeneutics balances efforts to protect the interests of women. This assertion of local context compensates for an emerging radical feminist consensus that overwhelmingly ignores the incommensurability of cultural motivations and meanings by projecting Western understandings of female circumcision onto African cultures.

This chapter argues that positions opposed to the modification of female circumcision are more appropriate for drastic forms of the practice. Although there is a dearth of scientific research on female circumcision, the available data do not implicate mild forms of the practice as dangerous. Without compelling health hazards, the case for total prohibition loses its force. This chapter will demonstrate that the value of eliminating mild forms of circumcision, in spite of the affirmative meanings they may express for the women and the cultures concerned, remains to be seen.

II. DEFINITIONS

A. WHAT IS FEMALE CIRCUMCISION?

The ritualized marking of female genitalia begins with the mildest forms of the procedures, where the clitoris is barely nicked or pricked to shed a few drops of blood. This procedure is innocuous and has a strictly symbolic connotation.[7] The next range of surgeries extends to the removal of the clitoral prepuce, hood, or outer skin.[8] This is the form that ritual Muslims refer to as *sunna,* and medical data indicate that it poses minimal health risks if scientifically performed and monitored.[9] *Sunna* is most comparable to male circumcision, and there is some suggestion that it may serve the purpose of hygiene and cleanliness.[10] A more radical form of female genital surgeries is known as excision or clitoridectomy. In this procedure, the clitoral glans and some of the nympha or labia minora, the narrow lip-like enclosures of the genital anatomy, are severed. The most extreme form of the surgeries is called infibulation, and it has been identified as the form that presents the most significant risks and hazards. This procedure entails scraping the labia majora, the two rounded folds of tissue that contour the external boundaries of the vulva, and stitching the remaining raw edges together in a manner that ensures that only a tiny opening will be left after the surgery heals.[11]

B. THE AURA OF A NAME

The debate over the nomenclature of African genital surgeries reveals that Western-biased themes of bodily "integrity" and tightly bounded individuality tend to confuse and distort the issue. Several critics quarrel with the term "female circumcision," insisting that it is a misnomer for the more extensive practices of clitoridectomy and infibulation.[12] Pontificating that any irreversible removal of a healthy organ or tissue is inherently mutilative, many of these critics maintain that "female genital mutilation" is the only appropriate characterization.[13] Mary Daly, caught in a hyperbole of monocultural indignation, even goes so far as claiming that the varied surgeries all share the "common (slashing and mutilating) features of contemporary gang rape."[14]

Describing a vital aspect of African cultural identity as "mutilation" has proven offensive, if not psychically mutilating, to critical African constituencies like the Premier Group des Femmes d'Afrique who prefer to employ the term "female circumcision."[15] This semantic tug-of-war is emblematic of the constellation of misunderstandings that surround the practice. Ironically, the catchall phrase "genital mutilation" favored by Western-influenced critics is potentially as much a misnomer as "female circumcision," because not all forms of the genital surgeries are impairing. "Circumcision," which literally means "cutting around,"[16] accurately describes *sunna* and actually overstates symbolic prickings. In light of the relative inadequacies of the terms "mutilation" and "circumcision," more than comity and expedience urge deference to the euphemism that resonates with the affected population. The perception and meaning of the practices for the women who exist within the domain they define are of utmost relevance for deliberating constructive nomenclature and strategy. Consequently, I will use the term "circumcision," which indigenous African coalitions prefer. Where necessary for emphasis, a differentiation will be made between the respective forms of circumcision.

III. THE QUEST FOR LOST ORIGINS

A. THE FETISHIZATION OF SEXUALITY: FEMALE GENITAL RECONSTRUCTION IN THE WEST—A SOURCE OF BIAS

Female circumcision is not the African "anomaly" that critics would have one believe. Practices of genital alteration have existed in recent times in Australia, Asia, Latin America, America, and Europe. In fact, Western surgeons claimed to have invented clitoridectomy. The English gynecologist Isac Baker Brown, notable for his innovative acumen, promoted excision in the early nineteenth century. Although the practice was repudiated by the British medical establishment in 1867, it persisted in the United States through the 1950s. Clitoridectomies are currently infrequent in the West, but in rare instances they are inappropriately prescribed as treatment for sexual dysfunction.[17]

Most commentators are unanimous that in the West, circumcision was implemented for patriarchal control of female sexuality.[18] It was also foisted as a "remedy" for female masturbation, which some believed to be a cause of insanity. The removal of the clitoral prepuce is sometimes performed in the United States to counter failure to attain orgasm, a failure associated with redundancy or phimosis of the female prepuce. During the 1970s, "clitoral relocation" or "love surgery" was employed by some medical practitioners, supposedly to enhance sexual pleasure.[19]

The focus of Western feminists on sexuality and gender can be understood as part of a historical preoccupation with male control of sexuality in the industrialized world. The peculiar power that men wield over social relations in this region has been developed through rigid separations of domestic and public life. The bifurcation of public and private life into hierarchized yet relatively autonomous "spheres" clearly has origins in the onset of modernization in Western Europe.[20] The functionalist bent of much feminist analysis of how the dichotomized structure organizes the sexualization of bodies orients the perception of rituals that give form to the meaning of sex and sexuality as inherently about male social control. In the final analysis, however, blind assertions of female subordination and male control may not adequately describe the complexity of gender relations in other worlds.

B. THE PATRIARCHAL EXPLANATORY PARADIGM

Although customs and ritual processes are founded on a mirror of accepted usage, they are by definition not static, but organic and dynamic in terms of rationale, significance, social function, and ideology.[21] A commonality of form is not self-explanatory or determinative of substance. As noted above, circumcision is subject to considerable variation; different forms of the operation affect the genitalia differently, even though some people regard the differences as immaterial "accidents."[22] Furthermore, at the same time, in closely situated localities, female circumcision can mean different things to different actors and subjects. While it may indicate both privilege and prestige in one historic moment or geographic point, it may signify low female social status and deprivation in another regime. The absence of historical records and other relevant data to verify assertions as to the origin and purpose of the practice poses an insurmountable constraint. Even retroactive reconstruction via circumstantial extrapolation is problematic because an almost infinite variety of meanings can be projected on almost any complex of circumstances. Regardless of the diversity of context and meaning, some feminists campaigning against female circumcision explain the origin of the practice monolithically in terms of sexual politics and patriarchal control.[23]

The charge of patriarchy is used to explain a purportedly universal devaluation of women's status in societies. "Patriarchy" is said to be a structure that constrains agency and determines behavior.[24] This thesis postulates that the patriarchal social structure ultimately survived because of a whole range of cruel and ingenious devices that restrained the sexuality of women and assured genealogy.[25] In discussions about circumcision, the argument is expatiated with allegations that in polygamous societies it is physically impossible for a man to satisfy his numerous wives; therefore, he resorts to drastic mutilation of the genitals to stymie their sexual appetites. An analogue of this claim is that circumcision ensures that any child born by a woman is a legitimate child of her husband.[26] This claim is tenuous because some polyandrous and matrilineal societies observe the practice. The idea that the concept of legitimacy, to the extent that it obtains in any particular indigenous African context, provides a universal justification for the practice must be examined in light of cases that demonstrate the continuing negotiation over the affiliation of children. In most communities, the rights of a person are not predicated on or jeopardized by the marital status of the mother. Indeed, there are established traditions that celebrate childbearing out of wedlock.[27]

It is certainly curious that female circumcision has endured the test of time, despite its allegedly endemic gynecological and obstetrical sequelae that are fundamentally irreconcilable with, and regressive of, the natalistic orientation of African value systems. Allegations that a man proves his masculinity and virility by achieving the difficult act of penetrating a circumcised woman pale against the backdrop of widely documented accounts of reciprocal male frustration. Furthermore, the explanation for the practice must be sought elsewhere in areas where it obtains in mild forms that do not interfere with the penetration of the vagina. It stands to reason that invoking a conflating abstraction such as "patriarchy" neither captures nor explains the complexity of circumcision.

The patriarchal paradigm can be criticized for contradictory and circular propositions that are intrinsic in the idea that men exert a totalized control over the construction of social life. It obscures the variable ways men and women are bound together in social units, institutions, and categories that crosscut gender divisions. It essentializes social tensions even when they defy gender boundaries and manifest along generational, socioeconomic, or other lines. The intricate meshing of gender, age, and rank is particularly apparent in initiation rites. In gerontocratic settings, ritual circumcision may connote age hierarchy. The physical hardship that both young men and women endure may essentially speak to them of the authority of age. Female circumcision may not be perpetuated just for its constrictive effect, but for its cohesive effect. Women's control over rituals can be located as a source of strength and power. This control is particularly apparent in initiation societies that have a reputation for acting as a religious counterbalance to the secular male power.

Despite abundant evidence to the contrary, Western analyses continue to be informed by misconceived notions of African women as nothing but subjugated and devoid of agency. They are objectified "only as victims and preyers-upon each other"[28] in negation of their "old traditions of power and strength and nurturance found in the female bonding."[29] Myths about their complacency and passive submission perpetuate the stereotype of the quintessential African woman as a beast of burden.

Most of these sentiments allude to the role of African women as wives and mothers. It may be true that this is the key role of the women, but it is not necessarily a subordinate role. It has led to a strong self-concept among many of the women; it has been a source of strength and impetus. Efforts to analyze gender stratification may be seriously flawed by uncritical ratifications of the female subordination and male control theories that erroneously assume that contemporary relationships between men and women replicate the past. Such theories are better qualified in terms of women's relative authority, rights, and responsibilities as well as the ritual and ideological dimensions of women's social roles and of gender relations. Even where they operate within the clearly defined parameters of a male-dominated homestead system, women's enculturated qualities of initiative and self-reliance motivate them to play vital roles in politics, production, accumulation, and the many exchanges that constitute social relations.

Research demonstrates the extent to which the entangled reality of many African women has been reconstituted by a multitude of contradictory structures and processes. Primarily, it is evident that the political economy of European patriarchal and colonialist hegemony restructured indigenous African sex-gender systems and transformed the significance of the "domestic" sphere.[30] Accordingly, some scholars take issue with the radical feminist "since the beginning of humankind male supremacy" doctrine. They argue that although the doctrine may be applicable writ large to Western societies, the historical data on Third World social structures refute the universality of the stereotype of female dependency and male monopoly of the "public" realm.[31]

Rosaldo, on the other hand, quarrels with the view that the relegation of women to the domestic sphere was invented by capitalist relations of production. Instead, she contends that although capitalism intensifies the domestic/public asymmetry, the asymmetry is a universal characteristic of human economic organization; despite cross-cultural variations in sex roles, the roles and activities of men are held in higher esteem than those of women.[32] In this vein, notwithstanding functionalist interpretations that often stress ritual and gender relational ideals, it is conceivable that female circumcision may be susceptible to flagrant abuse and that rationalizing it solely as an expression of "female power" may precipitate oppression. Along these lines, some writers psychologize that the reason it is predominantly women themselves who perpetuate the practice relates to their own past suffering.[33]

The failure of "patriarchy" as an explanation for sexual stratification reveals the absence of a pragmatic dimension in monocausal accounts of human motivation and behavior, accounts that do not consider the social refraction of symbols and their meaning. The implicit functionalism of the patriarchy thesis ignores the dynamism and feedback between norms and performance that characterize symbolic ritual. Even in those cases where the practice is prone to abuse, the "bottom line" of meaning cannot be drawn securely around the plans and techniques that are used by a people to infer innate appetite for aggression or malice. Often these plans and techniques are tired responses to specific realities that are not always easy for outsiders to ascertain. From historic and cultural distance they may appear devoid of justification. That does not mean that they are not pursued in sincere belief of their benefits and necessity.

Arbitrary imputations of conscious malevolence or misogyny distort and misrepresent the issue.[34] Such insinuations may only incite righteous indignation and thwart reformatory endeavors. Attitudes that have been misconstrued as evidence of malice may chiefly reflect the mindset that "nothing is being imposed on the young that their seniors have not fully and voluntarily assumed for themselves."[35] There are internal checks on bad faith, and violations of ritual procedures require ritual propitiation. The relative power of the collective of women, the belief and value systems, and the multiplexity and interdependence of relationships variously interact to curb abuse. Women may recognize the violent bent of a procedure like circumcision, but they generally deny that the violence is deliberately contrived and gender-biased. To this end, they are quick to emphasize repudiating comparisons between female and male circumcision and to underscore the point that in various African vernaculars the term for male and female circumcision is the same.[36]

C. AN ITINERARY OF CONTRADICTION

1. Situating the Anti-Circumcision Campaign in Feminist Critique

The raison d'être of feminism is compromised when, in its name, the ground-level realities of women are betrayed or a process that pawns the actual interests of women under the guise of protecting them is resurrected. Feminism emerged in opposition to patronizing and paternalistic politics predicated on phallocentric misconceptions of women's "nature" and "best interests."[37] The feminist critique seeks to redeem women's voices and realities from their eclipse by male-controlled social discourses and institutions. Insisting that no one community of norms is astute enough to trump the variegated values and standards of human experience, feminists argue that the white male ideal marginalizes, disempowers, and renders the "other" invisible.[38] Instead of predisposing women to uncritically adopt male standards, feminism validates the significance, strengths, values, and positive functions of women's experiences and perceptions. Because it grows out of direct experience and consciousness, feminism emphasizes context and the importance of identifying experience and claiming it for one's own. As a mode of analysis, feminism rejects elitism and vanguardism, on the basis that people are imbued with transformative capacities and are best suited to champion their own revolution.[39]

Nevertheless, whether out of arrogance or fear of fracturing the base for mobilization, feminism manifests a tendency that betrays the partiality of its makers and entertains a party line that muzzles the merits of voices that do not simply echo the mainstream sentiments. Assuming that women are a determinate group with identical interests and desires risks deteriorating feminist inquiries into the suppression of differences. Even if sincere, the assumption highlights the hypocrisy inherent in professing high-sounding principles of global sisterhood and the politics of experience while meting out a double standard that reinstates the very silencing and stigmatization of women that feminism challenges. Owing to their attraction to essentializing categories, their unconscious attachment to stereotypes, and their participation in a culture in which power is enforced by dominance over definitions and truth claims, some feminists renege on the principal insights that animate their initiatives— insights about the problems of unstated reference points and about how privileging a particular experience mystifies difference.

2. Co-opting Imperialist Discourses

In a "relentless depiction" of the practice of female circumcision in Africa, Mary Daly alleges that among the Nandi, a girl is mutilated and converted to the property of her husband when "stinging nettles are applied to the clitoris, so that it swells and becomes unimaginably large" before it is charred off with glowing coal.[40] In the overwhelming majority of practicing communities, however, Daly reports that the ritual operation is effected by scraping the vulva raw with the broken neck of a bottle and tying the legs of the patient; she is immobilized for weeks, during which time excrement remains in the bandage. Daly further claims that persons who survive this unspeakable atrocity are condemned to a life of repeated encounters with "the little knife."[41] In blind attempts to penetrate quasi-occluded vaginas, frustrated partners typically stretch and lacerate it with sharp instruments; alternatively, excisors specially tailor clay or wooden phalluses to the measurement of a "master's member," which they insert in circumcised orifices to facilitate intercourse.[42] Continuing, Daly notes that further incisions have to be made in order for the woman to be delivered of a child. She must then be resewn to renew her virginity after each birth. Thus, she relives this painful experience with each delivery.

More than a decade after Daly's work was published, Alice Walker's critically acclaimed "factual-fiction" *Possessing the Secret of Joy* chronicled the particular ordeals of generations of women from a misogynistic Olinka tribe at the hands of the *tsunga,* or circumcisor. The *tsunga* mutilates the Olinka women in mass ceremonies with unwashed and unsterilized sharp stones, tin tops, bits of glass, and rusty razors or dirty knives.[43] During prepubescence, the novel's protagonist, Tashi, voluntarily submits to the *tsunga,* who scrapes her clitoris clean, inserts a straw to prevent the adhesion of the traumatized flesh, and fastens the raw edges together with thorns. Tashi's determination to be "bathed" is portrayed as a manifestation of her dire need to assert her African identity. She eventually realizes that succumbing to nationalist sentiments eradicated her sense of self and crippled her hopes for a good life. The excruciation of circumcision reduces her to a psychotic state and corrupts her gait into what Walker describes as a "classic Olinka shuffle." Her urination and menstruation are inordinately prolonged. She reeks incessantly and is incapacitated by cramps caused by the near impossibility of discharging through the pinhole-like aperture that remains from the operation; to crown it all, the aperture is so tiny that the obstetrician breaks several instruments in a bid to enlarge it for her son's birth. Consequently, the son ends up deformed and developmentally disabled. In search of her vindication, Tashi travels out of Africa to the pristine shores of the West, where she receives intense psychotherapy; she eventually returns to Africa and murders the *tsunga.*[44]

Daly's and Walker's accounts are profoundly sobering, and are exemplary of the genre of works that have engendered chills and provoked Western indignation about female circumcision in Africa. Female circumcision has been so highly touted that it has become the prime point of reference in the West vis-à-vis African women. Yet some of the most critically acclaimed research on the subject is little more than the imaginings of "armchair" theoreticians.[45] Some of the more rigorous ones rely on selective samples that, even if painstakingly accomplished, are not validly generalizable to transcend the complex heterogeneity of Africans.[46] Inadequate sampling is often compounded by the fact that some of the studies involve minimal control-group representation. Incomparable results of misconceived criteria are further skewed by ideologically loaded research instruments and procedures. What is typically reflected is expected behavior born of the particular circumstances of the survey that largely serves to reinforce the investigators' preconceptions rather than to communicate observed realities.

Conveniently, critics of circumcision tend to extract the practice from its overwhelmingly developmental and cultural contexts in a manner analogous to "refusing to see the sun in the middle of the day."[47] The conceptual and methodological flaws of the anti-circumcision campaign are especially evident in the respective works of Mary Daly and Alice Walker. It does not require a rigorous exercise of what Mary Daly considers the "mind's imaginative and critical powers" to reckon that the grievous and rampant circumstances she and her cohorts vividly capture should result in phenomenal catastrophe, even the extinction of generations or races.[48] Curiously enough, Daly concludes that infections, but not death, are a characteristic aftermath of the operation.[49]

At various points, Daly denounces other researchers' "negation of the complexity of female experience, the poverty of imagination about the feelings of other women, fixation on sensational materials, maze of deceptive expressions, lack of social perspective, crass indifference, arrogance and ignorance."[50] Yet, although she may be unconscious of her complicity in what she criticizes in others, she is not exempt from her own reproach. Daly relies on and reinforces overt and subliminal racist sentiments by paying homage to the work of Felix Bryk, who invalidated the very basis of his own findings when he surmised that Africans "like to lie—particularly to whites—just as children do, because, like children, they cannot comprehend the moral necessity for truthfulness."[51]

Similarly, Alice Walker, oblivious to the elusiveness and inherent ambiguity of behavioral transcripts, bemoans what she perceives as the pathetic demeanor of the women she encountered on the streets of Africa. She assumed that these women, without exception, were reeling from "genital mutilation." It is not a surprise that her protagonist, Tashi, whom she first described as having hands like that of a monkey, was the one to epitomize the classic "Olinka shuffle" by preferring a Western identity over an African one. Nonetheless, the woes of this maladjusted character are depicted as representative of the objective realities of African women.

Much like Mary Daly's and Alice Walker's exposés, the debates that have ensued on their heels tend, regrettably, to be dogmatic, insulting, and ethnocentric. Apparently, Western feminist interventions are motivated by the concept of "sisterhood" that Daly equates to the mandate for "naming the crimes against (these African) women without paying mindless respect to the social fabric."[52] At the very least, "sisterhood" equally counsels sensitivity to the dignity and intricate realities of the women. The Association of African Women for Research and Development (AA-WORD) echoes a similar sentiment in its stern condemnation of uninformed propagandists who, in a desperate appeal to Western audiences, are "insensitive to the dignity of the very women they want to 'save.'"[53]

IV. ORCHESTRATING CHANGE: EXTRALEGAL ALTERNATIVES

A. EDUCATION

As noted earlier, effective legal engineering can hardly occur in a social vacuum or without public support. Meaningful change requires specific conditions. It is in this regard that education for critical consciousness becomes relevant as both a prerequisite and a complement to legislation. By virtue of education for critical consciousness, women can articulate and assess the burdens and benefits of circumcision in order to determine how best to serve their interests. One way of maximizing critical consciousness may be to integrate circumcision into a mainstream discourse of health.

Several authorities hail education as the single most important factor in combating the practice. The noble efforts of the IAC merit special attention. The IAC is constituted primarily, if not exclusively, of men and women from many African countries. The initiatives of the IAC are on a continuum with the struggles of African activists and scholars against various manifestations of gender-based prejudice. By disseminating information to foster awareness, mass mobilization, and local outreach, the IAC enhances the attitudinal foundation for change. The committee emerged, in part, as a reaction against efforts, mounted largely by Western feminists and WHO specialists, to abolish the practice.

In its educational efforts, the committee adopts a global approach and its programs strive to blend old and new. Instead of focusing on female circumcision in isolation, the IAC programs situate it in the context of other health-endangering traditional practices, including early marriage, nutritional taboos, and scarification.

B. CLINICALIZATION

Just as education is contingent, it is organic. It is a process of incremental effect that presupposes a temporal dimension. An urgent question, therefore, concerns interim transformational strategies that will address the needs of the women who are at risk before education is fully implemented. On this point, it might be illuminating to consider whether a proposal to prohibit female circumcision would be readily entertained if circumcision were an innocuous surgery. What would be the competing arguments for and against state intervention? The case for immediate prohibition is viable for persons who are persuaded by the premise implicit in statements such as Pat Schroeder's that "the girl who suffers genital mutilation is subject to a permanent, irreversible choice made by her parents."[54] Closer scrutiny precludes uncritical acceptance of the premise as applicable to various forms of practices that come under the rubric of female circumcision. While existing data are deficient, there is sufficient evidence to suggest that health complications are more characteristic of the drastic forms of circumcision, especially infibulation.[55]

The condemnation of medicalization as regressive partly results from the fact that it presents a slippery slope. The term "mild circumcision" is ambiguous and can be interpreted as encompassing a wide range of operations. Medicalization has also not precluded the risk of death. Just recently, a fourteen-year-old Egyptian girl died from the administration of anesthesia in the process of circumcision.[56] It is arguable that death from anasthetic complications is an inherent risk of many surgical procedures. It is not peculiar to circumcision and it is distinguishable from death on account of circumcision. Experiments with medicalization have also failed on some occasions to dissuade those committed to circumcision from pursuing more drastic procedures. A team of UN representatives visited a clinic in Djibouti where traditional circumcisors performed mild circumcision under local anesthesia. The team found that grandmothers often quarreled with the fact that the procedure was not complete since it was short of infibulation. The implicit concern was that disgruntled patrons may go elsewhere to perfect an infibulation.[57]

"Clinicalization" seems uncritically accepting of medicine and education. In material respects, however, medical and educational reforms are not the optimal avenues to depoliticize the regulation of female circumcision. Modern medical science, for example, is supposedly more value-neutral, objective, and transcendental of boundaries and differences than law and custom. Yet medicine has been analyzed as constitutive of hegemonic social practices.

Sanitization may not be the ultimate solution, but neither is abolition. The former remains the lesser of two evils, an interim measure targeted at attenuating potentially dire consequences until such a time that adequate groundwork is laid for eradication. Where not being circumcised is perceived as a transgression of social mores, to attempt a full-fledged and undifferentiated assault is to jeopardize enduring reform. It is more likely that reform will be coherent and successful if it is based on identifiable principles and concepts that command general acceptance, particularly as legal sanctions compete and conflict with social sanctions and self-interest. Modification is not only the least restrictive means; it is the path of least resistance and the more efficient and humane strategy.

It cannot be overemphasized that a mild form of female circumcision, such as the one described as entailing symbolic pricking, is largely inconsequential from a health standpoint. Medical science and technology have facilitated and reduced the risk of far more delicate and intricate surgeries than the circumferential excision of the clitoral prepuce.

Sanitization ameliorates mutilation, morbidity, and mortality. It is compatible with preexisting community values and agendas for welfare. Some of the rationales for the practice are lost in the abyss of historical uncertainties, but it appears that sanitization would cater to various concerns implicit in different strands of discernible rationales. It aligns the practice with official objectives for the protection of the integrity of women and children, while striking a balance with the competing interests that sustain the practice. Sanitization holds promise as a viable option for both Africa and the West. The point of extending the proposal for modification to the West is not to dictate how it should deal with matters within its jurisdiction. It is rather to explore how best to ensure the welfare of the affected population who, in the wake of the recent wave of intercontinental migrations, now reside in the West.

It is evident that there will be additional costs associated with clinicalization and the initiation of educational programs that expose the dangers and dysfunctions of female circumcision. Realizing any plan of attack involves costs, with or without harsh budgetary and economic realities. Many studies demonstrate that the ineffectiveness of prohibition is related to the prohibitive cost of stringent enforcement. Prosecution and punishment require a significant expenditure of time, energy, and other resources, and the expenditure may not translate into optimum effectiveness. Moreover, most jurisdictions adopt twin policies of prohibition and education, so that the case against the cost of education for critical consciousness is redundant. It is not obvious that clinicalization entails more expenses than prosecution and monitoring. More important, its short-term costs may well be long-term gains, especially in terms of protecting human life and relieving court schedules.

V. CONCLUSION

Beginning with a description of practices of female circumcision, which notes its variability across different cultures, this chapter systematically explores the theoretical and normative bases for transcultural critique and interrogates the circumstances under which "outsiders" can validly evaluate or condemn any cultural practice. More precisely, it discusses the campaign against female circumcision and the data on which the campaign is based. In highlighting the medical, social, sexual, and psychological consequences of the practice, the chapter offers a critical analysis of the empirical and methodological flaws in the data on which the anti-circumcision campaign rests.

Ultimately, the chapter investigates the conditions for reformist intervention and underscores the types of intervention that are likely to be effective. The analysis asserts the importance of indigenous hermeneutics and nuanced contextualism in response to an emerging consensus that overwhelmingly disregards the incommensurability of cultural motivations and meanings. As postcolonialist critiques of Western rights ideology demonstrate, the discourse of absolute rights offers little help for the resolution of the competing claims of cultural and individual autonomy. Accordingly, the chapter explores the possibility of a bottom-up transitional transformation, and its potential for bridging the rift between polarized views of relativism (read as custom) and universalism (read as law) with regard to female circumcision. In articulating the requisite dimensions for sustainable change, the chapter suggests that "clinicalization" or "medicalization" is an apparent (but only apparent) way of circumventing the tension between "custom" and "law" in the circumcision debate.

Regulating female circumcision, even as an interim response, reconciles the need to protect women with a respect for embodied sociocultural identities. It also underscores the relevance of claims of cultural specificity to overriding questions of justice, liberty, and diversity. In conclusion, it is important to emphasize that the argument for a middle course that this chapter espouses is neither a case for nor a case against female circumcision. Essentially, the argument seeks to give voice to perspectives that have heretofore remained unarticulated or muted, and to enrich pertinent academic debates and policy strategies.

NOTES

1. *See* Asthma El Dareer, Women Why Do You Weep? 48 (1982).
2. *See* Marie Bassili Assaad, *Female Circumcision in Egypt: Social Implications, Current Research and Prospects for Change*, 11 Stud. Fam. Plan. 3, 5 (1980).

3. *See* Henrietta Boas, *Problem of Female Circumcisions in Holland*, Jerusalem Post, May 10, 1992, at Features.

4. *See* Guido de Bruin, *Women: Dutch Government Ends Debate on Circumcision Proposal*, Int'l Press Service, Nov. 11, 1992.

5. *See id.*

6. *See* World Health Organization, Female Genital Mutilation: World Health Assembly Calls for the Elimination of Harmful Traditional Practices (Geneva: WHO Office of Information, Press Release WHA/10, May 12, 1993).

7. *See* Belke Wold Giorgis, Female Circumcision in Africa: Research and Social Implications (1981).

8. *See* Nahid Toubia, *Female Circumcision as a Public Health Issue*, 331 New Eng. J. Med. 712, 712 (1994).

9. *See* Amna Elsadik Badri, Female Circumcision in the Sudan 9 (1984).

10. *See* Robert Cook, *Damage to Physical Health from Pharonic Circumcisions in Infibulation of Females, in* World Health Organization, Seminar on Traditional Practices Affecting the Health of Women and Children 145 (Taha Baasher et al. eds., 1982).

11. *See* Hanny Lightfoot-Klein, Prisoners of Ritual: An Odyssey into Female Genital Circumcision in Africa 33 (1989).

12. *See* Paula Giddings, *Alice Walker's Appeal*, Essence, July 1992, at 59 (book review and interview).

13. *See* Mary Daly, Gyn/Ecology: The Metaethics of Radical Feminism (1978).

14. *Id.* at 155, 172.

15. *See* Marie-Angelique Savanne, *Why We Are Against the International Campaign*, 40 Int'l Child Welfare Rev. 37 (1979).

16. Webster's New Universal Unabridged Dictionary 328 (2d ed. 1983).

17. *See* Lightfoot-Klein, *supra* note 11, at 179–81.

18. *See, e.g., id.*

19. *See* Outrageous Acts and Everyday Rebellions 296 (Gloria Steinem ed., 1983).

20. *See* Rosaling Coward, Patriarchal Precedents: Sexuality and Social Relations 7, 17, 253 (1983).

21. *See* L. Amede Obiora, *Reconsidering African Customary Law*, 17 Legal Stud. F. 217, 217 (1993).

22. *See* Victor W. Turner, The Forest of Symbols: Aspects of Ndembu Ritual 153 (1967).

23. *See* Daly, *supra* note 13, at 157–60; Alice Walker, Possessing the Secret of Joy (1992); Steinem, *supra* note 19, at 295.

24. *See* Gerda Lerner, The Creation of Patriarchy 239 (1986).

25. *See* Nawal Saadawi, The Hidden Faces of Eve: Women in the Arab World 41 (1980).

26. *See* Raqiya Haji Dualeh Abdalla, Sisters in Affliction: Circumcision and Infibulation of Women in Africa 52–60 (1982).

27. *See* Ify Amidiume, Male Daughters, Female Husbands: Gender and Sex in African Society 31–34, 94 (1987).

28. Audre Lorde, *An Open Letter to Mary Daly, in* Sister Outsider 67 (1984).

29. *Id.* at 69.

30. *See* Women and Gender in Southern Africa to 1945, at 27 (Cheryl Walker ed., 1990).

31. *See generally* Ester Boserup, Woman's Role in Economic Development (1970); Eleanor B. Leacock, *Women's Status in Egalitarian Society: Implications for Social Evolution*, 19 Current Anthropology 247, 250 (1978).

32. *See* Women, Culture, and Society 17–42 (Michelle Zimbalist Rosaldo and Louise Lamphere eds., 1974).

33. *See* Scilla McLean and Stella E. Graham, Female Circumcision, Excision and Infibulation: The Facts and Proposals for Change 8 (Minority Rights Group Report, no. 47, 1980).

34. *See* Kay Boulware-Miller, *Female Circumcision: Challenges to the Practice as a Human Rights Violation*, 8 Harv. Women's L.J. 155, 166 (1985).

35. *See* Loren E. Lomasky, Persons, Rights, and the Moral Community 182 (1990).

36. *See* Taha Baasher et al., *Psycho-Social Aspects of Female Circumcision, in* Baasher et al., *supra* note 10, at 165.

37. *See* Mary E. Hawkesworth, *Knowers, Knowing, Known: Feminist Theory and Claims of Truth*, 14 Signs 533 (1989).

38. *See* L. Amede Obiora, *Neither Here Nor There: Of the Female in American Legal Education*, 1996 L. and Soc. Inquiry 355.

39. *See* Nancy Hartsock, *Fundamental Feminism: Process and Perspective*, 2 Quest: A Feminist Quarterly 67–80 (Fall 1975).

40. *See* Daly, *supra* note 13, at 166.

41. *Id.* at 157.

42. *See id.* at 156, 164 (relying on Jacques La Lantier, La cite magique et magie en Afrique noire 279 (1972)).

43. *See* Walker, *supra* note 23.

44. *See id.*

45. *See* Filomina C. Steady, *Research Methodology and Investigative Framework for Social Change: The Case for African Women, in* Association of African Women for Research and Development, What Type of Methodology 12 (1983).

46. *See* Arthur Phillips, *Introduction* to Lucy Mair, African Marriage and Social Change viii (1969).

47. *See* Association of African Women for Research and Development (AAWORD), *A Statement on Genital Mutilation, in* Third World: Second Sex 217, 219 (Miranda Davies ed., 1983) (hereinafter AAWORD).

48. Daly, *supra* note 13, at 155.

49. *See id.* at 156.

50. *Id.* at 170.

51. *See* Felix Bryk, Dark Rapture: The Sex-Life of the African Negro 28 (Arthur J. Norton trans., 1939).

52. Daly, *supra* note 13, at 172.

53. *See* AAWORD, *supra* note 47, at 218.

54. Patricia Schroeder, *Female Genital Mutilation: A Form of Child Abuse*, 331 (11) New Eng. J. Med. 739, 740 (1994).

55. *See* Efua Dorkenoo and Scilla Elworthy, Female Genital Mutilation: Proposals for Change 8–9 (1992).

56. *See* Independent, Aug. 25, 1996.

57. *See* Halima Embarek Warzazi, Study on Traditional Practices Affecting the Health of Women and Children, U.N. Doc. E/CN 4/Sub.2/1991/6 at 19 (1991).

18 | Uneasy Alliances and Solid Sisterhood

A Response to Professor Obiora's "Bridges and Barricades"

Isabelle R. Gunning

Professor Leslye Amede Obiora's article "Bridges and Barricades: Rethinking Polemics and Intransigence in the Campaign against Female Circumcision" is an incisive, compelling, and in some respects disturbing argument for the clinicalization or medicalization of female genital surgeries.[1] This chapter is a reaction piece. It will explore the most persuasive of Professor Obiora's points. Where we most agree is on the racist and hypocritical manipulation of the imagery and lives of African women so frequently on display in the anti–female circumcision campaign. But it will also explore our points of disagreement—on the static and monolithically oppositional ways she juxtaposes the lives of African and Western women. It will end, ultimately, with my uneasiness with, if not wholehearted opposition to, her proposal.

Obiora raises several substantial criticisms of the anti–female circumcision campaign. Her article raises immediately the fundamental question in international human rights discourse of how to define in concrete terms the meanings of cherished human rights "in a universe of competing values and moralities,"[2] a universe made even more problematic when so many of these human rights "bear a Western imprint."[3] This is a fitting introduction to her sections "The Fetishization of Sexuality: Female Genital Reconstruction in the West—A Source of Bias"[4] and "The Patriarchal Explanatory Paradigm."[5] These sections focus on the insistence of Western commentators and feminists on imposing a particular and monolithic framework upon the African experience of female genital surgeries without regard for the differences and complexities of the Western and African experiences with the surgical manipulation of the female genitalia. Western bias—frankly, racism—in the misuse of static and denigrating imagery of African cultures and African women in

Reprinted by permission from 47 *Case Western Reserve Law Review* 445 (1997).

order to forward the movement against female genital surgeries is a long-standing concern of my own.[6] This is a point well taken, and still not well incorporated by much of the general anti–female circumcision discourse one reads.

Most pointedly, Obiora largely ignores the more liberal, general "do-gooder" commentators who might be expected to turn up in mainstream media venues to articulate the offensive and tired "white man's burden to save these colored savages from themselves" line of self-righteous argument. She focuses, instead, on people who should know better: feminists. Her critique is targeted on the functionalist bent of much of feminist analysis, and she makes quite clear that she means "Western" feminism. Moreover, her most stinging criticism is aimed at two well-known and well-respected feminists, Mary Daly and Alice Walker.[7] She entitles the section on these two women "Co-opting Imperialist Discourses," and her well-chosen quotes and unadorned summary of the arguments that the two advance make clear that "the master's tools will never dismantle the master's house."[8] The reinvigoration of racist and imperialist imagery is glaringly exposed in Obiora's rendition of their works.[9] Unfortunately, it is not the feminists who have co-opted the imperialist discourses; it is the imperialist discourse that has co-opted the feminists. Obiora invokes Daly's own "mind's imaginative and critical powers" to explain the "conceptual and methodological flaws" in these works.[10]

Obiora's ultimate point here is a compelling one. Daly and Walker are thoughtful intellectuals and feminists. Daly has herself been critical of other writers' "negation of the complexity of female experience, the poverty of imagination about the feelings of other women (and the) fixation on sensational materials."[11] Walker is progressive, feminist, and African American, and has herself been so critical of the marginalization of the experiences of any woman who is not white in the common understanding of the term "feminism" that she has coined a related term, "womanist," to denote the inclusion of women of color.[12] Knowing Professor Obiora as I do, I can say that these are women with whom she would, and has been, otherwise allied. Their stumbling here represents a warning. Good intentions are not enough. Constant vigilance and self-criticism are required for the feminist or progressive who truly intends to bridge the multicultural divides to create sisterhood.

Beyond the imperialism and racism that are employed by feminists, Obiora points out as well the hypocrisy. In her well-documented section "Situating the Anti-Circumcision Campaign in Feminist Critique," she describes one of the primary aims of feminism as

> [T]o redeem women's voices and realities from the eclipsing of male controlled social discourses and institutions. . . . [F]eminism validates the significance, strengths, values and positive functions of women's experiences and perceptions. Because it grows out of direct experience and consciousness, feminism emphasizes context and the importance of identifying experience and claiming it for one's own.[13]

Obiora underscores the hypocrisy of the anti–female circumcision campaign when its feminist advocates employ "male-controlled social discourses" like racism and imperialism to "eclipse" the voices of African women who continue to value the experience of circumcision.[14] While one view of the surgeries may be their location in an array of patriarchal control devices, Obiora notes that it is both politically disrespectful and intellectually compromising to ignore the complex layers of symbolism attached to the surgeries for African women; to see nothing of what women find positive in the ritual and symbol is to violate one's own premise to contextualize and to take women's experiences seriously. Obiora's astute observations represent a challenge. The process by which we struggle for the rights of women is important. There is a long patriarchal history, much critiqued and criticized by feminists, of people doing "what was best" for women with little input, and less consent, from us. If feminists in the anti–female circumcision campaign are to distinguish themselves from that history, then the voices and experiences of all women will have to be heard.

Obiora's feminist critique of feminists' approaches in the anti–female circumcision campaign is one of her strongest points, yet it is also where I found the beginnings of my differences with her. While Obiora rightly criticizes Western feminists for viewing female genital surgeries as rooted "monolithically in terms of sexual politics and patriarchal control"[15] regardless of evidence of the diversity of contexts and meanings for the practices, she herself begins to treat the views and experiences of Western feminists monolithically and as if they were diametrically opposed to those of African women. Part of her criticism of "much feminist analysis" is that "the blind assertions of female subordination and male control may not adequately describe the complexity of gender relations in other worlds."[16] She argues, essentially, that Western cultures may be well understood by simple explanations of sexual politics and patriarchal control. She cites, as an example, feminist scholars who contend that the devaluation of women's work and subordination to men are historical realities, "since the beginning of humankind"; their work, she agrees, is true for Western cultures.[17] However, she suggests that African cultures are different in this particular respect on male and female roles and valuation. African women's experiences involve a more "entangled reality" that has been "reconstituted by a multitude of contradictory structures and processes."[18] Frankly, this "multitude of contradictory structures and processes" sounds like a fine general description of the lives of most women. The particularities of these processes and structures will of course vary around the culture, class, race, sexual orientation, age, and other individual and social characteristics and circumstances of the women involved, but ultimately the history and lives of Western women are not fairly characterized by monolithic terms either. Scholars have disputed the notion that women's work was always of little or no value during other historical times in Western contexts.[19] Some Western feminists have raised issues about the fundamental nature of class in the actual lives of poor and working-class Western women and how this complicates simplistic notions of patriarchal control; men and women in the same class may have a number of substantial ties and alliances that in many contexts may be more significant and binding than the ties or interests that connect women across class lines.[20]

Similarly, Western feminists of color have rejected a monolithic "patriarchal control" explanation of the lives of women of color, given the continuing vitality and virulence of racism.[21] When Obiora criticizes the patriarchal paradigm for obscuring "the variable ways in which men and women are bound together in social units, institutions, and categories that cross cut gender divisions. . . . [and] essentialize social tensions even when they defy gender boundaries and manifest along generational, socio-economic or other lines,"[22] she is not talking just about the African cultures, or "other worlds" to which she refers, she is talking about all cultures. Her overall criticism of the simple patriarchal control model holds not just as to the complex lives of African women, but also as to the complex lives of Western women. Employing a purely patriarchal control model has been politically useful in Western contexts for sharpening and defining the contours of debates around women's rights, but acknowledging that usefulness is not the same as arguing that the model accurately frames the multifaceted lives of Western women.

In oversimplifying the lives and experiences of Western women to make her point in contrasting Western feminism and culture with African women and culture, Obiora does a certain amount of oversimplification of African women's lives. This simplification is, perhaps, deliberate. Her argument is that millions of women support some form of female circumcision, and feminists who are a part of the anti–female circumcision campaign need to listen to, not dismiss, these voices and experiences. She wants to show solidarity with these voices that are often overlooked or ignored; indeed, her very choice of the terminology "circumcision" as opposed to "female genital mutilation" is a part of her determination to make central the "perception and meaning of the practices for the women who exist within the domain they define."[23] Obiora wants to respect and demand respect for primarily the women who support the surgeries; clinicalization is a solution designed to acknowledge the complex and cherished symbolism that the surgeries represent and at the same time confront and cure the physical damage the surgeries can cause. But, of course, the voices of support for the surgeries are not the only voices emanating from "the women who exist within the domain they define";[24] there are also voices of opposition. Some of these opponents Obiora mildly denigrates by characterizing them as "Western-influenced critics" because of their willingness to characterize the surgeries as mutilations.[25]

I understand Obiora's intent and purpose in muting all (and, let us say, chastising some) of the voices of opposition. To some extent it can be said that opponents are "heard" all the time in and by the anti–female circumcision campaign. Still, I feel compelled, in reacting to Obiora's approach, to talk about the resistor voices. It is not to remind Obiora of their existence; she flags that in her work. Rather, it is because African opponents of the surgeries do have a difficult time getting "heard."

As critical as Obiora and others have been of the work of Alice Walker, it is not an accident that it is her work that has been frequently identified as having elevated the surgeries in the popular consciousness of Western feminists; African activists whose concern and activity preceded Walker's were not heard. And even when

African feminists speak, their words can be distorted. For example, Soraya Mire is a young, circumcised Somalian American filmmaker who created a documentary of the surgeries in Somalia called *Fire Eyes*.[26] The film is a highly contextualized piece that portrays the specificity of a particular African culture (Somalian) and the nuances, tensions, and ambivalences of an array of Somalian people, men and women, who discuss the surgeries. Although Mire continues her career as a filmmaker, she has spent, and continues to spend, some time showing *Fire Eyes* and speaking out against the surgeries. Despite the thoughtful, complicated, and loving perceptions and voice that Mire has, when she appeared, for example, on the *Oprah Winfrey Show*, she had to address a set of eurocentric questions posed, ironically, by an African American woman who has been identified with the fight for women's issues.[27] Winfrey's somewhat disruptive questioning was designed to contain Mire's complex answers into a simplistic "but oh, how barbaric! this is so unusual for us Americans!" box. Even when people say they are listening, it is not clear that they actually hear anything more than what they want to hear. I do not mean to belabor the point, for Obiora and I, an African feminist and an African American feminist, have lived through this particular problem.

Perhaps, as I think Obiora subtly suggests when she characterizes them as "Western-influenced critics," those opponents who are willing to describe the surgeries with harsh language like "mutilations" or "torture" are "heard" because they are saying just what Westerners want to hear; they pander or perhaps they have been co-opted. Still I want to judge them more gently. When I read about Mimi Ramsey, a circumcised Ethiopian American nurse who speaks with other Ethiopian immigrants against the surgeries and is reported to pray aloud, "Please, God, save girls from being tortured. Please, God. Please. Thank you";[28] or when I read a report from a United Nations–sponsored regional conference on damaging traditional practices held in Burkina Faso and see that the participants, largely African activists, recommend that the term "female genital mutilation" be used in place of "female circumcision,"[29] I believe something more complex is going on than Western influence. I do not mean to suggest that Western influence cannot be tainting; I struggle against the negative parts within myself all the time. But it is Obiora herself who strongly argues against the trap of denying the agency of African women. Be it "Western feminist influence" or "African patriarchal influence," most African women cannot be free of either. But neither do such influences totally dictate their thoughts and actions.

Moreover, she is also clear about the dynamic nature of culture: "[C]ulture is a set of interpretive understandings and aggregate consciousnesses under active construction. Just as it is always practiced, it is never neutral. It integrates and incorporates inequalities."[30] She recognizes that the process of hegemony makes inequalities appear natural, normal, traditional, inviolate, and that what lies beneath this are profound layers of influences on individual life. Both the supporters of the surgeries, whose voices Obiora elevates, and the opponents are a part of this dynamic nature of culture that she describes. The entire range of "perceptions and meanings"—the supporters who are angry with opponents for blaspheming treasured traditions; the supporters who are bemused, perhaps annoyed, with their opposing sisters for falling under the spell of foreigners; the opponents who are angry at supporters and want to shock sense into them with blunt language; the opponents who want to be gentle with their supporting sisters and nurture and educate them to a different view—are an important part (and, I confess, to this feminist the most important part) of the lively mass of voices contesting the past, current, and future meanings of the range of African, and in many instances Western, cultures of which they are a part. The resistor voices are necessary complements and contestants to supporter voices; Obiora herself notes that "it is conceivable that female circumcision may be susceptible to flagrant abuse and that rationalizing it solely as an expression of 'female power' may precipitate oppression."[31]

Noting the dynamic, process nature of culture and cultural change reveals some of the compelling rationales for Obiora's proposal. Obiora underscores that as a matter of respect and consistency, feminists need to acknowledge the perceptions and experiences of the women who support the surgeries; and one way to meet them part of the way is through the clinicalization of the surgeries. Once clinicalized, the surgeries will lose the bulk of the physical health hazards that they can pose in their most invasive forms. If there are no major health risks, arguably they will be no worse than "trimming," breast implants, or, the rage of the younger generation, body piercing (including the genitalia of both men and women).[32]

Even if one were to refuse to acknowledge the agency and self-determination rights of African women who support the surgeries and take the more imperialistic or maternalistic (depending on one's degree of anger at such arrogance) approach, one might still support clinicalization for practical reasons. Especially if one's focus is on the most severe health consequences that can occur (deaths, infections, long-term menstrual problems, complications in birthing), then some intermediate intervention would save the lives and health of women who continue to want the surgeries performed.

While Obiora notes that in the Netherlands a proposal for clinicalization was too politically hot to be executed,[33] in some African countries some forms of clinicalization are occurring. Obiora mentions areas of the Sudan and Egypt, although as she noted, in Egypt political struggle continues over whether to allow modern health care practitioners to continue to perform some form of the surgeries and under what circumstances. In Djibouti the main women's, and primary anti–female circumcision, organization, the Union Nationale des Femmes de Djibouti (UNFD), has a clinic where traditional circumcisers perform a form of the surgery that is less invasive than the more popular infibulation form, under sterile conditions.[34] I have to respect the decision by anti-circumcision activists to pursue this intermediary step, especially the UNFD activists who include the retraining of traditional circumcisers as part of their plan. Still, the Djibouti example raises a troubling issue that Obiora does not starkly confront: if the physical health problems are minimized, is any degree of removal (not just nicking) of the female genitalia, which possibly, though not conclusively, may affect women's sexual health acceptable?

Since the Djibouti feminists are focused on a shift from infibulation to anything less, it seems that a considerable amount of the genitalia is removed under this clinicalization procedure. In many ways, Obiora does not focus on this aspect of her proposed solution. In my own writings on female genital surgeries, Obiora had been instrumental in reminding me, as is also evidenced in this essay, that the surgeries (emphasis on the plural) are a range of surgeries. She criticizes the ways Western feminists tend to conflate all the surgeries into infibulation and assume that all of the worst-case physical, sexual, and psychological health problems, which are not unambiguously or universally documented in all cases of infibulation and not necessarily existent in less invasive surgeries, occur virtually all the time in every type of surgery. While Obiora raises a brilliant critique of the flaws in such conflation toward the most severe form of the surgeries, I think she tends to encourage us to conflate toward the opposite end. She raises a range of issues that rightly complicate notions of female sexuality and sexual pleasure that assume that the physical is primary and unrelated to the psychological, social, and cultural notions of sexuality and that the particular part of the physical female anatomy that is key is the clitoris.[35] She again argues that feminists are refusing to take the voices and experiences of African women seriously if they ignore reports of sexual pleasure or satisfaction from circumcised women. Still, I sense that Obiora suggests that clinicalization will not just reduce the physical health risks, but will also reduce the amount of the female body that is removed during the operations; she imagines, and I want to imagine with her, that clinicalization will mean, by and large, the performance of some minor and ritualistic pricking that could not possibly pose any physical or sexual impairments. It is not clear that is what is occurring in countries, like Djibouti, where the clinicalization route is being used. Nor is it necessarily likely, given some evidence that suggests that the more ritualized forms of the surgeries are more common for Asian female circumcisions than for African circumcisions, that the very mild form of the surgeries will be likely in the near future.[36] It may well be that whatever likelihood and degree of sexual impairment might occur due to a clinicalized intermediate form of the surgeries would be no worse than the impact of "trimming" the clitoris or reshaping the genitalia of intersexed people or any number of patriarchally shaped psychological notions of what women should or should not do or feel (and with whom) in bed. All of these raise some issues of sexual impairment even within the culturally defined confines of sexual pleasure. While the "mere" possibility of sexual impairment might reduce the surgeries to a lower level of priority on the "feminist agenda," where African feminists have long thought it belonged (behind, say, physical health issues and economic development), I still think that the preservation of corporeal integrity, especially but not exclusively for women, and the promotion of positive psychological notions regarding sexuality are important feminist goals. Consequently, I find the notion of the clinicalized intermediate form troubling.

The UNFD clinicalization approach involves the retraining of traditional circumcisers, who are largely women. But other approaches involve what Obiora largely focuses on—the training of modern health care practitioners. This approach raises its own set of troublesome issues. Opponents of female circumcision have denounced the supporting voices of traditional circumcisers by noting that they have a personal, perhaps selfish, and economic interest in the perpetuation of the surgeries; in some cultures the job of circumciser may be one of the few ways women can earn money and status on their own.[37] In countries where modern health care professionals have participated in the performance of the surgeries, critics have charged that they now have acquired an economic stake, greed, in the perpetuation of the surgeries.[38] Medicalization could just substitute modern, Western-trained health care professionals for traditional circumcisers. Two problems might develop. One, already mentioned, is that these health care workers could become professionally invested in the perpetuation of the surgeries and thus become a powerful opposition voice to the long-term abolition of the surgeries. Perhaps, between the fact that these professionals have a broader range of health care skills than just the surgeries to rely on for their economic survival, and Obiora's hope that, ultimately, the "surgery" performed would be merely ritualistic, this is either an unlikely consequence or a benign one. The second problem involves the fact that the transfer of authority to circumcise from traditional circumcisers to modern health care practitioners may also, in effect, become a transfer of the provision of health care for women from a more female-dominated and traditional model to a more male-dominated and Western model. Western feminists have found that the domination of health care by men has, in some instances, had a detrimental effect on the health care and needs of women.[39]

In addition, although some traditional health care practices have been determined to be detrimental to health, Western medicine is increasingly realizing that some traditional, more natural approaches and remedies ("old wives' tales") are in fact quite beneficial to human health and, indeed, preferable to more chemically or surgically oriented approaches.[40] Creating a health care institutional structure that emulated Western approaches in these regards could be, in the long run, detrimental to women, indeed to everyone, in the cultures involved.

All these concerns underscore my unease with the clinicalization or medicalization approach. That unease is increased by another aspect of Obiora's approach. While I respect the fact that Obiora has her thoughtful reasons for resisting efforts to force her to position herself as "for" or "against" the surgeries, I view the clinicalization approach in the absence of a clear articulation of opposition to the surgeries as particularly disquieting. Without being firmly situated in an overall anti–female circumcision campaign, like the UNFD approach, clinicalization risks becoming "regulation," a tolerable goal and end in and of itself. I am unwilling, at least at this juncture in the conversation and struggle, to believe that this is all that we as women and feminists must accept.

Still, I am pleased to see Obiora's article and to be a part of this particular conversation. Her work and insights challenge me. Some I do not really want to hear; but I must. After all, no one said that multicultural dialoguing or alliances would be easy. They are just the necessary prerequisites to solid sisterhood.

NOTES

1. L. Amede Obiora, *Bridges and Barricades: Rethinking Polemics and Intransigence in the Campaign against Female Circumcision*, 47 Case W. Res L. Rev. 275 (1997) (also chapter 17 in this volume).

2. *Id.* at 277.

3. *Id.*

4. *See id.* at 298.

5. *See id.* at 299.

6. *See* Isabelle R. Gunning, *Arrogant Perception, World-Traveling and Multicultural Feminism: The Case of Female Genital Surgeries*, 23 Colum. Hum. Rts. L. Rev. 189 (1992).

7. *See* Obiora, *supra* note 1, at 323–28.

8. Audre Lorde, Sister Outsider 112 (1984) (emphasis in original omitted).

9. *See* Obiora, *supra* note 1, at 323–28 (critiquing Mary Daly, Gyn/Ecology: The Metaethics of Radical Feminism (1978); Alice Walker, Possessing the Secret of Joy (1992)).

10. *See* Obiora, *supra* note 1, at 326 (quoting Daly, *supra* note 9, at 155).

11. *See id.* at 326–27 (quoting Daly, *supra* note 9, at 170).

12. *See* Alice Walker, In Search of Our Mothers' Gardens xi (1983).

13. *See* Obiora, *supra* note 1, at 311–12 (footnotes omitted).

14. *Id.* at 311.

15. *Id.* at 301.

16. *Id.* at 299.

17. *Id.* at 304.

18. *Id.*

19. *See* Angela Y. Davis, Women, Race and Class 224 (1983).

20. *See, e.g.*, Marion Crain, *Between Feminism and Unionism: Working Class Women, Sex Equality and Labor Speech*, 82 Geo. L.J. 1903 (1994).

21. *See, e.g.*, Taunya Lovell Banks, *Two Life Stories: Reflections of One Black Woman Law Professor*, 6 Berkeley Women's L.J. 46 (1991).

22. *See* Obiora, *supra* note 1, at 302.

23. *Id.* at 290.

24. *Id.*

25. *Id.*

26. Videotape: Fire Eyes (Sonya Mire, Filmakers Library 1994).

27. *Oprah Winfrey Show* (ABC television broadcast, Sept. 14, 1995).

28. *See* Linda Burstyn, *Female Circumcision Comes to America*, Atlantic Monthly, Oct. 1995, at 34.

29. Report of the United Nations Seminar on Traditional Practices Affecting the Health of Women and Children, Sub-comm'n on Prevention of Discrimination and Protection of Minorities, Comm'n on Human Rights, 43d Sess., at 32, U.N. Doc. E/CN.4/Sub.2/1991/48 (1991) [hereinafter 1991 Report on Traditional Practices].

30. *See* Obiora, *supra* note 1, at 314 (citations omitted).

31. *Id.* at 305.

32. *See* Patrick Rogers and Rebecca Crandall, *Think of It as Therapy: Even the Suit-and-Tie Set Is into Body Piercing*, Newsweek, May 31, 1993, at 65.

33. *See* Obiora, *supra* note 1, at 285.

34. *See* Study on Traditional Practices Affecting the Health of Women and Children: Final

Report of Special Rapporteur, Mrs. Halima Embarek Warzazi, Sub-Comm'n on Prevention of Discrimination and Protection of Minorities, Comm'n on Human Rights, U.N. ESCOR, 43d Sess., at 17, U.N. Doc. E/CN.4/Sub.2/1991/6 (1991).

35. *See* Obiora, *supra* note 1, at 307–10.

36. *See* Preliminary Report of the Special Rapporteur on Traditional Practices Affecting the Health of Women and Children, Mrs. Halima Embarek Warzazi, Sub-Comm'n on Prevention of Discrimination and Protection of Minorities, Comm'n on Human Rights, U.N. ESCOR, 47th Sess., at 5, U.N. Doc. E/CN.4/Sub.2/1995/6 (1995).

37. *See, e.g.*, Gunning, *supra* note 6, at 222–23.

38. *See* 1991 Report on Traditional Practices, *supra* note 29, at 4, 7.

39. *See* Jonathan M. Eisenberg, *NIH Promulgates New Guidelines for the Inclusion of Women and Minorities in Medical Research*, 10 Berkeley Women's L.J. 183 (1995).

40. *See* Jeanne Achterberg, *Forging a Sisterhood of Women Healers*, East West, Nov. 1990, at 56; Chris Bird, *Medicines from the Rainforest*, New Scientist, Aug. 17, 1991, at 34.

19 Families, Fatherlessness, and Women's Human Rights

An Analysis of the Clinton Administration's Public Housing Policy as a Violation of the Convention on the Elimination of All Forms of Discrimination against Women

Lisa A. Crooms

I. INTRODUCTION

The fathers' rights movement and related activism have been credited with helping to focus public attention on the social crisis of "fatherlessness." While this movement appears to be overwhelmingly white and fairly affluent, strains of its rhetoric are ubiquitous. From the Nation of Islam's Million Man March and the Institute for Responsible Fatherhood to the Promise Keepers, a diverse group of men are intent on reclaiming their patriarchal authority, both in the family and in society. Their shared rhetoric identifies the twin scourges of fatherlessness and single motherhood as the root causes of the poverty, violence, and criminality that mar life in the inner city. Society must correct these maladies, they contend, by reinstating the social and cultural importance of fatherhood, marriage, and the traditional two-parent family.

In many ways, the call for fathers' rights is a reaction to the perceived fragmentation of fatherhood at the hands of legal reformers and public policy pundits. Many bemoan the public sector's role in the marginalization of fathers through regulations, laws, and policies advanced under the guise of progress. Responsible policies and programs, as these commentators see it, must reverse the dangerous practice of volitional fatherlessness. The social and cultural phenomenon of poverty, in their view, must be reversed by a modification of the terms of the social contract. They declare that the poor can no longer be rewarded for the socially and culturally dysfunctional conduct of their poverty, and they reserve particular disdain for childbearing and rearing outside the traditional two-parent family. They conclude that irresponsible government policies and programs that have enabled the poor to engage in reckless, volitional fatherlessness must end.

Reprinted by permission from 36 *Brandeis Family Law Journal* 1 (1997–98).

What follows is a discussion of fatherlessness in the context of U.S. poverty policy as a violation of the Convention on the Elimination of All Forms of Discrimination against Women (Women's Convention).[1] This essay begins with a brief overview of the public discourse about fatherlessness in the United States. Then it considers the Clinton Administration's position on fatherlessness, as expressed in former Housing and Urban Development (HUD) secretary Henry G. Cisneros's essay, "Fathers and Families: Changing the Rules."[2] Cisneros uses this essay to sketch the contours of the Clinton administration's public housing policy and its central objective of reuniting poor and working poor fathers with their families in public housing projects. Next, the discussion turns to the Women's Convention and the Reservations, Understandings, and Declarations (RUDs) proposed by the Clinton administration.[3] Although the United States has failed to ratify the Women's Convention, this essay uses the rights set forth in that treaty, particularly those regarding family, marriage, and reproduction, as the norms against which to assess the legitimacy of HUD's focus on fatherlessness. The discussion, however, also considers the impact of the proposed U.S. RUDs, which represent the extent of the duties the United States is likely to assume should it ratify the Women's Convention before 2000. As such, this analysis of women's rights is grounded in U.S. public housing policy, the unadulterated norms of the Women's Convention, and the treaty obligations likely to be assumed by the United States.

The central thesis of this essay is that both the fatherlessness initiatives and the Clinton Administration's proposed RUDs offend the general principles of the Women's Convention. The Clinton Administration's fixation on fatherlessness is fundamentally patriarchal because its policy initiatives, government programs, and laws designed to cure fatherlessness by encouraging traditional fatherhood and marriage rely on sex and gender stereotypes prohibited by the Women's Convention. Moreover, the RUDs offered by the Clinton Administration threaten to foreclose the Convention as a source of justiciable rights for women in the United States. Furthermore, should the United States ratify the Convention, subject to these RUDs, it will insulate efforts such as HUD's fatherlessness initiatives from international scrutiny and permit the United States to avoid both assuming and being held accountable for the full range of government obligations under the Women's Convention.

II. THE SOCIAL/CULTURAL CRISIS OF FATHERLESSNESS

In his book *Fatherless America: Confronting Our Most Urgent Social Problem*, David Blankenhorn makes the following diagnosis: the United States is in the midst of a fatherhood crisis marked by a severe case of fatherlessness. According to Blankenhorn, through a process that started about two hundred years ago, "fatherhood has lost, in full or in part, each of its traditional roles: irreplaceable caregiver, moral educator, head of family, and family breadwinner."[4] He contends that the social/cultural crisis of fatherlessness is evidenced by the social/cultural narrative's marginalization of fatherhood. The narrative has diminished, devalued, and decultured fatherhood to the point that, for most, it is no more than an economic obligation. "[F]athers' roles as nurturers, teachers and mentors are overlooked."[5]

Blankenhorn opines that the most severe manifestations of this crisis are the scores of families disabled by volitional fatherlessness, particularly among the poor. He sees these families as victimized by the choices made by men whose biological connection to their offspring is different from that binding mothers and children. To compensate fathers for this biological disadvantage, Blankenhorn believes fathers need the social construct of fatherhood in the context of traditional, heterosexual, two-parent families. This will force men to channel their natural male aggressions into prosocial behavior for the benefit of familial dependents.

According to Blankenhorn, contemporary fatherhood can have at least three attributes, all of which contribute to the social/cultural crisis of fatherlessness. First, fatherhood includes biological fathers who neither marry the biological mothers of their children nor cohabitate with their biological offspring and the mothers of these children. In Blankenhorn's view, cohabitation and parental alliances between mothers and fathers are the two structural preconditions for effective fatherhood, and the absence of both evinces a "transmogrification" that deprives fatherhood of "any coherent structure."[6] Second, biological and social/cultural fatherhood are not, a priori, consanguineous. The disconnect of the biological from the social/cultural is manifested in, inter alia, laws and policies that accept that the rights of biological fatherhood and social fatherhood need not be held by the same individual. Third, fatherhood is defined as neither necessary nor desirable. Evidence of this phenomenon includes laws and policies that purport to support degendered breadwinning and make marriage an option to be exercised, rather than a choice compelled by circumstance.

For the poor, the social/cultural crisis of fatherlessness, to which each of the three attributes of fatherhood contributes, is borne out by both the disproportionate representation of single mothers and their children living in poverty and the violent and destructive communities in which many of these families reside. These are communities where the residents are more than likely Black and Latino, and where families are headed by single mothers to which men appear largely irrelevant. The seemingly "transmogrified" fatherhood that features prominently in these communities is thought not only to deprive children of the opportunity to be fathered, it also robs the communities to which these "defathered" men and "unfathered" children belong of the benefits derived from the presence of engaged, productive, and committed fathers. Fatherhood, as bifurcated, contributes to contemporary confusion about fathers and fatherhood, which renders traditional heterosexual two-parent families optional. Fatherhood, as either unnecessary or despised, makes fathers a liability and men largely superfluous in the raising of children by poor single mothers.

In Blankenhorn's estimation, the misogyny and hyper- or protest masculinity, which he calls the "primary generator of violence among [poor] young men," is directly linked to chronic fatherlessness.[7] Using the mainstream's cultural narrative of inner-city poverty, Blankenhorn describes the apocalypse of chronic fatherlessness in communities where

> the idea of "being a man" is increasingly identified with violence, materialism, and predatory sexual behavior. I am a man because I will hurt you if you disrespect me. I am a man because I have sex with lots of women and my girlfriends have my babies. I am a man because I have more money and more things than you do.[8]

Blankenhorn blames the government for what he contends is its complicity in destroying the moral fiber of the inner city through government entitlement programs, the adult recipient population of which is disproportionately Black and Latina—overwhelmingly female. The problem, as he sees it, is that these programs have made marriage an option to be exercised by the poor, pregnant women who both populate and propagate these devastated communities. To solve this problem, he favors curbing chronic fatherlessness by forcing the poor to make different decisions about marriage, family, and reproduction in a scheme that rewards patriarchal choices. That is, the poor must be compelled both to marry and to limit their childbearing and child rearing to traditional two-parent families.

To this end, Blankenhorn calls for a rewriting of the cultural narrative to stem the tide of fatherlessness. He advocates abandoning programs that, at least in theory, recognize that virtually all custodial parents are women. Instead, Blankenhorn favors forcing women to take a cold, hard look at the consequences of refusing to refrain from extramarital childbearing and child rearing. Accordingly, he urges the government to stop "subsidizing out-of-wedlock births" and other threats to fatherhood. Simply put, he wants the government to create incentives for marriage and traditional, heterosexual, two-parent families, in which the complementary gender roles of husband/father and wife/mother create one, unified, natural whole.

III. HUD, HOUSING, AND FATHERLESSNESS

Blankenhorn ends his book with proposals for how the United States might address its crisis of fatherlessness. Chief among his proposals is one that both requires all men to pledge themselves to patriarchal principles within traditional two-parent families and allows married fathers to end the chronic fatherlessness plaguing inner-city public housing projects and experienced by people who are overwhelmingly Black and Latino. Transformed by both the presence and the efforts of married men, the projects will no longer be the site of "[r]outine violence, intimidation by gangs, destruction of property, teenage childbearing, an ethos of fear and fatalism," all caused by an apparent lack of "responsible male authority."[9] In this way, "married fathers [might] do what mothers, the police, social workers, and public housing officials are now manifestly unable to do: turn public housing developments into reasonably hospitable environments for raising children."[10]

To make this a reality, Blankenhorn calls on responsible public officials to reverse the chronic fatherlessness caused by irresponsible public policies and programs.

Public monies would be used to better poor communities by encouraging marriage and traditional two-parent families while discouraging fatherlessness and single motherhood. For public housing policy, Blankenhorn's proposals mean that the government must end marriage disincentives and give married couples housing priority, create more opportunities for tenant management and ownership, and increase funds for housing vouchers for all eligible poor and working poor families.[11] If these three policy changes are made, he believes, the United States might turn the corner on fatherlessness. Although he offers no guarantees, Blankenhorn suggests that these communities have nothing more to lose.

As if responding to Blankenhorn's challenge, the Clinton Administration has made addressing fatherlessness a policy objective of the highest order. Central to these efforts is redefining the public sector's role to encourage fatherhood and heterosexual marriage. Like Blankenhorn's proposals, the Clinton Administration's reforms assume that the lack of fatherhood and proper marriage is the crux of many of the seemingly intractable maladies experienced by the poor. Current efforts to reform both the law and the policy of welfare and public housing blame not only the public sector for using cash and other benefits to destroy inner-city families and communities, but also the poor for their poverty.

An example of the Clinton Administration's thinking in this regard is former HUD Secretary Henry G. Cisneros's essay "Fathers and Families: Changing the Rules." Cisneros's essay outlines a plan to reverse the fatherlessness/single motherhood phenomenon plaguing inner-city public housing projects. Central to this plan is redefining the public sector's role to encourage both marriage and complementary, gender-bound parental roles. He advocates changing HUD's approach "to discourage the destruction of the American family by creating policies and programs that are family-friendly and encouraging to fathers within families."[12]

To achieve these objectives, Cisneros proposes "[r]emoving the disincentive from work . . . ; [p]utting a ceiling on [public housing] rents . . . ; [and] [e]ncouraging a mix of incomes by repealing the Federal preference rules that mandate [public housing authorities] to house only the poorest Americans."[13] These minimal changes, Cisneros contends, "would ease the plight of some [poor] families and make it easier for fathers to stay within them."[14] His new scheme of heterosexual marriage and patriarchal gender conventions is offered as a policy option to address the extreme problems of poverty and housing, particularly for those in inner-city public housing projects.

Cisneros also uses his essay to highlight HUD's achievements and goals in its effort to make public housing "family friendly." He praises HUD's efforts to raze unprecedented numbers of existing public housing units and replace them with mixed-income, commercial/residential developments. He also applauds the agency for having changed public housing rules not only to make the projects safer, but also to encourage the poor to behave responsibly. For Cisneros, economic self-sufficiency, marriage, and educational achievement are the tenets on which this responsibility depends. Cisneros specifically commends the work of two demonstration projects aimed directly at the problem of fatherlessness. These projects, one in Hartford,

Connecticut, and the other in Baltimore, Maryland, "use a combination of job opportunities and housing benefits to encourage the unification of families and the more active participation of fathers in their families."[15] Believing that both projects can be duplicated, Cisneros identifies a number of fundamental policy changes needed to make this possible. First, welfare rules must be changed to encourage ousted fathers to return to those welfare-reliant families headed by single mothers. Second, reasonable schedules for child support arrearage payments must be developed. Third, the services provided to at-risk males enrolled in these programs must be bolstered by both case managers and support groups, with particular attention to the emotional and physical challenges of the men's "new" roles as fathers, husbands, and providers. Finally, any model of family reunification on which the program relies must avoid forcing incompatible parents to live together.

Cisneros's essay rests on a preference for programs that reintroduce fathers into the poor families from which they are absent over those designed to increase the life chances and earning potential of poor single mothers. Apparently ignoring the fact that the poverty of many single mothers stems from their inability to secure employment at a living wage, Cisneros uses the mere existence of single mothers and their children to prove the need for gender-exclusive programs aimed at poor fathers. He joins those who want to pass off teaching fathers how to provide for and protect their families as responsible public policy to curb the irresponsibility of poor single mothers. To this end, encouraging the poor to adopt patriarchal gender conventions, under which men are providers and women are domestic caretakers within traditional two-parent families, is offered as a panacea for poverty, particularly for those living in inner-city public housing projects.

IV. WOMEN'S HUMAN RIGHTS AND THE WOMEN'S CONVENTION

In 1979 the United Nations General Assembly unanimously adopted the Women's Convention; in 1981 it was entered into force.[16] The treaty enumerates the full panoply of women's human rights to be free from sex- and gender-based discrimination.[17] It calls for the "full and complete development of . . . countr[ies], the welfare of the world and the cause of peace [which] require the maximum participation of women on equal terms with men in all fields."[18]

In the area of sex and gender stereotyping, the Women's Convention includes broad provisions that set the stage for the specific government obligations and individual rights enumerated elsewhere in the treaty. At the outset, the Convention acknowledges that while "the great contribution of women to the welfare of the family and to the development of society" has not been appreciated fully, "the social significance of maternity" has taken on mythic proportions as the construct by which the fullness and quality of women's lives are judged.[19] It also warns "that the role of women in procreation should not be a basis of discrimination"; rather, "the upbringing of children requires a sharing of responsibility between men and women and society as a whole."[20] Finally, it mandates that traditional gender roles, in both the family and society, be changed to achieve full equality between men and women.[21]

Turning from the general to the specific, Article 2 requires signatory States Parties both to "condemn discrimination against women in all its forms" and to "agree to pursue by all appropriate means and without delay a policy of eliminating discrimination against women."[22] It imposes on governments a duty to eliminate discrimination against women by both public and private actors. Specifically, Article 2(d) requires governments "[t]o refrain from engaging in any act or practice of discrimination against women and to ensure that public authorities and institutions shall act in conformity with this obligation." Article 2(e) mandates States Parties "[t]o take all appropriate measures to eliminate discrimination against women by any person, organization or enterprise." Article 2(f) orders governments "[t]o take all appropriate measures, including legislation, to modify or abolish existing laws, regulations, customs and practices which constitute discrimination against women."

Article 5 compels States Parties to

> take all appropriate measures . . . [t]o modify the social and cultural patterns of conduct of men and women, with a view to achieving the elimination of prejudices and . . . all other practices which are based on the idea of the inferiority or the superiority of either of the sexes or *on stereotyped roles for men and women.*

It imposes an additional duty on governments

> to ensure that family education includes a proper understanding of maternity as a social function and the recognition of the common responsibility of men and women in the upbringing and development of their children, it being understood that the interest of the children is the primordial consideration in all cases.

Both of these provisions have been interpreted as "promotional" in the sense that States Parties are urged "to adopt education and public information programmes, which will help eliminate prejudices and current practices that hinder the full operation of the principle of the social equality of women."[23] That is, the government must use measures such as public education to promote Article 5's changes in gender roles and ungendered parenting.

Finally, Article 16 defines equality before the law as including marriage and family law.[24] It requires States Parties to "take all appropriate measures to eliminate discrimination against women in all matters relating to marriage and family relations."[25] Sections (d) and (e) of Article 16 identify the specific rights to which both women and men are entitled, which include "[t]he . . . rights and responsibilities as parents, irrespective of their marital status, in matters relating to their children," and "the . . . rights to decide freely and responsibly on the number and spacing of their children and to have access to the information, education, and means to enable them to exercise these rights," respectively.

V. THE UNITED STATES AND THE WOMEN'S CONVENTION

In 1980 President Jimmy Carter signed the Women's Convention, and it has awaited Senate ratification since that time. After it languished in virtual obscurity during both the Reagan and Bush Administrations, however, Executive branch advocacy around the Women's Convention was revived during the first Clinton Administration. This renewed attention also reinvigorated nongovernmental organization activism aimed at securing Senate ratification.

In a letter dated September 13, 1994, Secretary of State Warren Christopher not only affirmed the Clinton Administration's support for the Women's Convention, but also outlined the Administration's proposed RUDs to the treaty.[26] The following discussion is limited to those RUDs that are relevant to the rights and obligations set forth in Articles 2, 5, and 16 of the Convention. Specifically, it focuses on the Clinton Administration's proposed reservation to Articles 2 and 5 based on concerns about the regulation of private conduct, the proposed understanding of Article 5 regarding freedom of speech, expression, and association, the proposed understanding regarding U.S. federalism, and the proposed declaration rendering the treaty non–self-executing. This discussion concludes that the U.S. position on women's human rights, which is reflected in these proposed RUDs, violates the terms and conditions of its membership in the international community. They evince this country's particular brand of cultural relativism anchored by both the Constitution and the traditional two-parent, patriarchal family.

The Clinton Administration's proposed privacy-based reservation states, in pertinent part,

> [t]he United States understands that by its terms the Convention requires broad regulation of private conduct, in particular under Articles 2 . . . and 5. The United States does not accept any obligation under the Convention to enact legislation or to take any other action with respect to private conduct except as mandated by the Constitution and laws of the United States.[27]

This reservation relies on the constitutional right to privacy which it interprets as shielding much conduct from government regulation. According to the reservation, "individual privacy and freedom from government interference in private conduct are . . . recognized as among the fundamental values of our free and democratic society."[28] Hence the United States attempts to balance the requirements of Articles 2 and 5 against the domestic mandates of the U.S. Constitution. Seen in this way, these international obligations give way when the Constitution conflicts with the requirements of the Women's Convention. With this reservation, the United States rejects any obligation to regulate purely private conduct that the constitutional right to privacy renders unregulable.[29]

The administration's proposed speech-based understanding provides that

> the United States does not accept any obligation under this Convention, in particular under Article[] 5 . . . to restrict [speech] rights through the adoption of legislation or

any other measures, to the extent that they are protected by the Constitution and laws of the United States.[30]

As it relates to Article 5, this understanding appears to reject any government duty to engage in content-based regulation of speech that advocates traditional "social and cultural patterns of conduct of men and women."[31] In this way, the First Amendment protection of free speech remains untrammeled by any obligations under the Women's Convention that might be imposed on the United States.

Under the proposed, federalism-based understanding, the federal government intends to enforce the Convention

> to the extent that it exercises jurisdiction over the matters covered therein, and otherwise by the state and local governments. To the extent that state and local governments exercise jurisdiction over such matters, the Federal Government shall, as necessary, take appropriate measures to ensure the fulfillment of this Convention.[32]

This understanding directly impacts Article 16, which defines equality before the law as including marriage and family law because matters such as marriage, divorce, and child custody have historically been subject to state regulation. From the perspective of the Clinton Administration, imposing an international obligation on the federal government in this area risks offending traditional principles of federalism. Therefore, the scope of the federal duties recognized under Article 16 is limited by doctrinal ideas about the proper division of authority and power between the federal and state governments.

Finally, the non–self-executing declaration provides, "[t]he United States declares that, for the purposes of its domestic law, the provisions of the Convention are non–self-executing."[33] This declaration seeks to avoid the Women's Convention's obligation to take all appropriate measures to ensure and protect the rights contained in the treaty. Consequently, this broad declaration may prove fatal to the recognition of rights beyond those granted under U.S. domestic law.

VI. FATHERLESSNESS AS PUBLIC POLICY, THE WOMEN'S CONVENTION, AND THE PROPOSED U.S. RUDS

As a policy objective, fighting fatherlessness requires the government to engage in three different activities. First, it must evaluate existing policies, programs, rules, and regulations to determine if they inadvertently interfere with the privacy of family life. Second, it must change any policies, programs, rules, and regulations found to interfere with that privacy. Third, it must promulgate policies, programs, rules, and regulations designed to achieve the underlying objective of curbing fatherlessness and encouraging traditional patriarchal fatherhood. Although these three activities involve different types of government conduct, their relationship to the norms articulated in the Women's Convention is plagued by a common problem. To the extent that the activities share a common patriarchal objective, they violate both the spirit and the letter of the Women's Convention.

Although the preamble of the Women's Convention neither imposes duties on States Parties nor grants individuals substantive, treaty-based rights, it does, at the very least, express the spirit of the treaty. In the areas implicated by HUD's policies on fatherlessness, this spirit reflects a vision of full sex and gender equality that considers the ways both women and men have been thwarted by stereotypical notions about their proper cultural and social roles in families and communities. According to this vision, women have been disabled by not only the historical failure to recognize their contribution to families and societies, but also the social significance of maternity and its role as a basis for discrimination. For men, the disabilities stem from views of manhood and fatherhood that limit men to economic providers for the families over which they exercise virtually unchallenged authority. To correct the inequities borne of these constructions, we must rescript family life and child rearing so that parenting is a nongendered and collective responsibility shared by women, men, and society. To this end, full sex and gender equality requires abandoning traditional patriarchal gender roles.

Moving from the Convention's spirit to its letter, HUD's fatherlessness policy appears to violate Articles 2, 5, and 16. As an initial matter, the agency's fatherlessness initiatives contravene the Women's Convention's basic obligations to "condemn discrimination in all its forms" and "to pursue policies designed to eliminate [this] discrimination."[34] To pursue a policy explicitly based on a traditional, patriarchal social/cultural construct of fatherhood approves, rather than condemns, the types of discrimination targeted by Article 2. This appears inconsistent with the requirements of the Women's Convention that States Parties use government programs and policies to end all forms of discrimination against women.

In addition, Article 5 obligates States Parties to "take all appropriate measures . . . [t]o modify social and cultural patterns of conduct of men and women . . . to . . . eliminat[e] . . . all . . . practices . . . based on . . . stereotyped roles for men and women."[35] It also requires States Parties to "take all appropriate measures . . . [t]o ensure that family education includes a proper understanding of . . . the recognition of the common responsibility of men and women in the upbringing and development of their children."[36] In the context provided by the explicit requirement that parental rights not be contingent on the parents' marital status, these provisions appear to require States Parties, at a minimum, to refrain from any activities that might further entrench the gender stereotypes they are obligated to challenge. Article 5 obliges States Parties "to adopt educational and public information programmes, which will help eliminate prejudices and current practices that hinder the full operation of the principle of social equality of women."[37] Fighting fatherlessness, as envisioned by HUD, clearly works against States Parties' Article 5 duties.

This conclusion draws further support from the domestic discourse's construction of gender roles as complementary, and its accompanying gender-role zero-sum game. In this game, "gains" for women translate into "losses" for men, both of which contribute to the fragmentation of fatherhood, masculinity, marriage, and family.[38] These views, as expressed by Cisneros and others, are patently incongruous with the idea that patriarchal gender stereotypes are inconsistent with sex and gender equality. Indeed, to focus on traditional patriarchal fatherhood manifests the patriarchal desire to return to the types of gender stereotypes condemned in Article 5.

It must be noted that curbing fatherlessness need not conflict with Article 5. The only point made here is that the fatherhood preferred by Cisneros and others as the solution to the poverty of fatherlessness privileges the patriarchal notions supporting the traditional two-parent family. Under this model, men must not only be primed to work for wages (which they are presumed not to do) but also be reintroduced into families to which both ultimate male authority and marriage are central. Women are given primary responsibility for tending to domestic matters, and any income earned from their own outside employment is treated as supplemental. Parental responsibilities follow these gendered divisions of labor, and child care is among the domestic matters for which women remain primarily (although not ultimately) responsible. In this way, relying on the traditional two-parent family model makes HUD's ideas about curbing fatherlessness inharmonious with Article 5's norm regarding the "common [parental] responsibility of men and women in the upbringing and development of their children."[39] Moreover, the privileging of marriage over single parenthood, in effect, makes the treaty's family-based rights contingent on the marital status of the parents rather than the interests of the children.

Article 16 defines "equality before the law," within the meaning of the Convention, to include marriage and family law.[40] It guarantees women parental, family-based, and reproductive rights that are equal to those held by men.[41] Setting aside any problems with the equality paradigm, particularly in the context of reproductive rights and the reality of biological differences, fighting fatherlessness remains a troubling policy objective. Specifically, the model of the traditional, heterosexual, two-parent family, on which HUD's new policy initiatives are based, is inherently discriminatory in a way that offends Article 16's equality provision. HUD's family model casts men in the role of patriarchs who wield ultimate authority in both traditional two-parent families and communities. It also casts women in the supporting roles of mother and wife with penultimate and derivative authority. As such, the patriarch retains the discretion to determine the conditions under which intergender power delegation is legitimate and appropriate. Rather than taking "all appropriate measures to eliminate discrimination against women in all matters of marriage and family relations," HUD's fatherhood policy, as well as the executive's general concern about fatherlessness, perpetuates this type of discrimination.

The obligations the United States is likely to assume under the Women's Convention prove to be a mixed bag. Of the four proposed RUDs that are relevant to Articles 2, 5, and 16, it appears that only the non–self-executing declaration will prove fatal to women seeking to vindicate their right to be free from traditional gender stereotypes in both public and private life. In effect, this declaration evinces the Executive Branch's intent to treat the rights in the Women's Convention as gifts to be bestowed on women when one of the three branches of government sees fit to act.

By declaring the Convention to be non–self-executing, the United States also avoids having to "take all appropriate measures" to make the Convention's rights real. Rather, even if the Women's Convention is ratified, it is likely that the United States will remain obligated to do only that which the Constitution compels it to do.

The remaining RUDs are additional subterfuge for U.S. unwillingness to accept the full responsibility of membership in the international community. They, however, may not necessarily insulate efforts, such as HUD's fatherlessness initiatives, from the limited norms likely to be embraced by the United States should it ratify the Women's Convention under the watch of President Clinton. Concerns about the impermissible regulation of private conduct and speech, as well as those regarding federalism, should be irrelevant to those Women's Convention rights implicated by public programs designed to encourage fatherhood and traditional, heterosexual, two-parent families.

Challenging HUD's fatherlessness initiatives need not implicate private conduct that the Constitution places beyond regulation. In proposals such as Cisneros's, the offensive conduct at issue is that of the government in general and HUD in particular. More important, it is facilitated, in part, by the availability of federal monies. This is true even in cases of public/private partnerships involved in efforts such as those championed by Cisneros. Moreover, to the extent that private conduct is implicated, it appears that HUD's proposed initiatives are, at the very least, equally offensive. That is, if governmental "interference" is permissible when curbing fatherlessness is the objective to be achieved, then it should also be permissible when protecting women's rights in matters of family, marriage, and reproduction is the governmental objective being pursued.

Furthermore, speech-based concerns appear unwarranted. The government's authority to make decisions about social welfare and the use of public largesse do not infringe on the individual right to hold, without government interference, patriarchal views about fatherlessness. Accordingly, the Convention need not impinge this right because the treaty is aimed at establishing the boundaries within which both gender roles and States Parties should operate. While the Convention limits the range of legitimate policy objectives to be pursued by the government, individuals remain free to disagree with the government's objectives. The effect of the Convention is to prohibit the government from relying on stereotypical notions of motherhood and fatherhood to encourage marriage and the formation of traditional two-parent families.

In addition, the federalism-based declaration need not deny women their rights to be free from gender stereotyping in the areas of marriage, family, and reproduction. Although federalism is fundamental to the structure of U.S. government, federal authority over matters previously regulated by the states is not unprecedented. In addition to the apparent understanding of the nature of federalism in the context of the fatherlessness initiatives promoted by HUD, the passage of measures such as the Personal Responsibility and Work Opportunity Reconciliation Act of 1996, the Violence against Women Act of 1994, and the Child Support Enforcement Act of 1994–95, are measures through which the federal government has thrust both itself and its authority into areas traditionally reserved for state regulation. More important, however, the proposed public housing policy outlined in Cisneros's essay appears to be an example of the type of federal action in the area of marriage, family, and reproduction that the Clinton Administration's proposed declaration seeks to avoid. The extent to which those same concerns were raised and addressed in the context of the initiatives forwarded by the Administration, such as HUD's fatherlessness programs, makes this point particularly salient.

VII. CONCLUSION

The proposed RUDs to the Women's Convention make it clear that the United States is unwilling to change its laws to conform to international human rights norms. This intransigence is exacerbated by the blatantly patriarchal policies advanced by the Clinton Administration, such as the fatherlessness initiatives being pursued by HUD. These types of programs rest on views of manhood and fatherhood, as well as of marriage and families, that are linked to the types of traditional cultural and social norms prohibited by the Women's Convention. They are nothing more than pseudosolutions doomed to fail because they misdiagnose the causes of poverty as largely behavioral and linked to personal choices about sex, parenthood, and marriage. It is not surprising that the disproportionate representation of Blacks and Latinos among the very visibly poor infuses these policy proposals with a heavily raced discourse. It is bound up in the iconography of inner-city projects that serves as a shorthand for the nadir of social and cultural values thought to threaten the very existence of the United States. From this position, very little attention is paid to the structural causes of poverty, the manifestations of which include the disproportionate representation of single mothers and their children among the poor. Rather, these policy initiatives desperately cling to cultural and social practices that violate international human rights norms. Public policies, such as that proposed by Cisneros, demonize single mothers as the progenitors of the moral and social decay thought to be represented by poor, inner-city public housing projects. This demonization stems from the blaming, at some level, of single mothers and the welfare state for creating the conditions in which men willfully and recklessly practice highly volitional fatherlessness. In this way, welfare-reliant single mothers are viewed as culpable in ways that absent fathers are not. In this poverty paradigm, absent fathers are victimized by both the failure of single mothers to abide by traditional gender conventions and the availability of cash benefits for those whose failures are most visible. Against the backdrop of this demonization, initiatives such as HUD's fatherlessness efforts strive to coerce the poor to form traditional two-parent families in which men and women assume the complementary gender roles of husband/father and wife/mother.

HUD's emphasis on fatherlessness, however, imperils the basic human rights of poor women in the United States. Those rights set forth in the Women's Convention, specifically in the areas of procreation, reproductive choice, and marriage, as well as the general obligation to avoid traditional patriarchal gender stereotyping, could provide poor women, who rely on HUD's assistance, with some protection against the regressive measures being passed off as poverty policy. Rather than a good-faith effort to respond to the devastating impact of poverty on sex and gender equality, as defined in the Women's Convention, policies such as those being pushed by HUD change issues of women's rights into concerns about the threats to manhood and fatherhood in a male-dominated, patriarchal society. Unless and until the United States abandons its reactionary and conservative brand of cultural relativism, the integrity of the rights of women within its borders, particularly poor women, will remain compromised.

NOTES

1. Convention on the Elimination of All Forms of Discrimination against Women, G.A. Res. 34/180, U.N. GAOR, 34th Sess., Supp. No. 46, at 193, U.N. Doc. A/34/36 (1980) [hereinafter Women's Convention].

2. Henry G. Cisneros, U.S. Dept. of Housing and Urban Development, *Fathers and Families: Changing the Rules* (1996).

3. Under Article 2(d) of the Vienna Convention on the Law of Treaties, a reservation is "a unilateral statement, however phrased or named, made by a State, when signing, ratifying, accepting, approving or acceding to a treaty, whereby it purports to exclude or to modify the legal effect of certain provisions of the treaty in their application to that State." Vienna Convention on the Law of Treaties, 1155 U.N.T.S. 331 (entered into force Jan. 27, 1980) (May 23, 1969). Reservations are subject to the general proviso that they be compatible with the object and purpose of the treaty. Understandings and declarations, however, are statements of a state's interpretation of a treaty provision.

4. David Blankenhorn, Fatherless America: Confronting Our Most Urgent Social Problem 16 (1996).

5. Cheryl Wetzstein, *Focus on Fatherhood to Fight Society's Problems, Group Urges*, Wash. Times, Mar. 8, 1995, at A2. *See also* Blankenhorn, *supra* note 4, at 16–17.

6. Blankenhorn, *supra* note 4, at 18–19.

7. *Id.* One cannot credibly dispute the fact that Blankenhorn's description parallels that of many "gangsta" rappers. It is also indisputable that this music reflects the norms, mores, and experiences of a segment of those people of color who are poor and live in violent, inner-city communities. The flaw in Blankenhorn's analysis, however, is his conclusion that patriarchal conventions and institutions will solve the seemingly intractable problems faced by these communities. He fails to consider the equally plausible explanation of hypermasculinity as a reaction of an acculturated but disadvantaged group in a materialist society. Being disadvantaged, in this context, refers to both (1) being ill-equipped to maximize the limited number of legal opportunities that might be available; and (2) recognizing that, for many, there are no opportunities for employment, particularly employment that pays a living wage. *See generally* Michael Eric Dyson, *When Gangstas Grapple with Evil*, N.Y. Times, Mar. 30, 1997, at 34 (Arts and Leisure).

8. Blankenhorn, *supra* note 4, at 224. *See also* Robert Rector, *A Comprehensive Urban Policy: How to Fix Welfare and Revitalize America's Inner Cities*, Memorandum from Her-

itage Foundation to President-Elect Clinton, Jan. 18, 1993, *available in* LEXIS, News Library, Hfrpts File (discussing "young males [who] enhance their macho image by siring children out of wedlock whom they have no intention of supporting").

9. Blankenhorn, *supra* note 4, at 229.

10. *Id.* at 230.

11. *Id.*

12. *Id.* at 7.

13. *Id.* at 9–10.

14. *Id.* at 9.

15. Cisneros, *supra* note 2, at 14.

16. Women's Convention, *supra* note 1.

17. Article 1 of the Women's Convention defines "discrimination against women" as follows:

any distinction, exclusion or restriction made on the basis of sex which has the effect or purpose of impairing or nullifying the recognition, enjoyment or exercise by women, irrespective of their marital status, on a basis of equality of men and women, of human rights and fundamental freedoms in the political, economic, social, cultural, civil or any other field.

Id., at Part 1, art. 1. *See also* U.N. Charter, at pmbl; Universal Declaration of Human Rights, G.A. Res. 217, U.N. Doc. A/810, at 71 (1948), at pmbl, Arts. 2 and 7; Intl. Women's Rights Action Watch, *CEDAW and the Platform for Action*, 9 Women's Watch 1 (1996) (discussing the role of the Committee on the Elimination of All Forms of Discrimination against Women in implementing the Platform for Action adopted at the Fourth World Conference on Women in Beijing, China, in 1995). *See generally* Kathleen Mahoney, *Theoretical Perspectives of Women's Human Rights and Strategies for Their Implementation,* 21 Brook. J. Int'l L. 799, 839–42 (1996).

18. Women's Convention, *supra* note 1, at pmbl.

19. *Id.*

20. *Id.*

21. *Id.*

22. *Id.,* at Part 1, art. 2.

23. Committee on the Elimination of All Forms of Discrimination against Women (CEDAW), General Recommendation No. 3 (6th Sess. 1987), Compilation of General Comments and General Recommendations Adopted by Human Rights Treaty Bodies, at 63, U.N. Cod. HRI/GEN/1 (1992).

24. "Equality before the law," as guaranteed in Article 15(1), is defined broadly to include legal capacity in civil matters including those involving contracts and property. Women's Convention, *supra* note 1, at Part 4, art. 15, paragraphs 2–4.

25. *Id.,* at Part 4, art. 16.

26. Letter from Secretary of State Warren Christopher to Claiborne Pell, chairman, Committee on Foreign Relations, U.S. Senate (Sept. 13, 1994) (on file with author).

27. *Id.,* at Enclosure 1, at 1.

28. *Id.*

29. Article 28(2) states that "[a] reservation incompatible with the object and purpose of the present Convention shall not be permitted." Women's Convention, *supra* note 1, at Part 6, art. 28, sec. 2. *See also* Vienna Convention, *supra* note 3 (prohibiting reservations that are incompatible with the object and purpose of a treaty).

30. Christopher, *supra* note 26, at 2.

31. Women's Convention, *supra* note 1, at Part 1, art. 5(a).

32. Christopher, *supra* note 26, at Enclosure 1, at 2.

33. *Id.* at 3. This is especially true in light of the proposed dispute settlement declaration, which removes the United States from the jurisdiction of the International Court of Justice. *Id.* In addition, this is exacerbated by the Convention's lack of an enforcement mechanism such as an Optional Protocol. *See generally* International Human Rights Law Group, Action Alert: An Optional Protocol to the Women's Convention (Aug. 1995) (on file with author).

34. Women's Convention, *supra* note 1, at Part 1, art. 2, paragraphs (d)–(f).

35. *Id.* at Part 1, art. 5, paragraph (a).

36. *Id.* at Part 1, art. 5, paragraph (b).

37. CEDAW, *supra* note 23.

38. Although much of the imagery used in this discourse, particularly by HUD, features poor, inner-city communities of color, it is apparent that the implications of these types of policies are foreboding to all women, regardless of race, ethnicity, national origin, class, marital status, or sexual orientation.

39. Women's Convention, *supra* note 1, at Part 1, art. 5, paragraph (a).

40. *Id.*, at Part 4, art. 16, paragraph (1). *See also id.* at Part 4, art. 15.

41. *Id.*, at Part 4, art. 16, paragraph (1).

5 | Violence against Women
Family Terrorism, Rape, and Sexual Harassment

20 Violence against Aboriginal Women in Australia

Possibilities for Redress within the International Human Rights Framework

Penelope E. Andrews

> It was a cold winter night in 1989 in a Central Australian Aboriginal community. Although late, muted sounds of fighting could still be heard coming from the camps. Suddenly the screams of a woman rented the air as she ran towards the nurses' quarters and hammered desperately on the locked gate. Blood poured down her face and her left arm hung limp and broken. In close pursuit was a man brandishing a star picket. As the nurse struggled to open the gate to admit the woman, at the same time excluding her attacker, she noticed the woman's T-shirt. Emblazoned across the front was the statement: "We have survived 40,000 years." Yes, but will they survive the next 40, she wondered.
>
> —Audrey Bolger, *Aboriginal Women and Violence*

For Australia's indigenous population there is a desperate struggle for survival: cultural, physical, and economic. For Aboriginal women, the struggle for physical survival has taken on a greater urgency.[1] The violence to which Aboriginal women are subjected has reached epidemic proportions, and it has been argued that it constitutes a continuing violation of human rights.[2]

The problem of violence against Aboriginal women incorporates an array of factors: race, gender, the aftereffects of colonialism, the minority status of Aboriginal people, the unequal access to societal resources, and consequent unequal development of Aboriginal communities. In addition, addressing this problem demands an appreciation of the differing roles and status of Aboriginal people, ranging from a separate or fringe community to an integrated part of Australian society. This great variety of factors complicates considerably the analysis of the issue of violence against Aboriginal women, because it involves an interplay of all these factors.

Reprinted by permission from 60 *Albany Law Review* 917 (1997).

All social and economic indicators suggest that Aborigines are the most disadvantaged Australians. Within Aboriginal communities, women fare the worst. This is despite the fact that the role of Aboriginal women was significant in both the public and private spheres of Aboriginal society.[3]

Our knowledge of violence against Aboriginal women has until recently been quite precarious; this subject has been taboo for many reasons, some obvious. Aboriginal women have been reluctant to expose conflict within their communities to outside scrutiny that might not always be sympathetic. They have perceived that such exposure runs the risk of further denigration of their communities from the larger white society. White feminists have been reluctant to engage this issue for fear of accusations of prioritizing sexism over racism or for creating divisions within Aboriginal communities, and for fear of accusations of perpetuating the stereotype of the predatory and violent Aboriginal male. However, recent reports suggest that the statistics of violence against Aboriginal women require urgent attention. They indicate that Aboriginal women are at far greater risk than non-Aboriginal women of being the victims of homicide, rape, and other assaults.

A consequence of the limited knowledge of violence against Aboriginal women is the scant public attention or education directed to this issue. Moreover, statistics concerning efforts by Aboriginal women to organize against violence are also quite sparse. So too is a thorough assessment of whether the violence against Aboriginal women is increasing, decreasing, or taking other forms.[4]

INTRODUCTION

This chapter addresses the issue of violence against Aboriginal women. Section 1 concerns the historical violence against Aboriginal people generally, and Section 2 concerns violence against Aboriginal women in particular. Section 3 considers how the priorities and perspectives of Aboriginal women and non-Aboriginal women differ in significant ways despite their congruence in others. In particular, the chapter evaluates the awkward relationship between Aboriginal women and the largely white feminist movement in Australia as a consequence of these different priorities and perspectives, and suggests how political victories for white or non-Aboriginal women could be translated into gains for Aboriginal women. The fourth section refers to the advantages or possibilities, on the one hand, and the limitations on the other, of the utilization of international human rights law and policy by Aboriginal women to confront these questions in a satisfactory manner. The conclusion suggests that local programs and projects, buttressed by a global human rights discourse that is more accessible than ever before, are far more likely to deal with the issue of violence comprehensively and satisfactorily.

In Australia the narratives of colonialism and racism take a peculiar shape, a distinctly Australian one encumbered by the tyranny of distance. For Aboriginal people, who are marginalized in this geographically marginalized society, the struggle for land rights, recognition of cultural rights, self-management, or other permutations of sovereignty involves an increasing engagement with the international human rights framework. This marginalization has many sources, a significant one being the demographic statistics. Aboriginal people make up less than 2 percent of the total Australian population. Their influence in the political process is extremely limited, and they are to a large measure dependent on the support of the larger Australian population. This support reached its zenith on two occasions in recent history. One occurred in 1967, when a national referendum empowered the Australian Commonwealth government to legislate on all matters pertaining to the indigenous population. The second occasion was a 1992 Australian High Court land rights decision, *Mabo v. State of Queensland,* in which the doctrine of terra nullius, which had been sustained for over two hundred years, was finally jettisoned and the claims of the Murray Islanders to rights to their land were recognized.[5]

But for the most part, the political fortunes of Aboriginal people oscillate between dependence on a benign government often politically stifled by mining interests and conservative groupings (as has been the case for the past two decades) and a government somewhat unsympathetic or outright hostile to Aboriginal interests. The latter scenario is the current situation.

I. HISTORICAL VIOLENCE AGAINST ABORIGINAL PEOPLE

It has been noted that Aboriginal occupation of Australia dates back to approximately forty thousand years ago, during which time Aborigines settled and continuously traversed the continent. It has also been noted that the invasion of Australia and the brutal decimation of the Aboriginal population commenced just over two hundred years ago. The history of colonization and the subsequent dispossession of the indigenous population has been well documented. Most of these texts bear testimony to, and suggest reasons for, the dire circumstances in which Aborigines find themselves. Contact with Europeans resulted in the near annihilation of Aboriginal communities, and it has been argued that what underpinned the activities of the settlers (both official and unofficial) was the idea that Aboriginal people would die out as a race.[6]

The literature on the history of colonization points to substantial resistance on the part of Aboriginal people. However, this did not prevent drastic reductions of their numbers from disease. The denial of access to their land deprived them of food and resources, and interfered with the ceremonial religious practices that were part of their culture and identity. White intrusion on the land made it extremely difficult for Aboriginal people to protect their sacred sites.

The basis of Aboriginal society and the traditional systems of Aboriginal law—spirituality and kinship—were completely disrupted. The effect of the implementation of the British system of laws was to render Aboriginal people aliens in their own land. More significantly, where they were once self-sufficient, nomadic and hunting peoples, who lived in spiritual as well as economic harmony with the land, this British feat left them without the independence and mobility that were their lifeblood.[7] This forced immobility resulted in a dependency on European food and welfare rations for survival. With their cultural integrity completely undermined, Aborigines became increasingly vulnerable to European influences, in particular alcohol.[8]

For women, in addition to the ravages on their communities, colonization deprived them of their status and role in their respective communities. Their status as women also made them more vulnerable to sexual exploitation from the settlers. Most important, though, the imposition of a highly patriarchal European legal and value system ensured that Aboriginal women would be relegated to second-class status in their communities.

With its patriarchal attitudes, the British colonial administration largely rendered Aboriginal women invisible. If traditional Aboriginal society harbored gender inequality, the imposition of the colonial policies cemented this inequality by ensuring that the Aboriginal male view was the dominant reflection and interpretation of Aboriginal society. The situation has continued to the present, and in most of the areas of concern to Aboriginal communities, it is the Aboriginal male perspective that is sought after and considered. In the area of land rights, this situation is most stark, and has resulted in profound injustice to Aboriginal women. In short, Aboriginal women in Australia must contend not only with the legacy of cultural destruction, but with the double bind of racism and sexism as well.[9]

The situation of Aboriginal women in Australia today reflects a great diversity in geographic location, economic status, lifestyle, and age. General observations, therefore, need to be contextualized and nuanced to reflect this reality. Empirical observations are further complicated by the fact that it is unclear how many Aboriginal women continue to have large parts of their personal lives governed by aspects of traditional law.

Questions bearing on differential experiences and location, in particular with respect to access to traditional structures and systems of conflict resolution, are significant in an appraisal of the validity of suggested mechanisms to deal with violence against Aboriginal women. In the wider society, this traditional (spiritual) realm coexists with the harsh economic and social realities of Aboriginal women's lives. This combination of somewhat contradictory factors provides a formidable challenge for Aboriginal women activists and their allies in the international human rights arena.

A significant impediment for Aboriginal women in their quest for equality is the privileging of the male Aboriginal voice in all matters of concern to their communities. Until the mid-1980s it was uncommon for women to be consulted about their needs, preferences, or life choices. The many fact-finding missions that regularly visited Aboriginal communities simply ignored women's voices; their opinions appeared not to matter. And yet numerous programs and policies on health, housing, education, and other important community concerns were predicated on the findings of these missions. In all these programs, women's voices were simply absent.

II. VIOLENCE AGAINST ABORIGINAL WOMEN

A. VIOLENCE FROM OUTSIDE THE ABORIGINAL COMMUNITY

The Australian Law Reform Commission's 1994 Report on equality and justice issues for women has noted the overrepresentation of Aboriginal women in the Australian prison population. The report referred to the 1992 National Prison Census, which stated that 14.1 percent of male prisoners and 18 percent of female prisoners are Aboriginal. Considering that Aboriginal people comprise less than 2 percent of the total Australian population, the number is disturbing.[10]

A further disturbing fact is the harassment and abuse that Aboriginal women suffer while in police custody. An inquiry into violence in Australian society a few years ago revealed evidence suggesting widespread sexual abuse of indigenous women at the hands of police officers. More disturbingly, this abuse was not confined to women in custody. Testimony was provided describing the police practice in one town of detaining young Aboriginal women patrons at a bar and then offering them to white male patrons for sex.

In 1991 the Royal Commission into Aboriginal Deaths in Custody, reporting on the disproportionate number of Aboriginal people who die in police custody, lamented the overwhelming lack of confidence that Aboriginal people have in the Australian legal system. Even though the report included the death of twelve Aboriginal women in police custody, it paid scant attention to the needs of Aboriginal women in their interaction with the criminal justice system. Aboriginal activists have commented on the report's paucity of specific recommendations to deal with violence against women.

This lack of confidence or disillusionment that Aboriginal people exhibit toward the Australian legal system has its origins in a variety of sources, but an obvious one is the legacy of brutality and dispossession sanctioned by law during the colonial period. Although the consequences of this wholesale legal disenfranchisement impact enormously on most Aboriginal people, Aboriginal women are the "least well served by the legal system," a factor that correlates with the appalling conditions of social and economic disadvantage in which they find themselves. In this particular context, their race, class, and gender intersect in ways that ensure that the violence to which they are exposed receives scant attention. This is reflected in two major reports on violence in Australia and Aboriginal societies, in which the issue of violence against Aboriginal women in the criminal justice system was almost completely ignored.[11] The Royal Commission into Aboriginal Deaths in Custody investigated these matters between the periods January 1, 1980, and May 31, 1989. In the Northern Territory, where a large proportion of Aboriginal people live, the commission reported nine deaths. During the same period in the Northern Territory, the police crime records reported thirty-nine homicides of Aboriginal women.[12]

B. VIOLENCE FROM WITHIN THE ABORIGINAL COMMUNITY

The cultural devastation, as well as the resulting pathologies of alcoholism and violence, in many Aboriginal communities has been noted. Diane Bell has analyzed the involvement of Aboriginal women both as initiators and victims of physical attacks.[13] Katherine Burbank's observations about physical disputes in the Aboriginal communities that she analyzed indicate that women are by no means passive victims of physical attacks, and, as the title of her book *Fighting Women* suggests, they engage in widespread aggression.

But these accounts also observe that although a woman might at times engage in aggressive behavior, for example, by hurling abuse or an object, her partner would often launch an immediate physical attack and she was more likely to suffer greater physical injury than her male partner. In fact, a study conducted in Victoria in the southeast of Australia in early 1996 indicated that 46.9 percent of all Aboriginal female victims of crime were violently assaulted, compared to 11.4 percent of non-Aboriginal women. The study also showed that Aboriginal women were 3.6 times more likely to be victims of rape. Earlier studies have highlighted the incidence of sexual abuse in the Aboriginal community and the silence surrounding this problem.

The causes of violence against indigenous women are complex; the research suggests a combination of factors. The first is the system of sexual subordination that exists in traditional Aboriginal society and is buttressed in the wider Australian society. Although Aboriginal scholars and activists and white anthropologists differ among themselves as to the role and status of Aboriginal women in traditional society and the extent of this sexual subordination, there appears to be a general consensus that a combination of colonial attitudes toward all Australian women, patriarchal values prevalent in Australian society, and the differing sex roles and status in indigenous society have resulted in the subordinate status of Aboriginal women. Marcia Langton, a prominent Aboriginal anthropologist and activist, refers to "the ability of men to use force in the final analysis, to preserve male dominance in ideology, in structures and relationships. This was so in traditional times and remains so, but in vastly changed circumstances."[14]

The second factor is the breakdown of traditional social control due to the imposition of foreign influences and societal structures. For example, Bolger describes the inability of tribal elders to control younger men, who appear to have abandoned traditional values.[15] A third factor noted is the appalling socioeconomic conditions in which many Aborigines find themselves, and which have been mentioned earlier in this chapter.

By far the most devastating factor highlighted is the abuse of alcohol in many communities. Although the research is inconclusive on the role of alcohol in the incidence of violence, there appears to be a general recognition of the association of excessive alcohol consumption and violence. It is significant that a substantial number of Aboriginal women interviewed for different research purposes identify their abuser's consumption of alcohol with the violence. It is also worth noting that Aboriginal women have been active in local campaigns to designate their communities alcohol-free zones.

Audrey Bolger, in her comprehensive study of violence against Aboriginal women, found that Aboriginal people prefer the term "family fighting" to "domestic violence."[16] It has been poignantly noted that the "relatively suburban term 'domestic violence' does not come close to adequately describing the levels of violence perpetrated on Aboriginal women—typically by male perpetrators (not only the spouse), over a longer period, more commonly with weapons and more frequently resulting in severe injury."[17] Bolger has demonstrated that the nature of the injuries inflicted on Aboriginal women is much more egregious because of the use of weapons and the range of individuals who appear to take license to attack them. Bolger cites a litany of the most horrendous incidents of weapon-inflicted violence, involving hammers, knives, sticks, stones, and pickets, which results in a frightening number of homicides of Aboriginal women.[18] Other research has documented the number of young Aboriginal females who are subjected to rape, incest, and other forms of sexual abuse by a variety of male family members.

III. THE RELATIONSHIP OF ABORIGINAL WOMEN TO THE FEMINIST MOVEMENT IN AUSTRALIA

Much of the writings by Aboriginal female scholars and activists suggest a significant wariness by Aboriginal women of the feminist movement.[19] Some of this wariness can be traced to the history of colonialism and racism, and the resultant different worlds occupied by Aborigine and other communities. Hester Eisenstein has documented the significant gains that Australian feminists (particularly those located in the public sector, the so-called femocrats, and those in the tertiary education system) have achieved in Australia in the last fifteen years.[20] The various pieces of legislation—the Sex Discrimination Act, the Affirmative Action for Women Act, the legislative incursions into violence against women, and pay equity—all bear testimony to these achievements. But these gains for non-Aboriginal women have not necessarily translated into gains for Aboriginal women.

The focus of the feminist movement has generally been on reproductive rights, sexuality, equity in employment, sufficient child care, and freedom from sexual harassment and violence. For Aboriginal women, these struggles have often been seen as irrelevant and sometimes antithetical to their needs. They have merely highlighted for Aboriginal women the glaring contradictions of experience and reality. Reproductive rights and child care issues represent for Aboriginal women vivid memories of struggles to end forced sterilization and a not too distant reminder of children being removed from mothers in an almost genocidal fervor.[21]

Employment equity and freedom from sexual harassment are hollow victories when statistics suggest that a disproportionate number of Aboriginal women do not have the means to enter the workforce due to insufficient education. The much-heralded legislative inroads into family violence, after persistent deflation of the public/private distinction, are arguably an ominous sign to Aboriginal women that the state once more has the power to invade that private space only recently regained after the zealous pursuit of protectionism and assimilation. The public/private distinction for Aboriginal women has been ephemeral; the state has persistently been an invasive and intrusive presence.[22]

Feminist analyses and praxis in Australia have inadequately addressed the racialized nature of violence against women. This has resulted in a serious lapse in addressing the racial or cultural context of the kinds of violence perpetuated against Aboriginal women, and has also vitiated a comprehensive inquiry into the causes of violence and strategies of intervention aimed at stemming such violence.

Recent developments in Aboriginal women's organizations and writings by Aboriginal activists suggest that Aboriginal women are becoming amenable to the incorporation of feminist analyses in their broader struggles. Conversely there appears to be an increasing recognition of the multiple political and personal goals of Aboriginal women by white feminists.

But the feminist paradigm raises for Aboriginal women profound questions about Aboriginal identity, that is, broader communitarian concerns on the one hand, and the pressing issue of the violence to which they are subjected as women on the other. Although certain Aboriginal women are sympathetic to or see the need to embrace the full panoply of feminist issues dealing with the problem of violence, they also regard the issue of violence as connected to a more general set of issues relating to the role of Aboriginal women in their society, as well as outside their society. Unlike the situation of other women, and particularly white women in the wider Australian society, the focus of combating violence against Aboriginal women involves stemming violence from outsiders as well.

This poses somewhat of a challenge for Australian feminists. Although the priorities and strategies of Aboriginal women and white feminists have overlapped only rarely, there is room for some convergence of strategies to overcome violence against all women.[23] Such a challenge might require some deference and understanding by white feminists, but in the process might allow the organizational space for Aboriginal women to set the agenda and determine strategies that have the likelihood of the most beneficial outcomes.

IV. THE INTERNATIONAL HUMAN RIGHTS FRAMEWORK AND ITS RELEVANCE

The international human rights framework provides an empowering point of reference for human rights activists in the local setting. Aboriginal people have utilized this human rights environment to internationalize their struggle and garner strategic victories. Specifically, the United Nations Working Group on Indigenous Populations has served as an important international forum to pursue political and legal strategies alongside indigenous peoples from around the globe.[24]

Aboriginal women have been actively involved in these campaigns, but their efforts have targeted the transformation of their communities as a whole. There has thus far been no concerted effort by Aboriginal women to address the question of public and private violence against Aboriginal women in the international human rights context. Despite this, the recent incursions in international law by feminist scholars and activists provide both a symbolic and substantive backdrop. Women's rights have shifted from the margins to the center of discourse in international law. This changing universe is marked by significant signposts: the United Nations Decade for Women, the Vienna Declaration on Violence against Women and the Fourth World Conference on Women in Beijing, to mention a few. These events manifest the need to place the realities and experiences of women's lives in the center of human rights practice.[25]

But the utilization of international law poses some significant challenges for women activists. These challenges are represented by two major underpinnings of international law, and specifically international human rights law and practice. The first is the quest for universality, and the second is a certain formalism that typifies the substance and procedures of international law and the United Nations system.[26]

A. CHALLENGES OR LIMITATIONS OF THE INTERNATIONAL LAW FRAMEWORK

In the international law arena, the feminist project burst onto the scene with the pioneering writings of Hilary Charlesworth and others who posed a significant challenge to the structures, institutions, procedures, and essentially male cast of international law. These writings coincided with emerging struggles for democracies in which women increasingly demanded a central place in the transformation project. But the ascendancy of these feminist analyses soon became subjected to a thorough critique, centered on their essentialist focus and their failure to incorporate the economic, ethnic, racial, religious, and cultural factors that impinge on women's identity and their consequent engagement in political struggle.[27]

The voices of women in Africa, Asia, South America, and the Islamic world have raised questions concerning the universality of rights and remedies. They have located theoretical discrepancies in feminist analyses relating to the cultural determination of rights, as well as socioeconomic and political imperatives.

The response, a feminist critique that recognizes and incorporates these issues of intersectionality, is now more apparent. But recognition and incorporation do not necessarily mean an engagement with other beacons of identity. The paradigm still remains the quest for a universalism, with the "other" constituting an additional analytical component.[28]

The second challenge, the arcane world of international law, represents a perennial preoccupation. For Aboriginal women, the symbolism and substance of human rights provide a useful backdrop for buttressing these issues locally. But serious engagement as a form of legal redress necessitates overcoming formidable obstacles; cumbersome enforcement mechanisms locked in a truly distant world. Although the pursuit of human rights through United Nations or regionally mandated procedures is theoretically possible and symbolically positive, the enforcement procedures provided in various human rights instruments are constrained by lengthy time periods between initial reporting and final outcome. The paradigm designed to ensure a thorough investigation of all the relevant facts and local exhaustion of remedial procedures renders swifter conclusion of the complaints procedure almost impossible. Moreover, the process demands access by individuals who are schooled in, or at least familiar with, this formal, legalistic paradigm. The inability to acquire such access is a formidable obstacle for many women trapped in dire economic and social circumstances and who conduct their lives in a foreign language.[29]

This dissonance between the universe of formal law and rights and the material reality of marginalized peoples is stark in the Australian context. For reasons mentioned earlier in this chapter, Aboriginal women display little faith in the criminal justice system. They constantly face the dilemma of negotiating the daily exigencies of violence and needing some form of protection, in a context of deep skepticism of official (police) interference in their communities.

B. POSSIBILITIES OF INTERNATIONAL LAW

What perspectives might be brought to bear on international legal discourse that will enable Aboriginal women to utilize the substance and symbolism in a more empowering manner? Put another way, are there alternative approaches or strategies in light of the foregoing critiques?[30]

Women engaged in feminist struggles must move beyond the paradigm that pits the universalist aspirations of feminism and its human rights vision against the continuing recognition of cultural difference, now incorporated in postmodern discourse. This bipolar paradigm increasingly distorts the discourse and thwarts significant programs that have a potentially transformative capacity to improve women's lives. We must engage in human rights discourse that does not shun the notion of the particular (products of divergent cultural, racial, economic conditions), but will recognize at times the requirement to engage in what Gayatri Spivak refers to as "strategic essentialism."[31]

We have to promote and engage in a human rights discourse that recognizes multiple identities and multiple agendas, that enables an Aboriginal woman to utilize an international agenda to end violence in her community, while simultaneously demanding some semblance of self-determination for her people. Tentative steps toward this ideal are slowly permeating human rights practice, as evidenced by developments leading to the World Conference on Human Rights in Vienna and the Fourth World Conference on Women in Beijing. Of particular significance was the lobbying efforts of women from developing and Islamic countries.

Feminism needs to embrace a discourse that envelops a nuanced sense of the articulation of rights. This approach incorporates the compounded layers of oppression and confronts totally the "compartmentalized selves,"[32] of which critical theory reminds us. This approach more comprehensively articulates women's lives, and has enormous implications for the international political and legal agenda. In essence we need to engage in a different kind of discourse even while we aspire to an agreed universalism, one that builds from the particular.

Commencing with the particular necessitates a theoretical reorientation of the starting point of women's struggle; an involvement in overcoming racism, economic exploitation, patriarchy, and religious and cultural prejudice. Thus far, the feminist input into international law has mediated the imperative to overcome the male-centered universe of international law while accommodating the demands of "other" voices to incorporate issues of race, class, ethnicity, culture, and religion. But the very act of incorporation still perpetuates marginalization of those variables, and the standard still remains the universalist assumptions located within Western feminist discourse. In short, the elimination of patriarchy is placed at the center of feminist human rights discourse, tempered by voices of the "other" at the margins.[33]

A reconstituted human rights discourse will locate the "other" at the center, with the elimination of patriarchy and sexism as part of the overall agenda. In other words, one could imagine the metaphorical narrative of women's struggle as a sprawling tree, with different branches representing the confluence of theoretical influences. In such a construction, the elimination of patriarchy is a powerful branch, as powerful as the branch for the elimination of poverty or the branch for the recognition of cultural rights. Such an approach should not be interpreted as an erosion of the feminist project; rather, it is a bold assertion of a feminism centered on the particular, which utilizes strategic essentialism at necessary points of intervention.

CONCLUSION

Aboriginal women are engaged in local initiatives that represent a nascent but growing determination to confront the violence to which they are exposed, both from within their communities and from the criminal justice system. In these endeavors Aboriginal women can draw on international human rights laws, procedures, and structures to bolster their struggles. In concrete terms, the Australian government's ratification of a plethora of human rights instruments relevant to Aboriginal women suggests that the legal groundwork has been laid, and that an official human rights atmosphere amenable to local initiatives has been provided.

For Aboriginal women, as indeed for all women on the margins, the process should be a circuitous one: extrapolating from both indigenous or local methods and an expanding global human rights framework, and simultaneously influencing the content, enforcement mechanisms, and indeed the tone of the human rights infrastructure. The purpose of the presentation of these issues in this chapter is a plea for such a possibility.

Aboriginal people as marginal members of Australian society constantly have to struggle against the majoritarian political instinct to submerge indigenous interests. For Aboriginal women, their quest is one of full membership in the Australian polity; not at sufferance, but as entitlement and in celebration. At the aspirational level, and indeed in substance, the international human rights framework provides the prism for local articulation of such possibility.

NOTES

1. I use the term "Aboriginal" to describe all of Australia's indigenous population, including Torres Strait Islanders.

2. *See* Diane Bell, *Representing Aboriginal Women: Who Speaks for Whom?*, in The Rights of Subordinated Peoples 221 (Oliver Mendelsohn and Upendra Baxi eds., 1994).

3. *See* Sharon Payne, *Aboriginal Women and the Law,* in Aboriginal Perspectives on Criminal Justice 31 (Chris Cuneen ed., 1992).

4. Audrey Bolger, Aboriginal Women and Violence 22 (1991).

5. (1992) 175 C.L.R. 1 (Austl.).

6. *See* Charles Rowley, The Destruction of Aboriginal Society, at 6. *See also* Iris Clayton, *Anybody Could Afford Us,* in Being Aboriginal 74 (Ross Bowden and Bill Bunbury eds., 1990).

7. *See* Henry Reynolds, The Other Side of the Frontier 114 (1982).

8. *See* C. D. Rowley, Outcasts in White Australia 42, 51 (1972). The choices of survival for Aboriginal people were slim. *See* Rowley, *supra* note 6, at 31. The settlers wanted control of their land, not their labor, which was provided for by convicts. They were, therefore, of absolutely no economic value to the settlers. *See* Colin Bourke, *Economics: Independence or Welfare,* in Aboriginal Australia 179 (Colin Bourke et al. eds., 1994). The ideology of racism, and the particularly obnoxious stereotype of Aborigines that prevailed then, meant that Aboriginal people were, at best, a source of irritation and, at worst, a scourge to be eliminated. *See* Tony Austin, Simply the Survival of the Fittest: Aboriginal Administration in South Australia's Northern Territory 1863–1910, at 10 (1992).

9. The literature about Aboriginal people is voluminous. Indeed, Aboriginal people have continually complained of being the most widely researched community in Australia, without the concomitant benefits of such endless inquiry. However, most of the research has focused on Aboriginal society from the perspectives of males in the communities, and very often authored by male anthropologists. *See* Jocelynne Scutt, *Invisible Women?: Projecting White Cultural Invisibility on Black Australian Women*, 2 Aboriginal L. Bull. No. 46, at 4 (1990).

10. For an extended discussion on this issue, see generally Marie Brooks, *Aboriginal and Torres Strait Islander Women in Custody,* in Aboriginal Justice Issues II (Australian Institute of Criminology ed., 1994).

11. *See* Royal Commission into Aboriginal Deaths in Custody (1991) (overwhelmingly concerned with the incarceration and deaths of Aboriginal males). *See also* National Com-

mittee on Violence, Violence: Directions for Australia (1990) (largely ignoring the violence against Aboriginal women).

12. Australian Law Reform Commission, Equality before the Law: Justice for Women 120 (1994) [hereinafter 1994 Report].

13. *See* Diane Bell, Daughters of the Dreaming 100, 172 (1983).

14. Marcia Langton, *Feminism: What Do Aboriginal Women Gain?*, Broadside National Foundation for Australian Women Newsletter 1989, *quoted in* Bolger, *supra* note 4, at 53.

15. *See* Bolger, *supra* note 4, at 56.

16. *Id.* at 6.

17. 1994 Report, *supra* note 12, at 119.

18. *See* Bolger, *supra* note 4, at 16.

19. *See* Larissa Behrendt, *Aboriginal Women and the White Lies of the Feminist Movement: Implications for Aboriginal Women in Rights Discourse*, 1 Australian Feminist L.J. 27 (1993).

20. *See generally* Hester Eisenstein, Inside Agitators: Australian Femocrats and the State (1996).

21. *See* Margaret Tucker, If Everyone Cared 91–96 (1977).

22. *See* Jan Pettman, *Gendered Knowledge: Aboriginal Women and the Politics of Feminism, in* Power, Knowledge and Aborigines 120 (Bain Attwood and John Arnold eds., 1992).

23. Although the causes and manifestations differ, domestic violence is a serious problem in Australian society. *See generally* Jocelynne A. Scutt, Even in the Best of Homes (1983).

24. *See* Tony Simpson, *On the Track to Geneva, in* Voices of Aboriginal Australia 170 (Irene Moore ed., 1995).

25. These developments raise similar questions highlighted in the previous section regarding the relationship between Aboriginal women and white feminists in Austra'ia.

26. The purpose of this point is not to debunk the idea of formal procedures—they are a vital component of substantive rights. The question is raised to highlight the dissonance between the arcane world of legal rights and the harsh socioeconomic and political realities of most women's lives. *See* Peter Vale, *Engaging the World's Marginalized and Promoting Global Change: Challenges for the United Nations at Fifty*, 36 Harv. Int'l L.J. 283 (1995).

27. *See* Rebecca Cook, *Women's International Human Rights: A Bibliography*, 24 N.Y.U. J. Int'l L. and Pol. 587 (1992); Third World Women and the Politics of Feminism (Chandra Talpade Mohanty et al. eds., 1991).

28. *See also* Mridula Udayagiri, *Challenging Modernisation: Gender and Development, Postmodern Feminism and Activism, in* Feminism/Postmodernism/Development 159 (Marianne H. Marchand and Jane L. Parpart eds., 1995).

29. *See* Tom J. Farer, *The United Nations and Human Rights: More Than a Whimper Less Than a Roar*, 9 Hum. Rts. Q. 550 (1987). *See also* Tokel Opsahl, *Instruments of Implementation of Human Rights*, 10 Hum. Rts. L.J. 13 (1989).

30. The following approach is not proffered in the prescriptive sense of offering solutions, nor is it exhaustive; it is an attempt to influence the discourse and practice of human rights law so that Aboriginal women, and indeed all female victims of violence, may benefit from that legal and aspirational framework. *See* Marysia Zalewski, *Feminist Standpoint Theory Meets International Relations Theory: A Feminist Version of David and Goliath?*, 17 Fletcher Forum of World Affairs, Summer 1993, at 13.

31. *See* Gayatri Chakravorty Spivak, Address at the Center for Humanities, Wesleyan University (Spring 1985), *cited in* Vasuki Nesiah, *Toward a Feminist Internationality: A Critique*

of U.S. Feminist Legal Scholarship, 16 Harv. Women's L.J. 189, 203 (1993) (also chapter 2 in this volume).

32. *See* Celina Romany, *Themes for a Conversation on Race and Gender in International Human Rights Law*, chapter 3 in this volume; *see also* Angela P. Harris, *Race and Essentialism in Feminist Legal Theory*, 42 Stan. L. Rev. 581 (1990); and Mari Matsuda, *When the First Quail Calls: Multiple Consciousness as Jurisprudential Method*, 11 Women's Rts. L. Rep. 7 (1989).

33. *See generally* Comparative Perspectives of Third World Women: The Impact of Race, Sex, and Class (Beverly Lindsay ed., 1980) (providing theoretical perspectives that place the concerns of "Third World" women and minority women in the United States at the center of the discourse and focusing on issues of economic exploitation, development, race, and gender, which provides a more comprehensive picture of the situation of the women concerned and possible steps to redress these issues).

21 Domestic Violence in Ghana

An Initial Step

Rosemary Ofeibea Ofei-Aboagye King

This chapter focuses on and attempts to expose the anxiety of abused women in Ghana. This project is ambitious in that it names, isolates, and defines domestic violence in Ghanaian culture.[1] The first section focuses on the need to do research on domestic violence in Ghana. The second section addresses the "invisible" nature of domestic violence in Ghana and some of the possible reasons for this invisibility. The third section looks at the ways domestic violence could be examined and addressed in Ghana. While there is no clear-cut definition of domestic violence in Ghana, it is important to identify the fact that the phenomenon exists.

I. THE NEED FOR RESEARCH AND SOME INITIAL EFFORTS

This segment of the chapter focuses on the void in the documentation and research on the problem of domestic violence in Ghana. The challenging concepts that I identify and discuss result from the very rudimentary nature of research on domestic violence in Ghana. There are no studies on this problem, nor has any publication addressed it. This lack of attention has made writing this essay a challenge. Moreover, I have had to rely on alternative sources of evidence to buttress my assertion that domestic violence, by whatever name, in fact exists in Ghana. The absence of research findings indicates that research on women and the status of law must become an urgent priority in Ghana.

Significant inroads into the identification and resolution of domestic violence disputes in the United States and Canada increase the need to identify and resolve issues of domestic violence in Ghana. The recognition of "battered women" (or

Reprinted by permission from 4 *Columbia Journal of Gender and Law* 1 (1994).

indeed, the existence of domestic violence) is rare in Ghana. Even I have known women who clearly fit the definition of "battered women," yet I had never thought of them as such. Certainly Ghanaian law has never recognized them as such.

However, is the examination of battered women a possible (and plausible) area of research in Ghana? The largest problem in (not) talking about domestic violence is its nonproblem status. Ghanaians wish it out of existence and deliberately downplay its visibility. This denial stems from women's (and some men's) pain in recounting the violence and the victim's embarrassment in being a "bad" wife, according to her husband's standards—for being slothful, lazy, and argumentative. For many, deviance from a husband's expectations is an acceptable reason for punishing a recalcitrant wife. A woman's vulnerability comes from being exposed as a "bad wife" as well as from the fact that there is no place for her to turn: society believes that this is the way that things are and will always be.

Moreover, defining domestic violence is further complicated by the difficulty in identifying the actors. Domestic violence may include many different kinds of activities and victims, including the abuse of children, the elderly, cohabitants, and so on. For simplicity's sake, I have limited the scope of this chapter to physical abuse of women by their male partners. For the most part, and unless otherwise stated, these are women who are married to their abusers under the customary law or the marriage ordinance.

The following discussion is based on the responses of fifty women clients of the Legal Aid Clinic of the International Federation of Women Lawyers in Ghana (Federación Internacional de Abogadas, or FIDA) to an informal survey on domestic violence. The questionnaires were administered to the women when they came to the clinic for their first (previously scheduled) appointment between the months of May and August 1991. Women were selected solely on the basis of their willingness to answer questions on domestic violence.

In spite of assurances about anonymity, out of approximately two hundred domestic violence clients, only fifty women agreed to be interviewed. All the others refused because they did not wish to have any answers recorded "against them." Those who did agree to do the interviews felt they had "nothing to lose" if their views were recorded.

The respondents came from many different backgrounds. They did not belong to a particular income bracket, did not have a common educational background, nor did they belong to one particular tribe. What these women did have in common was the fact that they all consulted FIDA about marital problems. This, in itself, is quite unusual as women are discouraged from discussing their domestic affairs with anyone other than family members. Yet all these women had suffered some form of abuse at the hands of their partners, to the point at which they felt that they had to seek recourse from the Legal Aid Clinic of FIDA.

Based on my interviews with fifty Ghanaian women, I realize that women in my country are beaten by their husbands every day. Incredibly, neither the men nor their wives seem to question the categorization of beating as discipline and thus acceptable. This provides food for thought. What about the women who are being hurt? Where is the justice for them—not only for North American women but for their Ghanaian (and African) counterparts as well? For all women?

II. THE INVISIBLE NATURE OF DOMESTIC VIOLENCE IN GHANA

Of course, as long as the women who are being hurt remain invisible, their problems are likely to continue. However, I have found that women will talk about domestic violence if sufficiently persuaded that their accounts of violence will remain anonymous.

A. WOMEN'S EXPERIENCES AND REACTIONS

Contours of domestic violence can be gleaned from excerpts of interviews held with battered women in Ghana.

> He would beat me whenever he was drunk. . . . When I confronted him with evidence of his sleeping with another woman. . . . When I asked him for chop-money. . . . When I refused to have sex. . . . There was no particular reason. . . . Because I was pregnant. . . . He accused me of sleeping with another man. . . . Because my cooking was not to his taste. . . . He said I was rude in public. . . . I had insulted his mother. . . . I spent too much money. . . . He links giving me maintenance money with whether or not I have sex with him. . . . He's violent with the children. . . . He even attempts to sleep with our daughters. . . . We should know people for a long time before we marry them.[2]

But one woman who accepts that beating is a part of married life had this comment to make: "It happens to a lot of people. If your husband gets annoyed, don't respond to him. Just leave him and go out. If you reply, he might beat you. So, do not give him the opportunity to beat you."[3]

When asked, "In your culture/tribe, is it usual/accepted for a woman to be beaten by her husband?" only five women out of the fifty answered yes. The remaining forty-five women stated that it was not the norm of their tribe. However, this response was not supported by their answers to the question, "When does it transcend the norm and become a violent action . . . , assuming that it is the usual thing for a woman to accept some disciplining at the hands of her husband?"

The answers reflected the existence of a norm—a view that some beating is acceptable, even expected, to keep the woman in line.[4] But when "[h]e injures her. . . . She is hurt or experiences any pain. . . . He beats her to leave a scar or deformity. . . . He leaves her with a fracture. . . . He beats her publicly. . . . The beating is more than three slaps or he beats her three or four times," then it transcends the norm. Only two women emphatically stated that "any beating" at all transcends the norm. The discrepancy between the stated disapproval and the tacit acceptance of some form of violence may relate to the framing of the question. The women were asked whether beating was the norm; if they had been asked whether disciplining was the norm, more might have replied yes. Most of the women surveyed accept some level of beating as discipline. All the women considered the excessive beating of a woman by her husband to be a deplorable action.

All the respondents had been struck by their partners during the course of their marriages. Only four women called the beating an isolated incident, while five of them had endured more than ten years of beating. Most women had lost count of the number of times they had been beaten.

For a variety of reasons, none of the women had left her abusive marriage:

> I felt shy at my "failure" to keep my husband happy. . . . I would not be able to keep the children in the comfort to which they were accustomed. . . . So long as the danger to my health was not so bad I felt that I could manage. . . . My family would not support me if I left. . . . I did not want my children to have different fathers. . . . I had no money to sue him in court. . . . We have to be obedient to our husbands. . . . I know of no organization that could advise and support me if I left.[5]

All the women who had been beaten believed that the beatings were serious enough to warrant some outside action. However, they responded that they had never really thought about serious action, typically because they felt that it was just not the way things were done and that it could be worse.

The question becomes what action these women can take against domestic abuse. Generally, the women had little or no information as to what they could do or whether, indeed, they had the "right" to do anything. Each woman had reported the incidents at some point to relatives. Ten had chosen to report the abuse to their priests. Nine women had reported their husbands to the chief of the village where he came from, but they all said that it did not help much. Out of fifty women, only four perceived reporting the violence to the police to be an option. Two had reported the incidents to their husbands' superiors at work. Two had sought the assistance of the Department of Social Welfare, but neither received a meaningful response. Interestingly, none attempted to report it to their doctors, typically because they felt shy. All the women felt that they could now seek advice from FIDA lawyers as to possible legal redress.

While no woman had left her abuser, each felt that she had endured enough pain and humiliation to come out of her silence, report the abuse, and possibly leave the relationship. When asked why they now felt they could break their silence, all the women expressed fears that their health was in danger from the abuse likely to result from continued silence. More than half felt that the repeated abuse to them was detrimental to the atmosphere in which their children were growing up.

Finally, when asked whether they would consider mediation or counseling to repair their marriages, most of them found that such a step would be useless since they felt they would be blamed for the breakdown in the relationship by their partners and both families. Though most of them wanted the violence to stop, they were not aware of their alternatives. Except for three who planned to leave their marriages, the women had never considered leaving their partners to be an option.

The only firm conclusion that we can draw from such a limited study is that domestic violence exists in Ghana. There remains, as yet, no sense of how to deal with it.

B. THE CHALLENGE

The difficulty in speaking about the domestic violence faced by African women is the risk of importing Western values that conflict with traditional African culture. Many Africans perceive Western feminist analysis as anathema to the culture in that it questions the status quo and ripples the smooth surface of tradition. Similarly, any attempt to address domestic violence seems like an invasion of "foreign" values into deeply rooted tradition.

Despite any conflict between feminist reform and Ghanaian culture, there remains the need to address the conditioned helplessness that seems to pervade the spirits of most Ghanaian women regardless of their differing levels of education or social status. As Justice Anne Jiagge (the first female judge of the Court of Appeal of Ghana) states,

> [W]omen have accepted the inferior status imposed on them as an inescapable fact of life. Wives are proud to be treated as appendages of their husbands. A wife will bask in the glory of her husband's achievements without giving a thought to her own capabilities and native wisdom. Even where the creative urge is strong and she is aware of her own potential she is inhibited within herself and suppresses what is crying to be let out for fear of being regarded as out of the ordinary.[6]

Marilyn Frye compares the oppression of women to the structure of a birdcage.[7] She notes that if one closely examines the wires individually and in sequence, one will not be able to figure out why the bird cannot escape. If, however, one stands back and views the cage as a whole, it becomes perfectly obvious that the bird is surrounded by a network of systematically related barriers. No one wire in itself would hinder the bird's flight, but by their interwoven relations, the wires become as confining as the solid walls of a dungeon.

This graphic description applies just as powerfully to the situation of a Ghanaian woman. "Cage wires" include the factors of ostracism by her family, economic hardships if she seeks independence, fear of further abuse if she attempts to leave, loss of custody, and importantly, the "learned helplessness" an abused woman is likely to feel.[8] Perhaps taken individually, each factor might not bar escape. Taken as a whole, however, the cage becomes a prison from which escape seems impossible.

Despite the power of Frye's analogy, the average Ghanaian woman probably does not see herself as a bird in a cage. First, she is not aware of confinement. She would interpret what Frye describes as "a network of systematically related barriers" as a way of life—*the* way of life.[9] Second, she may see the individual strands (the factors discouraging her from leaving her abuser) as merely the hazards to be expected in a marriage. Hence the initial barrier to reform is that the people to be freed do not perceive themselves to be in bondage.

Although there is no one answer to this dilemma, we must focus primarily on changing the social order that teaches a woman that she is incapable of even small decisions and confines her to waiting for her husband to lead the way in all that she does. To this end, we must examine the customs and folklore that reinforce the idea that wife beating is acceptable.

C. IMAGES OF GHANAIAN WOMEN: THE ROLE OF TRADITION AND FOLKLORE

By examining entrenched social practices, Takyiwaa Manuh identifies the reasons it is difficult to resolve questions about gender roles in Ghana.[10] Tradition is the single most important reason Ghanaian women accept the fact that there is an obvious disparity between their lifestyles and that of their male counterparts, and consequently have not been able to lift the shackles of inequality. Manuh observes that all ethnic groups within Ghana believe, to some extent, that a woman is in need of protection and is under the authority and control of someone, usually a male, throughout her life. In reality, power and independence are possessed by only a tiny percentage of women, and even these women suffer from the traditional prejudices and beliefs. The majority of Ghanaian women live in the rural areas and are engaged in farming and other activities that bring few economic rewards and give little or no power.

Traditional Ghanaian folklore includes stories that most children are told just before they go to bed, often by their grandmother (or Nana). These stories cover a wide range of issues about our ways of life. Children assimilate the lessons of these stories and understand them to be illustrations of how people in the culture should act. Although there are no stories that label beating "domestic violence," there are stories about a man beating his wife to maintain "law and order." The Anansesem folktales illustrate this pattern.[11]

Ghanaian children's stories and traditional songs usually revolve around Ananse. He is the spider-man figure in Ghanaian mythology who has an overworked, hapless wife, Yaa, and a brood of malformed children. Several stories depict Ananse as an inept, bumbling, greedy man—full of cunning with which he attempts to cheat the rest of the world. His pranks are often traced back to him, but he always manages to escape by the skin of his teeth, leaving his wife to take the blame. Despite his conniving nature, he is a formidable disciplinarian to his wife, Yaa, and their children, and they stand in awe of him. The underlying message must be that the man of the house, regardless of his social position or personal faults, has the untrammelled authority to control the household as he chooses.

Children often accept the underlying messages of such stories without question. Ghanaian children laugh at the amusing incidents that occur in Ananse's colorful existence, but do not question Yaa's role as his stoic and uncomplaining wife. In many stories, the family's seemingly endless poverty and hunger would have ended if Yaa's ideas had been accepted by Ananse.[12] Instead, Ananse's grand gestures always take precedence. When things go wrong, Yaa always takes a beating, for Ananse is quick with his fists and never accepts his faults.

This chapter indicates the unwillingness of most Ghanaian women to step out of trends created by culture, yet this is what must be done. A culture that teaches male mastery and domination over women must be altered. The changes in Ghanaian culture that I envision can be compared in a way to the weaving of the traditional Ghanaian kente.[13] We must add to and subtract from the fabric of our society in order to create a masterpiece. I think we can accomplish this by undoing some of the cultural norms and replacing them with others, different but beneficial and equally strong.

This process is like trying to grow a strong plantain tree—all the weak suckers are removed from around the mother and only the best left to flourish.[14] The popular expression "uprooting the sucker" is a traditional saying that describes a person's stubborn attempt to uproot and change the firmly entrenched status quo.

III. AN APPROACH TO THE PROBLEM OF DOMESTIC VIOLENCE

My aim is to draw attention to wife beating as one area of distress that requires rethinking and social change. While we cannot expect an instant solution, it is important that we begin to think about the need for social reform and substantive equality for Ghanaian women. Taking a look at efforts elsewhere will clarify the way we should approach domestic violence in Ghana.

In a study of housing for battered women in Canada, one author concludes that "woman battering is a crime and a social problem, not a private affair. Therefore all levels of government and society must share the responsibility to eliminate it."[15] Even in Canada, where efforts have been made to address domestic violence for the last fifteen to twenty years, we still hear pressing appeals such as this one.[16] Certainly in Ghana, where the issue has not even been addressed, there is an even greater need for such an appeal.

The following urgent questions come to mind: How can we identify and define the problems of wife beating in order to make them visible to Ghanaians generally? How can we bring the issue of domestic violence to the forefront of the social and political agenda? What social measures can we take to counter the problem? Additionally, how can we structure legislation that would eradicate it? Even if such legislation is passed, how can we ensure that its implementation will create peace for women?

A. INITIAL SOLUTIONS

I argue that an emphasis on public education is vital to the task of focusing attention on the problem of domestic violence in Ghana; women's organizations can be instrumental in this effort. I submit that only through some form of public education that fosters awareness and social change can we eradicate domestic violence and at the same time upgrade the status of Ghanaian women generally. I consider to what extent organizations that work within communities can disseminate the message of freedom from domestic violence. Such a community-based approach is necessary to educate the Ghanaian woman about her self-worth as an independent human being.

These projects should embrace the needs of Ghanaian women without tearing apart the fabric of Ghana's rich tradition in order to successfully encourage the de-velopment of Ghanaian women and bring domestic violence out into the open. Moreover, there can be no meaningful solution to the problem of wife beating un-less an entire community participates.

I base this belief on my knowledge that Ghanaians generally have a sense of their community's well-being. On the whole, society in Ghana is communal rather than individualistic; all members of a particular community stand ready for the most part to assist each other. I find it troublesome that the same community that takes a keen interest in a bereaved neighbor's plight may hesitate to intervene when a man is beating up his wife. Perhaps education can help the community to harness its en-ergies toward alleviating the anguish of a battered wife.

Strengthening women's organizations in Ghana will facilitate the achievement of self-awareness, and therefore self-help. Organizations established to meet the needs of women should be functional and technically competent and, most importantly, should reach rural women.

1. NCWD

The Ghana National Council on Women and Development (NCWD) fits these criteria.[17] Most women in Ghana belong to a local voluntary organization, either in their church or at their work place, be it a market, a factory, or an office. Thus, the NCWD tries to work through these organizations to reach women.

The first major task of the NCWD was to create public awareness about the plight of Ghanaian women. In 1975 it launched an education program that sought to eradicate prejudices through public lectures and discussions on radio and televi-sion in both English and the Ghanaian languages. One result of this program was a healthy debate in schools and in newspapers about women's capabilities and their role in society.

While the NCWD has never addressed domestic violence as a matter of primary consideration, it could provide one forum for the educational process by teaching that domestic violence should not be accepted in marriage in either rural or urban settings. Because women in Ghana would contribute more effectively to Ghana's development if they did not have to contend with the threat of domestic violence, the NCWD can also teach that domestic violence is a public development issue, within the province of national development organizations, and not a private mat-ter as previously assumed. If domestic violence is a reason for the failure of women to reach their full productive potential, then its eradication is necessary for opti-mum economic development. In other words, to the extent that wife beating detracts from women's self-confidence and assertion of their productivity, it detracts from the Ghanaian economy.

In other contexts the NCWD has understood the public and social consequences of seemingly private and individual matters. For instance, it has identified a need to change the attitudes of parents so that they will realize that, given the same opportunities, their daughters will do as well as their sons in school and will similarly benefit from higher education. Another goal of the NCWD is to create functional literacy programs for women who need them. In addition, the NCWD has made recommendations to the government about issues affecting the education and training of girls, including the creation of programs relevant to girls' needs and the diversification of vocational training programs to include nontraditional courses. They have also held a series of seminars, consultations, and public discussions to identify the needs of Ghanaian women regarding training, income generation, employment, health, and family welfare.

The illustration of some of the NCWD's other concerns may help to show how it could play an important part in domestic violence reform. Dolphyne sees some hope for women in the actions of the NCWD. She states that the cynicism that met the launching of the International Women's Year in Ghana soon gave way to sober reflection and understanding of issues highlighted by NCWD programs.[18] Similar changes could happen with the issue of domestic violence if it were given comparable exposure and coverage.

2. FIDA

I submit that FIDA could be an ideal organization for the exposure of domestic violence in Ghana. Like their colleagues elsewhere, FIDA's Ghanaian members, both lawyers and judges, are highly educated and powerful women who can propose many measures to stop the oppression of women.

At the moment, FIDA devotes its efforts primarily toward assisting women in dealing with their legal problems. Addressing domestic violence specifically as a legal problem would bring it to the forefront of public opinion. Moreover, recognizing domestic violence as a legal matter would further women's sense of self-worth.

The educational campaign would have to be massive in order to change beliefs and practices held since time immemorial concerning the place of a woman and the right of a husband to assault her as he wishes. This has to be done without unduly upsetting the tradition, as we would uproot the plantain sucker or change a strand in the kente fabric, altering the pattern without destroying the fabric.

Organizations like the NCWD and FIDA can educate Ghanaian communities on the harms of domestic violence. Similar efforts have been made by women and women's movements in the United States and Canada. Doubtless, such early efforts led to the exposure of domestic violence in these countries. The same can be accomplished in Ghana. If organizations such as the NCWD and FIDA help to deal with the issue of domestic violence, they could generate an awareness that might break through the culture of silence that surrounds this deeply private crime against women.

B. LONG-TERM SOLUTIONS

Once educational efforts have paved the way, long-term solutions to domestic violence can follow. These measures might include adopting legislation to help battered women as well as educating the police and the judiciary about domestic violence. I shall briefly discuss these courses of action.

1. Legislation

One of the greatest tensions in Ghanaian law has been between the retention of Ghanaian customary law and the incorporation of inherited British common law. The process of blending these two has led to some absurdities. Justice A. N. E. Amissah recounts how Lord Carnarvon, the British secretary of state for the colonies, told the House of Lords in 1874 that it would be "a mistake, and almost an absurdity, to apply to negroes the English Law of bankruptcy" and that he anticipated "a great simplification of this and other branches of law on the Gold Coast."[19]

Even though the promised "great simplification" of the laws of England was applied to the Gold Coast, it is unclear how much of the cultural norm remains and prevents change. Furthermore, it is unclear how much of the customary law should remain.

This uncertainty has led to inadequacy in the realm of criminal law. For example, there is no specific legislation in the Criminal Code of Ghana to punish husbands for beating their wives.[20] While assault is covered by three different headings in Section 85(1)—Assault and Battery, Assault without Actual Battery, and Imprisonment—none of these is clearly designed to cover the crime of domestic violence. The legislative body in Ghana should consider creating and defining the crime of wife beating within the Ghanaian Criminal Code as well as introducing mandatory prosecution for assault.

In addition, I believe that there should eventually be clear provisions in the Matrimonial Causes Act of Ghana to make battering a clear ground for divorce, regardless of the victim's status, educational or otherwise. Again, the dilemma of how far to follow either common law or customary law has perhaps made any meaningful or comprehensive legislation difficult. There must be ways to scrutinize and rectify this discrepancy.

The NCWD has documented the absence of women from the country's decision-making bodies at all levels. Few women hold positions of seniority or authority in any of the medical, legal, or educational fields or in the civil service. Legislative bodies must have representation of both women and men if laws are to take into account the position and well-being of women. The present government of Ghana pledges its commitment to women.[21] Regardless, only enhanced participation of women in all levels of the decision-making process will ensure that more will be done to alleviate the hardships facing women.[22]

2. The Police

Unless the police are enlisted to enforce the laws on behalf of battered women, there can be no meaningful eradication of domestic violence. As we have seen, Ghanaian women do not currently view the police as a resource. This stems in part from the women's own reluctance, which, as I have argued, can be addressed through public education efforts. However, to the extent that police indifference contributes to the problem, we can create awareness programs for the police. For instance, FIDA, in conjunction with the Police Service, could organize such programs to educate police officers about the need to treat domestic violence as a public matter and could engage them in discourse about the dangers and unfairness of the traditional idea of physical "discipline" for wives. While undoubtedly difficult, these tasks are crucial. The next step should be the compulsory charging of spousal abuse offenses in Ghana. A project such as the London, Ontario, Integrated Community Project might be of immense help in Ghana.[23] Ultimately, the Police Service Act of Ghana could be a medium for channeling the services of the police into restraining and controlling domestic violence.[24]

3. The Judiciary

There are hardly any reported cases in the Ghana Law Reports on domestic violence. However, reported cases in divorce law indicate that some judges making decisions in divorce cases believe that a woman's social standing and education should determine whether assaults by her husband are cruel or not. This is illustrated by statements in two cases.

In *Manu v. Manu*, a European wife petitioned for a divorce for cruelty, complaining of, among other things, that she was being beaten by her Ghanaian husband.[25] A deciding factor in the Chief Justice's ruling was his observation that "[t]he petitioner is a University graduate, and must be a person of considerable culture and intelligence. In our opinion, conduct of the kind complained of . . . having regard to her class and standing, amounted to intolerable mental cruelty."[26] The petitioner was then, in the opinion of the judge, subjected to the indignity of mental cruelty not befitting her status. His words seem to imply that such treatment might be more appropriate or less cruel to women who do not share Manu's class background and standing. In *Osei-Koom v. Osei-Koom*,[27] the court said, "Here are man and woman trained in the best traditions of English life and urbanity and their standard of culture, no doubt, is on a higher plane than that of a couple quartered in a remote Ghanaian village."[28]

In both cases, the battered wives got the divorces they sought. The judges' comments indicate that there are certain women who, by virtue of their status, should not be beaten; by implication, other women may be beaten. The women who are protected by these opinions are the ones farthest from the traditional lifestyle. They are foreigners, literally or metaphorically, and are more able than most women to leave an abusive marriage. Neither case reflects the possibility that battered women from rural, traditional, or underprivileged backgrounds would find any support from the judiciary. This assumes they could even bring a case to court; many economic and social barriers would stand in their way.

These cases indicate that we are far from reaching the point where all Ghanaian women are seen as equal, all deserving the basic freedom from domestic oppression, and not dichotomized by virtue of their position in Ghanaian society. When judges see people in terms of class and standing, it erodes any sense of an impartial referee dispensing justice and it detracts from the purpose of the law.

Here, as elsewhere, the judiciary must be educated to see Ghanaian women as equal to each other and entitled to equal protection of the laws. Even when courts reach the right outcome, if it is for the wrong reason we gain little. I would recommend that FIDA, in conjunction with the Judicial Service of Ghana, take on the project of educating the judiciary about the horrors of domestic violence. No woman should be excluded from legal protection from assault. This must be the premise of any policing of domestic violence for it to have any meaning.

IV. CONCLUSION

We must deal with the domestic violence that Ghanaian women face. The questions are many: What is the nature and incidence of domestic violence in Ghana? Why do the cases not get to the courts? What are the sociological and psychological constraints? What are the attitudes of the authorities—judges, police, lawmakers—and the extended family? What lessons can be learned from other jurisdictions that have taken the bold plunge to examine questions of domestic violence?

I hope that this chapter can generate serious and widespread interest in the issues surrounding the scourge of domestic violence. Perhaps the discussion can also focus on the practicality of possible solutions, such as educating the public about the right to freedom from such abuse, upgrading the educational and employment level of women to help reduce their economic dependence on their husbands, enacting provisions in the Ghanaian Criminal Code and the Matrimonial Causes Act to deter and punish wife battering, and educating the police and the judiciary on the concept of domestic violence and its attendant remedies.

At present the paucity of information on domestic violence in Ghana indicates how compelling the need is for research into this problem. This essay is based on information from interviews with Ghanaian women, examinations of divorce cases, and explorations of the patterns of Ghanaian folklore. Obviously, much work still needs to be done. Merely making pronouncements about how heinous the crime of domestic violence is will not begin to solve the problem. Rather, we must engage in research, teach methods of self-help, and establish a system of communal education that can acknowledge and incorporate Ghanaian traditions. Only after these measures have been undertaken will we fully understand the existence of domestic violence in Ghana and be able to demonstrate that it is wrong. Perhaps at that point we will be able to establish and enforce legislative, prosecutorial, and judicial controls.

Domestic violence in Ghana can no longer be accepted as an "occupational hazard" of marriage. Now is the time to begin addressing and eradicating it.[29]

NOTES

1. What I loosely describe as "Ghanaian culture" is actually a mosaic of many different tribal customs and beliefs. It would be a disservice to encourage readers to assume that there is a hegemony. Where I use a single description, I have been influenced by the mores and practices of the Akan tribe, because it is the largest tribe among the peoples of Ghana and is the tribe from which I come. The word Akan refers both to a group of intimately related languages found in West Africa and to the people who speak them. This ethnic group lives predominantly in Ghana and in parts of adjoining Côte d'Ivoire. In Ghana they inhabit most of the southern and middle belts and account for about half the national population of fourteen million. Best known among the Akan subgroups are the Ashantis. Closely cognate are the Denkyiras, Akims, Akuapims, Fantes, Kwahus, Wassas, Brongs, and the Nzimas, among others. Kwasi Wiredu, *An Akan Perspective on Human Rights, in* Human Rights in Africa 243 (Abdullahi Ahmed An-Na'im and Frances M. Deng eds., 1990).

2. Anonymous, Responses to Legal Aid Clinic of FIDA questionnaire (on file with author).

3. *Id.*

4. "Beating" was seen as any form of hitting. Slapping with the hands or with a weapon such as a belt, a cane, or shoes were all examples of beatings. In some cases, women admitted to being whipped or "booted," which is common slang in Ghana for kicking.

5. *Supra* note 2.

6. Hon. Anne Jiagge, Talk Given at the World Council of Churches' Fifth Plenary Presentation on "Women in a Changing World," 1975, in L. F. Arthur, *African Regional Conference of the International Federation of Women Lawyers (FIDA),* 8 Rev. Ghana L. 140, 142 (1976).

7. Marilyn Frye, The Politics of Reality: Essays in Feminist Theory 4–5 (1983).

8. *See* Lenore E. Walker, *How Battering Happens and How to Stop It, in* Battered Women 59–78 (Donna M. Moore ed., 1979).

9. Frye, *supra* note 7, at 5.

10. Takiyiwaa Manuh, Law and the Status of Women in Ghana 5 (1984).

11. Anansesem are the tales of Ananse, which literally means "spider" and, in the context of the stories, refers to a "spider-man."

12. One of these ideas was to cultivate a farm of their own instead of plundering their neighbor's; another was to engage in some profitable business venture instead of living on the gifts given to them by sympathetic passersby while Ananse pretended that all of his family were lepers and beggars.

13. Kente is the traditional cloth of Ghana, originating with the powerful Ashanti Empire. Colorful strands of thread are woven over and across each other on a broadloom with a shuttle until a broadcloth has been created that is intricate and original in design. In a sense, this is the nature of the culture: different strands intertwining and crossing each other, strips of fabric that the weaver can remove or add, to change the pattern until the quintessential piece is created. The kente cloth defies description entirely in the beauty of its weave. It is as

much a tradition as the very essence of the people themselves, and its mystery and beauty are handed down from generation to generation, not through words but through a picturesque weave that speaks for itself.

14. Plantain trees grow out of plantain suckers in tropical forests. There is usually a clump of suckers from which the strongest one will grow over and above the others to become the dominant tree. The plantain sucker is particularly difficult to uproot.

15. T. Don, An Introduction to the Ontario Association of Interval and Transition Houses 8 (1986).

16. Anne McGillivray, *Battered Women: Definition, Models and Prosecutorial Policy*, 6 Can. J. Fam. L. 15, 17 (1987).

17. Following the celebration of International Women's Year in 1975, with its focus on the need to integrate women into national development at all levels, the government of Ghana established the NCWD to advise government on all issues affecting the full participation of women in national development. National Redemption Council Decree 322 (1975). Strictly speaking, the organizations that I discuss are not community-based in the sense that they belong to any one community. However, these are the groups most likely to reach all women— urban and rural—in their own communities. Furthermore, they may be useful in fostering the creation of truly local organizations.

18. Florence Abena Dolphyne, *The Ghana National Council on Women and Development: An Example in Concerted Action, in* Sex Roles, Population and Development in West Africa 214 (Christine Oppong ed., 1987).

19. Justice A. N. E. Amissah, *The Supreme Court, A Hundred Years Ago, in* Essays in Ghanaian Law 2 (W. C. Ekow Daniels and G. R. Woodman eds., 1976).

20. *See* Criminal Code Act 29, Ghana (1960).

21. Indeed, the Head of State of Ghana, Jerry John Rawlings, said in August 1982 (nearly a year after assuming office) that "there is no way there will be a successful social change in the country without the effective participation of Ghanaian women." Daily Graphic, Accra, Aug. 2, 1982, at 1.

22. Of course, it is important to remember that the mere presence of women on decision-making panels is not sufficient to ensure the safeguarding of women's interests because, in a male-dominated society, these women might be present as tokens rather than as full participants.

23. In May 1981 the London, Ontario, City Police Force, the University of Western Ontario, and several community services came together to fight the problem of wife abuse. The participants in the project assumed that the community, with the leadership of criminal justice officers, could improve services to victims of family violence if people became aware of the nature of the problem and existing limitations.

> The policies put in place encouraged and empowered officers to lay charges of assault in domestic situations. [This effort] did not result from changes in legislation but was undertaken by the department in response to research which indicated that the victims wanted officers to lay charges and that the necessary grounds for laying the charges often existed. The Police perceived this policy as reflecting a change in attitudes about the seriousness of wife assault cases.

Carole Anne Burris and Peter Jaffe, *Wife Abuse as a Crime: The Impact of Police Laying Charges*, 25 Can. J. Criminology 309 (1983). This project is worth studying for its potential application to the Ghanaian situation.

24. Police Service Act 350, Ghana (1970), governing the organization and administration of the Ghana Police Force.

25. 1959 Ghana Law Reports 21.

26. *Id.* at 22.

27. 1967 Ghana Law Reports 274.

28. *Id.* at 278.

29. Since the writing of this article, the most prominent consciousness-raising women's group in Ghana—the 31st December Women's Movement—and the Ghana Federation of Women Lawyers have been working on promoting women's rights in Ghana through symposia and reading materials. The status of societal views on domestic violence has certainly hindered their work. Later research I have conducted emphasizes the enormity of the problem, but indicates that mechanisms for dialogue have been set in motion. *See* Rosemary Ofei-Aboagye, Ghanaian Women: Equality and Empowerment (1994)(unpublished thesis for D.Jur. degree, Osgoode Hall Law School, Toronto, Canada).

A Critical Race Feminist
Conceptualization of Violence

South African and Palestinian Women

Adrien Katherine Wing

INTRODUCTION

As the Introduction to this volume makes clear, Critical Race Feminism draws from Critical Legal Studies, Critical Race Theory, and feminist jurisprudence. It demarginalizes women of color and places them at the center of a multidisciplinary analysis that focuses on both theory and praxis. Within a global framework, it explores the lives of those women facing multiple discrimination on the basis of their nationality, ethnicity, race, gender, class, and other axes of identity, revealing how all these factors interact within conditions of patriarchy and racism. This chapter seeks to conceptualize violence against women, under both international and foreign domestic law, from the perspective of critical race feminism. Two groups of women, Black South African women and Palestinian women in the West Bank and Gaza Strip, are featured. Both groups of women have faced violence from multiple sources—external violence from the state and internal violence from the home.

CONCEPTUALIZING VIOLENCE USING A CRITICAL RACE FEMINIST APPROACH: OUTSIDE/INSIDE DICHOTOMY AND SPIRIT INJURY

In attempting to use a Critical Race feminist construct to conceptualize violence affecting South African and Palestinian women, this chapter will utilize two concepts: the outside/inside dichotomy and spirit injury. With respect to the first concept, I posit that under conditions of the "outside" violence of colonialism, neocolonialism, apartheid, or occupation, the men of an oppressed group are not allowed to be

Reprinted by permission from 60 *Albany Law Review* 943 (1997).

"men" in the culturally constructed use of the term. In effect, they are not allowed to dominate in the outside public sphere of government and business because of the influence and control of outsider men. One of the few areas where the oppressed men can exert some limited expression of their maleness is through oversight of their own women in the "inside" or private sphere. As one Palestinian man said, "What is left for us? We don't have land, homes or identity—at least let's have our honor."[1] The only sphere where the "emasculated" men can take out their frustration is the private one affecting their own women and children. Thus, their families are going to be disproportionately subject to domestic violence as they bear the brunt of frustration of male high unemployment and political impotence. Ironically, the oppressed male's ability to dominate even in the private sphere may be limited because the oppressor's police or army can intrude into this realm as well.

Custom, culture, and religion become psychological refuges for the oppressed against foreign penetration, providing the bases to at least try to survive the violent incursions. People may glorify the most ancient, and in many cases the most repressive, patriarchal traditions in order to restore and maintain a sense of manhood for the embattled men. Many women, as well as men, view these customs as "desirable, one area where their own culture [is] reaffirmed," even though this results in female subordination.[2] Most women, subject to the multiple burdens of their ethnicity and gender, would not even think of going to outsiders, that is, the police or other officials, to seek relief from repressive practices or to report their own men for abuse. This would make the women collaborators or traitors.[3] Thus, they suffer in silence, perhaps unaware of the "patriarchal bargain" they have made in their own subordination.[4] When evaluating their multiple oppression, many politically aware women in the developing world realize that even though they may join guerrilla movements, work outside the home, and enter politics, at the end of the day they are still inferior to men, fighting to be second- or third-class citizens.[5]

The multiple effect of violence on these women, simultaneously coming from outside and inside their culture, constitutes a "spirit injury" to women, and thus on the entire culture. Spirit injury is a Critical Race feminist term that contemplates the psychological, spiritual, and cultural effects of the multiple assaults on these women. Spirit injury "leads to the slow death of the psyche, of the soul, and of the identity of the individual."[6] Women come to believe in their own inferiority, and that there is justification for the violence against them, because "[a] fundamental part of ourselves and of our dignity is dependent upon the uncontrollable, powerful external observers who constitute society."[7] If society places a low value on certain members, they in turn will perceive themselves as having a lesser worth in that society. Because they are devalued by both the outside society of the oppressor and the inside society of their own culture, as well as by the intimate inside of their own family, women cannot help but be profoundly silenced and experience a loss of self-actualization. The spirit injury becomes "as devastating, as costly, and as psychically obliterating . . . as robbery or assault."[8] On the group level, the accumulation of multiple individual spirit injuries can "lead[ ] to the devaluation and destruction of a way of life or of an entire culture."[9] Neither international nor domestic law adequately remedies the spirit injuries that oppressed women or men face on an individual or group basis.

This chapter will now use this critical race feminist approach to the outside/inside dichotomy and spirit injury to conceptualize violence in two concrete applications. By placing Black South African women and Palestinian women at the center of the analysis, we can specifically examine how international and domestic law helps and hinders any improvement in the social and legal status of the women. Because CRF believes in evaluating women in their own cultural context rather than "essentializing" them as the universal woman, this chapter will now provide background on the current status of South African and Palestinian women.

SOCIAL AND LEGAL CONDITIONS IN SOUTH AFRICA

Black South African women, who constitute more than 36 percent of the South African population, are the most oppressed group in South Africa.[10] Even though legal apartheid has ended, Black South African women are still victimized on a de facto basis by whites, both male and female, on account of their race. White males still constitute the vast majority of employers or potential employers of Black women as well as professional service providers to these women. White women are also employers, especially of domestics—a profession that almost exclusively employs Black females. Additionally, Black and white men victimize Black women on the basis of gender. Because almost all Blacks are still of poor or working-class backgrounds, Black women are also oppressed on the basis of class. This oppression is perpetrated predominantly by whites, but also by Colored, Asian, and a few Black employers. Coloureds and Asians constitute a middle class of employers and service providers.

Despite a new constitution that grants equality to women, Black women are still affected by sexist presumptions found in African customary law as well as the Afrikaner, British, Colored, and Asian patriarchy of the employers of Black women. The customary law of each Black ethnic group affects marriage, divorce, guardianship, succession, contractual power, and property rights in that group. Women remain "perpetual minors and lifelong wards of their fathers, husbands, brothers, or sons. . . . [W]omen [cannot] engage in contracts of any kind, acquire property, inherit, or marry without . . . permission."[11] Thus, Black women are literally and figuratively male property.

VIOLENCE IN SOUTH AFRICA

South Africa's culture of the outside violence of apartheid has contributed to male and female acceptance of domestic violence in the private sphere as a fact of life. South African women have experienced a great deal of abuse as a result of both rape and domestic violence. One study estimates that in 1991 95 percent of rapes were unreported, and that 95 percent of all rapes were committed against Black women.[12] Some estimates say as many as one-third of the Black South African women will be raped, and as many as one-sixth of the women are in abusive relations.[13] Additionally, the legal definition of rape excluded spousal rape until the enactment of the Prevention of Family Violence Act.[14] However, the definition of rape still excludes same-sex rape. Thus, any sexual acts between people of the same sex, such as oral sex, anal sex, or the use of objects other than a penis, remain outside the scope of the law. Also excluded from the Act are incidents between people not living together.

Although the high prevalence of rape and abuse may be partially attributable to the outside violence of apartheid, customary law plays a role in domestic violence as well. Because customary beliefs include the idea that women are the property of males, many men believe that they have the right to batter and rape women. These patterns have continued despite the adoption of the permanent Constitution of South Africa in 1996. One recent study exposed the shocking fact that 70 percent of disabled women became disabled as a result of domestic violence.[15]

Female victims of domestic violence are unable to obtain much assistance from doctors, counselors, or the police. They must also undergo abuse from the legal system, which doubts their credibility. In the courtroom, women must deal with traditional stereotypes that depict women as seductive sex objects that men cannot resist. They must deal with the spirit injury that results when insinuations of promiscuity are made in brutal cross-examinations.[16] Prosecutors infer that such promiscuity leads to rape, which the victim must have resisted to the utmost to prove her nonconsent.[17]

The combination of the outside/inside violence of apartheid and customary practices constitutes a massive spirit injury for Black South African women. The symptoms of defilement, silence, sexuality, trespass, and emasculation are present. Since the legacy of apartheid has resulted in continued high unemployment and disempowerment for many Black males, these men continue to feel emasculated by the trespass on the control over their families and culture, even in the new South Africa. These men may take out their frustrations on their women. "Men's experience of racism and economic deprivation often causes a reactionary backlash within the family—to the detriment of women—rather than opening up the space for resistance to race and class oppression."[18]

Thus, the women are defiled by the multiple levels of abuse—abuse from the outside violence of the apartheid legacy, inside violence from their own men, and a legal system that re-rapes them if they attempt to seek justice. These women may prefer to suffer in silence as their men attempt to totally control their lives, including their sexuality.

Fortunately, there are a number of organizations dealing with domestic abuse, as well as some hotlines. Additionally, there is the Wynberg Sexual Offenses Court, and the acceptance of the rape trauma syndrome by courts in the Western Cape.[19] The Prevention of Family Violence Act is now several years in operation as well. These developments may hold substantial potential for the future.

SOCIAL AND LEGAL CONDITIONS IN PALESTINE

Palestinian women in the West Bank and Gaza Strip have lived under occupation for centuries. Ottoman Turks ruled the area for five hundred years until World War I, when they were ousted by the Allied forces. Then the British tried to govern an increasingly fractious region where Arab nationalism confronted Jewish Zionist nationalism. After the formation of the state of Israel, the West Bank came under the jurisdiction of Jordan, and Egypt took over the administration of the Gaza Strip.

In 1967 Israel started its military occupation. During the occupation, many women were among those arrested, imprisoned, and tortured. When their men were taken into administrative detention for long periods, the women became the bulwarks of the large and extended families. Many women worked only in the home and did not earn money to support the family. Many women and women's organizations played an increasingly visible and prominent role during the six-year uprising known as the *intifada* that began in 1987. The former minister of higher education Professor Hanan Ashrawi notes that "[i]n every confrontation, committee, project, or enterprise women took the initiative, stood up and stood out. Neither kitchen nor prison could contain or intimidate them. The first person pronoun was no longer the sole domain of the masculine."[20] Ashrawi is best known as the spokesperson for the Palestinians during the Madrid peace talks with Israel.

The peace process that started in 1993 has resulted in a high level of frustration among the Palestinians. Although the new Palestinian National Authority (PNA) government of President Yasser Arafat now controls 70 percent of the Gaza Strip, it controls only 3 percent of the entire West Bank.[21] Thus, a large number of Palestinian women and men remain under direct occupation, and the remainder under indirect occupation. There have been periodic closures, total and partial, on the area, which have resulted in Palestinians being unable to leave or enter Palestinian areas without difficult-to-obtain permits. Many Palestinians have characterized the Gaza Strip as a virtual prison for its nearly one million denizens. The Israelis have also occasionally cordoned off the various Palestinian cities in the West Bank from each other, which is reminiscent of the South African apartheid bantustan strategy. One Palestinian author has called these little patches of Palestinian-controlled territory "arabistans."[22] The net result of the violence of "peace" is an economy in shambles and a peace process in tatters.[23]

In addition to the external oppression of the outsider, Palestinian women face multiple burdens from the customary and Islamic heritages. Customary practices predate the introduction of Islam in the seventh century, yet current custom and Islam have mutually influenced each other. Both custom and Islam have also been affected by the various occupations.

Under current custom, women are considered repositories of family and clan honor.[24] Female chastity and purity must be maintained or the family will be disgraced. There is also the tradition of honor killings, in which male family members are justified in killing any female family member who they feel has besmirched the family's honor. Crimes for which women could be punished include dating, premarital sex, leaving home without permission, or marrying outside the faith or to someone not approved by the family. One human rights group estimates that nearly all of the 107 women killed as suspected Israeli informers during the uprising were in fact victims of honor killings.[25] Women activists see these killings as a means to prevent women from rebelling against a system in which they are dominated by male patriarchy from the cradle to the grave.[26]

Male children are preferred, and upon a son's birth the mother becomes known as Umm (mother of) her oldest son's name.[27] Girls are still likely to be married off in arranged marriages when they are teenagers. Thus, their completion of secondary school may not be a priority. As one woman said, "[i]f a family cannot educate all the children, the man must be chosen, because he will be the breadwinner and the head of the household."[28]

A bride price, *mahr,* is paid by the groom's family to the girl, for her own use. If divorce occurs, the woman goes back under the jurisdiction of her father or other male relatives. There is no independent living as there is in the United States. While these customs are more likely to be followed in rural or less well educated families, they have surprising resonance even in highly educated, elite families as well.[29]

The Islamic heritage that began in the seventh century was seen as an improvement over custom. Polygamy was limited to four wives in the *shari'a,* which is the Islamic law as found in the Koran. Now women are allowed to divorce on limited grounds and obtain maintenance. Women also gained the right to own and inherit property.[30]

Despite these improvements over custom, *shari'a* sanctions differential treatment for women. Women's inheritance share is limited to one half of a male's share. Only men can have more than one spouse, and men can freely divorce.[31] Muslim men can marry a Muslim, Christian, or Jewish woman, while a Muslim woman can only marry a Muslim. Furthermore, custody of children is awarded to the wife only when children are young.[32]

Most important for the purposes of this chapter, *shari'a* permits men to beat their wives if they do not submit, and the wives must endure the punishment.[33] The Jordanian Personal Status Law, which codifies many *shari'a* principles for the West Bank, makes clear that the wife has the duty to obey the husband (*taa*).[34] The net effect is that women are well aware of and feel their subordination, regardless of their age or educational status.

VIOLENCE IN PALESTINE

The symptoms of spirit injury manifest themselves in the area of violence among the Palestinians as well. Unfortunately, the silence of spirit injury is so profound that there are no reliable statistics on domestic violence or other violence against women, and public discussion on such issues is still relatively muted.[35] Alarming rates of domestic violence have been found in the West Bank.[36] According to one provider, domestic violence is also endemic in Gaza: "[M]en have a lot of aggression and very few channels for ventilating it. . . . Men . . . use women to ventilate, and beating is part of the culture."[37] Wife beating continues because of patriarchy and the way males are socialized to view women from an early age, and because of the custom of noninterference in domestic disputes.[38]

Reports have uncovered a few cases of classic torture in which men mimicked Israeli torture techniques that were used against them in prison. For example, one husband covered his wife's head with a sack and beat her with pipes and cable.[39] He was arrested, but released eighteen days later without being charged.

Victims feel the spirit injury of silence because they dare not speak for fear of hurting family honor. Many of them are blamed for the "shame" they have caused—that is, they are defiling the family honor if they complain. In the one major survey of women's attitudes, women indicated that they preferred to handle the situation within the family rather than seek outside assistance.[40] In a recent study, 35.2 percent admitted to psychological abuse, and 4.3 percent even admitted to being raped by their fathers.[41] When presented with hypothetical situations involving psychological and physical abuse, significant numbers of men and women blamed the woman as well as the man for the situation. Large numbers of men (50 percent) felt that disobedience by a woman would justify battery.[42]

In addition to the spirit injury, there are three major problems facing these women: continued economic dependence on the spouse; lack of protective services or shelters; and lack of legal protection. It simply is not a crime to beat one's spouse, and the legal system is unwilling to trespass on "inside" matters. Such interference would represent an emasculation of the men in the family, who would be seen as being unable to control female sexuality. Women's rights advocates claim that government and society are not interested in providing counseling or outreach.[43] There are only two hotlines and one counseling service in the entire West Bank.[44]

Now that this chapter has provided social and legal background about the two cultures and the nature of outside/inside violence and spirit injury that affects them, it will now discuss the remedial treatment for these women and their societies.

INTERNATIONAL LAW: CONVENTION ON THE ELIMINATION OF ALL FORMS OF DISCRIMINATION AGAINST WOMEN

While there are many human rights agreements, the Convention on the Elimination of All Forms of Discrimination against Women (CEDAW) represents a holistic approach to women's civil, political, economic, social, and cultural rights. Several sections of CEDAW may have some relevance to the situation of violence against women in South Africa and Palestine. Article 2 calls on states to "modify or abolish laws or practices which discriminate against women."[45] Another article calls upon states to "modify the social and cultural patterns of conduct of men and women, with a view toward achieving the elimination of prejudices and customary and all other practices which are based on the idea of the inferiority or superiority of either of the sexes or on stereotyped roles for men and women."[46] CEDAW also calls for men and women to have equality before the law[47] and for states to eliminate discrimination in all areas "relating to marriage and family relations."[48] These provisions could be interpreted to call for an end to domestic abuse on the patriarchal grounds of women's property status.

Because of the vagueness of the above provisions with respect to violence against women, the Committee on the Elimination of Discrimination against Women, which is the body charged with oversight of CEDAW, endorsed an explicit resolution on this point in 1992.[49] This resolution recognized that violence against women is a form of discrimination.[50] The Committee interpreted CEDAW to make explicit that gender-based violence is a violation of several articles. The Committee's action was followed up in 1993 when the United Nations General Assembly adopted the Declaration on the Elimination of Violence against Women, which defines violations of women's human rights to equality.[51]

South Africa has signed and ratified CEDAW, without lodging any reservations to it. Unfortunately, CEDAW's enforcement mechanisms are known to be notoriously weak, and thus South African women would be well advised to look to their own new constitution, which is more comprehensive in scope.[52]

With respect to Palestine, the draft constitution known as the Third Reading of the Basic Law of Palestine explicitly states that "[t]he Palestinian National Authority shall work, without delay, to incorporate international and national declarations and agreements which protect human rights."[53] While the Authority, as an autonomous entity, does not have the status of independent statehood and thus cannot join these agreements, it is highly significant that it is committing itself to these principles. An earlier draft of the Basic Law of Palestine specifically listed numerous conventions, including CEDAW.[54] The enumeration of all the conventions was eliminated for the sake of simplicity while the author was present as a foreign advisor at the deliberations of the Legal Committee of the Palestinian Legislative Council.

At this point, international law in the form of CEDAW has very limited direct applicability for either South Africa or Palestine. It is highly significant, however, that both societies agree to be bound by this important convention, something the United States has not yet committed to do. Since CRF is concerned with improving the status of women in a real-world sense, it is important to look next at the areas with the most potential to effect real change in the area of violence prevention—the domestic law of the jurisdictions.

DOMESTIC LAW OF SOUTH AFRICA

The 1993 interim constitution of South Africa provided a positive step forward in improving the legal and social status of Black women.[55] The Equal Protection Clause guaranteed that "Every person shall have the right to equality before the law and to equal protection of the law."[56] Additionally, the interim constitution went beyond the Constitution of the United States by outlawing discrimination on a wide range of grounds: "race, gender, sex, ethnic or social origin, colour, sexual orientation, age, disability, religion, conscience, belief, culture, or language."[57] The entire human rights chapter bound all legislative and executive organs, but was not directly applicable to private parties.[58] Additionally, under the interim constitution, a Gender Commission was created whose function is to advise and make recommendations to Parliament about laws and proposed legislation.[59]

In order to avoid the question of reverse discrimination that has plagued discussions in the United States about equality, the interim constitution contained an affirmative action clause: "[The Equal Protection Clause] shall not preclude measures designed to achieve the adequate protection and advancement of persons or groups or categories of persons disadvantaged by unfair discrimination, in order to enable their full and equal enjoyment of all rights and freedoms."[60] The government has proceeded to implement affirmative action measures. Unfortunately, as a result of the apartheid and customary legacies, few Black women have the educational and employment prerequisites to benefit from affirmative action programs.

The interim constitution affirmed the right to have one's dignity respected and protected, as well as the right not to be subjected to torture of any kind.[61] Unfortunately, the clauses were limited in their impact to the public sphere, since they bound only the executive and legislative branches. Most such violence occurs in the private sphere; thus, the physical and spirit injuries remain unaddressed.

To deal with some of the perceived inadequacies of the interim constitution, the Women's National Coalition (WNC) adopted a Charter, which they hoped would influence the drafters of the permanent constitution, that is, the newly elected Parliament sitting in its dual role as constituent and assembly.[62] Going far beyond the interim constitution, the Charter has specific provisions on sexual and physical violence.[63] Article 10 declares that "[v]iolence in all its forms is endemic to South African society. Both sexual and domestic violence are pervasive and all women live under the threat of or experience violence." Article 10 also affirms the constitutionally protected right to security and integrity of the person, which is the "right to be free from all forms of violence in the home, in communities, in the workplace and in public spaces." Furthermore, the state must provide facilities, public education, and training for police, judges, and others. Article 6 of the Charter demands the provision of accessible social welfare services, which of course would greatly benefit women who suffer abuse. Since a prime area where women suffer abuse has to do with sexual activity and men's patriarchal presumptions about women's duty to submit, the Charter states that "[w]omen must have the right to decide on the nature and frequency of sexual contact within marriage and intimate relationships."[64]

The Charter deals specifically with the relationship between customary law and constitutional rights. The Charter calls for equality in areas of family life and partnerships, as well as equal access to decision making, all areas that are under the sole authority of the husband under customary law. It makes clear that cultural and religious practices should be subject to the Equality Clause.

In 1996 a permanent Constitution was adopted by the new Parliament sitting in its role of constitutional assembly, and ratified by the Constitutional Court. The new Article 8 now makes clear that the Bill of Rights provisions will be binding on private persons as well as the government.[65] Article 8 thus may have profound implications for women suffering abuse, since they will now be able to go after private actors, no longer having to endure in silence. Since legal apartheid is over and the police are now controlled by the government of President Mandela, more women may feel able to report abuse to the authorities. They will no longer be considered traitors when seeking relief from the oppressor.

Additionally, the revised article on freedom and security of the person, Article 12, now makes clear that everyone has a right "to be free from all forms of violence from either public or private sources" as well as a right not to be tortured in any way.[66] The revised article on language and culture now states that while everyone has the right to participate in the culture of their choice, no one can do so "in a manner inconsistent with the Bill of Rights."[67] Finally, the new constitution clarifies that courts must consider international law when interpreting the Bill of Rights.[68] These revised articles should augment the constitutional protections available to abused women.

DOMESTIC LAW OF PALESTINE

The Third Reading of the Basic Law of Palestine contains fundamental rights and freedoms that may assist women in the struggle to lessen domestic violence. The Equality Clause states that everyone is equal before the law without regard to "descent, gender, color, religion, political opinion, or disability."[69] Another article makes clear that no person shall be subjected to coercion or torture.[70] This article, however, is located in a series of provisions pertaining to criminal due process rights, so it may ultimately be found inapplicable in the domestic violence context. Additionally, the Constitution states that Islam is the official religion.[71] Since Islamic *shari'a* law permits the beating of a wife, there is an inherent contradiction and tension with the Equality Clause.

In 1994 the General Union of Palestinian Women published a Declaration of Principles on Palestinian Women's Rights, which goes beyond anything proposed in the Basic Law of Palestine.[72] Its general provision on civil rights states that "the law should stand next to the woman to protect her family from violence and practices that infringe on any of her guaranteed rights, . . . by guaranteeing her right to go to a court as a citizen with full rights."[73] Could this be interpreted to protect her from domestic violence? The provision on economic, social, and cultural rights "affirms the importance of equality in social welfare . . . and the guarantee of her full equality regarding issues pertaining to personal status."[74]

Palestinian police have begun to go after the perpetrators of honor killings,[75] but there are still no battered women's shelters in the West Bank and Gaza Strip. Perhaps as the new government gains legitimacy and gains control over more of the territory, it will expand its outreach into a sensitive area like domestic violence. Right now, the government is still fundamentally concerned with outsider violence perpetrated by the Israeli government, Israeli settlers living in the West Bank and Gaza, and Islamic fundamentalists. If the situation normalizes in the future and the Palestinian police gain respect along with a reconstituted court and legal profession, more women would dare to think to approach authorities with their domestic concerns.

CONCLUSION

We can assist the women of Palestine and South Africa with their legacies of inside/outside violence and spirit injury if we adopt a "world-traveling" methodology.[76] This Critical Race feminist approach allows us to identify our interconnectedness, even as we respect the independence of others. We must first see ourselves in our own historical context, and then see ourselves as another might see us. Finally, we must see the other in her own cultural context and offer humble thoughts.[77] As an African American Critical Race feminist from the United States—a nation that has often sided with oppressors of South Africans and Palestinians—I must be careful in my assessment. I do not want to be seen as a cultural and legal imperialist, blindly accepting the ancient customs of my white male international and comparative law colleagues that have often called for adopting a Western, specifically American, approach to problem solving. Nor do I want to be seen as my white feminist colleagues often are—culturally insensitive to the views of women in the developing world and their concrete life experiences. Thus, in formulating my opinion, I have humbly sought out the opinions of my sisters in both countries, who must live out their choices on the ground.

With these thoughts in mind, I offer some policy recommendations. Because the problem of violence against women is affected by multiple sources, the solutions must be multiplicative as well. No single solution is the solution, and it is critically important that women, especially women who have been abused, be involved in crafting the solutions. I realize that South Africa is further along in its transformation process than Palestine, and thus may be able to consider some of these ideas at an earlier point than Palestine.

With respect to the legal arena, both South Africa and Palestine could seek to implement some of the proposals of the United Nations Declaration on the Elimination of Violence against Women. These proposals include developing adequately funded national plans of action to promote the protection of women against any form of violence. Such plans should include collecting data and promoting research in the area as to the causes, nature, seriousness, and consequences of such violence, as well as the effectiveness of preventive and remedial measures.[78]

Additionally, Palestine could follow the lead of South Africa and adopt a specific constitutional provision on domestic violence, since the Basic Law has not yet been ratified by President Arafat.[79] Two Latin American countries provide examples for Palestinian drafters. Brazil has a provision that states that "[t]he State shall assure assistance to the family in the person of each of its members and shall create mechanisms to suppress violence in the ambit of family relationships."[80] Colombia goes a step further. Its constitution provides that "[f]amily relations are based on the equality of rights and duties of the couple and on the reciprocal respect of all of its members. Any form of violence in the family is considered destructive of its harmony and unity, and will be sanctioned according to law."[81]

Equality between men and women cannot remain a paper right found only in constitutions. Thus, changes in the various personal status laws are required in both societies so that these laws conform with the new constitutions. Also, changes in penal laws are needed to ensure that domestic abuse is recognized as a crime and that batterers are arrested, tried, convicted, and sentenced. The improved South Africa Prevention of Family Violence Act is a step in the right direction, one that Palestine might consider at some future time.

A Critical Race feminist humbly realizes that law is only one facet of problem solving. Thus, with respect to education, there is a profound need to train police, judges, lawyers, teachers, and medical professionals in both societies. Community education is also needed in schools, religious places, women's centers, and so forth, so that men, women, and children learn that violence against women is inappropriate behavior for the twenty-first century. There is also the need for sensitive individual and family therapy in societies that shun this alien Western approach.

The batterer must not be left out of the counseling loop. Anonymous hotlines and shelters are essential as well, so that women may dare to think of leaving violent situations. Shelters may be a particularly difficult option for Palestine since there is no cultural norm that permits women and children to live independently, outside the context of a male-headed family. All these suggestions are mere band-aid solutions unless women are given sufficient economic and educational opportunities to enable them to have realistic options if they do decide to leave abusive relationships.

There also must be programs that focus not only on domestic violence but on the legacy of outsider violence that affects women, who have been the mothers, wives, and daughters of prisoners and martyrs, as well as prisoners themselves during the liberation struggle. The controversial Truth Commission of South Africa was an attempt to deal with the cultural spirit injury of outsider violence. The Commission permitted human rights violators from the apartheid era to confess their crimes. If a violator's effort was viewed as genuine, a pardon may have resulted. At some point far in the future, Israel and Palestine might consider such a Commission as an attempt at mutual healing.

Finally, responsible United States foreign aid might support some of the above endeavors to make up for past American support of outsider violence against the South African and Palestinian peoples. Perhaps this sort of aid might begin a process of addressing our own spirit injuries, leading to bilateral spirit healing and spirit warming.

NOTES

1. Paul Cossali and Clive Robson, Stateless in Gaza 38 (1986).
2. Adrien Katherine Wing, *Custom, Religion and Rights: The Future Legal Status of Palestinian Women*, 35 Harv. Int'l L.J. 149, 157 (1994).

3. *See* Jenny Rivera, *Domestic Violence against Latinas by Latino Males: An Analysis of Race, National Origin and Gender Differentials,* 14 B.C. Third World L.J. 231, 234 (1994); *see* Kimberlé Crenshaw, *Mapping the Margins: Intersectionality, Identity Politics, and Violence against Women of Color,* 43 Stan. L. Rev. 1241, 1257 (1991).

4. Devon W. Carbado, *Motherhood and Work in Cultural Context: One Woman's Patriarchal Bargain,* chapter 7 in this volume.

5. *See generally* Miranda Davies, Third World—Second Sex (1987).

6. *See* Adrien Katherine Wing, *Brief Reflections toward a Multiplicative Theory and Praxis of Being,* 6 Berkeley Women's L.J. 181, 190 (1991).

7. Patricia Williams, *Spirit-Murdering the Messenger: The Discourse of Fingerpointing as the Law's Response to Racism,* 42 U. Miami L. Rev. 127, 151 (1987).

8. *Id.* at 129.

9. Adrien Katherine Wing and Sylke Merchán, *Rape, Ethnicity and Culture: Spirit Injury from Bosnia to Black America,* 25 Colum. Hum. Rts. L. Rev. 1 (1993).

10. This section draws heavily from Adrien Katherine Wing and Eunice P. de Carvalho, *Black South African Women: Towards Equal Rights,* 8 Harv. Hum. Rts. J. 57, 87–90 (1995).

11. *Id.* at 64.

12. *See* John Carlin, *After Violation, There Is Only Fear,* Indep. (London), May 30, 1992, at 14.

13. *See* Paula Johnson, *Danger in the Diaspora: Law, Culture and Violence against Women of African Descent in the United States and South Africa,* 1 Iowa J. Gender, Race and Just. 471 (1998).

14. *See* section 5 of Prevention of Family Violence Act 133 of 1993. For a brief discussion of this Act, see Vivienne Goldberg, *South Africa: Private Law in Transition/The Effect of the New Constitution,* 33 U. Louisville J. Fam. L. 495, 499–500 (1995).

15. *See* Cindy Shiner, *The Silent Struggle,* Afr. Rep., July–Aug. 1994, at 44.

16. *See* Fatima Meer, *Women in the Apartheid Society, in* The Struggle for Liberation in South Africa and International Solidarity: A Selection of Papers Published by the United Nations Centre against Apartheid 160, 169–71 (E. S. Reddy ed., 1992).

17. Navi Pillay, *Judges and Gender: Wife Battery and Child Abuse,* 16 Agenda 62, 65 (1993).

18. Lloyd Vogelman and Gillian Eagle, *Overcoming Endemic Violence against Women in South Africa,* 18 Soc. Just. 209, 214 (1991).

19. *See* Johnson, *supra* note 13.

20. Hanan Ashrawi, This Side of Peace 47 (1995).

21. *See* Chandra Muzaffar, *Israel: The Root Cause of Violence,* New Straits Times (Malaysia), Apr. 15, 1996, at 12.

22. Mouin Rabbani, *Palestinian Authority, Israeli Rule: From Transitional to Permanent Arrangement,* Middle East Rep., Oct.–Dec. 1996, at 2, 6.

23. *See* Eugene Bird, *Since Oslo, U.S. Has Provided $17 Billion to Israelis, $50 Million to Palestinians,* Wash. Rep. on Middle East Aff., Oct. 1996, at 13.

24. *See* Philippa Strum, The Women Are Marching: The Second Sex and the Palestinian Revolution 26 (1992).

25. *See* Scheherezade Faramarzi, *Sins Cost Druse Women Their Lives,* Rocky Mountain News, Dec. 24, 1995, at 25A.

26. *See id.*

27. *See* Angela Bendt and James Downing, We Shall Return: Women of Palestine 89 (1980).

28. Cossali and Robson, *supra* note 1, at 35.

29. *See* Amal Kawar, Daughters of Palestine 20 (1996).

30. *See, e.g.*, Abdullahi An-Na'im, *The Rights of Women and International Law in the Muslim Context*, 9 Whittier L. Rev. 491, 493–97 (1987).

31. *See* Abdullahi Ahmed An-Na'im, *Human Rights in the Muslim World: Socio-Political Conditions and Scriptural Imperatives*, 3 Harv. Hum. Rts. J. 13, 39 (1990).

32. *See* Ann Elizabeth Mayer, *Law and Religion in the Muslim Middle East*, 35 Am. J. Comp. L. 127, 144 (1987).

33. *See* An-Na'im, *supra* note 31, at 39 n.112.

34. *See* Jordanian Personal Status Law, Temporary Law No. 61/1976, Official Gazette No. 2668 of Dec. 1, 1976, at arts. 36, 66, 67.

35. *See* United States Dep't of State Dispatch, Occupied Territories Human Rights Practices 1995 Section 5 (Mar. 1996). There are few empirical studies in the Arab world. *See* Jamileh Abu-Duhou, Report on Services Available for Victims of Violence and the Attitude of Service Providers: In the West Bank/Palestine 1995–1996, at 11 (on file with author).

36. *See* M. Al-Haj Yahia et al., Bisan Center for Research and Development, Attitudes of Palestinian Girls and Women Concerning the Issues of Domestic Violence 3 (1995), *cited in* Abu-Duhou, *supra* note 35, at 11.

37. Esther Hecht, *Therapy for Society*, Jerusalem Post, July 26, 1996, at 11.

38. *See* Abu-Duhou, *supra* note 35, at 9.

39. *See* Hecht, *supra* note 37, at 11.

40. *See* Al-Haj Yahia et al., *supra* note 36, at 12.

41. *Id.*

42. *Id.* at 35.

43. *See* United States Dep't of State Dispatch, *supra* note 35, Section 5.

44. *See* Abu-Duhou, *supra* note 35, at 25.

45. *See* Convention on the Elimination of All Forms of Discrimination against Women, G.A. Res. 34/180, U.N. GAOR, 34th Sess., Supp. No. 46, at art. 2, U.N. Doc. A/34/830 (1979).

46. *Id.* at art. 5.

47. *Id.* at art. 15.

48. *Id.* at art. 16.

49. *See* General Recommendation No. 19: Report of the Committee on the Elimination of Discrimination against Women, 11th Sess., Agenda Item 7, U.N. Doc. CEDAW/C/1992L.1/Add.15 (1992).

50. *See id.* at para. 1.

51. *See* Declaration on the Elimination of Violence against Women, G.A. Res. 104, U.N. GAOR, 48th Sess., Supp. No. 49, at art. 3, U.N. Doc. A/RES/48/104 (1994).

52. *See* Theodor Meron, Human Rights Law-Making in the United Nations: A Critique of Instruments and Process 212–13 (1986).

53. Third Reading of the Basic Law of Palestine art. 10 (1997) (translation on file with author).

54. Basic Law of Palestine art. 8 (1994) (4th draft) (translation on file with author). Ironically, the English version of the draft omitted mention of CEDAW.

55. *See* S. Afr. Const. (1993) (interim).

56. *Id.* at art. 8(1) (1993).

57. *Id.* at art. 9.

58. *Id.* at art. 7(1).

59. *Id.* at art. 119.

60. *Id.* at art. 8(3)(a).

61. *Id.* at arts. 10–11(2).

62. Women's Charter for Effective Equality (1994).

63. *Id.* at art. 10.

64. *Id.* at art. 8.

65. *See* S. Afr. Const. art. 8(2) (1996).

66. *Id.* at art. 12(1)(c).

67. *Id.* at art. 30.

68. *Id.* at art. 39(b).

69. Third Reading of the Basic Law, *supra* note 53, at art. 9.

70. *Id.* at art. 13.

71. *Id.* at art. 4.

72. Declaration of Principles on Palestinian Women's Rights, *reprinted in* 24 J. Palestine Stud. 137 (1994).

73. *Id.* at para. 7.

74. *Id.* at para. 4.

75. *See* Faramarzi, *supra* note 25, at 25A.

76. Maria Lugones, *Playfulness, World-Traveling and Loving Perception*, 2 Hypatia 3, 3 (1987).

77. *See* Isabelle R. Gunning, *Arrogant Perception, World Traveling, and Multicultural Feminism: The Case of Female Genital Surgeries, in* Critical Race Feminism: A Reader 352 (Adrien Katherine Wing ed., 1997).

78. *See* Declaration on the Elimination of Violence against Women, *supra* note 51, at art. 4.

79. The reasons for President Arafat's refusal to ratify the Basic Law are beyond the scope of this chapter.

80. Constituticao Federal [Constitution] [C.F.] art. 226, Section 8 (Braz.).

81. Constitución Política de Colombia art. 42.

23 Puerto Rico's Domestic Violence Prevention and Intervention Law

The Limitations of Legislative Responses

Jenny Rivera

> [O]ur judicial systems are currently ineffective instruments in their intervention in situations of domestic violence against women. They do not offer, for now, alternatives or remedies to women victimized by this form of violence.
> —Sylvia Bonilla, "Ay! Ay! Ay! Amor no me quieras tanto"

INTRODUCTION

Annually, three to four million women in the United States are targets of violence by their intimate partners or spouses.[1] The women who survive this violence endure physical, verbal, emotional, and psychological abuse that threatens their health and often their lives. The daily incidences of violence include severe physical abuse.[2] Even more alarming is the number of women who die at the hands of their intimate partners: violence against women by spouses or intimate male companions accounts for 30 percent of all homicides of women.[3] There is no avoiding or denying the prevalence and nondiscriminative nature of this violence, for it "cuts across all racial, ethnic, religious, educational and socio-economic lines."[4]

Violence against women by their former and current male partners is commonly referred to as domestic violence, partially because it involves the personal dynamics of intimate relationships. The effects of this violence, nevertheless, extend beyond the confines of the domestic sphere.[5] First, because family members, neighbors, and law enforcement officials may have direct or indirect knowledge of this violence, it cannot be summarily categorized as strictly private. Second, because of its detrimental impact on women's lives and on the social and human services that bind society, it has larger social and political implications.

This chapter considers the current and potential success of a recently enacted statutory effort to address intimates' violence against women, Puerto Rico's Domestic

Reprinted by permission from 5 *Columbia Journal of Gender and Law* 78 (1995).

Violence Prevention and Intervention Law, commonly referred to as Ley 54 (Law 54).[6] Puerto Rico's Law 54 is considered a model internationally because of its ambitious and comprehensive approach to domestic violence, its recognition of the seriousness of violence against women, and its criminalization components.[7] Hence, Puerto Rico's legislation is a useful source of information and a model for legislative structure. This legislation, however, has engendered mixed responses from Puerto Rico's legal community. The experiences of government officials and advocates in Puerto Rico have caused them to forge opinions about the efficacy of Law 54 and reflect underlying presumptions and concerns about domestic violence legislation that may be useful in the design and implementation of other legal strategies in other jurisdictions.

Law 54 was enacted in the wake of a massive effort by women activists, including lawyers, who sought to codify women's rights and to establish sanctions for domestic violence.[8] As I will discuss in Section 1, enactment of the statute was the beginning of another struggle, presaged by government officials' publicly voiced opposition to the statute. This struggle reveals the need for community and professional education in order to ensure the adequate utilization of the statute.

Section 2 discusses the potential for social reform under Law 54. Unlike other criminal legislative initiatives, which focus on the defendant's conduct, Law 54 provides women with both legal shelter from intimate partner violence, especially physical abuse, and the opportunity for self-development and personal empowerment.

I. PUERTO RICO'S DOMESTIC VIOLENCE PREVENTION AND INTERVENTION LAW

With the passage of Law 54 in 1989, Puerto Rico ushered in a new era of legal and social reform with respect to domestic violence. The international legal community has acknowledged the legal and political importance of Law 54: "Within the international legal community, [Law 54] is recognized as one of the most advanced legal efforts, globally, and as an effort to address domestic violence in an integral and complete manner."[9]

Despite the fanfare and enthusiasm that accompanied the enactment of the legislation, the pre- and post-enactment periods have been plagued by controversy and tainted by criticism. Evaluations of the Law's impact reveal that the legislation has encountered ongoing resistance and skepticism from law enforcement officials and politicians. Legislation alone, therefore, has done little to change officials' opinions concerning the importance of and need for a systemic legal response to domestic violence. Nevertheless, Law 54 has engendered positive social and legal change as the number of women utilizing Law 54's provisions has increased, and as police, prosecutors, and the courts have grappled with the penalogical components of the legislation.

A. THE LANGUAGE OF LAW 54

The purpose of Law 54 and the public policy at its core are set forth in its preamble. The preamble reads like a political diatribe on the need for a comprehensive legislative response to domestic violence. The legislature used the preamble to emphasize its commitment not only to the protection of the life, security, and dignity of women and men, but also to the protection of the family unit. As discussed further herein, this emphasis on the family unit has hampered the effectiveness of Law 54's implementation.

Law 54 assumes a progressive posture in defining domestic abuse. It states that domestic violence includes physical and nonphysical methods of abuse:

> [Domestic abuse is] a constant pattern of conduct involving physical force or psychological violence, intimidation, or persecution against a person by his/her spouse, former spouse, a person with whom he/she cohabits, or has cohabited, with whom he/she has, or has had, a consensual relationship, or a person with whom a son or daughter has been procreated, to cause physical harm to their self, their property, or another's self, or to cause him/her grave emotional harm.[10]

This definition is legally and politically important for several reasons. First, Law 54 places responsibility for the illegal conduct on the abuser. It rejects the notion that women cause or provoke the violence. As such, it removes the philosophical and political justification for treating women as the instigators (whether passive or aggressive) rather than the targets of domestic violence.

Second, Law 54 attaches legal responsibility to abusers, regardless of the status of the relationship of the parties. Current and former spouses as well as intimate partners are recognized as abusers under Law 54. The statute focuses on the acts of violence rather than the "domestic" quality of the relationship. This focus avoids disparate treatment of abusers simply because the relationship has ended, and ensures that all abusers and, a fortiori, all types of abusive conduct are addressed. This is critical because, as research has shown, violence escalates once the woman attempts to leave a violent environment, or after the relationship ends.[11] Law 54, therefore, aptly reflects women's experiences and the violent consequences of their relationships.

Third, the Law's definition of violence facilitates the provision of comprehensive legal protection for women against a range of abusive tactics. For example, the Law defines "psychological abuse" as

> a constant pattern of conduct performed to the dishonor, discredit, or scorn of personal worth, unreasonable limitation to access and handling of common property, blackmail, constant vigilance, isolation, deprivation of access to adequate food or rest, threats of deprivation of custody of sons or daughters, or destruction of objects held in esteem by the person, except those that privately belong to the offender.[12]

By penalizing emotional and psychological abuse, Law 54 responds to women's experiences and ensures that all types of harms and injuries may be addressed through legal interventions.

Successfully providing opportunities for self-development to women who are the targets of domestic violence is perhaps Law 54's most ambitious intent. According to its "Statement of Purpose for Law 54,"

> [Law 54 will contribute to] the development, establishment, and strengthening of effective measures to give protection and help to the victims, options for the rehabilitation of the transgressors, and strategies for the prevention of domestic abuse.[13]

Thus, based on its language, Law 54 is a legislative empowerment model. It includes statutory mandates to prevent and penalize abuse and incorporates procedural and substantive self-development methodologies.

B. THE STRUCTURE OF THE LAW

Law 54 promotes legal and policy strategies through a triadic structure composed of criminal sanctions, civil remedies, and preventive measures. The criminal sections of the statute identify five crimes and their corresponding penalties; the civil sections address orders of protection; and the preventive measures focus on education and government organizational development.

1. Criminal Provisions

Law 54 limits the discretion of law enforcement personnel in domestic violence cases. The most obvious examples are the Law's mandatory arrest provisions and the sections that mandate particular conduct in the preparation of law enforcement reports and in the treatment of domestic violence survivors by law enforcement personnel.[14]

Law 54 authorizes public officials, police officers, and prosecutors to issue complaints and to arrest an assailant without the benefit of a warrant, so long as the officials have a well-founded belief that the person has committed an act, even if committed outside the officials' presence, or is committing an act in violation of Law 54.[15] Any public official who intervenes in a domestic altercation must prepare a written report that includes the allegations and the conducted investigations, even if no criminal charges are issued.[16] The names of persons implicated in domestic violence cases are kept confidential.[17] The Law further directs public officials to take all necessary steps to avoid another violent altercation and to provide medical and social services, as well as full information to the woman about her rights.

Courts may release a person charged under Law 54 pending trial and courts may condition bail on a prohibition against contact with the complainant or persons providing her with shelter or refuge, and may mandate that the abuser abandon the residential premises, if shared with the complainant.[18] Finally, courts may also grant the accused release from prison on his own recognizance after considering the defendant's prior history of violence and whether the accused represents a potential threat to any other person.[19]

An abuser may be charged with up to five crimes under Law 54: abuse; aggravated abuse; threat to abuse; abuse and kidnapping; and marital rape. These five crimes constitute serious offenses carrying severe prison sentences.[20] Provisions for the reduction or increase in sentences are based on mitigating or aggravating circumstances.

In a limited number of cases, which are characterized by certain mitigating circumstances, and as a one time option, Law 54 provides for alternative punishment to incarceration.[21] The defendant's release is contingent on his participation in a program of reeducation and rehabilitation for batterers. The charging complainant has the right to state her opinion to the court regarding the appropriateness of this alternative release program.

The court may, at its discretion, supersede the case against the abuser. In such cases, no sentence is entered and the record of the charges and proceedings may be sealed. The convicted abuser is exonerated and avoids any and all legal ramifications associated with a criminal conviction.[22]

While flexibility and the development of individualized responses are positive aspects of a democratically instituted criminal justice system, a blanket provision allowing for the complete exculpation of an abuser, at best, is antithetical to efforts to criminalize domestic violence, and, at worst, undermines Law 54's legislative goals. Even where, as in the case of Law 54, legislative standards limit judicial discretionary action favoring exculpation, the very recognition of such exculpatory provisions negates Law 54's severity and exigency, and is therefore detrimental to the Law's success. It allows, even encourages, resistance to criminalization of abusive conduct between intimate partners.

2. Civil Provisions

Chapter 2 of Law 54 contains civil provisions for securing and enforcing orders of protection. An order of protection is defined as

> [a] written court mandate that sets forth the manner by which the assaulter must cease, or prevent from occurring, certain conduct or acts that constitute domestic violence.[23]

A woman may obtain an order of protection, without filing criminal charges or a complaint, at her own request, at the request of her legal representative, or through a public official.[24] A court shall issue an order of protection if there is sufficient evidence that the petitioner is a victim of domestic violence. The court of first instance or municipal judge is further authorized to issue orders to promote the goals and public policy of Law 54.[25] Orders may be revised by the appropriate higher court or, where necessary, by the family court.[26]

3. Statutorily Prescribed Preventive Measures

Chapter 4 sets forth three preventive measures for implementation of Law 54 on a macrolevel. The implementation of the preventive measures and responsibility for reporting on the progress of the Law fall directly within the duties of Puerto Rico's Commission for Women's Affairs, a government agency whose members are appointed by the Governor of Puerto Rico.[27] The Law's stated objectives include the establishment, in collaboration with other governmental departments, of a package of preventive and prescriptive measures to address domestic violence.[28] Thus, Law 54 assigns the Commission oversight responsibility and authorizes it to direct certain programs and initiatives, in furtherance of the statute's public policy.[29]

The Commission's twelve distinct responsibilities fall within four general categories: (1) educational—providing information to the Puerto Rican community on domestic violence and on the scope and applicability of Law 54; (2) investigative—studying, investigating, and publicizing reports on domestic violence in Puerto Rico,[30] including an annual report to the Governor of Puerto Rico and the Legislature on the progress of Law 54;[31] (3) Program and Service Development—developing direct service projects and strategies to promote political and procedural changes in government agencies, in order to improve those agencies' responses to domestic violence survivors;[32] and (4) Service Provision—providing training and orientation services for counselors, concerning treatment and counseling of domestic violence survivors.[33]

II. ANALYSIS OF LAW 54

A. LAW 54, PUBLIC POLICY, AND GENDER ROLES

The tension in Law 54 is juxtaposed between the Law's legal and political promises: criminalization of violence against women by current and former lovers and spouses, as well as the empowerment of women achieved through the development of women's self-esteem, in the context of a self-help legislative model.

Concern over the expansive nature of domestic violence and its concomitant devastating effects on women is partly the social and moral basis for the legislation. This legislation, Law 54, is thus unique and ambitious in its political and legal approach to violence against women. Nevertheless, the statute's Statement of Purpose places doubt on whether the status of women as independent members of Puerto Rican society is part of the legislative concern. The language suggests that concern for women's rights and women's opportunities to participate fully in Puerto Rico's political, legal, and social domains is inextricably intertwined with the concern for the well-being and continued existence of the traditional family structure.[34]

The Government of Puerto Rico reaffirms its constitutional commitment to protect the life, safety, and dignity of men and women. It also recognizes that domestic abuse violates the integrity of the family and its members and is a serious threat to the stability and preservation of the civilized conviviality of our people.[35]

The theme of the preservation and solidification of the family extends legislative intervention beyond male-female relationships to include "traditional" parent-child and spouse-caretaker relationships. So long as domestic violence is viewed as a danger because it threatens the traditional family structure and values, the impact of violence on women's lives, autonomy, and independence remains secondary to, or in conflict with, societal objectives.[36]

The fear that attacks on domestic violence will destroy the family unit clashes with feminist agendas. Feminists address violence in the context of women's struggles for recognition as individuals and as a community. To the extent that feminists define women as standing outside or beyond the family infrastructure, feminist ideas cannot coexist with legislative and political strategies based on well-entrenched gender roles.

The tenuous nature of women's rights and women's entitlement to full protection of the laws is revealed by the limited enforcement of legal mandates. As described in the Commission's evaluation of Law 54's implementation, the purposeful inaction of officials has obstructed the full implementation of Law 54 in Puerto Rico.

Even when cases are prosecuted, the courts are not "safe havens" for women. Judicial resolutions of factual situations, in which the philosophical bases of Law 54 challenge established gender roles and male dominance, evidence the social and legal reform potential and limitations of Law 54.

B. THE COMMISSION REPORTS ON THE STATUS OF LAW 54

The First Commission Report, issued in 1991, was the first evaluation and analysis of the Law's implementation. In addition to including summaries of the reactions of the Puerto Rican legal community, it provides a historical and sociopolitical sketch of the Law's legislative and political past, and stands as the seminal work on the Law's status in Puerto Rico. The Second Commission Report, issued in April 1993, further advances the analysis of Law 54's effectiveness by presenting a detailed discussion of the implementation of Law 54 during the interim two years between the issuance of the First and Second Reports.

Three themes predominate in the Commission's reports. First, Law 54 represents a radical change in Puerto Rico's social and legal fabric. Second, law enforcement officials have resisted the change in legal and social culture envisioned by Law 54. Third, patriarchal ideologies threaten the Law's implementation and the criminalization of domestic violence.

1. Law 54 Changes the Legal and Social Landscape

Law 54 is not only a political effort to ensure justice for domestic violence survivors but also a vehicle for social reform and women's empowerment.

[E]mphasis on the responsibility for the consequences of violent conduct is transferred from the victim to the entire community. It is no longer "her problem," rather it is ours. By converting physical and psychological violent conduct into serious offenses, society not only ratifies its repudiation of this behavior, but also sends a clear message about the social value of an individual's integrity and dignity in intimate relationships.[37]

The data confirm that women rely on Law 54 as the legal vehicle to protect themselves from abusers. In fact, during the early months of Law 54's implementation, Puerto Rico experienced a dramatic increase, approximately 44 percent, in domestic violence cases.[38]

From November 1989 to December 1990, Puerto Rico's Department of Justice initiated investigations in 9,095 domestic violence cases, found probable cause to arrest in 6,168 cases, and had probable cause to go to trial in 2,422 cases. Of the 1,529 cases in which there were final determinations, defendants were convicted in 72.5 percent of the cases and acquitted in 6.1 percent of the cases.[39]

The Commission opined that this increase was directly attributable to Law 54 and to public education on conduct constituting domestic violence and how to avoid this violent behavior.[40] Nevertheless, much work remains to be done.

2. Officials' Resistance to Law 54

As detailed in both reports, the reactions and concerns of government and legal officials and advocates are mostly negative, often unabashedly contrary to the letter and spirit of Law 54. Indeed, the Commission found that several officials charged with the Law's implementation have expressed vitriolic anti–Law 54 attitudes.

The Second Commission Report presents a disturbing picture of official resistance to, and rejection of, legislative action and criminalization of domestic violence. This situation has generally failed to improve since it was first documented in the First Commission Report. According to the Commission, government insiders who support Law 54 are "isolated, fragmented and delicately sustained."[41]

The opposition has been diverse and expansive, and even includes individual resistance entrenched within the institutions charged with enforcing Law 54. At the forefront of the resistance are government leaders and agency heads who continue to orchestrate opposition to domestic violence legislation.

> The [Commission] understands that the obstacles that impede the implementation of Law 54 for the chief benefit of persons who suffer the impact of domestic violence are the result of a persistent strategy (at times public and at other times discreet) of the functionaries and leaders at the highest level in the system's agencies who do not accept the mandate for change which [Law 54] imposes.[42]

This "officials' resistance" has continued to be the single most serious impediment to implementation. According to the Commission, "the Justice Administration System's agencies' leadership is the factor that has most adversely affected and impeded the progress of the implementation of Law 54."[43] The resistance by officials has been proactive and incessant, fostering gender-based attitudes that are antifeminist and antiwoman.

During the first, and critical, years after Law 54's enactment, two of the most ardent and visible opponents of the Law were the Superintendent of Police and the Administrator for Corrections. Rather than commend the implementation of Law 54, they argued that the growing numbers of complaints of domestic violence and the increased incarceration of abusers revealed the weakness of any criminalization effort and indicated that Law 54 is ineffective. In support of their universal condemnation of the Law, they highlighted the inability of the Puerto Rican criminal justice system to manage a burgeoning caseload. While they made sweeping statements about the system's overall weaknesses, however, they did not point to specific deficiencies in the statute.

Supporters of Law 54 maintained that government officials had mischaracterized the nature of the problem by confusing lack of resources and insufficient fiscal appropriations with substantive problems in the legislation. Supporters argued that while the former concerned problems with the criminal justice system and its capacity to handle the effects of any criminal statute, regardless of the subject matter, the latter dealt with the underlying philosophical premises of Law 54: criminalization as an appropriate and primary response to domestic violence.

The negative views of Law 54 voiced by these officials had debilitating effects on efforts to propagate a public education campaign and reform movement. In addition, these opinions sent a message to other officials in their departments that Law 54 was an ill-conceived and misguided legislative effort.[44] As a result, the police continue to trivialize the seriousness of domestic violence.[45]

As the First Commission Report details, law enforcement officials were critical of the Law and outwardly opposed it. A significant segment of the police vehemently disapproved of Law 54, believing that neither Law 54 nor any other legislation could resolve a fundamentally "social" problem like domestic violence.[46] Prosecutors opposed criminalization because domestic violence was perceived as a social problem that required the infusion of social services targeted at the family, rather than the imposition of criminal penalties on the abuser.

Prosecutors also relinquished responsibility for the implementation of Law 54 by focusing on the lack of follow-up by abused women, and on some women's unwillingness to pursue prosecution of the abuser. Prosecutors concluded that many women survivors lacked interest in and commitment to criminal prosecution. Frustrated by the numbers of incomplete or abandoned prosecutions, prosecutors blame women because they do not cooperate or desire prosecution.[47]

While government agencies also blame one another for the poor implementation of the Law,[48] women's failure to prosecute abusers remains a constant theme throughout agency descriptions of the problems associated with Law 54. The majority of prosecutors still consider women's lack of interest in prosecution to be the main obstacle to the implementation of the Law.[49]

Service providers once again paint a different picture of the dynamic between prosecutors and survivors and focus on prosecutorial blameworthiness. Providers claim that prosecutors are abusive themselves. They assert that prosecutors openly blame women for the abuse and chastise them for failing to cooperate with the criminal prosecution of the abuser.

Moreover, Law 54's supporters assert that insufficient resources exist in the criminal justice system to adequately respond to the Law's requirements for mandatory arrest and the resultant increase in incarcerations and convictions. Rather than blame survivors, advocates charge that government officials responsible for the proper funding and implementation of Law 54 should be held accountable for failing to direct adequate resources toward the efficacious use of the legislation. They maintain that a lack of sensitivity and informed understanding of the nature of domestic violence, institutional resistance, and misinformation are the true culprits, not women.[50]

Women survivors of domestic violence also complain that the police do not know what to do with an order of protection, or that they doubt the veracity of the women or the severity of the problem. They complain that judges issue dual orders of protection and refuse to recognize orders of protection from other jurisdictions, or that superior court judges refuse to take these cases because they incorrectly believe they should be handled by the lower courts.[51]

The system's opposition to the implementation of Law 54 is also manifested in more subtle but no less pernicious ways, as is illustrated by the low number of men who are convicted under Law 54, and by the disproportionately high number of women, when compared to men, who complete their jail terms for violations of Law 54. It is further demonstrated by the number of men actually convicted for violations of Law 54 who are then granted release on parole by the court. These men are never required to participate in reeducation or retraining programs.[52]

3. Ideology as a Practical Threat to Law 54

According to the Commission, institutional sexism undermines the implementation of Law 54 and the goal of empowering women.

> The sexist attitudes of some functionaries . . . [and] a view of the traditional right that places the responsibility on the victim, . . . and that prefers to continue seeing the problem of domestic violence only in a sociocultural dimension, without recognizing the criminal dimension of the Law . . . impedes the . . . implementation of this legislation. The Commission takes the position that persons charged with violating the domestic violence law should be treated no differently than others charged with committing a crime.[53]

In opposition to traditional theories of abuse modalities, the Commission rejects the proposition that alcohol and drug abuse are the true roots of the problem, or that domestic violence is a pathological condition that justifies excusing the abuser's conduct. The Commission's position reaffirms Law 54's contextual framework; Law 54 holds the abuser responsible for his or her violent conduct, regardless of the use of drugs or alcohol.[54]

From a critical perspective, the officials' oppositional views of Law 54 and domestic violence reflect well-entrenched gendered visions of the nature of "violence" and women's roles in Puerto Rican society. Moreover, the officials' characterizations cast domestic violence within the sphere of private conduct. By relegating the violent acts of intimate partners and ex-partners to the private sphere, officials propose to legitimate limited interventions that further goals of maintaining a family structure. The goal of punishing the abuser is devalued and seen as conflicting with the goal of family unification.

The Second Commission Report concludes that the core of the resistance is based on patriarchal stereotypes and gender-specific norms opposed to feminist concepts of liberation and empowerment. "The resistance of the functionaries is marked by a tradition of patriarchy within the justice system's agencies which tends to privilege [a male-centered world vision] and which challenges the importance of crimes against women and undervalues [women's] credibility and claims."[55]

C. *PUERTO RICO V. LACROIX CORREA*

A 1990 decision of the Supreme Court of Puerto Rico illustrates the philosophical struggle and norm-reference tensions inherent in the current jurisprudence on Law 54. In *El Pueblo de Puerto Rico v. Lacroix Correa*,[56] the Supreme Court of Puerto Rico overturned a lower court conviction under Law 54. Lizette Malcun Valencia, the complainant, and Alejandro Lacroix Correa, the defendant, had been involved in an intimate personal relationship until 1988.[57] They had lived together for one year when their relationship ended because of Lacroix Correa's unbearable conduct toward Malcun Valencia when he became drunk. One day, Lacroix Correa saw Malcun Valencia on a public street and physically and verbally accosted her. He stuck his hand through the car window where she was seated, punched her below the right cheekbone, and called her a dirty whore. As a result of her injuries, Malcun Valencia had to get nine stitches and was placed on antibiotics.

At the plea colloquy, Lacroix Correa pleaded guilty to the lesser charges of aggravated assault and disturbance of the peace. In return, and pursuant to a plea agreement, the prosecutor recommended that the court impose a suspended sentence. The lower court rejected the recommendation and sentenced Lacroix Correa to two consecutive six-month terms of incarceration, one on each count.

In overturning the lower court's decision, the Supreme Court reviewed the appropriate circumstances in which a suspended sentence should be granted and concluded that Lacroix Correa qualified for a suspended sentence. The Supreme Court examined the various mitigating factors specific to Lacroix Correa's case and emphasized his character. He did not have a prior criminal record; he held a degree in accounting; he was employed as an automobile leasing company sales representative with a $1,580 monthly salary; and he was the father of two dependent teenage children from a prior marriage. The report from the probation officer also noted that he has an adequate social conduct, except for some adulterated images of the female as a result of his prior marital experiences. This induces him to be aggressive with women when he comes into contact with liquor.[58]

On the basis of this information, the Supreme Court concluded that the lower court acted beyond the scope of its discretion in refusing to consider suspending the sentence. The Supreme Court's only tacit modifications to the sentence were directions that Lacroix Correa abstain from drinking alcohol, enter a treatment program for his alcohol problem, and have no contact with Malcun Valencia.

The majority opinion assumes that the abuser can be excused for his conduct based on such factors as his prior experiences with women and the impact of alcohol on his behavior toward women. The majority defines violent behavior in male-female intimate relationships as a form of aberrational and uncontrollable conduct. Such a definition falls within the discourse that such behavior is "pathological" in nature and downplays the significance of patriarchy and patriarchal structures in male-female relationship dynamics.

The dissent strongly opposed the suspended sentence.[59] In striking contrast to the majority opinion, the dissent approached the appeal as a violation of Law 54, rather than as an issue of abuse of discretion. It specifically rejected the significance of the proposed "mitigating" circumstances. In fact, it argued that the proposed mitigating factors demonstrated the nature of Lacroix Correa's aggressive behavior toward women, and therefore justified imposing a heavier penalty than a suspended sentence and an alcohol treatment program.[60]

In support of its position, the dissent referred to Lacroix Correa's abusive and deprecating attitude. It noted that he admitted to committing the assault, that he justified his behavior on the ground that Malcun Valencia provoked him, and that he exhibited no remorse for his actions.[61]

The dissent argued that Lacroix Correa's actions must be viewed as related to the larger problem of violence against women and that the case must be considered in the context of the role of the courts in stemming such violence. The dissent refused to excuse Lacroix Correa, and perceived a more active role for the court in addressing violence against women.[62]

While the dissent's recommendations for the proper treatment of Lacroix Correa reemphasizes Law 54's mandate to penalize abusers, the dissent did not go far enough. Although clearly more sympathetic to the struggles of domestic violence survivors than the majority, the dissent treats violence against women as unique, and a fortiori outside the category of other violent crimes. Moreover, the dissent succumbs to the prevalent theory that domestic violence can be addressed through alternative rehabilitative techniques. For the dissent, the need for rehabilitation is obvious because domestic violence is a societal problem that pervades and infects the social structure, threatening both men and women. In the specific case of *Lacroix Correa*, the dissent concluded that there was a need for psychological treatment to address Lacroix Correa's problems relating to women.

Rehabilitation or alternative sentencing programs do have a place in the domestic violence discourse. They can be useful for domestic abuse survivors. However, rehabilitative remedies and criminal penalties are not mutually exclusive and rehabilitation should not be presumed preferable to criminalization merely because the persons involved have or had an intimate relationship. The better approach is to replicate society's and the criminal justice system's treatment of other violent or criminal acts. The system should first penalize and then determine whether rehabilitation is useful or worthy of application under the circumstances.

III. CONCLUSION

Puerto Rico's Law 54 has been the basis for a wide range of social, political, and legal reform in Puerto Rican society. It has also been the target of resistance by government officials and agencies to its implementation. Indeed, official and public reactions to the Law have been major obstacles to securing the protections the Law intended to afford female targets of domestic violence. Moreover, while the Law is progressive in seeking to protect women and provide them with services to assist them in escaping violent intimate relationships, the Law nevertheless reflects traditional notions of family and the role of women in the family. Thus, the Law's potential for true empowerment of women is limited.

Control over the lives of women remains dependent on external factors—for example, rehabilitation of male batterers, judicial commitment to appropriate sentencing, and societal recognition of the need to address violence against women because it harms women collectively. As long as the legislative strategies, be they legal or nonlegal, perpetuate this external control and favor male status and the family structure over women's status, domestic violence will continue to tear at the social fabric. As one commentator has stated, "the inadequacy of resources becomes the smokescreen for maintaining the preeminence of the social over the criminal nature of violence."[63]

NOTES

1. Nancy Kathleen Sugg and Thomas Inui, *Primary Care Physician's Response to Domestic Violence: Opening Pandora's Box,* 267 JAMA 3157, 3157 (1992); N.Y. Senate Comm. on Investigations, Taxation, and Government Operations, Domestic Violence: The Hidden Crime 1 (1992).

2. Over half of the survivors of attacks by intimates are "seriously injured," and at least 25 percent require medical care. Antonia C. Novello, *From the Surgeon General, U.S. Public Health Service,* 267 JAMA 3132, 3132 (1991).

3. *Id.*

4. Ronet Bachman, U.S. Dept. of Justice, Office of Justice Programs, Bureau of Justice Statistics, Violence against Women: A National Crime Victimization Survey Report, NCJ-145325, Jan. 1994, at 7.

5. As I have stated in my other articles on this issue, I consider the term "domestic violence" a misnomer, and prefer the term "interpersonal violence." Nevertheless, I will continue to use the more commonly known term in this chapter.

"Domestic spheres" in this context refers to the home, as well as the "private sphere" of intimate relationships. These concepts contrast with the "public sphere," which the law has often treated as a more appropriate area for legislative intervention.

6. P.R. Laws Ann. tit. 8, sections 601–708 (1991). Translations from Spanish to English contained in this chapter are by the author, unless otherwise specified.

7. Commission for Women's Affairs, Office of the Governor of Puerto Rico, Second Report on the Progress of the Implementation in Puerto Rico of the Domestic Violence Prevention and Intervention Law (Law 54 of Aug. 15, 1989) (1993) [hereinafter Second Commission Report].

8. *See* Commission for Women's Affairs, Office of the Governor of Puerto Rico, First Report on the Progress of the Implementation in Puerto Rico of the Domestic Violence Prevention and Intervention Law (Law 54 of Aug. 15, 1989) 7 (1991) [hereinafter First Commission Report].

9. Second Commission Report, *supra* note 7, at 153.

10. P.R. tit. 8, section 602(k).

11. *See, e.g.,* Novello, *supra* note 2, at 3132.

12. P.R. tit. 8, section 602(1).

13. *Id.* section 601.

14. P.R. tit. 8, sections 638, 640, 641.

15. *Id.* section 638.

16. *Id.* section 641.

17. *Id.*

18. *Id.* sections 637(b)(1), (b)(3).

19. *Id.* sections 637(c)(1)–(3). The court must also consider the complainant's opinion concerning release or that of others who testified, as well as any other pertinent circumstances. *Id.* section 637(c)(4).

20. *See id.* sections 631–635.

21. *Id.* section 636.

22. The exonerated abuser, for example, has the option to secure any fingerprints or photographs related to his conviction under Law 54 that are in the custody of the Puerto Rico police. *Id.* section 636.

23. *Id.* section 602(e).

24. *Id.* section 621.

25. *Id.* section 621(j).

26. *Id.* section 622.

27. P.R. Laws. Ann. tit. 1, section 301 (1991).

28. P.R. tit. 8, section 653.

29. *Id.* section 651. Law 54 guarantees confidentiality for the Commission's service population. *Id.* section 652.

30. *Id.* section 651(b).

31. *Id.* section 651(j).

32. *Id.* section 651(e).

33. *Id.* section 651(i).

34. *See* Celina Romany, *Killing "the Angel in the House": Digging for the Political Vortex of Male Violence against Women, in* The Public Nature of Private Violence 285, 293 (Martha Albertson Fineman and Roxanne Mykitiuk eds., 1994) (focus on violence toward women and children compromises the position of women's experiences and gender-based violence).

35. *Id.*

36. Romany, *supra* note 34, at 293 (women's experiences of gender-based violence are submerged and concealed by focus on violence against the family).

37. First Commission Report, *supra* note 8, at 16.

38. According to the First Commission Report, prior to the Law's enactment in 1988 there were only 772 documented domestic violence cases per month. In 1990, however, the number had increased by 44.3 percent to 1,114, and another slight increase followed in 1991. *Id.* at 34; Second Commission Report, *supra* note 7, at 25. During the first fourteen months following Law 54's enactment, there were 15,594 calls related to domestic violence made to the police.

39. Second Commission Report, *supra* note 7, at 55.

40. First Commission Report, *supra* note 8, at 36.

41. Second Commission Report, *supra* note 7, at 9.

42. *Id.* at 8.

43. *Id.* at 7.

44. Romany, *supra* note 34, at 294.

45. *See* Second Commission Report, *supra* note 7, at 131.

46. *See* First Commission Report, *supra* note 8, at 55, 56.

47. *See id.* at 77–80.

48. *See, e.g.,* Second Commission Report, *supra* note 7, at 66.

49. *Id.* at 64.

50. *Id.* at 99–102.

51. All courts have jurisdiction, under Law 54, to consider charges of domestic violence and to issue orders of protection. P.R. tit. 8, section 622.

52. Second Commission Report, *supra* note 7, at 11–12.

53. *Id.* at 147, 151.

54. *See id.* at 151.

55. *Id.* at 10 (footnote omitted).

56. 90 JTS 124 (Sup. Ct. P. Rico 1990).

57. All facts are taken from the dissent in *Lacroix Correa. Id.* at 8217–18.

58. *Id.*

59. The dissent was authored by Associate Judge Hernández Denton and joined by Associate Judge Naveira de Rodon. Judge Naveira de Rodon is the only woman on the Court.

60. The dissent indicated that Lacroix Correra had a history of allegations of aggressive behavior toward other women with whom he had lived. *Id.* at 8218.

61. *Id.* at 8219.

62. *See id.* at 8220.

63. Romany, *supra* note 34, at 291.

24 Sexual Harassment and Human Rights in Latin America

Gaby Oré-Aguilar

INTRODUCTION

Sexual harassment is one of the most tolerated human rights violations against women in Latin American societies. Because it is often a hidden crime, Latin American governments have not specifically penalized sexual harassment in their domestic legislation. In fact, laws on sexual harassment in the region are primarily incorporated into general labor or penal code provisions. These laws rarely apply to educational establishments or other spheres of women's lives. Furthermore, no Latin American government has passed a national law defining sexual harassment as a human rights violation.

This chapter will analyze existing regional laws and international human rights treaties aimed at eradicating sexual harassment. Section 1 describes the current state of regional sexual harassment legislation in Latin American countries. The section concludes that, because most relevant legislation is contained primarily within broader labor legislation or penal codes, it is often inadequate in addressing the problem of sexual harassment. Section 2 introduces the international human rights perspective by reviewing varying definitions and conceptual models relevant to the issue of sexual harassment. In so doing, it analyzes international treaties and other international human rights instruments as they contain aspects of the conceptual models. Section 3 advocates for treating the issue of sexual harassment as a gender-based act of violence. The chapter concludes that such treatment is necessary for the recognition of sexual harassment as a human rights violation.

Reprinted by permission from 66 *Fordham Law Review* 631 (1997).

I. NATIONAL LAWS ON SEXUAL HARASSMENT

Sexual harassment is a form of discrimination against women on the basis of their gender. In Latin America sexual harassment is a particular problem because certain groups of Latin American women are more vulnerable to sexual harassment due to their social and economic conditions. Furthermore, because such women have limited access to redressive mechanisms, the need for regional or international protections is increased.

In Latin America there are few specific laws or other legislation penalizing sexual harassment. Most countries only prohibit sexual harassment in the workplace in the context of broader labor legislation.[1] Uruguay, El Salvador, and Mexico, however, regulate sexual harassment in their broader penal codes,[2] while Costa Rica has a special law that protects against sexual harassment in the workplace and educational establishments. This section examines various aspects of these laws and the degree to which they vary within the region.

In 1993 Argentina enacted a narrowly tailored law prohibiting sexual harassment. The Argentine legislature defines sexual harassment as a situation where "a public official, [in] the performance of his or her functions, takes advantage of a hierarchical relationship by inducing another person to accede to his or her sexual demands, whether or not a carnal act."[3] Although the definition may seem broad in theory, it is fairly limited in practice. First, it only prohibits sexual harassment at the workplace between civil servants in the executive branch and its decentralized entities. Second, the law contains exemptions for many public officials, including ministers and secretaries of the executive branch, secretaries of the presidency, subsecretaries, and persons of equivalent level.[4] The law also excludes diplomatic personnel, active members of the security and police forces, official clerics, teachers, and upper-level managers of decentralized entities. Because of these extensive exemptions, it would be interesting to know who, if anyone, the Argentine legislators had in mind when they promulgated this law.

Peru offers even less protection because sexual harassment is not considered an act of discrimination on the basis of sex. Instead, the Employment Promotion Law has established sexual harassment as an act of hostility on the part of the employer against an employee, defining it as a "dishonest act" that affects the dignity and the moral values of the workers.[5] Thus, sexual harassment differs from "acts of discrimination on the basis of sex," despite a different clause of the same law that defines discrimination as an act of hostility as well.[6] Logistically, a claim of sexual harassment offers the employee two mutually exclusive paths of action within thirty days of the alleged act. She or he may (1) solicit the labor court to order the employer to cease the sexual harassment, or (2) decide to terminate his or her work contract and demand compensation for unjustified dismissal.[7] In both cases, the plaintiffs must endure proceedings that are difficult, costly, and time-consuming.[8] Moreover, if the plaintiff reaches the damages stages, his or her damages may be limited. Because the law distinguishes between acts of harassment and acts of discrimination, the employee is precluded from using the compensation mechanisms established for discriminatory acts, which, while limited, are more favorable to workers.[9] Such obstacles create real disincentives: to date, no employee has filed a claim of sexual harassment—or at least presented a claim as such—in the Peruvian labor court system. To address this problem, the Peruvian Congress has recently proposed a specific bill to prevent and penalize sexual harassment in the workplace.[10] While this bill is an improvement over existing law,[11] it has some questionable aspects both in the definition of the crime and the procedural aspects. For example, the bill states that the complaint must be dismissed if the defendant proves during the proceedings that he or she was "encouraged through insinuations, poses, attitudes, and expressions of a sexual nature" or if "the victim of harassment accepted expensive gifts or invitations to recreation activities."[12] It also allows the defendant to bring charges and even to terminate the work contract if the judge determines that the claim is without merit.[13] Inexplicably, the bill also exempts those who have been elected to public office.[14]

In contrast, Costa Rica has fashioned a comprehensive law that extends beyond the workplace. More specifically, the Costa Rican legislature has enacted a specific law that penalizes sexual harassment both in the workplace and in educational establishments.[15] This law broadly defines sexual harassment as "all sexual conduct that is unwanted by the person to whom it is directed, that is recurring, and that provokes harmful effects in: a) the material conditions of the workplace or the educational establishment; b) the victim's working or educational performance, or; c) the general state of personal well-being."[16] It provides for legal recourse while enabling employers to establish internal procedures to independently investigate and resolve sexual harassment disputes.

In addition to these various civil approaches, certain Latin American countries discourage sexual harassment with criminal penalties. In El Salvador the recently approved Penal Code broadly defines sexual harassment as all sexual behavior that is unwanted by the person to whom it is directed.[17] The penalty ranges from six months to two years imprisonment.[18] Furthermore, if the perpetrator uses his or her position of authority or superiority to harass the victim, he or she may be subject to an additional fine of thirty to fifty days' wages.[19]

The Mexican Penal Code has also criminalized sexual harassment, categorizing it as a "Crime against Liberty and Normal Psychosexual Development."[20] Although it does not provide for imprisonment, it does demand a fine of forty days' wages from "any person who, with lustful intentions, repeatedly harasses a person of any sex, and who takes advantage of their hierarchical position deriving from relationships in the workplace, educational establishments, or in the domestic arena, or from any other relationship that implies subordination."[21] Under this law, sexual harassment is subject to such penalty only when the victim requests the prosecution and when the act of harassment causes harm to the victim.[22] The most notable aspect of the Mexican legislation is that it specifically provides protection against sexual harassment for domestic workers.[23] While other generic laws may include this category of women workers in their provisions, the specific Mexican criminal law underscores the vulnerability of domestic workers.

No matter what the type, these legislative proposals aimed at discouraging sexual harassment have become increasingly popular among the legislatures of several Latin American countries. Although these bills are needed to address the high rates of sexual harassment in the region,[24] they receive popular support and widespread media coverage only in cases of sexual harassment involving high-ranking officials. For instance, in June 1997 a Panamanian public official was dismissed for sexually harassing a secretary of the Central American Parliament based in Guatemala.[25] This case sparked debate over a 1996 bill that addressed the problem of sexual harassment in the workplace and educational establishments in Guatemala. If the bill passes, Guatemala would join Peru and Argentina as the only Latin American countries with specific laws on sexual harassment. Guatemala's law, however, unlike Peru's and Argentina's, would extend beyond the workplace.[26]

Thus, Latin American countries have developed different approaches to sexual harassment. The most traditional approach is to include sexual harassment legislation within labor-based legislation. Another common approach is to criminalize sexual harassment. Both of these institutional approaches, however, fail to specifically address the problem; rather, they categorize sexual harassment as a subset within broader laws. This response is inadequate—these countries instead should enact specific regional laws outlawing sexual harassment within and beyond the workplace. The next section will discuss how international instruments can complement such specific laws to provide comprehensive protections against sexual harassment.

II. THE REGULATION OF SEXUAL HARASSMENT IN INTERNATIONAL TREATIES AND DOCUMENTS

A. CONCEPTIONS AND DEFINITIONS

Before analyzing the international instruments developed to combat sexual harassment in Latin America, this section will review various definitional and conceptual models. These models, as they correspond to the appropriate spheres of action or the governing jurisdiction, represent an international effort to develop a unified approach to sexual harassment. This section introduces the theory behind the international approaches.

Both regional and international bodies have proffered definitions of sexual harassment. For example, the European Economic Community defines sexual harassment in a somewhat broad manner. Accordingly, sexual harassment includes all verbal or physical conduct of a sexual nature that the actor knows or should know is offensive to the employee.[27] Such conduct is considered illegal when (1) the rejection or acceptance of such conduct is used or invoked as a threat regarding a decision that affects the employee's employment or work conditions, or (2) such conduct prejudices the victim's work environment.[28] In March 1997 the Council of the European Union initiated the second phase of a consultation process with social interlocutors to establish a preventative common system regulating such incidents in the workplace.[29] Some of the issues submitted to consultation include the definition of sexual harassment, measures to be adopted to prevent sexual harassment, and the responsibility of employers to implement such measures.

International human rights organizations have tried to formulate a definition of sexual harassment. For example, in the 1988 Meeting of Experts, the International Labor Organization (ILO) established that the action must assume certain characteristics to constitute sexual harassment.[30] First, the employee must perceive the action as a condition of continued or secured employment. In addition, the incident must influence decisions affecting the employee, undermine the employee's professional performance, or humiliate, insult, or intimidate the employee.

The United Nations Commission on Human Rights, in its Preliminary Special Report on Violence against Women, states that to fight sexual harassment, authorities must establish a proper definition of what constitutes sexual harassment.[31] The report emphasizes that actions that fall within this category are very diverse, ranging from actions that may be considered "normal" in a particular social context to actions that are legally categorized as sexual crimes. As a result, the report states, cultural factors are critical in determining a definition of sexual harassment.[32]

The issue of sexual harassment is complicated not only by different definitions but by varying conceptual models. These models are contained in both the regional laws and international treatises and embody different perspectives on sexual harassment. The first model, the cultural values model, treats sexual harassment as an attack against social and cultural values such as decency, modesty, and good morals.[33] This model is evidenced in antiquated regional laws that define harassment as "offensive gallantry," a "malicious" or "dishonest" act that attacks the dignity and integrity of the employee.[34] Such an approach reflects the underlying humanistic and paternalistic vision that characterizes the labor legislation of the early nineteenth century. Although this model is reflected in the domestic laws of some countries, it is not reflected in international standards.

In contrast, the other two models are represented in both international and regional capacities. First, the antidiscrimination model calls for laws that penalize sexual harassment as an attack against the principles of equality and nondiscrimination. The second model, the gender-based violence model, considers sexual harassment one of several forms of violence against women. This model, although less represented, promises to be a useful tool in eradicating sexual harassment. In reviewing the regional laws and international instruments, the following section will further illustrate the impact of these conceptual models.

B. INTERNATIONAL EFFORTS

International treaties and documents have attempted to provide a complementary safeguard to regional laws that are often inadequate. This section briefly analyzes regulatory models based on treaties adopted by the universal and regional systems of human rights protection, including the treaties adopted by the ILO. The international approaches, for the most part, embody either the antidiscrimination model or the gender-based violence model.

The ILO Discrimination (Employment and Occupation) Convention (Discrimination Convention) has created a conceptual framework based on equal, nondiscriminatory treatment in the workplace without specifically addressing the issue of sex discrimination.[35] In 1979 the Convention on the Elimination of All Forms of Discrimination against Women (CEDAW) likewise contributed to the effort, offering a broad understanding of the problem of sex discrimination by addressing discrimination in all facets of women's lives.[36] CEDAW explicitly defined sexual harassment as a violation of the principle of equality in the workplace, noting that "discrimination against women . . . constitutes an obstacle to the full realization of the potentialities of women."[37] Thus, in effect, the resolution demands equality-promoting policies, including measures specifically aimed at eradicating sexual harassment.

Although many Latin American governments have created a standard of protection in the workplace by adopting the terms of the Discrimination Convention, CEDAW provisions are proving to be more effective. First, the local rules of domestic procedure often preclude seeking redress under both the regional employment laws and the Discrimination Convention provisions. Second, the Discrimination Convention provisions apply only to the workplace, while CEDAW provisions afford protection to women against discriminatory acts in and outside the workplace.[38] CEDAW provisions also have the power to expand protection in countries like Argentina, whose law governs only public sector employees. To illustrate, an employee in the private sector could invoke the Law of Employment Contracts, which protects the physical and psychological integrity of employees[39] via the provisions of CEDAW,[40] which have constitutional status in Argentina.[41] This could serve as a strategic alternative to Argentina's lack of specific legislation dealing with sexual harassment in the private sector.

Thus, while CEDAW has contributed much to the development of the antidiscrimination model, it also has been involved in the development of the gender-based violence model. This model became the center of international attention when the international women's movement demanded that women's human rights, including the right to be free from gender-based violence, be considered an integral and indivisible part of those fundamental human rights recognized by the universal system. In 1993 the World Conference on Human Rights (Vienna Conference) declared for the first time that "[g]ender-based violence and all forms of sexual harassment and exploitation" constitute attacks against the dignity of the individual and must be eliminated.[42] Only a few months thereafter, the General Assembly of the United Nations echoed the international consensus manifested at the Vienna Conference by adopting the Declaration on the Elimination of Violence against Women, articulating existing standards for combating gender-based violence in the form of sexual harassment in the workplace and the educational system.[43] The Declaration supports a broad conception of violence that "implies the right to inquire against all forms of action which disempower women because of the fear of violence, whether the fear is instilled by the State, actors in the community, or members of the family."[44]

Amidst this movement, CEDAW became particularly instrumental in advancing the gender-based violence model. In 1992 the Committee on the Elimination of Discrimination against Women established that gender-based violence—violence resulting in physical, mental, or sexual harm, the threat to commit such acts, and other coercive acts that deprive women of their freedom—is discrimination as described in Article 1 of CEDAW.[45] On this basis, the Committee recommended that national governments report on the status of sexual harassment under the norms of CEDAW, and revise their laws and policies accordingly. This initiative by the Committee created the possibility of developing legislation and other mechanisms to penalize sexual harassment in the spheres within CEDAW's reach. In doing so, the Committee successfully created an instrument that regulates gender-based violence as an act of discrimination.

In addition to the efforts of the United Nations, the Inter-American Convention on the Prevention, Punishment, and Eradication of Violence against Women (Convention of Belém do Pará), which was adopted by the Organization of American States (OAS) in 1994, has made significant strides against sexual harassment as a gender-based act of violence.[46] The Convention of Belém do Pará requires member states to adopt effective measures to prevent, penalize, and eliminate violence against women. More specifically, it includes examples of "sexual harassment in the workplace, as well as in educational establishments, health facilities, or any other place . . . that is perpetrated or condoned by the State and its agents regardless of where it occurs."[47]

In addition to the substantive provisions on sexual harassment, the Convention of Belém do Pará provides procedural mechanisms to carry out its provisions. Primarily, it provides that any person, group, or nongovernmental organization associated with any member state of the OAS may lodge petitions against a member state that fails to fulfill its duties under the established norms.[48] Thus, the Convention of Belém do Pará is the most advanced regional tool in preventing violence against women because it is the only international human rights treaty that specifically requires the states to eliminate sexual harassment in the public and private sphere.[49]

C. INTERNATIONAL EFFORTS SPECIFIC TO POOR LATIN AMERICAN WOMEN

International efforts have also focused on addressing sexual harassment in terms of its disproportionate impact on poor indigenous women in Latin America. Gender-based violence, while it affects all women because of their gender, is more likely to occur to these groups of women due to their socioeconomic status, their educational levels, their age, or their ethnic background.[50] Sexual harassment against domestic workers, for example, is a widespread phenomenon in Latin American societies, affecting mostly working women who are indigenous and poor.

In 1989 the ILO adopted the Indigenous and Tribal Peoples Convention,[51] which includes a provision specifically designed to protect indigenous working women against sexual harassment in the workplace.[52] This convention establishes that governments must create mechanisms to protect indigenous workers against sexual harassment with the aim of ensuring equal treatment.[53] Given that 59 percent of the forty million indigenous people of Latin America are women, these provisions against sexual harassment are of great importance for the protection of indigenous women and rural workers, at least in the workplace.

In addition, Article 9 of the Convention of Belém do Pará likewise recognizes the necessity of creating special protections for certain groups of women. In doing so, it notes "the vulnerability of women to violence by reason of, among others, their race or ethnic background or their status as migrants, refugees, or displaced persons."[54] The Convention of Belém do Pará urges governments to be especially aware of the specific situation of minority women and women in disadvantaged socioeconomic conditions.[55]

III. FUTURE STRATEGIES

Sexual harassment acts as a permanent warning to women that their gender, and often their socioeconomic background, makes them vulnerable to harassment and other forms of sexual violence. In all its forms, sexual harassment is a demonstration of power on the part of the aggressor aimed at subordinating the victim, thereby violating her human rights. Sexual harassment is also linked to social understandings of sexuality based on gender-based sexual stereotypes in which women are seen as engaging in behavior that "provokes" harassment or violence, while men who respond to such provocation by harassing women are excused because they must "fulfill their sexual role" or face scrutiny about their virility.[56]

In light of these findings, how should the law address the issue of sexual harassment? Should it be considered an act of gender discrimination or a mode of sexual and gender-based violence? As already discussed, as countries and international human rights organizations adopt one or the other approach, different procedures, outcomes, and remedies result in varying degrees of success.

Because sexual harassment often constitutes a kind of "preliminary phase" of sexual assault, the gender-based violence model holds the most promise.[57] It provides a useful framework because it successfully portrays sexual harassment as a violation of women's human rights. This approach encourages the development of effective strategies in two ways. First, it legitimizes the incorporation of measures against sexual harassment into the domestic human rights legislation of each country. Second, it allows victims of sexual harassment to seek compensation for damages using domestic and international mechanisms of protection.

Latin American countries and international organizations must adopt effective and comprehensive measures to counteract the harm that results from sexual harassment. Evidence shows that in countries that penalize sexual harassment by specific laws or human rights legislation, complaints are more frequent[58] and damages include compensatory damages.[59] In some cases, compensation for sexual harassment under such specific statutes does not exclude other means of compensating for damages provided by domestic law. Thus, both regional laws and international instruments can work in concert to provide a comprehensive system of protection. In this respect, the gender-based violence model offers an effective solution because it protects against sexual harassment in the spheres of public and private life outside the workplace without affecting the validity of antidiscriminatory laws in the workplace.

Within the Inter-American system of human rights and in Latin America in general, the Convention of Belém do Pará is the only tool that specifically addresses the problem of sexual harassment in terms of gender-based violence. These norms must be respected in those countries that ratify it. As of the date of publication of this essay, twenty-five member states of the OAS have signed the Convention, and almost all of them have ratified it.[60]

Progress may also come in the form of model legislation that has been proposed for countries belonging to the Caribbean Community and Common Market (CARICOM). The proposed legislation regulating sexual harassment in the workplace and educational establishments would include provisions for monetary compensation,[61] including compensation for emotional distress.[62] It also proposes the creation of a special tribunal to settle cases of sexual harassment.[63]

CONCLUSION

Sexual harassment is a violation of human rights based on the gender of the victims. The impact of sexual harassment on women's lives makes it a form of sexual and gender-based violence regardless of where it takes place.[64] Consequently, the most effective approach for reform in Latin America is to pass laws that define sexual harassment as a form of gender-based violence that infringes on the fundamental human rights of women. These laws have the potential to penalize sexual harassment in spheres of public and private life outside the workplace without affecting the antidiscriminatory model of protection. The framework of the gender-based violence model can open access to more effective procedural mechanisms than those established by Latin America's labor laws. Such mechanisms provide a more effective and comprehensive way of compensating victims of sexual harassment.

The Latin American countries that have ratified the Convention de Belém do Pará have the obligation to incorporate the norms of this convention into their domestic legislation and to seek out solutions and preventive strategies to the problem of sexual harassment. Latin American countries must respond to the crucial need to develop educational strategies to eradicate social and cultural patterns that subordinate women and their rights to equality and freedom.

NOTES

1. For example, Argentina and Peru regulate sexual harassment in their respective labor legislation.

2. Uruguay's Penal Code defines sexual harassment as a crime of "offensive gallantry." *See* Organización Internacional del Trabajo, Regulación del trabajo de la mujer en América Latina [Regulation of Work of Women in Latin America] 40 (1993). El Salvador and Mexico have treated sexual discrimination as a sex crime.

3. Decreto 2385/93 del 18.11.93 [Decree 2385/93 of Nov. 18, 1993] (visited Sept. 3, 1997) <http://infoleg.mecon.ar/perl/norma.pl?19028> (citing Decreto 2385/93, B.O. del 23.11.1993).

4. Ley 22140 del 14.01.80 [Law 22140 of Jan. 14, 1980] (visited Sept. 3, 1997) <http://infoleg.mecon.ar/txnorma/16169.HTM> (citing Ley 22140, B.O. del 25.01.80).

5. Texto Unico Ordenado de la Ley Fomento del Empleo [Unified Text of the Employment Promotion Law] art. 63.

6. *Id*. art. 63(f).

7. *Id*. art. 68.

8. In Peruvian labor proceedings, the burden of proof falls on the party who alleges that an illegal act has occurred. *Id*. art. 70. The act of sexual harassment is difficult to prove because an employer may use various justifications to fire a worker who refuses his sexual demands. The law does not provide for the inversion of the burden of proof in such cases, nor does it protect witnesses in subordinate positions from dismissal.

9. *Id*. art. 62. "Any dismissal is null and void when its motive is: . . . d) discrimination on the basis of sex, race, religion, opinion or language." *Id*. Thus, in effect, the worker has the right to be rehired. *Id*. art. 67.

10. The bill was presented to the Congressional Labor Committee by the Women's Committee of the Congress of the Republic on July 10, 1997. *See* Se Propone Ley para Prevenir y Sancionar el Hostigamiento Sexual en el Empleo [Law for the Prevention and Punishment of Sexual Harassment in the Workplace], Con Copia No. 2842/96-CR (1997).

11. The bill includes several new positive aspects. For example, it considers sexual harassment as a violation of the principle of equality and the right to security, health, and physical and moral integrity. *Id*. Exposicion de Motivos [Statement of Motives]. It also includes workers in all sectors and levels of employment and regulates sexual harassment between individuals of the same sex. *Id*.

12. *Id*. art. 23(a)–(b).

13. *Id*. art. 24.

14. *Id*. ch. V.2.

15. 1995-CRI 1. *Hostigamiento sexual* [Sexual Harassment] (visited Sept. 6, 1997) <http://www.oit.or.cr/Hp-oit/natlex/S95CRI01.HTM> (citing Ley Num 7476, de 3 de febrero de 1995, La Gaceta, 3 de Marzo de 1995, num 45, pags. 1–2).

16. *Id*.

17. Código Penal [C.P.] [Penal Code] art. 165.

18. *Id*.

19. *Id*.

20. *See* Código Penal para el Distrito Federal [C.P.D.F.] [Penal Code for the Federal District] arts. 259–62 (Porrora ed., 1995). In addition to sexual harassment, this title includes

sexual abuse, rape of a minor, and rape. *Id.* tit. 15 (Delitos Contra la Libertad y el Normal Desarrollo Psicosexual) [Crimes against Liberty and Normal Psychosexual Development].

21. *Id.* art. 259. For public servants, the penalty for such conduct is dismissal from their post. *Id.*

22. *Id.* Although the law does not specify the type of harm that makes sexual harassment a criminal act, analogous guidelines in other laws suggest that it encompasses harm against the victim's physical integrity.

23. *Id.*

24. *See generally* Red entre Mujeres, Las mujeres y los derechos humanos en América Latina (1994) [Women and Human Rights in Latin America] (describing acts of violence against women in Latin America in preparation for the Beijing Conference of 1995).

25. Silvio Hernandez, *Panama-Women: Immunity No Longer the Norm for Sexual Harassment,* Inter Press Serv., June 2, 1997, available in WL 7075711:

> Parlacen Deputy Emiliano Aguilar was the second high-level government official to be ousted by President Ernesto Pérez Balladares. . . . The measure against Aguilar was taken after a Parlacen secretary denounced him before the governing body of the Guatemala-based regional integration forum for repeated sexual harassment. The former deputy also reportedly abused a woman in Guatemala.

26. The bill on sexual harassment is applicable in the workplace and in educational establishments. This bill was approved by Congress, and must be approved in a plenary session of the Guatemalan Congress. *See Satisface a diputadas dictamen favorable del proyecto sobre acoso sexual* [Congress Women Are Satisfied with the Proposal against Sexual Harassment] (visited July 16, 1997) <http://www.lahora.com.gt/08101996/paginas/nacil1.htm>.

27. Resolution of 29 May 1990, 1990 O.J. (157) (regarding the protection of the dignity of women and men in the workplace).

28. *Id.*

29. 1997-3 E.C. Bull., no. 1.3.157, at 58.

30. Equality in Employment and Occupation: General Survey of the Reports on the Discrimination (Employment and Occupation) Convention (No. 111) and Recommendation (No. 111), 1958, International Labor Conference, Committee of Experts on the Application of Conventions and Recommendations, 75th Sess., rep. III, pt. 4B, para. 45 (1988).

31. Preliminary Report Submitted by the Special Rapporteur on Violence against Women, Its Cause and Consequences, Ms. Radhika Coomaraswamy, in accordance with Commission on Human Rights Resolution 1994/45, U.N. ESCOR, Comm'n on H.R., 50th Sess., Agenda Item 11(a), para. 190, U.N. Doc. E/CN.4/1995/42 (1994) [hereinafter Preliminary Report on Violence against Women].

32. *Id.*

33. The penal code of Uruguay, for example, considers "offensive gallantry" a crime and penalizes it with a fine and/or a prison sentence. In India the penal code penalizes the act of insulting a woman's modesty through words, gestures, or actions. Similarly, the Metropolitan Council of Delhi penalizes "malicious annoyance," defined as written or spoken words, signs, or visible representations or gestures, the act of reciting or singing indecent words in a public place, or acts or poetry or songs, carried out by a man in order to upset or offend a woman. *See* Preliminary Report on Violence against Women, *supra* note 31, para. 193.

34. *See, e.g., supra* note 5 and accompanying text (Peru's civil law).

35. Discrimination (Employment and Occupation) Convention, adopted June 15, 1960,

ILO, 42d Sess., 4th Agenda Item (1958), II ILO, International Labor Conventions and Recommendations 1952–1976, at 176 (1996).

36. G.A. Res. 34/180, U.N. GAOR, 34th Sess., Agenda Item 75, U.N. Doc. A/RES/34/180 (1979).

37. *Id.* para. 5.

38. *Id.* art. 1.

39. Ley de Contrato de Trabajo [Law of Employment Contracts] (Astrea ed., 1981).

40. G.A. Res. 34/180, *supra* note 36, art. 81, 172.

41. Const. Arg. art. 75(22).

42. Report of the World Conference on Human Rights, U.N. GAOR, U.N. Doc. A/Conf. 157/24 (1993).

43. G.A. Res. 48/104, U.N. GAOR, 48th Sess., Agenda Item 111, U.N. Doc. A/RES/48/ 104 (1994).

44. *See* Preliminary Report on Violence against Women, *supra* note 31, para. 98 (reviewing the progress of the Declaration on the Elimination of Violence against Women).

45. *See* General Recommendation No. 19 (11th Session, 1992): Violence against Women, U.N. CEDAW, 11th Sess., Agenda Item 7, para. 8, U.N. Doc. CEDAW/C/1992/L.1/Add.15 (1992) ("Gender-based violence which impairs or nullifies the enjoyment by women of human rights and fundamental freedoms under general international law or under specific human rights conventions is discrimination within the meaning of article 1 of the Convention.").

46. Inter-American Convention on the Prevention, Punishment, and Eradication of Violence against Women (Convention of Belém do Pará), adopted June 9, 1994, G.A. OAS, Inter-American Comm'n of Women, 24th Sess. [hereinafter Convention of Belém do Pará].

47. *Id.* art. 2(b)–(c).

48. *Id.* art. 12.

49. *Id.* arts. 2, 7, 12.

50. Glenn Welker, *Indigenous Women* (last modified Sept. 6, 1996) <http://www.indians.org/welker/indwomen.htm>.

51. Convention Concerning Indigenous and Tribal Peoples in Independent Countries, adopted June 27, 1989, ILO, 76th Sess., III ILO, International Labor Conventions and Recommendations: 1977–1995, at 324 (1996).

52. *Id.* art. 20.3.

53. *Id.* art. 20.

54. Convention of Belém do Pará, *supra* note 46, art. 9.

55. *Id.*

56. Interviews of Peruvian men convicted of rape reveal that the offenders do not consider as crimes non-violent sexual aggression, such as "abuse or illicit pressure by an individual in a position of authority or superiority." On the contrary, the rapists constructed "discourses of exoneration" that denigrated their victims as human beings and sought to explain the crime based on the actions of the victims. *See* Abraham Siles Vallejos, *Apuntes sobre lo hallado* [Notes on the Findings], *in* Yo actuaba como varón solamente . . . [I was Just Acting Like a Man] 170, 172–73 (Rafael Leon and Marga Stahr eds., 1995).

57. A Federal Bureau of Investigation study of repeat offenders revealed that crimes of sexual harassment, such as voyeurism, obscene phone calls, or exhibitionism, are often precursors to more violent crimes. *See* Mary Becker et al., Cases and Materials on Feminist Jurisprudence: Taking Women Seriously 203 n.6 (1994) (citing The Serial Rapist: His Characteristics and Victims, FBI L. Enforcement Bull., Feb. 1989, at 18, 21).

58. For example, in Canada,

the system of specific human rights statutes which is also seen at the state level in the U.S., avoids the difficulties inherent in the British system because the violation of a right labeled a "human right" emphasizes the egregious nature of harassing conduct. While the level of compensation seems relatively modest, the Canadian response seems to have been to increase the seriousness of the tort, allowing the victim to attain psychological vindication by being able to show that the harasser has infringed her or his human rights. This may explain why sexual harassment litigation seems more frequent in Canada than in Britain, even though the damages awarded in such litigation are broadly comparable.

Joseph Kelly and Bob Watt, *Damages in Sex Harassment Cases: A Comparative Study of American, Canadian and British Law*, 16 N.Y. L. Sch. J. Int'l and Comp. L. 79, 133 (1996) (footnote omitted).

59. *Id.* at 89 n.70.

60. OAS, Inter-American Commission on Human Rights, Documentos Basicos en Materia de Derechos Humanos en el Sisterna Interamericano [Basic Documents Pertaining to Human Rights in the Inter-American System] 160 (1997).

61. Protection against Sexual Harassment Act para. 16.-(1) (Model legislation proposed by CARICOM secretariat).

62. *Id.* para. 16.-(2).

63. *Id.* para. 6.-(1) (providing two options—either the establishment or the appointment of a tribunal).

64. *See* ILO, *Unwelcome, Unwanted, and Increasingly Illegal*, World of Work, March 1997, at 7, 8 ("The studies are striking. Millions of women are suffering sexual harassment, as we speak. The problem is how to point them out.").

6 | The Global Workplace

25

(Dis)Assembling Rights of Women Workers along the Global Assembly Line

Human Rights and the Garment Industry

Laura Ho, Catherine Powell, and Leti Volpp

My sisters make my blouse . . . . [A]re my hands clean?
—Sweet Honey in the Rock, "Are My Hands Clean?"

INTRODUCTION

On August 2, 1995, a multi-agency raid found sixty-seven Thai women and five Thai men kept in slave-like conditions in an apartment complex in a Los Angeles community called El Monte. Under the constant surveillance of armed guards and confined behind a ring of razor wire, they had been held for several years and had been forced to work as garment workers up to eighteen hours per day for far less than the minimum wage. They were refused unmonitored contact with the outside world and threatened with rape or harm to themselves and their families if they tried to escape. On one occasion, a worker who tried to escape was brutally beaten; his photograph was taken and shown to the other workers as an example of what might happen to them if they too tried to flee.[1]

Such conditions constitute the essence of slavery.[2] An ideological remnant of Black slavery that has survived despite the enactment of the Reconstruction amendments is the misguided notion that certain categories of people can be mistreated through employment arrangements aimed at placing them beyond legal protections as well as through constructs of citizenship that deny them full enjoyment of human rights. The fact that immigrant women, Black women, and women of color generally continue to occupy disproportionately the most degraded positions on the economic ladder triggered the search for collaborative strategies that spawned this chapter.[3]

Some observers would like to explain away sweatshops as immigrants exploiting other immigrants, as "cultural,"[4] or as the importation of a form of exploitation

Reprinted by permission from 31 *Harvard Civil Rights–Civil Liberties Law Review* 383 (1996).

that normally does not happen here but occurs elsewhere, in the "Third World." While the public was shocked by the discovery at El Monte, garment workers[5] and garment worker advocates have for years been describing abuses in the garment industry and have ascribed responsibility for such abuses to manufacturers and retailers who control the industry.[6]

Sweatshops, like the one in El Monte, are a homegrown problem with peculiarly American roots.[7] Since the inception of the garment industry, U.S. retailers and manufacturers have scoured the United States and the rest of the globe for the cheapest and most malleable labor—predominantly female, low-skilled, and disempowered—in order to squeeze out as much profit as possible for themselves. Along with this globalization, the process of subcontracting, whereby manufacturers contract out cutting and sewing to contractors to avoid being considered the "employer" of the workers, has made it extremely difficult for garment workers in the United States to assert their rights under domestic law.[8]

This chapter examines the challenges garment workers in the United States face in asserting their rights in the global economy and investigates how transnational advocacy can be deployed to compensate for the inability of U.S. labor laws to respond to problems with international dimensions. Using a purely domestic U.S. legal framework, advocates can attack the problem of transnational corporations' (TNCs) subcontracting in the United States.[9] Such efforts, however, will have limited effect because of the global nature of the garment industry. Most efforts to change the structure of the garment industry have occurred within the limitations of U.S. law, even while there has been a predominant failure of the U.S. legal system effectively to utilize a human rights framework.[10]

While the nation-state has traditionally been viewed as the locus for the development and enforcement of rights-creating norms, it cannot adequately respond to all the dynamics that now arise from markets that cut across borders. Violation of workers' rights on the global assembly line calls for strategies that are transnational, and this chapter highlights past successes and suggestions in this vein. Because of the difficulty of restraining TNCs in a global economy, no strategy used in isolation will be successful. We present here alternative strategies that can be used in multiple and flexible ways in the struggle for human rights.[11]

I. HISTORY AND CURRENT STATUS OF THE GARMENT INDUSTRY IN THE UNITED STATES

Women workers have formed the backbone of the U.S. garment industry throughout its history. The geographic location and racial composition of this workforce has varied as retailers and manufacturers have shifted location of production to lower their labor costs. During the nineteenth and early twentieth centuries, the industry was centered primarily in New York City, where a large influx of White immigrants provided a vast supply of inexpensive labor.[12]

The success of unions in northern industrial centers and immigration restrictions imposed by the 1924 Immigration Act led to the relocation of the garment industry to southern states that offered large economic incentives to firms willing to relocate, as well as a workforce of rural White women who were an unorganized and inexpensive source of labor.[13] After the civil rights movement succeeded in opening up manufacturing jobs previously unavailable to Blacks, companies turned to Black women in the 1970s as the newest source of cheap labor in the U.S. South.[14] Meanwhile, New York and California developed as the twin centers of the U.S. garment industry, where a new influx of immigrants provided low-wage labor. California has capitalized on its large Asian[15] and Latina[16] immigrant populations to become, today, the largest site of garment production in the United States.[17]

In addition, garment facilities along the U.S.–Mexico border in Texas have incorporated immigrant labor, primarily from Mexico and other parts of Latin America. While garment employment in Texas has dropped, the garment sector has expanded on the other side of the border in *maquiladora* factories in Mexico,[18] largely due to the Mexican government's establishment of the Border Industrialization Program in 1965.[19] Lower wages and less stringent labor law enforcement than in the United States make *maquiladoras* in Mexico and Central America attractive sites for off-shore production. Drawing from a pool of women of Mexican descent as their primary source of labor, garment factories on both sides of the U.S.–Mexico border are paradigmatic examples of the increasingly transnational nature of corporations and of labor.

While the garment industry has provided women, particularly women of color and immigrants, access to the manufacturing workforce, job access has been accompanied by a downward spiral of wages and consistent exploitation.[20] Wages are especially low in thriving "underground" economies in such cities as Los Angeles and New York, where garment workers usually make much less than the federal minimum wage, and work ten- to twelve-hour days without the overtime compensation mandated by federal law.

As predominantly working-class women of color, garment workers face severe structural barriers to exercising their rights.[21] Positioned at the intersection of race, gender, class, and frequently immigrant status, these women workers must also struggle against the power of international capital.[22] Their organizing attempts are often met by a shift to offshore production, where their counterparts—primarily low-wage women workers in developing countries—are paid even less for the same work.[23]

II. THE CREATION OF THE GLOBAL SWEATSHOP AND THE NEED FOR AN ALTERNATIVE STRATEGIC PARADIGM

The garment industry is one of the most global industries in the world.[24] The proliferation of industrial garment production follows broader patterns in trade globalization and economic restructuring.[25] This trend has been accompanied by a paradigm shift in economic development. Many developing countries have switched from the model of "import substitution"—industrialization through substituting imports with goods produced domestically—to a model of "export promotion"—export-led industrialization.[26] Export promotion typically involves strategies that attract foreign investment through such incentives as tax holidays, the promise of cheap, controllable labor for transnational corporations,[27] and the establishment of export-processing zones (EPZs) that ease importing/exporting restrictions.

In addition to engaging in direct foreign investment (for example, through their own branch offices), TNCs also arrange arm's-length relationships through subcontracting and licensing agreements, which often allow them to limit their liability for labor violations. TNCs benefit from their ability to scour the globe for the cheapest sources of labor in developing countries, as well as in advanced industrialized countries, where extensive immigration from less-developed countries has created a "Third World within."[28]

The transnational structure of garment production trade highlights the fact that the concept of the nation-state is becoming an increasingly ineffective model for designing market-controlling mechanisms. While the nation-state traditionally has been viewed as the locus for the declaration of rights-based norms (through courts) and their enforcement (through police and army), the state cannot adequately respond to dynamics that arise from markets that cut across borders. This effacement of sovereignty at the national level is accompanied by the emergence of regional and world trade agreements and bureaucracies that seek to mediate the new global space where transnational economic transactions rule, and markets generally triumph over governmental action. The decline of geographic sovereignty and conceptual boundaries such as the traditional public/private, state/market, political/economic, and national/international dichotomies testifies to the fact that simplistic, nationalistic approaches for securing worker rights are no longer viable.

Thus, more sophisticated approaches that are transnational in scope and that explore the interplay of labor rights and free trade must be examined. Labor, environmental, and other types of human rights discourses have begun to penetrate free trade discussions, although purist free traders object to this infiltration. More often than not, the free trade debate has a dichotomous quality—in its starkest form breaking down between free traders who value complete economic liberalization and protectionists who want to shield certain industries and their workers from unfettered competition—neither of which adequately frame a space within which transnational strategies that protect workers can be developed.

An alternative paradigm to the free trade/protectionist paradigm is a post–free trade approach, which posits transnational mechanisms through which to harmonize labor, environmental, and human rights standards. Such mechanisms allow for trade liberalization while offering protections to workers both at home and abroad. While in theory these mechanisms are attractive, in practice they have often failed to live up to their mission because of inadequate resources, investigatory capability, and enforcement powers.

Putting a transnational, post–free trade approach into practice requires thinking *and* acting globally *and* locally, in contrast to the popular aphorism "Think Globally, Act Locally." But even when restated, the "global-local" distinction does not reflect the way parameters of the "local" and "global" are often indefinable, indistinct, or intermingled, due to the transnational flows of culture and corporations.[29] Any attempts to change working conditions in the "local" will be largely fruitless without improved conditions in other sites. We therefore need to engage in transnational solidarity. In doing so, we must take care to acknowledge differences in women's lives—specifically with regard to the geographic distribution of power and privilege, as well as the ways other structures of dominance and subordination, for example, class or race, crosscut gender. We must make sure that the various experiences of women inform the category "women" in order to avoid implying that the category is monolithic and homogeneous, as well as to avoid rendering women of color invisible.[30] Special care must be taken when working transnationally to negotiate around discourses of cultural relativism and universalism that do not reflect the needs of women workers of color.

III. PRAXIS: LABOR PROTECTION VIA FORMAL LEGAL REGIMES

Combating TNC tactics necessitates coupling U.S. legal strategies with transnational ones, such as deploying the extraterritorial application of U.S. laws, public international law, U.S. trade laws, and multilateral trade agreements. This section surveys the possibilities for applying various permutations of these legal strategies to the situations presented on the global assembly line.

A. EXTRATERRITORIAL APPLICATION OF U.S. LAWS

One of the drawbacks involved in the extraterritorial application of U.S. laws is the secondary boycott prohibition of the National Labor Relations Act (NLRA).[31] While most groups outside unions arguably fall beyond the NLRA's reach, the more a group looks and acts like a union, the more a court may interpret its activities as proscribed by the NLRA's secondary boycott prohibitions.[32]

More promising is the extraterritorial application of Title VII, which clearly provides antidiscrimination protection for garment workers in U.S. plants overseas. In 1991, in response to the Supreme Court's refusal to extend Title VII of the Civil Rights Act extraterritorially, Congress specifically amended Title VII to have such reach.[33] For workers employed by U.S. companies in factories outside U.S. borders, the law provides a way to combat the sexual harassment as well as other forms of discrimination common in many factories both domestically and abroad.

Garment workers, however, are not always well served by the extraterritorial application of U.S. laws. To the extent U.S. labor law is an amalgamation of corporate and labor interests, specific provisions may be the product of political deal making rather than concern for the protection of workers' rights. Moreover, the extension of U.S. laws to the activities of U.S. companies in other national jurisdictions could be viewed as a form of neocolonialism. As such, more cooperative approaches to developing and enforcing transnational labor standards should be explored.

B. THE USES OF PUBLIC INTERNATIONAL LAW

Internationally recognized worker rights have long been part of the regime of international human rights law. The International Bill of Human Rights, composed of the Universal Declaration of Human Rights,[34] the International Covenant on Civil and Political Rights,[35] and the International Covenant on Economic, Social and Cultural Rights,[36] declares core labor rights, which include freedom from slavery,[37] freedom of association including organizing trade unions,[38] and fair wages and equal pay to be universal human rights.[39]

The ILO, now a part of the United Nations, sets international labor standards through the passage of conventions and recommendations, supervision of implementation of those standards, provision of technical assistance, information, and aid, and enforcement by means of reporting requirements and moral suasion.[40] While the lack of effective enforcement mechanisms is a general weakness of international law, the incorporation and acceptance of these internationally recognized rights into labor-protective regimes in the United States have allowed such rights to be accessed and enforced more effectively by garment workers and their advocates.

C. U.S. TRADE LAWS

Of all U.S. trade laws available to assert labor rights, worker advocates have used the Generalized System of Preferences (GSP) petition process most frequently.[41] The GSP provides duty-free tariff treatment on certain products for designated "beneficiary developing countries" (BDCs) in order to promote economic development in those countries. When the GSP program was renewed in 1984, section 502(b) of the Renewal Act added mandatory worker rights criteria to the statute. Furthermore, section 502(b)(7) of the Renewal Act mandated that "the President shall not designate any country a beneficiary developing country under this section . . . if such country has not taken or is not taking steps to afford internationally recognized worker rights to workers in the country (including any designated zone in that country)."[42] Those internationally recognized worker rights are (1) freedom of association; (2) the right to organize and bargain collectively; (3) a prohibition on the use of forced or compulsory labor; (4) a minimum wage for the employment of children; and (5) acceptable conditions of work with respect to minimum wages, hours of work, and occupational safety and health.[43]

Following a review of BDCs in 1985–86, the United States Trade Representative issued regulations that allow "any person," on an annual basis, to "file a request to have the GSP status of any eligible beneficiary developing country reviewed with respect to any of the designation criteria."[44] Pursuant to these regulations, at least thirty-four petitions were filed challenging BDCs on worker rights grounds as of the beginning of the 1991–92 review cycle.[45] Eight countries have been suspended or terminated.[46] Because the United States imports garments from many BDCs, the GSP can and has been a useful tool for garment workers. BDC countries include Bangladesh, the Dominican Republic, Guatemala, El Salvador, and Haiti.

D. MULTILATERAL TRADE AGREEMENTS

1. GATT/WTO

The successor to the General Agreement on Tariffs and Trade (GATT), the World Trade Organization (WTO) is the primary multinational regulator of trade. While neither the provisions of the GATT nor the mandate of the WTO protects workers' rights explicitly, some commentators have suggested utilizing the unfair trade practices provisions under GATT/WTO to vindicate certain labor rights. For instance, the use of forced and child labor, which artificially lowers production costs, arguably violates the antidumping provisions of GATT/WTO and may also be considered a prohibited subsidy, which could lead to countervailing duties.[47] Similarly, the practice of denying labor rights that are otherwise generally applicable in a country in export-processing zones arguably confers an unfair trade advantage by effectively subsidizing exports to other countries.[48]

Such assertions of unfair trade practices, if successful, would thus subject the offending countries to economic sanctions, providing a powerful disincentive to exploit workers in their own countries. For U.S. garment workers, however, the GATT has posed a threat to their job security with its plan to phase out the Multi-Fiber Agreement (MFA) over a ten-year period.[49] When the MFA expires in 2005, the U.S. textile and apparel industry could suffer job losses of anywhere from 72,000 to 168,000.[50] Moreover, because many trade agreements do not protect worker rights or improve working conditions directly, the solutions they offer usually can do no more than protect U.S. industries generally against lower-priced imports and thus only indirectly protect workers' jobs.

2. NAFTA

Unlike GATT/WTO, the North American Free Trade Agreement (NAFTA) contains labor and environmental side agreements and thus affords worker rights greater protection.[51] These standards, however, are merely hortatory. The labor side agreement provides for enforcement of each country's existing labor laws in only three areas: (1) occupational health and safety, (2) child labor, and (3) minimum wages.[52] Significantly, the right to organize and bargain collectively is listed only in the aspirational Annex 1 rather than as an enforceable obligation governed by the procedures in the side agreement.

Worker advocates have put the NAFTA labor rights regime into immediate use and have begun testing its parameters, including pushing it to promote worker organizing. For example, U.S. unions have brought submissions against Mexico for antiunion discrimination in violation of Mexican law at Honeywell, General Electric, and Sony factories.[53]

IV. LESS FORMAL TERRAIN: USING NONLEGAL STRATEGIES TO FIGHT THE MIGHT OF GARMENT TRANSNATIONALS

Notwithstanding the few successes of the application of U.S. laws or the use of international law in protecting workers' rights, the persistent shortcomings of such formal legal mechanisms demand an alternative approach to advocacy on behalf of garment workers. Such advocacy should employ tactics that do not rely solely on the state or formal legal mechanisms, but rather combine them with worker organizing, consumer pressure, and other "nonlegal" strategies.

A. VOLUNTARY CODES OF CONDUCT

Voluntary codes of conduct provide one such layer of nonlegal worker protection. Four types of voluntary codes of conduct have developed in the garment industry: (1) corporate codes of conduct, where manufacturers and retailers set out guidelines for their business partners;[54] (2) union codes of conduct won through union contracts that apply to any overseas vendor with which the manufacturer and retailer do business; (3) community/labor partnership codes such as the Maquiladoras Standard of Conduct, which addresses pollution, worker safety, employment, and community impact; and (4) industry-wide codes of conduct such as the Apparel Partnership Initiative, developed by a coalition of business, labor, and human rights groups. Advocates should pressure TNCs to adopt and comply with these codes.

B. WORKER ORGANIZING

Unions and other worker advocacy groups have begun to respond to global economic restructuring through transnational organizing. For instance, unions are strengthening ties among workers of different countries so that when a plant announces that it is closing in the United States, workers at the relocation site can put concerted and simultaneous pressure on the manufacturer.[55]

Another kind of transnational worker organizing is accomplished through support committees that, based in the global North, pressure U.S.-based transnationals to a degree impossible for workers to achieve in the global South. The National Labor Committee's campaign on behalf of *maquiladora* workers in Central America is an example.

C. CONSUMER STRATEGIES: WATCHING THE CLOTHES WE BUY

TNCs are susceptible to pressures from consumers in the global North who inform retailers and manufacturers that their purchasing decisions will be affected by workplace conditions. A survey released in November 1995 found that 78 percent of U.S. consumers would avoid retailers if they knew they were dealing in sweat-shop goods.[56]

Building on consumer concern, groups are raising consumer awareness of the exploitation that pervades the garment industry through the use of informational cards and newsletters. For example, Sweatshop Watch issues a periodic newsletter designed to educate consumers about violations in the United States and overseas.

On a related note, advocates have explored the idea of positive buying campaigns, which encourage consumers to selectively purchase goods based on their knowledge of the conditions of production. It is extremely difficult, however, to find or create a "clean label," given the endemic violations that exist and the reluctance of garment retailers and manufacturers to admit any liability for workplace conditions.

D. ORGANIZING ACTIVISTS

Cross-border solidarity organizations and networks exist to create alliances and facilitate links between communities across national borders. Many engage in transnational feminist and cross-racial or ethnic solidarity, explicitly drawing links among women. Mujer a Mujer, which started as a Mexico-based group, subsequently spawned a Canadian counterpart and then expanded to the United States and Central America. Another example is STITCH, the Support Team International for Textileras, which seeks to unite the struggles and interests of women *maquila* workers in Guatemala with those of women workers, activists, union organizers, and feminists in the United States. The Maquila Solidarity Network, formed in the wake of NAFTA, promotes solidarity between Canadian labor and social movement groups and their Mexican and Central American counterparts that are organizing to raise standards and improve conditions in *maquiladora* zones. A final example is the Committee for Asian Women, a regional workers' organization that assists in raising consciousness among women workers in the formal and informal employment sectors of Asia, about the commonalities of their situations and problems.

E. UN FOURTH WORLD CONFERENCE ON WOMEN: BEIJING AS A SITE FOR MOBILIZING WOMEN WORKERS

Although the Platform for Action adopted at the 1995 UN Fourth World Conference on Women in Beijing, China, provided major breakthroughs in terms of the articulation of standards of economic justice, it is still painfully inadequate.[57] The Platform for Action is not a treaty, nor does it have the status of any other legally binding instrument. Moreover, the United Nations has not designated a lead agency with adequate resources to implement the Beijing platform.

Despite these shortcomings, many women's human rights advocates view the document as a politically binding contract between governments and the world's women.[58] It represents an interpretative text that informs human rights norms in legally binding instruments. Finally, the platform and other outcomes of Beijing present an enormous potential for grassroots organizing.

Coinciding with the UN conference was the 1995 Nongovernmental Organization (NGO) Forum—the largest gathering of women in history—held in Huairou, China. The authors, along with other garment worker advocates from the United States, organized the only workshop specifically addressing the garment industry among the five thousand events and activities organized at the NGO Forum. At the workshop, entitled "The Struggle of Garment Workers on the Global Assembly Line," garment workers and worker advocates from countries including the Philippines, Thailand, Bangladesh, and the United States spoke of conditions they found in their regions and different strategies they had pursued. After the workshop, several informal discussions took place in which advocates learned more about country conditions and discussed ways to collaborate transnationally in assisting workers to assert their rights. A joint statement, titled "The Global Assembly Line," was prepared and distributed to NGO Forum participants to build their awareness as consumers and to increase worker solidarity.

CONCLUSION

We, as consumers, too often fail to engage in conscious reflection about the hands that sewed our clothes. We thus live with and normalize everyday violations of workplace rights of garment workers. This is facilitated by society's historical and persistent dehumanization of and lack of concern for poor women of color workers.

If we, as advocates, neglect to develop and implement new strategies that reveal and contest the adverse consequences of economic globalization, more sweatshops will undoubtedly proliferate along the global assembly line. Unless we radically redefine the terms of the debate, violations will continue. The widespread abuse of garment workers across the globe will not automatically be eliminated by the removal of unnecessary fetters on free trade or immigration; for instance, violations of workplace rights would not end if national borders were opened. It is not simply the relative immobility of workers and unions in contrast to the increasing mobility of capital that puts workers at a severe disadvantage, nor is the ultimate source of the problem insufficient state-sponsored protectionism in the United States, contrary to xenophobic claims that have permeated political discourse of late.

The endemic and systematic violations of workplace rights of garment workers in the United States and overseas result primarily from the overriding lawlessness of transnational corporations, whose pursuit of profit runs roughshod over the human rights of those whose labor allows them to thrive. Garment worker advocates must attempt transnational strategies to fight such corporations through both formal legal mechanisms and strategies that use the pressure of consumers, workers, and the community. Political lawyers must envision creative strategies that move beyond traditional legal frameworks that dichotomize civil and political from economic and social rights, and U.S. domestic law from international law.

Garment worker advocacy must recognize the outdated nature of separately constructing a "global" and a "local" and look to the way specific strategies will impact transnational flows of capital and culture across borders. This praxis may, admittedly, appear a difficult task, but neither working within the confines of national borders nor focusing only on the global "North" will result in the ultimate restraint of transnational corporations.

We must embrace an international perspective that recognizes and values the humanity and the human rights of workers in the United States and overseas. Our hope is that this chapter spurs creative thinking on multiple levels in the search for new ways to build transnational solidarity among workers, among women, and among communities. Only by realizing our common interests and uniting in the struggle against abusive practices of garment industry manufacturers and retailers will we achieve lasting change.

NOTES

1. First Amended Complaint, Bureerong v. Uvawas, No. 95-5958 (C.D. Cal., filed Oct. 25, 1995) (Collins, J.) [hereinafter El Monte Complaint]; *see also* Kenneth B. Noble, *Thai Workers Are Set Free in California*, N.Y. Times, Aug. 4, 1995, at A1.

2. *See* Slaughter-House Cases, 83 U.S. (16 Wall.) 36, 72 (1872) ("While negro slavery alone was in the mind of the Congress which proposed the thirteenth article, it forbids any other kind of slavery . . . [for instance, slavery in the] Mexican peonage or the Chinese coolie labor system."); United States v. Booker, 655 F.2d 562, 565 (4th Cir. 1981) (upholding conviction for migrant farm labor abuses under 18 U.S.C. section 1583 and describing "the broad and sweeping intention of Congress during the Reconstruction period to stamp out the vestiges of the old regime of slavery and to prevent the reappearance of forced labor in whatever new form it might take").

3. For the purpose of this chapter, we use the term "Black" rather than "African American" because the former is more inclusive of peoples from Africa and the Caribbean living in the United States who do not necessarily identify as "African American." At the same time, our intention is not to elide significant cultural differences through this transnational gesture, nor to de-emphasize the importance of personal agency in self-identification.

4. For an example of this view, see Jane H. Lii, *Week in Sweatshop Reveals Grim Conspiracy of the Poor*, N.Y. Times, Mar. 12, 1995, at A1, 40 (describing exploitation in a contract shop and noting, "Everyone quotes a Chinese saying: 'The big fish prey on the little fish, the little fish in turn prey on the shrimp, and the shrimp can only eat dirt.'"). *See also* Laura Ho and Leti Volpp, *Look Also Who Profits from Sweatshops*, N.Y. Times, Mar. 19, 1995, at 14 (criticizing article for laying blame for violations solely on contractors and failing to explain the role of manufacturers and retailers in the industry); Leti Volpp, *(Mis)Identifying Culture: Asian Women and the "Cultural Defense,"* 17 Harv. Women's L.J. 57 (1994) (discussing the depoliticizing effect of using "culture" to explain behavior).

5. We use the term "garment workers" in this chapter to refer to workers engaged in the production of clothing. A synonymous term is "apparel workers." We generally do not use

the term "textile," referring to the manufacture of cloth, because we are limiting the scope of this chapter to workers who cut and assemble clothing.

6. *See* Lora Jo Foo, Laura Ho, and Leti Volpp, *Manufacturers and Retailers Must Be Liable*, L.A. Times, Aug. 24, 1995, at B9 (describing El Monte factory as "more egregious than most" but stating that "sweatshops flourish throughout . . . the underground economy").

7. Disconnecting the United States from the exploitation of workers like those in El Monte—who were "liberated from slavery" only to be placed into Immigration and Naturalization Service (INS) detention—also raises many immigration-related contradictions. The prevalent hatred of immigrants that has swept the country has been a major factor in facilitating violations of workplace rights, as has the problematic collaboration between labor law enforcement agencies and the INS.

Characterizing the United States as a site not of exploitation but of liberation raises complex questions. Advocates for political asylum, for example, must argue that their clients will be free from persecution here, and in so doing, may make it more difficult to criticize repression in the United States and by its agents in other contexts. *See* Cathy Powell, *"Life" at Guantánamo: The Wrongful Detention of Haitian Refugees*, 2 Reconstruction 58 (1993); Victoria Clawson and Laura Ho, *Litigating as Law Students: An Inside Look at Haitian Centers Council*, 103 Yale L.J. 2337 (1994) (describing problems and contradictions raised by such advocacy).

8. *See generally* Dennis Hayashi, *Preventing Human Rights Abuses in the U.S. Garment Industry: A Proposed Amendment to the Fair Labor Standards Act*, 17 Yale J. Int'l L. 195 (1992).

9. The El Monte workers, for example, hope to hold six manufacturers legally liable under U.S. domestic law for the extreme labor law violations the workers endured in the slave sweatshop. *See* El Monte Complaint, *supra* note 1. Their complaint relies on both federal and state law claims. Two of the authors, Laura Ho and Leti Volpp, were part of the legal team representing the workers.

10. *See generally* Human Rights Watch and American Civil Liberties Union, Human Rights Violations in the United States (1993) (joint report on U.S. compliance with the International Covenant on Civil and Political Rights); Dorothy Thomas, *Advancing Rights Protection in the United States: An Internationalized Advocacy Strategy*, 9 Harv. Hum. Rts. J. 15 (1996).

11. In calling for enforcement of rights, we are mindful of the critique of rights-based strategies as well as the countercritique that posits rights, and specifically civil rights laws, as important in creating formal equality. *See* Kimberlé W. Crenshaw, *Race, Reform, and Retrenchment: Transformation and Legitimation in Antidiscrimination Law*, 101 Harv. L. Rev. 1331 (1988). While the defense of civil and political rights through judicial interpretation has failed to address adequately structural inequality and poverty, we believe that rights enforcement is an important endeavor. Moreover, our definition of "human rights" in this chapter is not limited to civil and political rights, but includes social and economic rights that aim to eradicate material and cultural bases of marginalization and oppression.

12. Evelyn Blumenberg and Paul Ong, *Labor Squeeze and Ethnic/Racial Recomposition in the U.S. Apparel Industry, in* Global Production: The Apparel Industry in the Pacific Rim 309, 313 (Edna Bonacich et al. eds., 1994) [hereinafter Global Production].

13. *Id.* at 316–18.

14. *Id.* at 318.

15. We use the term "Asian" here in a descriptive sense, to reflect how communities are

perceived by mainstream society, which appears to reserve the appellation "American" for those who are assumed to have "assimilated" into mainstream culture. Of course, whether to use the terms "Asian" or "Asian American"—or whether to use the categories "Thai," "Chinese," and so on—is a political question entailing both risks and advantages. *See* Volpp, *supra* note 4, at 61.

16. The Latina Rights Initiative of the Puerto Rican Legal Defense Fund defines "Latinas" as "women of Latin American birth or descent living in the U.S." Telephone interview with Nina Perales, former coordinator, Latina Rights Initiative (Feb. 2, 1996). "For me, the more exciting question than which term to use—Hispanic, Latina, Hispana—is whether you use the term to refer to a race, ethnicity, or national origin because this choice has implications for law, politics, and culture." *Id.*

17. Blumenberg and Ong, *supra* note 12, at 321.

18. *Maquiladora* factories, sometimes referred to as *maquilas*, are defined as assembly plants that produce for export. *See* Jorge Carrillo V., *The Apparel Maquiladora Industry at the Mexican Border, in* Global Production, *supra* note 12, at 217, 218.

19. *Id.* at 217. Pregnancy discrimination, sexual harassment, and other gendered forms of exploitation are not uncommon in these factories. *See* Sex Discrimination in Maquiladoras (Human Rights Watch, 1996).

20. Blumenberg and Ong, *supra* note 12, at 312.

21. On the race, class, age, and gender effects of global coproduction and deindustrialization, see generally Teresa L. Ammott and Julie Matthaei, Race, Gender and Work: A Multicultural Economic History of Women in the United States (1991).

22. The concept of intersectionality, which refers to the interplay and interlocking nature of various forms of oppression, can provide a useful analytical tool. Living at the intersection of multiple burdens subjects garment workers to compounded experiences of marginalization and dehumanization. *Cf.* Kimberlé W. Crenshaw, *Demarginalizing the Intersection of Race and Sex: A Black Feminist Critique of Antidiscrimination Doctrine, Feminist Theory and Antiracist Politics*, 1989 U. Chi. Legal F. 139; Elizabeth M. Iglesias, *Structures of Subordination: Women of Color at the Intersection of Title VII and the NLRA. Not!*, 28 Harv. C.R.-C.L. L. Rev. 395 (1993); Volpp, *supra* note 4.

23. *See generally* Rachel Kamel, American Friends Service Comm., The Global Factory (1990).

24. *See* Edna Bonacich and David V. Waller, *The Role of U.S. Apparel Manufacturers in the Globalization of the Industry in the Pacific Rim, in* Global Production, *supra* note 12, at 21, 90–91.

25. *See* Bonacich et al., *Introduction to* Global Production, *supra* note 12, at 3, 3–18.

26. *Id.* at 3, 5.

27. Edna Bonacich et al., *The Garment Industry, National Development, and Labor Organizing, in* Global Production, *supra* note 12, at 365, 370.

28. Bonacich et al., *supra* note 12, at 7.

29. *See* Inderpal Grewal and Caren Kaplan, *Introduction to* Scattered Hegemonies: Postmodernity and Transnational Feminist Practices 10–11 (Inderpal Grewal and Caren Kaplan eds., 1994).

30. *Id.* at 27. The creation of transnational solidarity along gender lines poses a question regarding how to deploy identity-based affiliations that are useful bases for organizing without eliding difference. For a criticism of how U.S. feminist legal analysis has used the identity "women" as a transnational suspect class, see Vasuki Nesiah, *Toward a Feminist*

Internationality: A Critique of U.S. Feminist Scholarship, 16 Harv. Women's L.J. 189 (1993) (also chapter 2 in this volume).

31. The NLRA's secondary boycott prohibition makes it an unfair labor practice for a labor organization or its agents to engage or encourage an employee to engage in a strike or work stoppage. 29 U.S.C. section 158(b)(4)(B) (1994).

32. Most community and labor support organizations may evade the NLRA restrictions. Support for a cause, no matter how active it may become, does not rise to the level of representation unless it can be demonstrated that the organization in question is expressly or implicitly seeking to deal with the employer over matters affecting the employees. Center for United Labor Action, 219 N.L.R.B. 873 (1975).

33. EEOC v. Arabian Amer. Oil Co., 499 U.S. 244 (1991). *See* 42 U.S.C. section 2000e(f) (1994) (defining a covered "employee" to include U.S. citizens working abroad); Roy L. Brooks et al., Civil Rights Litigation Cases and Perspective 358 (1995). Title VII of the Civil Rights Act now applies extraterritorially in the absence of contrary foreign law. 42 U.S.C. section 2000e-1(b) (1994).

34. G.A. Res. 217A, U.N. Doc. A/810, at 71 (1948) [hereinafter Universal Declaration].

35. G.A. Res. 2200A, U.N. GAOR, 21st Sess., Supp. No. 16, at 52–53, U.N. Doc. A/6316 (1968) [hereinafter ICCPR].

36. G.A. Res. 2200A, U.N. GAOR, 21st Sess., Supp. No. 16, at 49, U.N. Doc. A/6316 (1968) [hereinafter ICESCR].

37. Universal Declaration, *supra* note 34, art. 4; ICCPR, *supra* note 35, art. 8.

38. Universal Declaration, *supra* note 34, arts. 19, 20, 23; ICCPR, *supra* note 35, art. 22; ICESCR, *supra* note 36, art. 8.

39. Universal Declaration, *supra* note 34, art. 23; ICESCR, *supra* note 36, art. 7.

40. For an in-depth discussion of the ILO process, see Daniel S. Ehrenberg, *The Labor Link: Applying the International Trading System to Enforce Violations of Forced and Child Labor*, 20 Yale J. Int'l L. 361 (1995).

41. International labor law standards are reflected in a number of U.S. trade laws that include workers' rights provisions, including the Caribbean Basin Economic Recovery Act, 19 U.S.C. sections 2701, 2702(c)(8) (1994), the Generalized System of Preferences, 19 U.S.C. sections 2461, 2462(b)(7) (1994), the Overseas Private Investment Corporation, 22 U.S.C. sections 2191, 2191a(a) (1994), and section 301 of the Trade Act, 19 U.S.C. sections 2411–2420, 2411(d)(3)(B)(iii) (1994). For discussion of these trade laws, see Karen Travis, *Women in Global Production and Worker Rights Provisions in U.S. Trade Laws*, 17 Yale J. Int'l L. 173 (1992).

42. 19 U.S.C. section 2462(b)(7) (1994).

43. *Id.* section 2642(a)(4).

44. 15 C.F.R. section 2007, 2007.0(b) (1996).

45. Travis, *supra* note 41, at 183.

46. *Id.*

47. Ehrenberg, *supra* note 40, at 393–96.

48. *See* Travis, *supra* note 41, at 174.

49. The MFA has allowed countries to negotiate bilateral agreements or impose unilateral restraints on textile and apparel imports that disrupt domestic markets, and its phaseout is now deemed necessary to bring the two industries in line with GATT's free trade principles. 2 General Accounting Office, Report to the Congress, Uruguay Round Final Act Should Produce Overall U.S. Economic Gains 146–47 (1994).

50. *Id.* at 151.

51. North American Agreement on Labor Cooperation, Sept. 14, 1993, U.S.–Can.–Mex., art. 1(b), H.R. Doc. No. 160, 103d Cong., 1st Sess. 48, 50, 32 I.L.M. 1502, 1503 (1993).

52. North American Agreement on Labor Cooperation, *supra* note 51, arts. 4–5, 49, H.R. Doc. at 52, 76–78, 32 I.L.M. at 1503–04, 1513–14.

53. In the first two submissions, the U.S. GAO has already concluded that it was "not in a position to make a finding that the Government of Mexico failed to enforce the relevant labor laws." Richard Alm, *Union Leaders Upset after Labor Complaints on Mexico Shunned*, Dallas Morning News, Oct. 14, 1994, at 1D.

54. On corporate codes of conduct, see generally Lance Compa and Tashia Hinchliffe-Darricarrere, *Enforcing International Labor Rights through Corporate Codes of Conduct*, 33 Colum. J. Transnat'l L. 663 (1995), which examines several private-sector initiatives embracing codes of conduct for labor and employment practices in international commerce.

55. For a description of this tactic, see Ruth Milkman, *Organizing Women in New York's Chinatown: An Interview with Katie Quan, in* Women and Unions: Forging a Partnership 297 (Dorothy Sue Cobble ed., 1993).

56. Charles Kernaghan, *A Call to Action/We Have More Power Than We Realize, in* The U.S. in Haiti: How to Get Rich on Eleven Cents an Hour 51, 55 (Nat'l Labor Comm. Educ. Fund 1996).

57. The Platform includes recognition of the value of women's unwaged and undervalued work, and the impact of globalization on women's employment. Further, the document encourages women's self-help groups, cooperatives, and workers' organizations, and endorses parental leave for both mothers and fathers to promote equal sharing of family responsibilities, as well as the review and reformulation of wage structures in female-dominated professions. The Platform also states that governments should provide social security to homeworkers, extend additional labor protections to part-time workers and homeworkers; implement and enforce laws; and encourage codes of conduct to facilitate equal rights. The majority of governments, however, refused to agree to any form of protection for workers in free trade zones, most of whom are women workers. In short, while claiming to support women's economic employment, signatory governments refused to address the structural causes of women's poverty and marginalization. *See Focus: Working Women*, Asian Lab. Update (Asia Monitoring Resource Ctr., Kowloon, H.K.), Aug.–Oct. 1995, at 1, 3 (on file with authors).

58. *See, e.g.*, Bella Abzug, Statement on "Contract with Women of the USA" Campaign, Women's Environment and Development Organization (Mar. 6, 1996) (on file with authors).

26 Holding Up More Than Half the Sky

Marketization and the Status of Women in China

Anna M. Han

I. INTRODUCTION

As China approaches the new millennium, much is made of the direction its economic policies have taken and how these changes affect its people. While these changes impact everyone in China, half of its population, the female half, should be especially concerned about how these shifting policies affect their place in society. In this inquiry, Chinese women have found that they have come a long way from the feudal days when they were little better than property and that communism has improved their status dramatically, making them legally equal to men. However, the future of Chinese women may be much less promising. China is going through tremendous changes politically, socially, and economically. The question that Chinese women should ask is, will these developments make it easier or more difficult for them to achieve the promised equality?

Despite the failings of communism, as evidenced by the collapse of the former Soviet Union and other Eastern European governments, China continues to adhere to the principles of Marxism while gradually introducing market concepts to its economy.[1] While most Chinese and foreign observers are encouraged by China's experimentation with capitalism, they ignore the adverse effects these policy changes have on Chinese women. To date, no other system of government has benefited Chinese women more than communism. Under this system, which stressed equality and theoretically eliminated all social and economic class structures, tremendous strides in gender equalization were realized.[2]

As China makes its evolutionary transition from a centrally controlled economy to a market-based one, the Chinese government and the Western world have ob-

Reprinted by permission of the author.

served for some time that the resulting economic boom has not benefited everyone equally.[3] While the world media, including China's, seem to focus their attention on the ever-widening social and economic gap between the urban dwellers in the coastal cities and the agricultural workers of the inner regions, the pervasive division between the sexes is being overlooked. The purpose of this chapter is to examine generally how Chinese women fared under communism and, more specifically, delve into marketization's adverse impact on the status of women in China. It is this author's contention that despite the overall improvements in the standard of living, Chinese women are increasingly being marginalized economically. The long-term effects of subjugating the advancement of women for the immediate benefits of China's experimentation with a market economy hold vast implications for the future of the country. As China progresses economically, politically, and socially, it cannot afford to leave half of its population behind as it marches toward the next century.

II. HISTORICAL PERSPECTIVE

To gain a greater understanding of the implications of marketization, we must first discuss the roles women have played historically in Chinese society. This chapter divides the historical discussion into two periods: pre-1949, which was marked by agrarian life and feudalism; and post-1949, which captures the era of Maoism and Marxism, followed by Socialism with Chinese Characteristics.[4] In the post-1949 era, there have been significant constitutional, legal, and social changes in China that have advanced the rights of women throughout the country's socioeconomic evolution.

A. CHINESE WOMEN PRE-1949

Images of traditional Chinese women, particularly as portrayed in films, often focus on the powerful (e.g., the Empress Dowager),[5] the unusual (e.g., prostitutes),[6] or the strong (e.g., martial artists).[7] However, the reality is far less glamorous. Historically, the great majority of Chinese women were peasant farmers who lived in the countryside, tied to their land. Until this century, however, women were never allowed to own the land they tilled. Property, including the women themselves, belonged to the fathers, husbands, brothers, or sons.[8]

In an agrarian society, the physical demands and rigors of eking out a living created the social hierarchy. In this hierarchy, children served not only as farmhands, but also as old-age social security plans. Reinforced by a patriarchal system, the second-rate status of women was further perpetuated in feudal society by the fact that females could not hold title to property and that marriage meant that females became legally divorced from their birth families.[9] As such, families diverted their property and other resources to their sons, ensuring that the investment remained in the family.[10] The inability to hold property meant that women could never accumulate wealth and wield any economic influence on society. This left them economically powerless and dependent upon men.

The Chinese family unit, being patrilineal, also reinforced the notion that wealth left to the males stayed in the family and wealth given to daughters benefited others. Additionally, the Chinese practiced primogeniture for centuries, where property was left to the eldest son and not to the daughters. Usually, younger sons were provided for if the family had sufficient assets. These practices continued the cycle of gender discrimination based on the ability of sons to continually contribute to the family's wealth and to continue the family name. In Chinese culture the basic social unit is the family. In an agrarian society, it was crucial that every member contributed its labor for the survival of the family. Grandparents helped with child care as adults worked in the field. Children who were old enough worked with the parents. "Social security" to the Chinese meant having enough children to support the parents in their old age. To the extent that a son could contribute a greater amount of labor in the fields than a daughter, he received more food and other resources. When a son reached marrying age and took a wife, this brought an extra worker to the family and the ability to have more sons. A daughter's contribution was perceived as outweighed by the economic burden on the family. Having a daughter of marriageable age was considered a sign of poverty. Not only did the family lose a worker to the groom's family, but the parents also had to provide a dowry. A daughter's value depended on her contributions to domestic work and as a possible source of a bride price. However, since the family also needed to pay a corresponding dowry upon marriage, this tended to offset the bride price gained. The economic aspect of marriage was clear; a bride's reception and subsequent treatment by the groom's family often directly corresponded to the amount of her dowry. A woman who married without a dowry was essentially "sold" for the bride price. Often their treatment was little better than that of a slave. Once a woman was married, any economic resources invested in raising a daughter were considered lost. The Chinese saying "[a] married daughter is like water spilling out of a bucket" reflects this sentiment.[11]

Chinese philosophy and culture further reinforced this gender-based view of women as second-class citizens. Signs of this prejudice permeated every facet of society.[12] The Confucian doctrine of the "Three Followings" mandated that daughters were to honor and obey their fathers until married, heed their husbands upon marriage, and yield to their sons if widowed. Girls were also taught the "Four Virtues" based on *Nuer Jing* (The Classics for Girls).[13] A woman must revere her husband as she does heaven and be compliant, silent, clean, and diligent. The accepted practice of polygamy also insured that a woman's position in her husband's household was precarious at best.[14] For periods in Chinese history, the custom of foot binding prevented daughters from pursuing any education and career options outside the home.[15] The education of daughters was considered a waste since it was unnecessary for child rearing and housekeeping, the primary responsibilities of Chinese women.[16] Girls were taught basic vocabulary and mathematics, sufficient for managing the household. Since women were not allowed to participate in the Imperial Exams, which were the only route to civil service and possible upward mobility for the poor and the middle-class, education of women was considered a poor investment. Viewed as economic burdens, women were naturally treated as second-class citizens. As such, abuse and violence against females became acceptable.[17] The most extreme form of violence, killing of females, remains prevalent even today.[18]

Through the ages, Chinese women survived as second-class members of society. Without any political power and lacking economic clout, Chinese women were powerless to elevate their status. With the 1911 Revolution, which overthrew the Manchu Dynasty, the possibility of improvement surfaced in China.[19] At the turn of this century, Chinese women were employed in certain positions such as textile workers and domestic servants, jobs that required no education. During the early years of the Republic, women began to receive education outside the home, and a few pioneers secured professional jobs.[20] Foot binding was outlawed and polygamy discouraged.[21] Universal education was first promoted in the Republic. However, few families allowed their daughters to receive an education. Most educational institutions open to women were all-girl schools sponsored by missionaries in major cities. Even the more educated women were often not allowed to pursue a career after marriage. Due to its tenuous political hold on China, equality of the sexes was never a high priority of the Nationalist government.[22]

B. CHINESE WOMEN POST-1949

To achieve victory against the ruling Nationalists, the Chinese Communist Party (CCP) believed that the existing social order needed to be undermined. Recognizing the need to equalize the status of all, the fledgling CCP focused on the majority of the Chinese population, who were peasant farmers. While Marxism does not explicitly address the issue of equality between the sexes, the CCP recognized that women, disproportionately underprivileged, needed to be included. Half of the peasants were women. Upon its establishment in 1921, the CCP adopted a policy of mobilizing peasant and working-class women. The CCP gained these women's support by promising legal rights, educational opportunities, and legal accountability.[23] Moreover, these opportunities were not limited to the political arena. The party encouraged women to contribute to the economic development of the new China; in response, women joined the workforce in record numbers under CCP rule.[24]

III. LEGAL DEVELOPMENTS POST-1949

When Mao introduced Marxist reform, it did little to change the status of Chinese women culturally. What it did accomplish was the elimination of legal discrimination against women. Through constitutional reforms in 1949, Mao succeeded in turning women into full-fledged citizens with all the attendant rights therein. Among these changes were laws that allowed females to own property, to obtain a divorce, and to seek a formal education and training.[25] It also provided regulation aimed at preventing females from becoming child brides brokered through marriage.[26] While the immediate impact was not sweeping or drastic, the legislation enacted did serve to lay the foundation for providing and protecting basic rights for Chinese women for the first time in Chinese history.

Over the years, the CCP would reaffirm the rights first created in the 1949 Constitution.

In 1954, when the Chinese Constitution was rewritten, Article 91 acknowledged the contributions of Chinese women by "guaranteeing women equal rights with men in all areas of political, economic, cultural, social and domestic life."[27] Despite these assurances in the constitution, women in China had yet to enjoy "equal rights with men in all spheres" of life. Many of the promises laid out in the constitution were aspirational and seldom enforced. Many of the so-called rights detailed in the constitution were not accepted by society.[28] The best evidence of the disparity between what the laws promised and what society was willing to tolerate was the periodic need to enact more laws to address specific areas of discrimination.

A. MARRIAGE LAW

Before 1949 Chinese women did not have the right to choose their own marriage partner and once married, could not initiate divorce.[29] A marriage was seen as an alliance of two families. The decision was made by the parents of both the bride and the groom. Most couples never met until the wedding night. Although a man also did not have much say in the selection of his partner, he had the option of taking concubines or divorcing his wife if he were unhappy with her. A woman did not have this option. The custom of extracting money from the groom's family as a bride price resulted in the widespread practice of "mercenary marriages," in which women, especially from poor families, were bought and sold as commodities.[30] To address these issues, China passed the Marriage Law of the People's Republic of China in 1950.[31] This Marriage Law abolished all laws allowing arranged marriages and introduced the concept that marriage is a contract of choice. The Marriage Law grants "full rights to the individual to handle his or her own matrimonial affairs without any interference or obstruction from third parties and without regard to social status, occupation or property."[32] Despite the proclamations in the 1950 Marriage Law, considerations of class, social status, and property continued to influence decisions on marriage. The consideration of "class" was especially important as marriage to a person with a "bad" social background virtually guaranteed that one would be denied access to good housing, jobs, and education for the children.[33]

In 1980 a new Marriage Law was enacted to promote certain government policies. This new version not only covers the legal formation and dissolution of a marriage, it also includes pronouncements on inheritance, family planning, custody, adoption, and support obligations of an extended family.[34] The drafters of this law gathered input from such diverse groups as the All-China Women's Federation, the Ministry of Public Health, and the People's Liberation Army.[35]

The Marriage Law of 1980 reaffirms the principles of free choice in marriage and equal rights to divorce.[36] Under this new Marriage Law, Chinese women gained greater freedom to determine their fate in marriage.[37] Clearly, the pressures from family and society to marry the "right" person persisted. This is particularly evident when Han Chinese and minority Chinese intermarry. During the Cultural Revolution, it was also important to consider the "class background" of a spouse. Working-class backgrounds were considered the most desirable, and former landowners and capitalists were the worst candidates. Similarly, even though the right to divorce was granted, social pressure and practical considerations often prevent couples from divorcing. One such consideration is the couple's housing. Housing in China is assigned from the couple's work unit. If the housing was assigned by the husband's employer, as is often the case, a divorce would leave the wife homeless. This problem is especially acute for couples in crowded urban areas. Often, estranged couples will stay married to preserve their housing.

The Marriage Law also clarifies that a man can become a member of a woman's family and vice versa.[38] This provision is a break from the centuries-old custom that once a woman marries, she is automatically a member of her husband's family. Since family members have a legal obligation of support, including support of one's parents, this classification is vital.[39] The significance of this provision is especially notable in a country practicing a one-child policy. If the only child is female, the prospect of being left childless and without old-age support is lessened with the possibility of the man becoming a member of the woman's family. In allowing a man to be "adopted" into the family by marriage, the drafters hoped to lessen the instances of female infanticide. Unfortunately, this provision may not be sufficient to overcome age-old prejudices.

B. THE INHERITANCE LAW

In addition to marriage, another area where women fared far worse than men was in their ability to inherit property. Chinese custom, reinforced by laws that did not allow women to own property, traditionally favored male heirs. Families sometimes provided for female heirs by granting them a stipend or the right to live in the family home. However, they did not inherit property outright.[40] While the 1980 Marriage Law does briefly state that husbands and wives may inherit property from each other, the law does not specify any details.[41] This issue was finally addressed with the passage of the Inheritance Law.[42] This law gave both men and women the right to dispose of their property in a will.[43] In the absence of a will, the Inheritance Law gave daughters and sons an equal right to inherit their parent's property.[44] The Inheritance Law also provided protection for widows, granting them the right to inherit from their deceased husband's estate. The protections granted to women under this law were further reinforced through the creation of laws such as the Law of the People's Republic of China on Protection of Rights and Interests of Women.[45] Chapter 5 of this law provides that "the state guarantees that women will enjoy equal right to property."[46] More specifically on the issue of inheritance, Article 31 provides that in the case of intestate succession, women shall enjoy equal rights as men.[47] Although the laws provide for equality in the case of intestate succession, there is nothing to prevent a testator from discriminating based on the sex of the beneficiaries in a will.[48]

C. EMPLOYMENT LAWS

From 1949 to the late 1970s, Chinese women were incorporated into the workplace in record numbers. During this era, women were encouraged to take on nontraditional jobs outside the home.[49] The work assignment system responsible for assigning high school and college graduates was administered by bureaucrats who had little concern with matching the students' talents to the demands of the job. Men and women were often randomly assigned regardless of gender considerations.[50] Once assigned, however, women often received lower work points for the same job as their male counterparts.[51]

In the workplace, women found employment conditions to be harsh. To address these workplace conditions, the Chinese government enacted the Regulations Governing Labor Protection for Female Staff and Workers in 1988.[52] These regulations address such details as how intense the labor may be, depending on specific physical conditions of women such as menstruation, pregnancy, and the postpartum period. The laws limit the type of work an employer may assign to a woman employee during these periods and require them to provide maternity leave and child care facilities.[53]

D. WOMEN'S PROTECTION LAW

The above laws address specific issues that affect women, such as marriage, inheritance, and labor. But despite prohibitions on discrimination and pronouncements about equality, vast differences between how men and women fared in each of these areas continued. As part of an effort to eliminate continuing discriminatory practices, China enacted a law for the protection of Chinese women. This law reiterates the equality of women with men in political, economic, social, and family life and prohibits discrimination in any manner.[54] In fifty-four articles, this law essentially repeats rights that Chinese women should already be enjoying. Although the intent of these laws is to protect women, their impact may be very different.[55]

Despite the assurances of these laws, equality of treatment remained illusive to Chinese women. Women continued to face many more obstacles to upward mobility than men. For example, for daughters, household chores were more important than homework; and private tutoring was almost always reserved for sons.[56] Although education was compulsory, females accounted for approximately 70 percent of China's illiterate and semiliterate population.[57] This disparity was even more acute in the rural communities.[58] As there is a direct relationship between education and economic empowerment, women still found themselves in lower-skilled and lower-paying jobs. Moreover, while the effort to assimilate women into the workforce was successful, women were not relieved of their traditional duties of cooking, housekeeping, and child care.[59] Thus, gender discrimination was never eliminated under CCP rule. However, it was the CCP's reforms to the Chinese Constitution that, at least legally, promised equality between men and women. This was the legacy of the Marxist movement. The movement eliminated discrimination in theory, if not in practice, against women. This protective legislation, coupled with the new movement toward market practices, has led to unforeseen results for Chinese women in the workplace. These results will be explored in the next section.

IV. MARKETIZATION AND DISCRIMINATION

If the gains for women under communism were more theoretical than real, under marketization the gains are anomalous at best. The resurgence of gender discrimination in China can be linked to the abandonment of strict economic controls following the death of Mao.[60] The subsequent movement from communism to privatization has given rise again to the subordination of women.

A. HIRING PRACTICES

Before China's experimentation with market concepts, Chinese enterprises were not particularly concerned with whether a man or a woman was assigned to the job. Employers had very little control over the nature of their workforce. Under communism, the economy was fully centralized and government administrators exercised full control over most of China's enterprises.[61] The government micromanaged these enterprises, deciding purchasing, production, and labor practices. Managers lacked the authority to hire or fire workers.[62] Workers were assigned based on the government's need to place graduates, not on the enterprise's labor requirements. Although both men and women were often misassigned under the poorly administered system, the work assignment system did have one merit: its very randomness was nondiscriminatory. Workers and managers received comparable wages, despite differences in job demands. Hard work did not produce more pay and incompetence did not result in firing. Under this planned economy, the government took away any profits and subsidized any losses.[63] This system took away incentives for enterprises to be profitable. In turn, the costs of labor and the efficacy of the workers were unimportant to these enterprises. Furthermore, because workers enjoyed the "iron rice bowl," or lifelong employment, once women secured a job, they enjoyed job security and its benefits.[64] As China's economy continues to make its transition from state-owned enterprises into competitive businesses, profitability is now of paramount concern.

Discrimination against women in hiring has been on the rise as enterprises reform and management is decentralized. Control is shifting from government bureaucrats to individual managers of the enterprises.[65] State cooperatives and private enterprises are now assuming primary responsibility for recruitment and organization of their labor force.[66] Since enterprises face the prospect of either going extinct or surviving by being profitable, and since selection of employees now bears a direct relationship to the bottom line, employers are seeking the cheapest labor.

With the focus on profitability, women are finding it more difficult to find employment that utilizes their training. Employers frequently refuse to hire women, or create obstacles by artificially raising entry requirements for female applicants. In a survey conducted by the All-China Federation of Trade Unions, of 660 factories with 15,000 workers, only 5.3 percent of the employers indicated that they were willing to hire a woman for positions that are suitable for either a woman or a man.[67]

The explanation for this resurgence of discrimination against women is primarily economic. The benefits accorded to women under the various laws, such as maternity leave, on-site child care facilities, and exemption from hard labor during certain periods,[68] are viewed as legitimate reasons to favor male employees.[69] These costs are often considered burdensome by the employer. One survey estimated that the cost of pregnancy, medical care for childbirth, and maternity leave would cost 1,259 yuan per worker.[70] Another survey showed that a male worker could earn 10,600 yuan more than his female counterpart if she were pregnant and involved in childbearing and caring over a period of two years.[71] These numbers actually demonstrate that despite all the government subsidies, the female worker and her family bear the majority of the burden for having a child. While there is paid maternity leave in China, it is not at full salary. Although these numbers have never been verified, the benefits and rights conferred on women workers are now excuses for not hiring them. Without the government supplementing their coffers, companies have taken the position that the economic disincentives of hiring females outweigh their productivity. Even when employers hire women, employers use the added costs of these benefits to justify paying women less than their male counterparts.[72]

Whether Chinese women work on a farm, in a factory, or in an office, they still carry the primary responsibility of housekeeping and child care. This societal expectation in turn leads to the perception that once married, a woman will be less career-oriented. Whereas the communist system provided some support for working mothers in the form of "complete care" for children, the shift to marketization means an end to these government-subsidized programs.[73] With the elimination of government subsidies, day care centers were one of the first things abolished by work units in order to control costs. Now women must not only enter the job market at lower wages than men, they do so without any of the previous child care support from the state. If a woman demands her lawful benefits, the private employer is likely to view the added cost as another reason to not hire or to fire a woman. Efforts by Chinese women to assert their rights have met with very little success in Chinese courts.[74]

Employers also have the perception that once married, a woman employee will have a child immediately. Often they force women to sign contracts promising not to get pregnant for a specified time.[75] If a woman breaks this contract, she is fined heavily for her pregnancy, even if it is illegal to do so under Chinese law. Ironically, the employer's assumption might be valid in China, where government policy allows only one child to every couple in most parts of the country. The one-child policy increases the pressure on married couples to have an heir as soon as possible.[76] This will be especially true as the first generation born under the one-child policy comes of age. The responsibility to produce a grandchild for both the husband's and the wife's family now rests solely on one couple. The couple does not have siblings who could provide the same result. As a result, a Chinese woman worker faces a conundrum: her employer wants her to refrain from becoming pregnant as long as possible and her family wants the opposite.

B. SURPLUS LABOR

As China moves to dismantle its bloated state-owned enterprises (SOEs), scores of redundant workers are being laid off. Women are bearing a disproportionate share of the cost of this reorganization. Married women, older women, and women with children are often the first to be dismissed.[77] Women account for a far greater percentage of workers labeled surplus than their actual representation in the industry.[78] At least one survey showed that of 660 enterprises that classified some workers as surplus, 64 percent of the surplus workers were women.[79]

In the past, the Chinese government controlled employment and accounted for all profits and losses of the state-owned enterprises. However, with marketization, private enterprises are no longer supplemented by the government, and the viability of a business depends on efficiency and profitability. As such, market forces have become the justification for employment discrimination against women. Often the elimination of surplus women workers is also justified on the grounds that they can be supported by their parents and husbands, making women economically dependent on others, mostly males, again. In a country where the labor supply exceeds employment opportunities and the majority of the decision makers are male, supply and demand have become the faceless perpetrators of the subjugation of Chinese women.

C. EDUCATION

The Chinese are not unaware of the disparity in pay and treatment of women workers. As such, this is the beginning of a vicious circle. Chinese families are working with declining resources and facing increasing costs of education. As they perceive the difference in earning powers between men and women, the emphasis on education has shifted to educating the males in each family.

Although education is compulsory in China, schools are charging ever higher fees for books and "extras." Unable to bear the brunt of these price increases, children in rural areas are dropping out of school at record rates.[80] Eighty percent of these dropouts are girls.[81] Furthermore, enrollment rates are not the same as attendance rates. There is evidence that sporadic attendance, dropout, and nonattendance rates of girls are significantly higher than those of their male counterparts.[82]

Women are also prevented from receiving higher education. At this level, discrimination takes the form of more stringent entrance exam requirements to educational institutions.[83] The higher requirements limit the number of female entrants and in turn limit the number of qualified women who are receiving more advanced education and training.[84] Once trained, they are also prevented from fully utilizing those skills due to employment discrimination.[85] The effect of these discriminatory practices in education is that half of China's population does not have the opportunity to learn the skills necessary to contribute to its economy to their maximum potential. The ability to academically excel and potentially be employed in a professional field is denied to these girls. As this cycle continues, the notion that girls should remain ignorant and are of little economic value will become a reality.

V. RAMIFICATIONS OF CAPITALISM

In addition to the bias in hiring, pay, and retention, emerging forms of discrimination against women have begun to sprout out of China's experiment with marketization. Communism discouraged makeup and fashion as bourgeois. Men and women wore the uniform of the Mao suit and generally had simple haircuts. The uniformity of dress promoted equality among women regardless of age and appearance.[86] With marketization, the notion of advertising to gain market share has become increasingly popular.[87] As companies, especially consumer-oriented ones, strive for their market share, there is an increased emphasis in hiring workers who are young and attractive. It is not unusual to see ads seeking employees specifying that the applicant must be "young, female and attractive."[88] While the introduction of individualism in clothing and appearance is not necessarily an evil in itself, this has led to discrimination based on appearance of the worker by employers, even when the worker's gender and appearance are unrelated to job performance. One ad indicated that women needed to be between the ages of eighteen and twenty-five for a waitress job.[89] Chinese women must compete with each other for jobs in a way that was not necessary under the earlier communist state.[90] Women in the workforce face not only bias based on gender, but also a prejudice centered on physical attractiveness. Attractive women are now considered commodities in Chinese society.[91]

Along with marketization, crimes against women are now on the rise. Abductions for prostitution and other forms of enslavement are among the many violations of rights women suffer under Mao's constitutional reforms. China's one-child policy coupled with its cultural bias toward males has refueled infanticide of females.[92] The resulting disproportion in marriageable females has in turn led to the abduction and sale of women.[93] As China's economy booms, women from rural areas, lured by the prospect of better job opportunities in the cities, migrate away from their families. They leave their families in part to alleviate a burden and in hopes of economic independence. They are the easiest targets for abduction into prostitution or forced marriage. Even when they obtain work, it is often at substandard wages because these women are not aware of their rights as employees. Since there is always another new worker ready to replace them, the women seldom complain of poor working conditions or other forms of exploitation. The legal system is also poorly equipped to enforce their rights. The workers' paradise envisioned by Marx is far from the reality in China.

VI. CONCLUSION

While the overall impact of China's economic experiment has been positive for the country as a whole and for the urban Chinese in particular, its impact on Chinese women is anomalous. Fifty years of communism with all its demands for equality was insufficient to eradicate discrimination and centuries-old prejudices, and the new marketization policy has served to rekindle these prejudices. Many advances made during the early years of communism have been negated by the introduction of a market-driven economy. Women are being deprived of their constitutional right to equality simply because market forces view them as more costly workers. In turn, education is being diverted away from girls. With lesser education, women will become less desirable workers and less likely to occupy higher-paid positions. Added to the mix is the increase in crimes and resurgence of exploitation of women in other areas. Chinese women must wonder whether this experiment is at their expense. The government has done little to study the ramifications of China's flirtation with marketization, specifically the long-term effects of economically marginalizing women. As China forges ahead, it can scarcely afford to ignore the widespread unemployment among women, exploitation, and the whole spectrum of social dysfunction that come with moving from a communist to a market economic system. At this stage in China's development, most women are not receiving their share of the benefits from China's new economic policies, and yet they must continue to hold up more than half the sky.

NOTES

This essay is dedicated to all the women who attended the UN Conference on Women in Beijing in 1995 for inspiring this topic and to the many scholars whose works are cited in this chapter. The author also wishes to thank her research assistant, Elizabeth Loh, for her help.

1. After the death of Mao in 1976, China, under the leadership of Deng Xiao Ping, adopted the "open door policy," which allowed for the introduction of foreign investment and the

accompanying capitalist concepts. China, however, still clings to Marxism politically, and terms the capitalist concepts "marketization" or "socialism with Chinese characteristics."

2. While clearly beyond the scope of this chapter, the benefits communism conferred on women in other countries are the subject of other scholarly research. *See* Barbara Jancar-Webster, Women under Communism (1978).

3. *See* Robert Weil, *China at the Brink: Class Contradictions of Market Socialism Part 2*, Monthly Review, Jan. 1995, at 11.

4. While it is true that China remains a primarily agrarian society and that some may argue that the advent of communism merely changes the ruler and not the form of the rule, the demarcation is nevertheless useful as the most dramatic changes in Chinese women's lives that have taken place in the last fifty years.

5. The Last Emperor (Bertolucci, 1988). For a more detailed explanation of the portrayal of Chinese women by the media, see Gina Marchetti, Romance and The "Yellow Peril" (1993).

6. The World of Suzie Wong (Richard Quine, 1960).

7. Mulan (Walt Disney Pictures 1998).

8. *See* Ann Jordan, *Women's Rights in the People's Republic of China,* 8 J. Chinese Law 47 (1994).

9. Under the Tang legal code, once a woman became betrothed to a man, she became a legal member of her fiancé's family. A betrothal was legally binding on both families. *See* Esther S. Lee Yao, Chinese Women: Past and Present 54–58 (1983).

10. *See* Jordan, *supra* note 8, at 73.

11. Yao, *supra* note 9, at 54–58.

12. Chinese literature does not always paint an accurate picture of the everyday life of women. Fiction tends to portray ideals for women: the mother who sacrifices herself for her children, the wife who waits years for a missing husband, the daughter who obeys all the commands of her parents. Historical accounts of women tend to focus on the few aberrant women rulers in China's history. The characters usually gain their positions by cunning and by elimination of their spouses or rivals. Such was the literary trend that when the book *The Dream of the Red Chamber* was published in 1791, it caused a major stir by portraying a family with many strong female characters. To date, the study of this novel still commands the intellectual interests of many Chinese scholars. Cao Xue Qin, Hong Lou Meng (1791, Translated as Dream of the Red Chamber, 1929).

13. *See* Confucius, Confucian Analects, The Great Learning and The Doctrine of the Mean (James Ledge trans., Dover Publications 1971) (1893).

14. Husbands were legally entitled to take concubines. Furthermore, concubines held a legal status in the family. *See* Kellee Tsai, *Women and the State in Post-1949 Rural China,* J. Int'l Aff., Winter 1996.

15. Ironically, the practice of foot binding, even at its zenith, was never popular in the rural areas, where women were expected to engage in physical labor outside the home. *See* Alison R. Drucker, The Influence of Western Women on the Anti–Foot Binding Movement 1840–1911, at 181 (1981).

16. Furthermore, even if a girl was taught to read and write, she was discouraged from reading anything but the prescribed classics such as *Nu Jie* (precepts for women) since it was believed that reading anything else could corrupt her morals. Stories of famous literate courtesans throughout Chinese history tended to reinforce this notion. *See* Yao, *supra* note 9, at 87–89.

17. One scholar argues that once a culture sees women as being an inferior social class, women become legitimate victims of abuse. *See* Nilda Rimonte, *A Question of Culture: Cultural Approval of Violence against Women in the Pacific-Asian Community and the Cultural Defense*, 43 Stan. L. Rev. 1311, 1315 (1991).

18. *See* Yao, *supra* note 9, at 90–96. For an excellent discussion of female infanticide in China, see Sharon Hom, *Female Infanticide in China: The Human Rights Specter and Thoughts towards (An)other Vision*, 23 Colum. Hum. Rts. Rev. 249 (1992) (also chapter 16 in this volume).

19. The 1911 revolution ended China's imperial rule. However, as political power was never consolidated in any one group, the Chinese government was fractionalized and regionalist. Even if there had been a policy to end discrimination against women, no one government was able to carry out the policy.

20. *See* Margaret Y. K. Woo, *Biology and Equality: Challenge for Feminism in the Socialist and the Liberal State*, 42 Emory L.J. 143 (1993).

21. *See* Olga Lang, Chinese Family and Society 45–46 (1946).

22. Janice A. Lee, *Family Law of the Two Chinas*, 5 Cardozo J. Int'l and Comp. L. 217, 224 (1997). The Nationalist, or the Kuomingtang, was the official government ruling China after the 1911 Chinese revolution that overthrew the Manchu Dynasty. However, parts of China were controlled by various military commands under regional warlords.

23. *See* Bobby Siu, Women in China 151 (1981).

24. *See* Patricia Beaver, *Rural Chinese Women: Two Phases of Economic Reform*, Modern China, Apr. 15, 1995, at 207.

25. The 1950 Marriage Law denounced patriarchal authority in the household, granted both sexes equal rights to file divorce, and outlawed marriage by sale and other venal practices involved in the negotiations of marriage; the Agrarian Reform Law recognized a woman's right to marry, divorce, and own property; and the Labor Insurance Regulations of 1951 made much of the same promises. *See* Henry R. Zheng, *China's New Civil Law*, 34 Am. J. Comp. L. 669, 671 (1986).

26. *See* Harriet Evans, Women and Sexuality in China 168 (1997).

27. The full text of the 1954 Constitution may be found in Zhonghua Remin Gongheguo Fagui Huician 4–31 (1956).

28. *See* Jordan, *supra* note 8, at 57.

29. *See* Elizabeth Croll, Changing Identities of Chinese Women 96 (1995).

30. *See* Elizabeth Croll, Chinese Women since Mao 74–75 (1983). For a different cultural perspective on "bride prices," see Adrien K. Wing and Eunice P. de Carvalho, *Black South African Women: Toward Equal Rights*, 8 Harv. Hum. Rts. J. 57, 64 (1995).

31. Croll, *supra* note 30, at 75.

32. Wu Zhangzhen, *The Principle of Freedom of Marriage Should Not Be Abused*, Guangming Ribao, 1957.

33. As a communist state, China was purging its upper and middle classes. Those with that type of family history were considered undesirable mates.

34. For the text of the 1980 Marriage Law, see SWB, 23 September, 1980 (FE6530/C/1); China Now, March–April 1982.

35. Explanations on the Marriage Law (Revised Draft) and the Nationality Law (Draft) of the People's Republic of China, Speech given at the Third Session of the Fifth National People's Congress on September 2, 1980 by Wu Xinyu, Vice-Chairman of the Commission for Legal Affairs of the Standing Committee of the National People's Congress.

36. *Id.*

37. *See China: Survey Reveals Problems with Marriage Law*, China Daily, Oct. 31, 1997.

38. Article 8 of the 1980 Marriage Law.

39. Article 15 of the 1980 Marriage Law.

40. *See* Jordan, *supra* note 8, at 73.

41. Article 18 of the 1980 Marriage Law.

42. Law of Succession of the People's Republic of China (Oct. 1, 1985), *trans. in* Laws of the People's Republic of China (1979–1982) (Beijing 1987).

43. *Id.* at Art. 16.

44. *Id.*

45. Law of the People's Republic of China on Protection of Rights and Interests of Women, Chapter 5, adopted Apr. 3, 1992.

46. *Id.*

47. *Id.* at Art. 31.

48. The right to inheritance was never a major issue in the early days of the People's Republic. Since there was little personal property to inherit and all real property was owned by the state, heirs had little to fight over. However, as China's economy progresses and the experiment with marketization has created a number of wealthy individuals, the issue of inheritance takes on new importance. With the one-child policy, the issue of discrimination among heirs based on sex may disappear of its own accord.

49. Although entry into the job market still depended upon the overall demand for labor, women were hired in factories and were assigned to work alongside men in the fields. For further information on Chinese women's entry into the workforce, see Woo, *supra* note 20, at 143.

50. The system created many mismatches: English majors were sent to botanical gardens and philosophy majors to toy factories. The author has met many of these assigned workers. For a discussion of the assignment system, see Hillary K. Joseph, Labor Law in China: Choice and Responsibility 21 (1990).

51. *See* Kang Keqing on Women's Role and Conditions, BBC Summary of World Broadcasts, March 9, 1979, at 1, available in LEXIS Asiapc Library, Arcnws File.

52. For the text of the Regulations Governing Labor Protection of Female Staff and Workers, see Croll, *supra* note 29, appendix I.

53. *Id.* at Art. 11.

54. Law of the People's Republic of China on Protection of Rights and Interests of Women, promulgated on April 3, 1992, by the 5th Session of the Seventh National People's Congress. Art. 1.

55. Margaret Woo has argued that these laws in fact legitimize the disparate treatment of women in the workplace by emphasizing women's biological differences. *See* Woo, *supra* note 20, at 143.

56. Many parents continue to see education as more valuable for boys than girls. Families with limited resources consider educating daughters to be a poor investment because traditionally daughters left their parents' home after marriage. Another factor that reinforces the notion of not spending scarce economic resources for a daughter's education is that women generally make less money than a man, so there is less of a return on the family's investment. *See* Nancy E. Riley, *Holding Up Half the Economy; Chinese Women*, China Business Review, Jan. 1996, at 22.

57. Zhonggong Funu Tongji Ziliao [Statistics on Chinese Women] 63 (1991).

58. The rate of illiteracy in 1982 among girls of fifteen in the rural areas was ten times as high as the male rate; between 1982 and 1990 female illiteracy as a percentage of the total rose from 69.2 percent to 73.49 percent, and in the same period the differential between urban and rural rates of illiteracy among girls increased considerably while among boys it remained stable. *See* Evans, *supra* note 26, at 227.

59. *See* Tsai, *supra* note 14, at 493–524.

60. *See* Sheryl WuDunn, *Profit and Loss: China's Affection for Capitalism Erodes Gains in Equal Rights*, Chi. Trib., Sept. 20, 1992, at 5.

61. *See* Peter M. Lichtenstein, China at the Brink 80 (1991).

62. *See* Chen Jiyan, *The Planning System, in* China's Industrial Reform (Gene Tidrick and Chen Jiyuan eds., 1987). *See also* Anna M. Han, *China's Company Law: Practicing Capitalism in a Transitional Economy*, 5 Pac. Rim L. and Pol'y J. 462 (1996).

63. *See* Zhou Shulian, *Reform of the Economic Structure, in* China's Economic Reform (George Totten and Zhou Shulian eds., 1992).

64. *See* Joseph, *supra* note 50, at 53.

65. *Id.* at 139.

66. *See* Croll, *supra* note 29, at 119.

67. *Id.* at 120.

68. As discussed earlier, the Regulations Governing Labor Protection of Female Staff and Workers provide very specific guidelines on the length and intensity of work during menstruation, pregnancy, and postpartum periods for women employees. *See* Croll, *supra* note 29, at 96.

69. Regulations Governing Labor Protection of Female Staff and Workers, 1988.

70. At the present exchange rate, the cost is approximately $130 in U.S. dollars. Since the survey was conducted in 1988, it can be assumed that inflation has increased this amount.

71. China Daily, Dec. 4, 1988.

72. It is a commonly held belief among employers and managers that women are less desirable workers because they will take advantage of the state-mandated maternity leave and take off from work for several months. This belief is undeterred by the lack of evidence for claims that firing or not hiring women has increased worker productivity. *See* Dusko Doder, *The Old Sexism in New China*, U.S. News and World Report, Apr. 24, 1989, at 36.

73. Working women were able to drop off infants and children at state-subsidized day care centers at their work unit for the day and sometimes for an entire week. *See* Weil, *supra* note 3.

74. *See* Dele Olojede, *Chinese Woman Fights Family Planning Laws*, S.F. Chron., Nov. 28, 1998, at C3.

75. *See* WuDunn, *supra* note 60.

76. The Chinese understanding of any policy is that it is subject to change. Therefore, to enjoy any permissive policy, one must always take full advantage before any change.

77. *See* Croll, *supra* note 29, at 120.

78. *See* Od Aslangeigi, Steven Pressman, and Gayle Summerfield, Women in the Age of Economic Transformation 121–22 (1994).

79. *See* Gale Summerfield, *Effects of the Changing Employment Situation on Urban Chinese Women*, Rev. Soc. Economy (1994).

80. In 1990, 4.8 million children, mostly in rural areas, dropped out of school.

81. *See* Croll, *supra* note 29, at 96.

82. *Id.*

83. *See* Croll, *supra* note 29, at 134.

84. Only one-third of the university slots are open to women. *See* WuDunn, *supra* note 60.

85. A woman who graduated from a well-respected university with an economics degree is teaching aerobics because she could not get employment in her field. *Id.*

86. Mao sought to eliminate class distinction and encourage equality though "socialist androgyny." Although this program was successful, it was at the cost of personal freedoms. *See* Evans, *supra* note 26, at 227.

87. A survey of 1,197 television commercials for two days each month from August 1 to December 31, 1991, showed that 33.7 percent were gender-biased, showing women as helpless without men, insatiable shoppers, and constantly worrying about their hair and makeup. Of 957 characters, 54 percent were female and of those, 87 percent were young, attractive females. *See* Xiong Lei, *China—Media: T.V. Ads Depict Women as Helpless and Weak*, Interpress Service, Apr. 29, 1997.

88. *See* WuDunn, *supra* note 60, at 5.

89. *See* Jennifer Lin, *Women Suffering High Unemployment in China*, News and Observer, March 24, 1998, at A6.

90. Mao and the CCP considered makeup and attention to physical appearance evils of a bourgeois society. *See id.*

91. For example, at the opening banquet of the Metal Exchange, a new commodities futures exchange, fifty attractive, seductively dressed women were brought in to dance with the guests. *See* WuDunn, *supra* note 60.

92. Through the advent of technology and the pressures of China's one-child policy, a new form of infanticide has been created. Now that families can determine the sex of the fetus, female fetuses are being aborted so that families can have male children. Hospitals in Shanghai deliver, on average, 125 male babies to every 100 female babies. As in feudal China, the reasons behind infanticide are economic. Men make more than women, so families believe that wealth accumulation and ensuring economic stability during old age are better served through the birth of boys. If only one child is allowed, for some Chinese families, the need to "carry on the family name" is also an important factor. Although Chinese women do not change their last name to that of their husband, the children (or in most cases, the child), carry the father's name. *See* Doder, *supra* note 72. As technology allows predetermination of the child's sex prior to insemination, it will be interesting to observe China's birth statistics.

93. Given the shortage of women of marriageable age, there has been an increase in the number of women abducted for sale into marriage and prostitution. As an example of the openness and acceptance of these crimes, one report indicates that women were lined up against a wall with prices written on them. Local villagers see nothing wrong with the sale of women or feel that the husband should not be penalized if he has already paid for a wife. *See* Evans, *supra* note 26, at 168–74.

27 Still Office Flowers

Japanese Women Betrayed by the Equal Employment Opportunity Law

Kiyoko Kamio Knapp

I. INTRODUCTION

Warriors or flowers—gender role stereotypes have forced the creation of two career paths in the Japanese corporate world. Under traditional Japanese management, guaranteed lifetime employment obligated men to work at the cost of their private lives. Some of these "corporate warriors"[1] put in more than three thousand work hours per year.[2] An increase in the number of victims of *karoshi*, a Japanese word for "death from overwork," symbolizes the dark side of Japan's economic success.[3] In contrast, women serve a mere ornamental role in the labor force as *shokuba no hana*, or "office flowers."[4] After female employees spend a few years performing clerical duties with little chance of promotion, employers often expect and sometimes force women to retire upon marriage or pregnancy. Japanese society traditionally allowed marriage and motherhood as the only source of fulfillment for women. Thus, the dominant gender bias has deprived both men and women of their freedom of choice; it has pushed men to climb up the corporate ladder while forcing women to stay away from it.

Recent social changes, such as a gradual collapse of lifetime employment and an anticipated labor shortage, have pressed Japan to evaluate critically its own management style. In particular, the increasing job mobility among men contradicts the norm that male workers alone exhibit corporate loyalty; this reality has bolstered the argument against reserving managerial positions for men. This all-or-nothing "warriors or flowers" approach should be replaced with a more flexible attitude reflecting the diversified values among today's workers.

Reprinted by permission from 18 *Harvard Women's Law Journal* 83 (1995). © 1995 by the President and Fellows of Harvard College.

Traditionally, Japanese men have perceived women's entry into the professional world as a threat. However, a sincere attempt to integrate more women into the core labor force will likely benefit men as well; women's participation will reduce the workload of men and allow them to gain satisfaction and fresh perspectives in their personal lives. The attainment of gender equality should also increase both efficiency and productivity in the Japanese labor force.

This chapter explores the most important source of legislative protection for equality in the Japanese workplace: the Equal Employment Opportunity Law (EEOL), enacted in 1985.[5] The EEOL emerged as more women began to protest discrimination during the United Nations Decade for Women (1976–85).[6]

On the whole, the EEOL has remained too weak to fight the gender bias deeply rooted in Japanese society. Considering the weak enforcement mechanisms of the law, one scholar describes the EEOL as an "heirloom sword that is no more than an ornament or a prestige symbol used to make Japan appear respectable in Western eyes."[7] The divergence of law and practice, which often occurs in Japan, is especially true of the law's application to women.

This chapter describes gender-based employment discrimination in Japan and discusses the failure of the EEOL to produce attitudinal changes in management. Section 2 illustrates common forms of gender discrimination, characteristics of Japanese employment, and social factors leading to the enactment of the EEOL. Section 3 discusses various laws concerning women's rights and the Japanese attitude toward litigation. Section 4 describes the basic principles embodied in the EEOL, and section 5 evaluates the effectiveness of the law. Finally, section 6 proposes amendments to the EEOL with an emphasis on challenging the societal bias inherent in the law.

II. WOMEN IN THE JAPANESE MARKETPLACE

A. GENDER-BASED EMPLOYMENT DISCRIMINATION

Japanese employers continue to push women aside to auxiliary positions in the labor force. As "office flowers" many women perform supplementary duties as men's assistants. Common forms of discrimination against women include the following: (1) hiring based on women's age, physical appearance, and ability to commute from their parents' homes; (2) assigning women to short-term, supplementary chores; (3) paying women lower wages; (4) limiting fringe benefits; (5) restricting promotions; and (6) requiring retirement upon marriage.[8]

Many Japanese companies have adopted gender-differentiated hiring practices, thereby excluding women from the initial stage of employment. While employers actively seek male university graduates, they recruit women mainly from high school and two-year colleges. This practice reflects a stereotype: less-educated women are more willing to perform menial tasks at lower wages.[9] In fact, intelligence or self-confidence may impair women's ability to perform their primary duty in the office: to maintain a pleasant manner and reduce tension in the harsh corporate world.

Seeking women for a decorative role at work, many employers use "blatantly biased hiring standards."[10] Many require that their female employees live with their parents because of their bias against "undisciplined" women without parental authority.[11] Some large trading and securities firms and banks hire women partly for their physical appearance.[12] This practice has motivated some women to turn to cosmetic surgery to enhance their career opportunities.[13]

Once hired, women receive training in various areas, ranging from telephone etiquette to tea service. Women are then assigned to pour tea, wipe off desks, clean ashtrays, water plants, and make copies.[14] Some employers expect women to retire upon marriage, pregnancy, or childbirth. In the past, women were forced to sign an agreement to resign either upon marriage or by a certain age. Employers have long justified this unfair treatment on the ground that women lack a serious commitment to work.[15] They regard women's view of work as a mere temporary stage before achieving their ultimate goal: to become a *ryosai-kenbo* (good wife and wise mother).[16] Such a stereotype has remained dominant in the Japanese corporate culture, despite a growing number of female career aspirants.

B. TRADITIONAL BUSINESS MANAGEMENT IN JAPAN

The unique nature of Japanese employment, most notably lifetime employment, profoundly affects the treatment of working women. Major firms hire fresh male graduates annually, train them to value corporate loyalty, and retain them until mandatory retirement at age sixty.[17] Wages rise according to length of service. Benefits include housing, transportation, meals, and vacation facilities. Termination occurs only under extraordinary circumstances, such as serious breaches of ethics.[18] The guarantee of job security, however, requires complete loyalty and commitment from employees in return. Men are obliged to put in extensive work hours, as much as one hundred hours of overtime monthly.[19] Harsh working conditions often dictate that men have full-time housewives totally responsible for household affairs. In other words, two groups of women support corporate warriors in Japan: assistants at work and wives at home. The enforcement of these gender role stereotypes has played a role in Japan's postwar economic performance by facilitating men's exacting work schedules.

Marriage, on the other hand, only increases responsibilities for working women. Among working couples, wives spend an average of three hours and thirty-one minutes daily on domestic chores and child care; in contrast, husbands spend an average of eight minutes.[20] Inevitably, most women fail to exhibit the high degree of loyalty to work expected of men. Thus, as a "policy of risk minimization," the companies refuse to invest in women.

C. TRANSITIONS IN THE WOMEN'S WORKFORCE

Despite continued discrimination, women are becoming more active in the Japanese labor force. Ministry of Labor statistics show a steady increase in the number of working women in Japan.[21] Increases in women's employment have resulted from a variety of social factors: an improved life expectancy; a decline in the fertility rate; reduced time spent on domestic chores; and higher academic credentials combined with women's greater self-awareness.[22] Perhaps most important, more women are now entering universities.

Opportunities for women have increased notably in the public sector. Some governmental positions, once reserved for men, began accepting female applicants in the late 1970s. These positions ranged from the controllers for the Transport Ministry to an "elite officer training course" in the National Defense Academy.[23] Other new career paths included national tax collectors, Imperial Palace guards, immigration officers, and prison officials. This increase in the influence of women in the workplace has served as a catalyst for gender equality.

III. GENDER EQUALITY IN JAPANESE LAW

A. SOURCES OF LEGAL PROTECTIONS FOR WORKING WOMEN

To understand the historical background of the EEOL, one must understand the legislative protections available for women before the passage of the law and how judges interpreted them in discrimination suits. Judges' weak enforcement of gender equality necessitated the implementation of a more comprehensive antidiscrimination law. Furthermore, the 1990 enactment of the Child Care Leave Law exemplifies how the Japanese government has responded to the changing pattern of the labor force.

1. Constitution

The present Japanese Constitution was adopted in 1946 under General Douglas MacArthur's influence after World War II. Article 14, also known as the Equal Rights Amendment, guarantees gender equality as follows: "All of the people are equal under the law and there shall be no discrimination in political, economic or social relations because of race, creed, sex, social status or family origin."[24] The following provisions also provide for equality: Article 13 (an individual's right to life, liberty, and the pursuit of happiness); Article 27 (all people's right to work); Article 24 (marriage based on mutual consent); and Article 26 (all people's right to an equal education).

Under both legal theory and court decisions, plaintiffs can invoke Article 14 only indirectly through private employment contracts.[25] In the public sector, however, courts can apply the provision directly, because the Government Official Act and the Local Government Official Act mandate gender equality with regard to all working conditions.[26] This constitutional guarantee has helped enhance women's status in the public sector. Nevertheless, observers describe the persistence of discrimination in the public sector.[27]

Judges have construed Article 14 of the Constitution as a "prohibition of unjustifiable discrimination, rather than a guarantee of absolute equality."[28] Thus, the Equal Rights Amendment has achieved little toward promoting gender equality in Japan.

2. Labor Standards Law

The Labor Standards Law (LSL) provides general guidelines regarding labor contracts, wages, work hours, safety, and health and accident compensation.[29] Article 4 of the LSL states, "An employer shall not engage in discriminatory treatment of a woman as compared with a man with respect to wages by reason of the worker being a woman."[30] Article 4 guarantees gender equality only with respect to wage differences. Court decisions suggest that the provision refers to "equal pay for equal work."[31] The guarantee of equal pay, however, remains irrelevant to many women workers who perform lower-level work in the first place.[32] As a basic principle, the LSL applies only to existing employment contracts and not to discrimination in recruitment and hiring.

3. Civil Code

Judges have often applied Article 90 of the Civil Code in discrimination cases, especially those involving mandatory retirement upon marriage or pregnancy. The article reads, "A juristic act which has for its object such matters as are contrary to public policy or good morals is null and void."[33] Furthermore, Article 1 indicates that the Civil Code is to be "construed from the standpoint of the dignity of individuals and the essential equality of the sexes."[34]

The Civil Code provisions apply to "any collective agreement, work rule, or individual labor contract."[35] Thus, using Article 90 provides a way around the indirect applicability of the Constitution to private employment contracts. Another advantage of Article 90 lies in its flexibility; with its broad language, the provision is applicable in a wide range of discrimination cases. On the other hand, some argue that this flexibility tends to give the court too much discretion.[36] The outcome of a case under Article 90 remains unpredictable because the standard for determining the reasonableness of the employer's conduct lies within the discretion of each judge. Moreover, because according to courts, only overt acts violate public policy, women may not use Article 90 to challenge subtle forms of discrimination, "as in job assignments and promotions, where policies may not be announced explicitly."[37]

The failure of the Civil Code, as a whole, to specify appropriate standards has provoked criticism. One scholar states that "[t]he formal neutrality of the Civil Code has done practically nothing to enhance equality between men and women."[38]

4. Child Care Leave Law

The 1990 enactment of the Child Care Leave Law reflects the Japanese government's concern for the steady decline in the birth rate.[39] The mounting anxiety of a severe labor shortage created the need to assist working parents. The Child Care Leave Law, which became effective in 1992, "grants a 'parent' (not just a 'mother') a decrease in working hours or up to a year's unpaid leave of absence to take care of a child under one year old."[40] This provision is a marked contrast to the prior Child Care Leave Law, adopted in 1975, which "(applied) only to female teachers and nurses in the public sector."[41] Critics, however, have challenged the practical application of such a seemingly liberal provision. Gender role stereotypes are most likely to dictate that only women benefit from child care leave.

B. THE JAPANESE ATTITUDE TOWARD LITIGATION

A basic understanding of the Japanese attitude toward law and litigation brings to light the cultural framework within which the Japanese government enacted the EEOL and partially explains the limits of litigation as a reform tool. The Japanese tend to share an aversion to law and conceive of litigation as a threat to society.[42] Instead of a formal legal order, the Japanese have "relied on indirect rule, local autonomy, vicarious liability, and shared responsibility."[43] Scholars assert that Confucian and Buddhist teachings have influenced the Japanese view of law and litigation.[44] Confucianism teaches the absoluteness of the hierarchical order of a society and sees "willing obedience [as] the principal human virtue."[45] On the other hand, Buddhism embraces submission to fate as "the source of all true happiness."[46] In addition, the spirit of *wa* (harmony) characterizes Japanese behavior: people strive to maintain harmony among themselves, even to the detriment of self-interest. Because an employee's community is defined by her company, she risks disrupting harmony by confronting her superiors. Japanese society views legal battle against one's own employer as a "radical, threatening act to fellow employees as well as to management."[47] Tatsuo Inoue observes that the "primacy of group loyalty" has resulted in "a weak commitment to such universal principles as human rights, justice, and fairness—principles that theoretically do not discriminate between insiders and outsiders."[48]

The embarrassment and humiliation that accompany litigation often discourage potential litigants. These consequences discourage women from going forward with their claims and instead force them to internalize their grievances. The Westernization of Japanese society may heighten people's awareness of individual legal rights, and discrimination suits may thereby slowly gain social approval.[49] Nevertheless, a strong cultural preference for informal dispute resolution will likely remain in force.

IV. THE EEOL AND ITS LIMITED EFFECT

A. OVERVIEW OF THE EEOL

The Diet enacted the EEOL on May 17, 1985, and it became effective on April 1, 1986.[50] The law proclaims that its goal is to assist women in harmonizing career and family.[51] The EEOL provides standards for treatment of women workers in the following five categories: (1) recruitment and hiring; (2) assignment and promotion; (3) vocational training; (4) fringe benefits; and (5) compulsory retirement age, resignation, and dismissal. Discrimination in the last three categories (Articles 9–11) is explicitly prohibited. In contrast, there is a mere "duty to endeavor" not to discriminate in the first two categories (Articles 7 and 8). The law provides no private cause of action. Moreover, lack of sanctions, a common feature of Japanese law, renders compliance with the EEOL entirely voluntary. For dispute resolution, the EEOL prescribes three steps: (1) in-house settlements; (2) resolution with assistance from the prefectural Women's and Young Workers' Office; and (3) mediation by the Equal Opportunity Mediation Commission.

B. OVERALL EFFECTS OF THE EEOL

More than a decade has passed since the passage of the much debated law. Today many observers, most notably Japanese women themselves, claim that the EEOL has failed to achieve its stated goal.[52] As a positive effect of the EEOL, some advocates point to a decrease in discriminatory language, such as "men only" and "women only" designations in help-wanted advertisements.[53] On the negative side, many women still serve only an auxiliary function in the office. Some employers still impose mandatory retirement upon marriage. Although the court held in 1966 that such mandatory retirement violates good public order, this practice continues more than three decades later. The current Japanese recession has greatly restricted employment opportunities for female university graduates as well.[54]

V. EVALUATION OF THE EEOL

A. "DUTY TO ENDEAVOR" PROVISIONS

Among the five employment categories under the EEOL, the first two (recruitment and hiring and job assignment) state that employers have the "duty to endeavor" to provide equal opportunity. Articles 7 and 8 read as follows:

> Article 7. With regard to the recruitment and hiring of workers, employers shall endeavor to provide women equal opportunity with men.
> Article 8. With regard to the assignment and promotion of workers, employers shall endeavor to treat women equally with men.[55]

These two categories have a lower standard than the other three categories, which explicitly prohibit discrimination. The use of the word "endeavor" in Articles 7 and 8 encourages a flexible approach based on the conditions of each workplace. Lack of objective standards, however, hinders the process of evaluating the treatment of women. The ambiguity of the "endeavor" provisions has allowed employers to justify continued discrimination. Employers who lack the sincere intent to comply with the EEOL have easily found ways around Articles 7 and 8. Combined with lack of sanctions, the "endeavor" provisions remain too ineffective to regulate employers' acts.

The conspicuous absence of prohibitory language has received criticism from various sources. On December 17, 1996, the Ministry of Labor announced its plan to replace the "duty to endeavor" provisions with prohibitory language. The ministry submitted the report documenting proposed amendments to the Diet in 1997, and the amended law will go into effect on April 1, 1999.[56] It remains to be seen how these amendments will help eliminate discrimination.

B. EXCLUSION OF MEN

By protecting women only, the EEOL fails to address any discriminatory practices against men. The EEOL completely disregards the possibility that men may be placed in a disadvantageous position because of their gender. In other words, the EEOL, which could help women become construction workers or investment bankers, remains entirely powerless to help men become nurses or flight attendants. This one-sidedness has harmful implications for women as well. In her article on the inattention to oppression of men, Nancy Levit emphasizes that "any discrimination against men may ultimately result in harm to women."[57] Similarly, Deborah A. Calloway argues that "[e]quality in one dimension means inequality in another dimension."[58] The EEOL's wholesale exclusion of men works to perpetuate a prevailing norm that nurturing roles are properly reserved for women.

C. DISPUTE RESOLUTION THROUGH
ADMINISTRATIVE GUIDANCE

The EEOL provides neither private causes of action nor criminal sanctions. For dispute resolution, the Ministry of Labor empowers the Women's and Young Workers' Office or upon their referral, the Equal Opportunity Mediation Commission to conduct administrative guidance for the parties. In the context of the minimal role that litigation plays in Japan, the law's exclusion of private causes of action may be a peripheral issue. From a woman's perspective, however, it is desirable to obtain the right to seek redress in court as an alternative. The possibility of a lawsuit could lead to more efficient dispute resolution by providing a reason to settle. Nonetheless, even if the right to litigate were granted, it would be unlikely to trigger a notable increase in discrimination suits. To avoid the adversarial nature of lawsuits, most Japanese would still choose negotiations or consultations. Additionally, two major obstacles inherent in the Japanese judicial system would discourage many potential litigants: the prolonged nature of trials and the substantial legal fees.[59] A lack of reliable information makes an evaluation of the effectiveness of administrative guidance difficult. The Ministry of Labor does not disclose detailed explanations of the procedure used by the office in providing advice, guidance, and recommendations.

D. TWO-TRACK HIRING POLICY

The enactment of the EEOL encouraged many employers, particularly banks and large firms, to adopt a new personnel policy, known as a two-track hiring system.[60] This system enables women to apply for either the *sogo-shoku* (management track) or *ippan-shoku* (standard/general track). Before the passage of the EEOL, the management track was essentially reserved for men. Most women remained on the standard track with no prospects for switching to the other. Under the new two-track system, the management track accepts a few women based on their qualifications and their willingness to accept transfers, including overseas assignments. The management track includes duties related to planning, development, and negotiations. On the other hand, the standard track involves traditional duties of women: copying, serving tea, and clerical work. The two tracks also differ in terms of wages, promotion, vocational training, and fringe benefits. For instance, a thirty-year-old woman on the management track at a bank receives 8.5 million yen a year (about $85,000); another on the standard track receives four million yen (about $40,000) a year.[61]

VI. POSSIBLE AMENDMENTS TO THE EEOL

Amending the EEOL will become crucial as Japan prepares for an acute labor shortage. The declining birthrate and the rapidly aging population will profoundly affect the Japanese labor force in the near future.[62]

A. ELIMINATION OF ONE-SIDEDNESS

Numerous scholars have criticized the EEOL's failure to enhance working women's status; in contrast, critics have given little attention to the law's silence on equal treatment of men. The lack of protection for both genders merits reevaluation, especially in light of a growing trend among young Japanese men: Outside the corporate world, Japanese men are now entering into a broader array of occupations, including traditionally female arenas. The November 1994 issue of *Nikkei Woman*, a monthly magazine for working women in Japan, featured an article on some of these men, who had chosen jobs as a dog groomer, a nurse, a nurse's aid, and a kindergarten teacher.[63] Entitled "Onna no Shigoto-ni Tsuku Otoko-tachi" ("Men Who Enter Women's Fields"), this article conveys a powerful message: More men are now refusing to choose the path to corporate success simply to fulfill their culturally expected role as breadwinners. The gradual shift in men's labor consciousness will necessitate the expansion of the EEOL to protect both genders. The dominant gender bias has deprived men, as well as women, of their right to be treated as individuals with varied career aspirations. Full attainment of equality would be possible only if both men and women gain equal access to employment.

B. IMPROVEMENT OF ADMINISTRATIVE GUIDANCE

The EEOL should prescribe a more effective means of dispute resolution, requiring a thorough investigation by the Women's and Young Workers' Office. Next, the Women's and Young Workers' Office must be able to refer cases to the Equal Opportunity Mediation Commission without significant procedural restrictions such as the requirement of consent by both the woman and her employer. Last, the Ministry of Labor should publish a more detailed and fact-specific annual report on the involvement of the Women's and Young Workers' Office. The new report should include statistics detailing the actual number of cases handled by each prefectural office, the number of cases in each of the five employment categories under the EEOL, and the overall results of these cases. Moreover, the report should contain any specific guidelines the ministry has developed for the Women's and Young Workers' Office to use in resolving disputes.

C. AN ALTERNATIVE APPROACH TO THE TWO-TRACK SYSTEM

The Ministry of Labor has recognized various problems with the two-track system. To consider an alternative approach to the current two-track system, one must first challenge the stereotypes inherent in the creation of this system. Employers should ask themselves: how can women prove their aspirations and capabilities when they are denied entry into the professional world in the first place? Likewise, employers should question the stereotype about men's attitudes toward work. Asked why the standard track purports to accept women only, Shun Arakawa, the director of the Japanese Management Federation, simply replied, "No men would choose that track."[64] Contrary to his assertion, an increasing number of men are hoping to free themselves from the constraints and stress inherent in the core labor force. Regardless of their individual desires, however, Japanese management invariably subjects men to the rigor of the corporate life. In this respect, men become victims of reverse discrimination through the two-track system.

Last, the Ministry of Labor should evaluate the two-track system in light of the most critical issue facing the Japanese labor market today: excessive work hours, a target of mounting international criticism. In recent years, *karoshi*, death from overwork, has emerged as a serious social problem. Some women are now beginning to question the way professionals have sacrificed their private lives to build their careers. Most younger women reject such a lifestyle in which work and family remain mutually exclusive.[65] A change in men's labor consciousness should become an essential step toward eliminating gender discrimination. Warriors or flowers—it is time for men and women to make a joint effort to abandon these two paths and to create a new workplace based on respect for diversity.

VII. CONCLUSION

Not only has the EEOL failed to eliminate the gap between gender-based career paths, it has yet to narrow it. Many superficial efforts have been made in the name of equality. Some employers have struck down the phrase "men only" in their help-wanted advertisements. Some have opened managerial positions to a few women by giving them inflated titles. These acts, often unsupported by genuine intent, do not amount to a meaningful step toward equal opportunity. The EEOL has allowed employers to modify the surface of their traditional personnel policies, while continuing to exploit women. Passed under both domestic and international pressure, the EEOL may be best described as a mere ornament embodying equality as an idealistic doctrine inapplicable to real life.

One scholar argues that the noncoercive nature of the EEOL can bring a lasting change in Japan through the patience of evolution.[66] On the other hand, another argues that a more forceful approach would benefit Japanese women, while no law can completely transform traditional patriarchy.[67] Given the severity and pervasiveness of gender bias in Japanese society, use of some force is necessary. Stronger enforcement mechanisms will be one important step to heighten societal awareness of equality. The Ministry of Labor should enforce the EEOL more vigorously by extending the law's protection to men as well; actively involving the Women's and Young Workers' Office in dispute resolution, by requiring full disclosure of information; and adopting a more flexible hiring system that would enable employees, irrespective of gender, to combine family and career. Harmonizing work life with family life should be a true goal for both men and women.

NOTES

1. "Corporate warrior" is a term often used to describe a Japanese businessman. Tatsuo Inoue, *The Poverty of Rights-Blind Communality: Looking through the Window of Japan*, 1993 B.Y.U. L. Rev. 517, 528 (1993) (illustrating how Japanese workers devote themselves to work). The "spirit" of corporate warriors manifests elements such as "stamina, intestinal fortitude, and dogged loyalty." Takada Masatoshi, *Woman and Man in Modern Japan*, 16 Japan Echo 39, 42 (1989).

2. A major newspaper in Japan reports that one out of every six Japanese employees works more than three thousand hours annually. *Karoshi Nintei Kanwa-o* [Death from Overwork: The Need to Relax the Standard of Proof], Asahi Shimbun [Asahi News], Jan. 7, 1994, at 4.

3. Kawahito Hiroshi, *Death and the Corporate Warrior*, 37 Japan Q. 149, 150–51 (1991) (citing National Defense Counsel for Victims of Karoshi, When the Corporate Warrior Dies

8 (1990)). Kawahito, secretary general of the National Defense Council for Victims of Karoshi, estimates that more than ten thousand Japanese workers become victims of *karoshi* every year. He further notes that this figure equals the number of traffic fatalities in one year. Many die from subarachnoidal hemorrhage, heart failure, cerebral hemorrhage, or myocardial infarction. *Id.*

4. William H. Lash III, *Unwelcome Imports: Racism, Sexism, and Foreign Investment*, 13 Mich. J. Int'l L. 1, 21 (1991); Catherine W. Brown, *Japanese Approaches to Equal Rights for Women: The Legal Framework*, 12 Law in Japan: An Annual 29, 30 (1979) (citing James Abegglen, Management and Worker: The Japanese Solution 45 (1973)).

5. The official title of the law is Koyo no Bunya ni Okeru Danjo no Kinto na Kikai Oyobi Taigu no Kakuho nado Joshi Rodosha no Fukushi no Zoshin ni Kansuru Horitsu [Law Respecting the Improvement of the Welfare of Women Workers, Including the Guarantee of Equal Opportunity and Treatment between Men and Women in Employment][hereinafter EEOL]. The law was passed on May 17, 1985, and went into effect on April 1, 1986.

6. World Conference of the International Women's Year, G.A. Res. 3520, U.N. GAOR, 30th Sess., 2441st plen. mtg., Supp. No. 34, at 95, U.N. Doc. A/10034 (1975).

7. Jan M. Bergeson and Kaoru Yamamoto Oba, *Japan's New Equal Employment Opportunity Law: Real Weapon or Heirloom Sword?*, 1986 B.Y.U. L. Rev. 865. *See also* John O. Haley, *Sheathing the Sword of Justice in Japan: An Essay on Law without Sanctions*, 8 J. Japanese Stud. 265 (1982).

8. Nancy Patterson, *No More Naki-Neiri? The State of Japanese Sexual Harassment Law*, 34 Harv. Int'l L.J. 206, 207–11 (1993); Alice H. Cook and Hiroko Hayashi, Working Women in Japan: Discrimination, Resistance, and Reform (1980).

9. Robert J. Smith, *Gender Inequality in Contemporary Japan,* 13 J. Japanese Stud. 1, 14 (1987).

10. Lash, *supra* note 4, at 20–21.

11. "A single woman who does not live with her parents is regarded as morally suspect." *Japanese Women: A World Apart*, Economist, May 14, 1988, at 19.

12. *See* Leslie Helm, *Women Fight Stereotypes*, Daily Yomiuri, July 3, 1993, at 10(a).

13. An unemployment rate increased by a prolonged recession has motivated even more job seekers to have cosmetic surgery: "At Jujin, probably Japan's oldest and largest hospital for cosmetic surgery, officials report a noticeable increase in the number of young [female] university students coming in for operations—a trend comparable to one the hospital noted after a recession in 1982." Helm, *supra* note 12.

14. Many employers consider it simply wasteful to place women in managerial positions. They especially view serving tea as an "established practice" for women, including university graduates. Takeuchi Hiroshi, *Working Women in Business Corporations,* 34 Japan Q. 320 (1982).

15. *See* Cook and Hayashi, *supra* note 8, at 28.

16. *See* Takeuchi, *supra* note 14, at 321.

17. *See* Kokusei-Sha, Nippon: A Chartered Survey of Japan 52–66 (Tsuneta Yano Memorial Society ed., 1989) (discussing general aspects of Japanese employment).

18. Japan: A Country Study 217 (Ronald E. Dolan and Robert L. Worden eds., 5th ed. 1992).

19. Japan Travel Bureau, Salarymen in Japan 26 (1986).

20. Nihon Keizai Shimbun-Sha [Japan Economic Journal], Josei-Tachi Wa Ima: Yureru Kintoho Sedai [Women Today: A Shaken EEOL Generation] 203 (1992).

21. Rodo-Sho: Fujin-Kyoku [Ministry of Labor: Bureau of Women's Affairs], Sei Ni Torawarezu Ikiiki To Kuraseru Jidai O Kizuko-o [Let Us Build a Society Free from Gender Role Stereotypes] 5 (1994) [hereinafter Women's Bureau].

22. Tadashi Hanami, Danjo Koyo Byodo No Shin-Jidai [New Era for Equal Employment] 200 (1989).

23. Japan Information Center, *Women to Be Admitted to Japan's Defense Academy,* 36 Japan Rep. 8 (1990).

24. KENPO [Constitution] art. 14 (Japan).

25. Hiroko Hayashi, *Japan, in* Women Workers in Fifteen Countries: Essays in Honor of Alice Hansen Cook 60 (1985).

26. *Id.*

27. Masako Kamiya, *Women in Japan,* 20 U.B.C. L. Rev. 447, 454 (1986). Kamiya states that "more than one third of municipal bodies discriminate against female job applicants even though (or perhaps because) women perform better than men on recruiting examinations." *Id.*

28. Kodansha, Kodansha Encyclopedia of Japan 230 (1983) (citing Judgment of May 27, 1964, Saikosai [Supreme Court], 18 Minshu 676 (Japan)).

29. Rodo Kijun Ho [Labor Standards Law], Law No. 49 (1947).

30. *Id.* art. 4.

31. *See* Cook and Hayashi, *supra* note 8, at 38.

32. *See* Linda Edwards, *Equal Employment Opportunity in Japan: A View from the West,* 41 Indus. and Lab. Rel. Rev. 240 (1988).

33. MINPO [Civil Code], art. 90, Law No. 89 of 1896 and Law No. 9 of 1898.

34. *Id.* art. 1.

35. Cook and Hayashi, *supra* note 8, at 48.

36. *See* Bergeson and Oba, *supra* note 7, at 871.

37. Brown, *supra* note 4, at 34.

38. Kamiya, *supra* note 27, at 455.

39. In 1992, the birthrate averaged 1.5 children per woman. Women's Bureau, *supra* note 21, at 8. It was 3.55 in 1950 and 2.0 in 1960.

40. Satomi Ban, *Fast Track,* 37 Look Japan 36 (1991).

41. Omori Maki, *Gender and the Labor Market,* 19 J. Japanese Stud. 79, 98–99 (1993).

42. Yoshiyuki Noda, Introduction to Japanese Law 14 (A. Angelo trans., 1976).

43. Robert J. Smith, *Lawyers, Litigiousness, and the Law in Japan,* 11 Cornell L.F. 53, 54 (1985). A low rate of litigation results in a small number of lawyers (16,000). The United States has seventeen times more lawyers per capita than Japan. The pass rate of the Japanese bar examination remains at less than 2 percent. Despite the small number of qualified lawyers, many "quasi-lawyers," such as those employed by corporate legal departments, perform legal tasks (e.g., drafting contracts); Donald L. Uchtmann et al., *The Developing Japanese Legal System: Growth and Change in the Modern Era,* 23 Gonz. L. Rev. 349, 357–58 (1988).

44. Noda, *supra* note 42, at 173.

45. *Id.*

46. *Id.*

47. Frank Upham, Law and Social Change in Postwar Japan 140 (1987).

48. Inoue, *supra* note 1, at 527.

49. The following case may be used as one example of heightened legal awareness among

Japanese women. This ten-year legal battle, which ended in 1990, became a focus of national attention. Eighteen women workers sued their employer, the Social Welfare Medical Treatment Compensation Fund, for its gender-based denial of promotion. For ten years, the plaintiffs vigorously protested discrimination at numerous meetings. They collected nearly 290,000 signatures in support of their claims. In 1990 the Tokyo District Court found for the plaintiffs, awarding them 124 million yen in total. Given societal pressure against litigants in Japan, the fact that these female plaintiffs persisted and finally prevailed after ten years of litigation is noteworthy. For a fuller discussion of this case and current issues on women's rights in Japan, see Lash, *supra* note 4, at 23. More recently, victory in another suit initiated by a woman captured national attention. In April 1992 a plaintiff won the nation's first "hostile environment" sexual harassment case in the Fukuoka District Court. Plaintiff, who worked for a publishing company, asserted that her editor had spread rumors about her private life. The court decision urged many employers to implement sexual harassment policies to prevent potential claims. In describing this case and its impact on Japanese society, Patterson concludes that the decision represents an important step for women's rights in Japan. *See generally* Patterson, *supra* note 8.

50. Loraine Parkinson, *Japan's Equal Employment Opportunity Law: An Alternative Approach to Social Change*, 89 Colum. L. Rev. 604, 606 (1989) (citing Rodo-Sho Fujin-Kyoku [Ministry of Labor Bureau of Women's Affairs], Shinpan Danjo Koyo Kikai Kintoho-Kaisei Rodo Kijunho No Jitsumu Kaisetsu [Explanation of Procedures Required by the Equal Employment Opportunity Law and Labor Standards Law as Amended] 25–26 (1986)).

51. The law aims to achieve the following three primary goals: (1) to promote equal opportunity and treatment between men and women in employment in accordance with the principle contained in the Constitution of ensuring equality under the law; (2) to foster measures for women workers, including the development and improvement of their vocational abilities, the provision of assistance for their reemployment, and efforts to harmonize their working life with family life; and (3) thereby to further the welfare and improve the status of women workers. EEOL, *supra* note 5, art. 1.

52. "A Letter from Japanese Women" Circle, Counter-Report to the Japanese Government's Second Periodic Report as a State Party to the Convention on the Elimination of All Forms of Discrimination against Women (July 9, 1992) (1994) [hereinafter Women's Circle].

53. *See* Parkinson, *supra* note 50, at 645.

54. *See Syusyoku Zensen Dosha-buri de Tairyo Joshi Gakusei-no Mushoku-Tosei* [Raining Cats and Dogs for Female Students: Grim Career Prospects and Unemployment], Sh-Unkan Shinch-O [Weekly Shinch-O], Dec. 2, 1993, at 138–42.

55. EEOL, *supra* note 5, arts. 7–8.

56. Ministry of Labor, Kintoho-Ga Kawarimasu [The EEOL Will Change] 18–24 (1998).

57. Nancy Levit, *Feminism for Men: Legal Ideology and the Construction of Maleness*, 43 UCLA L. Rev. 1037, 1052 (1996)(stating that both men and women can be victimized by gender role stereotypes).

58. Deborah A. Calloway, *Dealing with Diversity: Changing Theories of Discrimination*, 10 St. John's Legal Comment. 481, 491 (1995).

59. *See* Women's Circle, *supra* note 52, at 45 (discussing why there are still few discrimination suits in Japan).

60. *See* Sugeno Kazuo, Japanese Labor Law 129, 132 (Leo Kanowitz trans., 1992).

61. Teichaku Suruka, *Josei Sogo-shoku* [Women's Management Track: Is It Going to Take

Root?], Asahi Shimbun [Asahi News], July 1, 1993, at 13 [hereinafter Women's Management Track].

62. As of 1991, the life expectancy was 76.11 years for men and 82.11 years for women, both the highest in the world. In June 1990 the Ministry of Labor raised the minimum retirement age from fifty-five to sixty. Employers may rehire workers over sixty on a commissioned basis. The ministry said in its report, "The Japanese economy must adapt to include elderly, experienced workers." Akwi Seo, *Work Keeps Them Healthy*, 37 Look Japan 12 (1991).

63. *Onna-no Shigoto-ni Tsuku Otoko-tachi* [Men Who Enter Women's Fields], Nikkei Woman, Nov. 1994, at 138–43.

64. Women's Management Track, *supra* note 61, at 13.

65. *See* Takada, *supra* note 1, at 41.

66. *See* Parkinson, *supra* note 50, at 661.

67. M. Diana Helweg, *Japan's Equal Employment Opportunity Act: A Five-Year Look at Its Effectiveness*, 9 B.U. Int'l L.J. 293, 320 (1991).

Selected Bibliography

The sources listed here constitute a significant number of relevant materials on the global legal status of women of color published in English since 1980.

Abu-Odeh, Lama. *Comparatively Speaking: The "Honor" of the "East" and the "Passions" of the West,* 1997 Utah L. Rev. 287.

————. *Post-Colonial Feminism and the Veil: Considering the Differences,* 26 New Eng. L. Rev. 1527 (1992).

Afkhami, Mahnaz. Faith and Freedom: Women's Human Rights in the Middle East (1995).

Agarwal, Bina. A Field of One's Own: Gender and Land Rights in South Asia (1994).

Agimba, Christine, Florence Butegwa, Grace Osakue, and Sydia Nduna. Legal Rights Awareness among Women in Africa (1994).

al-Hibri, Azizah. *Islam, Law and Custom: Redefining Muslim Women's Rights,* 12 Am. U. J. Int'l L. and Pol'y 1 (1997).

Ali, Shaheen Sardar. A Comparative Study of the United Nations Convention on the Elimination of All Forms of Discrimination against Women, Islamic Law and the Laws of Pakistan (1995).

Amin, Sajeda, and Sara Hossain. *Religious and Cultural Rights: Women's Reproductive Rights and the Politics of Fundamentalism: A View from Bangladesh,* 44 Am. U. L. Rev. 1319 (1995).

Andrews, Penelope. *Aboriginal Women and Human Rights: A Survey, in* Women's International Human Rights (Kelly Askin and Dorean Koenig eds., 1998).

————. *Affirmative Action in South Africa: Some Theoretical and Practical Issues, in* The Constitution of South Africa from a Gender Perspective 49 (Sandra Liebenberg ed., 1995).

————. *Not White Enough, Not Black Enough: The Twilight World of Half-Caste Women in Australia, in* Women and Notions of Property: An Anthology of Interdisciplinary Readings (Patricia Williams ed., 1998).

————. *Spectators at the Revolution: Gender Equality and Customary Law in a Post-Apartheid South Africa,* 7 Law and Anthropology 261 (1994).

Andrews, Penelope. *Striking the Rock: Confronting Gender Equality in South Africa*, 3 Mich. J. Race and L. 308 (1998).

———. *Uhuru at Last! Now What about the Women: Women and Rights in the New South Africa*, *in* The South African Constitution and the Enforcement of Rights (Penelope Andrews and Stephen Ellman eds., 1998).

———. *Violence against Aboriginal Women in Australia: Possibilities for Redress within the International Human Rights Framework*, 60 Alb. L. Rev. 917 (1997).

An-Na'im, Abdullahi Ahmed A. *Human Rights in the Muslim World: Socio-Political Conditions and Scriptural Imperatives*, 3 Harv. Hum. Rts. J. 13 (1990).

———. *The Rights of Women and International Law in the Muslim Context*, 9 Whittier L. Rev. 491 (1987).

Annas, Catherine L. *Irreversible Error: The Power and Prejudice of Female Genital Mutilation*, 12 J. Contemp. Health L. and Pol'y 1325 (1996).

Armstrong, Alice K. Gender and the New South Africa Legal Order (1994).

———. *Zimbabwe: Away from the Customary Law*, 11 J. Fam. L. 339 (1987).

Armstrong, Alice K., and Welshman Ncube. Women and Law in Southern Africa (1987).

Banwell, Suzanna Stout. Law, Women's Status, and Family Planning in Sub-Saharan Africa (1993).

Barbieri, Catherine T. *Women Workers in Transition: The Potential Impact of the NAFTA Labor Side Agreements on Women Workers in Argentina and Chile*, 17 Comp. Lab. L.J. 526 (1996).

Bashir, Layli Miller. *Female Genital Mutilation in the United States: An Examination of Criminal and Asylum Law*, 4 Am. U. J. Gender and L. 415 (1996).

Boulware-Miller, Kay. *Female Circumcision: Challenges to the Practice as a Human Rights Violation*, 8 Harv. Women's L.J. 155 (1985).

Brandt, Michele, and Jeffrey A. Kaplan. *The Tension between Women's Rights and Religious Rights: Reservations to CEDAW by Egypt, Bangladesh and Tunisia*, 12 J. L. and Religion 105 (1995–96).

Brems, Eva. *Enemies or Allies? Feminism and Cultural Relativism as Dissident Voices in Human Rights Discourse*, 19 Hum. Rts. Q. 136 (1997).

Brennan, Katherine. *The Influence of Cultural Relativism on International Human Rights Law: Female Circumcision as a Case Study*, 7 Law and Ineq. J. 367 (1989).

Bryant, Taimie L. *For the Sake of the Country, for the Sake of the Family: The Oppressive Impact of Family Registration on Women in Japan*, 39 UCLA L. Rev. 109 (1991).

Burton, Eve B., and David B. Goldstein. *Vietnamese Women and Children Refugees in Hong Kong: An Argument against Arbitrary Detention*, 4 Duke J. Comp. and Int'l L. 71 (1993).

Callaway, Barbara J., and Lucy E. Creevey. The Heritage of Islam: Women, Religion, and Politics in West Africa (1994).

Carbado, Devon W. *Motherhood and Work in Cultural Context: One Woman's Patriarchal Bargain*, 21 Harv. Women's L.J. 1 (1998).

Carroll, Lucy. *Daughter's Right of Inheritance in India: A Perspective on the Problem of Dowry*, 25(4) Modern Asia Studies (1991).

———. *Law, Custom and Statutory Social Reform: The Hindu Widow's Remarriage Act of 1856, in* Women in Colonial India (J. Krishnamurty ed., 1988).

Cervenak, Christine. *Promoting Inequality: Gender Based Discrimination in UNRWA's Approach to Palestine Refugee Status*, 16 Hum. Rts. Q. 300 (1994).

Chandra, Sudhir. Enslaved Daughters: Colonialism, Law and Women's Rights (India) (1998).

Chandy, Anna. A Community in Peril: Christian Women's Struggle for Equal Inheritance Rights in Kerala (India) (1995).

Chanock, Martin L. *Neither Customary nor Legal: African Customary Law in an Era of Family Law Reform,* 3 Int'l J.L. and Family 72 (1989).

Chen, Mai. *Discrimination in New Zealand: A Personal Journey,* 23 Victoria U. Well. L. Rev. 137 (1993).

Cheng, Lucie. *Women and Class Analysis in the Chinese Land Revolution,* 4 Berkeley Women's L.J. 62 (1988).

Chigwedere, A. Lobolo: The Pros and Cons in Relation to the Emancipation of Women in Zimbabwe (1988).

Cho, Mi-Kyung. *Korea: The 1990 Family Law Reform and the Improvement of the Status of Women,* 33 U. Louisville J. Fam. L. 431 (1994–5).

Cisse, Bernadette Passade. *International Law Sources Applicable to Female Genital Mutilation: A Guide to Adjudicators of Refugee Claims Based on a Fear of Female Genital Mutilation,* 35 Colum. J. Transnat'l L. 429 (1997).

Cole, Melissa. *"Inthuthuko Means That We Are Going Forward": Hearing the Voices of Domestic Workers in South Africa,* 1 Colum. J. Gender and L. 61 (1991).

Colloquium. *International Law, Human Rights, and LatCrit Theory,* 28 U. Miami Inter-Am. L. Rev. 177 (1997).

Combrinck, Helene. *Positive State Duties to Protect Women from Violence: Recent South African Developments,* 20 Hum. Rts. Q. 666 (1998).

Cook, Alice H., and Hiroko Hayashi. Working Women in Japan: Discrimination, Resistance and Reform (1980).

Coomaraswamy, Radhika. *To Bellow Like a Cow: Women, Ethnicity and the Discourse of Rights, in* Human Rights of Women: National and International Perspectives 39 (Rebecca Cook ed., 1994).

Cossman, Brenda. *Turning the Gaze Back on Itself: Comparative Law, Feminist Legal Studies, and the Post-Colonial Project,* 1997 Utah L. Rev. 525.

Crossman, Brenda, and Ratna Kapur. *Women and Poverty in India: Law and Social Change,* 6 Canadian J. Women and L. 278 (1993).

Cotran, E. Casebook on Kenya Customary Law (1987).

Crooms, Lisa A. *Families, Fatherlessness and Women's Human Rights: An Analysis of the Clinton Administration's Public Housing Policy as a Violation of the Convention on the Elimination of All Forms of Discrimination against Women,* 36 Brandeis Fam. L.J. 1 (1997–98).

———. *Indivisible Rights and Intersectional Identities or, "What Do Women's Human Rights Have to Do with the Race Convention?",* 40 How. L.J. 619 (1997).

Culliton, Katherine M. *Legal Remedies for Domestic Violence in Chile and the United States: Cultural Relativism, Myths, and Realities,* 26 Case W. Res. J. Int'l L. 183 (1994).

Davis, Kirsten K. *Equal Protection for Women in India and Canada: An Examination and Comparison of Sex Equality Provisions in the Indian and Canadian Constitutions,* 13 Ariz. J. Int'l and Comp. L. 31 (1996).

Davison, J. Agriculture, Women and Law: The African Experience (1988).

Dengu-Zvogbo, Kebokile. Inheritance in Zimbabwe: Law, Customs, and Practice (1994).

De Silva, Rangita. Women and Violence: A Socio Legal Study (Sri Lanka) (1993).

Dow, Unity. Women, Marriage, and Inheritance (Botswana) (1994).

Dudziak, Mary. *Josephine Baker, Racial Protest and the Cold War*, 81 J. Am. Hist. 543 (1994).

Engineer, Asghar Ali. The Rights of Women in Islam (1992).

———. The Shah Bano Controversy (1987).

Engle, Karen. *Female Subject Parts of Public International Law: Human Rights and the Exotic Other Female*, 26 New Eng. L. Rev. 1509 (1992).

Figueroa, Evelyn. *Disarming Nicaraguan Women: The Other Counterrevolution*, 6 Colum. J. Gender and L. 273 (1996).

Freeman, Marsha. *Measuring Equality: An International Perspective on Women's Capacity and Constitutional Rights*, 5 Berkeley Women's L.J. 110 (1989–90).

———. *Women, Law, and Land at the Local Level: Claiming Women's Human Rights in Domestic Legal Systems*, 16 Hum. Rts. Q. 559 (1994).

Freeman, M. D. A. *Botswana: Bucking the Backlash*, 33 U. Louisville J. Fam. L. 293 (1994–95).

Friedman, Lawrence M. *The War of the Worlds: A Few Comments on Law, Culture, and Rights*, 47 Case W. Res. L. Rev.(1997).

Funder, Anna. *De Minimus Non Curat Lex: The Clitoris, Culture and the Law*, 3 Transnat'l L. and Contemp. Probs. 417 (1993).

Gana, Ruth. *Which "Self"? Race and Gender in the Right to Self Determination as a Prerequisite to the Right to Development*, 14 Wis. Int'l L.J. 133 (1995).

Ghodsi, Tamilla F. *Tying a Slipknot: Temporary Marriages in Iran*, 15 Mich. J. Int'l L. 645 (1994).

Gifford, Eugenie Anne. *The Courage to Blaspheme: Confronting Barriers to Resisting Female Genital Mutilation*, 4 UCLA Women's L.J. 329 (1994).

Gilbert, Kate. *Women and Family Law in Modern Nepal: Statutory Rights and Social Implications*, 24 N.Y.U. J. Int'l L. and Pol. 729 (1992).

Goff, Helen A. *Glass Ceilings in the Land of the Rising Sons: The Failure of Workplace Gender Discrimination Law and Policy in Japan*, 26 Law and Pol'y in Int'l Bus. 1147 (1995).

Goldberg, Vivienne. *South Africa: Private Law in Transition/The Effect of the New Constitution*, 33 U. Louisville J. Fam. L. 495 (1994–95).

Gomez, Anne M. *The New INS Guidelines on Gender Persecution: Their Effect on Asylum in the United States for Women Fleeing the Forced Sterilization and Abortion Policies of the People's Republic of China*, 21 N.C.J. Int'l L. and Comm. Reg. 621 (1996).

Goodall, Heather, and Jackie Huggins. *Aboriginal Women Are Everywhere: Contemporary Struggles, in* Gender Relations in Australia: Domination and Negotiation (Kay Saunders and Raymond Evans eds., 1992).

Gopal, Gita, and Maryam Salim. Gender and Law: Eastern Africa Speaks (1998).

Graves, Alison E. *Women in Iran: Obstacles to Human Rights and Possible Solutions*, 5 Am. U. J. Gender and L. 57 (1996).

Griffiths, Anne. *Women, Status, and Power (Botswana)*, 22 Cornell Int'l L.J. 575 (1989).

Guitron, Julian. *Mexico: A Decade of Family Law 1983–1993*, 33 U. Louisville J. Fam. L. 445 (1994–95).

Gunning, Isabelle. *Arrogant Perception, World Traveling and Multicultural Feminism: The Case of Female Genital Surgeries*, 23 Colum. Hum. Rts. L. Rev. 189 (1991–92).

———. *Uneasy Alliances and Solid Sisterhood: A Response to Professor Obiora's Bridges and Barricades*, 47 Case W. Res. L. Rev. 445 (1997).

Guyer, Jane I. Women and the State in Africa: Marriage Law, Inheritance, and Resettlement (1987).

Hahlo, H. R. The South African Law of Husband and Wife (1985).

Haroz, Audrey E. *South Africa's 1996 Choice on Termination of Pregnancy Act: Expanding Choice and International Human Rights to Black South African Women,* 30 Vand. J. Transnat'l L. 863 (1997).

Harries, Catherine. *Daughters of Our Peoples: International Feminism Meets Ugandan Law and Custom,* 25 Colum. Hum. Rts. L. Rev. 493 (1994).

Hay, Margaret Jean, and Marcia Wright. African Women and the Law: Historical Perspectives (1984).

Helton, Arthur C., and Alison Nicoll. *Female Genital Mutilation as Grounds for Asylum in the United States: The Recent Case of In re Fauziya Kasinga and Prospects for More Gender Sensitive Approaches,* 28 Colum. Hum. Rts. L. Rev. 375 (1997).

Helweg, M. Diana. *Japan's Equal Employment Opportunity Act: A Five-Year Look at Its Effectiveness,* 9 B.U. Int'l L.J. 293 (1991).

Hernández-Truyol, Berta Esperanza. *Tracing the LatIndia: Erasures, ReDiscoveries, and Re-Constructions—Claiming Our Mestizaje, a Human Rights Approach, Symposium: Critical Race Feminism: Preparing Legal Thought for the Twenty-first Century,* 3 Iowa J. Gender, Race and Just. (1999).

———. *Women in Castro's Cuba: A Myth of Equality, in* Encyclopedia of Third World Women (Nelly Stromquist ed., 1998).

Hernández-Truyol, Berta Esperanza, and Kimberly A. Johns. *Global Rights, Local Wrongs, and Legal Fixes: An International Human Rights Critique of Immigration and Welfare "Reform,"* 71 S. Cal. L. Rev. 547 (1998).

Hinz, Manfred O. *Law Reform from Within: Improving the Legal Status of Women in Northern Namibia,* 1997 J. Legal Pluralism 69.

Hirsch, Susan E. Pronouncing and Preserving: Gender and the Discourses of Disputing in an African Islamic Court (1998).

Ho, Laura, Catherine Powell, and Leti Volpp. *(Dis)Assembling Rights of Women Workers along the Global Assembly Line: Human Rights and the Garment Industry,* 31 Harv. C.R.-C.L. L. Rev. 383 (1996).

Holm, Gretelise. Women and Law in Southern Africa (1995).

Hom, Sharon. *Female Infanticide in China: The Human Rights Specter and Thoughts toward (An)other Vision,* 23 Colum. Hum. Rts. L. Rev. 249 (1992).

———. *Law, Ideology and Patriarchy in the People's Republic of China: Feminist Observations of an Ethnic Spectator,* 4 Int'l Rev. Comp. Pub. Pol'y 173 (1992).

Hom, Sharon, and Robin Paul Malloy. *China's Market Economy: A Semiosis of Cross Boundary Discourse between Law and Economics and Feminist Jurisprudence,* 45 Syr. L. Rev. 101 (1995).

Howard, Rhoda. *Women's Rights in English-Speaking Sub-Sahara Africa, in* Human Rights and Development in Africa 46 (R. I. Meltzer and C. E. Welch eds., 1984).

Human Rights in China. *Caught between Tradition and the State: Violations of the Human Rights of Chinese Women,* 17 Women's Rts. L. Rep. 285 (1996).

Human Rights Watch. Criminal Injustice: Violence against Women in Brazil (1991).

———. Discrimination in Maquiladoras (1996).

Human Rights Watch Africa Staff and Human Rights Watch Women's Rights Project Staff. South Africa: Violence against Women in South Africa: State Response to Domestic Violence and Rape (1995).

Human Rights Watch Africa Staff, Human Rights Watch Women's Rights Project Staff, and

Federation Internationale des Ligues des Droits de l'Homme Staff. Rwanda—Sexual Violence during the Rwandan Genocide and Its Aftermath: Shattered Lives (1996).

Human Rights Watch Asia Staff. India—Rape for Profit: Trafficking of Nepali Girls and Women to India's Brothels (1995).

Human Rights Watch Staff. Double Jeopardy: Police Abuse of Women in Pakistan (1992).

———. Trafficking in Burmese Women and Girls in Thailand (1993).

Human Rights Watch Women's Rights Project and Human Rights Watch Staff. The Human Rights Watch Global Report on Women's Human Rights (1995).

Hussain, S. Jaffer. Marriage Breakdown and Divorce Law Reform in Contemporary Society: A Comparative Study of USA, UK and India (1983).

Ilumoka, Adetoun O. *African Women's Economic, Social and Cultural Rights—Toward a Relevant Theory and Practice, in* Human Rights of Women: National and International Perspectives 307 (Rebecca Cook ed., 1994).

Inigo, Delia B. *Argentina: Cohabitation and Assisted Human Fertilization,* 33 U. Louisville J. Fam. L. 267 (1994–95).

Jagwanth, Saras, and Pamela-Jane Schwikkard. Women and the Law (South Africa) (1994).

Jenefsky, Anna. *Permissibility of Egypt's Reservations to the Convention on the Elimination of All Forms of Discrimination against Women,* 15 Md. J. Int'l L. and Trade 199 (1991).

Jewett, Jennifer. *The Recommendations of the International Conference on Population and Development: The Possibility of the Empowerment of Women in Egypt,* 29 Cornell Int'l L.J. 191 (1996).

Johnson, Kevin R. *Public Benefits and Immigration: The Intersection of Immigration Status, Ethnicity, Gender, and Class,* 42 UCLA L. Rev. 1509 (1995).

Johnson, Paula. *Danger in the Diaspora: Law, Culture, and Violence against Women of African Descent in the United States and South Africa,* 1 Iowa J. Gender, Race and Just. 471 (1998).

Jordan, Anne D. *Human Rights, Violence against Women, and Economic Development (The People's Republic of China Experience),* 4 Colum. J. Gender and L. 216 (1994).

Kabeberi-Macharia, Janet W. Women, Laws, Customs, and Practices in East Africa: Laying the Foundation (1995).

Kameri-Mbote, Patricia. The Law of Succession in Kenya: Gender Perspectives in Property Management and Control (1995).

Kamiya, Masako. *Women in Japan,* 20 U. British Columbia L. Rev. 447 (1986).

Kapur, Ratna. Feminist Terrains in Legal Domains: Interdisciplinary Essays on Women and Law in India (1996).

Kapur, Ratna, and Brenda Cossman. Subversive Sites: Feminist Engagement with Law in India (1996).

Kassindja, Fauziya, and Layli Miller Bashir. Do They Hear You When You Cry (1998).

Kelly, M. Patricia Fernandez. *Underclass and Immigrant Women as Economic Actors: Rethinking Citizenship in a Changing Global Economy,* 9 Am. U. J. Int'l L. and Pol'y 151 (1993).

Kerr, Joanna. Ours by Right: Women's Rights as Human Rights (1993).

Kibwana, Kivutha. Women and Autonomy in Kenya: Policy and Legal Framework (1995).

King, Rosemary Ofeibea Ofei-Aboagye. *Domestic Violence in Ghana: An Initial Step,* 4 Colum. J. Gender and L. 1 (1994).

———. *Domestic Violence in Ghana: A Preliminary Look, in* The Public Nature of Private Violence (Martha Fineman and Roxanne Mytikuk eds., 1994).

————. *Tradition or Tribulation? Thoughts on Women's Oppression and Wife Abuse in Ghana, in* A Cross-Cultural Exploitation of Wife Abuse (Aysan Sev'er ed., 1997).

Knapp, Kiyoko Kamio. *Still Office Flowers: Japanese Women Betrayed by the Equal Employment Opportunity Law*, 18 Harv. Women's L.J. 83 (1995).

Knowles, Jane. *Women's Access to Land in Africa*, Third World Legal Stud. 1 (1991).

Kozlowski, Gregory. *Muslim Women and the Control of Property in North India, in* Women in Colonial India (J. Krishnamurty ed., 1988).

Krikorian, Jacqueline. *A Different Form of Apartheid? The Legal Status of Married Women in South Africa*, 21 Queens L.J. 221 (1995).

Krotoszynski, Ronald J. *Building Bridges and Overcoming Barricades: Exploring the Limits of Law as an Agent of Transformational Social Change*, 47 Case W. Res. L. Rev. 423 (1997).

Langley, W. *The Rights of Women, the African Charter and the Economic Development of Africa*, 7 B.C. Third World L.J. 215 (1987).

Law, Sylvia A., and Lisa F. Rackner. *Gender Equality and the Mexico City Policy*, 20 N.Y.U. J. Int'l L. and Pol. 193 (1987).

Lee, Janice. *Family Law in the Two Chinas: A Comparative Look at the Rights of Married Women in the People's Republic of China and the Republic of China*, 5 Cardozo J. Int'l and Comp. L. 217 (1997).

Lee, Kay C. *Confucian Ethics, Judges, and Women: Divorce under the Revised Korean Family Law*, 4 Pac. Rim. L. and Pol'y J. 479 (1995).

Leites, Justin. *Modernist Jurisprudence as a Vehicle for Gender Role Reform in the Islamic World*, 22 Colum. Hum. Rts. L. Rev. 251 (1991).

Levinson, David. *Societies without Family Violence, in* Domestic Violence Law: A Comprehensive Overview of Cases and Sources (Nancy Lemon ed., 1996).

Lewis, Hope. *Between Irua and Female Genital Mutilation: Feminist Human Rights Discourse and the Cultural Divide*, 8 Harv. Hum. Rts. J. 1 (1995).

————. *Lionheart Gals Facing the Dragon: The Human Rights of Inter/National Black Women in the United States*, 76 Ore. L. Rev. 567 (1997).

————. *Women (Under)Development: The Relevance of the "Right to Development" to Poor Women of Color in the United States*, 18 Law and Pol'y 281 (1996).

Li, Xiaorong. *License to Coerce: Violence against Women, State Responsibility, and Legal Failures in China's Family Planning Program*, 8 Yale J. Law and Fem. 147 (1996).

Liebenberg, Sandra, ed. The Constitution of South Africa from a Gender Perspective (1995).

Lopez, Antoinette Sedillo. *Comparative Analysis of Women's Issues: Toward a Contextualized Methodology*, 10 Hastings Women's L.J. 101 (1999).

————. *Two Legal Constructs of Motherhood: "Protective" Legislation in Mexico and the United States*, 1 S. Cal. Rev. L. and Women's Stud. 239 (1992).

Mackay, Michael, and Sonia Smallacombe. *Aboriginal Women as Offenders and Victims: The Case of Victoria*, 3 Aboriginal L. Bull. No. 80, at 17 (1996).

Macklin, Audrey. *Foreign Domestic Worker: Surrogate Housewife or Mail Order Servant?*, 37 McGill L.J. 681 (1992).

Martin, Dianne L., and Janet E. Mosher. *Unkept Promises: Experiences of Immigrant Women with the Neo-Criminalization of Wife Abuse*, 8 Canadian J. Women and Law 3 (1995).

Martin, Maria Sol. *Women in Mexican Labor Law*, 23 Revue Generale de Droit 235 (1992).

Mathangani, Mumbi. *The Triple Battle: Gender, Class and Democracy in Kenya*, 39 How. L.J. 287 (1995).

Matsushima, Yukiko. *Japan: Continuing Reform in Family Law,* 33 U. Louisville J. Fam. L. 417 (1994–95).

Mbeo, M. A., and O. Ooko-Ombaka. Women and Law in Kenya (1989).

McKenzie, Paul D. *China and the Women's Convention: Prospects for the Implementation of an International Norm,* 7(1) China L. Rep. 23 (1991).

Mcnamara, Eve. Women and Law in Southern Africa: An Annotated Bibliography (1991).

Medina, Ceilia. *Women's Rights as Human Rights: Latin American Countries and the Organization of American States (OAS), in* Women, Feminist Identity and Society in the 1980s: Selected Papers (M. Diaz-Diocaretz and I. Zavala eds., 1985).

Mernissi, Fatima. The Veil and the Male Elite (1991).

———. Woman and Islam (1991).

Mikell, Gwendolyn. *African Structural Adjustment: Women and Legal Challenges,* 69 St. John's L. Rev. 7 (1995).

Miller, Kristin J. *Human Rights of Women in Iran: The Universalist Approach and the Relativist Response,* 10 Emory Int'l L. Rev. 779 (1996).

Mitter, Dwarka Nath. The Position of Women in Hindu Law (1984).

Mohanty, Chandra T. *Under Western Eyes: Feminist Scholarship and Colonial Discourses, in* Third World Women and the Politics of Feminism 51 (1991).

Mohanty, Chandra T. et al., eds. Third World Women and the Politics of Feminism (1991).

Mohite, Vijayrao. Law of Cruelty, Abetment of Suicide, and Dowry Deaths (India) (1993).

Morgan, Martha. *The Bitter and the Sweet: Feminist Efforts to Reform Nicaraguan Rape and Sodomy Laws,* 26 U. Miami Inter-Am. L. Rev. 439 (1995).

———. *Founding Mothers: Women's Voices and Stories in the 1987 Nicaraguan Constitution,* 70 B.U. L. Rev. 1 (1990).

———. *Taking Machismo to Court: The Gender Jurisprudence of the Colombian Constitutional Court,* 30 U. Miami Inter-Am. L. Rev. 253 (1999).

Morgan, Martha, and Mónica María Alzate Buitrago. *Constitution-Making in a Time of Cholera: Women and the 1991 Colombian Constitution,* 4 Yale J. L. and Feminism 353 (1992).

Murray, Christina. Gender and the New South African Legal Order (1994).

Nair, Janaki. Women and Law in Colonial India: A Social History (1996).

Nangia, Anshu. *The Tragedy of Bride Burning in India: How Should the Law Address It?,* 22 Brook. J. Int'l L. 637 (1997).

Nasir, Jamal J. The Status of Women under Islamic Law (1990).

———. The Status of Women under Islamic Law and under Modern Islamic Legislation (1990).

Ncube, Welshman. Family Law in Zimbabwe (1989).

———. *Released from Legal Minority, in* Women and Law in Southern Africa 193 (Alice Armstrong and Welshman Ncube eds., 1987).

Ncube, Welshman, and Julie Stewart. Widowhood, Inheritance Laws, Customs and Practices in Southern Africa (1995).

Ndulo, Muna. *Widows under Zambia Customary Law and the Response of the Courts,* 18 Comp. and Int'l L.J. S. Africa 90 (1988).

Nesiah, Vasuki. *Towards a Feminist Internationality: A Critique of U.S. Feminist Legal Scholarship,* 16 Harv. Women's L.J. 189 (1993).

Ngwafar, Ephraim. *Cameroon: Property Rights for Women—A Bold Step in the Wrong Direction,* 29 U. Louisville J. Fam. L. 297 (1990–91).

Nhlapo, R. T. *International Protection of Human Rights and the Family: African Variations on a Common Theme*, 3 Int'l J. L. and Fam. 1 (1989).

———. *The Situation of Women in Swaziland and Some Thoughts on Research, in* The Legal Situation of Women in Southern Africa (J. Stewart and A. Armstrong eds., 1990).

Obermeyer, Carla Makhlouf. *A Cross-Cultural Perspective on Reproductive Rights,* 17 Hum. Rts. Q. 366 (1995).

Obiora, L. Amede. *Bridges and Barricades: Rethinking Polemics and Intransigence in the Campaign against Female Genital Circumcision,* 47 Case W. Res. L. Rev. 275 (1997).

———. *Feminism, Globalization and Culture: After Beijing,* 4 Ind. J. Global L. Stud. 355 (1997).

———. *The Little Foxes That Spoil the Vine: Revisiting the Feminist Critique of Female Genital Circumcision,* 9 CJWL/RFD 46 (1997).

———. *New Skin, Old Wine: (En)Gaging Nationalism, Traditionalism and Gender Relations,* 28 Ind. L. Rev. 575 (1995).

Ojwang, J. B., and J. N. K. Mugambi. The S. M. Otieno Case: Death and Burial in Modern Kenya (1989).

Okumu Wengi, Jennifer. Women, Inheritance Laws and Practices (1994).

Oloka-Onyango, Joseph, and Sylvia Tamale. *"The Personal Is Political," or Why Women's Rights Are Indeed Human Rights: An African Perspective on International Feminism,* 17 Hum. Rts. Q. 691 (1995).

Ong, Aihwa. *Strategic Sisterhood or Sisters in Solidarity? Questions of Communitarianism and Citizenship in Asia,* 4 Ind. J. Global Leg. Stud. 107 (1996).

Oré-Aguilar, Gaby. *Sexual Harassment and Human Rights in Latin America,* 66 Ford. L. Rev. 631 (1997).

Parashar, Archana. Women and Family Law Reform in India (1992).

Pardee, Laurel Remers. *The Dilemma of Dowry Deaths: Domestic Disgrace or International Human Rights Catastrophe?,* 13 Ariz. J. Int'l and Comp. L. 491 (1996).

Pardo de Carvallo, Ines. *Chile: Tentative Steps toward Equality for Women,* 29 U. Louisville J. Fam. L. 317 (1990–91).

Parkinson, Loraine. *Japan's Equal Employment Opportunity Law: An Alternative Approach to Social Change,* 89 Colum. L. Rev. 604 (1989).

Pasqualucci, Jo M. *Sonia Picado, First Woman Judge on the Inter-American Court of Human Rights,* 17 Hum. Rts. Q. 794 (1995).

Patel, Rashida. Socio-economic Political Status, and Women and Law in Pakistan (1991).

Payne, Sharon. *Aboriginal Women and the Law, in* Aboriginal Perspectives on Criminal Justice 31 (Chris Cuneen ed., 1992).

Poinsette, Cheryl L. *Black Women under Apartheid: An Introduction,* 8 Harv. Women's L.J. 93 (1985).

Pseawa, Feoni P. *Values for Policies and Laws Affecting Women: Asia Pacific Forum on Women, Law and Development Regional Conference,* 1:2 Forum News (1988).

Raghu, Maya. *Sex Trafficking of Thai Women and the United States Asylum Law Response,* 12 Geo. Immigr. L.J. 145 (1997).

Rahman, Anika. *Religious Rights versus Women's Rights in India: A Test Case for International Human Rights,* 28 Colum. J. Transnat'l L. 473 (1990).

———. *A View towards Women's Reproductive Rights Perspective on Selected Laws and Policies in Pakistan,* 15 Whittier L. Rev. 981 (1994).

Raina, Dina Nath. Uniform Civil Code and Gender Justice (India) (1996).

Ralston, Julie Yuki. *Geishas, Gays and Grunts: What the Exploitation of Asian Pacific Women Reveals about Military Culture and the Legal Ban on Lesbian, Gay and Bisexual Members,* 16 Law and Ineq. J. 661 (1998).

Ranjana, Kumari. Brides Are Not for Burning: Dowry Victims in India (1989).

Razack, Sherene. *Domestic Violence as Gender Persecution: Policing the Borders of Nation, Race, and Gender,* 8 Canadian J. Women and L. 45 (1995).

Riles, Annelise. *Spheres of Exchange and Spheres of Law: Identity and Power in Chinese Marriage Agreements,* 19 Int'l J. Sociology of L. 501 (1991).

Rivera, Jenny. *Puerto Rico's Domestic Violence Prevention and Intervention Law and the United States Violence against Women Act of 1994: The Limitations of Legislative Responses,* 5 Colum. J. Gender and L. 78 (1995).

Romany, Celina. *Black Women and Gender Equality in a New South Africa: Human Rights Law and the Intersection of Race and Gender,* 21 Brook. J. Int'l L. 857 (1996).

———. *On Surrounding Privilege: Diversity in a Feminist Redefinition of Human Rights Law (From Vienna to Beijing), in* Basic Needs to Basic Rights (1994).

Russell, Jim. *Reproductive Health: The United Nations Convention on the Elimination of All Forms of Discrimination against Women as a Catalyst for Change in Colombia,* 49 U. Toronto Fac. L. Rev. 106 (1991).

Rwezaura, B. *Tanzania: Building a New Family Law Out of a Plural Legal System,* 33 U. Louisville J. Fam. L. 523 (1994–95).

———. *Tanzania: Family Law and the New Bill of Rights,* 29 U. Louisville J. Fam. L. 453 (1990–91).

———. Traditional Family Law and Change in Tanzania: A Study of the Kuria Social System (1985).

Saint-Germain, Michelle, and Martha I. Morgan. *Equality: Costa Rican Women Demand the Real Thing,* 11 Women and Pol. 23 (1991).

Saxena, Shobha. Crimes against Women and Protective Laws (India) (1995).

Scales-Trent, Judy. *African Women in France: Immigration, Family and Work,* 24 Brook. J. Int'l L. 705 (1999).

Schuler, Margaret. Employment and the Law: Strategies of Third World Women (1986).

Scott, Edith E. *Married Women's Rights under the Matrimonial Regimes of Chile and Colombia: A Comparative History,* 7 Harv. Women's L.J. 221 (1984).

Shenje-Peyton, Angeline. *Balancing Gender, Equality, and Cultural Identity: Marriage Payments in Post-Colonial Zimbabwe,* 9 Harv. Hum. Rts. J. 105 (1996).

Sheridan, Mary M. *In re Fauziya Kasinga: The United States Has Opened Its Doors to Victims of Female Genital Mutilation,* 71 St. John's L. Rev. 433 (1997).

Sinclair, June D. The Law of Marriage (South Africa) (1996).

———. *South Africa: Children and the Political Violence,* 29 U. Louisville J. Fam. L. 411 (1990–91).

Singh, Alka. Women in Muslim Personal Law (1992).

Singh, Indu Prakash. Women, Law and Social Change in India (1989).

Skrobanek, Siriporn. The Traffic in Women: Human Realities of the International Sex Trade (1997).

Slack, Alison T. *Female Circumcision: A Critical Appraisal,* 10 Hum. Rts. Q. 437 (1988).

Smith, J. Clay, Jr. *United States Foreign Policy and Goler Teal Butcher,* 37 How. L.J. 139 (1994).

Smith, Robin Cerny. *Female Circumcision: Bringing Women's Perspectives into the International Debate*, 65 S. Cal. L. Rev. 2449 (1992).

Somswadi, Virada. *Women in the Constitution of Thailand: A Far-Fetched Hope for Equality, in* Women's Legal Position in Thailand 1 (1991).

Splittgerber, Scott. *The Need for Greater Regional Protection for the Human Rights of Women: The Cases of Rape in Bosnia and Guatemala*, 15 Wis. Int'l L.J. 185 (1996).

Srivastava, T. N. Women and the Law (India) (1985).

Stairs, Felicite, and Lori Pope. *No Place Like Home: Assaulted Migrant Women's Claims to Refugee Status and Landings on Humanitarian and Compassionate Grounds*, 6 J.L. and Soc. Pol. 148 (1990).

Stephens, Beth. *A Developing Legal System Grapples with an Ancient Problem: Rape in Nicaragua*, 12 Women's Rts. L. Rep. 69 (1990).

Stewart, Julie, and Alice Armstrong. The Legal Situation of Women in Southern Africa (1990).

Stoner, K. Lynn. From the House to the Streets: The Cuban Women's Movement for Legal Reform 1898–1940 (1991).

Stromquist, Nelly, ed. Encyclopedia of Third World Women (1998).

Sullivan, Donna J. *Gender Equality and Religious Freedom: Toward a Framework for Conflict Resolutions*, 24 N.Y.U. J. Int'l L. and Pol. 795 (1992).

Telesetsky, Anastasia. *In the Shadows and behind the Veil: Women in Afghanistan under Taliban Rule*, 13 Berkeley Women's L.J. 293 (1998).

Temngah, Joseph N. *Customary Law, Women's Rights and Traditional Courts in Cameroon*, 27 Revue Generale de Droit 323 (1996).

Travis, Karen. *Women in Global Production and Worker Rights Provisions in U.S. Trade Laws*, 17 Yale J. Int'l L. 173 (1992).

Uzodike, Eunice. *Nigeria: Defining the Ambit of Custom*, 29 U. Louisville J. Fam. L. 399 (1990–91).

Vaidya, Shanta Arvind. Women and Labour Laws (India) (1993).

Vaz Ferreiral, Eduardo. *Uruguay: Ending Discrimination between Birth in and out of Wedlock and the Surviving Spouse's Right of Occupation and Use*, 33 U. Louisville J. Fam. L. 555 (1994–95).

Venter, Christine Mary. *The New South African Constitution: Facing the Challenges of Women's Rights and Cultural Rights in Post-Apartheid South Africa*, 21 J. Legis. 1 (1995).

Wadud, Amina. *Towards a Qur'anic Hermeneutics of Social Justice: Race, Class and Gender*, 12 J.L. and Religion 37 (1995–96).

Waisman, Viviana, and Anika Rahman. Women of the World: Laws and Policies Affecting Their Reproductive Lives: Anglophone Africa (1997).

Walker, Cheryl, ed. Women and Gender in Southern Africa to 1945 (1990).

Wani, Mohammad Afzal. The Islamic Law on Maintenance of Women, Children, Parents and Other Relatives: Classical Principles and Modern Legislation in India and Muslim Countries (1995).

Webber, Kathryn J. *The Economic Future of Afghan Women: The Interaction between Islamic Law and Muslim Culture*, 18 U. Pa. Int'l Econ. L. Rev. 1049 (1997).

Welch, Claude E., Jr. *Human Rights and African Women: A Comparison of Protection under Two Major Treaties*, 15 Hum. Rts. Q. 549 (1993).

Wells, Allison J. *Chinese Women Experience a Negative Side Effect of the Growing Private Sector in Gender-Based Employment Discrimination,* 6 Ind. Int'l and Comp. L. Rev. 517 (1996).

Welsh, G. H., F. Dagnino, and A. Sachs. *Transforming Family Law: New Directions in Mozambique, in* Women and Law in Southern Africa 105 (Alice Armstrong and Welshman Ncube eds., 1987).

Wing, Adrien Katherine. *Critical Race Feminism and the International Human Rights of Women in Bosnia, Palestine and South Africa: Issues for Lat-Crit Theory,* 28 Miami Inter-Am. L. Rev. 337 (1997).

———. *A Critical Race Feminist Conceptualization of Violence: South African and Palestinian Women,* 60 Alb. L. Rev. 943 (1997).

———. *Custom, Religion and Rights: The Future Legal Status of Palestinian Women,* 35 Harv. J. Int'l L. 149 (1994).

———. Democracy, Constitutionalism and the Future State of Palestine: With a Case Study of Women's Rights (1994).

———. *Gender Equality and Governance in Africa: A Critical Race Feminist Perspective, in* Cornell Institute for African Development, Governance in Africa: Building the Capable State (1997).

———. *The New South African Constitution: An Example for Palestinian Consideration,* 7 Pal. Yrbk Int'l L. 105 (1992–94).

Wing, Adrien Katherine, and Eunice de Carvalho. *Black South African Women: Towards Equal Rights,* 8 Harv. Hum. Rts. J. 57 (1995).

Wing, Adrien Katherine, and Shobhana Kasturi. *The Palestinian Women's Charter: Beyond the Basic Law,* Third World Legal Stud. 141 (1994–95).

Wing, Adrien Katherine, and Sylke Merchán. *Rape, Ethnicity and Culture: Spirit Injury from Bosnia to Black America,* 25 Colum. Hum. Rts. L. Rev. 1 (1993).

Women's Rights and Traditional Law: A Conflict?, 1994–5 Third World Legal Studies Special Issue.

Woodman, G. *Unification or Continuing Pluralism in Family Law in Anglophone Africa: Past Experience, Present Realities, and Future Possibilities,* 4 Lesotho L.J. 33 (1988).

Yu, Tong. *Reparations for Former Comfort Women of World War II,* 36 Harv. Int'l L.J. 528 (1995).

Zolan, Alexandra J. *The Effect of Islamization on the Legal and Social Status of Women in Iran,* 7 B.C. Third World L.J. 183 (1987).

Contributors

AzizaH Y. al-Hibri is a professor at the T. C. Williams School of Law, University of Richmond, where she teaches Islamic jurisprudence and corporate law subjects. She holds a B.A. from the American University of Beirut, Lebanon, an M.A. from Wayne State University, and a Ph.D. in philosophy and a J.D. from the University of Pennsylvania. Prior to attending law school, al-Hibri was an assistant professor at Texas A and M University and a visiting associate professor at Washington University in St. Louis, teaching courses in logic, ethics, feminism, and philosophy of technology. After completing law school she spent a semester as a visiting scholar at Harvard Divinity School and Center for the Study of World Religions. Al-Hibri then worked as an associate attorney at two major New York law firms. She is the founder and current President of Karamah: Muslim Women Lawyers for Human Rights and serves on the Advisory Board of both the Public Religion Project of the University of Chicago and the Pluralism Project of Harvard University. Al-Hibri also currently serves on the editorial boards of the *Journal of Law and Religion* and *Hypatia: A Journal of Feminist Philosophy*. Her edited books include *Women and Islam* (1982) and *Hypatia Reborn: Essays in Feminist Philosophy* (1990).

Penelope E. Andrews is an associate professor at the City University of New York School of Law at Queens College, where she teaches courses in International Human Rights Law, Torts, and Lawyering. She earned a B.A. and LL.B. from the University of Natal in Durban, South Africa. She also holds an LL.M. from Columbia Law School. Andrews has been the Chamberlain Fellow in Legislation at Columbia Law School, and has worked at the Legal Resources Center in Johannesburg and the NAACP Legal Defense Fund in New York. She has also been on the faculty at the Department of Law and Legal Studies at la Trobe University in Melbourne, Australia, and has visited at the University of Maryland School of Law. She currently serves as secretary/treasurer of the International Third World Legal Studies Association.

Taimie L. Bryant, a professor at the University of California at Los Angeles School of Law, writes and teaches courses about Japanese law based on seven years of research experience in

Japan. With special permission of the Japanese Supreme Court, she conducted research in the Japanese family court for four years. She earned a B.A. from Bryn Mawr College, a Ph.D. in anthropology from UCLA, and a J.D. from Harvard Law School. Her other scholarship and teaching interests include legal advocacy for animals and American legal concepts of property ownership.

MÓNICA MARÍA ALZATE BUITRAGO, an assistant professor in the Family Studies Department of the University of Caldas, in Manizales, Colombia, teaches research methods and research design. She received a B.A. from the Universidad Externado de Colombia, an M.A. in women's studies, and an M.S.W. in Social Work from the University of Alabama. Her Master's Thesis, "Free Motherhood in Colombia: Between the Catholic Church and the Law," won the Outstanding Thesis Award. Alzate's previous positions include consultant for the FES Foundation's Training Project for Female Heads of Households, research department coordinator for Fundación Sí Mujer, instructor of social work for the Universidad Externado de Colombia, and social worker in Butler County, Ohio.

DEVON W. CARBADO is an acting professor at the University of California at Los Angeles School of Law, where he teaches Criminal Procedure, Criminal Adjudication, and Critical Race Theory. He received a B.A. from UCLA and a J.D. from Harvard Law School, where he was Editor in Chief of the *Harvard Blackletter Law Journal*. Carbado then worked as an associate attorney at the law firm of Latham and Watkins in Los Angeles before being appointed Faculty Fellow and visiting associate professor at the University of Iowa College of Law. He is the editor of *Black Men on Race, Gender, and Sexuality: A Critical Reader* (1999).

MAI CHEN is a founding partner of Chen and Palmer, Barristers and Solicitors, New Zealand's first public law specialist firm. She holds an LL.B. (Hons) (First Class) from the University of Otago in Dunedin. After teaching as an assistant lecturer at the Otago Law Faculty, she completed an LL.M. at Harvard Law School, winning the Irving Oberman Memorial Award for the best human rights thesis. Chen also won the Ferguson Human Rights Scholarship to work as a fellow at the International Labour Office in Geneva. She then took up a lectureship at the Law School at Victoria University of Wellington, and wrote her first book, *Women and Discrimination: New Zealand and the United Nations Convention* (1989). In 1992 she became the youngest senior lecturer in New Zealand. She later coauthored *Public Law in New Zealand* with Sir Geoffrey Palmer, the former prime minister. Chen left full-time teaching to start the law firm, but continues to serve as honorary lecturer at Victoria University. She also has a regular program on TVNZ's *Breakfast Show*, where she talks about topical public law issues.

BRENDA J. COSSMAN is an associate professor at the Faculty of Law, University of Toronto. She earned a B.A. from Queens University, an LL.B. from the University of Toronto, and an LL.M. from Harvard Law School. Previously she was an associate professor at Osgoode Hall Law School, York University, where she was director of the Institute of Feminist Legal Studies. She teaches in the areas of family law, feminist theory, and international and comparative law. She is the coauthor of *Subversive Sites: Feminist Engagement with the Law in India* (1996); *Bad Attitude/s on Trial: Pornography, Feminism and the Butler Decision* (1997); and *Secularism's Last Sigh: Hindutva and the (Mis)Rule of Law* (1999).

LISA A. CROOMS, an associate professor at Howard University School of Law, teaches Contracts, Constitutional Law, and Legal Theory. She holds a B.A. from Howard and a J.D. from the University of Michigan Law School. Prior to joining the faculty, she was an associate attorney with Crosby, Heafey, Roach, and May, P.C. in Oakland, California, where she practiced in the areas of employment and labor law. An international human rights activist since 1984, Crooms has worked with the Washington Office on Africa and the American Committee on Africa. She has also participated in international human rights consultations in the United States, United Kingdom, Malaysia, Zimbabwe, and South Africa. Crooms is currently a member of the Advisory Committee for the Women's Rights Division of Human Rights Watch, for which she helped document state responses to domestic violence and rape in South Africa.

ANGELA Y. DAVIS is known internationally for her ongoing work to combat all forms of oppression in the United States and abroad. She is currently a professor in the History of Consciousness Department at the University of California at Santa Cruz. In 1994 she received the distinguished honor of an appointment to the University of California Presidential Chair in African American and Feminist Studies. Davis holds a B.A. from Brandeis and an M.A. and Ph.D. from the University of California. She has previously taught at UCLA and several other institutions. She is a member of the Advisory Board of the Prison Activist Resource Center, and is currently working on a comparative study of women's imprisonment in the United States, the Netherlands, and Cuba. Her books include *Women, Race and Class* (1983); *Angela Davis: An Autobiography* (1990); *Women, Culture and Politics* (1990); and *Blues, Legacies and Black Feminism: Gertrude "Ma" Rainey, Bessie Smith and Billie Holiday* (1998). She is also the editor of *If They Come in the Morning: Voices of Resistance* (1971).

MARY L. DUDZIAK is a professor of law at the University of Southern California. She received an A.B. from the University of California at Berkeley and an M.A., M.Phil., J.D., and Ph.D. from Yale. She then clerked for Judge Sam J. Ervin III on the U.S. Court of Appeals for the Fourth Circuit. She previously taught at the University of Iowa College of Law. Her subjects include Constitutional Law, Procedure, The Constitution in the Twentieth Century, The Civil Rights Movement and Civil Rights Law, and Law and Social Change in Postwar America. Dudziak is active in a wide variety of law and history organizations. She has served as a board member and member of the Executive Committee of the American Society for Legal History. She is the author of the forthcoming *Cold War Civil Rights: Equality as Cold War Policy, 1946–68*.

ISABELLE R. GUNNING is a professor at Southwestern University School of Law. She teaches courses on International Human Rights, Women and the Law, Immigration Law, Evidence, and Lawyering Skills. She received a B.A. and J.D. from Yale University. Upon graduation, Gunning clerked for the U.S. District Court for the District of Columbia, then served as a staff attorney for the D.C. Public Defender Office. She next worked as a staff attorney for the Southern Africa Project of the Lawyers Committee for Civil Rights under the Law. Prior to joining the faculty at Southwestern, Gunning was an acting professor at the University of California at Los Angeles School of Law. Her current Board memberships include the African Community Resource Center in Los Angeles and the ACLU of Southern California. Gunning is a former board member and cochair of the Asian Pacific American Dispute Resolution Center.

ANNA M. HAN is an associate professor at Santa Clara University School of Law, where she teaches Chinese Trade and Investment Law, Technology Licensing Contracts, Business Organizations, and Legal Issues of Start-up Business. She holds a B.A. from the University of California at Berkeley and a J.D. from University of California, Hastings College of Law. Prior to teaching, Han was an international lawyer, first as an associate attorney at Heller, Ehrman et al. in San Francisco, and then as a partner at McCutcheon, Doyle et al. in San Francisco and Shanghai, China. At Santa Clara she has served as Director of the Hong Kong/Beijing/Shanghai Summer Program and Chair of its HiTech Program. She currently is Chair of the China Law Committee for the Bar Association of San Francisco, and has served on the Executive Committee of the International Law Section of the California Bar Association as its Secretary and Treasurer.

BERTA ESPERANZA HERNÁNDEZ-TRUYOL, a professor at St. John's University School of Law, teaches, writes, and lectures widely on International Law, Issues of Race and Gender in the Law, and International Human Rights. She also teaches Property law. Hernández-Truyol received an A.B. from Cornell University, a J.D. from Albany Law School, and an LL.M. in International Legal Studies from New York University. Upon graduation, she worked at the Department of Justice, Antitrust Division, and also has practiced law with Milgrim, Thomajan et al. and Proskauer, Rose et al. in New York. She has taught at De Paul Law School and the University of New Mexico, as well as visited at Georgetown Law School. She was appointed by Chief Judge Judith Kaye to the New York State Commission on Judicial Nomination, served on the Second Circuit Task Force on Race, Gender, and Ethnicity, and currently serves as a special advisor to the Women's Rights Project of the ACLU. From 1993 to 1995 she was the Director of the International Women's Human Rights Project, and had the opportunity to represent that group at the Cairo, Copenhagen, and Beijing conferences. Her current book projects include *Trespassing Borderlands: Sovereignty, Citizenship, and Human Rights;* and *Moral Imperialism: A Critical Anthology.*

LAURA HO is an attorney at the Oakland, California, law firm of Saperstein, Goldstein, Demchak and Baller. The firm specializes in class action litigation on behalf of plaintiffs in employment and environmental lawsuits. Ho obtained a B.A. from the University of Washington and a J.D. from Yale Law School. Since graduation, Ho also has worked as a NAPIL Fellow at the Asian Law Caucus, a staff attorney at the ACLU National Immigrants' Rights Project, and a judicial law clerk for the U.S. District Court for the Western District of Washington.

SHARON K. HOM is a professor at the City University of New York Law School at Queens College, where she teaches Contracts, International Human Rights, Feminist Jurisprudence; she also teaches in the Immigration and Refugee Rights Clinic. She earned a B.A. from Sarah Lawrence College and a J.D. from New York University School of Law, where she was also a Root-Tilden Scholar. Hom served as a Fulbright Scholar in residence at the China University of Politics and Law in Beijing in 1986–88. For the past ten years, she has been active with U.S.–China legal exchange work and is a member of the Committee for Legal Exchange with China. She has also served as Co-Chair of the Society of Chinese Women's Studies in the United States. In 1995 Hom acted as a judge for the Global Tribunal on Violence against Women convened for the Fourth World Conference on Women and the NGO Forum in Beijing. She sits on the Advisory Board of Human Rights Watch/China, the Executive Committee of Human Rights in China, and the Asian Affairs Committee of the Bar of the Association of the City of New York. She is the coauthor of *Contracting Law* (1996); coeditor of the *Chinese-English Lexicon on Women and the Law (Yinghan funu yu falu cihuishiyi)* (1995); and the editor of *Chinese Women Traversing Diaspora: Memoirs, Essays, and Poetry* (1998).

ROSEMARY OFEIBEA OFEI-ABOAGYE KING is an adjunct assistant professor and Director of the Education Equity Program of the Faculty of Law at Queen's University, Kingston, Ontario. She teaches in the areas of Contracts, Torts, and Health Law. She holds an LL.B. (Hons) and B.L. from the University of Ghana, an LL.M. from Queen's University, and a D.Jur. from Osgoode Hall Law School of York University in Toronto.

KIYOKO KAMIO KNAPP was born and raised in Japan, where she lived for twenty-four years before moving to the United States. Her degrees include a bachelor's from Kansai Gaidai College in Osaka, Japan, and a J.D. from the Northwestern School of Law of Lewis and Clark College. She has clerked for the U.S. District Court for the Western District of Washington. Knapp is currently enrolled in the LL.M. program in Asian and Comparative Law at the University of Washington School of Law. Her current book project is *Warriors or Flowers Betrayed: Challenges Facing the Japanese Workplace.*

HOPE LEWIS is a professor at Northeastern University School of Law. She teaches courses on Gender and Human Rights, Human Rights and Development, Securities Regulation, and Corporations. She received an A.B. and J.D. from Harvard University. Prior to joining the faculty, she worked on gender and development issues as a research fellow for Transafrica Forum, and as an Attorney-advisor in the office of Chief Counsel of the U.S. Securities and Exchange Commission. She has also served on the Transafrica Forum Scholars Council.

ANTOINETTE SEDILLO LOPEZ is a professor at the University of New Mexico School of Law, where she teaches Comparative Law, Women's Legal Issues, Family Law, Law and Reproductive Technology, Civil Procedure, and Clinic. She earned her undergraduate degree from the University of New Mexico and a J.D. from the University of California at Los Angeles. She clerked for the U.S. Court of Appeals for the D.C. Circuit and worked as an associate attorney at Modrall, Sperling et al. in Albuquerque. Sedillo Lopez is a former President of the New Mexico Hispanic Bar Association. She is the editor of *Latina Issues: Fragments of Historia (Ella) (Herstory)* (1995); and *Latinos in the United States: History, Law and Perspective* (1995). She is the series editor of the Garland series, Latino Communities: Emerging Voices: Political, Cultural and Social Issues (1998).

MARTHA I. MORGAN is the Robert S. Vance Professor of Law at the University of Alabama School of Law, where she teaches courses in Constitutional Law, Civil Rights Litigation, and Gender Law. She received a B.S. from the University of Alabama and a J.D. from the George Washington University National Law Center. After graduation, Morgan clerked for Judge James R. Miller, Jr., of the U.S. District Court for Maryland, before joining the law faculty in 1979. She was a W. K. Kellogg Foundation National Fellow from 1985 to 1988. Since 1990 she has been part of the legal team representing Alabama schoolchildren seeking to establish and enforce their rights to an adequate and equitable public education. She serves on the Boards of Directors of the Equal Justice Initiative of Alabama and of the American Civil Liberties Union and its Alabama affiliate.

ZORICA MRSEVIC is a senior science associate at the Belgrade Institute of Criminological and Sociological Research and a lecturer in Women's Studies. She holds an LL.B., M.A., and Ph.D. from the University of Belgrade. She has also been a visiting professor at the University of Iowa College of Law. Mrsevic currently serves as Editor in Chief of the *Yugoslav Review for Criminal Law and Criminology*. She is a member of the Executive Board of the Yugoslav Lawyers Committee for Human Rights and a member of the editorial boards of the *Human Rights Journal*, *Women Studies Review*, and *Feminist Notebooks*. She continues to volunteer with the SOS Hotline for Women and Children as well. Her recent books include *Women's Rights Are Human Rights* (1993); *Women's Rights: A Legal Guide for Battered Women* (1995); *Incest between Myth and Reality* (1997); and *Women's Rights in International Law* (1998).

VASUKI NESIAH holds a B.A. from Cornell and a J.D. and S.J.D. from Harvard Law School.

Leslye Amede Obiora is an Igbo woman who is an associate professor of law at the University of Arizona, where she teaches International Law, Gender and the Law, Jurisprudence, Property, and Corporations. She holds an LL.B. from the University of Nigeria, an LL.M. from Yale, and is an J.S.D. candidate at Stanford. Her work has earned her several recognitions and awards, including a fellowship from the Institute for Advanced Studies at Princeton.

GABY ORÉ-AGUILAR is a program officer for Human Development and Reproductive Health at the Ford Foundation in Santiago, Chile. She received a B.A. and J.D. from the National University of San Marcos in Lima, Peru, and a Diploma in Gender Studies from the Catholic University of Peru. She earned an LL.M. from Columbia University. Oré-Aguilar wrote the article featured in this collection while she was a staff attorney responsible for Latin American projects at the Center for Reproductive Law and Policy in New York. She is the editor of *Mujeres trabajadores y políticas de empleo en el Perú* (Women Workers and Employment Policies in Peru) (1993); and *Women of the World: Laws and Policies Affecting Their Reproductive Lives—Latin America and the Caribbean* (1997).

CATHERINE POWELL is an associate clinical law professor at Columbia University. She joined the faculty in 1998 to found the Human Rights Clinic and serve as acting Executive Director of the Human Rights Institute. Her degrees include a B.A. from Yale, an M.A. from the Woodrow Wilson School at Princeton, and a J.D. from Yale. Upon graduation, she served as a Ford Fellow in Public International Law at Harvard, and then as a clerk with the U.S. District Court for the Southern District of New York. Powell spent nearly four years as an assistant counsel at the NAACP Legal Defense and Education Fund. She currently serves on the Advisory Committee of the Women's Rights Division of Human Rights Watch, and was a consultant for the organization during a fact-finding mission to South Africa to examine the government's response to domestic violence. Powell also was a member of the Lawyers Committee for Civil Rights delegation to the United Nations Fourth World Conference on Women in Beijing, China.

JENNY RIVERA is an associate professor at the City University of New York at Queens College Law School. She teaches Antidiscrimination Law, Civil Procedure, Property, Administrative Law, and State and Local Government Law. Her degrees include an A.B. from Princeton, a J.D. from New York University, and an LL.M. from Columbia. Prior teaching experience includes serving as an assistant professor at Suffolk University Law School. Rivera previously worked as a staff attorney for the Homeless Family Rights Project of the Legal Aid Society of New York and as associate counsel for the Puerto Rican Legal Defense and Education Fund. She currently serves as Co-Chair of the Advisory Committee for the Latina Rights Initiative. She was a member of the Initiative's delegation to the United Nations Fourth World Conference on Women in Beijing, China. A former law clerk for Judge Sonia Sotomayor of the U.S. District Court for the Southern District of New York, Rivera herself was an administrative law judge for the New York State Division on Human Rights. She is a former board member of the Latina Roundtable on Health and Reproductive Rights.

CELINA ROMANY is a professor at City University of New York Law School, where she was Co-Director of the International Women's Human Rights Program. She holds a B.A. from Trinity College, a J.D. from the University of Puerto Rico, and an LL.M. from New York University. Romany teaches in the areas of International Human Rights, Jurisprudence, Feminist Jurisprudence, Employment Law, and Civil Rights. She sits on the boards of several public interest organizations, including the Center for Constitutional Rights, the Women's Advisory Board of Human Rights Watch, and the Puerto Rican Legal Defense and Education Fund, where she is Co-Chair of the advisory board of its Latina Rights Initiative. Romany has been a visiting professor at Inter-American University, the University of Puerto Rico, and the University of Pennsylvania law schools.

JUDY SCALES-TRENT is a professor at the State University of New York at Buffalo Law School, where she teaches courses in Legal and Policy Issues Affecting Women of Color, Law and Literature, Constitutional Law, and Employment Discrimination. She earned a B.A. from Oberlin College (French), an M.A. from Middlebury College (French), and a J.D. from Northwestern University. After graduation she worked as an attorney for twelve years at the Equal Employment Opportunity Commission. This article is her tenth publication on legal and policy issues affecting women of color. She is also the author of *Notes of a White Black Woman: Race, Color, Community* (1995).

J. CLAY SMITH, JR., is a professor at Howard University School of Law, and has served as Dean of the Law School. He received a B.A. from Creighton University, a J.D. from Howard Law School, and an LL.M. and S.J.D. from George Washington National Law Center. He has served as Associate General Counsel of the Federal Communications Commission and was appointed to the Equal Employment Opportunity Commission by President Jimmy Carter and as Acting Chair of the EEOC by President Ronald Reagan. Smith was the first African American President of the Federal Bar Association. He has also been the President of the Washington Bar Association and a member of the House of Delegates of the American Bar Association. His books include *Emancipation: The Making of the Black Lawyer, 1844–1944* (1993); and *Rebels in Law: Voices in the History of Black Women Lawyers* (1998).

LETI VOLPP is an assistant professor at American University, Washington College of Law, where she teaches courses on Immigration Law, Asian Pacific Americans and the Law, and Property. Her degrees include an A.B. from Princeton, an M.S.P.H. from the Harvard School of Public Health, an M.S. from the University of Edinburgh, and a J.D. from Columbia University. After graduation, she clerked for the U.S. District Court for the Northern District of

California. Volpp was a Skadden Fellow and worked as a staff attorney at the Equal Rights Advocates and at the ACLU Immigrant's Rights Project, both in San Francisco. She also worked as a trial attorney for the U.S. Department of Justice Civil Rights Division as well as the National Employment Law Project in New York. Volpp has been a member of the Board of Directors of the San Francisco Asian Women's Shelter and the New York Asian Women's Center.

ADRIEN KATHERINE WING, a professor at the University of Iowa College of Law since 1987, teaches courses in Comparative Law, Critical Race Theory, Human Rights, and Constitutional Law. She holds an A.B. from Princeton University, an M.A. in African Studies from the University of California at Los Angeles, and a J.D. from Stanford Law School. While in law school, Wing was an editor of the *Stanford Journal of International Law* and winner of the Stanford African Students Association Award. Upon graduation, she practiced international law in New York with Curtis, Mallet-Prevost et al. and the Rabinowitz, Boudin et al. firm. Her civic activities have included serving on the boards of the Iowa Peace Institute, the National Conference of Black Lawyers, the Transafrica Forum Scholars Council, the International Third World Legal Studies Association, the American Association of Law Schools Minority Section, and the Executive Committee of the American Society of International Law. Wing was an advisor to the African National Congress Constitutional Committee in the years leading up to the adoption of the first democratic constitution in South Africa. She also served as a consultant to the Palestinian Legislative Council with respect to the drafting of the Basic Law. She is the editor of *Global Critical Race Feminism: An International Reader* and *Critical Race Feminism: A Reader* (1997).

Index

AAWORD. *See* Association of African Women for Research and Development

ABA. *See* American Bar Association

Abella, Aida, 205

Aboriginal people, 305; and colonial violence, 305, 306

Aboriginal women, xi, 17, 303–14; and violence, 303–9

Abortion, 74–78; law in Colombia, 211, 212; law in Mexico, 69, 75; law in U.S., 75

Abortionist, 247

Accommodation, 130, 137

Acculturation, 78

Activists: African, 270, 278, 279; anti-circumcision, 280; female, 75; FMC, 90; human rights, 99; political, 123; union, 211; women's rights, 103, 204, 254

AD M-19. *See* Alianza Democratica M-19

Adoption, 235, 236, 238, 246, 247

Adultery, 84, 92

Affirmative action, 5, 14, 60; in Colombia, 213–14; in France, 142; in South Africa, 340

Africa, 141, 192, 199–200, 260–72, 275–82; black, 194; and human rights, 195, 196

African, 141, 192, 260; francophone, 155; North, 143; sub-Saharan, 144, 147

African Americans, 3, 162, 163, 200, 279, 377, 379; and racial discrimination, 180

African immigrant, 143–44; and racism, 147–48

African immigrant women, 141–53; and racism, 147–48; and unemployment, 148–49

Africare, 200

Agence pour le Developpement des Resources Interculturelles (ADRI), 142

Alcoholism, 75; and violence against women, 308

Algeria, 141, 147–48

Algerian War of Independence, 33, 142, 148

Al-Hibri, Azizah, 15

Alianza Democratica M-19, 205

Alienation, 58

Aliens, 66, 117

Allen, Paula Gunn, 115

Alzate, Mónica María. *See* Buitrago, Mónica María Alzate

American: anti-, 184; Black, 190, 194, 199, 200; un-, 182, 186; white, 163, 200. *See also* African Americans

American Bar Association (ABA), 198, 199, 202

American Embassy: in Havana, 184–85; in Moscow, 180

American feminist, 43, 49, 50

Amparo, 74, 209

Andrews, Penelope, 17

Androcentric, 57, 65

Angelou, Maya, 137

Anti-apartheid. *See* Apartheid

Anti-discrimination law: in New Zealand, 137

Apartheid, 193, 198, 199, 201, 202, 334–35; anti-, 199, 200, 202

Arab, 147, 156

Arafat, President Yasser, 336

Argentina, 183, 363, 367

Arresto, 212

Ashrawi, Hanan, 336

Asia, 130, 244; South, 39

Association of African Women for Research and Development (AAWORD), 269, 274

Australia, 303–14

Authoritarian, 225, 227
Ayah, 225–28
Ayatollahs, 146

Babies, 166, 169, 236, 251, 288
Baker, Jean-Claude, 189
Baker, Josephine, 15, 179; and Cold War, 179–188; and racial protest, 179–188
Bar Association: Tokyo, 242. *See also* American Bar Association (ABA)
Bar groups: black, 198. *See also* American Bar Association (ABA)
Basta, 164
Battered women, 317–19
Bell, Derrick, 5
Bell, Diane, 308
Biko, Steve, 196
Bima, 227, 228
Birth, 208, 211, 217, 235, 256, 257, 268; out-of-wedlock, 288; rate, 206
Black Americans. *See* African Americans
Blackness, 218
Black women, 53, 55, 56, 59, 60–65, 84, 124, 379
Blankenhorn, David, 286–89, 298–99
Bolger, Audrey, 303
Boserup, Ester, 98
Bouillon, Jo, 181
Bowles, Ambassador Chester, 188, 191
Boxer Rebellion, the, 258
Brandt Commission, the, 196
Branton, Wiley Austin, Sr., 198
Brazil, 342
Breast implants, 280
Bride, 162
Bride price, 337, 394
Brown v. Board of Education, 188
Bryant, Taimie, 2, 3, 16
Bryk, Felix, 269
Buchanan, Bessie, 181
Buitrago, Mónica María Alzate, 78, 215, 217
Buraku, 250
Burakumin, 16, 234, 242, 245, 250
Burbank, Katherine, 308
Business, 99–102, 110; cooperative, 102; small, 99; women-owned, 100
Butcher, Goler Teal, 192–200

Caballero, Judge Alejandro Martinez, 211–12
Cabral, Amilcar, 3
Cain, Patricia, 71, 79
Capitalism, 125, 266, 402
Caraway, Nancie, 58, 66
Carbado, Devon, 2, 14
Carbonell, Judge Antonio Barrera, 211, 217
Careers, 187, 189, 192, 193, 222, 241, 244; academic, 135, 237

Caregiver, 286
Caretakers: domestic, 290; primary, 115, 235
Caribbean, the, 97, 101, 107, 108, 126, 127, 186
Carranza, María Mercedes, 205
Carter, President Jimmy, 195–97
Castro, Fidel, 82, 85–87, 90–91, 93–94
Catholicism, 80, 211
CEDAW. *See* Women's Convention
CERD. *See* Race Convention
Charlesworth, Hilary, 57, 311
Chen, Mai, 14
Chiapas, 76, 79
Chicanos, 80
Chihuahua, 79
Child: female, 257; girl, 256; legitimate, 264; male, 257
Childbearing, 264, 285, 288; extra-marital, 288; teenage, 288
Childcare, 97, 102, 104, 105, 124, 125, 295, 414
Childrearing, 122, 123, 125, 288, 294
Children: abducted, 151; female, 253, 257; Gypsy, 162; illegitimate, 234; immigrant, 132; male, 253, 257; minor, 237, 243, 247, 250; nonmarital, 245
Child support, 290, 296
Chile, 216, 258
China, 251–57, 392–403
Chinese, 130–32, 134, 138, 252–59
Chinese Communist Party (CCP), 395
Chinese immigrants: in New Zealand, 131
Chinese women, 18, 133, 392–403
Chodorow, Nancy, 125, 128
Chores, 123; domestic, 83, 89, 92
Christian, 247
Christianity, 49
Christopher, Warren, 292, 299, 300
Cigan, 162–63
Cigan mala, 164
Circumcised women, 264
Circumcision, 16, 260–72, 275–84; anti-, 260, 266, 268, 272, 275, 276; anti-female, 276–78, 280, 282
Cisneros, Henry G., 286, 289, 290, 295–99
City, inner, 285, 288–90, 297–300
Civil liberties, 174
Civil rights movements, 2, 96
Class: economic, 66; middle, 3, 72; privilege, 47; under, 66; upper, 239, 248; working, 124
Clinicalization, 270–72, 275, 278, 280–82
Clinton, Hillary Rodham, 99
Clinton, President William Jefferson, 99, 192
Clinton Administration, 286
Clitoridectomy, 262, 263
Cohen, Vincent, 198
Cold War, 105, 179, 183
Cólera, 205, 215, 216
Colombia, 205

Colombian Constitution, 206–8
Colombian women, 204–15; Black, 206, 214; and constitutional reform, 205; and constitution making, 205–6
Colonialism, 40, 108, 222; anti-, 188–89; neo-, 108
Color, 134, 155
Colorism, 119
Coloured, 117, 136
Commonalities, 55, 62
Commonwealth, 118, 126, 127
Communal, 164
Communism, 180, 182, 392, 399, 402
Communitarian, 245
Companies, 243, 247; Japanese, 237; transnational, 46. *See also* Transnational corporations
Comparative analysis, 34, 67–77, 129
Comparative law, 13, 27, 28, 29, 30, 37
"Compartmentalized selves," 313
Confucian ideology, 238, 394, 414
Conseil d'Etat, 144, 145, 146
Constitutional Assembly, the, 206
Constitutional Court, Colombian, 204, 207–8, 211–12; and affirmative action, 213; and gender law, 214; and diverse family structure, 212
Constitutionalism, 231
Constitutionality, un-, 208–10, 212, 214
Constitution making, 204
Constructive engagement, 198
Consultation, 224
Contextualism, 272
Contraception, 77
Convention of Belém do Pará, 368, 369
Cooperative Economics for Women (CEW), 102–4
Cooperatives, 99; business, 102
Co-ops, 102–4, 106–7
Cordoba de Castro, Senator Piedad, 214
"Corporate warriors," 409
Corporation. *See* Transnational corporation
Cossman, Brenda, 2, 13
Costa Rica, 364
Crenshaw, Kimberle, 5
Critical Legal Studies(CLS), 1, 4; Conference on, 4
Critical Race Feminism (CRF), 1, 2, 4–7, 68, 332
Critical race praxis, 6
Critical Race Theory(CRT), 1, 4, 5
Crocker, Chester, 198
Crooms, Lisa A., 16
Cuba, 13, 81–91, 184–85; constitution, 84, 86
Cuban military police, 185
Cuban Negro, 185
Cuban Women, Federation of (FMC), 86. *See also* Activists, FMC
Cultural relativism, 12, 16, 47, 67
Customary law, 334, 336, 397

Daly, Mary, 267–69
Declaration on the Right to Development, 98
Delgado, Richard, 1, 3
Democracy, 180
Derrida, Jacques, 4
Development, right to, 95–108. *See also* Declaration on the Right to Development
Diaz, Judge Carlos Gaviria, 210
Diggs, Congressman Charles Coles, 194; and "Study Mission to Africa," 194
Discrimination: in Britain, 119; employment, 197, 410; employment, in China, 392, 399–403; employment, in France, 149–50; employment, in Japan, 409–11; employment, in Serbia, 167–68; race, in France, 144; race, in New Zealand, 129; race, in Serbia, 160, 162–63; racial, in U.S., 179–81; sex, in New Zealand, 134; sexual, in China, 392–98; social, in Serbia, 160
Distinctive voice, 3
Divorce, 39
Djibouti, 280–81
Domestic violence: in Australia, 17, 308–9; in Colombia, 209–10; in Ghana, 17, 317–23; in Palestine, 17, 336–38; in Puerto Rico, 347–59; in Serbia, 161, 170–72; in South Africa, 17, 336–38. *See also* Family fighting; Violence against women
Domestic Violence Law, Puerto Rico, 348–57
Dowry. *See* Bride price
Du Bois, W. E. B., 180
Dudziak, Mary, 2, 6, 17
Duque, Gloria Guzman, 210

EEOL. *See* Equal Employment Opportunity Law
Egoyan, Atom, 27, 37
El Salvador, 364
Employment discrimination. *See* Discrimination
Employment law, 398
England, 116–25; and racism, 117–19
Epstein, Richard, 136
Equal Employment Opportunity Law (EEOL), 409, 415
Essentialism, 55–57, 85, 115: anti-, 1, 7; strategic, 312–13
Ethnocentric, 28
Ethnocentrism, 29
European Parliament, 152
European Union, 144

Factory workers, in Sri Lanka, 46–48
Familial ideology, 30–33
Family: Hindu, 40; joint, 40; nuclear, 39; two-parent, 287–90, 295–97
"Family fighting," 309
Family registration, 234–46
Family registry, 234
Fanon, Frantz, 3

Fatherhood, 115–16, 124–25, 285–90
Fatherlessness, 285–90
Federal Bureau of Investigations (FBI), 179, 182
Federation of Cuban Women (FMC), 86–87
Female circumcision. *See* Circumcision
Female genital mutilation, 78, 262, 273–74, 278–79. *See also* Circumcision
Female genital surgeries. *See* Circumcision; Female genital mutilation
Female infanticide, 16, 251–57, 402
Femicide, social, 252, 253, 257
Feminism: and Australia, 309–10; and Cuban culture, 81–91; and Jamaican culture, 121; and Mexico, 75; Western, 6, 28, 31, 34, 42–50, 71, 81, 263, 266–67, 276, 278, 311
Feminist: Black, 55–57; African, 281
Feminist internationality, 42–50
Feminist jurisprudence, 1, 7, 38
Feminist legal theory, 38; and praxis, 14, 16, 310
Feminist practices, 34, 38, 39, 40
Feminist scholarship, 35, 38, 39, 42
Feminist theory, 38, 56
Ferguson, Clarence Clyde, Jr., 199
FIDA. *See* International Federation of Women Lawyers in Ghana
Fire Eyes, 279
Folklore, Ghanaian, 322
Footbinding, 394–95
Foreign policy. *See* United States foreign policy
Foreign relations, 179, 183, 201, 299
Foucault, Michel, 4
Founding mothers, 204
Fourth World, the, 173–74
France, 14, 141–53, 181, 187; and African immigration, 143–44; and racism, 146–47
Frankenberg, Ruth, 33, 40
Free South Africa Movement, 198
Frye, Marilyn, 321
Fundamentalism, Islamic, 153

Gandhi, Mahatma, 3
Gangs, 167, 173, 288
Garces, Maria Teresa, 205
Garment industry, 377–79
GATT/WTO, 383
Gaviria, President Cesar, 205, 214
Gender: and the Colombian constitution, 206–8; discrimination, in Japan, 409–10; equality, 39, 412; in France, 141; relations, 34, 35, 39, 226, 229
Gender and Development(GAD), 99–101
Generalized System of Preferences (GSP), 382
Ghana, domestic violence in, 317–23
Ghana National Council on Women and Development (NCWD), 324
Gilligan, Carol, 115
Glendon, Mary Ann, 69

Global South, 96
Globalization, 5
Gordon, Ruth E., 5
Grassroots organizations, 106
Gray, Congressman William H., III, 199
Guatemala, 365
Gunning, Isabelle, 16, 121
Gypsies, Serbian, 161–62
Gypsy women, 15, 160–74; and domestic violence, 170; and employment discrimination, 167–68; and incest, 172–73

Habeas corpus, 209, 217
Hadiths, 232
Haiti, 157
Han, Anna, 18
Harkis, 141, 153
Harris, Angela P., 38
Hastie, Judge William Henry, 193
Havana Herald, 184–85
Head scarf, Islamic, 145–47
Health, women's sexual, 280
Hernández Truyol, Berta Esperanza, 13
Herran, Helena, 205
Ho, Laura, 18
Hom, Sharon, 17
Homelands policy, 198–99
Homemaker, 123, 128, 244
Honor killings, 336–37, 341
Honseki, 236, 240
hooks, bell, 58, 124, 128, 258
Hoover, J. Edgar, 182, 186
House system, 238, 240
Househead registration, 243
Household, 244
Household registration, 238
Household registry, 242–43
Housewives, 89, 98, 122
Housing, 163; government, 120; public, 120, 127, 285
Housing and Urban Development (HUD), 286, 289, 294–98
Howard, Rhoda, 101
Howard University School of Law, 192, 198, 200
Human rights, 312, 362; gender specific, 260; international law, 310–13; and sexual harassment, 362. *See also* International human rights; Women's human rights

Iblis (Satan), 226
ICCPR. *See* International Covenant on Civil and Political Rights
ICESCR. *See* International Covenant on Economic, Social and Cultural Rights
Ihtibas, 224–25
Ijma', 222
Ijtihad, 222, 230

Immigrant women, 144, 379
Immigration: in France, 143–44; and gender, 142
Immigration and Naturalization Service (INS), 186
Imperialism, 42, 44, 276
Incest, 172–73
India, 29–32, 38–41; colonial, 39; Government of, 32
Indigenous women, 368; violence against, 308
Infanticide. *See* Female infanticide
Infibulation, 145, 155, 261, 270, 280
Inheritance law, 397
Inner-city. *See* City, inner
International Bill of Human Rights, 97, 382
International Covenant on Civil and Political Rights (ICCPR), 55, 59, 63, 65
International Covenant on Economic, Social and Cultural Rights (ICESCR), 59, 63
International Federation of Women Lawyers in Ghana (FIDA), 318, 325, 328
International human rights, 53–65, 310–13. *See also* International Bill of Human Rights
International Labour Organization (ILO), 355, 367, 369, 382
International law, 53–65, 193; and racial and gender discrimination, 311–13, 338–39
International trade law, 383–84
Intersection methodology, 60, 63–64
Intifada, 336
Irua, 78
Islam, 9, 15, 16, 145–46, 337, 341; law, 221–29

Jamaican culture, 119, 121–23
Japan, 234–46, 409–19; and constitution, 412
Japanese women, 16, 18, 234–46, 409–19
Jaramillo, Isabel Cristina, 214
Jiagge, Justice Anne, 321
Job discrimination. *See* Discrimination, employment
Johnson, Cora Lee, 95
Johnson, Dean George Marion, 200
Johnson, Rebecca, 104
Jordanian Personal Status Law, 337
Jus cogens, 63–64
Justice system, 215

Kangwane, 198, 199, 202
Kaplan, Caren, 34, 38–41
Kapur, Ratna, 29, 37, 39, 40
Karamah, 230
Khadijah, 224–25
Kikuta, Noboru, 236–37
King, Reverend Dr. Martin Luther, 3, 101
King, Rodney, 3
King, Rosemary Ofei-Aboagye, 17
Kissinger, Henry, 194
Knapp, Kiyoko Kamio, 2, 18

Koran. *See* Islam
Kusturica, Emir, 162

Lacroix Correa, Puerto Rico v., 357
LatCrit Theory, 92
Latin America, 204, 362–70
Law: China, 395–99; Japan, 412–14; Palestine, 341; South Africa, 339
Law 54, 348–59
Legal education, 135
Legal research and writing, 136–38
Legislation, 326, 348–52; in Japan, 415–19
Lesbian, 10–11
Lewis, Hope, 14
Ley 54, 348
Like Water for Chocolate, 72–73
Location: domestic political, 36; geopolitical, 36; politics of, 34–36, 38–40
Lopez, Antoinette Sedillo, 13
Lorde, Audre, 127, 273, 283
Lusaka speech, the, 194–95

Mabo v. State of Queensland, 305
Machismo, 67, 204
MacKinnon, Catharine A., 44
Madonna, Catholic Virgin, 83, 92
Mambisas, 83, 85, 86, 90, 92
Mandela, Nelson, 3, 200
Mandovs, 161
Mani, Lata, 30, 33, 38–41
Manu v. Manu, 327
Mao, 395, 399
Maquiladora, 379, 384, 385
Marginalization, 55
Marianismo, 83, 85, 91, 92
Marital duties, 39
Marketization, in China, 392, 399–402
Marquez, Gabriel Garcia, 205
Marriage law, 396
Matsuda, Mari, 1, 2, 3, 130
May, Elaine Tyler, 188
M'Baye, Keba, 95, 97
McDougall, Gay J., 198
McHenry, Donald F., 199
Mesas de trabajo, 205–6
Mestre, Goar, 184–85
Mexican feminism, 75
Mexico, 13, 67, 72–74, 364, 379
Microenterprise for women, 99
Minority, 54
Mohanty, Chandra Talpade, 2, 30, 31, 38, 39
Moraga, Cherríe, 43
Morena, Mercedes Moya, 206
Morgan, Martha, 2, 15
Moser, Carolyn, 99
Motherhood, 10, 115–25, 188; and patriarchy, 121–23; and work in cultural context, 115–25

Mrsevic, Zorica, 2, 15
Multiplicative identity, 7–11, 13, 17
Multiple consciousness, 1, 7
Muñoz, Judge Eduardo Cifuentes, 210
Muslim, 221–29. *See* Islam
Muslim women, 221–29
Myrdal, Gunnar, 179

Nagle, Professor Luz Estella, 215
Namibia, 195
Narratives, 5, 129, 160
Nesiah, Vasuki, 13
New Zealand, 129–39
Nissan Motor Company, 242–43
Nongovernmental organizations (NGOs), 54–55
North American Free Trade Agreement (NAFTA), 383
Nurturer, 115

Obiora, Leslye Amede, 16, 275–82
Ofei-Aboagye, Rosemary. *See* King, Rosemary Ofei-Aboagye
"Office flowers," 409–10
Olinka women, 268
One-child policy, 401
Oppression, 1, 2, 3; gender, in Serbia, 160; racial, in Serbia, 160
Oré-Aguilar, Gaby, 17
Organization of American States (OAS), 368, 370
Orientalism, 47, 222
Osei-Koom v. Osei-Koom, 327

Palestinian women, 332, 336–37, 339, 341; and Basic Law, 339, 341
Palmer, Rt Hon Professor Sir Geoffrey, 138
Papon, Maurice, 142
Paris, 181
Patriarchy, 14, 40; and Africa, 264–66; and fathers, 123–25; and Gypsy women, 15, 169, 170; and Islam, 221–29; in Jamaica, 121–23
Patterson, William, 180
Paz, Octavia, 81
People of color, 2, 3, 96, 127
Perez, Alicia Elena, 74, 76, 79
Perkins, Edward J., 199
Peru, 363–64
Politburo, 86
Polygamy, 337, 394
Population control, 59
Pornography, 44
Positive discrimination. *See* Affirmative action
Posner, Richard, 3
Postcolonialism, 14, 29, 33, 39
Postcolonial theory, 1, 12, 13, 32, 35
Poverty, 54; feminization of, 53
Powell, Catherine, 18

Pregnancy, 77, 82, 210–11
Primogeniture, 394
Pro-choice, 77
Pro-life, 77
Propaganda, 183
Public housing. *See* Housing
Puerto Rico, 347–59

Qur'an. *See* Islam

Race: in France, 144; relations, 127, 182–83, 186–87
Race Convention (CERD), 55, 63–65
Race discrimination. *See* Discrimination
Racism: American, 45, 180; in Britain, 117–19; in France, 144, 152; in Serbia, 162–63
Rainbow Tribe, the, 15, 187
Ramirez, Socorro, 214
Rape, and slavery, 61
Reproductive rights, 210
Richardson, Henry J., III, 198
Rico, Roger, 181
Rifkind, Simon, 200
Riviera, Jenny, 17
Roberts, Dorothy, 61
Robeson, Paul, 180
Roe v. Wade, 77, 212
Romani. *See* Gypsies, Serbian
Romany, Celina, 13

Sahel development program, 197
Salome, 27, 28, 37
Samper, Jacquin de, 210
Scales-Trent, Judy, 14, 15
Sekiguchi, Reiko, 236–37
Self-determination, right to, 98
Serbia, 160–74
Sexual harassment, 362; definition, 11, 365–66; and international law, 366–68; and Latin America, 17, 362–70
Sexual orientation, 10
Shari'a. See Islam
Smith, J. Clay, 2, 6, 17
South Africa, 8, 194–96, 198–200, 334–35, 339–41; constitution, 60, 339–41. *See also* Free South Africa Movement
South African women, 60, 62, 332, 334–35
South Pacific, 181
Soviet Union, 180
Spirit injury, 14, 135, 332, 333, 338, 343
Spirit murder, 134–35
Spivak, Gayatri, 312
Sri Lankan women, 45–48
State Department, the, 179, 182, 183, 187
Stork Club, 181, 189
Strauss, Richard, 27
Sullivan, Reverend Leon H., 196, 199

Surname, 241
Sweat shops, 377–79

Taiwan, 130
Taiwanese immigrant woman, in New Zealand, 129
"Third World" women, 2, 39, 48, 49, 50, 68
Title VII, 381
TNCs. *See* Transnational corporations
Traditions, 40, 322
Transnational corporations, 42, 45–46, 378, 380, 386
Tutela, 208–10, 214–15

Union Nationale de Femmes de Djibouti (UNFD), 280–82
United Nations, 12, 106, 367; Charter 64, 98; Commission on Human Rights, 366; Declaration on Elimination of Violence Against Women, 342, 367; Fourth World Conference on Women (Beijing), 58, 222, 312, 385–86
United States Agency for International Development (AID), 192, 196; and Africa, 196–97
United States Constitution, 292
United States foreign policy: and Africa, 192; and human rights, 195
United States Information Service (USIS), 183
Universal Declaration on Human Rights, 97, 134
Universalism, 16, 311
Uruguay, 182

Vance, Cyrus, 196
Violence against women: in Australia, 303–10; in Palestine, 332, 336–37; in Puerto Rico, 347–48; in South Africa, 332–35; in U.S., 347. *See also* Domestic violence
Volpp, Leti, 18

Walker, Alice, 127, 268–69
Welfare: assistance, 61; benefits, 101; dependency, 100; queen, 11; recipients, 110; reform, 11, 99–100
Wells, Ida B., 124
West, Cornel, 4, 5
Western feminist, 321
West Indian, 117–20, 124
Wharton, Clifton R., Jr., 200
White, Curtis T., 199
Williams, Dean Gregory, 9
Winchell, Walter, 181, 182, 186
Wing, Adrien Katherine, 68, 134
Wives, 32, 39, 83
Women-in-development (WID), 98, 100
Women of color, 2, 53–54; in U.S., 96
Women's Convention (CEDAW), 55, 64–65, 147, 207, 254, 256, 258, 286, 290–300, 338–39, 367–68
Women's human rights, 290
Women's movement, in Cuba, 83–85
Workfare, 109
Working women, 411
Workplace, 364
World Bank, 99
World traveling, 13, 121, 342

Young, Andrew, 199
Young, Robert, 33, 40